Rise Up, O Judge

Rise Up, O Judge

A Study of Justice in the Biblical World

ENRIQUE NARDONI
Translated by Seán Charles Martin

English translation © 2004 by Hendrickson Publishers, Inc.
P. O. Box 3473
Peabody, Massachusetts 01961-3473

ISBN 1-56563-530-2

Translated from Enrique Nardoni, *Los que buscan la justicia: Un studio de la justicia en el mundo bíblico*, © 1997, Editorial Verbo Divino, Estella (Navarra), Spain.

All rights reserved. No part of this book may be reproduced or transmitted in any form or by any means, electronic or mechanical, including photocopying, recording, or by any information storage and retrieval system, without permission in writing from the publisher.

Printed in the United States of America

First Printing — August 2004

Cover Art: Marc Chagall. "Prayer of Solomon." 1956.
Credit: © 2001 Artists Rights Society (ARS), New York / ADAGP, Paris.
Used with permission.

Library of Congress Cataloging-in-Publication Data

Nardoni, Enrique, 1924–2002.
    [Que buscan la justicia. English]
    Rise up, o judge : a study of justice in the biblical world / Enrique Nardoni; translated by Seán Charles Martin.
       p. cm.
    Includes bibliographical references and index.
    ISBN 1-56563-530-2 (alk. paper)
    1. Justice—Biblical teaching. I. Title.
    BS680.J8N3713 2004
    241'.622—dc22
                     2004009608

Contents

Foreword	xi
Introduction to the English Edition	xiii
Abbreviations	xvii
Chapter 1: Justice in Ancient Mesopotamia	1
Introduction	1
1. Mesopotamia before social reforms	2
2. The social reforms of Entemena, Urukagina, and Gudea	2
3. The codes of Ur-Nammu, Lipit-Ishtar, and Eshnunna	5
4. The Code of Hammurabi	8
5. Proclamations of mercy	12
6. Texts of faith in the protective divinities of justice	15
Conclusion	17
Bibliography	18
Chapter 2: Justice in Ancient Egypt	21
Introduction	21
1. Justice in the Old Kingdom (2700–2130 B.C.E.)	22
2. Justice in the First Intermediate period (2130–1940 B.C.E.)	27
3. Justice in the Middle Kingdom (1940–1570 B.C.E.)	30
4. Justice in the New Kingdom (1570–1070 B.C.E.)	32
5. Justice in popular religion	37
Conclusion	38
Bibliography	39
Chapter 3: Exodus as an Event of Liberating Justice	42
Introduction	42
1. The Exodus in the Bible	43
2. The Exodus in the Bible's sources and traditions	47
3. The Exodus in history	50
3.1. The Exodus event and its religious dimension	51

3.2. Exodus and the revolutionary model	53
3.3. Exodus and egalitarian society	55
3.4. Exodus as the first revelation	56
3.5. Exodus as a paradigm of liberation	57
Conclusion	61
Bibliography	62

Chapter 4: Norms of Justice in the Laws of the Covenant — 68

Introduction	68
1. The laws of Sinai in Exodus	68
2. The Ten Commandments	69
2.1. "Remember the Sabbath day and keep it holy"	70
2.2. "Honor your father and your mother"	72
2.3. "You shall not kill"	73
2.4. "You shall not commit adultery"	76
2.5. "You shall not steal"	77
2.6. "You shall not bear false witness against your neighbor"	77
2.7. "You shall not covet your neighbor's house"	78
3. The Covenant Code	79
3.1. The social groups and the treatment of the slaves	80
3.2. Concern for the needy	80
4. The social laws of Deuteronomy	82
4.1. Humanitarian justice for Israelite slaves	83
4.2. Humanitarian justice for the needy	83
5. The Holiness Code	85
5.1. The social groups	85
5.2. Social justice as an imitation of the sanctity of God	86
5.3. The sabbatical institutions	86
Conclusion	89
Bibliography	90

Chapter 5: Justice, Monarchy, and Prophecy — 95

Introduction	95
1. Kingship in ancient Israel	95
1.1. The monarchy in ancient Israel	95
1.2. The king's power	97
2. Prophecy in ancient Israel	99
2.1. The prophets Nathan and Elijah	100
2.2. The prophet Amos in the northern kingdom	100
2.3. The prophet Hosea in Samaria	104
2.4. Isaiah of Jerusalem	106
2.5. Micah of Moresheth in the southern kingdom	108
2.6. Jeremiah and the last decades of Jerusalem	109
2.7. Ezekiel during the Babylonian exile	110
2.8. Second Isaiah and the liberation from the exile	111

2.9. Third Isaiah and the postexilic community	115
Conclusion	117
Bibliography	118

Chapter 6: Justice in the Psalms and Wisdom Books — 122
Introduction — 122
1. Justice in the Psalms — 122
   1.1. Justice, order, right conduct, and saving action — 123
   1.2. God, the source and model of justice — 124
   1.3. Justice and the poor — 124
   1.4. Identification of the poor — 125
   1.5. The enemies of the poor — 128
   1.6. Reflections on the prosperity of the wicked — 130
   1.7. Eschatological expectations of the poor — 131
2. The book of Proverbs — 132
3. The book of Job — 135
4. The book of Ecclesiastes — 138
5. The book of Sirach — 141
6. Wisdom of Solomon — 143
Conclusion — 146
Bibliography — 147

Chapter 7: Justice in Apocalyptic Writings — 151
Introduction — 151
1. The Book of the Watchers — 152
2. The Book of the Epistle of Enoch — 155
3. The book of Daniel — 158
4. The Book of the Similitudes — 163
5. The second book of Esdras — 165
Conclusion — 169
Bibliography — 170

Chapter 8: Justice in the Ministry of Jesus of Nazareth — 173
Introduction — 173
1. The quest for the historical Jesus — 174
2. The social and historical context of Jesus of Nazareth — 178
3. Jesus of Nazareth's social condition and public action — 181
4. Jesus' expectation of the imminent coming of the eschatological kingdom — 183
5. Jesus and the social and familial dimensions of the kingdom — 186
6. The social dimension of Jesus' sapiential sayings — 187
7. The social aspect of Jesus' prophetic sayings and actions — 189
8. The promotion of women — 191
9. Jesus and nonviolence — 193

Conclusion	196
Bibliography	196

Chapter 9: Justice in the Gospel of Mark — 201
- Introduction — 201
- 1. Jesus as Messiah, spokesman, and agent of God's kingdom — 202
- 2. Jesus as the crucified Messiah and the cornerstone of the new community — 204
- 3. Reordering power in the world — 206
- 4. Power as a service for the community — 208
- 5. Liberation from the slavery of wealth — 209
- 6. A family of disciples on equal conditions — 210
- 7. Reshaping the center of purity — 211
- 8. The dignity of women — 213
- Conclusion — 214
- Bibliography — 215

Chapter 10: Justice in the Gospel of Matthew and the Letter of James — 217
- 1. Justice in the Gospel of Matthew — 217
  - 1.1. Justice in the Beatitudes — 218
  - 1.2. Justice in the antitheses of the Sermon on the Mount — 225
  - 1.3. Justice in the trilogy: almsgiving, prayer, and fasting — 227
  - 1.4. Justice in the parable of the Two Sons — 230
  - 1.5. Justice in the option for the poor and the afflicted — 231
- 2. Justice in the Letter of James — 235
- Bibliography — 239

Chapter 11: Justice in the Gospel of Luke and the Acts of the Apostles — 242
- Introduction — 242
- 1. Jesus in the synagogue of Nazareth — 242
- 2. The Beatitudes — 247
- 3. The rich man and the alternative offered him by Jesus — 250
- 4. A banquet for the poor and a call to share — 252
- 5. A new map of relationships — 255
- 6. Promotion of women — 256
- Conclusion — 259
- Bibliography — 259

Chapter 12: Justice in Paul's Letters — 263
- Introduction — 263
- 1. The Roman Empire in the first Christian century — 263
- 2. Paul of Tarsus and his background — 264
- 3. Paul as apostle of Christ — 265
- 4. The social dimension of God's justice — 266
- 5. God's justice and the dignity of women — 270
- 6. God's justice and slavery — 273

7. God's justice and the Pax Romana	276
8. Paul and civil government	278
9. God's justice and the collection for the Jerusalem church	280
10. Justice and the exercise of authority in the Pauline Letters	282
Conclusion	285
Bibliography	286

Chapter 13: Justice in the Johannine Writings   290
  Introduction   290
  1. The Fourth Gospel   290
    1.1. An oppressed community, confident of divine vindication   291
    1.2. An oppressed community experiencing Christ's liberation   295
    1.3. An oppressed community fostering inner solidarity and equality   297
  2. Justice in the Johannine Letters   300
    2.1. The saving justice   300
    2.2. Righteous works, product of God's children   301
    2.3. Equality in the community   304
  3. Justice in the book of Revelation   304
    3.1. The critical situation of Christians   305
    3.2. Revelation's purpose and approach   306
    3.3. Revelation's alternative to the Roman Empire   308
    3.4. Christian participation   311
  Conclusion   313
  Bibliography   313

Chapter 14: Overall Conclusion   317
  Bibliography   323

Glossary of Frequently-Used Ancient Words   325

Index of Modern Authors   327

Index of Ancient Sources   333

Foreword

With the allusion to the fourth beatitude in Matthew's Sermon on the Mount (Matt 5:6), Professor Nardoni undertakes the very difficult task of following the theme of the pursuit of justice from the dawn of humankind in the Middle East to the New Testament period. Such an endeavor ought to be appreciated for three reasons. First, Professor Nardoni's analysis of the concern for justice in the biblical world helps us to situate and understand the quest for justice in the rest of history; indeed, such concern appears for the first time in the documents that come down to us from ancient Mesopotamia and the Nile Valley. Second, the ancient concerns of Mesopotamia and Egypt are closely related to the context in which the biblical revelation geminates and matures, which itself culminates in Christ "our justice" (or "righteousness") as Saint Paul puts it (1 Cor 1:30). And third, if there is an essential concern in the worlds of economics and political science, it is certainly that of justice—not so much the justice called (in the classical distinction) commutative, but rather that justice that is distributive or social. There is presently intense scrutiny in regard to the quest for the rational foundations and imperative character of justice, as well as in regard to the ways and means to put justice into practice, even in the very midst of modern (or postmodern) relativism and historicism. The light that this book is capable of throwing on the question will enlarge the present discussion by opening up a new perspective that is not only historical but also human and thus religious, or in other words, transcendent.

Justice, according to Professor Nardoni's analysis, is not limited to relations between individuals, or relations between the individual and society, or even relations between societies. It is grounded, rather, in the divine image found in man and woman and looks ahead to their divine destiny. That is why justice can be identified with Jesus Christ. In this identification, however, justice is transfigured and becomes an absolute. It is justice coming from God himself, and it confers justice on us and makes us just. Thus we come to the full understanding of justice and its faithful observance in ordinary human affairs.

In this context, I think of some reductive readings of the Bible that were in vogue during the seventies and that are perhaps to some extent still alive. According to such readings, the justice that really counts (and indeed, the only justice claimed to be found in the Bible) worked in but one direction, unilaterally, from the rich to the poor. It was merciless toward the former and almost exclusively for the benefit of the latter. According to such views, the practice of justice required, in the dynamics of history, the promotion of revolution, if not for the immediate installation of the kingdom of justice, at least as the condition for its possible advent against an otherwise remote and uncertain future. The mystery of the life, death, and resurrection of Christ was read and interpreted in this light.

Among the many merits of Professor Nardoni's book, one should be underlined. He has not avoided the challenge posed by this reductionist understanding of justice. The destitute and their concerns certainly belong among the main concerns of this study. But instead of taking his cue from any ideology whatsoever, Nardoni starts from the texts and makes each speak for itself. Not every text communicates the same message. It is simply honest, however, to hear what each has to say, to note it carefully, to place it in its proper context, and thus to try to show how a certain trajectory of thought emerges. Such a trajectory begins with the extrabiblical texts, allowing us to discern points of convergence and divergence with the Torah, the Prophets, and the Writings, then culminates in the message of the New Testament. There exists, therefore, and this may be one of the implications of this remarkably serious work, a kind of paradigm of justice that is not subject to the variations of history but that remains the same forever. Professor Nardoni does not explicitly affirm, much less emphasize, such a conclusion but is content to let it flow from these carefully written pages. Such care in writing is another of the merits of his book, along with his mastery of linguistic and bibliographic scholarship.

For all these reasons, let me express the hope that Professor Nardoni's book will be often read and carefully studied. He is well aware of what he calls, in the last sentence of the book, "the *elusive* character of justice" (emphasis mine). Yet, in spite of this, he qualifies this by saying that "the Christian community does not lose hope, because it trusts deeply in the power of the Spirit. . . ." Justice in our world, on *this* side of the coming of the Kingdom, will never be perfect but is always unstable. It is in perpetual need of rediscovery and restoration. Thus, one needs always to know what justice is and in what it consists, or rather, in *whom*. In view of this, I believe that Professor Nardoni's book has made a decisive contribution, and I am happy to express here, as a former colleague and as a friend, my heartfelt gratitude.

Jorge M. Mejía
Archivist and Librarian of the Holy Roman Church

INTRODUCTION TO THE ENGLISH EDITION

Readers may understand this book better if they know how and why it originated, and for whom it was written. As I explained in the introduction to the Spanish edition, what prompted its writing was a discussion on evangelization and justice during the eleventh annual meeting of the Argentinean Theological Society in Córdoba (Argentina) during August 1992. At that meeting, I presented two papers on social justice in the Bible. During our discussion I was encouraged to expand my research and to prepare a book-length study. It would provide college and seminary teachers and students, religious education moderators, and leaders of grass-roots or basic ecclesial communities *(comunidades de base)* a guide to the various biblical texts concerning social justice in their historical contexts, viewed from a social, political, and economic perspective. The intention of this book would be to counteract a reading of these biblical texts dominated by ideological interests in which eisegesis is more prominent than exegesis.

The need for such a book-length study was urgent. There was no other Spanish-language publication that could provide a competent guide for teachers and readers of the Bible in Latin America and that could encourage them toward further study. These are the circumstances in which the Spanish edition of this book was born. The University of Dallas granted me a sabbatical in the academic year 1995–1996 to work on this project. The book was published at the end of that sabbatical year in 1997 by La Editorial Verbo Divino as *Los que buscan la justicia: Un estudio de la justicia en el mundo bíblico.*

For this book and for brevity, I selected relevant passages on social justice from both the Old and New Testaments for analysis. The selection emphasized the continuity of concern for social justice over a period of centuries in the biblical world, a continuity that showed growth in motivation and changes in approach. The origin and development of the concept of social justice in the biblical world interested me, so I traversed the history and literature of ancient Mesopotamia and Egypt. Then, in the Old Testament, I studied the biblical narratives of Israel's exodus from Egypt and the oracles of the prophets. I listened to the psalms and the instructions of the wise, and gazed at the visions of the apocalypticists. In the New Testament, I examined the words and deeds of Jesus of Nazareth, and I analyzed the message of the Synoptics and the insights of the Pauline and Johannine literature.

Over the course of this journey, I read ancient texts from a social perspective. My predominant interest was in studying regulations and practices that concern the poor and oppressed as they are represented in laws issued on their behalf, in dicta concerning the fair and impartial exercise of justice, in critiques on abuses of power and authority, in condemnations of oppressive structures, in amnesties that offer new opportunities, in modes of philanthropic behavior, and in words and actions that seek to form a new society of justice and peace. I wanted to understand the texts in their own historical contexts and to establish a dialogue with leading scholars who have commented on the subject of justice and peace in the biblical world.

However, my concern for the original historical context of the texts was not solely historical. On the contrary, I had a strong interest in relating the biblical texts to our present situation. These concerns and interests permeate and give a sense of unity to the thirteen chapters of this book. The texts are not merely paraphrased but are placed in their own historical, social, and intellectual context; they are made alive for the reader. The purpose of this study is not to have readers as mere spectators but to prepare them to be actors, to allow them to be transformed from spectators into participants. The title of the book, *Rise Up, O Judge*, is inspired by Psalm 94:2, and understands justice in all of its dimensions—commutative, distributive, legal—as the express will of God. Since this book shows a development of the concept of social justice over the centuries in the biblical world, the reader is advised not to read an isolated chapter before perusing the overall conclusion that offers an overview of the process.

Why this English edition? This book is not a mere translation of the original Spanish work. Rather it is a revised edition—footnotes have been appended to each chapter, occasionally new paragraphs have been inserted improving the text, and the bibliography to each chapter has been updated. Teachers such as Thomas Cumiskey and Michael Duggan suggested that this would be a resource for a great variety of teaching and discussion activities on the issue of social justice. I hope that it serves as a textbook for workshops, seminars, and various courses. Whether they have themes of social justice and human development, or have social teaching in the Church, or biblical theology as topics, I have written it with parish, congregational, and ecumenical Bible study groups in mind. It is also a resource for pastors, homilists, and liturgists who want to develop themes of justice throughout the liturgical year. Indeed, I hope it will be used as a foundation both for discussions of cooperation between Jews and Christians in their pursuit of social justice and for discussions of the contribution of the Judeo-Christian tradition to issues of human development.

This book deals with a subject of great importance today. At the beginning of the new millennium, Christians are called to "discern Christ's voice in the cry for help that rises from this world of poverty" and are exhorted to engage in "a new 'creativity' in charity, not only by ensuring that help is effective but also by 'getting close' to those who suffer, so that the hand that helps is seen not as [offering]

Introduction to the English Edition

a humiliating handout but as . . . sharing between brothers and sisters."[1] May this book help them to achieve this calling.

I am grateful to the late Raymond E. Brown for his encouragement to publish the book in English. I am grateful to Anthony R. Ceresko and Fernando Segovia for their stimulating observations on some chapters. My gratitude is also due to Francis Swietek, for his stylistic corrections, and to Jorge M. Mejía, who wrote a prologue for the Spanish edition and agreed to do it again for the English edition. I am especially grateful to Seán Charles Martin for his invaluable collaboration in the work of the English translation.

Easter, 2001
Enrique Nardoni
University of Dallas
Irving, Texas

---

[1] John Paul II, "Apostolic Letter *Novo Millennio Ineunte*" 50 (6 January, 2001). Online: http://www.vatican.va/holyfather/johnpaulii/apostletters/documents/hfjpii.htm.

Abbreviations

General

Akk.	Akkadian
B.C.E.	before the Common Era
ca.	circa
C.E.	Common Era
ch(s).	chapter(s)
ed(s).	editor(s), edited by
Eg.	Egyptian
Gk.	Greek
Heb.	Hebrew
LXX	Septuagint (the Greek OT)
n(n).	note(s)
NAB	New American Bible
NIV	New International Version
NRSV	New Revised Standard Version
NS	new series
NT	New Testament
OT	Old Testament
repr.	reprinted
RSV	Revised Standard Version
Sum.	Sumerian
trans.	translator, translated by; transitive
v(v).	verse(s)
vol(s).	volume(s)

Hebrew Bible/Old Testament

Gen	Genesis
Exod	Exodus
Lev	Leviticus
Num	Numbers

Deut	Deuteronomy
Josh	Joshua
Judg	Judges
1–2 Sam	1–2 Samuel
1 Kgs	1 Kings
2 Chr	2 Chronicles
Ezra	Ezra
Ps/Pss	Psalms
Prov	Proverbs
Eccl	Ecclesiastes
Isa	Isaiah
Jer	Jeremiah
Ezek	Ezekiel
Dan	Daniel
Hos	Hosea
Mic	Micah
Zeph	Zephaniah
Zech	Zechariah

New Testament

Matt	Matthew
Acts	Acts of the Apostles
Rom	Romans
1–2 Cor	1–2 Corinthians
Gal	Galatians
Eph	Ephesians
Phil	Philippians
Col	Colossians
1 Thess	1 Thessalonians
1–2 Tim	1–2 Timothy
Jas	James
1–2 Pet	1–2 Peter
Rev	Revelation

Apocrypha and Septuagint

Bar	Baruch
1–2 Esd	1–2 Esdras
1–2 Macc	1–2 Maccabees
Sir	Sirach/Ecclesiasticus
Tob	Tobit
Wis	Wisdom of Solomon

Old Testament Pseudepigrapha

2 Bar.   *2 Baruch (Syriac Apocalypse)*
1 En.   *1 Enoch (Ethiopic Apocalypse)*
4 Ezra   *4 Ezra*
Jub.   *Jubilees*
Sib. Or.   *Sibylline Oracles*
T. Dan   *Testament of Dan*
T. Levi   *Testament of Levi*
T. Job   *Testament of Job*

Dead Sea Scrolls and Related Texts

1QH^a *Thanksgiving Hymns*^{a}
1QM   *War Scroll*
4Q525   *Beatitudes*
11Q13   *Melchizedek*
4QpPs 37   *Commentary to Ps 37:11*
4Q521   *Messianic Apocalypse*

Philo

Mos. 2   *De vita Mosis* II

Josephus

Ant.   *Jewish Antiquities*
J.W.   *Jewish War*

Apostolic Fathers

Mart. Pol.   *Martyrdom of Polycarp*

Classical Writings

Aelius Aristides
   Eulogy   *Eulogy of Rome*
Cicero
   Att.   *Epistulae ad Atticum*
Ovid
   Pont.   *Epistulae ex Ponte*
Pliny the Younger
   Ep.   *Epistulae*

Tacitus
   Ann.   *Annales*
   Hist.   *Historiae*
Virgil
   Aen.   *Aeneid*
   Ecl.   *Eclogae*

Secondary Sources

AB	Anchor Bible
ABD	*Anchor Bible Dictionary.* Edited by D. N. Freedman. 6 vols. New York, 1992
ABRL	Anchor Bible Reference Library
AER	*American Ecclesiastical Review*
AnBib	Analecta biblica
ANET	*Ancient Near Eastern Texts Relating to the Old Testament.* Edited by J. B. Pritchard. 3d ed. Princeton, 1969
AOAT	Alter Orient und Altes Testament
AS	Assyriological Studies
BA	*Biblical Archaeologist*
BAR	*Biblical Archaeology Review*
BASOR	*Bulletin of the American Schools of Oriental Research*
BBB	Bonner biblische Beiträge
BHT	Beiträge zur historischen Theologie
Bib	*Biblica*
BJS	Brown Judaic Studies
BTB	*Biblical Theology Bulletin*
BZ	*Biblische Zeitschrift*
BZAW	Beihefte zur Zeitschrift für die alttestamentliche Wissenschaft
CBQ	*Catholic Biblical Quarterly*
CNT	Commentaire du Nouveau Testament
CP	*Classical Philology*
CRINT	Compendia rerum iudaicarum ad Novum Testamentum
DBSup	*Dictionnaire de la Bible: Supplément.* Edited by L. Pirot and A. Robert. Paris, 1928–
EB	Echter Bibel
EcumRev	*Ecumenical Revue*
EHPhR	Études d'histoire et philosophie religieuses
EKKNT	Evangelisch-katholischer Kommentar zum Neuen Testament
ErIsr	*Eretz Israel*
EstBib	*Estudios bíblicos*
EstEcl	*Estudios eclesiásticos*
ETL	*Ephemerides theologicae lovanienses*
EvT	*Evangelische Theologie*

ExpTim	*Expository Times*
FB	Forschung zur Bibel
FRLANT	Forschungen zur Religion und Literatur des Alten und Neuen Testaments
Greg	*Gregorianum*
HÄB	Hildesheimer ägyptologische Beiträge
HNT	Handbuch zum Neuen Testament
HNTC	Harper's New Testament Commentaries
HSM	Harvard Semitic Monographs
HTKNT	Herders theologischer Kommentar zum Neuen Testament
HTR	*Harvard Theological Review*
HTS	*Harvard Theological Studies*
HUCA	*Hebrew Union College Annual*
IBC	Interpretation: A Bible Commentary for Teaching and Preaching
ICC	International Critical Commentary
IDBSup	*Interpreter's Dictionary of the Bible: Supplementary Volume.* Edited by K. Crim. Nashville, 1976
Imm	*Immanuel*
Int	*Interpretation*
IThSSup	Indian Theological Studies Supplements
JAAR	*Journal of the American Academy of Religion*
JAARSup	*Journal of the American Academy of Religion, Supplement Series*
JAC	Jahrbuch für Antike und Christentum
JANESCU	*Journal of the Ancient Near Eastern Society of Columbia University*
JAOS	*Journal of the American Oriental Society*
JAOSSup	*Journal of the American Oriental Society, Supplement Series*
JBL	Journal of Biblical Literature
JCS	Journal of Cuneiform Studies
JEA	Journal of Egyptian Archaeology
JESHO	Journal of the Economic and Social History of the Orient
JLR	Journal of Law and Religion
JNES	Journal of Near Eastern Studies
JNSL	Journal of Northwest Semitic Languages
JQR	Jewish Quarterly Review
JSJ	Journal for the Study of Judaism in the Persian, Hellenistic, and Roman Periods
JSNTSup	Journal for the Study of the New Testament: Supplement Series
JSOTSup	Journal for the Study of the Old Testament: Supplement Series
JTS	Journal of Theological Studies
KlPauly	*Der kleine Pauly*
LCL	Loeb Classical Library

List	*Listening: Journal of Religion and Culture*
NCBC	New Century Bible Commentary
NewDocs	*New Documents Illustrating Early Christianity.* Edited by G. H. R. Horsley and S. Llewelyn. North Ryde, N.S.W., 1981–
NIGTC	New International Greek Testament Commentary
NJBC	*The New Jerome Biblical Commentary.* Edited by R. E. Brown et al. Englewood Cliffs, 1990
NovT	*Novum Testamentum*
NTS	*New Testament Studies*
NTTS	New Testament Tools and Studies
OBO	Orbis biblicus et orientalis
OBT	Overtures to Biblical Theology
OGIS	*Orientis graeci inscriptiones selectae.* Edited by W. Dittenberger. 2 vols. Leipzig, 1903–1905. Reprinted 1960
OrAnt	*Oriens antiquus*
ÖTKNT	Ökumenischer Taschenbuch-Kommentar zum Neuen Testament
OTL	Old Testament Library
OTM	Old Testament Message
OTS	Old Testament Studies
RA	*Revue d'assyriologie et d'archéologie orientale*
RB	*Revue biblique*
REg	*Revue d'égyptologie*
RelSRev	*Religious Studies Review*
RevExp	*Review and Expositor*
RevistB	*Revista bíblica*
RIDA	*Revue internationale des droits de l'antiquité*
RivB	*Rivista biblica italiana*
RlA	*Reallexikon der Assyriologie.* Edited by Erich Ebeling et al. Berlin, 1928–
RSO	*Revista degli studi orientali*
RSPT	*Revue des sciences philosophiques et théologique*s
SBEC	Studies in the Bible and Early Christianity
SBLDS	Society of Biblical Literature Dissertation Series
SBLMS	Society of Biblical Literature Monograph Series
SBLSCS	Society of Biblical Literature Septuagint and Cognate Studies
SBLSP	Society of Biblical Literature Seminar Papers
SBS	Stuttgarter Bibelstudien
SBT	Studies in Biblical Theology
SemeiaSt	Semeia Studies
SJ	Studia judaica
SJLA	Studies in Judaism in Late Antiquity
SJT	*Scottish Journal of Theology*
SNTSMS	Society for New Testament Studies Monograph Series
SNTSU	Studien zum Neuen Testament und seiner Umwelt

SP	Sacra pagina
ST	*Studia theologica*
Str-B	Strack, H. L., and P. Billerbeck. *Kommentar zum Neuen Testament aus Talmud und Midrasch.* 6 vols. Munich, 1922–1961
SVTP	Studia in Veteris Testamenti pseudepigraphica
TB	Theologische Bücherei: Neudrucke und Berichte aus dem 20. Jahrhundert
TDNT	*Theological Dictionary of the New Testament.* Edited by G. Kittel and G. Friedrich. Translated by G. W. Bromiley. 10 vols. Grand Rapids, 1964–1976
TDOT	*Theological Dictionary of the Old Testament.* Edited by G. J. Botterweck and H. Ringgren. Translated by J. T. Willis, G. W. Bromiley, and D. E. Green. 8 vols. Grand Rapids, 1974–
THAT	*Theologisches Handwörterbuch zum Alten Testament.* Edited by E. Jenni, with assistance from C. Westermann. 2 vols., Stuttgart, 1971–1976
TS	*Theological Studies*
USQR	*Union Seminary Quarterly Review*
VS	Beauchesne, Gabriel, ed. *Verbum salutis. Commentaire du Nouveau Testament.* 16 vol. Paris: Beauchesne, 1927–1951
VT	*Vetus Testamentum*
VTSup	Vetus Testamentum Supplements
WUNT	Wissenschaftliche Untersuchungen zum Neuen Testament
ZAW	*Zeitschrift für die alttestamentliche Wissenschaft*
ZBAT	Zürcher Bibelkommentar, Altes Testament
ZNW	*Zeitschrift für die neutestamentliche Wissenschaft und die Kunde der älteren Kirche*
ZTK	*Zeitschrift für Theologie und Kirche*

CHAPTER ONE

JUSTICE IN ANCIENT MESOPOTAMIA

Introduction

Any study of justice in the Bible must begin with ancient Mesopotamia because the concept and the vocabulary of biblical justice are rooted in that culture. To uncover these roots, this chapter will explore justice in ancient Mesopotamia from the Sumerian culture to the Neo-Babylonian. Although the scope of this chapter seems ambitious, its purpose is limited. The structure of judicial power and the general administration of justice in these cultures will not be treated here.[1] This chapter restricts itself rather to the analysis of certain aspects of justice: the problem of the poor and the oppressed, the action of the government in response to them, and the reflection of such a problem in popular piety.[2]

The concept of justice in ancient Mesopotamia embraces a broader meaning than our concepts of commutative, distributive, or social justice. It is not enough for the governor to promulgate good laws and supervise the keeping of these laws; in order for justice to have its place in the Mesopotamian world, he must also issue decrees of mercy that allow the restoration of a destabilized equality.

This chapter studies the texts in chronological order. After an overview of early social and economic development in ancient Mesopotamia, it analyzes the first of social reforms undertaken there. It then goes on to consider the various Mesopotamian law codes, the decrees of mercy ("justice"), and the religious texts that reflect the situation facing the underclasses of Mesopotamia.[3]

---

[1] For a study of the characteristic structures of judicial power as well as the administration of justice in general within the societies of ancient Mesopotamia, see Hans J. Boecker, *Law and the Administration of Justice in the Old Testament and Ancient East* (trans. J. Moiser; Minneapolis: Augsburg, 1980).

[2] This chapter takes a point of view similar to that taken by Léon Epzstein, *Social Justice in the Ancient Near East and the People of the Bible* (London: SCM, 1986), even though Epzstein does not undertake a conceptual analysis of the texts, or examine the "decrees of mercy," or refer to religious texts in connection with the question of justice.

[3] In Mesopotamian texts the decrees of mercy embrace acts of liberative justice. See below, §5.

1. Mesopotamia before social reforms

An earlier generation of scholars held that as long as the national religious socialism of ancient Sumer existed, there were no major problems that would have moved the governors to undertake social reforms. According to this view, the political and economic system orbited around the temple in the old city-state of the Sumerians. The temple owned the land and the ENSI (Sumerian for governor or king of the city) was its administrator. The citizens would serve their gods by cultivating their assigned fields for the granary, and they would draw from the grain reserves of the temple.[4] Recent investigations have somewhat changed our understanding of the Sumerian situation.[5] It is possible that at the beginning, the first Sumerian settlers owned the land in a communitarian form; but very soon thereafter, with economic development, the land passed into the hands of three owners: the temple, the most powerful families, and the ENSI. The ENSI, besides securing his political power by establishing a dynasty, increased his economic position primarily through the control of commerce and the collection of taxes. Later on, he added another source of wealth, namely, the exploitation of the land that belonged to the temple, which the ENSI arrogated as his own property. This economic development produced a rich class that prospered, thanks to the work of the poor. Social conflict soon appeared. The complaints were directed against the ENSI and the wealthy members of society. Complaints were raised against the ENSI because he was illegally expropriating land that belonged to the temple and was imposing excessive tributes. Similar complaints were raised against the wealthy because they were oppressing the poor and seizing their properties. When social conflict began to threaten the stability of the dynasty, the ruling class felt the need to introduce social reforms.

2. The social reforms of Entemena, Urukagina, and Gudea

The oldest social reform known goes back to the year 2420 B.C.E. Entemena, governor *(ENSI)* of the state-city of Lagash, undertook it. He is celebrated in a text that says: "He [Entemena] restored the mother to her own son; restored the son to his own mother; freed [the population] of [oppressive] interest rates." Entemena extended the reestablishment of social order beyond the limits of his own city and glorified himself by "having given liberty" *(ama-gi₄ e-gar)* to other cities dependent on Lagash.[6]

---

[4] See H. W. F. Saggs, *The Greatness That Was Babylon* (New York: Hawthorn, 1962), 38–47, 157–63.

[5] See the second, revised edition of Saggs, *The Greatness That Was Babylon* (London: Sidgwick & Jackson, 1988), 41–43.

[6] M. Lambert, "L'expansion de Lagash au temps d'Entéména," *RSO* (1972): 1–22; Niels P. Lemche, "*Andurārum* and *Mīšarum:* Comments on the Problem of Social Edicts and their Application in the Ancient Near East," *JNES* 38 (1979): 16.

The expression "having given liberty," in the context of Entemena's reform, designates a legal act that, in general, can signify the restitution of lost liberty, and in particular, can include the legal emancipation of a citizen reduced to slavery by insolvency, the return of confiscated property, the abolition of debts to the state, and the derogation of oppressive taxes. The purpose of Entemena's action was the reestablishment of just order. To do this he issued an act of liberation that in the future turned out to be very important, since it became the starting point a legal institution, designated in Akkadian with the terms *mīšarum* and *andurārum*.

Fifty years later in Lagash, around 2370 B.C.E., another social reform took place, this time under Urukagina.[7] Even though noble families saw Urukagina as a usurper, history views him as a great social reformer.[8] An accomplished politician and man of decision, Urukagina appealed to the values of his society at that time in order to legitimize his authority and to strengthen his power. As such, he appealed to Sumerian legal tradition and used a theological argument in his appeal to Ningirsu, protective god of Lagash. He substantiated his declarations with deeds promoting prosperity, order and peace.[9] In the same way, he showed religious and social sensitivity by giving primacy to his divine mission of legally protecting the oppressed and forsaken. Thus, referring to his reforms, Urukagina says of himself in his inscriptions:

> He [Urukagina] cleansed the domiciles of the habitants of Lagash of usury, hoarding, famine, robbery, and the aggressions and established [their] liberty *[ama-gi₄–bi e-gar]*. He made Ningirsu to seal the declaration that he [Urukagina] would not put the widow and the orphan in the hands of the rich. . . . [When Urukagina] received the royal dominion of Girsu, he established liberty [for the inhabitants of Lagash].[10]

Those inscriptions refer to a liberty that is probably an exemption granted from the payment of taxes and amnesty from debts. In his reform, Urukagina proposed reestablishing the order of Ningirsu, an order revealed by his Sumerian gods, by which society had to integrate itself into the harmony of the cosmos.

---

[7] *See* Boecker, *Law*, 53–54; M. Lambert, "Les 'reformes' d'Urukagina," *RA* 50 (1956): 169–84; Alexander Scharff and Anton Moortgat, *Ägypten und Vorderasien im Altertum* (Munich: F. Bruckmann, 1950), 241–45.

[8] Ferris J. Stephens, "Notes on Some Economic Texts of the Time of Urukagina," *RA* 49 (1955): 129–36.

[9] Some elements of Urukagina's reform are worth mentioning. He was, for instance, zealous in his efforts to preserve the traditional theocratic structure of Sumerian society, insisting that land was neither the property of the king, nor of the queen, but of the god of the city. In his effort to "establish freedom," Urukagina followed the example of Entemena. To that end, after assuming office, he freed the population from the oppressive taxes that had been previously imposed on them. He likewise reduced governmental fees, especially those exacted when marriages were solemnized, writs of divorce obtained, or funerals celebrated. He decreed that public officials should be satisfied with the remuneration they received, and he forbade them from demanding direct compensation from the citizenry. Moreover, he prohibited noblemen from confiscating the crops of the peasants and the catch of the fishermen. *See* Lambert, "Reformes," 169–84; Scharff and Moortgat, *Ägypten*, 241–45.

[10] Lambert, "Reformes," 183.

According to this revelation and in agreement with the myth of *Atrahasis*, humanity had been created to substitute for subordinate deities in the service of the divine world. They served by obeying the will of the gods in their private and civil lives,[11] and above all, by celebrating religious feast days and by performing rituals.[12] In the light of these objectives of creation, the primary obligation of the Sumerian governors was to create conditions of life that would facilitate the service of the community to the divine world. By keeping this service, society was integrating itself into the cosmic harmony and also was acquiring solidarity. In this context, the law's ultimate purpose was to make integration possible, and as the *ensi*, it was the king's duty to promulgate and execute the law. This was how the king executed the integration of society into universal harmony.[13] In this case universal harmony does not include the modern cosmic concept in which internal laws of nature rule over the unity and harmony of the whole. Here, the harmony imagined is that which is imposed over chaos by the will of the gods.

Urukagina's reform was brief; it lasted just seven years, and ended with his death. But his reforming reign was not simply a shooting star. It demonstrates, rather, the traditional tendency to create and reform legal structures so that citizens can easily fulfill their purpose in life, which was to serve the divine world. Urukagina's reform was fleeting, but it made a permanent contribution to the culture of the ancient Near East: it reinforced the tradition to give justice a legal base, so that all citizens might have a healthy and prosperous life.

A few centuries later, again in Lagash, towards the middle of the twenty-first century, another reformer ascended the throne—Gudea, "the shepherd elected by Ningirsu." An excerpt of Gudea's Cylinder B may be translated as follows:

> He [Gudea] removed (all) injustice in (their) households. He gave care to the laws of Nanshe and Ningirsu. To the orphan, the rich man could do no evil. To the widow, the powerful man could do no evil. In a household without male heir, the daughter came to be the heir. He [Gudea] made justice to shine [and thus] the Sun god (Utu) crushed iniquity.[14]

---

[11] It was a common conviction in ancient Mesopotamia, as Bottéro has noted: "Just as all social restrictions came forth from the royal will and received their obligatory strength and, if needed, their sanctions from it, all the imperatives of life, both communal and individual, received their value from the fact that they represented the explicit will of the gods." See Jean Bottéro, *Mesopotamia: Writing, Reasoning, and the Gods* (trans. Z. Bahrani and M. Van De Mierrop; Chicago: University of Chicago Press, 1992), 227.

[12] Important parts of the liturgical celebrations and rites celebrated in the temples included processions with the statues of the gods, various recitals of cosmogonic and anthropogonic myths, sacred marriages, sacrifices of animals and agricultural produce, libations and the daily offerings in order to feed the gods, and the careful and expensive care of the statues. In order to sustain this onerous cult it was necessary that the community be prosperous. The active participation of all the members of the community was required for the common good. See Bottéro, *Mesopotamia*, 225–26; Georges Contenau, *La civilisation d'Assur et de Babylone* (Paris: Payot, 1951), 90–123.

[13] See Franco Pintore, "La struttura giuridica," in *L'Alba della Civiltà* (3 vols.; ed. S. Moscati; Turin: UTET, 1976), 1:420.

[14] M. Lambert and R. Tournay, "Cilindre B de Gudéa," *RB* 55 (1948): 534.

Utu was the Sumerian sun god; Nanshe and Ningirsu were the protective divinities of Lagash. According to this text, chaos and darkness rule when the powerful exercise iniquity against the humble. By contrast, the sun of justice reigns when iniquity is crushed and when the order presided over by Utu and revealed by Nanshe and Ningirsu is reestablished. The sun of justice shines brightest when the orphan and the widow are protected and when relations between the powerful and humble remain fair.

3. The codes of Ur-Nammu, Lipit-Ishtar, and Eshnunna

The Sumerian king Ur-Nammu (2064–2046 B.C.E.), contemporary of Gudea and founder of the third dynasty of Ur, left us the oldest known legal code. In the royal inscriptions it is said of him that "by the firm judging of Utu, he [Ur-Nammu] has made the light advance and has established peace."[15]

The code of Ur-Nammu, originally written in the Sumerian language, is known to us only through fragments of a copy made at the time of Hammurabi (1728–1686 B.C.E.). To judge from the fragments we have today, the code consisted of a prologue that contained theological, ethical, and historical considerations and a body of at least twenty-two articles.[16] This code describes its purpose in the prologue: "The orphan was not delivered up to the rich man; the widow was not delivered up to the mighty man; the man of one shekel was not delivered up to the man of one *mina*."[17]

The code of Ur-Nammu was once considered the oldest legal document written in conditional form. In legal texts written in the conditional form, every article has a protasis and an apodosis; the protasis is introduced by the conditional particle *if* and describes a concrete situation either in the present or in the past. Although the situation envisioned in the protasis is concrete, its description takes typical and essential elements extracted from particular cases. It is a generalization of the particular. The apodosis that follows is put in the future tense and determines what must be the juridical consequences of such an action. The connection between the apodosis and the protasis is based on legal custom or on the explicit will of the authority.[18] An example is the following article: "If a man, in the course of a scuffle, smashed the limb of another man with a club, he will pay one *mina* of silver."[19]

---

[15] George A. Barton, *The Royal Inscriptions of Sumer and Akkad* (New Haven, Conn.: Yale University Press, 1929), 273.

[16] See "The Laws of Ur-Nammu," translated by J. J. Finkelstein (*ANET*, 523–25). For commentary, see Boecker, *Law*, 56–78.

[17] "The Laws of Ur-Nammu" (*ANET*, 524). A *mina* is equivalent to sixty shekels. The text contrasts the one who possesses sixty shekels to the one who possesses only a single shekel.

[18] Bottéro, *Mesopotamia*, 170–73.

[19] "The Laws of Ur-Nammu" (*ANET*, 524).

Since the translation of texts found at Ebla (Tell Mardikh, Syria) following its discovery in 1968, Ur-Nammu's code is no longer considered to be the oldest known legal text written in the conditional form. The archives of Elba, dated between the years 2400 and 2250 B.C.E., also present conditional formulations of legal norms.[20] In addition, as J. Bottéro has observed, the conditional style is not only found in juridical collections but also in the treaties of divination and medicine. It seems as though the conditional style was the way ancient Mesopotamians thought about such matters, and the way they expressed what they deduced from reality, or the steps they had to take to confront the situation. It has been said that conditional formulations were to ancient Mesopotamians what the syllogism was to the ancient Greeks. Ancient Mesopotamians gave primacy to the observation of concrete reality, and from this they would deduce analogous models of conduct and judgment.[21]

The articles from these codes do not really contain universal imperative rules for social conduct, imposed and sanctioned by the legitimate authority. Rather, they are solutions for concrete cases. These are not laws that emanate from the legislator but rather judgment sentences that presuppose a universal law. The ancient compiler has not constructed a code of laws; his work is, instead, an anthology of jurisprudence.[22] The attribution of a code to a specific king may suggest that the collection reflects the practice of jurisprudence during his reign, though the degree to which these "law codes" were used as a basis for actual jurisprudence is debated.[23] The collection offers a model of jurisprudence following the spirit of reform that the king had decided to establish.[24]

A few centuries after Ur-Nammu, another code appeared in the Sumerian language. It was promulgated by Lipit-Ishtar, who reigned in the Sumerian city of Isin between the years 1875 and 1865 B.C.E. This code presupposes a society in which the Akkadians have already assimilated themselves to the Sumerian civilization and are living with them. In the prologue, King Lipit-Ishtar calls himself a "wise and humble shepherd" and declares that his purpose is that the Akkadians and the Sumerians have a happy life:

---

[20] See Reuven Yaron, *The Laws of Eshnunna* (Jerusalem: Magnes and Leiden: Brill, 1988), 106–13.

[21] Bottéro, *Mesopotamia,* 35, 130–37, 158, 170–79.

[22] Bottéro, *Mesopotamia,* 161–69.

[23] Since these law collections were not comprehensive, the term "code" may be misleading. See Samuel Greengus, CANE, 471–72.

[24] The role of the king in the formulation and codification of Mesopotamian law is much debated. Some scholars are inclined to think that the law codes are collections of traditional norms. This is the position taken by Roland de Vaux, *Ancient Israel* (2 vols.; New York: McGraw-Hill, 1965), 1:145. Other scholars allow for more influence on the part of the king in the formulation of the laws. This influence would show in the modification and in the abrogation of traditional norms, as well as in the introduction of new norms. According to this opinion, the codes would then be the result of such a reformation. So Jacob. J. Finkelstein, "On Some Recent Studies in Cuneiform Law," *JAOS* 90 (1970): 243–53. Bottéro leans more toward the second opinion.

When Anu (and) Enlil had called Lipit-Ishtar . . . to the princeship of the land in order to establish justice *[níg-si-sá]* in the land, to banish complaints, to turn back enmity and rebellion by the force of arms, (and) to bring well-being to the Sumerians and Akkadians, then I, Lipit-Ishtar . . . [estab]lished [jus]tice *[níg-si-sá]* in [Su]mer and Akkad in accordance with the word of Enlil. Verily, in those [days] I procured . . . the [fre]edom *[ama-ar-gi₄]* of the [so]ns and daughters . . . of [Sum]er (and) Akkad *upon whom . . . slaveship . . . had been imposed.*[25]

The administrative action of Lipit-Ishtar is described with traditional Sumerian concepts: to do justice is to free the members of society from the burdens and bonds that prevent them from having a healthy and prosperous life in the service of the gods.

Lipit-Ishtar's code reflects a society that is controlled by an economy of private property and is composed of the enslaved and the free, and those who are free are divided between patricians and plebeians.[26] It is interesting to observe that the code balances two aspects of private property. On the one hand, it protects property from possible violators; but, on the other hand, the code also defines the responsibilities of the owners. According to the code of Lipit-Ishtar, any legitimate use of property must take into account its effect upon one's neighbors.[27]

Approximately one and a half centuries after Lipit-Ishtar, and a few years before Hammurabi (1728–1686 B.C.E.), the first code in the Akkadian language appeared, the code of Eshnunna. This code is very similar to those of Sumer. Like them, the code of Eshnunna does not offer a systematic and complete group of laws; rather, it contains a loose collection of precedents and ordinances.

The similarities among ancient Mesopotamian codes are many. These similarities appear because, in ancient Mesopotamia, as F. Pintore says, "there existed a patrimony of statements and solutions, permanent through time and space, tenacious but flexible, whose context was the oral tradition."[28] Justice was

---

[25] "Lipit-Ishtar Lawcode," translated by S. N. Kramer (*ANET*, 159).

[26] The Sumerian law codes make no reference to resident aliens, but it is certain that they did not enjoy the same rights as citizens. Aside from the prisoners of war, who were subjected to perpetual slavery, the Sumerians took a pragmatic attitude toward resident aliens. In spite of their inveterate prejudices against them, the Sumerians tolerated them because they needed them as mercenaries or because they facilitated trade relations. For such services the diplomats received them favorably. It is important to note, however, that in Sumer, aliens could absorb the language and the culture of the region and thus become citizens, a possibility that did not exist in ancient Egypt. See Henri Limet, "L'étranger dans la société sumérienne," in *Gesellschaftsklassen im Alten Zweistronland* (ed. D. O. Edzard; Munich: Verlag der bayerischen Akademie der Wissenschaften, 1972), 123–38.

[27] Boecker, *Law*, 58–59.

[28] Pintore, "Structura giuridica," 1:440. This patrimony of law and legal decisions is, according to E. A. Speiser, one of the major factors that contributed to the unification of the diverse Mesopotamian cultures, in spite of differences in language, distances in space and time, and political divisions. This unifying factor allows cultures as diverse as those of Sumer, Babylon, and Assyria to be considered part of the greater Mesopotamian civilization. See Ephraim A. Speiser, "Authority and Law in Mesopotamia," *JAOSSup* 17 (1954): 14.

transmitted from generation to generation and was assimilated by the peoples who integrated themselves into the life of Mesopotamian cities.

Both codes, that of Eshnunna and that of Hammurabi, assume a society divided into three classes: that of *awīlum* (patrician), that of *muškēnum* (plebeian), and that of *wardum* (slave). The *awīlum* enjoyed the fullness of liberty with all the rights that the city could give; the *muškēnum*, since he had originally been emancipated or a foreign slave, enjoyed some degree of liberty, but his rights were limited: he could not become a state employee.[29] The society that the code of Eshnunna reflects is essentially agricultural. But, in this society, an economy based on the notion of payment in kind is beginning to give way to an economy based on currency (silver). The code, on the one hand, establishes a relation between currency (silver) and merchandise (barley), which was traditionally used as a medium of exchange; on the other hand, it fixes maximum prices for the basic consumer goods, establishes low salaries, and freezes leasing and interest rates.[30] These measures, designed to respond to an economy of inflationary tendencies, manifest the governor's preoccupation with social well-being. This preoccupation tends to protect the less powerful and to relieve the poor.

4. The Code of Hammurabi

At the beginning of the third millennium, when the Akkadians began to settle themselves in cultivated land, they assimilated the Sumerian patrimony to their own concept of justice, bringing, as one might expect, the characteristics of their own traditions. In the same way later on, at the end of the third millennium, when the Amorite tribes infiltrated Mesopotamian cities, they assimilated, along with the culture, the Sumerian-Akkadian juridical patrimony. In the process of infiltration and assimilation, one of those Amorite tribes succeeded in establishing itself in Babylon. Hammurabi (1728–1686 B.C.E.) was a distinguished descendent of this tribe. Thanks to his unstoppable tenacity and his unique political sagacity, Hammurabi extended his dominion to other Mesopotamian cities and created an empire that would survive for more than a millennium until it lapsed into political decadence.

From the earliest years of his reign, Hammurabi was preoccupied with the issues of internal stability of his dominion and the reinforcement of his own power. From this preoccupation, his famous code developed.[31] One purpose Hammurabi had in this work, as H. J. Boecker says, was to give a uniform law to the

---

[29] See Sabatino Moscati, *Ancient Semitic Civilizations* (London: Elek Books, 1957), 70; Guillaume Cardascia, "Les droits cunéiformes," in *Histoire des institutions et des faits sociaux des origines à l'aube du Moyen Age* (eds. R. Monier et al.; Paris: Montchretien, 1956), 17–68.

[30] "The Laws of Eshnunna," translated by Albrecht Goetze (*ANET*, 161–63); Yaron, *Eshnunna*, 223–56; Boecker, *Law*, 59–64; Epzstein, *Social Justice*, 8.

[31] "The Code of Hammurabi," translated by Theophile J. Meek (*ANET*, 163–80). For text with annotations, see André Finet, *Le code de Hammurapi: introduction, traducion et annotation* (Paris: Cerf, 1983).

empire he had created through his political and military actions.[32] A group of specialized jurists must have worked on the code, and poets from the court probably composed the prologue and the epilogue. Toward the end of his reign, once he had finished the composing the code, Hammurabi, king of Sumer and Akkad, finally promulgated it for his empire.

We tend to talk of the Code of Hammurabi but, as in the case of the other Mesopotamian codes already mentioned, it is not strictly a code; it is, rather, jurisprudence, a collection of judicial sentences given for particular cases, founded on a universal law and inspired by the spirit of equity that had guided Hammurabi in his governing. The code is intended to be Hammurabi's legacy. As the epilogue of the codes ays: "[These are]t he laws of justice *[dīnāt mīšarim]*, which Hammurabi, the efficient king, set up, and by which he caused the land to take the right way and have good government."[33]

This code presents a new synthesis of the cultural juridical patrimony of Sumerian–Akkadian traditions. Hammurabi makes this synthesis by appropriating to himself the royal Sumerian title "shepherd and elected of Enlil" and by claiming to have been inspired, as the prologue to his code says, by his god Marduk,t he god of the state of Babylon,a s well as by Enlil,t he chief god of the Sumerian pantheon.[34] In addition to the political reasons for its composition, Hammurabi's code was motivated by social concerns. In the prologue, as well as in the epilogue, Hammurabi glorifies himself for having established justice in his empire. The epilogue, for example, says "In my bosom I carried the peoples of the land of Sumer and Akkad; they prospered under my protection . . . In order that thes trongm ight noto ppresst he weak, thatj ustice mightb ed ealt theo rphan (and) the widow."[35] He finishes by stating on the stone column into which his code was carved "I wrote my precious words on my stela . . . to give justice to the oppressed."[36] The protection of the weak is thus an important motive in the context of the code. Examples of such motives are articles referring to the small farmer, the salaries of manual workers and day laborers, and the fixing of interest rates. However, as N. Lohfink observes, the body of the code makes no reference to the widow or the orphan.[37]

The code reflects a monarchical political structure, because this supposedly represents the immutable divine cosmic order. In this structure, as in the code of Eshnunna, society was divided into the three social classes of the *awīlum* (patrician), *muškēnum* (plebeian), and *wardum* (slave). The *awīlum* could be a dependent of the monarch, occupying a position in the bureaucracy, the army, the clergy, or the administration of finance, justice, and commerce. He could also be

---

[32] Boecker,*L aw*, 73.
[33] "The Code of Hammurabi" (*ANET*, 177); Bottéro, *Mesopotamia*, 164.
[34] "The Code of Hammurabi" (*ANET*, 164).
[35] Ibid., 178.
[36] Ibid., 178.
[37] Norbert F. Lohfink, "Poverty in the Law of the Ancient Near East and of the Bible," *TS* 52 (1991): 43.

an independent professional, such as a doctor, architect, or craftsman. The *muškēnum* were an intermediate class between the patricians and the slaves, but closer to the former than to the latter so that there was no legal impediment preventing them from ascending to the category of the *awīlum*. But in fact, the *muškēnum* constituted a part of the population exploited by the nobility and the powerful. The *wardum* (slave) could have been originally a prisoner of war or a free person subjected to slavery because of insolvency. Debt-slaves only served for a limited period of time. Article 117 of this code states that a slave of this kind must be declared free after the fourth year of service.[38] All slaves could marry free citizens and have free children.[39]

The code offered protection to the weak, such as the *muškēnum*, defended the small farmer against the exploitation of the landowner, determined an equitable salary for craftsman and laborers of different kinds,[40] and fixed tolerable rates of interest as well.[41]

It is important to observe that in all these administrative measures, social class determines the way in which the person is treated: "If a seignior *[awīlum]* has destroyed the eye of a member of the aristocracy *[awīlum]*, they shall destroy his eye."[42] But, "if he has destroyed the eye of a commoner *[muškēnum]* . . . he shall pay one mina of silver" and "if he has destroyed the eye of a seignior's slave *[wardum]* . . . he shall pay one half his value."[43] This kind of justice implies that equity does not mean all persons have the same rights, but rather individuals enjoy rights appropriate to their own social level.

The efforts of Hammurabi to overcome abuses and establish justice can be seen in his official correspondence. Hammurabi's letters to Sin-Idinnam illuminate his efforts. Sin-Idinnam was a vassal-king who occupied positions of high authority during the reign of Hammurabi. Much of the correspondence that survives refers to the administration of justice. The king supervised not only the cases treated in Babylon but also the decisions in the courts in the other large cities within the empire. Additionally, this correspondence shows that it was possible for a private citizen to appeal directly to the king. Hammurabi considered cases of appeal with the effort proper to an impartial judge who had no tolerance for corruption on the part of state employees. In cases of perjury or extortion, Hammurabi instructed Sin-Idinnam to examine the cases and send the guilty parties to Babylon, where they would be duly punished. Thus, for instance, was the case of Ani-Ellati, a shrewd money-lender, who advanced a person named Lalum money for sowing and harvesting, and charged him usurious rates of interest that were more than the farmer could pay. Ani-Ellati's purpose was to gain control over the harvest of his debtor. In considering Lalum's appeal, Hammurabi

---

[38] "The Code of Hammurabi" (*ANET*, 170–71).
[39] Finet, *Le code*, 12.
[40] "The Code of Hammurabi" (*ANET*, 177, §§273–77).
[41] Ibid., 169–70, §§88–102.
[42] Ibid., 175, §196.
[43] Ibid., 175, §§198–99.

declared the contract null and void, ordered Ani-Ellati's to forfeit the money that he had advanced, and sentenced him to punishment.[44]

In the prologue of his code, Hammurabi sums up what he had wanted to accomplish during his regime with the phrase "to establish *kittum u mīšarum* in the land." It has been often repeated that *kittum* represents the epitome of cosmic and unchanging truth, a divine order, established in the world in which Shamash, the sun god, exercises his divine hegemony. The king is not the owner of this order but its administrator, and his authority is made legitimate by his being loyal to the norms revealed by the gods throughout the law. The function of the king is to apply the law equally. He achieves this through a process called *mīšarum*. This process requires that the king have an attentive supervision of the political, economic, and social situation within his kingdom. This supervision can require that a situation be adjusted or corrected; it can also require that traditional norms be adapted to new necessities.[45]

H. Cazelles has persuasively argued that this conception of the bipartite phrase, *kittum u mīšarum*, makes, for the most part, a reference to Babylonian royal ideology. According to this ideology, kingship descended from the heavens after the great flood (of the myth of Atrahasis) as a gift from the gods. The purpose of this divine gift was to help human beings fulfill the task that had been imposed on them at creation, a task to act as substitutes for the subordinate deities in serving the divine world. To make this task possible, the king is supposed to bring about those conditions in which the subjects could have a healthy, prosperous, and long life. This is not a speculative theory that safeguards some sort of established cosmic order but a practical activity, insofar as it makes it possible for human beings to prosper in peace and harmony and to have a happy life. In developing this practical activity, the king integrates society into the cosmic order.[46]

To develop this activity and fulfill his commitment, the king received the gift of being strong and faithful, as well as the ability to create strength and fidelity. *Kittum* was the technical term for signifying the justice expressed by the king who had this gift and ability.[47] In addition, the king received the capacity to create the conditions that make the community's prosperity and progress possible, a capacity to place the life of the community in the direction of prosperity and harmony. The object of this capacity was expressed by the term *mīšarum*.[48] The king

---

[44] Leonard W. King, *The Letters and Inscriptions of Hammurabi* (3 vols.; London: Luzac, 1898–1900), 3:23–25.

[45] Speiser, "Authority," 12–13.

[46] Henri Cazelles, "De l'idéologie royale," in *Gaster Festschrift* (ed. D. Marcus; JANESCU 5; New York: ANE Society, 1974), 61–62, 73.

[47] *Kittum*, as Cazelles has observed ("Idéologie," 61), derives from *kânu*, a term that "evokes firmness, solidity and duration." So too Bottéro, *Mesopotamia*, 182–83.

[48] The word *mīšarum* derives from *ešērum*, which signifies "to walk rightly" or "to be in harmony." It refers to the order by which each thing occupies its own place according to its nature and function. According to this concept, "equity" would be a good translation of *mīšarum*. As an extension of its basic meaning, *mīšarum*, as related to *ešērum*, could indicate an action of reestablishing harmony, as in the decrees of mercy. See Bottéro, *Mesopotamia*, 182–83.

was legitimate or just *(šar mīšarim)* insofar as he put his abilities into practice to permit the community to enjoy the benefits of *kittum u mīšarum*.⁴⁹ The special responsibility of royal power was to attend to and protect the disadvantaged, who were the poor, the orphans, and the widows. The bipartite phrase *kittum u mīšarum* was extended from the Babylonian royal ideology to the Syrio-Palestinian region, where it took the west Semitic form of *ṣdk-m(y)šr* and in biblical Hebrew became *mišpāṭ-ṣedeq* ("law" and "justice").⁵⁰

Hammurabi glorifies himself for having provided for his citizens a life of prosperity, harmony, and equity or, as he himself says, for "having established *kittum u mīšarum*" in his reign. His work outlasted his reign. It was inscribed in his code, a monument of jurisprudence that circulated in Babylon and other countries for as long as ten centuries after the fall of his dynasty. So, for instance, there are numerous copies of the Code of Hammurabi in the library of Assurbanipal (668–627 B.C.E.). As G. Cardascia has noted, the widespread dispersal of the code cannot be explained solely from literary and linguistic motives. There must have been practical legal interest.⁵¹

5. Proclamations of mercy

There is an aspect of Hammurabi's code that deserves special attention. This code, like Eshnunna's code, opposes the practice of charging exorbitant rates of interest, which was a difficult practice to eradicate. This difficulty, among others, moved the kings periodically to promulgate decrees that annulled debts or obligations that had become otherwise impossible to pay.⁵² These periodic proclamations are sometimes referred to as "decrees of mercy" or "proclamations of remission," or even "edicts of grace." No one single word in English captures the full range of meaning of the Akkadian *mīšarum*. Hence, H. Petschow has observed that in the chronicles, legal writings, letters, and royal inscriptions of ancient Mesopotamia, there are reference in places like Isin, Babylon, Larsa, Eshnunna, or Hana, to the king's having "created justice in the land" and "destroyed the sealed documents and the tablets of debts."⁵³ The word "justice" in the phrase "he created justice in the land" is a translation of the Akkadian term *mīšarum*. The expression "he created justice," in connection with the action of the king who had destroyed the tablets of debts, signifies

---

⁴⁹ Cazelles, "Idéologie," 60–68.

⁵⁰ Ibid., 60–73.

⁵¹ Guillaume Cardascia, "La transmission des sources cunéiformes," *RIDA* 7 (1960): 31–50.

⁵² Jean Bottéro, "Désordre économique et annulation des dettes en Mésopotamie à l'époque paléo-babylonienne," *JESHO* 4 (1961): 113–64; Fritz R. Kraus, *Ein Edikt des König Ammi-saduqa von Babylon* (Leiden: Brill, 1958), 17–43; Kraus, "Ein Edikt des Königs Samsu-iluna von Babylon," in *Studies in Honor of Beno Landsberger* (AS 16; Chicago: Chicago University Press, 1965), 225–31.

⁵³ H. Petschow, "Gesetze," *RlA* 3:269–70.

without doubt a real act of justice. This favor included the remission of debts or other obligations, the return of property to the original owner, and liberation from debt slavery.

The significance of liberating justice given to the word *mīšarum* had its antecedents in the Sumerian tradition in which the equality that the king restored by decree was called *níg-si-sá* ("justice"). This can be seen in the code of Lipit-Ishtar. Parallel to *mīšarum* is another ancient technical term, *andurārum* ("liberty, liberation"), which was applied especially to the emancipation of slaves. This term had its antecedent in the Sumerian *ama-ar-gi₄*, as can be seen in the texts of the reform of Urukagina.[54]

It was the king's duty to promulgate decrees of mercy. The rationale for the exercise of liberating justice was founded on the notion that royal power, in accordance with Mesopotamian royal ideology, was a divine gift to human beings to help them with the work that had been entrusted to them when they were created as substitutes for inferior divinities.[55] It was essential that everyone could participate actively in this labor, according to his or her social status. The exercise of liberating justice was considered so important that Mesopotamian kings, following Hammurabi's example, gave themselves the title of *šar mīšarim* ("king of justice") or they called themselves "lover of justice" *(rā'im mīšari)*; in these phrases, justice included an action of support for the weak and of liberation for the oppressed.[56]

Antecedents of social proclamations of mercy appear very early in ancient Mesopotamia.[57] Urukagina, the last king of Lagash from the first dynasty of Ur (mid-twenty-fourth century B.C.E.) was known for having canceled unpaid taxes and interest. One of his predecessors, Entemena, glorified himself for having restored liberty to citizens and canceling tax debts. Lipit-Ishtar of Isin (1875–1865 B.C.E.), in the prologue of his code, alludes to decrees that he had issued both to liberate the habitants of Nippur, Ur, and Isin and to create justice in Sumer and Akkad. Scholars of the period have good reason for thinking that besides Lipit-Ishtar's code, the codes of Ur-Nammu, Eshnunna, and Hammurabi incorporated into their texts clauses from the edicts of *mīšarum* that earlier kings had promulgated.

Hammurabi introduced the practice of promulgating at the beginning of one's reign a declaration of justice or liberation *(mīšarum)*. He issued an edict that was to be repeated at the will of the king, without the existence of any law by

---

[54] With respect to the relationship between *andurārum* and *mīšarum*, R. Westbrook specifies that while the first term designates a specific act of liberation or amnesty, the second term refers to a general decree in which a king includes various liberating acts referring to groups or classes of people, rather than individuals. See Raymond Westbrook, *Property and the Family in Biblical Law* (JSOTSup 113; Sheffield: JSOT Press, 1991), 45.

[55] Cazelles, "Idéologie," 62; Speiser, "Authority," 8–15.

[56] See Lemche, "*Andurārum*," 11–22. Lemche cites important texts, one of which reads: "[He] who is the guardian of justice, the lover of justice, he who gives comfort, he who comes to comfort the invalid" (15).

[57] Lemche, "*Andurārum*," 13–17.

which to determine how often such decrees should be promulgated.[58] The only substantially complete text of this kind of edict is that of Ammi-Saduqa (1582–1562 B.C.E.), who was the tenth successor of Hammurabi to the throne of Babylon.[59] In this edict, Ammi-Saduqa canceled debts that the Akkadians and Amorites had had with the state and declared free those who had been made slaves by their creditors. When the text talks particularly of the emancipation of slaves, it uses the term *andurārum*, and when it includes the diverse measures of mercy shown by the king, it uses the word *mīšarum*.[60] Hence, the word *mīšarum* recurs frequently in the refrain: "Because the king has established liberating justice *[mīšarum]* in the country."

A similar edict preserved, albeit in fragmentary form, was first promulgated by Samsu-Iluna (1685–1648 B.C.E.), Ammi-Saduqa's great grandfather.[61] With this edict, the king established liberty for Sumer and Akkad. In this decree, the terms *mīšarum* and *andurārum* are found with a similar content to that of the edict of Ammi-Saduqa.

Liberation edicts continued to be promulgated in Babylon even after the city fell under Kassite rule. Thus, the Kassite king, Kurigalzu II (ca.1345–1324 B.C.E.), glorifies himself for having issued an edict of liberating justice for the Babylonians. The promulgation of these social edicts also occurs in the time of the Assyrian empire. Sargon II (721–705 B.C.E.) and Esarhaddon (680–669 B.C.E.) mention having made such decrees for parts of their empires.[62] A reference that may be purely literary is found in the Neo-Babylonian period, during Neriglissar's reign (559–555 B.C.E.), one of whose inscriptions says: "I permanently established *mīšarum* for the country (and) I let graze permanently in peace my far-extended people."[63]

---

[58] See Kraus, "Samsu-iluna," 225–31. For a study of the periodic practice of debt-forgiveness and manumission, see Westbrook, *Property*, 44–52; Jeffries M. Hamilton, *Social Justice and Deuteronomy: The Case of Deuteronomy 15* (SBLDS 136; Atlanta: Scholars Press, 1992), 48–72; Yairah Amit, "The Jubilee Law: An Attempt at Instituting Social Justice," in *Justice and Righteousness: Biblical Themes and their Influence* (ed. H. G. Reventlow and Y. Hoffman; JSOTSup 137; Sheffield: JSOT Press, 1992), 47–59.

[59] "The Edict of Ammisaduqa," translated by J. J. Finkelstein (*ANET*, 526).

[60] Kraus, *Ammi-saduqa*, 17–43.

[61] Kraus, "Samsu-iluna," 225–31.

[62] See Lemche, "Andurārum," 20–21.

[63] See Lemche, "Andurārum," 14. The words *mêšārîm* or *mîšôr* and *děrôr* found in the Hebrew Bible are cognate to the Mesopotamian terms *mīšarum* and *andurārum*. The words *mêšārîm* or *mîšôr* occur, e.g., in Pss 96:10; 98:9; 99:4; Isa 11:4, while the word *děrôr* is found in Lev 25:10; Jer 34:8; Isa 61:1; Ezek 46:17. It is worth noting that in the Hebrew Bible *děrôr* is used in connection with the Jubilee year but not with the sabbatical year. For the sabbatical year the Bible uses the term *šěmiṭṭâ* (Deut 15:2, 9; 31:10). Since the Hebrew *děrôr* is cognate to the Akkadian *andurārum* or *durāru*, it has been suggested that the biblical Jubilee should be correlated to the Mesopotamian proclamations of mercy. The difficulty with this opinion lies in the fact that the Hebrew *děrôr*, although part of the description of the Jubilee year *(yôbēl)*, is never used as a technical term to designate a general and periodic remission of obligations. See de Vaux, *Ancient Israel*, 1:173–77; Niels P. Lemche, "The Manumission of Slaves—the Fallow Year—the Sabbatical Year—the Jobel

The practice of starting a new regime with an edict liberating debts, besides having a probable social and political motivation, also had a theological motivation. At the beginning of a king's reign, the monarch actualizes the primitive myth of creation, establishing order in a world imprisoned by chaos with an edict of liberation. But perhaps the social and political motivations were more relevant because it was important for the new king to ingratiate himself to the people and to secure the support of the masses. For this there was nothing better than to clear the debts owed to his predecessor and to restore the lost rights of the citizens. With this the king could boast of "having established equity *[mīšarum]* in the land."[64]

6. Texts of faith in the protective divinities of justice

In the ancient Mesopotamian world, the concept of social justice and the aspiration for equity in society are found not only in legal texts but also in religious texts. These religious texts show that, in spite of the declarations made by the governors in favor of justice, there were people who found that justice was hard to obtain. These people would find in their religious faith refuge and support. In the following selections, we will see hymns and prayers that reflect an absence of trust in governors and a need to appeal to divinity.

One Sumerian hymn that survived was dedicated to Utu, the solar god and god of justice, who presides over the order of the universe. His Semitic counterpart was Shamash.

> Utu, you are the god of justice,
> Utu, (you are) the shepherd, the father of the "dark headed" (people).
> Utu, (you are) the principal judge of the land (of Sumer).
> Utu, to give judgment is in your power (right).
> Utu, to give decisions is in your power (right).
> Utu, justice is in your power (right).
> Utu, to lead in truthfulness and justice is in your power.
> . . . .
> Utu, the destitute girl, the forsaken woman (?) are in your power (care).
> Utu, to provide justice to the widow is in your power.
> Utu, if you do not come out (var., without you), no judgment is given, no decision is decided.[65]

In hymns such as this one, humble Sumerians, frustrated or uncertain of the efficacy of the authorities, appealed to the divine world as the primary source of order and justice. For them Utu was the primary divine representative of justice.

Year," *VT* 26 (1976): 38–59. On the Jubilee year, see Christopher J. H. Wright, "Jubilee, Year of," *ABD* 3:1025–30. See also the analysis of the Jubilee year below, ch. 4, §5.3.

[64] Bottéro, "Désordre," 159.

[65] Giorgio R. Castellino, "Incantation to Utu," *OrAnt* 8 (1969): 1–57, especially 9.

But the Sumerians also had a feminine representative of justice with outstanding maternal attributes in the goddess Nanshe. A Sumerian hymn acclaims the goddess Nanshe of Lagash as the mother of the orphan, the support of the widow, and the defender of the poor and the weak. According to S. N. Kramer, this hymn "includes some of the more explicit moral and ethical affirmations ever found in Sumerian documents."[66] The text describes Nanshe in the following terms:

> Who knows the orphan, who knows the widow
> Knows the oppression of man over man, the orphan's mother,
> Nanshe, who cares for the widow,
> Who seeks out (?) justice (?) for the poorest (?).
> The queen brings the refugee to her lap,
> Finds shelter for the weak ...
> To comfort the orphan, to make disappear the widow,
> To set up a place of destruction for the mighty,
> To turn over (?) the mighty to the weak, ... ,
> Nanshe searches the heart of the people.[67]

The Sumerians had a king from the third dynasty of Ur, who was deified as the prototype of the wise and just king. His name was Shulgi of Ur. The humble appealed to him in their sufferings. In his hymn the supplicant asks the divine Shulgi:

> Wise ruler, hero, come!
> Give rest unto the land!
> A faithful hero, a sun-god, who art just ...
> Who brings favor to man?
> Who brings justice?
> Who is like thee
> By whom the broad weapon is carried?[68]

A Babylonian hymn to Ishtar from the middle of the second millennium acclaims the attributes of the goddess: she is not only the patron of fertility and war; she is also the goddess of justice who protects the poor and oppressed. A passage of the hymn says:

> You are the one who pronounces judgments over your subjects with right and justice.
> You look at the oppressed and afflicted; you restore him every day.
> (Grant me) your grace, Queen of heaven and earth, Shepherd of the multitudes.[69]

---

[66] Samuel N. Kramer, "Sumerian Theology and Ethics," *HTR* 49 (1956): 58.

[67] Kramer, "Sumerian Theology," 58; see also Kramer, "'Vox populi' and the Sumerian Literary Documents," *RA* 58 (1964): 148–56.

[68] George A. Barton, *Miscellaneous Babylonian Inscriptions* (New Haven: Yale University Press, 1918), 27–28. Barton calls Shulgi, the second king of the third dynasty of Ur, by the name of Dungi, because this is how Sumerologists of the first half of this century read Shulgi's name. See, in this respect, Thorkild Jacobsen, "New Sumerian Literary Text," *BASOR* 102 (1947): 16.

[69] Marie-Joseph Seux, *Hymnes et prières aux dieux de Babylone et d'Assyrie: introduction, traduction et notes* (Paris: Cerf, 1976), 189. See also, 383–85.

From the Assyrian-Babylonian period, there is a hymn to Shamash, the Semitic sun god who was equivalent to the Sumerian god Utu. The hymn praises him for his beneficent action on the earth and in the underworld. The praise alternates with proclamation expressing the interest that the solar god has in justice and righteousness. The hymn contains phrases such as the following:

> Thou dost hold back the evildoer . . . by the true judgment, O Shamash, which thou hast spoken . . .
> The horn of the perpetrator of abominations thou dost destroy . . .
> The unrighteous judge thou dost make to see imprisonment
> The receiver of a bribe who perverts (justice), thou dost make to bear punishment . . .
>
> In his hollow voice the feeble man calls out to thee;
> The miserable, the weak, the mistreated, the poor man comes before thee faithfully with psalms (and) offerings.[70]

In the Babylonian epoch, Marduk, chief of the Babylonian pantheon since the eighteenth century, god of light, and conqueror of the monster of chaos in the Mesopotamian epic poem of creation, conquered the trust of the poor and forsaken. Marduk unites in himself the attributes that create hope in chaotic times, when those who suffer most are the poor: he was the supreme representative of justice and possessed the invincible power of the cosmogonic hero. A prayer of Marduk says:

> You, like Shamash, illuminate their darkness.
> Each day, you do justice to the oppressed and afflicted.
> You reestablish the disinherited, the widow, the one who moans and the one who cannot sleep.
> . . . .
> My lord, come near me today, and hear my prayer,
> Give a sentence for me, and pronounce a decision for me.[71]

Conclusion

It is worth noting that, in spite of changes in demography, in language, and in religion, a basic concept of justice with a strong liberating dimension developed over the centuries in Mesopotamia. In the social reforms, in the legal codes, and in the decrees of mercy, the mission of the king was to remove injustice from his territory and to liberate the oppressed and the forsaken so that they might render service to the gods. But, the reiteration of reforms, the promulgation of new codes, and the periodic announcement of decrees of mercy demonstrate how difficult it was to eliminate exploitation and oppression and to establish justice and equity. In addition, the texts of popular piety show how elusive justice was

---

[70] "Hymn to the Sun-God," translated by Ferris J. Stephens (*ANET*, 387–89).
[71] Seux, *Hymnes*, 445, 447.

and how almost inaccessible it was to the humble class. In spite of the difficulties, the Mesopotamian tradition kept the king's obligations alive with respect to justice: he was obliged to control the excesses of the state and the power of the oppressor and to reestablish violated rights; he was obliged to free his people from unsupportable and counterproductive obligations and burdens; he was obliged to protect those who, like the orphans and the widows, were forsaken for various reasons and who lacked the capacity to sustain themselves in society.

Bibliography

Amit, Yairah. "The Jubilee Law: An Attempt at Instituting Social Justice." Pages 47–59 in *Justice and Righteousness: Biblical Themes and their Influence*. Edited by H. G. Reventlow and Y. Hoffman. Journal for the Study of the Old Testament: Supplement Series 137. Sheffield: JSOT Press, 1992.

Barton, George A. *Miscellaneous Babylonian Inscriptions*. New Haven, Conn.: Yale University Press, 1918.

———. *The Royal Inscriptions of Sumer and Akkad*. New Haven, Conn.: Yale University Press, 1929.

Boecker, Hans J. *Law and the Administration of Justice in the Old Testament and Ancient East*. Translated by J. Moiser. Minneapolis: Augsburg, 1980.

Bottéro, Jean. "Désordre économique et annulation des dettes en Mésopotamie à l'époque paléo-babylonienne." *Journal of the Economic and Social History of the Orient* 4 (1961): 113–64.

———. *Mesopotamia: Writing, Reasoning, and the Gods*. Translated by Zainab Bahrani and Marc Van De Mierrop. Chicago: University of Chicago Press, 1992.

Cardascia, Guillaume. "Les droits cunéiformes." Pages 17–68 in *Histoire des institutions et des faits sociaux des origines à l'aube du Moyen Age*. Edited by R. Monier et al. Paris: Montchrestien, 1956.

———. "La transmission des sources cunéiformes." *Revue internationale des droits de l'antiquité* 7 (1960): 31–50.

Castellino, Giorgio R. "Incantation to Utu." *Oriens Antiquus* 8 (1969): 1–57.

Cazelles, Henri. "De l'idéologie royale." Pages 59–73 in *Gaster Festschrift*. Edited by D. Marcus. Journal of the Ancient Near Eastern Society of Columbia University 5. New York: ANE Society, 1974.

Contenau, Georges. *La civilisation d'Assur et de Babylone*. Paris: Payot, 1951.

Epzstein, Léon. *Social Justice in the Ancient Near East and the People of the Bible*. Translated from French. London: SCM, 1986.

Finet, André. *Le code de Hammurapi: introduction, traduction et annotation*. Paris: Cerf, 1983.

Finkelstein, Jacob J. "On Some Recent Studies in Cuneiform Law." *Journal of the American Oriental Society* 90 (1970): 243–53.

Greengus, Samuel. "Legal and Social Institutions of Ancient Mesopotamia." In *Civilizations of the Ancient Near East*. Edited by Jack M. Sasson; 4 vols.; New York: Scribners, 1995, 469–84; 2 vol. ed. Peabody, Mass.: Hendrickson, 2000.

Hamilton, Jeffries M. *Social Justice and Deuteronomy: The Case of Deuteronomy 15*. Society of Biblical Literature Dissertation Series 136. Atlanta: Scholars Press, 1992.
Jacobsen, Thorkild. "New Sumerian Literary Text." *Bulletin of the American Schools of Oriental Research* 102 (1947): 12–17.
King, Leonard W. *The Letters and Inscriptions of Hammurabi*. 3 vols. London: Luzac, 1898–1900.
Kramer, Samuel N. "Sumerian Theology and Ethics." *Harvard Theological Review* 49 (1956): 45–64.
———. "'Vox populi' and the Sumerian Literary Documents." *Revue d'assyriologie et d'archéologie orientale* 58 (1964): 148–56.
Kraus, Fritz R. *Ein Edikt des König Ammi-saduqa von Babylon*. Leiden: Brill, 1958.
———. "Ein Edikt des König Samsu-iluna von Babylon." Pages 225–31 in *Studies in Honor of Benno Landsberger*. Assyriological Studies 16. Chicago: Chicago University Press, 1965.
Lambert, M. "L'expansion de Lagash au temps d'Enténéna." *Rivista degli studi orientali* 47 (1972): 1–22.
———. "Les 'reformes' d'Urukagina." *Revue d'assyriologie et d'archéologie orientale* 50 (1956): 169–84.
——— and R. Tournay. "Cilindre B de Gudéa." *Revue Biblique* 55 (1948): 520–43.
Lemche, Niels P. "*Andurārum* and *Mīšarum*: Comments on the Problem of Social Edicts and their Application in the Ancient Near East." *Journal of Near Eastern Studies* 38 (1979): 11–22.
———. "The Manumission of Slaves—the Fallow Year—the Sabbatical Year—the Jobel Year." *Vetus Testamentum* 26 (1976): 38–59.
Limet, Henri. "L'étranger dans la société sumérienne." Pages 123–38 in *Gesellschaftsklassen im Alten Zweistronland*. Edited by D. O. Edzard. Munich: Verlag der bayerischen Akademie der Wissenschaften, 1972.
Lohfink, Norbert F. "Poverty in the Law of the Ancient Near East and of the Bible." *Theological Studies* 52 (1991): 34–50.
Moscati, Sabatino. *Ancient Semitic Civilizations*. London: Elek Books, 1957.
Petschow, H. "Gesetze." *Reallexikon der Assyriologie* 3 (1971): 269–70.
Pintore, Franco. "La struttura giuridica." Pages 417–505 in vol. 1 of *L'Alba della Civiltà*. Edited by S. Moscati. 3 vols. Turin: UTET, 1976.
Pritchard, James B., ed. *Ancient Near Eastern Texts Relating to the Old Testament*. 3d ed. Princeton: Princeton University Press, 1969.
Saggs, H. W. F. *The Greatness That Was Babylon*. New York: Hawthorn, 1962; 2d ed., London: Sidgwick & Jackson, 1988.
Scharff, Alexander, and Anton Moortgat. *Ägypten und Vorderasien im Altertum*. Munich: F. Bruckmann, 1950.
Seux, Marie-Joseph. *Hymnes et prières aux dieux de Babylonie et d'Assyrie: introduction, traduction et notes*. Paris: Cerf, 1976.
Speiser, Ephraim A. "Authority and Law in Mesopotamia." *Supplement to the Journal of the American Oriental Society* 17 (1954): 8–15.

Stephens, Ferris J. "Notes on Some Economic Texts of the Time of Urukagina." *Revue d'assyriologie et d'archéologie orientale* 49 (1955): 129–36.
Vaux, Roland de. *Ancient Israel.* 2 vols. New York: McGraw-Hill, 1965.
Westbrook, Raymond. *Property and the Family in Biblical Law.* Journal for the Study of the Old Testament: Supplement Series 113. Sheffield: JSOT Press, 1991.
Wright, Christopher J. H. "Jubilee, Year of." Pages 102–30 in vol. 3 of *Anchor Bible Dictionary.* Edited by D. N. Freedman. 6 vols. New York: Doubleday, 1992.
Yaron, Reuven. *The Laws of Eshnunna.* Jerusalem: Magnes; Leiden: Brill, 1988.

CHAPTER TWO

JUSTICE IN ANCIENT EGYPT

Introduction

Egyptian culture is important for the study of biblical justice because the wisdom of Egypt influenced the thinking of ancient Israel. In addition, the ancient Israelite concept of order, as well as the preoccupation with the poor and the oppressed, are analogous to what we find in Egypt from the earliest dynasties.

Until now, archeologists have not been fortunate enough to find ancient law codes in Egypt like those found in Mesopotamia. The legal texts from Egypt are few and fragmentary. Moreover, they belong to different epochs and different places, and they refer to particular cases and use imprecise legal language. The oldest extant Egyptian code is the work of Boccharis, who reigned around 715 B.C.E.[1] The second oldest one discovered is the code of Hermopolis, which probably dates from the third century B.C.E.[2] Despite the paucity of early legal texts, we can be certain, as A. Théodoriés says, that "a legal system existed in Egypt since the beginning of Pharaonic dynasties."[3]

The purpose of this chapter is to inspect important judicial texts dating from the Old to the New Kingdoms.[4] It does not pretend to study the structure of

---

[1] The existence of the Code of Boccharis is not directly known to us from Egyptian documentation, but Diodorus Siculus, an author of the first century B.C.E., makes mention of it. See Henri Cazelles, *Etudes sur le code de l'alliance* (Paris: Letouzey et Ané, 1946), 164.

[2] The text of the code of Hermopolis has been published by G. Mattha and G. R. Hugues, *The Demotic Legal Code of Hermopolis West* (Cairo: Institut français d'archéologie orientale du Cairo, 1975).

[3] Aristide Théodoridès, "A propos de la loi dans l'Egypte pharaonique," *RIDA* 14 (1967): 107–52, esp. 109; ET: Théodoridès, "The Concept of Law in Ancient Egypt," in *The Legacy of Egypt* (ed. J. R. Harris; Oxford: Oxford University Press, 1971), 291–322. See also Frank C. Fensham, "Widow, Orphan, and the Poor in Ancient Near Eastern Legal and Wisdom Literature," *JNES* 21 (1962): 132–34.

[4] In this chapter, I follow the chronology proposed by John Baines, "Dynastic Chronology," in *Religion in Ancient Egypt: Gods, Myths, and Personal Practice* (ed. B. E. Shafer; Ithaca, N.Y.: Cornell University Press, 1991), 201–3. See also R. Krauss, *Sothis- und Monddaten: Studien zur astronomischen und technischen Chronologie Altägyptens* (Hildesheimer ägyptologische Beiträge 20; Hildesheim: Gerstenberg, 1985).

judicial power and the exercise of general justice. It confines itself to the analysis of one aspect of justice, namely, the problem of the poor and the oppressed, as well as the governor's action toward them.

1. Justice in the Old Kingdom (2700–2130 B.C.E.)

Since the beginning of the Old Kingdom, it was believed in Egypt that the pharaoh possessed the power of *maat* (Egyptian *m3ʿt*).[5] *Maat* was the *ka* (moving and animating energy) of the pharaoh. This power found its personification in the goddess Maat, protector of stability, truth, order, and justice. The term *maat* is difficult to translate, because it includes many concepts whose extent is as broad as the range of protection that the goddess Maat offered. It is usually translated as "truth-justice." Originally, *maat* designated the concept of order, the order deriving from the foundation of the world and human society. This order included the indispensable harmony of maintaining the structure and the form of the universe and society. L. Ramlot compares the central position of *maat* in Egyptian civilization with the importance of the *logos* in Greek thought.[6] It must be kept in mind, however, that *maat* was not only truth and knowledge. The observation of M. Lichtheim is pertinent here: "Autobiographic texts in the tombs declare that *maat* is 'the good'; and 'to do *maat*' consists in doing deeds of honesty, justice, and benevolence."[7] L. Epzstein has observed that *maat* in the pharaoh had an ethical dimension, since he had to act according to his obligation to maintain and renovate the universal order.[8] *Maat* is comparable to the wisdom (*ḥokmâ*) of the Hebrew Bible. There is no doubt that Egyptian wisdom has exercised some influence over the Bible and that personified Wisdom in the Bible reflects certain attributes of *maat*.[9] But per-

---

[5] On *maat*, see Jan Assmann, *Maât: L'Egypte pharaonique et l'idée de justice sociale* (Paris: Julliard, 1989); Henri Cazelles, *Autour de l'Exode: Etudes* (Sources bibliques; Paris: Gabalda, 1987), 372–74; Léon Epzstein, *Social Justice in the Ancient Near East and the People of the Bible* (London: SCM Press, 1986), 18–20; I. Shirun-Grumach, "Remarks on the Goddess Maat," in *Pharaonic Egypt, the Bible and Christianity* (ed. Sara Israelit-Groll; Jerusalem: Magnes Press, 1985), 173–201; W. Helck, "Maat," *LÄ* 3: 1110–19; Siegfried Morenz, *Egyptian Religion* (Ithaca, N.Y.: Cornell University Press, 1973), 110–38; Hans H. Schmid, *Gerechtigkeit als Weltordnung: Hintergrund und Geschichte des alttestamentlichen Gerechtigkeitsbegriffes* (BHT 40; Tübingen: J. C. B. Mohr, 1968), 46–61; A. Moret, "La Doctrine de Maât," *REg* 4 (1940): 1–14.

[6] Léon Ramlot, "Prophétisme," *DBSup* 8 (1972): 822.

[7] Miriam Lichtheim, *Maat in Egyptian Autobiographies and Related Studies* (OBO 120; Freiburg, Schweiz: Universitätsverlag; Göttingen: Vandenhoeck & Ruprecht, 1992), 18, 145–53.

[8] Epzstein, *Social Justice,* 18.

[9] One demonstration of the influence that Egyptian wisdom had on biblical literature may be found in the similarities between Prov 22:17–24:22 and the Instruction of Amen-em-Opet. See Nili Shupak, "The 'Sitz im Leben' of the Book of Proverbs in the Light of a Comparison of Biblical and Egyptian Wisdom Literature," *RB* 94 (1987): 98–119; James L. Crenshaw, "Proverbs, Book of," *ABD* 5:516.

sonified Wisdom in the Bible has been transformed in the religious traditions of Israel. Hebrew *ḥokmâ* is not a goddess like Egyptian Maat. In the Hebrew Bible it is at most a personified divine attribute that, when directed to humans, takes on the modalities of one holding the prophetic office who issues threats and promises.[10]

The pharaoh participated in *maat* on earth because he was a god, the incarnation of Horus. Because of his divine birth, the pharaoh was called to establish and promote the order fixed in the universe since creation; he was to create in his kingdom the same harmony that the sun produced in nature's daily and seasonal rhythm. H. Cazelles states that *maat* was the foundation of the pharaoh's throne in Egypt in the way that *ṣedeq* was the foundation of the throne of Yahweh (Ps 89:14), as well as the foundation of the throne of the king of ancient Israel (Prov 16:12).[11]

This comparison of *ṣedeq* and the Israelite king helps us to clarify the relationship between *maat* and the pharaoh. In contradistinction to the Israelite king, who was invested with the power of justice at the time of his enthronement, the pharaoh possessed *maat* from the time of his birth because he was a god by nature—a god on earth conceived by a god in heaven. But, although the pharaoh possessed *maat* from the time of his birth, the pharaonic prince began the exercise of his power on the day of his enthronement. According to the texts of the royal coronation, on this day the country of Egypt experienced the restoration of *maat* by the effective coming to earth of the pharaoh god—in itself eternal but now rejuvenated—in the person of the new monarch. This restoration was like the renovation of the primeval act of creation, by which order had once been established in the world.[12] The pharaoh was a god in person, from whose mouth the law came forth, a law that renewed itself by the coming of the new king. Because of this, Egypt thought herself blessed.

The pharaoh's responsibility to produce order and prosperity for his subjects was not based on their rights or in the representative power they had given him. All power came directly from the gods; the citizens were just ordinary mortals. There is no doubt that it was important for the king to secure the support of his subjects. Nevertheless, what was more important in the conscience of the king was his responsibility to practice *maat* as an offering to the gods.[13] This practice assured the king divine protection over his realm and the privilege of eternal life. However, to maintain his eternal life, he needed the support of his subjects, since eternal life for the pharaoh involved their perpetual maintenance of his tomb and the daily offering of food to sustain his *ka*.[14]

---

[10] Ralph Marcus, "On Biblical Hypostases of Wisdom," *HUCA* 23 (1950–1951): 157–71; Roland E. Murphy, "Wisdom in the OT," *ABD* 6: 926–29.

[11] Henri Cazelles, "Royaté sacrale et la Bible," *DBSup* 10 (1984): 1062–63.

[12] See "Joy at the Accession of Mer-ne-Ptah," translated by John A. Wilson (*ANET*, 378).

[13] See Rudolph Anthes, "Die Maat des Echnaton von Amarna," *JAOSSup* 14 (1952): 3–7; John A. Wilson, "Authority and Law," *JAOSSup* 17 (1954): 4–7.

[14] Claire Lalouette, *Textes sacrés et textes profanes de l'ancienne Egypte* (Connaissance de l'Orient 54; Paris: Gallimard, 1984), 293, note 92. According to ancient Egyptian belief, the human being, after death, was individualized by its remains in the tomb together with

The pharaoh's concentration of the power of justice carried with it some risk. On one hand, the king ran the risk of abusing the divine power he claimed by using it to his own advantage. On the other hand, he ran the risk of failing to uphold that power and of becoming a pawn of the powerful who sought their own advantage, regardless of the standards of social justice.[15]

Theoretically, the pharaoh was the only source of law and authority; however, he ordinarily delegated his authority to the vizier, who administered the kingdom and supervised the bureaucrats in the numerous districts of Egypt's vast domain. It is a matter of historical record that from the Third Dynasty on, the pharaohs were assisted by their viziers.[16] A vizier was second in authority after the pharaoh. His power of government was so immense that he was revered as Maat, and his secretary was called the secretary of Maat.[17]

The autobiographic inscriptions of the viziers are instructive. For example, the inscription of vizier Kagemni survives on his tomb at Saqqara. Kagemni was vizier and supreme judge during the time of the Fifth Dynasty. In his inscription he boasts of being the man in whom his "king and great god" trusted. His boast is based on the fact that he practiced *maat*, because it was good and was what the god wanted. To practice *maat* included acts of honesty, justice, and benevolence. In one part of his inscriptions Kagemni says:

> His majesty relied on all that his majesty ordered done,
> because I was worthy and valued by his majesty.
> O you—do what is right *[bw m3ᶜ]* for the king,
> the right *[m3ᶜt]* which the god loves.
> Speak what is true to the king, what the king wants is the truth *[m3ᶜt]!*[18]

It is hardly strange, given the sort of ethical understanding the viziers possessed, that the oldest moral treatise that survives was written by a vizier, Ptahhotep. He was vizier under Isesi, the next to the last pharaoh of the Fifth Dynasty,

---

three active elements: the *akh,* the *ba,* and the *ka.* The *akh* was a divine power that joined the pharaoh's being only after death and gave it divine qualities by which it could exert influence on the living. The *ba* gave to the dead pharaoh the strength to move around, to participate in the activity of the cosmos, to ascend to the sky, and to travel with the sun god. The *ka* gave the pharaoh divine creative power and enabled him to relate to human society and to receive the food offering necessary for his sustenance. It is easy to see, given this conception of the afterlife, why the Egyptians evinced such great concern for funeral rites, the care of their tombs, and the food service for the dead. Life after death was conceived as an extension of earthly existence, with the same activities and needs. See J. Vandier, *La religion égyptienne* (Paris: Presses Universitaire de France, 1949), 131–34; Edward F. Wente, "Egyptian Religion," *ABD* 2:408–12.

[15] Helck, "Maat," *LÄ* 3: 1110–19; Epzstein, *Social Justice,* 22.

[16] Hans H. Schmid, *Wesen und Geschichte der Weisheit: Eine Untersuchung zur altorientalischer und israelitischer Weisheitsliteratur* (BZAW 101; Berlin: Töpelmann, 1966), 38.

[17] Aristide Théodoridès, "Les Egyptiens ancient 'citoyens' ou 'sujects de Pharaon'?" *RIDA* 22 (1973): 51–112, esp. 52–53.

[18] Lichtheim, *Maat,* 12.

around the year 2360 B.C.E. The treatise is known as the Maxims of Ptah-hotep and consists of thirty-seven considerably developed maxims that open with a prologue and conclude with a long epilogue. The Maxims of Ptah-hotep may be characterized by the importance they assign to moral values that elevate social interests over personal advantage. The fifth maxim says:

> If thou art a leader commanding the affairs of the multitude, seek out for thyself every beneficial deed until it may be that thy (own) affairs are without wrong. Justice [m3ᶜt] is great, and its appropriateness is lasting; it has not been disturbed since the time of him who made it, (whereas) there is punishment for him who passes over its laws. It is the (right) path before him who knows nothing. Wrongdoing has never brought its undertaking into port. (It may be that) it is fraud to gain riches, (but) the strength of justice [m3ᶜt] is that it lasts, and a man may say: "It is the property of my father."[19]

The theme of justice in the Old Kingdom appears not only in texts related to the mission and the activity of the vizier and in the sapiential texts of instructions, but it is also inscribed in autobiographical form on the tombs of high-ranking bureaucrats. The emphasis of these inscriptions is that practicing justice includes assisting the needy. Being compassionate with the weak is a particular form of *maat*. Nefer-seshem-Ptah, a high-ranking bureaucrat of the Sixth Dynasty, who declares in his autobiographical inscription on his tomb at Saqqara:

> I spoke the good, I repeated the good,
> . . . .
> I judged two parties so as to content them,
> I saved the weak from one stronger than he as best I could,
> . . . .
> [I gave bread to the hungry,] clothes to the naked,
> I landed one who was stranded,
> I buried him who lacked a son,
> I made a boat [for the boatless,]
> [and supported] the orphan.
> I never spoke evil against anyone to a potentate.[20]

The funerary inscription of Nefer-seshem-Re, chief of the priests of the pharaoh Teti's pyramid (*ca.* second half of the twenty-fourth century B.C.E.), also deserves to be mentioned. The text says:

> I spoke the truth and practiced justice . . .
> I exercised justice, so that the people would love me.
> I was judge between rivals so they would be appeased, one with the other.
> I did all that was possible to save the weak from the hands of the one stronger than him.
> I gave bread to the hungry and clothes [to the naked].

---

[19] "The Instruction of the Vizier Ptah-hotep," translated by John A. Wilson (*ANET*, 412); Lichtheim, *Maat*, 16; Lalouette, *Textes*, 238.
[20] Lichtheim, *Maat*, 13–14.

I permitted the one who did not have a boat to get on board.
I gave a tomb to the one who had no sons.
. . . .
I respected my father, I was sweet to my mother, and I brought up their children.
Thus speaks the one whose name is Sheshi.[21]

A similar autobiographical inscription is found on the tomb of Hirkhouf, prince of Aswan and African explorer (*ca.* 2300 B.C.E.). Part of the text says: "I am an excellent man . . . the favorite of his father, praised by his mother, the favorite of all his brothers. I gave bread to the hungry and clothes to the naked. I permitted the one who did not have a boat to get on board."[22]

These autobiographical declarations emphasize generous behavior toward the needy, repeating known formulas. Without doubt, such inscriptions were directed to those who visited the tombs—the families and relatives of the deceased, who presumably possessed the same social status.[23] The inscriptions provide testimony to the honest and generous life the individual had lived and thus proved that the deceased was worthy of respect and deserved a prayer. Holding up the life of the deceased as an example reinforced the prestige of his class and promoted the glory of being part of it. Such declarations were formulated following the pattern of a moral ideal sought by the Egyptian society of the Old Kingdom.[24] This ideal showed, according to F. Daumas, that "the society wanted to build its existence on high moral principles."[25] But it must be observed that the constant repetitive formulas, which allude to the neighbor in need (the widow, the orphan, the divorced woman, the hungry, the naked), show the social problem of the forsaken poor was a perennial reality.

The situation facing the poor in the Old Kingdom was exacerbated by class divisions in Egyptian society. The upper classes comprised a small number of select families. The lower classes were made up of a large number of craftsmen and an immense multitude of dependent laborers of various kinds. M. Liverani classifies the latter into three categories: wage earners, forced laborers, and slaves.[26]

---

[21] Lalouette, *Textes,* 163.

[22] Ibid., 169.

[23] Since the capacity to read was a skill reserved solely for those of a certain social class—it is thought, for instance, that less than 5 percent of the population could read—one may deduce that autobiographical declarations were principally directed to those who enjoyed the same social status as the deceased. See John Baines, "Society, Morality, and Religious Practice," in *Religion in Ancient Egypt: Gods, Myths, and Personal Practice* (ed. B. E. Shafer; Ithaca, N.Y.: Cornell University Press, 1991), 132.

[24] See Baines, "Society," 140–41.

[25] François Daumas, "La naissance de l'humanisme dans la littérature de l'Égypte ancienne," *OrAnt* 1 (1962): 160.

[26] Two large-scale projects give an idea of the magnitude of the Egyptian workforce. The first project involved the preparation of terraces of arable land in order to take advantage of the periodic flooding of the Nile. The relatively short time between floods required an enormous effort of collective work, which was organized under the control of a central power exercising jurisdiction over the whole valley of the Nile. The other project during the Old Kingdom was the construction of the pyramids. For the construction of the pyra-

Wage earners were hired to perform specific jobs and received a salary that exceeded by very little the daily needs of the family. Forced laborers were compelled by the state to work in public works projects; they were given food, clothes, and provisions for their families. Slaves—most of them foreigners—received only what was necessary to survive and be productive for their masters.[27] On the fringes of society, there were those who were unable to manage on their own and who lacked support from their families. These were orphans, widows, divorced and abandoned women, the disabled, and sick or aged persons without family. Their survival depended on the voluntary help they received from generous hands. In Egyptian society, there was a general sentiment of compassion toward the needy; helping them was a work of *maat*.

The Old Kingdom, in spite of its splendor, came to an end. The reasons for its fall were many, among which we must include political, economic, and judicial corruption. The Protests of the Eloquent Peasant refers to this sort of corruption:

> He who should have established a fair distribution is a robber. He who should have reduced scarcity is the one who creates it, and the city is caught in its flood. He whose duty is to eliminate evil deeds is the one who commits them.[28]

2. Justice in the First Intermediate period (2130–1940 B.C.E.)

At the time of the fall of the Old Kingdom, the First Intermediate period began, during which different royal houses competed for power. Among these the royal families of Heracleopolis were distinguished. According to some prestigious Egyptologists, the fall of the Old Kingdom was the fruit of a social revolution.[29] Some Egyptologists, such as J. Spiegel, reconstruct the details of such a revolution, identifying an ideological leader whom they called "the Reformer," who abolished differences between social classes and proclaimed the right for

---

mid of Cheops, for instance, about one hundred thousand workers were required—and for more than twenty years. See Epzstein, *Social Justice,* 24–25.

[27] See Mario Liverani, "Il modo di produzione," in *L'Alba della Civiltà* (3 vols.; ed. S. Moscati; Turin: UTET, 1976), 2: 82–84. With regard to slavery, there was a fundamental difference between the citizen and the foreigner. The citizen could be subjected to slavery but only for a limited period. The foreigner, however, could be enslaved in perpetuity. See too Mario Liverani, "Nationality and Political Identity," *ABD* 4:1031. It is interesting to observe how the ancient Egyptians compared themselves to foreigners. On the one hand, they thought that their land was the center of the world and that their language and culture were the only truly human ones. On the other hand, they knew of those who lived outside that center—foreigners, inferior beings that they could use as slaves.

[28] Lalouette, *Textes,* 202.

[29] Epzstein, *Social Justice,* 26; Alexander Scharff and Anton Moortgat, *Ägypten und Vorderasien im Altertum* (Munich: F. Bruckmann, 1950), 74–85. For a critical estimation of the theory of social revolution, see J. Vercoutter, "The Fall of the Old Kingdom and the First Intermediate Period," in *The Near East: The Early Civilization* (ed. J. Bottéro et al.; New York: Delacorte, 1965), 320–46.

everyone to share the goods of the earth.³⁰ Without getting into details difficult to prove, we may discuss a revolution that ended with the Old Kingdom. This affirmation is based on a combination of diverse factors.³¹ Among them, first of all, is the constant complaint about the corruption and oppression at the end of the Old Kingdom. The Admonitions of Ipu-wer, for example, strongly criticizes the situation of social disturbance at the end of the Old Kingdom. Ipu-wer was an erudite priest who complained about the arduous situation bearing upon the country to one of the last pharaohs of the Sixth Dynasty, probably Pepi II, toward the end of the twenty-third century B.C.E. In one of his lamentations Ipu-wer says: "The land spins around as a potter's wheel does. The robber is (now) the possessor of riches." Addressing himself to the pharaoh, Ipu-wer says: "Authority, Perception, and Justice [maat] are with thee, (but) it is confusion which thou would set throughout the land, together with the noise of contention."³²

A second factor that supports the thesis of a social revolution is the barbaric destruction of the tombs of the nobility, perpetrated in the north of Egypt in the First Intermediate period. This destruction was accompanied by the proliferation for simple people of mastabahs (Egyptian tombs with sloping sides and flat roofs), which were constructed of material from the violated tombs. The third factor is the democratization of pharaonic titles at the time of the First Intermediate period. The concept of being the image of god the creator, once reserved exclusively for the pharaoh, was now attributed to all human beings. Thus, the Instruction for King Meri-ka-Re says:

> Well directed are men, the cattle of the god. He made heaven and earth according to their desire, and he repelled the water-monster. He made the breath of life (for) their nostrils. They who have issued from his body are his images.³³

The titles and symbols of divine dignity that were exclusively the pharaoh's began to be applied to common people; thus, archaeological discoveries show that the crown, the scepter, and the hooked staff became symbols that adorned the coffins of common people.³⁴

M. Lichtheim states that, in spite of the destruction caused, the First Intermediate period was a time of creative energy in which Egyptians discovered the sources of subjectivity. In the search for themselves, they affirmed the heart and the character were powers that formed thoughts, aspirations, and the actions of the human individual.³⁵ Autobiographical inscriptions of this epoch testify to this new conscience. Thus, Rediu-khnum of Dendera said that it was "his heart which made him progress in society and was his character which maintained him

---

³⁰ J. Spiegel, *Soziale und weltanschauliche Reformbewegungen im Alten Ägypten* (Heidelberg: Kerle, 1950).

³¹ See Scharff and Moortgat, *Ägypten*, 74–85.

³² "The Admonitions of Ipu-wer," translated by John A. Wilson (*ANET*, 441–44, esp. 443).

³³ "The Instruction for King Meri-ka-Re," translated by John A. Wilson (*ANET*, 417).

³⁴ See Scharff and Moortgat, *Ägypten*, 79.

³⁵ Lichtheim, *Maat*, 23.

up front." Then he adds, referring to himself in the third person: "I am a knower of himself as leader of men, a costly timber made by the god."³⁶ In the same way, Henun, chamberlain of various pharaohs in the Eleventh Dynasty, said, again referring to himself in the third person: "There was no falseness that came from my mouth, no evil that was done by my hands. I am the maker of his character, one beloved of people each day."³⁷

With the affirmation of proper subjectivity, a humanitarian sense of moral action increased, and people sought reasons to elicit and direct the sentiment of compassion toward the needy. Thus Khety, from the First Intermediate period, said on his tomb at Siut: "[I did] what people love and gods praise: I have given bread to the hungry, clothes to the naked; I listened to the plea of the widow, I gave a home to the orphan."³⁸ According to this affirmation, to help the needy is part of the order that the gods want. Moreover, in accord with the consent of the people, the governor had an obligation to include this in his practice of *maat*. The ideal of humanitarian justice is also emphasized in the writings on the tombs of this epoch. A writing of Key, son of Nehri, represents, in autobiographical form, the virtues of the perfect governor: competence, courage, benevolence, and justice. To practice these virtues is to do *maat*. Key's inscription marries the gentle action of charity to the drastic deeds of justice when liberating the weak from the powerful: "I have done rightness razor-sharp, I have rescued the weak from the strong, I succored the widow bereft of her husband, I raised the orphan bereft of his father."³⁹ There is any number of texts from the First Intermediate period in which values were expressed in social and spiritual terms. Some of the most famous of these are The Instruction for King Meri-ka-Re, a Dispute over Suicide, and texts from the sarcophagi.

The Instruction for King Meri-ka-Re contains a series of counsels that a king gives to his son and successor. It is a political testament written at the end of the First Intermediate period. This instruction is one of the first examples of a doctrine that teaches that each individual is responsible for his own behavior before the divine tribunal. Such responsibility emphasizes the theme of social justice that ought to be practiced by the governor. The following text is a sample:

> Do justice *[maat]* whilst thou endurest upon earth. Quiet the weeper; do not oppress the widow; supplant no man in the property of his father . . . Be on thy guard against punishing wrongfully. . . . The council which judges the deficient, thou knowest that they are not lenient on that day of judging the miserable, the hour of doing (their) duty. . . . A man remains over after death and deeds are placed beside him in heaps. . . . (But) as for him who reaches it without wrongdoing, he shall exist yonder like a god, stepping out freely like the lords of eternity.⁴⁰

---

³⁶ Ibid., 23–24.
³⁷ Ibid., 24.
³⁸ Ibid., 21.
³⁹ Ibid., 31.
⁴⁰ "Instruction for King Meri-ka-Re," translated by John A. Wilson (*ANET*, 415).

A Dispute over Suicide is a didactic work dating from the First Intermediate period, according to J. A. Wilson.[41] This piece gives the social problem a psychological framework. The political and social disturbances that began in the First Intermediate period created a moral and spiritual crisis. The individual lost the framework of a hierarchical and balanced society, one that would give security to each member of the social body. Eliminating this framework left people on their own; they had to put aside the concept that the human being was an element of a collective society and adopt a new concept that the human being was an individual person.

A Dispute over Suicide presents a man arguing with his own soul. In the argument, he describes the tragedy of human life, in which the evil part of nature and destiny is compounded by the oppression of those who callously step on the rights of their neighbors in order to accomplish their own greedy desires. In the Dispute, the man expresses his conviction that death resolves the tragedy of the oppressed and restores his rights; he even affirms that death sets the oppressed as the judge of those who were once his oppressors. In this sense, referring to the poor oppressed one who enters into the kingdom of death, he says: "Why surely, he who is yonder will be a living god, punishing the sin of him who commits it.... he who is yonder will stand in the barque of the sun."[42]

The texts on the sarcophagi manifest a profoundly new aspect of the theme of rights and responsibilities held by the individual: all men are equal by divine creation. These texts date from around the end of the First Intermediate period and the beginning of the Middle Kingdom at the beginning of the twentieth century B.C.E. On six sarcophagi, the creator god speaks, affirming he made all men equal and they have violated what he established:

> I made the four winds that every man might breathe thereof like his fellow in his time.... I made the great inundation that the poor man might have rights therein like the great man.... I made every man like his fellow. I did not command that they do evil, (but) it was their hearts which violated what I had said.[43]

3. Justice in the Middle Kingdom (1940–1570 B.C.E.)

J. A. Wilson observed that during the First Intermediate period, social justice was for everyone, and the governor was required to practice *maat* with all the citizens of the kingdom. In keeping with this, the kings in the Middle Kingdom took names that expressed their desire to exercise justice *(maat)* toward the gods and mortals, such as "He Who Takes Pleasure in Justice," "The Just of Voice," "He Who

---

[41] "A Dispute over Suicide," translated by John. A. Wilson (*ANET*, 405).
[42] Ibid., 407.
[43] "All Men Created Equal in Opportunity," translated by John A. Wilson (*ANET*, 7–8); John A. Wilson, *The Culture of Ancient Egypt* (Chicago: University of Chicago Press, 1965), 117.

Makes Justice Appear."[44] Thus, animated by this intention of justice, the text of the Teaching of Amen-em-het I, written at the beginning of the Middle Kingdom, makes declarations such as the following: "I gave to the poor man. I cherished the orphan. I caused him who had nothing to attain (to wealth) like him who was wealthy."[45] State bureaucrats, for their part, echoed this idea of justice and typically referred to a triple obligation to the king, to the gods, and to the people.

But bringing *maat* to every individual was difficult to accomplish. In fact, the prosperity that the pharaohs were able to bring about caused the promotion of human rights for all individuals to be forgotten.[46] Prosperity created great opportunities, but in fact only the upper classes benefited from them.

The urgent theme of social justice is taken up in the literary work the Protests of the Eloquent Peasant, which puts the theme into a historical narrative framework. The narrative is the result of the interest of a wise man in the commoner. The narrative tells how a peasant went to make an exchange of his produce for groceries and how he was stripped of his goods by a bureaucrat of the public administration. The peasant did not remain silent; on the contrary, he turned out to be eloquent. Like the prophet Amos, the peasant criticized the corrupt administration and made his defense through an appeal to the principles of social justice. He claimed the right to justice (*maat*), and appealed to Rensi, principal administrator of the kingdom, explaining that he was coming to him because he was "the father of the orphan, the husband of the widow, the brethren of the divorced and the womb of the one without a mother." The administrator became interested in the case only after having heard nine discourses of the eloquent peasant. The story ends with a harsh sentence for the abuser and a favorable sentence for the abused: the former had to give back what had been stolen and was handed over to the latter as a slave.[47] By composing this story, the wise man gave commoners a voice to vindicate their rights. This story assures its readers that justice, although difficult and at a distance, was possible for the commoner. It teaches that the great titles the governors used for their political prestige ("the father of the orphan, the husband of the widow") could serve as motives for awakening the conscience of the powerful regarding their obligations to the weak.

The theme of justice also appears in many funerary inscriptions. The inscriptions of Beni Hasan are worth mentioning. On these, Khnum-hotep II, a local magistrate, refers to the social and political transformation that king Amen-em-het I (1938–1909 B.C.E.) brought about after overcoming the disturbances of the First Intermediate period, a period in which the state was buffeted by dynastic struggles and local wars. A phrase from the inscriptions says:

As his majesty came he expelled wrongdoing:
Risen like Atum himself,

---

[44] Wilson, *Culture*, 133.
[45] William K. Simpson, ed., *The Literature of Ancient Egypt: An Anthology of Stories, Instructions and Poetry* (New Haven, Conn.: Yale University Press, 1972), 136.
[46] Wilson, *Culture*, 143.
[47] "The Protests of the Eloquent Peasant," translated by John A. Wilson (*ANET*, 408).

he restored what he found in ruins,
what one town had snatched from another....
because he so greatly loved Maat.[48]

The so-called prophecy of Neferti likewise refers to this transformative action of Amen-em-het I, supposedly still off in the future.[49] This prophecy, actually a *vaticinium ex eventu*, speaks with assurance of a social order of justice and equity that a future monarch will firmly establish. Thus, it gives a vote of confidence in the reign of Amen-em-het I. These manifestations of confidence in the monarchy have their counterpart in the instructions of the same king Amen-em-het I that he left for his son Sesostris. Left as a political testament, these instructions affirm that a king, just though he may be, still may be betrayed by the people of his own court. Just order can be destroyed inside the institution of the monarchy, and evil can triumph even with monarchical titles.[50]

4. Justice in the New Kingdom (1570–1070 B.C.E.)

At the beginning of the eighteenth century B.C.E., the Middle Kingdom weakened, because of continuous internal fights among ambitious provincial lords who struggled to establish a central power. As a consequence, the kingdom dissolved, the economy degenerated, and the country was exposed to foreign aggression. In these circumstances, the invasion of the Hyksos took place, an invasion that created an interruption in the history of Egypt, an interruption now called the Second Intermediate period. With the expulsion of the Hyksos toward the middle of the sixteenth century B.C.E., however, Egypt recommenced its own history. The Eighteenth Dynasty reestablished continuity with the Middle Kingdom and initiated the New Kingdom, with one important addition: an extensive military conquest widened Egypt's borders and transformed its kingdom into an empire. The New Kingdom sustained the traditional concept of *maat* established in the Middle Kingdom: loyal service to the king and the gods, and a just and compassionate behavior toward the people. Moreover, in the service to the gods, the theme of gratitude toward the divinities of Egypt received a new accent and the practice of prayer among the people increased.

A testimony of the traditional teaching of *maat* during this period is found in the Instruction of Ani. Ani lived during the reign of Ah-mosis (1539–1514 B.C.E.), the first king of the Eighteenth Dynasty. His Instruction offers an extensive series of traditional teachings that encompass the principal aspects of human life. It is interesting to observe that the Instruction counsels generosity toward the poor while maintaining that the existence of misery is an inevitable evil:

---

[48] Lichtheim, *Maat*, 39.
[49] Lalouette, *Textes*, 70–74.
[50] Lichtheim, *Maat*, 43–44; Lalouette, *Textes*, 57–59.

Do not take bread, when someone stands before you, without extending your hand to give him bread also. This gesture will be known in eternity even if the man is no more. One is rich; another one is poor. But food will remain for those who share it. The one who was rich last year might be a wanderer this year. Do not be greedy to fill your belly without having in mind the needs of your neighbor. If some day scarcity reaches you, someone else will probably do you some good.[51]

The Instruction of Ani has an educational purpose. As Lalouette astutely observes, the instruction ends with "an almost philosophical discussion of the transformation that education can produce in human nature."[52] This purpose of the Instruction provides an optimistic vision regarding education. But it must also be observed that only a very few people had access to education.

The traditional concept of *maat*, including its obligations toward the king, the gods, and the people, also is found in the descriptions of the viziers. The description of the vizier Weser is inscribed on the tomb of his secretary and administrator, Amen-em-het, who lived during the reign of Thut-mosis III (ca. 1479–1426 B.C.E.). After describing his loyal conduct toward the king and his generous devotion to the gods, the inscription refers to the behavior of Weser toward the people and says:

The mayor of Thebes and vizier Weser did what nobles and folk love:
protecting the poor and the rich,
succouring the widow lacking a family,
pleasing the revered and old;
he placed sons on the fathers' seat
and put the whole land at ease.[53]

The description of the vizier Rekh-mi-Re, although longer, presents much the same perspective. This text is famous because it is part of a speech that Thutmosis III delivered on the occasion of Rekh-mi-Re's nomination as vizier, and the vizier wanted it to be recorded on his tomb. Among other things, the text instructs the vizier to be an impartial, fair, balanced, considerate, and accessible judge to all. One of the paragraphs says: "Do not judge unfairly, God abhors partiality. . . . He who does justice before all people, he is the vizier."[54]

The tradition of the New Kingdom was interrupted by the reform of Amarna, accomplished by Amen-hotep IV (Akh-en-Aton, 1353–1336 B.C.E.). This was a reform of an eminently religious character centered on the worship of Aton, the divine solar disk. The reform dethroned the god Amon and enthroned Aton in his stead. Amon, originally a secondary god of the Theban tradition, had gained prestige with the emergence of the Theban Dynasty at the beginning of the Middle Kingdom. He was installed as the main god in the New Kingdom and was

---

[51] Lalouette, *Textes*, 256–57.
[52] Ibid., 339, note 59.
[53] Lichtheim, *Maat*, 55–56.
[54] Miriam Lichtheim, *Ancient Egyptian Literature: The New Kingdom* (vol. 2 of *Ancient Egyptian Literature;* Berkeley: University of California Press, 1976), 23.

identified with Re, the creator god. The reform of Amarna tore down Amon's supremacy and established Aton's exclusive dominion. Akh-en-Aton opposed the distant and hidden character of the god Amon (whose very name means "Hidden") to the disposition of his visible and closer god Aton, the solar disk. The reform emphasized *maat* to an extraordinary degree, but it did not consider it so much under the aspect of righteousness and justice as under the aspect of truth. In this sense, truth should be understood as the disclosure of the hidden, including the family life of the pharaoh and the spontaneous forces of nature rather than an artificial world of the gods. The reform promoted art that accorded with its new conception of human life, which emphasized the aesthetic aspect of the created world; but it did not pay attention to the administration of justice and to political and economic needs. In this sense, it is not surprising that the texts of the reform, such as the famous Hymn to the Sun, make no reference to justice for mortals.[55] An echo of the Hymn to the Sun is found in Psalm 104 of the Hebrew Bible.

The reform of Amarna lasted only four decades. Although brief, its neglect of justice and political and economic administration brought serious consequences: the empire disintegrated, social order destabilized, and professional dishonesty infected the administration. Both kings who followed Akh-en-Aton, namely Tut-ankh-Amon and Ay, returned to the Theban tradition, but they were not strong enough to restore the kingdom. The strong man who made the restoration possible was Hor-em-heb. He reigned in the years 1319–1292 B.C.E. and was the last pharaoh of the Eighteenth Dynasty.[56]

Hor-em-heb's most famous edict contained a series of draconian amendments designed to correct abuse and restore order. Speaking of himself in the third person, Hor-em-heb (literally, "Horus is in celebration") congratulates himself because he has made the country happy: he has established justice. Thus he says:

> Righteousness has come; she has united [with it]. They [are] in exultation. Egypt, it is reborn; the whole of the Black Land, its heart is merry in jubilation. He has come in dignity. He has filled the Two Lands with his beauty, for the Good God, he was born to Re, doing righteousness throughout the Two Lands.[57]

Hor-em-heb reorganized the courts of law as a pivotal measure to establish justice in a country oppressed by a corrupt bureaucracy. He describes his reforms as follows:

> I have sought out people . . . of good character, knowing how to judge thought, listening to the words of the Palace (and) to the laws of the throne-hall. I have appointed them to judge the Two Lands and to satisfy [their] inhabitants. . . . I have set them in the great cities [of] Upper and Lower Egypt, every one of them, without exception, enjoying the benefit of a stipend. . . . I instructed them, saying "Do not associate with other people. Do not take a bribe from another."[58]

---

[55] Wilson, *Culture*, 214. See "The Hymn to the Aton," translated by John A. Wilson (*ANET*, 369–71).
[56] Wilson, *Culture*, 235–38; Epzstein, *Social Justice*, 26–42.
[57] See Kurt Pflüger, "The Edict of King Haremhab," *JNES* 5 (1946): 260.
[58] Pflüger, "Haremhab," 265.

Hor-em-heb's edict itemizes injunctions against specific abuses, including references to state employees who were stealing public goods, tax collectors who were abusing the defenseless, and soldiers who were extorting commoners. The edict establishes penalties against anyone who takes away transport vessels used for delivering dues: "The Law shall be applied against him by cutting off his nose, he being sent to Si[le]."[59] The same penalty is applied against anyone who interferes with the dues for the *harîm* (Arabic for "what is sanctified") and divine offerings. The edict also protects peasants who have had to endure the looting of their farms by those who were looking for hides, and it frees them from taxes. Referring to several cases of extortion, the edict states "My Majesty has commanded to prevent this from being done, starting from today."[60]

It is not easy to discern the motives that led Hor-em-heb to take such drastic measures. Some historians think his motives were humanitarian; others impute to him more utilitarian motives, such as those of assuring an income for the state treasury and of gaining popular support to consolidate his power.[61] The truth is Hor-em-heb's main preoccupation was the stability and prosperity of the state, a preoccupation that dominated the history of the New Kingdom. In weighing this preoccupation with the state's stability and prosperity against any interest in securing justice for the poor, it seems clear that the New Kingdom was far more interested in stability and prosperity. Furthermore, it can be said that the upper classes considered the practice of *maat* on behalf of the common people a way of securing their own success and happiness. Thus generosity and nobility in behavior are presented as means to having success in life. The Instruction of Amen-em-Opet provides a salient example of so generous and courteous an attitude animated by so utilitarian a purpose. Amen-em-Opet was a high-ranking bureaucrat, believed to have lived sometime during the second half of the New Kingdom, working in what may be termed the royal court's Ministry of Agriculture and Bureau of Properties. His Instruction is characterized by a concern to inculcate an honest attitude, just and generous in relation with others. Some of his proverbs referring to the poor are noteworthy:

> If thou findest a large debt against a poor man
> Make it into three parts,
> Forgive two, and let one stand.
> Thou wilt find it like the ways of life;
> Thou wilt lie down and sleep (soundly); in the morning
> Thou wilt find it (again) like good news.
> . . . .
> Do not recognize a widow if thou catchest her in the fields,
> Nor fail to be indulgent to her reply.
> Do not neglect a stranger (with) thy oil-jar,

---

[59] Ibid., 261.
[60] Ibid., 264.
[61] Epzstein, *Social Justice*, 37–38.

That it be doubled before thy brethren
God desires respect for the poor
More than the honoring of the exalted.[62]

These teachings are substantially traditional, but in the Instruction of Amen-em-Opet, they take an especial emphasis: they are considered as ways of making progress and of gaining individual prestige so as to be successful in society. This is seen in the prologue where the objective of the Instruction is expressed: "The beginning of the teaching of life, the testimony for prosperity . . . in order . . . to make [the courtier] prosper on earth."[63]

In this context of the theme of justice in the New Kingdom, the confessions of innocence in the Book of the Dead are worth mentioning. The Book of the Dead contains elements that date from the First Intermediate period and the Middle Kingdom, but as a collection it first appears during the New Kingdom, and it became popular thereafter.[64] These confessions of innocence deposited upon a mummy were part of a magic ritual that allowed the deceased to avoid negative judgment from the divine tribunal. This kind of personal apology says nothing about the actual conduct of the dead. It expresses, rather, the expectation of the bureaucrat or landowner to merit a good funeral and happiness in the afterlife. These declarations of innocence were for members of the upper and middle classes and express an attitude of security and self-confidence:

I have not committed evil against men.
I have not mistreated cattle.
I have not committed sin in the place of truth *[maat]*. . . .
I have not done violence to a poor man. . . .
I have not made (anyone) sick.
I have not made (anyone) weep.
I have not killed.
I have given no order to a killer.[65]

---

[62] "The Instruction of Amen-em-Opet," translated by John A. Wilson (*ANET*, 423–24). With respect to the advice given by Amen-em-Opet to forgive two parts of the debt of a poor person, we should mention the position of Moshe Weinfeld, who holds that in ancient Egypt, as elsewhere in the Middle East, there existed "proclamations of freedom." Since as yet no actual texts of Egyptian acts of liberation or bans of grace have been discovered, Weinfeld supports his thesis by pointing out parallel expressions found in ancient Mesopotamia. See Moshe Weinfeld, "Freedom Proclamation in Egypt and in the Ancient Near East," in *Pharaonic Egypt, the Bible and Christianity* (ed. S. Israelit-Groll; Jerusalem: Magnes, 1985), 317–27. See also H. S. Smith, "A Note on Amnesty," *JEA* 54 (1968): 212. But some of the texts seem to refer not to decrees of liberation from tax burdens but to permanent dispensations granted people living within the domain of a temple, since temple service was regarded as an extension of military service. The topic of "proclamations of freedom" in ancient Egypt requires more investigation and discussion.

[63] "The Instruction of Amen-em-Opet," translated by John A. Wilson (*ANET*, 421).
[64] "The Protestation of Guiltlessness," translated by John A. Wilson (*ANET*, 34–36).
[65] Ibid., 34.

5. Justice in popular religion

The attitude of the confessions of innocence finds its counterpart in the attitude of the poor in the texts of popular piety.[66] These texts belong to the Nineteenth Dynasty (1292–1190 B.C.E.). In these, we can sense the religious emotion of the powerless members of society, who have no personal security, and who put all their trust in the deity. Thus, a poor person, who had no money to pay a scribe to serve as a lawyer, asks for help from the god Amon, vizier of the poor, to obtain a favorable judgment from the tribunal:

> O Amon, give thy ear to one who is alone in the law court, who is poor; he is not rich. The court cheats him (of) silver and gold. . . . May it be found that Amon assumes his form as the vizier, in order to permit [the] poor man to get off. May it be found that the poor man is vindicated. May the poor man surpass the rich.[67]

A suppliant calls Amon "the pilot of the helpless," the only one who can be a secure guide and can offer true protection:

> Pilot who knows the water,
> Helmsman of [the weak];
> who gives bread to him who has none . . .
> I take not a noble as protector,
> I associate not with the man of wealth . . .
> My wealth is in the house of my [lord].
> My lord is my protector . . .
> Amun who knows compassion.
> Who hearkens to him who calls him.[68]

In the faith of the people, Amon possesses an extraordinary power to listen and a unique sense of compassion. That is why the needy place their trust in him and plead with him:

---

[66] A. I. Sadek, *Popular Religion in Egypt during the New Kingdom* (Hildesheimer Ägyptologische Beiträge 27; Hildesheim: Gerstenberg, 1987); Lynn H. Holden, "The People's Religion," in *Egypt's Golden Age: The Art of Living in the New Kingdom, 1558–1085 B.C.* (Boston: Museum of Fine Arts, 1982), 296–307; Battiscombe Gunn, "The Religion of the Poor in Ancient Egypt," *JEA* 3 (1916): 81–94; James H. Breasted, *Development of Religion and Thought in Ancient Egypt* (New York: Harper, 1912), 344–70.

[67] "A Prayer for Help in the Royal Court," translated by John. A. Wilson (*ANET*, 380). The god Amon, originally from Thebes, rose to prominence in the religious system of Egypt during the Middle Kingdom. After the expulsion of the Hyksos, Amon was amalgamated to Re, the ancient god of Heliopolis. Thanks to this amalgamation, the story of Amon was identified with that of Re, and he assumed the attributes of a creator-god. Consequently, Amon was said to have engendered himself in secret, proceeding out of the primordial egg atop the primordial hill, creating the world, and becoming the king of the gods. Amon was the principal god during the New Kingdom, and he was believed to listen to the prayers of each person, even those who were far off. See Vincent A. Tobin, *Theological Principles of Egyptian Religion* (New York: Peter Lang, 1989), 50–51.

[68] Lichtheim, *New Kingdom*, 112. Amun is an alternative spelling of Amon.

You are Amun, the Lord of the silent,
Who comes at the voice of the poor.
When I call to you in distress,
You come to rescue me.
To give breath to him who is wretched,
To rescue me from bondage.
You are Amen-Re, the Lord of Thebes,
who rescues him who is in *dat*.
For you are he who is [merciful].
When one appeals to you,
you are he who comes from afar.[69]

Another text that expresses the gratitude and the appreciation of the one who feels protected by the divinity says:

My heart longs to see you. My heart is glad, Amun, thou protector of the poor. You are the father of the orphan, the husband of the widow. How pleasant it is to speak your name! It is like the taste of life. It is like the taste of bread to a child, like a robe for the naked; like the scent of a blossoming bough in the time of the summer heat.[70]

Conclusion

There is an idea that ties together the disparate elements of this study of justice in ancient Egypt. It is the idea of *maat*, often translated into English as "truth-justice." Associated with *maat* is the figure of the king and his retainers, who were called to be mediators of *maat*. In the Old Kingdom, society was dominated by a collective monarchical structure; according to this understanding, the individual was an element in the community, was defined by a sense of belonging to this structure, and was fulfilled by service to the king. The function of the king and his associates was to activate individuals of different levels for the well-being and prosperity of the state. The action of the king had a cultic purpose: to offer the practice of *maat* as an offering to the gods. Indeed, the divine protection and the eternal life of the sovereign depended upon this offering. Within this conception, the forsaken poor, who had fallen into misery, were relegated to the margins of society. Their fate was delivered over to the generous compassion of their neighbors.

The First Intermediate period broke with the collective concept and gave to the common individual the consciousness of being a person. With this development, participation in the divine image ceased to be an exclusive privilege of the king, and was extended to everybody, even to the marginalized, who had been abandoned to their misery. This new awareness of the dignity of the other stressed the responsibility of helping the needy and the oppressed.

---

[69] Ibid., 106.

[70] The text is cited by Norbert Lohfink, *Option for the Poor: The Basic Principle of Liberation Theology in the Light of the Bible* (Berkeley: Bibal, 1987), 20.

The Middle and the New Kingdoms inherited the developed conscience of the First Intermediate period. The kings adopted names that reflected their concern to extend the practice of *maat* to everyone, especially to the poor. The prosperity of the Middle Kingdom and, most of all, that of the New Kingdom created new economic and social opportunities, but generally these proved to be profitable only for the nobles and powerful. Their prosperity placed justice for the poor into hibernation. Misery was regarded in a fatalistic way—an irremediable condition, an effect of uncontrollable causes. As a result the poor lost all confidence in those who on earth were supposed to be mediators of *maat* and reverted directly to the divine world as the last source of justice and compassion.

Bibliography

Anthes, Rudolph. "Die Maat des Echnaton von Amarna." *Supplement to the Journal of the American Oriental Society* 14 (1952): 1–36.

Assmann, Jan. *Maât: L'Egypte pharaonique et l'idée de justice sociale*. Paris: Julliard, 1989.

Baines, John. "Dynastic Chronology." Pages 201–3 in *Religion in Ancient Egypt: Gods, Myths, and Personal Practice*. Edited by Byron E. Shafer. Ithaca, N.Y.: Cornell University Press, 1991.

———. "Society, Morality, and Religious Practice." Pages 123–200 in *Religion in Ancient Egypt: Gods, Myths, and Personal Practice*. Edited by Byron E. Shafer. Ithaca, N.Y.: Cornell University Press, 1991.

Breasted, James H. *Development of Religion and Thought in Ancient Egypt*. New York: Harper, 1912.

Cazelles, Henri. *Autour de l'Exode: Etudes*. Sources bibliques. Paris: Gabalda, 1987.

———. *Etudes sur le code de l'alliance*. Paris: Letouzey et Ané, 1946.

———. "Royaté sacrale et la Bible." Pages 1056–78 in *Dictionnaire de la Bible: Supplément* 10 (1984). Edited by L. Pirot and A. Robert. Paris: Letouzey & Ané, 1926–.

Crenshaw, James L. "Proverbs, Book of." Pages 513–20 in vol. 5 of *Anchor Bible Dictionary*. Edited by D. N. Freedman. 6 vols. New York: Doubleday, 1992.

Daumas, François. "La naissance de l'humanisme dans la littérature de l'Égypte ancienne." *Oriens Antiquus* 1 (1962): 155–84.

Epzstein, Léon. *Social Justice in the Ancient Near East and the People of the Bible*. Translated from French. London: SCM, 1986.

Fensham, Frank C. "Widow, Orphan, and the Poor in Ancient Near Eastern Legal and Wisdom Literature." *Journal of Near Eastern Studies* 21 (1962): 129–39.

Gunn, Battiscombe. "The Religion of the Poor in Ancient Egypt." *Journal of Egyptian Archaeology* 3 (1916): 81–94.

Helck, W., E. Otto, and W. Westendorf, eds. *Lexicon der Ägyptologie*. 7 vols. Wiesbaden: Harrassowitz, 1972.

Holden, Lynn H. "The People's Religion." Pages 296–307 in *Egypt's Golden Age: The Art of Living in the New Kingdom, 1558–1085 B.C.* Boston: Museum of Fine Arts, 1982.

Krauss, R. *Sothis- und Monddaten: Studien zur astronomischen und technischen Chronologie Altägyptens.* Hildesheimer ägyptologische Beiträge 20. Hildesheim: Gerstenberg, 1985.

Lalouette, Claire. *Textes sacrés et textes profanes de l'ancienne Egypte.* Connaissance de l'Orient 54. Paris: Gallimard, 1984.

Lichtheim, Miriam. *Ancient Egyptian Literature: The New Kingdom.* Vol. 2 of *Ancient Egyptian Literature.* Berkeley: University of California Press, 1976.

———. *Maat in Egyptian Autobiographies and Related Studies.* Orbis biblicus et orientalis 120. Frieburg: Universitätsverlag; Göttingen: Vandenhoeck & Ruprecht, 1992.

Liverani, Mario. "Il modo di produzione." Pages 80–96 in vol. 2 of *L'Alba della Civiltà.* 3 vols. Edited by S. Moscati. Turin: UTET, 1976.

———. "National and Political Identity." Pages 1031–37 in vol. 4 of *Anchor Bible Dictionary.* Edited by D. N. Freedman. 6 vols. New York: Doubleday, 1992.

Lohfink, Norbert F. *Option for the Poor: The Basic Principle of Liberation Theology in the Light of the Bible.* Berkeley: Bibal, 1987.

Marcus, Ralph. "On Biblical Hypostases of Wisdom." *Hebrew Union College Annual* 23 (1950–1951): 157–71.

Mattha, G., and G. R. Hugues. *The Demotic Legal Code of Hermopolis West.* Cairo: Institut français d'archéologie orientale du Cairo, 1975.

Morenz, Siegfried. *Egyptian Religion.* Ithaca, N.Y.: Cornell University Press, 1973.

Moret, A. "La Doctrine de Maât." *Revue d'égyptologie* 4 (1940): 1–14.

Murphy, Roland E. "Wisdom in the OT." Pages 920–31 in vol. 6 of *Anchor Bible Dictionary.* Edited by D. N. Freedman. 6 vols. New York: Doubleday, 1992.

Pflüger, Kurt. "The Edict of King Haremhab." *Journal of Near Eastern Studies* 5 (1946): 260–68.

Pritchard, James B., ed. *Ancient Near Eastern Texts Relating to the Old Testament.* 3d ed. Princeton: Princeton University Press, 1969.

Ramlot, Léon. "Prophétisme." *Dictionnaire de la Bible: Supplément* 8 (1972): 811–1221.

Sadek, A. I. *Popular Religion in Egypt during the New Kingdom.* Hildesheimer Ägyptologische Beiträge 27; Hildesheim: Gerstenberg, 1987.

Scharff, Alexander, and Anton Moortgat. *Ägypten und Vorderasien im Altertum.* Munich: F. Bruckmann, 1950.

Schmid, Hans H. *Gerechtigkeit als Weltordnung: Hintergrund und Geschichte des alttestamentlichen Gerechtigkeitsbegriffes.* Beiträge zur historischen Theologie 40. Tübingen: J. C. B. Mohr, 1968.

———. *Wesen und Geschichte der Weisheit: Eine Untersuchung zur altorientalischer und israelitischer Weisheitsliteratur.* Beihefte zur Zeitschrift für die alttestamentliche Wissenschaft 101. Berlin: Töpelmann, 1966.

Shirun-Grumach, I. "Remarks on the Goddess Maat." Pages 173–201 in *Pharaonic Egypt, the Bible and Christianity*. Edited by Sara Israelit-Groll. Jerusalem: Magnes Press, 1985.

Shupak, Nili. "The 'Sitz im Leben' of the Book of Proverbs in the Light of a Comparison of Biblical and Egyptian Wisdom Literature." *Revue biblique* 94 (1987): 98–119.

Simpson, William K., ed. *The Literature of Ancient Egypt: An Anthology of Stories, Instructions and Poetry*. New Haven, Conn.: Yale University Press, 1972.

Smith, H. S. "A Note on Amnesty." *Journal of Egyptian Archaeology* 54 (1968): 212–14.

Spiegel, J. *Soziale und weltanschauliche Reformbewegungen im Alten Ägypten*. Heidelberg: Kerle, 1950.

Théodoridès, Aristide. "The Concept of law in Ancient Egypt." Pages 291–322 in *The Legacy of Egypt*. Edited by John R. Harris. Oxford: Oxford University Press, 1971.

———. "Les Egyptiens ancient 'citoyens' ou 'sujets de Pharaon'?" *Revue internationale des droits de l'antiquité* 22 (1973): 51–112.

———. "A propos de la loi dans l'Egypte pharaonique." *Revue internationale des droits de l'antiquité* 14 (1967): 107–52.

Tobin, Vincent A. *Theological Principles of Egyptian Religion*. New York: Peter Lang, 1989.

Vandier, J. *La religion égyptienne*. Paris: Presses Universitaire de France, 1949.

Vercoutter, J. "The Fall of the Old Kingdom and the First Intermediate Period." Pages 320–46 in *The Near East: The Early Civilization*. Edited by J. Bottéro et al. New York: Delacorte, 1965.

Weinfeld, Moshe. "Freedom Proclamation in Egypt and in the Ancient Near East." Pages 317–27 in *Pharaonic Egypt, the Bible and Christianity*. Edited by S. Israelit-Groll; Jerusalem: Magnes, 1985.

Wente, Edward F. "Egyptian Religion." Pages 408–12 in vol. 2 of *Anchor Bible Dictionary*. Edited by D. N. Freedman. 6 vols. New York: Doubleday, 1992.

Wilson, John A. "Authority and Law." *Supplement to the Journal of the American Oriental Society* 17 (1954): 1–7.

———. *The Culture of Ancient Egypt*. Chicago: University of Chicago Press, 1965.

CHAPTER THREE

Exodus as an Event of Liberating Justice

Introduction

The existence of widespread concern for the poor, the widow, and the orphan in Mesopotamia and ancient Egypt shows that similar concerns in ancient Israel were not innovations. Rather, Israel shared a social preoccupation common in the ancient Near East. From ancient Mesopotamia, Israel inherited the vocabulary of justice and law, the concept of liberating justice, as well as the conditional formulation of social laws. From ancient Egypt, she was enriched by the wisdom Egyptian sages had taught through their admonitions and instructions, in which consideration for the poor was prominent. But what was distinctive to ancient Israel was that the nation began its history as slaves, poor and oppressed, who were rescued by God through a powerful act of saving justice. This compassionate and saving action of God, which had given Israel existence and dignity, served as a model in ancient Israel in their efforts to assist the poor and oppressed in their own midst. The story and significance of this divine action, which is contained in the book of Exodus, is the subject of inquiry in this chapter.

The book of Exodus contains the narrative of the escape from Egypt, as well as laws revealed by God on Mount Sinai. Remarkably, the narratives and the laws are intimately intertwined, so that the narratives are not simply historical notes added to legal texts but are the matrix within which the laws were shaped. The Sinai laws originated in the liberating events and were molded according to the spirit of a compassionate and saving God. The entire purpose of God's liberating action was to make a covenant with Israel and thus lay down norms for her to follow in order to be a free nation at his service.

Both the narrative texts and the legal texts of Exodus are important for the study of justice in the Bible because they contain the mighty deeds of God's justice and the norms by which Israel was to serve God. This chapter is devoted to an analysis of justice in the narrative texts, and the next chapter will study justice in the legal texts. The present chapter is divided into three sections: the story of liberation in the text of Exodus, the story in the traditions that underlie the text as it now stands, and a historical reconstruction of the original event of Exodus.

1. The Exodus in the Bible

The story of the book of Exodus does not depict daily life within a world of ordinary experience. It goes beyond the ordinary and unveils the extraordinary and supernatural action of God who intervenes in history to fulfill his design. The story of Exodus resulted from discovering God's marks or vestiges in ordinary events and from shaping these findings into a narrative—both epic and mythopoetic in its scope—designed to display the purpose of God's intervention. The outcome is an epic work that exalts Yahweh's supremacy and his overwhelming punitive action against an earthly power that defied God by refusing to follow God's established order. In concrete terms, God punished Pharaoh in the book of Exodus because Pharaoh's cruel and despotic treatment of Israel defied Yahweh's established order. In punishing Pharaoh, God liberated Israel.[1] The extant text of Exodus contains a logical sequence of events, beginning with the entrance of Jacob's children into Egypt through the Exodus of the tribes of Israel and their arrival at Sinai, the place of the covenant. In the process, God granted Israel the elements that were considered essential, according to the ancient concept of nationhood: a leader, a law, a temple with rituals and ministers, and a land. Peculiar to the book of Exodus is the fact that Yahweh is both the protagonist who guides and performs the liberating action and the speaker who issues words and discourses mastering the whole story. This combination of narrative and discourse, in which Yahweh is both actor and speaker, seems to derive from the cultic setting in which the material of this book most probably had been formed.

The narrative of Exodus can be divided into two parts. The first part depicts an action located primarily in Egypt, the place where Pharaoh rules and Israel endures oppression (Exod 1:1–13:16). The second part locates the action at Sinai, which is under Yahweh's rule (Exod 15:22–40:38). Actually both parts are intertwined, since Yahweh, the Lord of Sinai, is active not only in the second but also in the first part. In the first part, Yahweh calls Moses twice, sending him on a mission to Pharaoh to request Israel's release. The implementation of each mission involves God's action through Moses and his confrontation with the Egyptian ruler. The confrontation is intensified in the story of the plagues, which shows the overwhelming action of Yahweh in Pharaoh's territory.

The second part portrays Yahweh acting at Sinai and making the liberated Israel his own people. God's action involves making two covenants, each with its own tablets of laws. Israel breaks the first covenant, and Moses shatters the law tablets into pieces. But God makes a second covenant with Israel and gives them new tablets. Within the structure of the book of Exodus, the two covenants, described in the second part of the book, correspond to the two missions of Moses in the first part. At the center of the structure lies the story of the crossing of the

---

[1] Walter Brueggemann, "Pharaoh as Vassal: A Study of a Political Metaphor," *CBQ* 57 (1995): 27–51.

sea (Exod 13:17–15:21), which contains the description of Yahweh's final victory over Pharaoh.[2]

The first manifestation of God's decision to liberate his people takes place in the theophany of the burning bush (Exod 3:1–12). Here, Yahweh breaks the ordinary and natural rhythm of history, introducing the extraordinary and supernatural (3:1–3); he goes beyond the sacred manifested in nature and introduces his creative word in history. He reveals himself in the burning bush and speaks from the midst of its fire. He is the God of the patriarchs who identifies himself as Yahweh—as the powerful God who creates unprecedented events in history and gives assurance that he is totally committed to rescuing his people from oppressive powers (3:7–10, 17, 19–20). Verbs of liberation dominate the dialogue between Yahweh and Moses (3:8, 10, 11, 12, 17, 20). After Moses failed in his mission (5:1–21), God renews his call to reassure him that his divine determination to liberate the chosen people remains as strong as ever. To this effect, he issues an emphatic statement of his resolve:

> I am the Lord, and I will free you from the burdens of the Egyptians and deliver you from slavery to them. I will redeem you *(wĕgāʾaltî ʾet(ĕ)kem)* with an outstretched arm and with mighty acts of judgment *(ûbiš(ĕ)pāṭîm gĕdōlîm)*. I will take you as my people, and I will be your God. You shall know that I am the Lord your God . . . I will bring you into the land that I swore to give to Abraham, Isaac and Jacob; I will give it to you for a possession. I am the Lord. (Exod 6:6–8)

God describes his liberating act as a redemption that is carried out through acts of judgment, namely, acts motivated by reasons of justice. It is a just redemption, but not necessarily because Israel deserves it on account of her merits. Rather, it is just because God has decided to conform his action, first, to the order that he himself had established as the creator and master of history, and second, to the obligation that he had assumed in the oath sworn to Abraham to protect him and his descendants (Gen 15:1, 13–21; 17:2–8). As creator, he had imposed upon himself the obligation to protect the dignity of human beings, and as protector of Israel, he had assumed the responsibility to defend his chosen people.

Now, after observing the misery and outcry of the elect, God decides that he has to intervene because it is a duty of justice for him to punish oppressive Pharaoh and to rescue oppressed Israel. By doing so, he shows that he is the indisputable sovereign of the cosmos and the redeemer *(gōʾēl)* of Israel.[3] Yahweh defeats Pharaoh by unleashing the powers of nature against him. The story of the plagues (Exod 7:8–11:10) shows the overwhelming supremacy of God who destroys any power that dares to defy his sovereignty. This story echoes the mythical battle be-

---

[2] Mark S. Smith, "The Literary Arrangement of the Priestly Redaction of Exodus: A Preliminary Investigation," *CBQ* 58 (1996): 25–50.

[3] See Jeremiah Unterman, "Redemption (OT)," *ABD* 5:650–54. The relationship of redeemer and redeemed is based on a social and legal practice of ancient Israel. In that culture, the redeemer was always the closest adult male relative, whose responsibility it was to look out for the well-being of his ward.

tween the God of order and life and the primordial monster which seeks destruction and death. In Exodus, the fight has its climax in the last plague, in which Yahweh, in the middle of the night, strikes the final blow—he defeats Egypt and its gods, and rescues Israel, fulfilling an action of justice that punishes the oppressor and saves the oppressed (ʾeʿĕśeh šĕpāṭîm, Exod 12:12). During that night, while Egyptian families mourn the death of their firstborn (12:30), the Israelite households enjoy the celebration of the Passover lamb (12:1–28). This celebration became a permanent institution, commemorating the liberation of Israel from Egyptian slavery and the birth of the nation as God's people (12:14). Through the ritual, the story became a memorial; reenacted yearly for each new generation, the event transcended its facticity.[4]

Yahweh's victory over Pharaoh culminates in the story of the crossing of the sea (Exod 14:1–15:19), in which God wins the final battle against a massive military operation that Pharaoh had marshaled in his last effort to seize Israel. In the battle, God splits the sea (14:21), an exploit that evokes the creation myth in which the Lord cut through the primeval sea monster (Isa 51:9; Job 26:13). The purpose of employing this mythical image is to emphasize that the birth of Israel is the effect of Yahweh's creation; it is the result of the creative victory of the God of order and justice over the monster of oppression and death.[5] While the prose narrative (Exod 14:15–31) underlines the reminiscences of the mythical and primordial victory, the following hymn (15:1–18) reenacts God's victory in the style of a liturgical celebration, instilling in every new generation trust in the indisputable power of God as the creator and liberator of Israel: "The Lord will reign forever and ever" (15:18).

After the liberation from Pharaoh's despotic power, Yahweh leads Israel to Sinai to conclude a covenant through which Israel becomes Yahweh's "treasury possession," called to be a holy nation (Exod 19:5–6). Yahweh, in turn, assumes the responsibility of protecting Israel, provided that the nation fulfill the duties stipulated in the agreement. The covenant results from Yahweh's merciful favor; hence, it is a combination of law and grace. In this vein, sharing in the gracious benefits of the covenant requires obedience to God's will expressed through the Ten Commandments (20:1–17) and the Code of the Covenant (21:1–23:19).

Yahweh's revelation to Israel continues after the covenant is concluded (Exod 24:1–11). Moses is called again to go up to the mountain to receive instructions for building the tabernacle and instituting the Aaronic priesthood (25:1–31:18). While

---

[4] See Bernard Sesboüé, "De la narrativité en théologie," *Greg* 75 (1994): 415–29.

[5] See Bernard F. Batto, *Slaying the Dragon: Mythmaking in the Biblical Tradition* (Louisville: Westminster/John Knox, 1992), 102–52. In devising his own historical-critical reconstruction of the crossing of the sea, Batto holds that the motif of crossing the sea dry-shod derived from ritual celebrations commemorating the conquest at Gilgal in the eleventh century B.C.E. These celebrations interpret the crossing of the Jordan River within the mythic scheme of the struggle of the creator-God with the primordial sea. This interpretation understood the Conquest as a result of the creative action of Yahweh. Gradually, with the passage of time, the liturgical celebration transferred these connections to the traditions of the Exodus associated with the Red Sea (140–44).

Moses is on the mountain with God, in the valley below an unexpected scene develops in violation of the covenant—the worship of the golden calf (32:1–35). This scene, which so enrages God, provides the occasion for Moses to intercede before God for Israel. As a result Moses obtains God's forgiveness for the people and the renewal of the covenant with new tablets. It is worth noting that Moses obtained from God not only forgiveness for this particular violation of the covenant but a permanent attitude of God's mercy toward Israel (33:12–17; 34:6–13).

The bestowal of new tablets and a new covenant, however, does not imply replacement of the apostate Israel by another people. In fact, Moses rejected the idea of replacement. He was ready to die rather than be a leader of another people, no matter how good they might have been (Exod 32:10, 31–32). He argued that the apostasy of the people cannot abolish the promise of the Lord, an argument of which God approves (Exod 32:11–14). In Moses' argument, the continuity of Israel is a question of justice in the biblical sense. It is rooted in the pledge that God gave to the ancestors. In accepting Moses' plea, then, God did not reject his people. Instead, he established his protecting and forgiving presence in the midst of a sinful people (Exod 33:19; 37:6–9). Paul follows Moses' position in the Letter to the Romans: "The gifts and the call of God are irrevocable" (Rom 11:19).[6]

The book of Exodus concludes with the construction of the tabernacle and the institution of the Aaronic priesthood (Exod 36:8–40:33). In this way, God establishes his presence in the midst of Israel and enables chosen priests to exercise their mediation on behalf of the elect. According to the story, once the tabernacle is completed, Moses inspects and certifies that everything has been done just as the Lord had commanded (39:43). These expressions are reminiscent of the scene in the Priestly school's creation narrative in which God, at the end of the sixth day, inspects what he had done and certifies that everything is very good (Gen 1:31). This verbal echo suggests that the building of the tabernacle is the climax of what God has done for Israel at Sinai, just as the Sabbath was the culmination of what he had done at the creation (Gen 2:1–3).

The narrative of the Exodus has an essential orientation toward the future. It narrates the foundational events for Israel's existence in history. Israel was liberated from Egyptian slavery not to wander the desert but to settle in the promised land and to grow as a free and holy nation at Yahweh's service. The protagonist of the narrative is the God of the ancestors who promised them a great posterity in the land of Canaan. The covenant code that God gave Israel through Moses is for her to prosper and live in justice and peace in the promised arable and fertile land. The establishment of God's presence in the tabernacle and the institution of the priestly mediation, of the mercy seat, and of the Passover celebration speak of the orientation of this narrative to the future of Israel. Most important in regard to this orientation is the fact that the extant book of Exodus was written during

---

[6] See Göran Larsson, *Bound for Freedom: The Book of Exodus in Jewish and Christian Traditions* (Peabody, Mass.: Hendrickson, 1999), 249–53; Norbert F. Lohfink, *The Covenant Never Revoked: Biblical Reflections on Christian Jewish Dialogue* (trans. J. J. Scullion; New York: Paulist Press, 1991).

the Babylonian exile and in the early postexilic period. In the perspective of this writing, the liberation from Egyptian slavery is an event that gives an anticipated assurance of the liberation of Israel from Babylonian captivity. The victory of Yahweh over the Egyptian monster gives believers the assurance of the defeat of the Babylonian oppressor. The religious and political structures that Moses prepares for the nation have a broad scope—they encompass the new community emerging from the Babylonian captivity, a community called to be "for me a priestly kingdom, and a holy nation" (Exod 19:6). In all this there is an encouraging message: God is carefully committed to protecting the elect from oppression and to inspiring them to grow in freedom, justice, and peace. However, the encouraging message of Exodus is not just for Israel, but for any human group under oppression. The God who defeated the oppressor and liberated the oppressed in Exodus is the creator who proves active in history on behalf of his creatures (humanity) and is committed to defeating any power that violates the order established in creation. Thus, the story of Exodus nurtures in oppressed people the desire to be free from oppression, giving them the assurance that God is moved by the cry of the afflicted. In this sense, the story of Exodus is a paradigm of liberation.

2. The Exodus in the Bible's sources and traditions

From the nineteenth century until the last quarter of this century, the hypothesis of sources in the Pentateuch enjoyed widespread acceptance. In the last decades, however, the situation has changed. A serious challenge has undermined the academic consensus. As a result, some scholars dismiss altogether the study of sources in the Pentateuch, devoting themselves exclusively to a synchronic analysis of the text, while others continue a diachronic study, but with some modifications. This latter group agrees in general on the important role of the Deuteronomic school and Priestly writers but disagrees with respect to the nature and even the existence of the Yahwistic and Elohistic sources or traditions.

Most of those who are interested in the formation of the text accept the traditional idea that the Priestly school gave the final shape to the text of Exodus.[7] The Priestly school adopted extant texts and added their own traditions. According to the Priestly tradition, the eternal promise given to Abraham is the reason for God's intervening in favor of Israel against Pharaoh. When Yahweh heard the cry of the oppressed people in Egypt, he remembered the oath he had sworn to Abraham and made the decision to free his people. In the process, he revealed to Moses his name, emphasizing his overwhelming and invincible power, and unveiled his determination to carry out his action of saving justice (Exod 6:2–8). This Priestly school, employing existing traditions, constructed the two calls and missions of Moses as parallels to the two covenants and completed the story of

---

[7] Smith, "Arrangement," 25–50.

the ten plagues that ends with Yahweh's victory on the last night of Israel in Egypt, a night that has become eternally memorialized in the annual celebration of the feast of Passover (Exod 12:14). The same school emphasized in the story of the crossing of the sea the splitting of the waters as an allusion to the victory of God the creator over the primordial chaos (Exod 14:15–18, 22–23, 26–27; see Isa 51:9–10).[8] In the story of Israel at Sinai, the Priestly school used the traditional stories of the two covenants to create a symmetrical correspondence to the two calls of Moses, and they added the construction of the tabernacle as the place of the merciful presence of God in the midst of Israel and the institution of the Aaronic priesthood to exercise its ministry of mediation between God and his chosen people.

In the last decades, some scholars have drawn attention to the important role played by the Deuteronomic school in the formation of the text of Exodus: in the story of the first call and mission of Moses (Exod 2:23–4:17), in the preparation and conclusion of the covenant (19:1–25; 24:1–14), and in the story of the golden calf and of the second covenant (32:1–35; 34:1–35).[9]

In the past, the supporters of the sources theory stressed the role of the Yahwist and the Elohist in their explanation of the formation of the book of Exodus. They singled out distinctive elements of Yahwistic tradition: Pharaoh's cruel treatment of Israel threatened God's blessing to Abraham by impeding Israel's growth and preventing her from taking possession of her own land. Yahweh intervened to allow the blessing to be fulfilled (Exod 3:7–8). He revealed to Moses, the messenger of liberation (3:16–17; 4:10–17), that he would use the plagues to convince Pharaoh to release Israel (3:19–20). In the plagues, Yahweh engaged Pharaoh in single combat, a fight between the God of life and the monster seeking Israel's destruction, ending with Yahweh's last blow in which he killed Pharaoh's firstborn together with all the Egyptian firstborn (12:29). In the crossing of the sea, Yahweh fought against Pharaoh's army, while Israel remained quiet. In his fight he used the waters of the sea and mastered the wind against his adversary, and from his throne of cloud and fire he threw the Egyptians into panic (14:13–14, 19–21, 24–25, 27). In the Yahwistic tradition, the destination of Israel's journey is the Promised Land (3:8, 17; 6:1). Sinai is only a stage, though it is an important one, because here, Israel worshiped Yahweh and received covenant stipulations, which are essentially cultic (Exod 34) and are designed for Israel to observe in recognition of Yahweh as the sole source of life and prosperity once she is settled in the land (34:11, 18–26).

In the past, many supporters of the sources theory identified the Elohistic tradition as parallel to the Yahwistic. In their opinions, the Elohist conveyed distinctive elements: God intervened on behalf of the oppressed Israelites in order to fulfill the promise given to the Patriarchs. To this end, God chose Moses as the

---

[8] See "The Creation Epic," translated by E. A. Speiser and A. K. Grayson (*ANET*, 60–72, 501–3).

[9] See Joseph Blenkinsopp, *The Pentateuch: An Introduction to the First Five Books of the Bible* (New York: Doubleday, 1992), 150–51, 194–97.

mediator of liberation (Exod 3:10) and revealed to him his name to render credibility to Moses' mission (3:13–15). Once the mission of liberation was accomplished, God bestowed on Moses a higher role—the mediator of the covenant. The Elohistic tradition stressed that the covenant was based on a union of wills. Hence, it was fundamental for Israel to conform her conduct to God's will, revealed in the covenant (19:5). Similarly, the Elohist understood sin as a rebellion against the covenant and stressed the need of conversion, as is shown in the story of the golden calf (32:7–10, 14, 30–34).

Today, however, scholars who are interested in the formation of the Pentateuch are divided regarding the existence of the Yahwist and Elohist. Most of them do not deny the existence of traditions previous to Deuteronomy and the Priestly school, but they question the existence of distinctive strings of traditions, clearly identifiable as full stories, that are recognized as Yahwistic or Elohistic. For instance, R. Rendtorff thinks that the Yahwist is not a full narrative that weaves through the Pentateuch, but an editorial reworking of individual passages.[10] Others, such as J. Blenkinsopp, think that passages that were attributed to the Yahwist are really the result of the accumulation of successive stages of interpretation (as in Exod 2:23–4:17) or are part of the editorial work done by the Deuteronomic school (as in Exod 19:1–25; 24:1–14; 32:1–34:35).[11] Others, such as J. Van Seters, think that the Yahwist is a postexilic work.[12] Finally, still others, including R. E. Murphy, H. Seebass, and J. Vermeylen, continue to affirm the existence of the Yahwist as a workable hypothesis, describing him as transmitter and interpreter of traditions and adding the explanation that it was an ancient writing that was open to further expansions and elaboration under prophetic influence.[13] In this vein, A. de Pury says: "The postexilic Pentateuch inherited centuries-old traditions."[14] The tradition of the Elohist, whose existence has always been a debatable issue, today is considered by many to be an editorial expansion of the Yahwist.[15]

---

[10] Rolf Rendtorff, *Das überlieferungsgeschichtliche Problem des Pentateuch* (BZAW 147; New York: De Gruyter, 1976), 80–111.

[11] Blenkinsopp, *Pentateuch*, 148–51; 186–90.

[12] John Van Seters, *Prologue to History: The Yahwist as Historian in Genesis* (Louisville: Westminster/John Knox, 1992) argues extensively for the exilic composition of the Yahwist writings. See Blenkinsopp, *Pentateuch*, 1–28.

[13] Roland E. Murphy, "Introduction to the Pentateuch," *NJBC* 3–7; Albert de Pury and Thomas Römer, "Le Pentateuque en question: position du probleme et brève histoire de la recherche," in *Le Pentateuque en question* (ed. Albert de Pury; MdB 19; Geneva: Labor et Fides, 1989), 9–80; Horst Seebass, "Que reste-t-il du Yahwiste et de l'Elohiste?" in *Pentateuque en question*, 199–230; Jacques Vermeylen, "Le premières étapes littéraires de la formation du Pentateuque," in *Pentateuque en question*, 149–97. See also Kaare Berge, *Die Zeit des Jahwisten: Ein Beitrag zur Datierung jahwistischer Vätertexte* (BZAW 186; Berlin: de Gruyter, 1990); Henri Cazelles, "Pentateuque," *DBSup* 7 (1966): 771–858; Robert B. Coote, *In Defense of Revolution: The Elohist History* (Minneapolis: Fortress, 1991); Richard E. Friedman, "Torah (Pentateuch)," *ABD* 6:605–22.

[14] de Pury, "Pentateuque en question," 80.

[15] For a defense of the Elohistic tradition see Alan W. Jenks, "Elohist," *ABD* 2:478–82; Terence E. Fretheim, "Elohist," *IDBSup* 259–63; Sean McEvenue, "The Elohist at Work," *ZAW* 96 (1984): 315–32.

3. The Exodus in history

The question about the historical nature of the Exodus from Egypt was raised in the nineteenth century, and the debate was rekindled especially in the last decades of the twentieth century under the influence of new archaeological discoveries in Palestine. The nature and significance of the original event have drawn the attention of scholars engaged in liberation theology. For the present chapter I will review three representatives of this trend: J. S. Croatto, G. Pixley and N. K. Gottwald.[16]

Croatto thinks that the recovery of the original event of the Exodus is pivotal because this was the first occurrence of God's revelation to Israel. In his opinion, the original event involved a mixed group of slaves, without common roots or aspirations, who, aware of the oppressive injustice they were suffering under Pharaoh's rule, united against their oppressor and became a people. They fought and won their sociopolitical freedom. This is the event that gave birth to Israel and imprinted in her the first revelation as a call to political liberty. According to Croatto, the story preserved in the book of Exodus is a religious interpretation of the historical event. As a result, the event of Exodus was associated with the yearly celebration of Passover, a ritual designed to keep alive in the people their original call to political freedom. In his opinion, the original fact of Exodus was a political event, full of implications. Its significance was not exhausted in Israel's history. It is a meaningful paradigm applicable to any socially oppressive situation in which a human community may be found.[17]

Pixley concurs with Croatto in emphasizing that those subject to forced labor in Egypt were a mixed group without common roots, who united under the experience of common suffering. He also concurs with Croatto in the description of the original event of Exodus; it was not an ethnic or religious struggle but a class struggle motivated by sociopolitical reasons. Pixley stresses that the religious interpretation was added later as an ideological justification for the political liberation.[18]

Gottwald leaves aside the biblical traditions of the Exodus from Egypt, because, on the one hand, he thinks that their historicity cannot be proved, and on the other, he is convinced that Israel was born in Canaan. Gottwald sees the Exo-

---

[16] J. S. Croatto and G. Pixley are chosen for this analysis of the Exodus event because they are the most representative exegetes of the book of Exodus among Latin American scholars. N. K. Gottwald is included because of his contribution to the study of the Exodus event, as well as his influence on Latin American readers of Exodus.

[17] J. Severino Croatto, "Liberación y libertad: reflexiones hermenéuticas en torno al Antiguo Testamento," *RevistB* 33 (1971): 4–5, 14; Croatto, *Liberación y libertad: pautas hermenéuticas* (Buenos Aires: Mundo Nuevo, 1973), 28–30, 55–59, 78–79, 142; Croatto, "El Dios en el acontecimiento" *RevistB* 35 (1973): 56–59. See also Croatto, *Biblical Hermeneutics: Toward a Theory of Reading and the Production of Meaning* (trans. R. R. Barr; Maryknoll: Orbis, 1987).

[18] Jorge V. Pixley, *On Exodus: A Liberation Perspective* (trans. R. R. Barr; Maryknoll: Orbis, 1987), xviii–xx.

dus as a social and political process—the movement from slavery to freedom, the transition from a collective life under foreign rulers to a social life under self-determination. This process becomes an event through a sociopolitical revolution, as was the birth of Israel in Canaan. In Gottwald's opinion, Israel was born as result of the victory of peasants, termed *ḫāpiru* who revolted against the oppressive regimes of the Canaanite cities. Those who revolted were ethnically mixed groups who united in the revolutionary movement and who gradually developed a new social system with an egalitarian basis.

Gottwald thinks that the early stories of Exodus contained the narrative of the revolution that had given Israel sociopolitical freedom. But in the premonarchic period, under the influence of the ideology of holy war, these stories were transformed into a religious epic, and later in the exilic and postexilic period, under the Priestly influence, the religious dimension became so prominent that the political aspect was altogether eclipsed. It is up to exegetes and historians to recover the fresh vitality of the original sociopolitical event. The purpose of such exegetical work is to offer a critically refined paradigm to those who seek a new experience of Exodus.[19]

Croatto, Pixley, and Gottwald concur regarding the importance of the search for the original Exodus and its reconstruction as an event of sociopolitical revolution. But they diverge in the identification of the place at which the event occurred. In order to evaluate their reconstruction and to suggest an alternative explanation, I shall develop my discussion in five points: the original event of Exodus and its religious dimension; Exodus and the revolutionary model; Exodus and egalitarian society; Exodus as the first revelation; and Exodus as a paradigm of liberation.

3.1. The Exodus event and its religious dimension

In the Exodus epic, Yahweh's victory over Pharaoh not only shows Yahweh's indisputable sovereignty, but also brings about the creation of Israel as an independent, free nation. Historians are eager to know the events that would have provided the basis for this epic. But the historicity of such events is a controversial issue among contemporary scholars. Many scholars, like N. P. Lemche and R. B. Coote, deny the historicity of the Exodus of Israelites from Egypt.[20] Because of the academic debate, Gottwald chose to consider Exodus not as an event but as a process—a journey from slavery to freedom. He applied this concept to the situation of Israel, not in Egypt, but in Canaan, and saw the process as developing in

---

[19] Norman K. Gottwald, "The Exodus as Event and Process: A Test Case in the Biblical Grounding of Liberation Theology," in *The Future of Liberation Theology: Essays in Honor of Gustavo Gutiérrez* (ed. Marc H. Ellis and Otto Maduro; Maryknoll: Orbis, 1989), 250–60.

[20] Niels P. Lemche, *Ancient Israel: A New History of Israelite Society* (Sheffield: JSOT Press, 1988), 89; Robert B. Coote, *Early Israel: A New Horizon* (Minneapolis: Fortress, 1990), 89–90.

accordance with a revolutionary model. Croatto and Pixley instead assumed the substantial historicity of the Exodus of Israel from Egypt. The three scholars concur, however, that originally the early existence of a sociopolitical event would have been disconnected from religious connotations.

The reconstruction of the exodus as a *secular event* does not seem to derive from the study of the cultural conditions of the Early Iron Age of the ancient Near East (*ca.* 1200–1000 B.C.E.), because in the ancient Near East, as H. Cazelles says, it was a common and indisputable assumption that nations and peoples understood themselves to be led by deities. It was completely normal, for instance, that the Assyrian king, after a victory against his enemies, would write down a report for the sovereign god of the nation.[21] As G. von Rad said: "The experiences of the world were for her [Israel] always divine experiences as well, and the experiences of God were for her experiences of the world."[22] The secular reconstruction of Exodus seems to derive from modern concepts of secularity. In fact, in the praxis of liberation theology, the interpretative process starts from below: the conscience-raising of an oppressed group and the analysis of the sociopolitical situation in which it lives.[23] In this process, the analysis of contemporary society and the modern concept of secularity seem to govern the reading of the text so strongly that it influences the reconstruction of the original event.[24] Gottwald, in particular, begins with a secular event because, in his opinion, religion depends on the socioeconomic structures of society.[25]

Moreover, the secular reconstruction regards the religious interpretation of the event as a subsequent addition to the original event. But the process that formed the story may be the exact opposite of what Gottwald, Croatto, and Pixley imagine. Indeed, it is far more probable that the biblical story of the Exodus begins with the discovery of God's influence on history, after which the mytho-

---

[21] Henri Cazelles, ed., *Introduction critique à l'Ancien Testament* (Paris: Desclée, 1973), 196.

[22] Gerhard von Rad, *Wisdom in Israel* (trans. James S. D. Martin; Nashville: Abingdon, 1972), 62.

[23] Gustavo Gutiérrez, *A Theology of Liberation* (trans. M. J. O'Connell; Maryknoll: Orbis, 1973), 203–8; Gutiérrez, "Notes for a Theology of Liberation," *TS* 31 (1970): 244–45.

[24] William C. Spohn, *What Are They Saying about Scripture and Ethics?* (New York and Ramsey: Paulist, 1984), 54–66, esp. 58.

[25] Norman K. Gottwald, *Tribes of Israel: A Sociology of the Religion of Liberated Israel, 1250–1050 B.C.E.* (Maryknoll: Orbis, 1979), 700–709. In an article published in 1983, however, Gottwald recognized that he should have paid more attention to religious factors in the process of liberation. He says: "It is evident that the specific thrust and intensity of Yahwism required more than frontier distance to come into play, since the new religion presupposes a powerful social impulse and effective organizational mechanisms. At this point the role of the Levites, or Yahwistic intellectuals, is probably of great importance, constituting one of the undeveloped aspects of my hypothesis that invites enlargement." See Gottwald, "Two Models for the Origins of Ancient Israel: Social Revolution or Frontier Development" in *The Quest For the Kingdom of God: Studies in Honor of George E. Mendenhall* (ed. H. B. Huffmon et al.; Winona Lake: Eisenbrauns, 1983), 16.

poetic story is reframed, so that the divine design might be disclosed. As P. Ricoeur says: "God's mark is in history before being in speech."[26]

The objection that during the time of Exodus there was not yet worship of Yahweh is not compelling. The belief in Yahweh goes back to the origins of Israel, as the Song of Deborah and Psalm 89 testify. Many scholars think that the worship of Yahweh was introduced into Canaan by some Israelite tribes coming from Sinai.[27] In this regard, the Song of Deborah is an important witness because, even though it was composed as early as the middle of the twelfth century B.C.E., it already identifies Israel as "the people of Yahweh" (Judg 5:11, 13) and associates this identity with the worship of Yahweh, the Lord of Sinai (5:5), suggesting the exclusive worship due him (5:8).[28] The Song of Deborah contains substantial elements of the relationship between Yahweh and Israel, which later would be described in terms of covenant.[29]

3.2. Exodus and the revolutionary model

Croatto and Pixley think that the original event was a revolutionary struggle. They reconstruct the Exodus from Egypt, employing the revolutionary model that had been used in explaining the conquest of the land. Gottwald, in turn, converts the Exodus into a revolutionary process that takes place in Canaan—not in Egypt. The probability of these theories essentially depends on the success of

---

[26] Paul Ricoeur, *Essays on Biblical Interpretation* (Philadelphia: Fortress, 1980), 79. In this regard R. E. Murphy says that in ancient Israel "the world is never experienced as purely secular, as apart from the Lord who controls it and who is revealed in it." See Roland Murphy, *The Tree of Life* (New York: Doubleday, 1990), 114.

[27] Graham I. Davies, "Sin, Wilderness of," *ABD* 6:49; David N. Freedman, "The Religion of Early Israel," in *Ancient Israelite Religion* (ed. Patrick D. Miller, Jr. et al.; Philadelphia: Fortress, 1987), 315–35; Edward Lipinski, "Judges 5,4–5 et Psaum 68,8–11," *Bib* 48 (1967): 185–200; P. K. McCarter, "The Origins of Israelite Religion," in *The Rise of Ancient Israel* (ed. H. Shanks; Washington, D.C.: Biblical Archaeology Society, 1992), 119–36; Ernest W. Nicholson, *God and His People: Covenant and Theology in the Old Testament* (Oxford: Clarendon, 1985), 196–97; Moshe Weinfeld, "The Tribal League at Sinai," in *Ancient Israelite Religion*, 304–14; Lemche, *Ancient Israel*, 253, 255, despite his skepticism with respect to the historicity of Moses, is attracted by the theory that the worship of Yahweh was introduced by a group of Levites coming from Sinai.

[28] On the dating of the Song of Deborah, see David N. Freedman, "Early Israelite Poetry and Historical Reconstructions," in *Unity and Diversity: Essays in the History, Literature, and Religion of the Ancient Near East* (ed. Hans Goedicke and J. J. M. Roberts; Baltimore, London: The Johns Hopkins University Press, 1975), 13; A. Globe, "The Literary Structure and Unity of the Song of Deborah," *JBL* 93 (1974): 495–97.

[29] See Nicholson, *God and His People*, 176–78; 184–87; John Day, "Pre-Deuteronomic Allusions to the Covenant in Hosea and Psalm LXXVIII," *VT* 36 (1986): 1–12. These two authors, together with many others, call into question the thesis of Lothar Perlitt, *Bundestheologie im Alten Testament* (Neukirchen-Vluyn: Neukirchener Verlag, 1969) who holds that the covenant, as a way of expressing the relationship between Yahweh and Israel, was an invention of the deuteronomistic authors. Nicholson and Day, instead, argue against this notion, on the basis that already in the eighth century B.C.E. Hosea makes reference to the covenant.

applying the revolutionary model to the conquest. In the past, this application enjoyed wide acceptance, but today it is dismissed by many historians and archaeologists. P. J. King, a Palestinian archaeologist, stresses three items in his report on the social and cultural reconstruction of the origins of Israel: (1) hundreds of sites throughout Palestine that were unoccupied in the Late Bronze Age, prior to ca. 1200 B.C.E., were settled peacefully in Iron Age I that immediately followed; (2) the architecture, agriculture, and ceramics of these settlements reflect a level of sophistication not associated with pastoral nomads; (3) those settlements, although located in vulnerable positions, remained unfortified. The peaceful character of these settlements shows that their inhabitants did not feel that their security would be threatened by eventual attacks or reprisals from enemies.[30] V. Fritz concurs with King in underlining the absence of fortifications in the hundreds of villages of Iron Age I and in dismissing the revolutionary model as an explanation of the conquest of the land. Fritz supports the theory of a symbiotic process by which seminomadic tribes, through long and intensive contact with the Canaanites, abandoned their nomadic life, adopted the culture of the land, and settled in the hilly areas.[31] The theory of symbiosis enjoys wide acceptance. In this regard, W. G. Dever says that the symbiotic model provides the best explanation for the archaeological data.[32]

In the light of such archaeological data, many historians today have discarded the revolutionary model as an explanation of the conquest of the promised land. Likewise, they reject as unfounded the thesis of the unrest and opposition of the ḫāpiru to authorities in Palestine, which had been understood as forming the historical background of the so-called Israelite revolution against the Canaanite regimes.[33] There is no evidence, either in the documents of Amarna or those of Byblos of a revolt of the ḫāpiru against the monarchies of Canaan.[34] Gottwald himself, who earlier had supported the theory of Israelite revolt against Egyptio-Canaanite regimes in Palestine, later became more cautious and labeled the thesis of Israelite revolt as a pure supposition.[35]

---

[30] The text of this report is in Philip J. King, "The Contribution of Archaeology to Biblical Studies," *CBQ* 45 (1983): 1–16, esp. 5–12. One may also read a summary in North, Robert and Philip J. King, "Biblical Archaeology," *NJBC* 1196–1218. In a recent book, the archaeologist A. Mazar also underlines the peaceful character of the Israelite population at the beginning of the Iron Age, highlighting the absence of fortifications. See Amihai Mazar, *Archaeology of the Land of the Bible: 10,000–586 B.C.E.* (New York: Doubleday, 1992), 334–45.

[31] Volkmar Fritz, "Conquest or Settlement?" *BA* 50 (1987): 96–98.

[32] William G. Dever, "How to Tell a Canaanite from an Israelite," in *The Rise of Ancient Israel* (ed. H. Shanks: Washington, D. C.: Biblical Archaeology Society, 1992), 27–56, esp. 30.

[33] Lemche, "Ḫabiru, Ḫapiru," *ABD* 3:6–10.

[34] Baruch Halpern, "Settlement of Canaan," *ABD* 5:1128–30; Halpern, *The Emergence of Israel in Canaan* (SBLMS 29; Chico, Calif.: Scholars Press, 1983), 63; Gösta W. Ahlström, *The History of Ancient Palestine from the Palaeolithic Period to Alexander's Conquest* (JSOTSup 146; Sheffield: JSOT Press, 1993), 344–45.

[35] Gottwald, *Tribes of Yahweh*, 398.

Contemporary historians relate Israel's consolidation in Canaan to the general collapse of the city-states of the Late Bronze Age, which collapse is still a perplexing phenomenon. Although they are divided in finding the factors that contributed to the formation of Israel, historians concur in dismissing the revolutionary model and in seeking other ways to explain Israel's origins. Many hold that a group coming from Sinai would have introduced the worship of Yahweh into Palestine, providing the Israelite tribes with a common religious bond.[36]

3.3. Exodus and egalitarian society

According to Croatto, Pixley, and Gottwald, the event of Exodus led to an egalitarian society. This statement assumes that premonarchical Israel historically was a community of equals. In this regard, some critiques of Gottwald's book, *The Tribes of Yahweh,* are most helpful. G. Lenski, for instance, says that, instead of speaking of an egalitarian society, Gottwald would have been more accurate if he had said "Israel constituted a society less stratified than her surrounding peoples."[37] After analyzing the mechanisms of judicial authority in early Israel, R. R. Wilson concluded that Israel did not organize herself as an egalitarian society, since the low strata of Israelite premonarchical society consisted of groups based on lineage relationship. In this system of lineage, differences in social status, political and economic power, and religious authority were expressed in genealogical terms. In this structure, the father of the family enjoyed virtually absolute power over members of his group, as can be seen in Genesis 31 and 38. Such power was exercised in the household over both family members and family retainers. In short, according to Wilson, the system of lineage, as it was practiced in premonarchical Israel, implied a principle of inequality.[38] In this vein, S. Bendor

---

[36] See Davies, "Sin, Wilderness of," 49; George E. Mendenhall, *The Tenth Generation: The Origins of the Biblical Tradition* (Baltimore: John Hopkins University Press, 1973), 12–31; McCarter, "Origins," 119–36; Freedman, "Religion," 329–31; Weinfeld, "Tribal League," 304–14; Nicholson, *God and His People,* 196–97.

[37] Gerhard Lenski, review of N. K. Gottwald, *The Tribes of Yahweh, RelSRev* 6 (1980): 276.

[38] Robert R. Wilson, "Enforcing the Covenant: the Mechanisms of Judicial Authority in Early Israel," in *The Quest for the Kingdom of God: Studies in Honor of George E. Mendenhall* (ed. H. B. Huffmon et al.; Winona Lake: Eisenbrauns, 1983), 59–76. See also Lawson G. Stone, "Ethical and Apologetic Tendencies in the Redaction of the Book of Joshua," *CBQ* 53 (1991): 25–36; Halpern, "Settlement," *ABD* 5:1120–42; C. J. H. Wright, "Family," *ABD* 2:762; Shunya Bendor, *The Social Structure of Ancient Israel: The Institutions of the Family from the Settlement to the End of the Monarchy* (Jerusalem: Simor, 1996), 173–204. With regard to the possession of the land, it would seem that it is necessary to keep in mind that the model of distribution by lots (Josh 14:1–5; Num 34:13–29), according to which each Israelite was assigned a parcel of land within the area of tribal patrimony, is artificial and unreal. In actuality, the occupation of the land was not made following a preset plan; rather, it was a slow and cautious process. See Yairah Amit, "The Jubilee Law: An Attempt at Instituting Social Justice," in *Justice and Righteousness: Biblical Themes and their Influence* (ed. H. Reventlow and Y. Hoffman; JSOTSup 137; Sheffield: JSOT Press, 1992), 57.

emphasizes the tension created in the family by the right of the firstborn to inherit a double portion (see Deut 21:15–16).[39] Since this system in ancient Israel was essentially patriarchal, we can understand, as P. A. Bird says, the subordinate place given to women.[40] In addition, we must keep in mind the practice of slavery in premonarchical Israel (Exod 21:1–11; Num 31:9–18).[41]

3.4. Exodus as the first revelation

According to Croatto and J. P. Miranda, the liberating event of Exodus from Egypt was the first revelation granted to Israel, and its content related exclusively to social justice. In their opinion, this revelation is prototypical; namely, it is the criterion by which all subsequent revelations must be understood. In this regard, Miranda is very assertive—any revelation involves a demand of social justice, and God is only known in the cries of the poor and afflicted asking for justice.[42]

The statement that the Exodus from Egypt is the first revelation to Israel assumes that the patriarchal stories are late creations of Israelite imagination. Their historical nature is indeed debatable, and scholars are divided on the subject. Some, such as T. L. Thompson and J. Van Seters, hold that they are fictions created during the monarchy or even during the postexilic period.[43] Others, including A. R. Millard and D. S. Wiseman, defend their historical value.[44] Finally, others, such as R. E. Murphy, J. M. Miller, J. H. Hayes, C. Westermann, R. S. Hendel, and J. J. Scullion, base their claims on studies of cultural anthropology and the nature of oral traditions. They discern various strata of traditions in the ancestral stories in which some historical elements may have been preserved.[45] Rejecting any historical value of patriarchal traditions goes beyond the academic state of the question.

---

[39] Bendor, *Social Structure,* 175–87.

[40] See Phyllis A. Bird, "Women (OT)," *ABD* 6:951–57.

[41] Muhammad A. Dandamayev, "Slavery (OT)," *ABD* 6:62–65.

[42] José P. Miranda, *Marx and the Bible: A Critique of the Philosophy of Oppression* (trans. J. Eagleson; Maryknoll: Orbis, 1974), 44–88, 146–150; Miranda, *Being and the Messiah* (trans. J. Eagleson; Maryknoll: Orbis, 1977), 30–39.

[43] Thomas L. Thompson, *The Historicity of the Patriarchal Narratives* (New York: De Gruyter, 1974); John Van Seters, *Abraham in History and Tradition* (New Haven, Conn.: Yale University Press, 1975).

[44] See A. R. Millard, "Abraham," *ABD* 1:35–41; A. R. Millard and D. S. Wiseman, ed., *Essays on the Patriarchal Narratives* (Winona Lake: Eisenbrauns, 1983); John Bright, *A History of Israel* (3d ed.; Philadelphia: Westminster, 1981), 67–103.

[45] Roland E. Murphy, "A History of Israel," *NJBC* 1224–25; James Maxwell Miller and John H. Hayes, *A History of Ancient Israel and Judah* (Philadelphia: Westminster, 1986), 74–79; Claus Westermann, "Promises to the Patriarchs," *IDBSup,* 690–93; Westermann, *Genesis 12–36: A Commentary* (Minneapolis: Augsburg, 1985), 23–121; Westermann, *The Promises to the Fathers: Studies on the Patriarchal Narratives* (trans. D. E. Gree; Philadelphia: Fortress, 1980); Ronald S. Hendel, "Finding Historical Memories in the Patriarchal Narratives," *BAR* 21 (1995): 52–55, 58–59, and 70; John J. Scullion, *Genesis: A Commentary for Students, Teachers, and Preachers* (OTS 6; Collegeville: Liturgical Press, 1992), 253–71.

The assertion that social justice was the sole theme involved in the revelation of Exodus might seem to be confirmed by those prophets who focused their messages on issues of social justice and condemned rituals and sacrifices as foreign to God's revelation at Sinai (Amos 5:21–23; Hos 6:6; Isa 1:12–15). The argument would be compelling if the prophetic oracles against rituals were an absolute condemnation of any type of ritual, as many nineteenth-century exegetes claimed. But this is not the understanding of contemporary exegetes who see homiletic hyperbole in those oracles which condemn particular forms of rituals and their demands, but not rituals as such.[46] In fact, the worship of Yahweh is a very ancient element in the stories of Exodus, and early traditions relate it to Sinai. The Song of Deborah refers to it, and the ritual of the Passover lamb preserves very primitive elements of worship practiced by early Israelite tribes.[47]

Although the story of Exodus is not necessarily the first divine revelation, and although God's revelation includes more than issues concerning social justice, the story of Exodus nevertheless emphasizes the liberating nature of divine revelation, which essentially involves a saving action through which God frees human beings from affliction and oppression and makes them members of his people. In reality, the story of Exodus stresses the social and political dimensions of God's revelation together with its religious aspect. Revelation happens in the historical context in which humanity experiences conflict and suffering. It is in this very context that God intervenes to restore human beings to their integrity and dignity. He does so not only to ensure their participation in the world to come but also to make them able to fulfill a mission in this world. The divine revelation holds the potential of liberation from any oppression that undermines human dignity and from any force that prevents human beings from reaching their full development in an environment of freedom, justice, and peace.

3.5. Exodus as a paradigm of liberation

In the opinion of Croatto, Pixley, and Gottwald, the event of Exodus seems to be a paradigm that, if followed, guarantees sociopolitical freedom. But what is the factor that activates the process and brings it to success? G. Gutiérrez stated that the commitment to transform sociopolitical structures is motivated by a hope for political utopia, a socialist view of a new humanity—a world of equality and

---

[46] John J. Schmitt, "Prophecy (Preexilic Hebrew)," *ABD* 5:486–89; Gary A. Anderson, "Sacrifice and Sacrificial Offerings (OT)," *ABD* 5:881–82; Michael Fishbane, *Biblical Interpretation in Ancient Israel* (Oxford: Clarendon, 1985), 529. Fishbane understands Jer 7:21–22 as an example of haggadic hyperbole that makes an apparent case against the laws of the covenant. This author is certain that in no case does homiletic exegesis propose to subvert the laws of the covenant revealed by God. For a study of contrast by negation as a literary form, see Michael L. Barré, "Fasting in Isaiah 58:1–12: A Reexamination," *BTB* 15 (1985): 94–97; T. Booij, "Negation in Isaiah 43:22–24," *ZAW* 94 (1982): 390–400; H. Kruse, "Die dialectische Negation als semitischen Idiom," *VT* 4 (1954): 385–400.

[47] Roland de Vaux, *Ancient Israel* (2 vols.; New York: McGraw-Hill, 1965), 2:484–93.

brotherhood, without oppression.⁴⁸ Croatto and Pixley share this position. But none of Croatto, Pixley, or Guttiérrez seems to think that the liberation process is ruled by an inner force that is built into history, as in the philosophical thought of historical materialism.

Gottwald, by contrast, has a clear philosophical stance in this regard—he interprets the historical process from the point of view of Marxist ideology. In Gottwald's opinion, history is moved by an inner process, one in which sociopolitical revolution is the crucial factor that unleashes the forces that completely transform society, bringing about the end of oppression and the beginning of egalitarian society. G. E. Mendenhall criticized Gottwald's position by saying that this trust in history is intrinsic to an ideology of historical materialism, but in reality this ideology is obsolete.⁴⁹ Historical facts show that history does not have the liberating power once credited to it. Hence, a movement or process inspired by such ideology cannot guarantee the success of a paradigm designed to create a free, just, and egalitarian society.

To find the validity of Exodus as a liberating paradigm we ought to turn to the way in which the biblical narrative presents the event. In fact, this narrative sees the event as a result of God's creative power that is extended over history. The power through which God destroyed the chaotic monster and established his divine order in creation now intervenes in history to save his elect. God's purpose in intervening is to destroy the primordial monster that revives through reincarnation in political, economic, and religious powers, and that threatens the life, dignity, and mission of the chosen people.⁵⁰

For the biblical authors, the Exodus was not an event that is unique and unrepeatable; it is a permanent task. So the postexilic psalmist affirms that "The Lord does righteous deeds *(ṣĕdāqôt)* and brings justice *(mišpāṭîm)* to all the oppressed" (Ps 103:6). The psalmist's reliance on the epic of Exodus is clear, since he says: "His ways were revealed to Moses, mighty deeds to the people of Israel" (Ps 103:7). Thus, B. F. Batto has put it very well when he says, "Yahweh continually redeems his people in an Exodus that never ends."⁵¹

Among the biblical witnesses of this concept are the second Isaiah, Psalm 74, and the Priestly editor. The second Isaiah, relying on the intervention of Yahweh

---

⁴⁸ Gutiérrez, *Theology of Liberation*, 232–39.

⁴⁹ George E. Mendenhall, "Ancient Israel's Hyphenated History," in *Palestine in Transition* (ed. D. N. Freedman and D. F. Graf; Sheffield: Almond, 1983), 91–103.

⁵⁰ Fishbane (*Biblical Interpretation*, 354) expresses this concept very well when he says: "In other instances where eschatological hope is enlivened by memories of creation, it is strikingly the *process* of primordial beginnings that is stressed—when *ab origine* YHWH destroyed the monsters of chaos in theomachian strife. For to the ancients, like Deutero-Isaiah, this event constituted a fundamental expression of divine power, one which was, moreover, re-expressed in historical forms, as at the time of the exodus. Indeed, it was the perceived typology between the constitutive power of primordial victory and its salvific reflex in history that established the basis for hope in a redemptive remanifestation of that same power."

⁵¹ Batto, *Slaying the Dragon*, 111.

to reenact the victory over the primordial monster in the Exodus from Egypt, invokes that same divine power to intervene against the Babylonian monster. He reminds Yahweh of the precedent that he had established by intervening in Egypt:

> Awake, awake; put on strength
> O arm of the Lord!
> Awake as in the days of old,
> in ages long ago!
> Was it not you who crushed Rahab,
> you who pierced the dragon?
> Was it not you who dried up the sea,
> the waters of the great deep,
> Who made the depth of the sea into a way
> for the redeemed to pass over? (Isa 51:9–11)

The psalmist, in the time of the exile, likewise speaks to God, reminding him of his commitment. In his lament, he cries out:

> Why draw back your right hand,
> why keep it idle beneath your cloak?
> Yet you, God, are my king from of old,
> winning victories throughout the earth.
> You stirred up the sea in your might;
> you smashed the heads of the dragons on the waters.
> You crushed the heads of Leviathan. (Ps 74:11–13)

In a similar fashion, the Priestly writer follows the outline of mythical combat when, at the time of the Babylonian exile, he rearranges the story of the Exodus in order to stir up hopes of a future Israel. This writer depicts Yahweh in the story of the plagues as the creator God who fights against the pharaoh, represented as the primordial monster. This theme of mythical combat takes on a special significance in the story of the crossing of the sea, in which Yahweh divides the waters as Marduk divided the aquatic monster in the Babylonian hymn of creation.[52] The Priestly writer stresses the mythical dimension of the Exodus from Egypt in order to emphasize that the God of order is present in history, ready to destroy any recurrence of the primordial dragon's threat against God's elect.

These texts show that the Exodus event proves and guarantees the presence of the creative God in history. By virtue of God's presence, the Exodus event transcends its supposed facticity and becomes a foundational event, a memorial, and a paradigm of liberation. One might even say that the biblical Exodus is not a paradigm in itself, rather it is the application of a paradigm—the fight of the God of order against the power of chaos. Since the Exodus from Egypt is, however, the event *par excellence* that embodies the extension of creative action into history,

---

[52] See "The Creation Epic," translated by E. A. Speiser and A. K. Grayson (*ANET*, 60–72, 501–3).

one could say that it is paradigmatic for any possible later Exodus. In fact, the mythical battle that pervades the narrative gives it a suprahistorical dimension, and it makes it applicable to similar situations. Moreover, since the struggle is that of God the creator against the power of chaos and because all people come from the hands of the same creator, the lessons of Exodus can be extended to all people who suffer the tragedy of oppression in its diverse forms.

The intervention of the creator in history, especially in the paradigm of the Exodus, communicates the conviction that human beings have not been created in order to be slaves or to live in oppression. Furthermore, it identifies oppression, be it social, economic, or political, as an injustice. The liberating event of Exodus also shows that God is with the oppressed and that he wants their liberation and integration into a society that protects and practices justice. In order to show the seriousness of his commitment, God himself acts in history; he does so in a creative action narrated as the fight of the God of order against the monster of chaos. In this mythopoetic narration, the plot is so dominated by the divine action that it leaves little place for the participation of human beings; the dynamic of the narrative emphasizes that the birth of Israel is the consequence of God's free and creative action in history. The action of God in the fight against pharaoh is, however, distinct from his action in holy war. In the fight against Pharaoh, God alone defeats the reincarnated primordial monster, while in holy war God directs the hosts of Israel, teaching them strategy so that they might defeat the enemy.[53] But this does not mean that the mythopoetic description of the Exodus eliminates any responsibility of human beings in history. This responsibility is a basic presupposition in the thought of the biblical thinkers—the biblical historians depicted the history of the monarchy as the result of human decisions; the prophets encouraged leaders to engage in religious and political action or judged their decisions; the sages instructed people to develop their abilities to be successful in life; and the lawgivers provided guidance in order to build a prosperous, just, and peaceful community.[54]

The story of the Exodus awakens an awareness of their own dignity in those who suffer a situation similar to that of the Israelites in Egypt, moving them to think of leaving the state of oppression and stimulating in them the responsibility to act. In the contemporary world, there are a number of situations similar to that of the Israelites in Egypt. Not only are there nations subjected to political and

---

[53] In holy war there was a fusion of divine and human activity. This is what P. D. Miller calls "synergism". See Patrick D. Miller, *The Divine Warrior in Early Israel* (Cambridge, Mass.: Harvard University Press, 1973), 156. But there is no such fusion or "synergism" in the motif of the mythical battle, in which only the divine action matters. An example of the mythical battle is the crossing of the sea, which presents the birth of Israel as the effect of God's creative action in history.

[54] See Roland E. Murphy, "Wisdom in the OT," *ABD* 6:925; Terence E. Fretheim, "Will of God in the OT," *ABD* 6:919; Walter Brueggemann, *Theology of the Old Testament* (Minneapolis: Fortress, 1997), 450–527; Brueggemann, *In Man We Trust: The Neglected Side of Biblical Faith* (Richmond: John Knox, 1972), 30; Gerhard von Rad, *Old Testament Theology* (2 vols.; Edinburgh: Oliver and Boyd, 1965), 1:129–305; 2:106–18.

economic slavery, there are also populations that live in subhuman conditions, people who are exploited or marginalized, and groups that experience societal discrimination. The *Document of Puebla* puts it this way:

> From the depths of the countries that make up Latin America a cry is rising to heaven, growing louder and more alarming all the time. It is the cry of a suffering people who demand justice, freedom, and respect for the basic rights of human beings and peoples.
>
> A little more than ten years ago, the Medellín Conference noted this fact when it pointed out: "A muted cry wells up from millions of human beings, pleading with their pastors for a liberation that is nowhere to be found in their case." (Med-PC:2) The cry may well have seemed muted back then. Today it is loud and clear, increasing in volume and intensity, and at times full of menace.[55]

In these situations, the story of the Exodus, reread in the cultural and religious atmosphere of our time, not only stimulates the prophetic word that criticizes the situation of injustice but also leads people to become aware of their dignity and their responsibility toward one another. It encourages resourceful people to undertake the task of cultural promotion so that those at the margins can participate in social and political life. Additionally, marginalized people are encouraged to leave behind deplorable conditions and equip themselves to participate in the life of the community. The story of the Exodus, culminating in the establishment of the covenant, contains formative principles that should encourage the political choices destined to produce the transition from oppression to freedom, from penury to well-being, from ignorance to culture, from social alienation to integration in political and social life. Without reference to moral norms, the praxis of liberation would remain exposed to the serious risk of abuses of violence and vengeance that blacken the process of liberation.[56]

Conclusion

The current text of the book of Exodus celebrates the deeds of Yahweh whose sovereign power defeats the pharaoh who seeks to establish a political order incompatible with that which God intends. This divine intervention has two facets to it; on the one hand, God defeats the pharaoh; on the other hand, he liberates Israel. The liberation of Israel is an act of justice inasmuch as it is an action

---

[55] Third General Conference of Latin American Bishops, *Evangelization at Present and in the Future of Latin America: Conclusions* (Washington, D.C.: National Conference of Catholic Bishops, Office for Publishing and Promotion Services, 1979), 48.

[56] See Spohn, *What Are They Saying*, 63. On the complexity of the moral problems surrounding the use of violence against institutionalized injustice, see John Langan, "Violence and Injustice in Society: Recent Catholic Teaching," *TS* 46 (1985): 685–99; J. Childress, "Just-War Criteria," in *War or Peace? The Search for New Answers* (ed. T. A. Shannon; Maryknoll: Orbis, 1980), 40–54.

adjusted to the order of the creation and adjusted to the promise—it puts Israel in the right position according to God's will. As a consequence, Israel becomes a free community and the special property of Yahweh. Therefore, the Exodus is the foundational event for Israel as a society, free to serve God, and her celebration of the Passover makes it possible for each new generation to participate in the power of the saving event. The Exodus is also a paradigm of hope for all oppressed peoples, assuring them they have not been created to be slaves but to be free in a society that should protect and practice justice.

With respect to the reconstruction of the original event of the Exodus, it is possible to offer the following conclusions. The secular reconstruction of the Exodus that follows a revolutionary model does not have the certainty that many attribute to it. A primitive narrative of the Exodus without any religious dimension is unlikely. Moreover, the Exodus as a secular event could not be a paradigm in a sense that would assure those in any analogous situation a similar outcome. What gives the Exodus from Egypt the force of paradigm is the active presence of the creative God in history, jealous of his sovereignty over the universe, and committed to exercising his liberating justice on behalf of an oppressed humanity who believe in him.

Bibliography

Ahlström, Gösta W. *The History of Ancient Palestine from the Palaeolithic Period to Alexander's Conquest.* Journal for the Study of the Old Testament: Supplement Series 146. Sheffield: JSOT Press, 1993.

Amit, Yairah. "The Jubilee Law: An Attempt at Instituting Social Justice." Pages 47–59 in *Justice and Righteousness: Biblical Themes and their Influence.* Edited by H. G. Reventlow and Y. Hoffman. Journal for the Study of the Old Testament: Supplement Series 137. Sheffield: JSOT Press, 1992.

Anderson, Gary A. "Sacrifice and Sacrificial Offerings." Pages 870–86 in vol. 5 of *Anchor Bible Dictionary.* Edited by D. N. Freedman. 6 vols. New York: Doubleday, 1992.

Barré, Michael L. "Fasting in Isaiah 58:1–12: A Reexamination." *Biblical Theology Bulletin* 15 (1985): 94–97.

Batto, Bernard F. *Slaying the Dragon: Mythmaking in the Biblical Tradition.* Louisville: Westminster/John Knox, 1992.

Bendor, Shunya. *The Social Structure of Ancient Israel: The Institutions of the Family from the Settlement to the End of the Monarchy.* Jerusalem: Simor, 1996.

Berge, Kaare. *Die Zeit des Jahwisten: Ein Beitrag zur Datierung jahwistischer Vätertexte.* Beihefte zur Zeitschrift für die alttestamentliche Wissenschaft 186. Berlin: de Gruyter, 1990.

Bird, Phyllis A. "Women (OT)." Pages 951–57 in vol. 6 of *Anchor Bible Dictionary.* Edited by D. N. Freedman. 6 vols. New York: Doubleday, 1992.

Blenkinsopp, Joseph. *The Pentateuch: An Introduction to the First Five Books of the Bible.* New York: Doubleday, 1992.

Booij, T. "Negation in Isaiah 43:22–24." *Zeitschrift für die alttestamentliche Wissenschaft* 94 (1982): 390–400.

Bright, John. *A History of Israel.* 3d ed. Philadelphia: Westminster, 1981.

Brown, Raymond E. et al., eds. *The New Jerome Biblical Commentary.* Englewood Cliffs, N.J.: Printice Hall, 1990.

Brueggemann, Walter. *In Man We Trust: The Neglected Side of Biblical Faith.* Richmond: John Knox, 1972.

———. "Pharaoh as Vassal: A Study of a Political Metaphor." *Catholic Biblical Quarterly* 57 (1995): 27–51.

———. *Theology of the Old Testament.* Minneapolis: Fortress, 1997.

Cazelles, Henri. "Pentateuque." *Dictionnaire de la Bible: Supplément* 7 (1966): 771–858.

———, ed. *Introduction critique à l'Ancien Testament.* Paris: Desclée, 1973.

Childress, J. "Just-War Criteria." Pages 40–54 in *War or Peace? The Search for New Answers.* Edited by T. A. Shannon; Maryknoll: Orbis, 1980.

Coote, Robert B. *In Defense of Revolution: The Elohist History.* Minneapolis: Fortress, 1991.

———. *Early Israel: A New Horizon.* Minneapolis: Fortress, 1990.

Croatto, J. Severino. *Biblical Hermeneutics: Toward a Theory of Reading and the Production of Meaning.* Translated by R. R. Barr. Maryknoll: Orbis, 1987.

———. "El Dios en el acontecimiento." *Revista Biblica* 35 (1973): 52–60.

———. *Liberación y libertad: pautas hermenéuticas.* Buenos Aires: Mundo Nuevo, 1973.

———. "Liberación y libertad: reflexiones hermenéuticas en torno al Antiguo Testamento." *Revista Bíblica* 33 (1971): 1–7, 14.

Dandamayev, Muhammad A. "Slavery (ANE): Old Testament." Pages 62–65 in vol. 6 of *Anchor Bible Dictionary.* Edited by D. N. Freedman. 6 vols. New York: Doubleday, 1992.

Davies, G. I. "Sin, Wilderness of." Pages 47–49 in vol. 6 of *Anchor Bible Dictionary.* Edited by D. N. Freedman. 6 vols. New York: Doubleday, 1992.

Day, John. "Pre-Deuteronomic Allusions to the Covenant in Hosea and Psalm LXXVIII." *Vetus Testamentum* 36 (1986): 1–12.

Dever, William G. "How to Tell a Canaanite from an Israelite." Pages 27–56 in *The Rise of Ancient Israel.* Edited by H. Shanks. Washington, D.C.: Biblical Archaeology Society, 1992.

Fishbane, Michael A. *Biblical Interpretation in Ancient Israel.* Oxford: Clarendon, 1985.

Freedman, David N. "Early Israelite Poetry and Historical Reconstructions." Pages 3–35 in *Unity and Diversity: Essays in the History, Literature, and Religion of the Ancient Near East.* Edited by Hans Goedicke and J. J. M. Roberts. Baltimore and London: The Johns Hopkins University Press, 1975.

———. "The Religion of Early Israel." Pages 315–35 in *Ancient Israelite Religion.* Edited by Patrick D. Miller, Jr. et al. Philadelphia: Fortress, 1987.

Fretheim, Terence E. "Elohist." Pages 259–63 in *Interpreter's Dictionary of the Bible: Supplementary Volume.* Edited by K. Crim. Nashville: Abingdon, 1976.

———. "Will of God in the OT." Pages 915–20 in vol. 6 of *Anchor Bible Dictionary.* Edited by D. N. Freedman. 6 vols. New York: Doubleday, 1992.

Friedman, Richard E. "Torah (Pentateuch)." Pages 605–22 in vol. 6 of *Anchor Bible Dictionary.* Edited by D. N. Freedman. 6 vols. New York: Doubleday, 1992.

Fritz, Volkmar. "Conquest or Settlement?" *Biblical Archaeologist* 50 (1987): 80–100.

Globe, A. "The Literary Structure and Unity of the Song of Deborah." *Journal of Biblical Literature* 93 (1974): 495–97.

Gottwald, Norman K. "The Exodus as Event and Process: A Test Case in the Biblical Grounding of Liberation Theology." Pages 250–60 in *The Future of Liberation Theology: Essays in Honor of Gustavo Gutiérrez.* Edited by Marc H. Ellis and Otto Maduro. Maryknoll: Orbis, 1989.

———. *Tribes of Yahweh: A Sociology of the Religion of Liberated Israel, 1250–1050 B.C.E.* Maryknoll: Orbis, 1979.

———. "Two Models for the Origins of Ancient Israel: Social Revolution or Frontier Development." Pages 5–24 in *The Quest For the Kingdom of God: Studies in Honor of George E. Mendenhall.* Edited by H. B. Huffmon et al. Winona Lake: Eisenbrauns, 1983.

Gutiérrez, Gustavo. "Notes for a Theology of Liberation." *Theological Studies* 31 (1970): 244–45.

———. *A Theology of Liberation.* Translated by M. J. O'Connell. Maryknoll: Orbis, 1973.

Halpern, Baruch. *The Emergence of Israel in Canaan.* Society of Biblical Literature Monograph Series 29. Chico, Calif.: Scholars Press, 1983.

———. "Settlement of Canaan." Pages 1120–43 in vol. 5 of *Anchor Bible Dictionary.* Edited by D. N. Freedman. 6 vols. New York: Doubleday, 1992.

Hendel, Ronald S. "Finding Historical Memories in the Patriarchal Narratives." *Biblical Archaeology Review* 21 (1995): 52–55, 58–59, 70.

Jenks, Alan W. "Elohist." Pages 478–82 in vol. 2 of *Anchor Bible Dictionary.* Edited by D. N. Freedman. 6 vols. New York: Doubleday, 1992.

King, Philip J. "The Contribution of Archaeology to Biblical Studies." *Catholic Biblical Quarterly* 45 (1983): 1–16.

Kruse, H. "Die dialectische Negation als semitischen Idiom." *Vetus Testamentum* 4 (1954): 385–400.

Langan, John. "Violence and Injustice in Society: Recent Catholic Teaching." *Theological Studies* 46 (1985): 685–99.

Larsson, Göran. *Bound for Freedom: The Book of Exodus in Jewish and Christian Traditions.* Peabody, Mass.: Hendrickson, 1999.

Lemche, Niels P. *Ancient Israel: A New History of Israelite Society.* Sheffield: JSOT Press, 1988.

———. "Ḥabiru, Ḥapiru." Pages 6–10 in vol. 3 of *Anchor Bible Dictionary.* Edited by D. N. Freedman. 6 vols. New York: Doubleday, 1992.

Lenski, Gerhard. Review of N. K. Gottwald, *The Tribes of Yahweh. Religious Studies Review* 6 (1980): 275–78.

Lipinski, Edward. "Judges 5, 4–5 et Psaum 68, 8–11." *Biblica* 48 (1967): 185–200.

Lohfink, Norbert F. *The Covenant Never Revoked: Biblical Reflections on Christian Jewish Dialogue.* Translated by J. J. Scullion. New York: Paulist Press, 1991.

Mazar, Amihai. *Archaeology of the Land of the Bible: 10,000–586 B.C.E.* New York: Doubleday, 1992.

McCarter, P. Kyle. "The Origins of Israelite Religion." Pages 119–36 in *The Rise of Ancient Israel.* Edited by H. Shanks. Washington, D.C.: Biblical Archaeology Society, 1992.

McEvenue, Sean. "The Elohist at Work." *Zeitschrift für die alttestamentliche Wissenschaft* 96 (1984): 315–32.

Mendenhall, George E. "Ancient Israel's Hyphenated History." Pages 91–103 in *Palestine in Transition.* Edited by D. N. Freedman and D. F. Graf. Sheffield: Almond, 1983.

———. *The Tenth Generation: The Origins of the Biblical Tradition.* Baltimore: John Hopkins University Press, 1973.

Millard, A. R. "Abraham." Pages 35–41 in vol. 1 of *Anchor Bible Dictionary.* Edited by D. N. Freedman. 6 vols. New York: Doubleday, 1992.

Millard, A. R., and D. J. Wiseman, eds. *Essays on the Patriarchal Narratives.* Winona Lake: Eisenbrauns, 1983.

Miller, James Maxwell, and John H. Hayes. *A History of Ancient Israel and Judah.* Philadelphia: Westminster, 1986.

Miller, Patrick D. *The Divine Warrior in Early Israel.* Cambridge, Mass.: Harvard University Press, 1973.

Miranda, José P. *Being and the Messiah.* Translated by J. Eagleson. Maryknoll: Orbis, 1977.

———. *Marx and the Bible: A Critique of the Philosophy of Oppression.* Translated by J. Eagleson. Maryknoll: Orbis, 1974.

Murphy, Roland E. "A History of Israel." Pages 1224–25 in *The New Jerome Biblical Commentary.* Edited by Raymond E. Brown et al. Englewood Cliffs: Prentice Hall, 1990.

———. "Introduction to the Pentateuch." Pages 1–14 in *The New Jerome Biblical Commentary.* Edited by Raymond E. Brown et al. Englewood Cliffs: Prentice Hall, 1990.

———. *The Tree of Life.* New York: Doubleday, 1990.

———. "Wisdom in the OT." Pages 920–31 in vol. 6 of *Anchor Bible Dictionary.* Edited by D. N. Freedman. 6 vols. New York: Doubleday, 1992.

Nicholson, Ernest W. *God and His People: Covenant and Theology in the Old Testament.* Oxford: Clarendon, 1985.

North, Robert and Philip J. King. "Biblical Archaeology." Pages 1196–1218 in *The New Jerome Biblical Commentary.* Edited by Raymond E. Brown et al. Englewood Cliffs: Prentice Hall, 1990.

Perlitt, Lothar. *Bundestheologie im Alten Testament.* Neukirchen-Vluyn: Neukirchener Verlag, 1969.

Pixley, Jorge V. *On Exodus: A Liberation Perspective.* Translated by R. R. Barr. Maryknoll: Orbis, 1987.

Pritchard, James B., ed. *Ancient Near Eastern Texts Relating to the Old Testament.* 3d ed. Princeton: Princeton University Press, 1969.

Pury, Albert de, and Thomas Römer. "Le Pentateuque en question: position du probleme et brève histoire de la recherche." Pages 9–80 in *Le Pentateuque en question.* Edited by Albert de Pury. Le Monde de la Bible 19. Geneva: Labor et Fides, 1989.

Rad, Gerhard von. *Old Testament Theology.* 2 vols. Edinburgh: Oliver and Boyd, 1965.

———. *Wisdom in Israel.* Translated by James S. D. Martin. Nashville: Abingdon, 1972.

Rendtorff, Rolf. *Das überlieferungsgeschichtliche Problem des Pentateuch.* Beihefte zur Zeitschrift für die alttestamentliche Wissenschaft 147. New York: De Gruyter, 1976.

Ricoeur, Paul. *Essays on Biblical Interpretation.* Philadelphia: Fortress, 1980.

Schmitt, John J. "Prophecy (ANE): Preexilic Hebrew Prophecy." Pages 482–89 in vol. 5 of *Anchor Bible Dictionary.* Edited by D. N. Freedman. 6 vols. New York: Doubleday, 1992.

Scullion, John J. *Genesis: A Commentary for Students, Teachers, and Preachers.* Old Testament Studies 6. Collegeville: Liturgical Press, 1992.

Seebass, Horst. "Que reste-t-il du Yahwiste et de l'Elohiste?" Pages 199–230 in *Le Pentateuque en question.* Edited by Albert de Pury. Le Monde de la Bible 19. Geneva: Labor et Fides, 1989.

Sesboüé, Bernard. "De la narrativité en théologie." *Gregorianum* 75 (1994): 415–29.

Smith, Mark S. "The Literary Arrangement of the Priestly Redaction of Exodus: A Preliminary Investigation." *Catholic Biblical Quarterly* 58 (1996): 25–50.

Spohn, William C. *What Are They Saying about Scripture and Ethics?* New York and Ramsey: Paulist, 1984.

Stone, Lawson G. "Ethical and Apologetic Tendencies in the Redaction of the Book of Joshua." *Catholic Biblical Quarterly* 53 (1991): 25–36.

Third General Conference of Latin American Bishops. *Evangelization at Present and in the Future of Latin America: Conclusions.* Washington, D.C.: National Conference of Catholic Bishops, Office for Publishing and Promotion Services, 1979.

Thompson, Thomas L. *The Historicity of the Patriarchal Narratives.* New York: De Gruyter, 1974.

Unterman, Jeremiah. "Redemption (OT)." Pages 650–54 in vol. 5 of *Anchor Bible Dictionary.* Edited by D. N. Freedman. 6 vols. New York: Doubleday, 1992.

Van Seters, John. *Abraham in History and Tradition.* New Haven, Conn.: Yale University Press, 1975.

———. *Prologue to History: The Yahwist as Historian in Genesis.* Louisville: Westminster/John Knox, 1992.

Vaux, Roland de. *Ancient Israel.* 2 vols. New York: McGraw-Hill, 1965.

Vermeylen, Jacques. "Le premières étapes littéraires de la formation du Pentateuque." Pages 149–97 in *Le Pentateuque en question.* Edited by Albert de Pury. Le Monde de la Bible 19. Geneva: Labor et Fides, 1989.

Weinfeld, Moshe. "The Tribal League at Sinai." Pages 304–14 in *Ancient Israelite Religion*. Edited by Patrick D. Miller, Jr. et al. Philadelphia: Fortress, 1987.

Westermann, Claus. *Genesis 12–36: A Commentary*. Translated by J. J. Scullion. Minneapolis: Augsburg, 1985.

———. *The Promises to the Fathers: Studies on the Patriarchal Narratives*. Translated by D. E. Gree. Philadelphia: Fortress, 1980.

———. "Promises to the Patriarchs." Pages 690–93 in *Interpreter's Dictionary of the Bible: Supplementary Volume*. Edited by Keith R. Crim. Nashville: Abingdon, 1976.

Wilson, Robert R. "Enforcing the Covenant: the Mechanisms of Judicial Authority in Early Israel." Pages 59–76 in *The Quest for the Kingdom of God: Studies in Honor of G. E. Mendenhall*. Edited by J. B. Huffmon et al. Winona Lake: Eisenbrauns, 1983.

Wright, C. J. H. "Family." Pages 761–69 in vol. 2 of *Anchor Bible Dictionary*. Edited by D. N. Freedman. 6 vols. New York: Doubleday, 1992.

CHAPTER FOUR

NORMS OF JUSTICE IN THE LAWS OF THE COVENANT

Introduction

After the analysis of the exodus as an event of liberating justice in the previous chapter, we now turn to the topic of justice in the laws of Sinai, focusing on the exercise of justice and of equity primarily towards the needy and the weak of society. This chapter first analyzes the laws contained in the book of Exodus: the Ten Commandments and the Covenant Code. Next, continuing a chronological approach, the chapter studies the social laws of Deuteronomy the purpose of which was to update the law given at Sinai in order to respond to the necessities created by a new time of crisis and transition in Moab. The chapter finishes with an analysis of the social dimension of the Holiness Code attributed to the Sinai revelation, according to Leviticus. Left aside is the cultural code of Exodus 34:10–26, since it makes no reference to the topic of justice.

1. The laws of Sinai in Exodus

The text of the book of Exodus establishes a strict connection between the departure from Egypt and the reception of the laws at Sinai. The connection may be summarized in the key phrase that introduces the Ten Commandments: "I am the LORD your God, who brought you out of the land of Egypt, out of the house of slavery" (Exod 20:2). The laws are included in the narrative of liberation and are meant to regulate and consolidate the life of Israel as a society free from Pharaoh, placed at the service of Yahweh. The connection between the legislative and the narrative puts the law in the framework of the covenant (19:5; 24:7), which includes characteristic elements such as election, promise, and blessing. Thus, in the preparations of the covenant, Yahweh addresses Israel as the house of Jacob since Israel is the elect lineage and her people are heirs to the promises already made to Abraham.[1] These promises are renewed in the covenant (Exod 23:27–31), and they are accompanied by the blessings that make prosperity and fertility possible

---

[1] See Exod 19:3; Gen 28:13–15; 35:10–12.

(23:25–26). The tableau of the covenant is infused with the atmosphere of a personal dialogue, enlivened by the warmth of God's faithful benevolence and deep appreciation for Israel. In this atmosphere the laws are expressions of the voice of God who addresses Israel with a preferential love (19:4–6) while the obedience of Israel is the concrete manifestation of her response to God's love (19:8; 24:3, 7). The laws indicate to liberated Israel the way her people must follow so that they may grow in friendship with Yahweh and increase their participation in the benefits of God's promises and blessings. Obedience is the key to the event: for the disobedient and those who are hardened in sin, there are threats and curses until the fourth generation;[2] for the obedient and those who are penitent, God maintains his kindness and fidelity until the thousandth generation.[3]

The narrative of the exodus event and the legislative texts contained in the book of Exodus are the result of the combination of old traditions and of a long editorial process; they received their definitive form during the exile and the postexilic era. The final edition of these texts, done by the Priestly writers, was destined for the community existing at the end of the Babylonian exile and the beginning of the restoration during the time of the Persian Empire. The pardon and the renovation of the covenant in the desert were typological anticipations of the pardon and the renovation of the covenant that the postexilic community went through in its own experience. This edition gave to postexilic Israel norms to follow in order to complete her mission as a sacred community among the nations (Exod 19:5–6) and to be a community loyal to Yahweh expressed by an uncontaminated worship and by a just and equitable social life.

The texts look toward the future. This look forward is an opening that facilitates the transfer of the religious and ethical spirit that animates the norms of the covenant to any new situation in which the community might find itself. What is important about these laws is not so much their embodiment of concrete social norms with cultural limitations peculiar to their time and culture as their spirit, which animates the whole legislative process of the covenant and its successive modernizations or adaptations to new circumstances. This spirit is used as a guide in order to answer the question, "What must a people do during the process of liberation and after it has been liberated from oppression?"

2. The Ten Commandments

The text of the Ten Commandments (Exod 20:1–17; Deut 5:6–21) is the result of the condensation of cultural and ethical norms concerning questions central to the life of the nation. By being associated with the theophany at Sinai, the Ten Commandments acquire divine origin. All the laws of the Pentateuch are attributed to God as their legislator. But among them the Ten Commandments occupy a unique position because they form the only body of law that claims to

---

[2] See Exod 20:5; 23:21; 34:7; Deut 5:9.
[3] See Exod 20:6; 34:6–7; Deut 5:10; Jer 32:18.

have been communicated by God directly, without an intermediary. This claim is expressed with the formula of self-revelation with which God introduces himself when he promulgates the commandments (Exod 20:1–2). He is the one who has been with his people, who has intervened directly in order to liberate them from their slavery in Egypt. Upon identifying himself as the redeemer of Israel, Yahweh expresses his authority and his right to make known his will in order to establish a covenant with the people he has redeemed.[4] In this scenario, the apodictic form of the commandments inculcates and reinforces the absolute obedience that is due Yahweh, an essential obedience because it refers to areas of activity that are central to Israel's life. The violation of these commandments is not only an offense against Yahweh but also a crime against the community because it puts their existence in danger.[5] The commandments are formulated in the second person masculine singular. The Hebrew is very clear on this point because Hebrew verbs distinguish the second person masculine from the second person feminine. The commandments go to the heads of Israelite households, who normally were males, given the patriarchal structure of the time. By way of the heads of households, the commandments then reach the entire community.[6] The Ten Commandments come to the biblical reader in two versions, substantially the same, albeit with certain differences in expression and in motivation. One version may be found in Exod 20:1–17 and the other in Deut 5:6–21. The origin of the Ten Commandments is controverted among contemporary exegetes. All agree, however, that they are the result of a long historical development. Probably, the basic structure as a collection of Ten Commandments was formulated in the eighth century, during the time of Amos and Hosea.[7]

The concern of this chapter is the social and humanitarian dimension that appears in the injunctions to observe the Sabbath and to respect one's parents and in the prohibitions of premeditated homicide, robbery, adultery, false witness, and greed for other people's goods.

2.1. "Remember the Sabbath day and keep it holy" (Exod 20:8–11; Deut 5:12–15)

Like all the other commandments, this one is also expressed in the second person masculine singular. Also, for the explanation, "your son or daughter, your

---

[4] See Walther Zimmerli, *I Am Yahweh* (Atlanta: John Knox, 1982), 82–87.
[5] Anthony Phillips, *Ancient Israel's Criminal Law: A New Approach to the Decalogue* (New York: Schocken Books, 1970), 10–13.
[6] Phyllis A. Bird, "Images of Women in the Old Testament," in *The Bible and Liberation: Political and Social Hermeneutics* (ed. N. K. Gottwald: Maryknoll: Orbis, 1983), 259.
[7] See Johann J. Stamm and M. E. Andrew, *Ten Commandments in Recent Research* (SBT 2nd ser. 2; Naperville: Allenson, 1967), 95–96; Erhard Gerstenberger, "Covenant and Commandment," *JBL* 84 (1965): 38–51; André Lemaire, "Le Décalogue: Essai d'histoire de la rédaction," in *Mélanges bibliques et orientaux en l'honneur de M. Henri Cazelles* (ed. A. Casquot and M. Delcor; AOAT 212: Neukirchen-Vluyn: Neukirchener, 1981), 258–95; Christoph Dohmen, "Der Dekaloganfang und sein Ursprung," *Bib* 74 (1993): 175–93.

male or female slave," the "you" to which the commandment refers is the head of the household. Not mentioned in this injunction is the wife or the matriarch, probably because she is included as an immediate dependent of the patriarch, participating with him in his reproductive function. The commandment goes to the father of the family because the family, not the individual, is the basic unit of society in ancient Israel. The head of the household is responsible not only for his own acts but also for those of his family.

The law of the Sabbath rest, addressed to the heads of households, is actually for the entire community. That includes sons and daughters, male and female slaves, resident aliens and domestic animals. All in the land of Israel should pause and take a rest from the fatigue and weariness caused by the daily and endless effort of human existence. It is an obligatory rest even in the busiest days of the year, such as the season of plowing and harvesting (Exod 34:21). The verbs "remember" (Exod 20:8) and "observe" (Deut 5:12), which express the precept, indicate that the community is called to fulfill a traditional obligation.

Many investigations were made in the last century in order to discover the provenance of the Sabbath, but in spite of much effort, its origins remain wrapped in mystery.[8] What is known at the present time is that the Sabbath was a characteristic celebration in Israel that had no parallel among neighboring peoples.[9] The particularity of the Sabbath in the rhythm of the week is that it broke with the rhythm of the month determined by the moon; neither did it continue the rhythm of the year fixed by the sun or the other stars. For ancient Israel, the Sabbath week had been instituted by God and contained a sense of independence from astral forces. Given this characteristic, its practice and celebration was very significant, religiously and politically, for the Israelite community in Babylonian exile. In that atmosphere, the Sabbath turned out to be a celebration that nurtured the sense of national and religious identity, and represented a silent protest against the structures of the subjugating Babylonian power, which was itself guided and sustained by astral divinities.

The commandment concerning the Sabbath is preserved in two versions (Exod 20:8–11; Deut 5:12–15), each of which contains a different motivation. The version in Deuteronomy alludes to the experience of the Exodus according to which Yahweh liberated Israel from Egyptian slavery, constituted her as a free people, and gave each member of the community the possibility of enjoying one day of rest in the rhythm of weekly work. In this sense, the Deuteronomic version considers the Sabbath rest to be a celebration of social and political liberation carried out by the redemptive intervention of Yahweh. The version in Exodus (Exod 20:8–11), however, makes reference to the divine model of the creation (Exod 20:11; 31:17). This reference, with its allusion to Gen 2:2–3, is the work of the Priestly writer who finished the Pentateuch during the Babylonian exile or at the beginning of the postexilic period. According to the Priestly conception,

---

[8] See Gerhard F. Hasel, "Sabbath," *ABD* 5: 850–51.
[9] See Roland de Vaux, *Ancient Israel* (2 vols.; New York: McGraw-Hill, 1965), 2:475–83.

human beings are made in the image and likeness of God; therefore, in their behavior they are called to imitate the activity first established by the creator: they should work six days and rest on the seventh. The Sabbath rest is the celebration of human beings who, as images of God, imitate their creator and rejoice in the gift of their endowed dignity.

The Priestly tradition transcends the particularist vision of Deuteronomy. While Deuteronomy considers Israel to be the object of Yahweh's liberating action, the Priestly tradition offers a universal vision that extends to the whole of humanity. In this universal focus, the Sabbath is the recognition of the sovereignty of the creator God who has made human beings participants in his own image. This universal vision has enormous potential for breaking the social structures that oppose the equality and the dignity of human beings. It is a vision that stimulates a thirst for justice in oppressed peoples and groups.

The Priestly writers, who worked during the Exile, undoubtedly knew the Babylonian explanation of work described in the myth of Atrahasis.[10] By comparison it is possible to discover, both in Genesis and in Exodus, a contrast between the Babylonian concept of work and the Priestly concept of work incorporated in the Bible.[11] According to the Babylonian conception, human beings engage in hard and unceasing chores because they were created to alleviate the oppressive work required of the subordinate gods. According to the Priestly conception, humans are called by God to imitate his work in creative action and to enjoy their rest. This concept of work contributes to the social and religious identity of the people of God and, during the exile, it reinforced the silent political protest that the outline of the week already contained as an institution independent of astral powers. The Babylonian perspective on work, in the form perceived by the exiled Israelites, finds its equivalent in the ideologies and economic praxis of our time in which the worker is exploited for the benefit of the powerful. For modern readers of the Bible in lands of oppression, the text awakens a consciousness of their exploitation as workers and it moves them to struggle together in order to achieve respect for their humanity as they work.[12]

2.2. "Honor your father and your mother" (Exod 20:12; Deut 5:16)

This commandment is also formulated in the second person masculine singular and likewise goes to the male heads of the community. It takes as its subject the respect due equally to fathers and mothers. Both share the responsibility of procreation, which was of supreme importance for the subsistence of the family and society, especially for the honored father in the patriarchal system. This com-

---

[10] See "Atrahasis," translated by Ephraim A. Speiser (*ANET*, 104–6).

[11] See J. Severino Croatto, "Cómo releer la Biblia desde su contexto socio-político? Ejercicio sobre algunos temas del Pentateuco," *RevistB* 53 (1991): 197–203.

[12] See Pope John Paul II, "Laborem Exercens (On Human Work)," *Origins* 11, no. 15 (1981): 225–44; Gregory Baum, *The Priority of Labor: A Commentary on "Laborem Exercens," Encyclical Letter of Pope John Paul II* (New York: Paulist, 1982).

mandment demands the respectful relationship of children toward their parents, from those who received life toward those who gave it to them. In ancient Israel, besides life, parents transmitted to their children the traditions that gave identity to the community (Prov 1:8–9; Sir 3:1–16). The commandment's text assures those who honor their ancestors—who have given them life—will enjoy longevity and will make a lasting name for themselves for generations to come. The honor that children owe their parents is a right that parents conserve until death.[13] The senility of parents does not exempt children from their obligation towards their parents, nor does it give society the right to eliminate the latter. The terms "parents and children" in this context should be understood in the widest sense, since the family system characteristic of ancient Israel was one in which several generations lived in the same premises.[14]

This commandment probably originated in the instructions imparted in the clans; this may be confirmed by the numerous references found in wisdom literature.[15] Besides the admonishments on respect and obedience owed parents, the biblical texts also contain punishments for children who fail in their respect toward their parents. The Covenant Code imposes capital punishment on the son who curses or hits his father or his mother (Exod 21:15, 17). Deuteronomy imposes capital punishment on a rebellious son (Deut 21:18–21). In Babylon, on the other hand, the penalty for such infractions was not as severe. The code of Hammurabi, for example, punished the son who attacked his father not with death but with the amputation of a hand.[16] The severity of the Israelite law is based on the understanding that respect for parents is an essential part of the covenant. The violation of the injunction is a crime against the author of the covenant and against the community. This concept of crime differentiates the laws of Israel from those of the neighboring countries of the ancient Middle East.[17]

2.3. "You shall not kill" (Exod 20:13; Deut 5:17)

This commandment uses the Hebrew verb $rāṣaḥ$, which has its own semantic history. In the prophetic and the wisdom literature from the eighth

---

[13] Prov 19:26; 20:20; Sir 3:12.

[14] C. J. H. Wright, "Family," *ABD* 2: 761–69; J. Gamberoni, "Das Elterngebot im Alten Testament," *BZ*, NS 8 (1964): 161–90; Heinz Kremers, "Die Stellung des Elterngebotes im Dekalog," *EvT* 21 (1961): 145–61. Premonarchical Israelite society was based on a threefold kinship system: the tribe (*šebet/maṭṭeh*), the clan (*mišpāḥâ*), and the father's house (*bêt ʾāb*), which was an extended family comprising all the descendants of a single living ancestor in a single lineage: the father with his wife/wives, his unmarried sons and daughters, his married sons with their wives and children, and his grandsons with their wives and children. Moreover, the *bêt ʾāb* comprised male and female slaves and their families, resident laborers, and sometimes resident Levites. They all resided in a cluster of dwellings. This arrangement continued during the monarchy.

[15] See, e.g., Prov 1:8; 4:1, 3–4; 6:20; 10:1; 15:20; 23:22.

[16] See "The Code of Hammurabi," translated by Theophile J. Meek (*ANET*, 175).

[17] Phillips, *Ancient Israel's Criminal Law*, 82.

century B.C.E. on, this verb invariably took the sense of intentional and malicious violence.[18]

This is the sense of the verb in this commandment: it prohibits intentional homicide, and it forbids one the right of taking the law in one's own hands in order to satisfy the desire for vengeance. In the same way, it prohibits abuses of power that result in the death of a person. In ancient Israel, this commandment did not exclude capital punishment, nor did it forbid killing enemies in time of war, including civilians.[19]

The commandment seems also to forbid indirect homicide. Texts such as Ps 94:6 and Job 24:14 probably refer to social situations that deprive the poor of life. So the Psalmist says:

> They pour out their arrogant words;
> all the evildoers boast.
> They crush your people, O LORD,
> and afflict your heritage.
> They kill the widow and the stranger,
> they murder *(yĕraṣṣēḥû)* the orphan. (Ps 94:5–6)

Job echoes this criticism when he says: "The murderer rises at dusk to kill *(rôṣēaḥ)* the poor and needy" (Job 24:14). In the New Testament, the sense of the prohibition is refined and the commandment prohibits all hurtful or injurious words said in anger or in hatred, inviting the hearer to take the first step in order to be reconciled with the offended neighbor (Matt 5:22–26).

The biblical laws punish intentional and malicious homicide with capital punishment.[20] Unlike other countries of the ancient Middle East,[21] Israel admitted no alternative in the form of physical punishment or monetary compensation.[22] Israel gave no advantage to the rich in permitting them to pay compensation

---

[18] See Isa 1:21; Hos 6:9; Job 24:14; Ps 94:6. In ancient Israel an unintentional murderer had the right to seek asylum (Num 35:9–15; Deut 4:41–43; 19:1–13). For this purpose six cities were set aside as Cities of Refuge. There the unintentional murderer could find protection against the summary proceedings of the blood avenger and wait until he could stand for judgment before the Elders of the community.

[19] See, e.g., Eccl 3:3, 8; Josh 6:17; 10:28–40. On war in ancient Israel, see Patrick D. Miller, *The Divine Warrior in Early Israel* (Cambridge, Mass.: Harvard University Press, 1973); Millard C. Lind, *Yahweh is a Warrior: The Theology of Warfare in Ancient Israel* (Scottdale: Herald, 1980); T. Raymond Hobbs, *A Time for War: A Study of Warfare in the Old Testament* (Wilmington: Glazier, 1989); Theodore Hiebert, "Warrior, Divine," *ABD* 6:876–80; T. B. Dozeman, *God at War: Power in the Exodus Tradition* (New York: Oxford University Press, 1996).

[20] See Exod 21:12–14; Lev 24:17; Num 35:16–21; Deut 19:11–13.

[21] In ancient Mesopotamia, Hammurabi introduced punishment by the *lex talionis*, including the death penalty, for personal injuries suffered by freemen, although he preserved the old practice of monetary compensation for injuries suffered by lower social classes or slaves. See Jacob J. Finkelstein, "Ammisaduqa's Edict and the Babylonian 'Law Codes,'" *JCS* 15 (1961): 98. The Assyrians practiced both compensation and blood revenge, while the Hittites used only compensation. See S. Greengus, "Law," *ABD* 4:249.

[22] See Num 35:31–32; Deut 19:11–13.

in lieu of death. The rich transgressor had to suffer the same punishment as the poor.

The biblical laws are distinguished for the preeminence they give to human life. Among these laws, those of the Priestly tradition stand out as giving an inestimable value to the life represented in human blood. Any premeditated violation of the law that forbade murder causes such contamination that it could not be cleansed save by the execution of the culprit (Num 35:33; Gen 9:5b–6). The inestimable value of the life of the human person is based on its character as formed in the image of God (Gen 9:6). Unjustifiable homicide is forbidden because it is a lethal blow, in effect, against the image of God that is the concrete life of the individual human. The foundation of this prohibition contains a universal conception of the dignity of the human being, which seems to be restricted to the physical life of the individual. But, for the modern reader who is conscious of the value of the human person, the text of the commandment opens all its moral potential to any effort that nourishes the sense of human dignity and helps change social and political structures that are discriminatory and oppressive.[23] After all, human beings can be killed not only by a lethal blow to the body or by denying them the physically necessary sustenance but also by depriving them of their legitimate rights.

In our century, a strong opposition to capital punishment has spread. Several factors contribute to such opposition, such as a deeper appreciation of the dignity of the human person, the consideration that the educational dimension of punishment should prevail over its vindictive aspect, the desacralization of political power, and an understanding of the limitations that promote error and abuse. It is necessary to add that today, the objectives of capital punishment, which theoretically could justify its application, could be achieved by other means.[24]

In our time the legitimacy of war has also been debated. Christians agree that true peace, the fruit of justice, is possible here and now, but it is not yet stable and complete. They correct the position taken in the Book of Ecclesiastes, which accepts war as an established and normal thing which has its place and time (Eccl 3:3, 8). One must not make a season for war, and if war is actually declared, not every means at the disposal of the combatants is morally licit for them to use. According to Catholic moral teaching, in the case of unjust aggression, the resort

---

[23] As the Second Vatican Council says: "All offenses against human dignity, such as subhuman living conditions, arbitrary imprisonment, deportation, slavery, prostitution, the selling of women and children, degrading working conditions where men are treated as mere tools for profit rather than free and responsible persons: all these and the like are criminal: they poison civilization; and they debase the perpetrators more than the victims and militate against the honor of the creator." See Vatican Council II, "Pastoral Constitution on the Church in the Modern World *(Gaudium et Spes)*" 27, in *Vatican Council II: The Conciliar and Post Conciliar Documents* (ed. Austin Flannery: Collegeville: Liturgical Press, 1975), 928.

[24] See P. Valadier, "Des évêques pour l'abolition de la peine de mort," *Études* 348 (1978): 683–91; Jean-Marie Aubert, *Chrétiens et peine de mort* (Paris: Desclée, 1978), 44–52, 85–144; John Langan, "Capital Punishment," *TS* 54 (1993): 111–24; Pope John Paul II, "Encyclical Letter: The Gospel of Life *(Evangelium Vitae)*," 56 in *Origins* 24, no. 42 (1995): 709.

to weapons of self defense can be made only after all other possible resources have been exhausted; and soldiers should observe a rigorous set of restrictions if the use of their weapons is to be morally legitimate.[25]

2.4. "You shall not commit adultery" (Exod 20:14; Deut 5:18)

This commandment, like the one that precedes it and the one that follows it, is laconic. It carries no explanation. It does not say what is understood by the term adultery. The understanding of the term is taken from Deut 22:22–24 and Lev 20:10–12. These texts define adultery as the sexual union of a man with a woman who is married or betrothed to another man. This understanding of the term does not include the sexual union of a married man and a single woman. The commandment is addressed to the male heads of households and refers to the violation of family law in a patriarchal society. In such a social setting, adultery was considered an attack on the exclusive property of the husband, who held the sexuality of his wife as a possession. The duty of the wife was to "build" the house of the husband with the procreation of legitimate children—to bear bastard children in a patrilineal society was abominable. In addition, adultery was an attack against the authority of the husband responsible for the solidarity and integrity of the family. In adultery, the two participants were condemned to capital punishment (Deut 22:22–24; Lev 20:10–12). The reason for the commandment is eminently social. But the social aspect of the sin was strengthened by its religious dimension. Adultery was a "big sin" (Gen 20:9), a "sin against God" (Gen 20:3; 39:9), and a sin of high treason (Jer 9:2). This sin placed those who committed it in the company of murderers (Job 24:14–15). The incorporation of the prohibition against adultery into the Ten Commandments makes adultery not only an injustice against an individual and an offense against God, it also constitutes a crime against the community. This is so because it injures the very existence of the people of the covenant and endangers their continued residence in the land given to them by God. Adultery was considered one of the crimes that so contaminated the land that the land would be forced to spit out its inhabitants (Lev 18:20, 24–25).[26] In the New Testament, the commandment was internalized and as a result attacks the very root of adultery. It prohibits both the desire for illicit sexual union and the intention of committing it (Matt 5:28–30). In the Christian understanding, which likens marriage to the covenant, and which recognizes the dignity of women, any act of adultery, by man or woman alike, is a serious sin against justice and matrimonial fidelity.

---

[25] Kenneth R. Himes, "War," in *The New Dictionary of Catholic Social Thought* (ed. J. A. Dwyer; Collegeville: Liturgical Press, 1994), 977–82.

[26] In the neighboring countries adultery was regarded as a grave offense against the husband and was punished by death. See "The Story of Two Brothers," translated by John A. Wilson (*ANET*, 24); "The Code of Hammurabi," 129–30, translated by Theophile J. Meek (*ANET*, 171); "The Hittite Laws," 195, translated by Albrecht Goetze (*ANET*, 196); "The Middle Assyrian Laws," 15, translated by Theophile J. Meek (*ANET*, 181); Phillips, *Ancient Israel's Criminal Law*, 110–29; Elaine A. Goodfriend, "Adultery," *ABD* 1:82–86.

2.5. "You shall not steal" (Exod 20:15; Deut 5:19)

This commandment prohibits robbery but makes no reference to the object that one is forbidden to steal. It prohibits, in general, the furtive or fraudulent appropriation of other people's possessions, whether these belong to an individual, a group, or an institution. The commandment is directed to the entire community by way of the head of the household. It obliges the rulers as much as those who are ruled, the rich as much as the poor. The laws of Mesopotamia had also prohibited robbery and punished it by making the thief pay the value of the stolen thing several times over.[27] A similar punishment is found in the Covenant Code (Exod 22:1–4). As distinct from the laws of Mesopotamia, however, the biblical commandment considers theft not only an injury against an individual but also as crime against the covenant, and therefore, an offense against the community itself. Consequently, according to this commandment, justice is done not only when the thief is forced to restore several times over the value of what was taken. Justice also requires that the community protect what belongs to people, groups, or institutions against all furtive or fraudulent damage, that it educate people to respect the goods of other people, that it punish the thief, and that it use appropriate means to prevent robbery. Evidently, the commandment requires that those who are in charge of the public administration give example of administrative honesty and that they show respect for the boundaries that exist against appropriating what they themselves do not own.

2.6. "You shall not bear false witness against your neighbor" (Exod 20:16; Deut 5:20)

This commandment presupposes a legal procedure in which one member of the community testifies against another in the court of the elders. The declaration of the witness is essential for the imposition of the sentence. A witness is capable of speaking the truth (Prov 14:25) or is capable of lying (Deut 19:18; Prov 6:19). In this legal situation, this commandment prohibits bearing false witness or lying against one's neighbor, which is to say, against either fellow citizen or resident alien.[28] This prohibition protects the right that the individual has to a just process that defends him or her against the threat of false accusation. It primarily protects the weak and the poor against the machinations of the powerful who have the means to buy or bribe witnesses. The story of the vineyard of Naboth (1 Kgs 21:1–16) is an example of the horrendous consequences of bearing false witness. This commandment makes false witness a crime against the covenant. It is an offense against the community itself, which therefore has the responsibility of punishing any violation and of discouraging any future transgression. Animated

---

[27] "The Code of Hammurabi," 254 (*ANET*, 176–77); "The Hittite Laws," 57–69 (*ANET*, 192).

[28] See Exod 22:21–22; 23:9; Deut 10:17–19; Lev 19:33–34.

by this spirit, Deuteronomy 19:19–21 requires capital punishment for a person whose false witness brings about the death of the accused.[29]

2.7. "You shall not covet your neighbor's house" (Exod 20:17; Deut 5:21)

This commandment prohibits the desire that initiates the action, underhanded or open, of taking something that belongs to another.[30] It attacks theft at its root. Like the other commandments, it is directed to the heads of households. Here, however, there seems to be a dual purpose. First, it assures that the heads of the household respect other people's property; and second, it assures that they make others respect the right of exclusive property that each head of the household has over his house—his wife, his slaves, and all his belongings. This right was inviolable. The commandment comes down to us in two versions, preserved in Exod 20:17 and Deut 5:21. Both versions contain a double prohibition. The version of Exod 20:17 repeats the same verb "covet" *(ḥāmad)* for both prohibitions: "you shall not covet your neighbor's house; you shall not covet your neighbor's wife." This version first prohibits coveting the house and then the wife of the neighbor, and it includes in the prohibition everything pertaining to this, naming his slaves, his ox, and his donkey especially. The second prohibition is probably a later addition that develops the concept of "house" in the first prohibition; it explains the "house" by what it contains: the wife, the male slave, the female slave, the ox, the donkey, and any another thing in the master's possession.[31]

The version of Deut 5:21, on the other hand, alternates "covet" *(ḥāmad)* with "want" *(hitʾawweh)*. The alternation is probably stylistic. It also inverts the location of the two terms, "house" and "wife." It puts the wife in the first prohibition and passes the house to the second. This inversion highlights the value of the woman and separates her from the goods that the Israelite could negotiate; hence, the commandment expresses the humanitarian concern of the Deuteronomic composition. Besides this inversion of terms, the commandment in Deuteronomy adds "his field" in the second prohibition in order to clarify that real estate is included in the commandment.

---

[29] The Mesopotamian codes devote special attention to false testimony. See, e.g., "The Code of Lipit-Ishtar," 17, translated by Samuel. N. Kramer (*ANET*, 160); "The Code of Hammurabi," 1–4, 11 (*ANET*, 166).

[30] Covetousness is amply testified in the literature of ancient Egypt. See "The Protestation of Guiltlessness," translated by John A. Wilson (*ANET*, 35); "The Instruction of the Vizier Ptah-Hotep," 295, translated by John A. Wilson (*ANET*, 413); "The Instruction for King Meri-ka-re," 40, translated by John A. Wilson (*ANET*, 415); "The Protests of the Eloquent Peasant," 290, translated by John A. Wilson (*ANET*, 409).

[31] William L. Moran argues that, according to the tenth commandment, the wife was not the mere chattel of her husband. He could not regard her as property that he could sell or bequeath at will. See William L. Moran, "The Conclusion of the Decalogue (Exod 20,17 = Dtn 5,21)," *CBQ* 29 (1967): 552. On the concept of household, family and the role of women in the patriarchal system see: Harry A. Hoffner, "tiyaB bayith," *TDOT* 2:107–16; Wright, "Family," 2:761–69; Phyllis A. Bird, "Women (OT)," *ABD* 6:951–57.

This commandment, on the one hand, protects the right of the Israelite family to have a home, a parcel of land, and the means to work it. On the other hand, it prohibits an immoderate and unjust accumulation of wealth for the benefit of the few, with the consequent impoverishment of the greater part of the population, an accumulation that requires the centralization of economic and political power in the hands of the rich for their own profit. In referring to the situation in which the powerful wrongly appropriate the goods of the poor, the prophet Micah says:

> They covet *(ḥāmĕdû)* fields and seize them;
> houses, and take them away;
> they oppress householder and house,
> people and their inheritance. (Mic 2:2; also see Isa 5:8)

The prophet attests, in fact, to the growing difference between classes that took place by the middle of the eighth century; wealth was consolidated in the hands of the few, justice was corrupted, and the powerful took possession of the lands of the poor. This commandment points out a factor of highest importance among the social problems of any time in its denunciation of the greedy and the unjust accumulation of wealth that increases the difference between the rich and the poor.

3. The Covenant Code

The Covenant Code (Exod 20:22–23:33) is not a law code in the modern sense of the word.[32] Besides being fragmentary and incomplete, it is a combination of laws and admonitions. One could call it a code in the ancient sense. It offers samples or examples of the divine will for the life of Israel. It may be divided into three sections: norms for worship (20:23–26), groups of laws reinforced with penalties (21:1–22:19), and exhortations of a moral, social, and religious character (22:20–23:19). The laws of Exodus 21:1–22:20 use the conditional form from ancient Mesopotamia and stem from a common Semitic tradition. The typical conditional laws begin with the formula: "If a man does thus and so . . ."[33] The laws of the Covenant Code are given to the community via its male leaders; the Code presupposes a patriarchal society in which the males are the only members of the society with full rights. As a whole, the laws presuppose a community which is at once pastoral (based on the herding of sheep and goats) and agrarian (based on the raising of crops). The legal material could have been in effect during the time before the advent of the monarchy in Israel. It is, however, difficult to

---

[32] On the Code of the Covenant, see Shalom M. Paul, *Studies in the Book of the Covenant in the light of Cuneiform and Biblical Law* (VTSup 13; Leiden: Brill, 1970); Jay W. Marshall, *Israel and the Book of the Covenant: An Anthropological Approach to Biblical Law* (SBLDS 140; Atlanta: Scholars Press, 1993); Joe M. Sprinkle, *The Book of the Covenant: A Literary Approach*. JSOTSup 174; Sheffield: JSOT Press, 1994.

[33] See, e.g., Exod 21:2, 7, 18, 20, 26, 28, 33.

determine the time of the literary composition of the actual body of laws. The admonitions, nevertheless, show prophetic and Deuteronomist influences.

3.1. The social groups and the treatment of the slaves

The Israelite community described in the Covenant Code was composed of both freeborn and slaves. Among the freeborn were the needy—the poor, the orphans and the widows. There were also the resident aliens living in the land, descendents of dispossessed Canaanites or of emigrants, whose economic condition was precarious. The slaves, on the other hand, had a more diverse origin. Insolvent debtors sold members of their own families and, sometimes, they even submitted themselves to slavery in the service of their creditors (Lev 25:39–41). Prisoners of war who were not put to the sword were reduced to slavery (Num 31:9–18, 32–35). One could also buy slaves from the neighboring nations (Lev 25:44–46; Eccl 2:7).[34]

The Covenant Code establishes norms for the emancipation of the "Hebrew slave" (that is to say, an Israelite) bought by a private person (Exod 21:2–11). If the slave were male, he could not be forced to serve as a slave for more than six years. During the seventh year of servitude, he should be set free unless he decided to remain a slave forever. The female slave was treated differently. Upon completing the six years of service, the owner could make her his wife, or he could give her to his son as a wife, or he could permit her redemption. The case of the emancipation of the Israelite slave after the sixth year of service is paralleled in the Code of Hammurabi, which provides that the debtor reduced to slavery for insolvency is freed at the end of the third year of service.[35]

In addition to the emancipation of the Israelite slave, the Covenant Code establishes means to moderate in general the treatment of slaves. For example, if a slave is disciplined, the punishment should be controlled by moderation. If the slave should die as a result of an owner's punishment, the owner himself should be punished (Exod 21:20–21). The text does not, however, clarify what sort of punishment the owner deserves. If the slave is mutilated, the owner should compensate for the ensuing damage by the emancipation of the slave (Exod 21:26–27). These measures of moderation, without parallel in the laws of the ancient Middle East, encompass the recognition of certain rights of the slaves. These measures protect the good of the slaves themselves as human beings more than they secure the profit that the masters could extract from them.

3.2. Concern for the needy

Besides these measures of moderation with regard to the slaves, the Covenant Code demonstrates humanitarian attention, above all, for the needy.[36] The

---

[34] See Muhammad A. Dandamayev, "Slavery (OT)," *ABD* 6:62–65.
[35] See "The Code of Hammurabi," 117 (*ANET*, 170–71).
[36] Exod 22:21–27; 23:3, 6–10, 12.

needy included three universal groups, that is, the poor, the widows, and the orphans. But the Covenant Code adds an additional group—the resident aliens (gērîm).[37] In treating the topic of the needy, the Code intends to suppress oppression and injustice, and remedy poverty. The Code of Hammurabi also uses the three-part expression "the poor, the orphan and the widow." This code makes use of the expression both in the foreword and in the epilogue, but makes no mention of the expression in the body of the code. Unlike the Code of Hammurabi, the collection of laws in the Covenant Code not only presupposes the existence of poverty, but also takes rather serious measures to eradicate it.

The code forbids abusing or being unjust to any needy person, be he or she poor, orphan, widow, or resident alien (Exod 22:21–22; 23:9). Abusing any needy person is prohibited as an extraordinarily serious matter because such abuse attracts the anger of God, who is extremely sensitive to the cry of the oppressed in the land of Israel, just as he was sensitive to the cry of his people in the land of Egypt (22:23–24). As examples of abuse and injustice, the code points out the perversion of justice against the needy, especially by bribing judges and purchasing false witnesses (Exod 23:1–3, 6–8). In answer to the cry of the oppressed, God uses destruction and death against the oppressor (Exod 22:21–24).

The code also orders compassion toward, and sharing with, the needy. Being compassionate is ceasing to observe a custom that oppresses the poor, such as charging interest on a loan (Exod 22:25).[38] Being compassionate is also knowing how to apply the law with moderation, such as ordering that the poor man's garment taken as collateral on a loan be returned before evening because it is the only thing that he has to ward off the cold of the night (Exod 22:26–27). Sharing is letting the poor make free use of the produce of the field and of the vineyard and olive orchard in the Sabbath year (Exod 23:10–11). An Israelite should be compassionate with the needy just as God has been, and presently is, compassionate with Israel.

It is worth noting that the Covenant Code frames many of the laws in favor of the needy within the prohibition of oppressing the resident alien: "You shall not wrong or oppress a resident alien, for you were aliens in the land of Egypt" (Exod 22:21; 23:9). Israelites should remember that they were foreigners in Egypt, and that God liberated them and made them free citizens in a land of their own. They should see on the face of the resident alien a memory of what they were in Egypt. That memory should lead them to imitate the compassion that God had with

---

[37] See Christoph Bultmann, *Der Frende in antiken Juda: Eine Untersuchung zum sozialen Typen-begriff 'ger' und seine bedeutungswandel in der alttestamentlichen Gesetzgebung*. FRLANT 153; Gottingen: Vandenhoeck & Ruprecht, 1992; Innocenzo Cardellini, "Stranieri ed 'emigrati-residenti' un una sintesi di teologia storico-biblica," *RivB* 40 (1992): 129–81; Christiana van Houten, *The Alien in Israelite Law*. JSOTSup 107; Sheffield: JSOT Press, 1991; and Norbert Lohfink, "Poverty in the Law of the Ancient Near East and of the Bible," *TS* 52 (1991): 34-50.

[38] All the countries surrounding ancient Israel charged interest on a loan. See C. Zaccagnini, "La circolazione dei beni," in *L'alba della civiltà* (3 vols; ed. S. Moscati; Turin: UTET, 1976), 2:528–31; R. de Vaux, *Ancient Israel*, 1:170–71; A. Kirk Grayson, "Mesopotamia, History of (Babylonia)" *ABD* 4:760.

them, and to practice this compassion in their dealings with the resident alien and with all the needy of their own people, like the poor, the orphans and the widows. To protect the needy is to celebrate the divine action of the exodus and to become instruments of liberation for other people. Within this ideational context, doing justice is restoring people to their rightful social condition so that they become active and free in society. It means enabling human beings to have the means in order to exercise their work and to develop their productivity. And it means making it possible for those who have been prevented from working to have what they need to get by. Justice is not restricted to a particular social class or to those who possess proof of citizenship. And it is not founded solely on fulfilling work. In the last analysis, justice is based on the will of Yahweh, who liberated Israel from slavery in Egypt. Yahweh does not want people who live within the territory of the community to suffer for want of necessities. He has given Israel a land flowing with milk and honey[39] so that all those who live within it might share its wealth.

4. The social laws of Deuteronomy

The Book of Deuteronomy underwent a long period of formation lasting from the mid-eighth until the mid-sixth centuries. The central part of the work (4:44–28:68) preserves, with some later additions, the oldest portions of the book composed in the second half of the eighth century, and discovered in the temple in the latter part of the seventh century. That first edition was used as the text for the reforms of Josiah. The book of Deuteronomy, finished during the Exile, presupposes that God communicated his will to Israel in the past by means of the Ten Commandments and the Covenant Code. Its purpose now is to update the expression of the divine will for the Israelite community in a new period of crisis and transition. In Deuteronomy, Moses continues to be the mediator but now he uses more authority in his style of speech. He wants to convince those who are in position of authority to modify the social configuration of society. In general, he calls upon all to reform their lives. The purpose of such a reform is to animate society with a spirit of loyalty toward Yahweh and of justice toward fellow human beings. In its final edition, Deuteronomy, through Moses, addresses Israel in exile, especially the pioneers engaged in the restoration of the community in its own land. Moses exhorts them that, in the process of that restoration, they shape a community in accordance with the ideals entrusted to them. The figure of Moses, who looks to the future and who communicates his ideals for a loyal and just society, is inspirational and provocative. He inspires leaders to undertake the task of shaping a society rooted in justice and calls people to join the effort of improving society on behalf of the poor and the needy.[40]

---

[39] See, e.g., Exod 3:8, 17; 13:5; 33:3; Lev 20:24; Num 13:27; 14:8; Deut 6:3.
[40] See Jeffries M. Hamilton, *Social Justice and Deuteronomy: The Case of Deuteronomy 15* (SBLDS 136; Atlanta, Ga.: Scholars Press, 1992), 143–44; Harry P. Nasuti, "Identity, Identification, and Imitation: the Narrative Hermeneutics of Biblical Law," *JLR* 4 (1986): 9–23.

4.1. Humanitarian justice for Israelite slaves

Deuteronomy picks up the law of emancipation of Israelite slaves after six years of service as expressed in Exod 21:2–11 and adds that the owner should not discharge the emancipated slave empty-handed, but rather, should weigh them down with gifts of livestock, grain, and wine (Deut 15:12–14). The reason for this precept is that God has liberated Israel from slavery in Egypt and has blessed them with every good thing. Israel should imitate God's liberating and generous act (Deut 15:14–15). If Israel does so, God will bless them and will make them wealthier still (15:4–5). Moreover, Deuteronomy gives the law of emancipation the permanent character of a sacred cycle, assimilating it to the law of the Sabbath day. It establishes a parallel between emancipation in the seventh year after six years of service (15:12) and the rest on the seventh day after six days of work (5:13–14). Something similar is done with the law governing the remission of debts (15:1). This assimilation shows that, for Deuteronomy, the problem of the poor and oppressed is of vital importance for the well-being of the community. It has as much importance as the Sabbath day observance.

4.2. Humanitarian justice for the needy

Deuteronomy makes no mention of the sabbatical year of the field after six years of cultivation (see Exod 23:10–11), probably because it concentrates its interest in the people. It does prescribe, however, a sabbatical year of debt-cancellation for Israelite debtors, although not for the aliens (Deut 15:1–6). Moreover, it exhorts those who possess the goods of the earth to be generous in lending without interest to the brother in need even when they know that the year of debt-remission approaches (Deut 15:7–11; 23:19–20). And, it institutes the triennial tithe to aid the Levite, the resident alien, the orphan, and the widow (Deut 14:28–29; 26:12–15).[41] Deuteronomy also exhorts harvesters not to be too thorough in the gathering of the sheaves but to leave something for the resident alien, the orphan, and the widow (Deut 24:19–21). During the festivals of Weeks and of Tabernacles, the Israelites are exhorted to share their offerings not only with members of the household, both free and enslaved, but also with the Levite, the resident alien, the orphan, and the widow (Deut 16:11–14). These measures are part of a system designed to provide help to all those who, for one reason or another, lack the necessities of life.

Justice in commercial transactions is important for all consumers but, above all, for those of limited resources. Deuteronomy mandates that merchants use

---

[41] To the traditional list of needy people (the poor, the orphan, the widow, and the resident alien) Deuteronomy adds a new group, the Levites (Deut 14:27, 29; 26:11–13) who seem to have been impoverished by Josiah's reform that centralized all sacrifice in Jerusalem. On the humanitarian dimension of Deuteronomy see Hamilton, *Social Justice;* and Moshe Weinfeld, *Deuteronomy and the Deuteronomic School* (Oxford: Clarendon, 1972), 282–97.

just weights and measures in their purchases and sales (25:14–15). In the structure of the society described by Deuteronomy, the justice of the nation is in the hands of the judges. Israel (probably the elders of the tribe) should name judges and magistrates in every city "so that they judge the people with justice" (16:18).[42] Those so named are charged with the grave responsibility of avoiding partiality and bribes (16:19). Their mission is described with one of the most emphatic imperatives of the book: "Justice, and only justice, you shall pursue" (*ṣedeq ṣedeq tirdōf,* 16:20). This mission is so important that both the prosperity of Israel and the possession of the land that God has given them (16:20) depend on its execution. The discharge of this mission is an essential part of the demands of the covenant. What God demands of Israel in the covenant is "to serve the LORD your God with all your heart and with all your soul, and to keep the commandments of the LORD your God and his decrees that I am commanding you today, for your own well-being" (10:12–13). The God whom Israel should serve is the "God of gods and Lord of lords, the great God, mighty and awesome, who is not partial and takes no bribe, who executes justice for the orphan and the widow, and who loves the strangers, providing them food and clothing" (10:17–18). Therefore, concludes Deuteronomy, "you shall also love the stranger" (10:19a). The model and the reason to follow in this love is the conduct of God toward Israel when they were resident aliens in Egypt (10:19b).

While Deuteronomy admits that it is not possible to eliminate the existence of the resident alien, the orphan, and the widow, it does claim that it is possible to create a system in which the immigrant, the orphan, and the widow do not suffer poverty. "Since there will never cease to be some in need on the earth, I therefore command you, 'Open your hand to the poor and needy neighbor in your land'" (Deut 15:11). The exhortation to generosity is accompanied by the promise that if one opens one's hand to the neighbor, God will greatly increase the prosperity of the nation. Such generosity creates a circulation of goods that favors the well-being of the community (Deut 15:14–15).

Deuteronomy determines the relationships between ruler and governed, between rich and poor, between the powerful and needy, not just on the basis of principles of commutative and distributive justice, but primarily on the basis of a

---

[42] Deuteronomy set up two courts of law: a local one in every town, comprising a corps of professional judges and officials, and the other in Jerusalem, comprising Levitical priests and lay judges. The latter dealt with difficult cases the local courts could not resolve (Deut 16:18–20; 17:8–13). According to the ancient Near East mores, the king was the judge *par excellence,* but in Deuteronomy he seems to be deprived of judicial jurisdiction. Instead, the emphasis is on his obligation to read and observe the law, with the understanding that his obedience is pivotal for the survival of the dynasty (17:14–20). In setting up two courts, Deuteronomy established a reform similar to Jehoshaphat's (2 Chr 19:4–11), but with the difference that the latter set up local courts only in fortified cities. Both reforms coincide in reducing the competence of the local courts of elders, probably because of their venality and abusiveness. See chapter 6, note 12. See Richard Clifford, *Deuteronomy: With an Excursus on Covenant and Law* (OTM 4; Wilmington: Michael Glazier, 1982), 98–100; Philips, *Ancient Israel,* 17–23; R. de Vaux, *Ancient Israel,* 1:150–55.

beneficent justice, suffused with a compassionate love in imitation of the love of God towards Israel. This beneficent justice manifests itself in the liberation of slaves and the cancellation of debts every seven years. It also manifests itself in a special manner by favoring the poor and indigent by allowing them to partake of the produce of the land. Deuteronomy emphasizes that this beneficent justice is an essential part of the order brought about by the liberation from Egyptian oppression and articulated under divine authority in the two ensuing covenants at Sinai and Moab. Such a beneficent justice is an essential element of the order Moses envisioned for the Israelites who would emerge from the severe trial of the Babylonian captivity. The execution of such order is the way to secure God's blessing (28:1–14), the way to life (30:15–20). It assures the survival of the nation, and for the community permanence in the land, prosperity, and peace. What is more, this beneficent justice, suffused with compassionate love, is a model for the nations of the world. Hence, Moses says, "What other great nation has statutes and ordinances as just as this entire law that I am setting before you today?" (4:8).

5. The Holiness Code

The collection of Deuteronomic laws finds a parallel in the Holiness Code (Leviticus 17–26). The age of the so-called Holiness Code is a much-discussed topic. The most common opinion is that it represents the oldest part of the Book of Leviticus. It was most likely composed by priests from Jerusalem at the close of the monarchy, though it is thought to contain post-Exilic additions such as the law of the Jubilee (Leviticus 25).[43] The authors of the Holiness Code share the understanding of Israel's mission affirmed in Exod 19:5–6. According to that mission, the legislation of Sinai is designed to teach the post-Exilic Israel how to live as a sacred community, different from all the nations, yet with a mission to them as they exercised a priestly function among the nations by being the very model of a just society.

5.1. The social groups

According to the Holiness Code, Israelite society was made up of both free people and slaves. The slaves were bought from the neighboring nations, acquired from among the resident aliens, or were descendents of slaves in perpetuity (25:44–46a). Leviticus 25, which is postexilic, repeatedly prohibits one Israelite from accepting or reducing another Israelite to slavery (25:39, 46b). This prohibition presupposes a practice, perhaps still extant, of taking Israelites as slaves. Free

---

[43] See J. Alberto Soggin, *Introduction to the Old Testament* (OTL; Philadelphia: Westminster, 1980), 138–44. For a more conservative position, see Jacob Milgrom, *Leviticus 1–16* (AB 3; New York: Doubleday, 1991), 27–37. For a reversal of the relationship of P to H, see Israel Knohl, *The Sanctuary of Silence: The Priestly Torah and the Holiness School* (Minneapolis: Fortress, 1995).

Israelites were divided between the wealthy and the poor. The poor together with the resident aliens were vulnerable to exploitation by the wealthy.[44] However, there were cases of resident aliens who came to Israel and made their fortunes (25:47). The Holiness Code mentions two groups with the names of *śĕkîrîm* and *tôšabîm*.[45] The *śĕkîrîm* were day laborers, numbered among the poor. The *tôšabîm* were assimilated aliens, a new category of dependents who did not own their own homes, and who were put up in the servants' quarters; they were similar to the resident aliens *(gērîm)*, but they were something more than these; it appears as though they were more socially and religiously assimilated.

5.2. Social justice as an imitation of the sanctity of God

Leviticus 19, the oldest part of the Holiness Code, offers an extremely close relationship between religious piety and social behavior. Indeed, in this chapter the norms for social life (vv. 3a, 9–18) are intertwined with the regulations governing public worship (vv. 3b–8). Moreover, both are located under the rubric: "Be holy as I am holy" (v. 2). This rubric is a call to imitate the sanctity of Yahweh as much in acts of worship as in social behavior. The call presupposes that the sanctity of God is imitated when his precepts are obeyed. It is worth noting that this chapter ends a long list of socially ethical obligations with the precept: "You shall love your neighbor as yourself" (v. 18b). In this context, to love one's neighbor is to take his part and make him better off. The neighbor, in turn, is identified in particular with the poor (19:10, 15, 39), the deaf and the blind (19:14), the destitute senior citizen (19:32), the day laborer (19:13), and the resident alien (19:10, 33, 34). The resident alien is included within the concept of neighbor indicating that love should be given to all those who live in the land of Israel—even if they are not Israelites. In order to highlight this idea, the text repeats the precept of love applying it particularly to the foreigner: "You shall love the alien as yourself" (19:34).[46]

5.3. The sabbatical institutions

Leviticus 25, the most recent part of the Holiness Code, treats two sabbatical institutions: the traditional sabbatical rest of the field (Lev 25:1–7; see Exod 23:10–11) and the Jubilee (Lev 25:8–17, 23–55), an institution not mentioned in

---

[44] For references regarding the poor and the resident aliens, see Lev 19:10, 15, 33, 34; 23:22; 25:35, 45.

[45] For *śĕkîrîm*, see Lev 22:10; 25:6, 40, 50, 53. For *tôšabîm*, see Lev 22:10; 25:6, 23, 25, 40.

[46] On the concept of love among human beings including political loyalty and commitment of one's mind and heart to pursue the chosen object and conquer it, see William L. Moran, "The Ancient Near Eastern Background of the Love of God in Deuteronomy," *CBQ* 25 (1963): 77–87; Hans-Peter Mathys, *Liebe deinen Nächsten wie dich selbst: Untersuchungen zum alttestamentlichen Gebot der Nächstenliebe (Lev 19,18)* (OBO 71; Freiburg: Universitätsverlag, 1986), 12–24; Abraham Malamat, " 'Love Your Neighbors as Yourself.' What It Really Means?" *BAR* 16 (1990): 50–51; Katharine D. Sakenfeld, "Love (OT)," *ABD* 4:376–78.

the previous codes. Leviticus makes no reference to the emancipation of the Israelite slave after six years of service (see Exod 21:2–11; Deut 15:12–18). The reason for the omission is simple: Leviticus 25 does not admit the possibility that one Israelite may be a slave of another Israelite (25:39). Neither does it mention the Sabbath remission of debts according to Deut 15:1–11, but in its place, Leviticus includes the remission of debts in the year of the Jubilee.

In the treatment of the sabbatical year of the field (25:1–7), Leviticus relates it to the obligation of the Sabbath day; the field should also observe the Sabbath as a sign of its ownership by Yahweh (25:2). In giving the social motive, the text does not allude to the poor, as the Covenant Code does (Exod 23:11). It assigns the natural produce of the field in the year of rest to the family with its male and female slaves, their day laborers, and their *tôšabîm* (assimilated foreigners, 25:6). This assignment is in all probability due to the fact that, in postexilic Israel, the text intends to promote the restoration of the unity of the family in an extended sense. As a whole, these Sabbath cycles base interpersonal relationships and social structures on social principles that guarantee social equality and ecological balance between humanity and the environment.[47]

The Jubilee, which appears for the first time in Lev 25:8–17, 23–55, is a law that prescribes a recurrent practice, which should be repeated every fifty years in the entire country at the same time. Every fifty years land must return to its original owners. In the same way, people who sell themselves into slavery, who consequently are removed far from their families, and who have not yet been ransomed, have the right to be ransomed during the Jubilee. Likewise, every fifty years, debts are remitted and fields should lie fallow.

The historical value and the practical application of this law have been discussed extensively. The authors who treat the topic could be divided in three groups. The first group holds that the social and economic atmosphere in which the Jubilee would have had a practical application can be reconstructed.[48] These authors locate the Jubilee in a primitive agrarian economy in which, for reasons of insolvency, one could lose one's property, and even run the risk of being reduced to slavery. The function of the law of the Jubilee was to restore the original situation, returning the field to its first owner and emancipating the slave. Its purpose was to safeguard the family. One of the criticisms against this theory is that it attributes the institution of the Jubilee back to the period of the occupation of the land, for which there is no documentation of any sort that may support the case.

The second group of scholars looks for parallels in the ancient Near East in order to prove the historical probability of the Jubilee.[49] These scholars see in the

---

[47] See Yairah Amit, "The Jubilee Law: An Attempt Instituting at Social Justice," in *Justice and Righteousness: Biblical Themes and their Influence* (ed. H. G. Reventlow and Y. Hoffman; JSOTSup 137; Sheffield: JSOT Press, 1992), 50.

[48] See Robert North, *Sociology of the Biblical Jubilee* (Rome: Pontifical Biblical Institute, 1954). J. P. M. van der Ploeg, "Studies in Hebrew Law," *CBQ* 13 (1951): 164–71; Edward Neufeld, "The Socio-Economic Background to Yobel and Šemitta," *RSO* 33 (1958): 53–124.

[49] See, e.g., Julius Lewy, "The Biblical Institution of Děrôr in the Light of Akkadian Documents," *ErIsr* 5 (1958): 21–31; Jacob. J. Finkelstein, "Some New Misharum Material

practice of the *mīšarum* and *andurārum* of the ancient Near East an excellent parallel. There is no doubt that incidental practice in the ancient Near East offers a parallel to the institution of the Jubilee. Cancellation of debts, emancipation of slaves, and restitution of fields to their original owners all happened in the ancient Near East. But these were not events that were fixed ahead of time by law; rather, they occurred at the beginning of the reign of a monarch, and they periodically recurred during a given regime. They entirely depended, however, on the will of the king. They were sporadic measures that addressed a given situation, lacking any force of law for the future. The biblical Jubilee does not depend, however, on the benevolence of the ruler; it is an institution, permanently established by God, which should apply in a recurrent, continuous, universal, and simultaneous form among the chosen people.

The third group thinks that the law of the Jubilee is a late and idealistic expression of a measure that was never put into practice. Rather, its objective was to maintain an ideal of social justice that served to shape the society of the future.[50] This thesis has several arguments in its favor. Besides the fact that the law seems to find insuperable obstacles in practice, there is no proof that any of its provisions were ever applied.[51] There is no mention of the Jubilee in the historical or prophetic books. Moreover, in order to understand the formation of the law of Jubilee it is necessary to keep in mind several factors. The law of Jubilee presupposes an experience of disappointment with the conduct of the Israelite kings. From the eighth century onward these kings favored the concept of land as merchandise over and against the concept of land as right of inheritance. The kings aided the division of the land into large estates, a policy which caused farmworkers to become increasingly impoverished and which attracted the denunciation of the prophets. That experience of disappointment also includes the resentment caused by noncompliance with the established sabbatical laws.[52] The law of Jubilee further presupposes the frustration of the postexilic community living in a reduced area of arable land in which there was insufficient room for each family to occupy its own acreage and take the harvest for its own good. The law of the Jubilee is an answer to these experiences and is formulated with nostalgia for a presumed socioeconomic equality of the tribal period when the land was being distributed. It is a nostalgia based on the fact that, in an agrarian society, access to arable land is the most important means by which a family could survive. The law of Jubilee outlaws gathering the land into large estates. It prohibits individuals from accumulating enormous extensions of arable land for their own exclusive profit. It restores the right of the person to his land. It is a concrete law. As

---

and its Implications," in *Studies in Honor of Benno Landsberger* (AS 16; Chicago: Chicago University Press, 1965), 233–46; C. J. H. Wright, "Jubilee, Year of," *ABD* 3:1025–30.

[50] See Eli Ginzberg, "Studies in the Economics of the Bible," *JQR*, NS 22 (1932): 343–408; R. de Vaux, *Ancient Israel*, 1:175–77; Raymond Westbrook, *Property and the Family in Biblical Law*, JSOTSup 113; Sheffield: JSOT Press, 1991; Y. Amit, "Jubilee Law," 47–59.

[51] Lev 27:16–25 and Num 36:4 both depend on Lev 25. See R. de Vaux, *Ancient Israel*, 1:175–77.

[52] See Exod 21:2–11; 23:10–11; Deut 15:1–6.

J. A. Fager says, this law declares that a person, a member of a particular family, has the right to occupy a certain parcel of arable land and harvest its produce for his own good.[53] Maintaining this law is crucial for the community to subsist in an agrarian society. Any noncompliance demolishes the order established by God and creates chaos. At bottom, the purpose of the law of Jubilee is to impede the perpetuation of socioeconomic discrimination and to diminish the causes that generate social conflicts. Every fifty years socioeconomic inequality must cease and each member of the society must begin with a new cycle of opportunity. The law of Jubilee is an ideal destined to motivate society to work for a better life so that each individual might have an honorable existence with a guaranteed minimum of economic means.[54] The Jubilee remains a powerful model in formulating Christian biblical ethics to protect people from the inequitable distribution of goods when the ownership of property accumulates in the hands of a wealthy few with the inevitable result of oppression and alienation. The motivations of the Jubilee law draw attention to situations that repeat in the history of humanity. Their significance for the present reader is brought to life not only by the sad spectacle of inequitable and monopolized distribution of goods within society, but also by the painful situation of many in poor or developing countries, who, oppressed by international debts, are kept under a yoke of slavery without any hope of relief.[55]

Conclusion

It is necessary to stress that the laws of the Pentateuch result from a change in structures; Israel passed from the oppressive structures of Egypt to those of a free society in service to Yahweh. The laws are part of the covenant in which one may distinguish two concepts that undergird the foundations of social justice. The first is particularistic and regionalistic, associated with ancient traditions and adopted by the Deuteronomist authors. The other is universalistic, and characteristic of the Priestly writers. The first concept plays the predominant role, while the second plays a role less outstanding.

The terms that are used in the first conception are Yahweh the liberator, Israel the liberated, and the land given by Yahweh. In this conception, the laws that regulate social justice are based on the nature of the society established at Sinai and in Moab. The motivations for Israel's observations of these laws are her

---

[53] Jeffrey A. Fager, *Land Tenure and the Biblical Jubilee: Uncovering Hebrew Ethics through the Sociological Knowledge* (JSOTSup 155; Sheffield: JSOT Press, 1933), 113.

[54] Amit, "Jubilee Law," 53–59.

[55] In this context, Pope John Paul II has stated, "In the spirit of the Book of Leviticus (25:8–12) Christians will have to raise their voice on behalf of all the poor of the world, proposing the jubilee as an appropriate time to give thought, among other things, to reducing substantially, if not canceling outright, the international debt." Pope John Paul II, *Tertio Millennio Adveniente* (1994), 52.

grateful appreciation for having been liberated from slavery and the honor bestowed on her of imitating the compassion of Yahweh toward her when under oppression. Additional motivations are, on the one hand, the promise of prosperity if Israel obeys the will of God, and on the other, the threat of great loss that results from the moral contamination of the land where the holiness of God dwells. Actions promoting social justice, in this concept, protect the freedom of the members of the Israelite community, safeguard the land as ancestral property of the family, and defend social and economic life against the oppression of creditors or harassment by the greedy. These social actions form a program designed to create a free, just, and prosperous society. In the final redaction of the Pentateuch, this program is projected toward the future with the hope that postexilic Israel carry out that ideal. This turning toward the future makes viable the application of the text to new critical situations by the chosen people. This turning toward the future suggests the attitude which must guide anyone in society who looks for sociopolitical liberation or wishes to consolidate a free sociopolitical existence.

A more recent, universalistic vision runs parallel to this. The terms used in this vision include the Creator, Israel, and humanity. The motivation for social action here is the neighbor as a human person created in the image of God. This concept played its part in the social action of ancient Israel though with restrictions owing to the cultural limitations of the time. In spite of this, Israel maintained faith that God created human beings according to his image and likeness, setting aside a remnant capable of thoroughly transforming human society. This equality is grounded in a participation in the divine image and is the root of contemporary thinking on human rights; it is the guide that inspires people to change discriminatory social structures, stimulates people to point out the injustice of ideologies and oppressive socioeconomic practices, and motivates those who struggle to develop awareness among those in underdeveloped regions in order to improve their economic and social condition.

These two concepts are integrated in the extant text of the laws as part of the covenant. Together, they offer a strong motivation to stir up awareness of the dignity and destiny of the chosen people. They create a sense of individual and social responsibility. The exilic editor combined both concepts and made them concrete in the figure of Moses, who looks toward the future of an Israel reestablished in the land. It is Moses who inspires in his people an ideal of justice, loyalty, and peace. The text of these laws is animated by a spirit of justice and equity that serves as direction and encouragement for all those who struggle for justice and peace in today's world.

Bibliography

Amit, Yairah. "The Jubilee Law: An Attempt Instituting at Social Justice." Pages 47–59 in *Justice and Righteousness: Biblical Themes and their Influence*. Edited by H. G. Reventlow and Y. Hoffman. Journal for the Study of the Old Testament: Supplement Series 137. Sheffield: JSOT Press, 1992.

Aubert, Jean-Marie. *Chrétiens et peine de mort.* Paris: Desclée, 1978.
Baum, Gregory. *The Priority of Labor: A Commentary on "Laborem Exercens," Encyclical Letter of Pope John Paul II.* New York: Paulist, 1982.
Bird, Phyllis A. "Images of Women in the Old Testament." Pages 252–88 in *The Bible and Liberation: Political and Social Hermeneutics.* Edited by N. K. Gottwald. Maryknoll: Orbis, 1983.
———. "Women (OT)." Pages 951–57 in vol. 6 of *Anchor Bible Dictionary.* Edited by D. N. Freedman. 6 vols. New York: Doubleday, 1992.
Botterweck, G. J., and H. Ringgren, eds. *Theological Dictionary of the Old Testament.* Translated by J. T. Willis, G. W. Bromiley, and D. E. Green. 8 vols. Grand Rapids: Eerdmans, 1974–.
Bultmann, Christoph. *Der Frende in antiken Juda: Eine Untersuchung zum sozialen Typen-begriff "ger" und seine Bedeutungswandel in der alttestamentlichen Gesetzgebung.* Forschungen zur Religion und Literatur des Alten und Neuen Testaments 153; Göttingen: Vandenhoeck & Ruprecht, 1992.
Cardellini, Innocenzo. "Stranieri ed 'emigrati-residenti' in una sintesi de teologia storico-biblica," *Rivista Biblica* 40 (1992): 129–81.
Clifford, Richard. *Deuteronomy: With an Excursus on Covenant and Law.* Old Testament Message 4; Wilmington: Michael Glazier, 1982.
Croatto, J. Severino. "¿Cómo releer la Biblia desde su contexto socio-político? Ejercicio sobre algunos temas del Pentateuco." *Revista bíblica* 53 (1991): 197–203.
Dandamayev, Muhammad A. "Slavery (OT)." Pages 62–65 in vol. 6 of *Anchor Bible Dictionary.* Edited by D. N. Freedman. 6 vols. New York: Doubleday, 1992.
Dohmen, Christoph. "Der Dekaloganfang und sein Ursprung." *Biblica* 74 (1993): 175–93.
Dozeman, T. B. *God at War: Power in the Exodus Tradition.* New York: Oxford University Press, 1996.
Fager, Jeffrey A. *Land Tenure and the Biblical Jubilee: Uncovering Hebrew Ethics through the Sociological Knowledge.* Journal for the Study of the Old Testament: Supplement Series 155. Sheffield: JSOT Press, 1933.
Finkelstein, Jacob J. "Ammisaduqa's Edict and the Babylonian 'Law Codes.'" *Journal of Cuneiform Studies* 15 (1961): 91–104.
———. "Some New Misharum Material and its Implications." Pages 233–46 in *Studies in Honor of Benno Landsberger.* Assyriological Studies 16. Chicago: Chicago University Press, 1965.
Flannery, Austin, ed. *Vatican Council II: The Conciliar and Post Conciliar Documents.* Collegeville: Liturgical, 1975.
Gamberoni, J. "Das Elterngebot im Alten Testament." *Biblische Zeitschrift,* New Series, 8 (1964): 161–90.
Gerstenberger, Erhard. "Covenant and Commandment." *Journal of Biblical Literature* 84 (1965): 38–51.
Ginzberg, Eli. "Studies in the Economics of the Bible," *Jewish Quarterly Review,* New Series, 22 (1932): 343–408.
Goodfriend, Elaine A. "Adultery." Pages 82–86 in vol. 1 of *Anchor Bible Dictionary.* Edited by D. N. Freedman. 6 vols. New York: Doubleday, 1992.

Grayson, A. Kirk. "Mesopotamia, History of (Babylonia)." Pages 755–77 in vol. 4 of *Anchor Bible Dictionary*. Edited by D. N. Freedman. 6 vols. New York: Doubleday, 1992.

Greengus, Samuel. "Law." Pages 242–52 in vol. 4 of *Anchor Bible Dictionary*. Edited by D. N. Freedman. 6 vols. New York: Doubleday, 1992.

Hamilton, Jeffries M. *Social Justice and Deuteronomy: The Case of Deuteronomy 15*. Society of Biblical Literature Dissertation Series 136. Atlanta: Scholars Press, 1992.

Hasel, Gerhard F. "Sabbath." Pages 849–56 in vol. 5 of *Anchor Bible Dictionary*. Edited by D. N. Freedman. 6 vols. New York: Doubleday, 1992.

Hiebert, Theodore. "Warrior, Divine." Pages 876–80 in vol. 6 of *Anchor Bible Dictionary*. Edited by D. N. Freedman. 6 vols. New York: Doubleday, 1992.

Himes, Kenneth R. "War." Pages 977–82 in *The New Dictionary of Catholic Social Thought*. Edited by J. A. Dwyer. Collegeville: Liturgical, 1994.

Hobbs, T. Raymond. *A Time for War: A Study of Warfare in the Old Testament*. Wilmington: Glazier, 1989.

Hossfeld, Frank-Lothar. *Der Dekalog. Seine späten Fassungen, die originale Komposition und seine Vorstufen*. Orbis biblicus et orientalis 45. Fribourg: Universitätsverlag, 1982.

Houten, Christiana van. *The Alien in Israelite Law*. Journal for the Study of the Old Testament: Supplement Series 107. Sheffield: JSOT Press, 1991.

Knohl, Israel. *The Sanctuary of Silence: The Priestly Torah and the Holiness School*. Minneapolis: Fortress, 1995.

Kremers, Heinz. "Die Stellung des Elterngebotes im Dekalog." *Evangelische Theologie* 21 (1961): 145–61.

Langan, J. "Capital Punishment." *Theological Studies* 54 (1993): 111–24.

Lemaire, André. "Le Décalogue: Essai d'histoire de la rédaction." Pages 258–95 in *Mélanges bibliques et orientaux en l'honneur de M. Henri Cazelles*. Edited by A. Casquot and M. Delcor. Alter Orient und Altes Testament 212. Neukirchen-Vluyn: Neukirchener, 1981.

Lewy, Julius. "The Biblical Institution of Dĕrôr in the Light of Akkadian Documents," *Eretz Israel* 5 (1958): 21–31.

Lind, Millard C. *Yahweh is a Warrior: The Theology of Warfare in Ancient Israel*. Scottdale: Herald, 1980.

Lohfink, Norbert. "Poverty in the Law of the Ancient Near East and of the Bible," *Theological Studies* 52 (1991): 34–50.

Malamat, Abraham. " 'Love Your Neighbors as Yourself.' What It Really Means?" *Biblical Archaeology Review* 16 (1990): 50–51.

Marshall, Jay W. *Israel and the Book of the Covenant: An Anthropological Approach to Biblical Law*. Society of Biblical Literature Dissertation Series 140; Atlanta: Scholars Press, 1993.

Mathys, Hans-Peter. *Liebe deinen Nächsten wie dich selbst: Untersuchungen zum alttestamentlichen Gebot der Nächstenliebe (Lev 19,18)*. Orbis Biblicus et Orientalis 71. Freiburg: Universitätsverlag, 1986.

Milgrom, Jacob. *Leviticus 1–16*. Anchor Bible 3. New York: Doubleday, 1991.

Miller, Patrick D. *The Divine Warrior in Early Israel.* Cambridge, Mass.: Harvard University Press, 1973.

Moran, William L. "The Ancient Near Eastern Background of the Love of God in Deuteronomy." *Catholic Biblical Quarterly* 25 (1963): 77–87.

———. "The Conclusion of the Decalogue (Exod 20,17 = Dtn 5,21)." *Catholic Biblical Quarterly* 29 (1967): 543–54.

Nasuti, Harry P. "Identity, Identification, and Imitation: the Narrative Hermeneutics of Biblical Law," *Journal of Law and Religion* 4 (1986): 9–23.

Neufeld, Edward. "The Socio-Economic Background to Yobel and Šemitta," *Rivista degli studi orientali* 33 (1958): 53–124.

North, Rorbert. *Sociology of the Biblical Jubilee.* Rome: Pontifical Biblical Institute, 1954.

Paul, Shalom M. *Studies in the Book of the Covenant in the light of Cuneiform and Biblical Law* (Vetus Testamentum Supplements 13; Leiden: Brill, 1970).

Phillips, Anthony. *Ancient Israel's Criminal Law: A New Approach to the Decalogue.* New York: Schocken, 1970.

Ploeg, J. P. M. van der. "Studies in Hebrew Law." *Catholic Biblical Quarterly* 13 (1951): 164–71.

Pope John Paul II. Apostolic Letter, *Tertio Millennio Adveniente* (10 November 1994). Online: http://www.vatican.va/holy_father/john_paul_ii/apost_letters/documents/hf_jp-ii_apl_10111994_tertio-millennio-adveniente_en.html.

———. Encyclical Letter, *Evangelium Vitae* (25 March 1995). Online: http://www.vatican.va/edocs/ENG0141/_INDEX.HTM

———. Encyclical Letter, *Laborem Exercens* (14 September 1981). Online: http://www.vatican.va/edocs/ENG0217/_INDEX.HTM

Pritchard, James B., ed. *Ancient Near Eastern Texts Relating to the Old Testament.* 3d ed. Princeton: Princeton University Press, 1969.

Sakenfeld, Katharine D. "Love (OT)." Pages 375–81 in vol. 4 of *Anchor Bible Dictionary.* Edited by D. N. Freedman. 6 vols. New York: Doubleday, 1992.

Soggin, J. Alberto. *Introduction to the Old Testament.* Old Testament Library. Philadelphia: Westminster, 1980.

Sprinkle, Joe M. *The Book of the Covenant: A Literary Approach.* Journal for the Study of the Old Testament: Supplement Series 174; Sheffield: JSOT Press, 1994.

Stamm, Johann J., and M. E. Andrew. *The Ten Commandments in Recent Research.* Studies in Biblical Theology, Second Series 2. Naperville: Allenson, 1967.

Valadier, Paul. "Des évêques pour l'abolition de la peine de mort." *Études* 348 (1978): 683–91.

Vaux, Roland de. *Ancient Israel.* 2 vols. New York: McGraw-Hill, 1965.

Weinfeld, Moshe. *Deuteronomy and the Deuteronomic School.* Oxford: Clarendon, 1972.

Westbrook, Raymond. *Property and the Family in Biblical Law.* Journal for the Study of the Old Testament: Supplement Series 113. Sheffield: JSOT Press, 1991.

Wright, Christopher J. H. "Family." Pages 761–69 in vol. 2 of *Anchor Bible Dictionary*. Edited by D. N. Freedman. 6 vols. New York: Doubleday, 1992.

———. "Jubilee, Year of." Pages 1025–30 in vol. 3 of *Anchor Bible Dictionary*. Edited by D. N. Freedman. 6 vols. New York: Doubleday, 1992.

Zaccagnini, C. "La circolazione dei beni." Pages 528–31 in vol. 2 of *L'alba della civiltà*. Edited by S. Moscati. 3 vols. Turin: UTET, 1976.

Zimmerli, Walther. *I Am Yahweh*. Atlanta: John Knox, 1982.

CHAPTER FIVE

JUSTICE, MONARCHY, AND PROPHECY

Introduction

The two preceding chapters were devoted to stories and legal texts taken from the books of the Pentateuch. The stories in Exodus described the action of God's justice that punished oppressive Pharaoh and liberated oppressed Israel. In doing so, the book depicted the exodus from Egypt as a paradigm of liberation and described the ritual that transformed a historical event into a memorial for future generations. The legal texts, on the other hand, expressed the norms of God's will, guiding Israel to behave as the chosen of God. Their purpose was to help Israel fulfill her mission as a community liberated to serve God and to be an example of justice for the world.

The present chapter deals with the monarchy and the prophets, two social phenomena important to our analysis of ancient Israel as a community called to serve God and practice justice. Our specific purpose is to inquire about justice during the monarchic period, studying both the role and conduct of monarchs and the preaching of prophets. The inquiry will continue into the exilic and postexilic periods, analyzing important prophetic figures who survived the monarchy. Central to our consideration are the relations between rulers and their subjects and among groups or individuals within society, with particular attention to the poor, the weak, and the oppressed.

1. Kingship in ancient Israel

1.1. The monarchy in ancient Israel

The biblical texts associate the beginning of the monarchy with Israel's struggle with surrounding peoples, particularly the Philistines, who were a threat to the nation's very existence.[1] Historically, however, the Israelite monarchy was

---

[1] It has been commonly imagined that the formation of the Israelite state took place after the settlement and expansion of the tribes. Within this framework, the thesis has

probably the result of a social and economic process that started very early within Israel, although we cannot deny the influence of external factors such as the threat from surrounding peoples.² In her search for a political model, Israel adopted the monarchic structure of its neighbors. Monarchy was a millennia-old institution in Mesopotamia and Egypt, although it appeared more recently in locales bordering on Israel. There was a common belief in those areas that monarchy was a venerable institution, brought down from heaven by divine beings. Hence, the monarch was an agent of deities, entrusted with the responsibility of maintaining or recovering on earth the harmony instituted by the god of order in his fight against the powers of chaos. In his mission as guardian of cosmic order, the king acted as warrior, judge, and priest. As warrior, the king protected and defended his kingdom against external and internal threats. As judge, he guaranteed order and established justice, paying particular attention to the poor. As priest, he insured proper and orderly worship of the deities by the community.³ In ancient Mesopotamia, the firmness of the divine order and the ability to maintain it were expressed by the couplet *kittum-mīšarum* ("firmness" and "equity"). Hence, the king, the guardian of order, was called the *šar mīšarim* ("prince of order" or "of equity").⁴ In ancient Egypt, the divine order and the power to maintain it were expressed by the word *maat,* and the pharaoh was called "the lord of *maat,*" since he was the son of Amon and the representative of Re, the creator, the god of order.⁵

In the Near Eastern world, the Mesopotamian vocabulary for power and order was more influential than the Egyptian. The terms *kittum* and *mīšarum*

---

arisen according to which the monarchy was imposed on Israel by aristocratic interests, thereby producing a foreign development in the history of Israel. One defender of this thesis is George E. Mendenhall. See, e.g., his publications *The Tenth Generation: The Origins of the Biblical Tradition* (Baltimore: Johns Hopkins University Press, 1973), 209; "The Monarchy," *Int* 29 (1975): 155–70; "Social Organization in Early Israel," in *Magnalia Dei, the Mighty Acts of God* (ed. F. M. Cross et al.; Garden City: Doubleday, 1976), 132–51.

² On the factors—economic, social, political, military, and international—that moved the tribes to establish a central power, see, e.g., Giorgio Buccellati, *Cities and Nations of Ancient Syria* (Rome: Istituto di Studi del Vicino Oriente, 1967), 240–41; J. Alberto Soggin, *A History of Ancient Israel* (Philadelphia: Westminster, 1985), 167–68; Niels P. Lemche, "Israel, History of," *ABD* 3:541–44; Marvin L. Chaney, "Systematic Study of the Israelite Monarchy," in *Social Scientific Criticism of the Hebrew Bible and Its Social World: The Israelite Monarchy* (ed. N. K. Gottwald; Semeia 37; Chico, Calif.: Scholars Press, 1986), 53–76; Robert B. Coote and Keith W. Whitelam, "The Emergence of Israel: Social Transformation and State Formation following the Decline in Late Bronze Age Trade," *Semeia* 37 (1986): 107–47, and *The Emergence of Early Israel in Historical Perspective* (Sheffield: Almond, 1987); Frank S. Frick, *The Formation of the State in Ancient Israel: A Survey of Models and Theories* (Sheffield: Almond, 1985); Jimmy J. M. Roberts, "In Defense of the Monarchy: The Contribution of Israelite Kingship to Biblical Theology," in *Ancient Israelite Religion* (ed. P. D. Miller et al.; Philadelphia: Fortress, 1987), 385–86.

³ See Keith W. Whitelam, "King and Kingship," *ABD* 4:40–48; Henri Cazelles, "Sacral Kingship," *ABD* 5:863–66.

⁴ See above, ch. 1, §4.

⁵ See above, ch. 2, §1.

spread over the Syro-Palestinian countries and were translated in the Northwest Semitic languages by the words *ṣdq* and *m(y)šr*. Hence the Hebrew *ṣedeq* and *mîšôr* with *mišpāṭ* added as parallel.[6]

The royal psalms in the Bible provide evidence that substantial elements of the royal ideology of the ancient Near East were assimilated to the Davidic monarchy.[7] In fact, according to these psalms, the Davidic king is the son of God, begotten on the day of enthronement (Ps 2:2), to be the representative or agent of God on earth.[8] That day, God gave the king the scepter of order (*mîšôr*, Ps 45:7; English Ps 45:6) and seated him on David's throne, with its foundation of equity (*ṣĕdāqâ*, Prov 16:12; 25:5), to dispense justice (*mišpāṭ*, Ps 122:5). In other words, God gave the king a share of his divine royal power, granting him the gift of political leadership in order to maintain and protect the harmony of the kingdom and of all creation (Ps 72:1–2). An essential part of this mission was the protection of the poor (*ʿānî*) and the oppressed (*ʾebyôn*).[9] The life and prosperity of the nation depended on the king's proper exercise of his power to protect order and justice (Ps 72:3). Likewise, on the day of enthronement, the king was given the promise of universal dominion and the total destruction of his enemies.[10] The same day, the king was invested with the priestly dignity forever (Ps 110:4).

In ancient Israel, the appointment of Davidic kings as agents of divine power on earth was the beginning of the messianic hope that was developed later. This appointment was associated with the election of Jerusalem as the Lord's dwelling place and the residence of his anointed. Such an election was, in turn, the basis for the vision of the holy city as the hub of order and peace for the world.

1.2. The king's power

In adopting the monarchic model of surrounding peoples, Israel introduced distinctive features. In Israel the king was not the son of God by birth but by adoption. In addition, order and justice, to be preserved and fostered by the king, were shaped in accordance with the theology of the peculiar relationship between Yahweh and Israel—Yahweh was the sole source of order and justice. This is why the prophets, in indicting the king and those who were powerful, did not appeal to the mores accepted in the ancient Near East but to the authority of Yahweh, the author of the moral tradition of Israel.[11] Furthermore, in Israel the power of justice, possessed by the king, was a participation in Yahweh's justice. Hence the

---

[6] See Henri Cazelles, "De l'idéologie royale," *JANESCU* 5 (1973): 60–68.
[7] See, e.g., Pss 2, 45, 72, 101, 110.
[8] See Pss 2:6; 45:7; 110:1.
[9] See Ps 72:2, 4, 12–14.
[10] See Pss 2:8–9; 110:1, 5–6.
[11] On the enthronement day, the new king was given a protocol containing the norms for him to follow. It is probable that 1 Sam 10:25 refers to it under the title "the rights and duties of the kingship." An allusion seems also to be found in Deut 17:14–20. See Baruch Halpern, *The Constitution of the Monarchy* (Chico, Calif.: Scholars Press, 1981), 140–44, 222–49; Whitelam, "King and Kingship," 4:46.

responsibility of the king before God: as his representative, the king ought to imitate the divine behavior, characterized by goodness (ḥesed) and faithfulness (ʾĕmet). Therefore, like the Mesopotamian king, the Israelite king ought to protect the established order, penalize offenders and delinquents, restore the destitute and oppressed to the social position suited to them according to the divine will, and foster peace and prosperity. But in addition, the Israelite king had to imitate God's behavior toward his people by enlivening his action of justice with love, compassion, and faithfulness.

For the modern reader used to the concept of nature, we must note that the ancient Israel did not embrace a concept of unity and harmony in the cosmos, which is seen to be ruled by inner laws; the Greek philosophers did, and used the order of nature to determine the right thing for a human being to do, both as an individual and as a member of society. In the Israelite understanding, however, the order of the world and the basis of justice were established by God's supreme will. Hence, a transgression against order and justice was a revolt against God. In addition, the transgression was regarded as a crime against the community, since the laws that were broken had been established by God as essential principles for communal life.

Scholars have raised doubts about whether the Israelite kings enacted laws. In the Bible there is no clear reference to lawgiving activity on the part of any king. This fact may be explained by the theological view that dominated the history of the law in ancient Israel—namely, that God himself was the lawgiver. This theological perspective might have overshadowed human intervention in the formation and promulgation of laws. One may, however, discover traces of the king's lawgiving action in such biblical episodes as the manumission by King Zedekiah (Jer 34:8–9) and King Jehoshaphat's reforms (2 Chr 19:4–11). On the other hand, it is hard to understand how a king might have governed his people guided only by the laws contained in the codes of the Pentateuch.[12]

Likewise, the question has been raised whether the Israelite king had judicial power, because it seems as though the administration of justice was in the hands of the elders and professional judges. Many hold, however, that the king not only appointed judges but himself exercised judicial functions; this is the view of K. W. Whitelam, G. C. Macholz, and H. Reviv.[13] These scholars find support for their thesis in a series of stories that assume that the king was invested with a judicial prerogative, such as the episode of the wise woman of Tekoa, who seems to appeal to the king against a judgment given by her clan (2 Sam 14:1–24). Also pertinent to the idea that the king had judicial power is the story of Absalom, who, in his eagerness to be David's successor, promised that he would expeditiously resolve any

---

[12] See Hanoch Reviv, *The Elders in Ancient Israel* (Jerusalem: Magnes, 1989), 87–97; Keith W. Whitelam, *The Just King: Monarchical Judicial Authority in Ancient Israel* (JSOTSup 12; Sheffield: University of Sheffield Press, 1979), 209–18; G. C. Macholz, "Die Stellung des Königs in der israelitischen Gerichtsverfassung," *ZAW* 84 (1972): 157–82.

[13] Whitelam, *Just King*, 123–97; G. C. Macholz, "Zur Geschichte der Justizorganisation in Juda," *ZAW* 84 (1972): 314–40; Reviv, *Elders*, 92.

lawsuit or complaint the people might have (2 Sam 15:1–6). The story of Solomon's judgment proved to all that "the wisdom of God was in him, to execute justice" (1 Kgs 3:28). Finally, King Jehoshaphat's reform established a balance between royal jurisdiction and communal jurisdiction, relieving the king of his office of supreme judge (2 Chr 19:4–11).[14] Even the psalmists, in Psalms 45 and 72, mention the king's judicial power and ask God that the king might exercise it to establish peace, justice, and prosperity for the nation. These psálms, written for the community, presupposed a widespread conviction that the king possessed the charism of justice, a conviction apt to generate hope in those disappointed with the local courts. Composed on the occasion of the wedding of a king and his enthronement respectively, these psalms renewed the hope of the people in their desire for a better world, since for them the king was the messiah of Yahweh, the bearer of peace and prosperity, and the protector of order and justice. Possessing the charism of justice, the king was nevertheless exposed to serious temptations to abuse his power for his own profit and was consequently subject to divine punishment. The kings' abuse of power earned sharp criticism from the prophets, which the Deuteronomistic writers summarized in Samuel's discourse against the monarchy (1 Sam 8:11–18).

2. Prophecy in ancient Israel

Prophecy is a religious phenomenon with political and social connotations. Its early existence in the ancient Near East goes back to the eighteenth century B.C.E. The letters of Mari testify to its presence in northern Mesopotamia during Zimri-Lim's reign (1779–1757 B.C.E.).[15] In Israel prophecy occurred for the first time at the close of the premonarchic period, in groups and itinerant individuals who were associated with Israelite places of worship and who defended Yahwistic religion against Canaanite religious practices. Prophets played a substantial role in establishing the monarchy and confronting the kings' errant conduct. They continued their influence on the leadership of the community until the postexilic

---

[14] Jehoshaphat's appointment of professional judges in the fortified cities may have been done in order to counteract the abuses of the local courts, comprised of elders who were subject to manipulation by powerful families. The fact that professional judges seem to have functioned only in fortified cities suggests that their judicial sentences were enforced with the support of the military authority. The appointment of professional judges implies a reduction of the jurisdiction of the local courts of elders, although these continued lending their services in the towns and smaller cities. See Whitelam, *Just King*, 196. Reviv maintains that the court of elders continued to function as an institution independent of the magistrates who were established by the state administration, although the former collaborated with the latter. See Reviv, *Elders*, 108–11. Jehoshaphat's reform has been compared with Horemheb's edict (see above, ch. 2, §4), and several similarities have been emphasized, but literary dependence remains a matter of controversy. See Whitelam, *Just King*, 203–5.

[15] Joseph Blenkinsopp, *A History of Prophecy in Israel: From the Settlement in the Land to the Hellenistic Period* (Philadelphia: Westminster, 1983), 53–58.

period, developing a deep and sharp sense of the personal and moral character of the divine reality and highlighting the connection between worship and social ethics. The prophets were the champions of social justice—the moral conscience of the kings and the powerful ones of society.[16]

2.1. The prophets Nathan and Elijah

The meeting of Nathan with King David after the king committed adultery and homicide (2 Sam 11:1–25) is well known. The prophet accused the king of a grave abuse of the power bestowed on him by God. Nathan judged David in accordance not with the mores accepted in the ancient Near East but with God's will as it had been revealed to Israel.

Equally famous is the role of Elijah the Tishbite, in the story of Naboth's vineyard; here the prophet condemned Ahab and Jezebel because of their manipulations of justice, manipulations that amounted to legalized crime (1 Kgs 21:1–29). The story shows the king's influence on the local courts of elders and highlights the abuse of power by the royal couple. It presents a case in which the royal administration legally murdered an innocent person for its own profit by using a puppet court. In human terms, once the royal sentence is executed the case is definitively closed. There is no higher authority to which one might appeal; the sentence has been determined absolutely by the supreme authority of the king. But the prophet emphasizes that although the king feels that he is supreme over any human court, he cannot escape God's judgment. God is actually the supreme judge.

2.2. The prophet Amos in the northern kingdom

Amos prophesied during Jeroboam II's reign (786–746 B.C.E.), in the northern kingdom, at a time when deep social differences were developing within Israelite society. His oracles reflect the sharp social contrast between the well-off, who lived in the cities, and the poor dwelling around cities or in small towns. In these circumstances, Amos persistently denounced violations of justice.[17] He addressed the citizens of the northern kingdom who regarded themselves as religious and faithful to their beliefs. Among these were the leaders of society (the king, priests, and judges) and upper-class and influential people (rich landowners, prosperous traders, and businessmen). The poor were often referred to in the oracles, but they were not directly addressed by the prophet.

---

[16] Bruce Vawter, "Introduction to Prophetic Literature," *NJBC* 196.

[17] See Moshe Weinfeld, "'Justice and Righteousness'—mišpāṭ ûṣĕdāqâ—the Expression and Its Meaning," in *Justice and Righteousness: Biblical Themes and Their Influence* (ed. H. Reventlow and Y. Hoffman; JSOTSup 137; Sheffield: JSOT Press, 1992), 228–46; Herbert B. Huffmon, "The Social Role of Amos's Message," in *The Quest for the Kingdom of God: Studies in Honor of George E. Mendenhall* (ed. Herbert B. Huffmon et al.; Winona Lake: Eisenbrauns, 1983), 109–16; Marlene Fendler, "Zur Sozialkritik des Amos," *EvT* 33 (1973): 32–53.

Amos directed his message to persons of a homogeneous religious character. They devoted themselves to sacrificial celebrations in Yahweh's temples, faithfully observed religious feasts, undertook pilgrimages to famous sanctuaries,[18] and honored the exodus, desert, and conquest traditions (Amos 3:1–2, 9–10). The prophet complained not because of the people's lack of religious practice but because of the abysmal gap that existed between their religious piety and their relationship to their neighbors, particularly the poor; in other words, Amos condemned the terrible disconnection between worship and ethics.[19] Amos criticized their worship because of this disconnection:

> I hate, I despise your festivals,
> and I take no delight in your solemn assemblies.
> Even though you offer me your burnt offerings and grain offerings,
> I will not accept them. . . .
> But let justice [*mišpāṭ*] roll down like waters
> and righteousness [*ṣĕdāqâ*] like an ever-flowing stream. (5:21–22, 24)

In these texts, Amos employs terms that require explanation: *mišpāṭ* and *ṣĕdāqâ*.[20] They sometimes occur in parallel construction.[21] Very often they are conjoined *(mišpat ûṣĕdāqâ)*.[22] Worth noting is that an analogous use, either in parallel or in a couplet, occurs also with the terms *mišpāṭ* and *ṣedeq*.[23]

The term *mišpāṭ* by itself has a wide range of meanings, such as "judgment," "judicial sentence," "verdict," "legal complaint," "decree," "bylaw," "order," and "custom."[24] The words *ṣedeq* and *ṣĕdāqâ*, in turn, derive from the same root, but it is not

---

[18] See Amos 4:4–5; 5:5, 21–22; 8:5.

[19] In his attack against the cult, Amos (5:21–25) uses a dialectic negation that contrasts morality with the cult (see also Jer 7:21–23; Isa 58:1–12). In fact, however, Amos does not reject the cult as such; he rejects, rather, worship empty of moral commitments. On the contrast by negation as an idiomatic form, see Michael L. Barré, "Fasting in Isaiah 58:1–12: A Reexamination," *BTB* 15 (1985): 94–97; T. Booij, "Negation in Isaiah 43:22–24," *ZAW* 94 (1982): 390–400; H. Kruse, "Die Negation dialectische als semitischen Idiom," *VT* 4 (1954): 385–400; M. Fishbane, *Biblical Interpretation in Ancient Israel* (Oxford: Clarendon, 1985), 292–307. Fishbane studies contrast by negation as a method of haggadic exegesis, a method that intends to emphasize the primary importance of what is stated positively without denying the validity, although secondary, of what is negated. Contrast by negation is a way of establishing a hierarchy of values.

[20] On "justice" in the OT, see John J. Scullion, "Righteousness (OT)," *ABD* 5:724–36; B. Mogensen, "*Ṣĕdāqâ* in the Scandinavian and German Research Tradition," in *The Productions of Time: Tradition History in Old Testament Scholarship* (ed. K. Jeppesen and B. Otzen; Sheffield: JSOT Press, 1984), 67–80; Alfred Jepsen, "*Ṣdq* und *Ṣdqh* im Alten Testament," in *Gottes Wort und Gottes Land* (ed. H. G. Reventlow; Göttingen: Vandenhoeck & Ruprecht, 1965), 78–89; H. J. Stoebe, "Die Bedeutung des Wortes ḥäsäd im Alten Testament," *VT* 2 (1970): 244–54; H.-J. Zobel, "ḥesed," *TDOT* 5 (1986), 44–64.

[21] See Amos 5:7, 24; 6:12; Isa 1:27; 56:1.

[22] See Isa 33:5; Jer 9:23; Prov 21:3. This set of terms is older than the Hebrew since it is already read in Ugaritic literature and in Phoenician inscriptions. See Cazelles, "Idéologie," 59–73.

[23] See, e.g., Ps 94:15; 97:2; Prov 1:3; 2:9.

[24] See G. Liedke, "*Špṭ*," *THAT* 2:999–1010.

clear whether both have the same meaning. Jepsen maintained that the former denotes "right order" and the latter signifies an action related to that order.[25] More recent scholars, however, think that both terms have substantially the same meaning. Both may denote "order," "uprightness," "justice," or "right conduct" and "saving action."[26] On the other hand, the terms ṣedeq and ṣĕdāqâ, when coordinated in a pair with mišpāṭ, can form hendiadys and designate the order established by God in human society, particularly in Israel.[27] This is the order that people ought to observe in order to behave rightly, and it is up to the king to preserve it and rule in conformity with it, so that the land may have peace, justice, and prosperity.

It is worth noting that these terms are sometimes parallel to ḥesed ("goodness") and ʾĕmet ("faithfulness").[28] In addition, the word ḥesed is occasionally associated with raḥămîm ("compassion").[29] These connections underline, in the terms mišpāṭ, ṣedeq, and ṣĕdāqâ, the meaning of a compassionate, generous, reliable, and faithful goodness, always ready to serve the needs of others and to foster their well-being. Therefore, the meaning of these terms goes beyond the limits of strict justice; the meaning expands to include a saving and liberating justice, connected especially to the need for the poor to improve their social condition. This type of justice should involve, on the governmental level, thoughtful plans not only to redress wrongs committed against the needy and weak but also to improve their material, intellectual, and spiritual conditions.[30] Within this context, we can understand better the call of Amos: "Let justice [mišpāṭ] roll down like waters and righteousness [ṣĕdāqâ] like an ever-flowing stream" (5:24).

Amos seems to have assumed widespread injustice through the various social strata. He not only accused judges and rulers of perverting justice (5:12, 15); he reproached his audience in general with unjust behavior toward the poor.[31] Instead of showing compassion and interest in helping the needy, they robbed them, stealing from them any possibility to obtain their just aspirations. They trampled over them, oppressing them to the point of selling them as slaves. In the eyes of the powerful and prosperous, the poor were cheap merchandise.[32] For Amos what caused the cup of wickedness to brim over was the arrogance of the powerful who prevented the prophets from speaking (2:12).

In Amos's understanding, this lack of justice and equity was a very serious matter, since Israel had been chosen by God to be a model of justice and equity

---

[25] Jepsen, "Ṣdq und Ṣdqh," 79–81.
[26] See Scullion, "Righteousness (OT)," 5:725–26, 735–36; Mogensen, "Ṣĕdāqâ," 67–80.
[27] See Scullion, "Righteousness (OT)," 5:735–36.
[28] See, e.g., Pss 89:15; 33:4–5; 37:28; Jer 9:23; Weinfeld, "Justice and Righteousness," 237.
[29] See, e.g., Zech 7:9; Hos 2:21; Jer 16:5.
[30] See Moshe Weinfeld, *Social Justice in Ancient Israel and in the Ancient Near East* (Jerusalem: Magnes, 1995), 237.
[31] The oppressors of the poor were people not only from the upper class but also from the middle class. See Fendler, "Sozialkritik," 48–52. And not altogether unknown were those in the poorer classes who, as in the contemporary world, took advantage of the poverty of their neighbors.
[32] See Amos 2:6–7; 4:1; 5:11, 12; 8:4, 6.

among the nations (3:1–2). Unfortunately, the reality was, as the prophet made it clear in the eight oracles against the nations (1:3–2:16),[33] that Israel was the apex of the pyramid of nations that had violated the principles of justice and equity. In this ascending incrimination against the nations, Israel is at the highest point:

> Thus says the LORD:
> For three transgressions of Israel and for four,
> I will not revoke the punishment;
> because they sell the righteous for silver,
> and the needy for a pair of sandals—
> they who trample the head of the poor into the dust of the earth
> and push the afflicted out of the way. (2:6–7)

The injustice in Israel was so serious, so contrary to God's will, that Amos foretold the destruction of the nation. In his vision, the Day of the Lord, expected by the people, will come soon. But it will not be in favor of Israel, as the people believe, but against it; it will be the day of Israel's judgment and destruction (5:18–20). None will be able to escape. The great house and the little one as well will be shattered to pieces (6:11), and those who are left will be killed by the sword (9:1). Through these predictions, Amos issued an insistent call to conversion (5:4, 6, 14). He spoke of a conversion that included the practice of justice and equity to the poor and the right functioning of the courts of justice, which would listen to the poor man's complaints and pass just sentences (5:7, 15, 24). Amos left us with a permanent call: "Let justice roll down like waters and righteousness like an ever-flowing stream" (5:24).

Postexilic editors added oracles of hope (e.g., 9:11–15) to balance Amos's oracles of destruction. The result is that the book of Amos, as edited in the postexilic era, offers a message of both judgment and redemption, a message that not only was valid for the postexilic community but also would be relevant for the believing community in the future. A caveat may be required in this regard. The prospect of redemption does not diminish the urgency of God's judgment, since God, the redeemer, makes permanent ethical demands on his elected people—namely, total faithfulness to Yahweh and conduct animated by the spirit of justice, equity, and compassion to our neighbors.

---

[33] On the type of authority under which the nations are accused, there are two primary scholarly positions. Some consider these nations to be members of the Davidic-Solomonic empire; consequently, God judges them as their supreme king (see J. Mauchline, "Implicit Signs of a Persistent Belief in the Davidic Empire," *VT* 20 [1970]: 287–303). The other opinion, which seems more probable, sees the nations as creatures of God; therefore God judges them because God is the judge of the whole earth (Gen 18:25). They are judged, however, not according to the divine will revealed to Israel but according to well-known moral principles binding all peoples, principles founded on the way things are. (See J. Barton, "Natural Law and Poetic Justice in the Old Testament," *JTS* 30 [1979]: 1–14; F. Horst, "Naturrecht und Altes Testament," *EvT* 10 [1950–1951]: 253–73; J. J. Collins, "The Biblical Precedent for Natural Theology," *JAARSup* 45 [1977]: 39–40.)

2.3. The prophet Hosea in Samaria

Hosea preached during the last decades of the northern kingdom, addressing a divided society. In Hosea's view, the inhabitants of Samaria had abandoned Yahweh and followed the Canaanite gods, ignoring the conditions of the covenant and violating the rights of God and their neighbors. In Hosea's book, God brings a lawsuit *(rîb)* against Israel[34] because of its violations of the covenant clauses:

> The LORD has an indictment *[rîb]* against the inhabitants of the land.
> There is no faithfulness *[ʾĕmet]* or loyalty *[ḥesed]*,
> and no knowledge *[daʿat]* of God in the land.
> Swearing, lying, and murder, and stealing and adultery break out;
> bloodshed follows bloodshed.
> Therefore the land mourns, and all who live in it languish;
> together with the wild animals and the birds of the air,
> even the fish of the sea are perishing. (Hos 4:1–3)

This oracle presupposes the Sinai covenant.[35] On its basis, Yahweh files a suit against Israel. The causes for complaint are the lack of *ʾĕmet, ḥesed,* and *daʿat,* three important terms that need elaboration. It is difficult to express all the connotations of each in a single English word. The first term *(ʾĕmet)* denotes the character of a person thought to be faithful to his neighbors, honest in his words, and reliable in his actions. The English word "faithfulness" would seem a sound translation. The second term *(ḥesed)* designates an essentially interpersonal relationship animated by an active, positive, and lasting attitude committed to the well-being of others, an attitude apt to strengthen the bond of friendship and always ready and willing to help neighbors in need. The English expressions "steadfast love" and "enduring loving-kindness" are very close to the Hebrew meaning of this term. The third word *(daʿat)* refers to God and denotes the practical acknowledgment of God's sovereignty and an attendant devotion to observe God's will. Hosea considers these three concepts the basic virtues reflective of the spirit of the covenant, and he accuses Israel of lacking them—a lack that has induced the nation to commit numerous and hideous crimes, which the prophet enumerates by way of example, ranging from false testimony to multiple homicides (4:3).

In Hosea's understanding, these crimes offend God, the author of the covenant; they violate the justice one owes to one's neighbors; and they damage all living beings. Because of these crimes, "the land mourns, and all who live in it languish" (4:3). The earth mourns because it feels frustrated in its mission of giving life and happiness to its inhabitants. Human beings are disappointed in their toil because they cannot harvest from the soil the products that provide well-

---

[34] See Herbert B. Huffmon, "The Covenant Lawsuit in the Prophets," *JBL* 78 (1959): 285–95; John Harvey, "'Le Rîb-Pattern,' réquisitoire prophétique sur la rupture de l'alliance," *Bib* 43 (1963): 172–96.

[35] See Ernest W. Nicholson, *God and His People: Covenant and Theology in the Old Testament* (Oxford: Clarendon, 1985); J. Day, "Pre-Deuteronomic Allusions to the Covenant in Hosea and Psalm LXXVIII," *VT* 36 (1986): 1–12.

being; they suffer the frustration of work undone, experiencing the result of the curse on the land. All of this is happening because God sees himself rejected by Israel, his partner in the covenant; as a result, Yahweh withdraws his assistance from the sources of sustenance to humans.[36] The blessings of the covenant cease to be active, and instead the curses are activated. In God's mind, the cessation of divine assistance is meant to move his people to acknowledge that God and only God is the true life-giver (2:9–13).

Like Amos, Hosea criticized the northern kingdom citizens' worship, placing his criticism in the context of the covenant: "I desire steadfast love [*ḥesed*] and not sacrifice, the knowledge [*daʿat*] of God rather than burnt offerings" (6:6). In this critique of worship, Hosea went further than Amos. While the latter had focused on social injustice as conduct incompatible with true worship, Hosea inquired into the inner dispositions necessary to acceptable worship, dispositions that emerge from the depth of a human being and lead one to make an enduring commitment regarding God and one's neighbors. In the name of God, Hosea accused Israel of lacking the three substantial dispositions. Now, criticizing their worship, he focused on two of them: "steadfast love" (*ḥesed*) and "knowledge [*daʿat*] of God." Their absence renders religious worship unacceptable to God.

As a result, great punishment is in store for Samaria. In Hosea's perception, however, Yahweh, the God of the covenant, is not only an angry husband demanding justice, a prosecutor seeking punishment, or a judge issuing a sentence. He is, above all, a father who cannot stop loving his favorite creature (11:1–9). This is why, unlike the original Amos, Hosea called Israel to conversion with full trust in the saving love of God: "Come, let us return to the LORD; for it is he who has torn, and he will heal us; he has struck down, and he will bind us up. After two days he will revive us; on the third day he will raise us up" (6:1–2).

Like Amos, Hosea stated that a true conversion includes the practice of equity (*ṣĕdāqâ*) and steadfast love (*ḥesed*) in social relations (10:12; 12:6). Such practices make it possible to have order (*ṣedeq*) in the community. In stressing the need for steadfast love, the prophet teaches that the exercise of justice is not merely a cold and impersonal action implementing an established norm but an action enlivened by the warmth of compassion and esteem toward the person in need, an action that can be creative in resolving his difficulty. The Gospel of Matthew takes up this concept of compassion and, quoting Hosea twice (Matt 9:13; 12:7), emphasizes compassion as an essential element both in God's relation to sinners and in the conduct of the disciples among themselves.

The book of Hosea underwent an expansive interpretative process. Although the original oracles were issued in the northern kingdom, they came later to be applied to the people of the southern kingdom. Finally their message was extended to the elect community at any time in its history. The last verses of the

---

[36] On the symbiosis between the physical order and the moral order, see H. Schmid, "Creation, Righteousness, and Salvation," in *Creation in the Old Testament* (ed. B. W. Anderson; Philadelphia: Fortress, 1984), 102–17; Terence E. Fretheim, "The Plagues as Ecological Signs of Historical Disaster," *JBL* 110 (1991): 285–96.

book are very significant in this regard. They include a wise call to future readers, encouraging them to discover in this book a valid message for their own historical situation (14:9). This message includes encouragement to practice justice which liberates the oppressed and promotes the poor, offering them the warm esteem of a steadfast love.

2.4. Isaiah of Jerusalem

Isaiah prophesied in Jerusalem in the period between 742 and 700 B.C.E. He cherished a deep trust in God's holiness and sovereign power on behalf of God's elected people. His preferred name for God was "the holy one of Israel." In employing it, the prophet proclaimed the transcendent and overwhelming power of Yahweh, who dwelled in Zion as the center of his universal dominion over the earth (Isa 6:3). For the prophet, however, the power of God's holiness had a clear moral dimension (6:5–7), particularly manifested in his demands for social justice. In this, Isaiah resumed the prophetic tradition (Amos 5:21–24; Hos 6:6) and the teaching of the sages.[37] Like them, Isaiah criticized worship that was dissociated from the practice of social justice (1:10–17). In this vein, he addressed the political and religious leaders ("rulers of Sodom") and the inhabitants of Jerusalem ("people of Gomorrah") and uttered an oracle of rejection against worship without ethical commitment (1:10–15). The oracle concludes with nine imperatives summarizing what people ought to observe:

> Wash yourselves; make yourselves clean;
> remove the evil of your doings from before my eyes;
> cease to do evil, learn to do good;
> seek justice [*mišpāṭ*], rescue the oppressed,
> defend the orphan, plead for the widow. (1:16–17)

Like Hosea (4:1–3), Isaiah spoke of a lawsuit (*rîb*) of Yahweh because of Israel's violation of the covenant. Yahweh filed suit against the inhabitants of Jerusalem because they oppressed the poor (Isa 3:13–15), freed the guilty through bribery, stripped the innocent of their rights (5:23), issued wicked rules, and wrote oppressive decrees to deprive the needy of justice (10:1–2). Isaiah said that Yahweh expected from the people of Judah "justice [*mišpāṭ*], but saw bloodshed [*miśpāḥ*]. He expected righteousness [*ṣĕdāqâ*], but heard a cry [*ṣĕʿāqâ*]" (5:7). It was the cry of those dispossessed from their land (see 5:8), probably because of their failure to pay the mortgage on it.[38] In Isaiah's eyes, such foreclosure was a violation of equity, since, instead of helping the poor to develop their own life within the society, it deprived their families of their source of sustenance. In an agrarian economy a family deprived of its land could barely find the wherewithal to survive.

---

[37] See, e.g., Prov 14:31; 15:8; 21:3, 27.
[38] See Weinfeld, "Justice and Righteousness," 239.

In Isaiah's view, Jerusalem, daughter of Zion and Yahweh's bride, once a faithful city and house of justice *(mišpāṭ)*, had become a whore and a lodge of murderers, dominated by the violence and oppression of its own rulers and judges. There was no defense for the orphan and no protection for the widow (1:21–23). In response, God would bring a purifying chastisement (1:25–26) and restore justice, establishing right judges and counselors to make Jerusalem "the city of righteousness, the faithful city" (1:26–27).

The contemporary violations of justice moved Isaiah to utter numerous oracles of condemnation foretelling punishment for the inhabitants of Judah and Jerusalem (e.g., 3:1–18; 5:26–30). Still, in spite of his announcement of punishment, the prophet cherished the hope that Jerusalem would not be destroyed, because Yahweh dwelled in it.[39]

Like Hosea, Isaiah hoped for the restoration of the country. Unlike Hosea, however, the prophet of Jerusalem founded his hope on the traditions of the unassailable Zion and the divine promises to David.[40] Isaiah hoped that Yahweh himself would carry out the saving action of justice: "The zeal of the LORD of hosts will do this" (9:7). Underlying his thought was the conviction that God guides history to God's own purpose through conflicts between human powers, energizing the desire for truth and justice that God had instilled in men. Thus God produces events in history that to the human mind seem to be impossible. Isaiah foresaw a new era, in which the king would actually be the mediator of justice and peace:

> He will establish and uphold [the throne of David] with justice and with righteousness. . . .
> With righteousness he shall judge the poor,
> and decide with equity for the meek of the earth. . . .
> Righteousness shall be the belt around his waist,
> and faithfulness the belt around his loins. (9:7; 11:4–5).

Isaiah predicts that the king will fulfill the prophetic ideal of social justice, moving beyond what each man deserves. He will make it possible for the poor to improve their condition within the community. The same concept of saving justice is endorsed by the psalmist: "May he [the king] defend the cause of the poor of the people, give deliverance to the needy, and crush the oppressor" (Ps 72:4).

Isaiah's oracles lead the reader to consider the need for a special intervention of God to establish a just society. But it is not a simple suggestion. The prophet assures us that God will intervene to meet those who seek justice, and will help them. Through this assurance, Isaiah encourages those who strive for justice, instilling in them the belief that God will transform the current unjust situation and implement the dream of the "city of justice" and "the faithful city" (1:26).

---

[39] See Isa 7:14; 8:9–10; Ps 46:5–8, 12.
[40] Isa 2:2–4; 8:23–9:6; 11:1–9; see Hans Wildberger, *Isaiah 1–12: A Commentary* (trans. T. H. Trapp; Minneapolis: Fortress, 1991), 81–96, 383–410, 459–81.

2.5. Micah of Moresheth in the southern kingdom

Micah preached in the southern kingdom (Judah) at the same time as Isaiah. He shared with the latter a belief in the divine election of the Davidic dynasty (Mic 5:1–3). But unlike Isaiah, Micah did not believe in the unassailability of Zion; on the contrary, he announced its destruction (3:12). The prophet, however, did not seem to consider the ruin of the city a definitive event, since in his book are some oracles of restoration that apparently derive substantially from Micah himself (e.g., 4:6–7).[41]

The book of Micah, in view of its size, offers extensive information on social justice, although there is some debate about the date of the material. It has been customary to speak of the work's expansion from a small primitive core, but without any consensus about the date of the material. In recent years, however, a new approach has emerged after models drawn from the social sciences, in particular the model of "revitalization."[42] The purpose is to identify, within the mass of variegated and disconnected material, a logical whole that would make sense within the life of the prophet. This logical whole seems to include oracles of both condemnation and salvation.

Concerning social justice, the book of Micah incorporates important elements of the prophetic tradition, such as Yahweh's suit against his people (Hos 4:1–3; Isa 3:13–15), the critique of worship,[43] and the concepts of justice and steadfast love.[44] Micah combines these traditions in his oracles, as we can see from phrases in Mic 6:1–8:

> The LORD has a controversy *(rîb)* with his people. . . .
> Will the LORD be pleased with thousand of rams,
> with ten thousands of rivers of oil? . . .
> He has told you, O mortal, what is good;
> and what does the LORD require of you
> but to do justice *[mišpāṭ]*, and to love kindness *[ḥesed]*, and to walk humbly with your God?

Micah underlines the concept of justice associated with steadfast love in order to support his effort to reintegrate the needy into society. In dealing with the poor, the prophet does not use different adjectives to identify them; he includes them all under one single title, "the weak," contrasting them to the powerful. The powerful include judges, royal functionaries, priests, and professional prophets, while the weak are the common people. Micah accuses the powerful of seizing the land and houses of the weak:

> Alas for those who devise wickedness and evil deeds on their beds!
> When the morning dawns, they perform it, because it is in their power.

---

[41] See Delbert R. Hillers, *Micah: A Commentary* (Hermeneia; Philadelphia: Fortress, 1984), 54.
[42] See ibid., 608.
[43] See Amos 5:21–24; Hos 6:6; Isa 1:12–17.
[44] See Amos 5:24; Hos 2:21; 12:6; Isa 5:7.

They covet fields, and seize them; houses, and take them away;
they oppress householder and house, people and their inheritance. (2:1–2)[45]

Such an accusation is similar to Isaiah's denunciation: "Ah, you who join house to house, who add field to field, until there is room for no one but you, and you are left to live alone in the midst of the land!" (Isa 5:8). Micah, however, surpasses Isaiah in his vivid description of oppression, using metaphors of cannibalism. Addressing rulers and judges, he says:

Should you not know justice?—you who hate the good and love the evil,
who tear the skin off my people, and the flesh off their bones;
who eat the flesh of my people, flay their skin off them,
break their bones in pieces, and chop them up like meat in a kettle,
like flesh in a cauldron. (Mic 3:2–4)

Micah threatens the powerful with divine punishment, predicting the radical reversal of their present social condition and describing the new era with images of agrarian culture. He says that, in the final redistribution, no land will be allotted to the covetous and their descendants (2:4–5). It will be allotted only to the weak, who will enjoy it in peace and prosperity: "They shall all sit under their own vines and under their own fig trees, and no one shall make them afraid" (4:4).

The book of Micah is not merely a document of oracles referring to the past. It was included in the canon as a valid message regarding God's plan for future Israel: a plan of punishment and redemption. The book has a liturgical conclusion, in which the believing community, reading the book, perceives itself as existing between God's judgment and his redemption, with its eyes fixed on God's compassion and faithfulness (7:18–20) as models for the powerful to imitate in their relations with the weak.

2.6. Jeremiah and the last decades of Jerusalem

Jeremiah was active during one of the most tumultuous periods in the history of the ancient Near East, the last decades of the southern kingdom, between 627 and 587 B.C.E. How Jeremiah's book was fashioned is a very difficult issue. A substantial core probably derived from the prophet himself, a core expanded with annotations of the Deuteronomistic editors. The predominant theme is the announcement of the imminent punishment of Jerusalem as a result of Yahweh's suit against Judah (Jer 2:9; 12:1). The cause of complaint is that Jerusalem has abandoned Yahweh and changed gods. In doing so, it has left "the way of the LORD," "the law [*mišpāṭ*, 'order'] of their God" (5:4–5), followed the opposing

---

[45] The greed for land should be understood in light of the situation created by the growth of the population of Jerusalem in the last decades of the eighth century. The growth was due to the immigration of Israelites who came from the northern kingdom after the fall of Samaria in 722 and to the affluence of the refugees from the cities taken by Sennacherib and given to the Philistines in 701. On the increase of the population in Jerusalem, see Moshe Kochavi, ed., *Judaea, Samaria, and the Golan: Archaeological Survey, 1967–1968* (Jerusalem: Magnes, 1972), 20–21.

way, the way of wickedness, and shed the lifeblood of the innocent poor *(ʾebyônîm)* (2:34). Jeremiah says that within the elected community there are scoundrels, who "like fowlers set a trap; they catch human beings" (5:26) to enslave them. "They have grown fat and sleek.... They do not judge with justice the cause of the orphan, to make it prosper, and they do not defend the rights of the needy" (5:28). In the eyes of Jeremiah, there is no one in Jerusalem who practices justice *(mišpāṭ)* and seeks faithfulness *(ʾĕmûnâ)*. If there were but one, God would forgive the city (5:1).

In accord with the prophetic tradition, Jeremiah condemns the worship of the people of Judah because their cultic actions do not include a commitment to obey the law of God (7:21–23), in which the prophet underlines ethical duties. In this vein, Jeremiah states before the people at the gate of the temple that the salvation of the sanctuary and the city depends on their practice of justice; they should stop oppressing strangers, orphans, and widows and shedding innocent blood (7:5–6). In his prophetic fearlessness, Jeremiah addresses the same message to the king, calling him to practice justice and equity *(mišpāṭ ûṣĕdāqâ)* in accordance with God's will (22:3, 16–17).

The prophet often predicted terror and ruin in punishment of the people's rebellion against Yahweh. The question has been raised whether he also uttered oracles of hope. Doubtless, the book attributes to him such oracles.[46] But their authenticity is doubtful. In the past, scholars usually dated them to exilic or postexilic times under Deuteronomistic influence.[47] In the last few decades, however, some prominent exegetes have reconsidered the subject and now attribute the beginning of the oracles of restoration to the prophet himself. They posit traditions that go back to the prophet and were then expanded in the exilic and postexilic times.[48] Be that as it may, the text extant since the exilic time explains the cause of the 597 B.C.E. catastrophe and instills into readers a hope for the restoration of the covenant. It bases this hope in the divine promise of a gracious and creative action of God, which will provide the Davidic dynasty with an offspring who will rule with wisdom and dispense justice and equity; his name will be "Yahweh is our righteousness" (23:5–6; 33:15–16). In addition, divine action will transform the hearts of the members of the elected people and pour into them a sense of social justice, a transformation that will make possible the implementation of the prophetic ideal of justice and peace (31:31–34).

2.7. Ezekiel during the Babylonian exile

In his first prophetic period in Babylon, before the destruction of Jerusalem, Ezekiel carried on the traditional prophetic critique about corruption in worship and the violations of social ethics, but he left aside the dialectical contrast between

---

[46] See, e.g., Jer 23:1–6; 30:1–31:40; 33:14–26.
[47] See Robert P. Carroll, *Jeremiah* (OTL; Philadelphia: Westminster, 1986), 46–50.
[48] See Douglas R. Jones, *Jeremiah* (New Century Bible Commentary; Grand Rapids: Eerdmans, 1992), 18–37; Lawrence Boadt, *Jeremiah 1–25* (OTM 9; Wilmington: Glacier, 1982), xviii–xxiii; Guy P. Couturier, "Jeremiah," *NJBC* 265–95.

cult and ethics emphasized by previous prophets.[49] Instead, like the Holiness Code (Lev 17–26; See esp. 19:2–18), Ezekiel combined the rules of worship with the demands of social ethics. In his view, ideal righteousness unites both demands. This combination emerges in the passages in which the prophet enumerates the virtuous acts of the practitioner of justice *(mišpāṭ)* and equity *(ṣĕdāqâ)* (Ezek 18:5–9, 14–17). The combination is also present in his description of abominable sins distinctive to evildoers (22:1–12). Here the prophet combines idolatry, a contempt for holy things (sanctuary, sacrifices, temple vessels), and the profanation of the Sabbath with scorn for one's parents, the abuse of aliens, orphans, and widows, sexual assault, slander, murder, bribery, usury, and extortion (22:6–7, 9, 12).

The prophet foresees an inevitable punishment because the misconduct is so deeply rooted in the heart of the people (20:1–21), but he is not disheartened. On the contrary, he promises that Yahweh on his own initiative will transform the hearts of the people, granting them a new heart (11:19; 36:25–27)—an inner transformation that will provide the spiritual strength to fulfill God's commands to practice justice and equity (11:20; 36:27).

A quarter century after Ezekiel was taken into exile, he returns to Jerusalem via visionary experience and is assured of the rebuilding of the temple and the redistribution of the land (Ezek 40–48). A paradise-like era is promised, when the twelve tribes will be reunited, the land definitively allotted to them, and each family granted divine blessings forever. The children of Israel, ruled by a theocracy with a new Jerusalem as their capital, will savor the matchless pleasure of a righteous, peaceful, and prosperous society. In Ezekiel's vision, the land plays an essential role: at its center lies the temple, where Yahweh dwells and whence flows the sacred river that transforms the earth; and being renewed, the land offers home, sustenance, and medication so that human beings may have a healthy, enduring, and happy life. This wonderful world will be brought about entirely by the saving justice of God.

The postexilic editors gave final shape to Ezekiel's book and imprinted on it an eschatological orientation by combining the vision of the temple (37:27; 43:7, 9) with the messianic promise of a King David *redivivus* (37:24–28). Within this perspective, although the divine judgment remains in the background, the predominant theme becomes the promise of a restored society, devoted to the worship of God and the practice of justice and equity. This promise supports the desire for a righteous society, which is deep-rooted in the heart of the oppressed, by offering assurance that God has a plan for mankind in history and will grant the spirit that transforms people and makes them seek justice and peace actively and responsibly.

2.8. Second Isaiah and the liberation from the exile

Second Isaiah's oracles, together with their subsequent literary expansions, are included in Isaiah 40–55. Second Isaiah preached his prophetic message

---

[49] See, e.g., Amos 5:21–25; Hos 6:6; Jer 7:21–23; Isa 58:1–12.

during the Babylonian exile after 547 B.C.E., when Cyrus the Persian defeated Croesus, king of Lydia, and began consolidating an empire capable of challenging the Babylonian power. Second Isaiah saw in Cyrus the agent elected by Yahweh to liberate Israel from exile (44:28–45:7, 13). With this conviction in mind, he proclaimed in God's name that Israel had paid twice the penalty she deserved because of her sins (40:1–2), and announced that her time of humiliation and oppression was ended. For the prophet, Cyrus's victories signaled the beginning of Yahweh's action of saving justice on behalf of his people, an action that Yahweh would carry out with unabated and overwhelming determination.

The prophet supported this message of liberation with theological arguments. He had to convince those who were skeptical and to encourage the disheartened. His arguments were rooted in the unsurpassable power of Yahweh. He argued considering various aspects of the divine power. Yahweh, the supreme ruler of the nations, particularly of Israel, comes with majesty and glory to establish his definitive dwelling in Zion.[50] He is the Creator and redeemer, who showed his overwhelming power in the exodus from Egypt (43:15–17; 51:9). He is the only God, the Creator of all, the Lord of history.[51] He is the sovereign who chose Cyrus to destroy the Babylonian Empire, liberate the captives, and rebuild Jerusalem.[52]

Through the words of the prophet, Yahweh speaks of his own power and encourages the exiles not to be afraid because Yahweh will control historical events in order to liberate his people: "Do not be afraid . . . for I am your God. . . . I will uphold you with my victorious right hand" (41:10). The right hand symbolizes the irresistible and overwhelming power of Yahweh and is equivalent to his "arm," the mighty arm of creation and exodus, which the prophet vividly calls to awaken it:

> Awake, awake, put on strength, O arm of the LORD!
> Awake, as in days of old, the generations of long ago!
> Was it not you who cut Rahab in pieces, who pierced the dragon?
> Was it not you who dried up the sea; the waters of the great deep;
> who made the depths of the sea a way for the redeemed to cross over?
> So the ransomed of the LORD shall return. (51:9–11)

God, who crushed the primordial monster and imposed order on creation, is the same God who defeated the Egyptian beast and ransomed his own people. God's unyielding commitment to Israel gives a solid basis for the exiles to hope he will now overthrow the Babylonian monster and redeem his people. The prophet fervently prays that God may repeat the saving action of justice he showed in Egypt and restore his people to their own land. He reiterates the theme of God's saving justice in various modes, but for the same purpose: to win the trust of the exiles, revive their hope, and make them active in the preparation of their return. Among the several passages where he employs the theme of liberation are the

---

[50] See Isa 40:10–11; 44:28; 45:13–14; 52:7–12.
[51] See Isa 40:12–26; 43:3; 44:6–7, 24–28; 45:18.
[52] See Isa 41:1–6; 44:28–45:4, 13.

oracles of the election of Cyrus and the oracles of salvation for those who seek justice. The oracles of the election of Cyrus (44:24–45:13) echo the creative commands in the first chapter of Genesis. The commands are repeated now in order to unleash the action that will restore Jerusalem and reshape the community in its own land: "He will say of Jerusalem, 'Let it be rebuilt,' and of the temple, 'Let its foundation be laid'" (44:26). After remembering that Yahweh created light and darkness, the oracle utters the final creative command:

> Shower, O heaven, from above,
> and let the skies rain down righteousness *[ṣedeq]*;
> Let the earth open, let salvation *[yešaʿ]* spring up,
> and let it cause righteousness *[ṣĕdāqâ]* to sprout up also;
> I, the LORD, have created it. (45:8–9)

In the metaphoric expressions of these creative commands, heaven and earth join as husband and wife to produce the redemption of the exile Israel. The whole process is Yahweh's creation. (In the oracle, the verb "have created" is in the past tense, but actually it is a prophetic past emphasizing the certainty of the future event.) Justice as a liberating action fertilizes the earth, which in turn gives birth to salvation. This is the happy result of the creative power of God, who leads history and overcomes human impotence, sterility, and desolation.

The theme of saving justice occurs also in the oracle of salvation in Isa 51:1–8, where the prophet, addressing those who pursue justice and seek the Lord, assures them that, in spite of their present humiliation, they will enjoy the fulfillment of promises rooted in the divine word given to the patriarchs. Just as God's power overcame their impotence and sterility and made them a great and numerous people in their own land (51:2), so those who now pursue justice will repossess the land and rejoice at the sight of Israel restored and of the nations subjected to Yahweh for the good of Israel:

> Listen to me, my people, and give heed to me, my nation;
> for a teaching will go out from me,
> and my justice *[mišpāṭî]* for a light to the peoples.
> I will bring near my deliverance *[ṣidqî]* swiftly,
> my salvation *[yišʿî]* has gone out, and my arms will rule the peoples;
> the coastlands wait for me, and for my arm they hope. (Isa 51:4–5)

In this text, *ṣidqî*, usually translated as "justice" or "righteousness," is well rendered in the NRSV by "deliverance," since it is parallel to "salvation." This includes the idea of the return to the land, the rebuilding of Jerusalem, and the restoration of Israel as a free nation. Then the promises given to David will be extended to every member of the community (55:3).[53] Yahweh's justice (*mišpāṭî*),

---

[53] Isaiah 55:3 promises that God will make an eternal pact with the people that will lead to the fulfillment of the promises made to David. The entire people will now participate in the privileges formerly granted to David. As Stuhlmueller has noted, Second Isaiah does not project a country without any political leadership or a society without any sort

an enlightening event for the nations, is the execution of God's design to liberate Israel, a mighty deed that will open the eyes of the nations so that they will glorify Yahweh. These ideas of saving justice fit well with the beginning of Isaiah 51, in which Yahweh addresses those who seek justice and await their liberation (51:1). To them the prophet assures God's consolation: "He will make her [Zion's] wilderness like Eden, her desert like the garden of the LORD; joy and gladness will be found in her, thanksgiving and the voice of song" (51:3). The whole context of 51:1–52:16 seethes with the idea of justice as liberation and restoration, which will not be transitory but permanent. God assures his people that although the heaven will vanish and the earth be destroyed, "my salvation [*yĕšûʿātî*] will be forever, and my deliverance [*ṣidqātî*] will never be ended" (51:6, 8). Yahweh addresses his words of consolation and hope to those who seek him, and Yahweh's action of saving justice meets the desire for justice cherished by his people.

Thus, according to the prophet, God's saving justice is able to emulate in the present the mighty deeds of the past, to transform the geography of the political and economic powers of the world, and to liberate Israel, restoring her in her own land. Even more, God's justice has the power to make Israel the center of a world established on peace and prosperity. Such a concept of justice is translated by the LXX with the Greek word *dikaiosynē*,[54] which in turn is very influential in the Pauline concept of God's justice.

In Second Isaiah, the Servant of the Lord is introduced. This Servant of the Lord plays a unique prophetic role. He was martyred in pursuance of his mission, and his martyrdom contributed in the liberation of Israel.[55] The Servant proclaimed that Cyrus was elected by Yahweh to liberate Israel. This proclamation must have generated hostility in Babylonian centers of power as well as the opposition of Jews who supported the imperial regime. In the fourth song (52:13–53:12), the persecuted Servant submits himself peacefully as a victim of governmental oppression (53:3–10). This song was composed by his disciples to honor the death he suffered in expiation of the sins of Israel to bring justification to his people (53:5, 8, 10–11). The disciples suggested that the suffering of the Servant was parallel to that of Israelites in Egypt. Both sufferings are caused by imperial violence: one under Pharaoh's reign and the other under Babylonian

---

of government but, rather, a society with a government less centralized than that at the time of the Davidic monarchy. See Carroll Stuhlmueller, "Deutero-Isaiah and Trito-Isaiah," *NJBC* 343; Otto Eissfeldt, "The Promises of Grace to David," in *Israel's Prophetic Heritage* (FS J. Muilenburg; ed. B. W. Anderson et al..; London: SCM, 1962), 196–207.

[54] See John W. Olley, *"Righteousness" in the Septuagint of Isaiah: A Contextual Study* (SBLSCS 8; Missoula: Scholars Press, 1979), 65–118.

[55] The identification of the Servant of the Lord with Second Isaiah is supported, among others, by Anthony R. Ceresko, "The Rhetorical Strategy of the Fourth Servant Song (Isaiah 52:13–53:12): Poetry and the Exodus–New Exodus," *CBQ* 56 (1994): 42–55; Richard J. Clifford, *Fair Spoken and Persuading: An Interpretation of Second Isaiah* (New York: Paulist, 1984), 57; Stuhlmueller, "Deutero-Isaiah," 330–31, 341–42; R. N. Whybray, *Thanksgiving for a Liberated Prophet: An Interpretation of Isaiah Chapter 53* (JSOTSup 4; Sheffield: JSOT Press, 1978), 25.

rule. Both end in a liberation exodus: one from Egypt and the other from Babylon. The first moves toward the settlement of the promised land, and the second toward the repossession of the land that had been lost. On the other hand, both liberations are conducted by Yahweh, the Creator, who effects human history and carries out his undertaking through human persons: through Moses in the exodus from Egypt and through Cyrus and the prophet martyr in the liberation from Babylonian captivity.

Distinctive to the Servant of the Lord is the suffering of the innocent one who, without exercising violence, submits himself to death as a sacrifice on behalf of the community. He defeated violence by refusing to respond and by submitting himself to the oppression that had been inflicted on him. The disciples of the Servant praised the service rendered by his preaching and martyrdom. In their eyes, what the Servant did on behalf of the Israelites is worth more than all Cyrus's victories. They composed the fourth song as a thanksgiving hymn for the divine vindication of the Servant. It was a way of exhorting the people to unite their efforts for the good of the postexilic community settled in the land and of encouraging them to develop the desolate soil and make it a source of life, prosperity, and happiness. The death of the prophet—who was executed by the rage of Babylonian power but nevertheless vindicated by God—is a consoling model for those today who, because of their dedication to the needy and oppressed, run the risk of falling under the deadly violence of repressive regimes.

Second Isaiah conveys to the reader the conviction that God, the Creator, is present in our history, always ready both to protect his sovereignty against any power that dares challenge it and to liberate his believers from the oppression of their adversaries. God's intervention in the exodus from Egypt gives the assurance of future liberation. His saving and creative commands are always present for the good of his people. The Servant's death is a great legacy to the people of God. It is an intercessory power and a model of dedication for those who work on behalf of the oppressed and look for the promotion of the weak and destitute.

2.9. Third Isaiah and the postexilic community

The community, reorganized in its own land after the exile, faced inner problems similar to those experienced during the monarchy. Among them were a lack of justice and the consequent oppression of one by another. Third Isaiah's preaching addressed these problems through four means. First, he exhorted his people to practice justice and equity (56:1). Second, he criticized the lack of concern about the killing of innocents (57:1). Third, he stressed that the practice of justice is necessary for the promise of restoration to be implemented (58:10–14). Fourth, he condemned the disconnection of religious practices from ethical obligations (58:3–5). After condemning these practices, the prophet described what authentic piety is:

> Is not this the fast that I choose:
> to loose the bonds of injustice, to undo the thongs of the yoke,
> to let the oppressed go free, and to break every yoke?

> Is it not to share your bread with the hungry,
> and bring the homeless poor into your house;
> when you see the naked, to cover them,
> and not to hide yourself from your own kin?
> Then your light shall break forth like the dawn,
> and your healing shall spring up quickly. (58:6–7; see also 58:9–10)

The description of oppression and the lack of justice in the postexilic community is similar to that of the prophets in the monarchic period. There are, however, some noticeable differences. The postexilic community was small, living in a desolate land, around a Jerusalem in ruins, under foreign rule. In these hard conditions, Third Isaiah, like other prophets, stressed promises of restoration over oracles of condemnation and, in spite of the lack of justice, showed God as more ready to heal than to punish (57:14–19). If God punishes, he does so in a restricted manner (65:8); generally speaking, he punishes those refusing to return to the Lord (65:11–12). In these circumstances, the attitude of God stressed by the prophet is God's making of a new creation, centered in a new Jerusalem, assuring that the faithful remnant of the people will be its beneficiary (65:13–25). Violence will be eliminated and justice established in a land that never will be expropriated (60:17–22). The community will have "Peace" as its overseer and "Righteousness" as its taskmaster (60:17). All its members will be clothed with garments of justice and salvation (61:10). A great social reversal will be carried out: "My servants shall eat, but you shall be hungry; my servants shall drink, but you shall be thirsty; my servant shall rejoice, but you shall be put to shame" (65:13). Third Isaiah felt himself called to be instrumental in God's final undertaking:

> The Spirit of the LORD God is upon me, because the LORD has anointed me;
> he has sent me to bring good news to the oppressed *[ᶜănāwîm]*,
> to bind up the brokenhearted,
> to proclaim liberty *[děrôr]* to the captives, and release to the prisoners;
> to proclaim the year of the LORD's favor, and the day of vengeance of our God;
> to comfort all who mourn; to provide for those who mourn in Zion—
> to give them a garland instead of ashes. (61:1–3a)

Third Isaiah's mission was to proclaim an extraordinary jubilee *(děrôr)*, an amnesty encompassing all levels of human existence: material and spiritual, economic and social. The prophet transformed the content of the jubilee law (Lev 25:8–17) into a promise. Instead of imposing an obligation on the community, he announced a promise of liberation that God would fulfill.

He addressed this announcement to the afflicted people of Zion, encompassing all of them under a single name, ᶜănāwîm ("afflicted"). According to the divine promise of liberty, the community of those now suffering deprivation, hostility, and oppression will experience a happy reversal of its situation forever. Then Jerusalem "shall be a crown of beauty in the hand of the LORD, and a royal diadem in the hand of your God" (62:3). The nations will be attracted by the new Jerusalem and bring their wealth to God's city (60:1–14).

Third Isaiah's oracles were appended to Isaiah's book by postexilic editors without providing any information on the occasion and time when they were issued. The disconnection from the historical context expanded the horizon of these oracles, and they became a revelation of God's plan for the elect in whatever circumstances they may live in the future. In God's plan both a threat of judgment and a promise of redemption exist—the threat for sinners and the promise for the repentant. In addition, the community awaiting its eschatological redemption is constantly encouraged to secure God's acceptance by producing works of compassionate and liberating justice (58:6–9).

Conclusion

During Israel's monarchic period, the king was the person responsible for the establishment and maintenance of order in society and the promotion of justice. But the practice of justice, necessary for the existence of order, was demanded not only from the king and his magistrates but also from all members of the community. Distinctive to Israel among the ancient Near Eastern nations was its belief in Yahweh, the Creator of order both in the universe by creation and in Israel by covenant. In the Israelite faith, Yahweh was active in history to punish lawbreakers and restore the order that had been damaged.

In prophetic thought, God implements his plans through human beings and powers. Therefore a promise that God will intervene to change the present situation includes a strong encouragement and an urgent invitation—encouragement both to those who suffer abuses and injustices and to those who work to correct them, and an invitation for people to participate in the implementation of God's plan.

The prophetic mission takes place within the framework of Israelite ideas about order and justice. The prophets indicted kings and magistrates not in the name of ancient Near Eastern mores but in the name of Yahweh's justice, namely, the moral order established by Yahweh's will. Nathan, Elijah, and the subsequent prophets acted in this way. In the name of Yahweh, Amos, Hosea, Micah, Isaiah, and Jeremiah denounced social injustices and religious practices disconnected from ethical obligations. They predicted punishment but also invited people to return to the Lord. Ezekiel issued similar accusations before the destruction of the temple but afterward focused his preaching on Yahweh's saving justice. Second Isaiah comforted Israel in exile, proclaiming that Yahweh had begun his saving action and would accomplish his redemption of Israel. Third Isaiah resumed the preaching of the preexilic prophets, emphasizing the need for the practice of social justice and for worship that included a commitment to social ethics. His threats of punishment were balanced by promises of a wonderful restoration of Jerusalem, with the announcement of a jubilee of endless liberty, peace, and prosperity.

It is remarkable that, in the course of Israel's history, in spite of critical times of unfulfilled oracles, the prophets untiringly persisted in reasserting the promises of justice and peace. The believing community in turn experienced a vehement desire for justice and, although perceiving it as humanly elusive, did not lose hope. Paradoxically, the more elusive justice was, the more attractive it became for believers. The factor that contributed to intensifying the desire for justice was faith in the committed and active presence of Yahweh, the God of order. The reader finds here an enduring lesson. The prophets' persistent hope for justice, in spite of its elusive character, instills encouragement and a sense of perseverance in those working to improve the miserable conditions of those suffering starvation, destitution, and oppression.

Bibliography

Barré, Michael L. "Fasting in Isaiah 58:1–12: A Reexamination." *Biblical Theology Bulletin* 15 (1985): 94–97.

Barton, J. "Natural Law and Poetic Justice in the Old Testament," *Journal of Theological Studies* 30 (1979): 1–14.

Blenkinsopp, Joseph. *A History of Prophecy in Israel: From the Settlement in the Land to the Hellenistic Period.* Philadelphia: Westminster, 1983.

Boadt, Lawrence. *Jeremiah 1–25.* Old Testament Message 9; Wilmington: Glacier, 1982.

Booij, T. "Negation in Isaiah 43:22–24." *Zeitschrift für die alttestamentliche Wissenschaft* 94 (1982): 390–400.

Botterweck, G. J., and H. Ringgren, eds. *Theological Dictionary of the Old Testament.* Translated by J. T. Willis, G. W. Bromiley, and D. E. Green. 12 vols. Grand Rapids: Eerdmans, 1974–.

Buccellati, Giorgio. *Cities and Nations of Ancient Syria.* Rome: Istituto di Studi del Vicino Oriente, 1967.

Carroll, Robert P. *Jeremiah.* Old Testament Library. Philadelphia: Westminster, 1986.

Cazelles, Henri. "De l'idéologie royale." *Journal of the Ancient Near Eastern Society of Columbia University* 5 (1973): 59–73.

———. "Sacral Kingship." Pages 863–66 of vol. 5 of *Anchor Bible Dictionary.* Edited by D. N. Freedman. 6 vols. New York: Doubleday, 1992.

Ceresko, Anthony R. "The Rhetorical Strategy of the Fourth Servant Song (Isaiah 52:13–53:12): Poetry and the Exodus–New Exodus." *Catholic Biblical Quarterly* 56 (1994): 42–55.

Chaney, Marvin L. "Systematic Study of the Israelite Monarchy." Pages 53–76 in *Social Scientific Criticism of the Hebrew Bible and Its Social World: The Israelite Monarchy.* Edited by N. K. Gottwald. Semeia 37. Chico, Calif.: Scholars Press, 1986.

Clifford, Richard J. *Fair Spoken and Persuading: An Interpretation of Second Isaiah.* New York: Paulist, 1984.

Collins, J. J. "The Biblical Precedent for Natural Theology." *JAARSup* 45 (1977): 39–40.

Coote, Robert B., and K. W. Whitelam. *The Emergence of Early Israel in Historical Perspective.* Sheffield: Almond, 1987.

———. "The Emergence of Israel: Social Transformation and State Formation following the Decline in Late Bronze Age Trade." *Semeia* 37 (1986): 107–47.

Couturier, Guy P. "Jeremiah." Pages 265–95 in *The New Jerome Biblical Commentary.* Edited by Raymond E. Brown et al. Englewood Cliffs: Prentice Hall, 1990.

Day, J. "Pre-Deuteronomic Allusions to the Covenant in Hosea and Psalm LXXVIII." *Vetus Testamentum* 36 (1986): 1–12.

Eissfeldt, Otto. "The Promises of Grace to David." Pages 196–207 in *Israel's Prophetic Heritage.* FS J. Muilenburg. Edited by. B. W. Anderson et al.. London: SCM, 1962.

Fendler, Marlene. "Zur Sozialkritik des Amos." *Evangelische Theologie* 33 (1973): 32–53.

Fishbane, M. *Biblical Interpretation in Ancient Israel.* Oxford: Clarendon, 1985.

Fretheim, Terence E. "The Plagues as Ecological Signs of Historical Disaster." *Journal of Biblical Literature* 110 (1991): 285–96.

Frick, Frank S. *The Formation of the State in Ancient Israel: A Survey of Models and Theories.* Sheffield: Almond, 1985.

Halpern, Baruch. *The Constitution of the Monarchy.* Chico, Calif.: Scholars Press, 1981.

Harvey, John. "'Le Rîb-Pattern,' réquisitoire prophétique sur la rupture de l'alliance." *Biblica* 43 (1963): 172–96.

Hillers, Delbert R. *Micah: A Commentary.* Hermeneia. Philadelphia: Fortress, 1984.

Horst, F. "Naturrecht und Altes Testament." *Evangelische Theologie* 10 (1950–1951): 253–73.

Huffmon, Herbert B. "The Covenant Lawsuit in the Prophets." *Journal of Biblical Literature* 78 (1959): 285–95.

———. "The Social Role of Amos's Message." Pages 109–16 in *The Quest for the Kingdom of God: Studies in Honor of George E. Mendenhall.* Edited by Herbert B. Huffmon et al. Winona Lake: Eisenbrauns, 1983.

Jenni, E., ed., with assistance from C. Westermann. *Theologisches Handwörterbuch zum Alten Testament.* 2 vols. Stuttgart, 1971–1976.

Jepsen, Alfred. "Ṣdq und Ṣdqh im Alten Testament." Pages 78–89 in *Gottes Wort und Gottes Land.* Edited by H. G. Reventlow. Göttingen: Vandenhoeck & Ruprecht, 1965.

Jones, Douglas R. *Jeremiah.* New Century Bible Commentary. Grand Rapids: Eerdmans, 1992.

Kochavi, Moshe, ed. *Judaea, Samaria, and the Golan: Archaeological Survey, 1967–1968.* Jerusalem: Magnes, 1972.

Kruse, H. "Die Negation dialectische als semitischen Idiom." *Vetus Testamentum* 4 (1954): 385–400.

Lemche, Niels P. "Israel, History of." Pages 541–44 of vol. 3 of *Anchor Bible Dictionary.* Edited by D. N. Freedman. 6 vols. New York: Doubleday, 1992.

Macholz, G. C. "Die Stellung des Königs in der israelitischen Gerichtsverfassung." *Zeitschrift für die alttestamentliche Wissenschaft* 84 (1972): 157–82.

———. "Zur Geschichte der Justizorganisation in Juda." *Zeitschrift für die alttestamentliche Wissenschaft* 84 (1972): 314–40.

Mauchline, J. "Implicit Signs of a Persistent Belief in the Davidic Empire." *Vetus Testamentum* 20 (1970): 287–303.

Mendenhall, George E. "The Monarchy." *Interpretation* 29 (1975): 155–70.

———. "Social Organization in Early Israel." Pages 132–51 in *Magnalia Dei, the Mighty Acts of God*. Edited by F. M. Cross et al. Garden City: Doubleday, 1976.

———. *The Tenth Generation: The Origins of the Biblical Tradition*. Baltimore: Johns Hopkins University Press, 1973.

Mogensen, B. "Ṣĕdāqâ in the Scandinavian and German Research Tradition." Pages 67–80 in *The Productions of Time: Tradition History in Old Testament Scholarship*. Edited by K. Jeppesen and B. Otzen. Sheffield: JSOT Press, 1984.

Nicholson, Ernest W. *God and His People: Covenant and Theology in the Old Testament*. Oxford: Clarendon, 1985.

Olley, John W. *"Righteousness" in the Septuagint of Isaiah: A Contextual Study*. Society of Biblical Literature Septuagint and Cognate Studies 8. Missoula: Scholars Press, 1979.

Reviv, Hanoch. *The Elders in Ancient Israel*. Jerusalem: Magnes, 1989.

Roberts, Jimmy J. M. "In Defense of the Monarchy: The Contribution of Israelite Kingship to Biblical Theology." Pages 377–98 in *Ancient Israelite Religion*. Edited by P. D. Miller et al. Philadelphia: Fortress, 1987.

Schmid, H. "Creation, Righteousness, and Salvation." Pages 102–17 in *Creation in the Old Testament*. Edited by B. W. Anderson. Philadelphia: Fortress, 1984.

Scullion, John J. "Righteousness (OT)." Pages 724–36 of vol. 5 of *Anchor Bible Dictionary*. Edited by D. N. Freedman. 6 vols. New York: Doubleday, 1992.

Soggin, J. Alberto. *A History of Ancient Israel*. Philadelphia: Westminster, 1985.

Stoebe, H. J. "Die Bedeutung des Wortes ḥäsäd im Alten Testament." *Vetus Testamentum* 2 (1970): 244–54.

Stuhlmueller, Carroll. "Deutero-Isaiah and Trito-Isaiah." Pages 329–48 in *The New Jerome Biblical Commentary*. Edited by Raymond E. Brown et al. Englewood Cliffs: Prentice Hall, 1990.

Vawter, Bruce. "Introduction to Prophetic Literature." Pages 186–200 in *The New Jerome Biblical Commentary*. Edited by Raymond E. Brown et al. Englewood Cliffs: Prentice Hall, 1990.

Weinfeld, Moshe. " 'Justice and Righteousness'—mišpāṭ ûṣĕdāqâ—the Expression and Its Meaning." Pages 228–46 in *Justice and Righteousness: Biblical Themes and Their Influence*. Edited by H. Reventlow and Y. Hoffman. Journal for the Study of the Old Testament: Supplement Series 137. Sheffield: JSOT Press, 1992.

———. *Social Justice in Ancient Israel and in the Ancient Near East*. Jerusalem: Magnes, 1995.

Whitelam, Keith W. *The Just King: Monarchical Judicial Authority in Ancient Israel.* Journal for the Study of the Old Testament: Supplement Series 12. Sheffield: University of Sheffield Press, 1979.

———. "King and Kingship." Pages 40–48 of vol. 4 of *Anchor Bible Dictionary.* Edited by D. N. Freedman. 6 vols. New York: Doubleday, 1992.

———. "The Semantic Range of ḥesed." *Biblica* 62 (1981): 519–26.

Whybray, R. N. *Thanksgiving for a Liberated Prophet: An Interpretation of Isaiah Chapter 53.* Journal for the Study of the Old Testament: Supplement Series 4. Sheffield: JSOT Press, 1978.

Wildberger, Hans. *Isaiah 1–12: A Commentary.* Translated by T. H. Trapp. Minneapolis: Fortress, 1991.

CHAPTER SIX

JUSTICE IN THE PSALMS AND WISDOM BOOKS

Introduction

The previous chapter focused particularly on three subjects: people's expectations regarding kings as mediators of justice on behalf of the poor and oppressed, royal abuse of power, and the prophets' critiques of rulers' abuses and their defense of the poor. The current chapter is devoted to the theme of justice and the condition of the poor in the Psalms and Wisdom books. These writings, while sharing common elements of the concept of justice as analyzed in previous chapters, have very distinctive features. The book of Psalms stands out among others books of the OT in the frequency with which the theme of justice is related to the poor and in the number of terms used to designate the poor and weak. The Wisdom books share these characteristics, though to a lesser degree; but they have their own distinctiveness because of their universal character. They are part of a literature that transcends national borders and ethnic groups, reflecting on general problems of human existence; they are open to the wisdom of the surrounding world. The distinctive features of the Psalms and the Wisdom writings encourage special curiosity to know their contribution to the subject of social justice in ancient Israel. The present chapter is divided into six sections, each devoted to one book: Psalms, Proverbs, Job, Ecclesiastes, Sirach, and Wisdom of Solomon.

1. Justice in the Psalms

Justice in the Psalms, as in the other OT books, is a complex and rich concept whose meaning in each case is determined by context.[1] Basically, it includes or

---

[1] See Moshe Weinfeld, *Social Justice in Ancient Israel and in the Ancient Near East* (Jerusalem: Magnes), 1995; John Scullion, "Righteousness (OT)," *ABD* 5:724–36; B. Mogensen, "*Ṣĕdāqâ* in the Scandinavian and German Research Tradition," in *The Productions of Time: Tradition History in Old Testament Scholarship* (ed. K. Jeppesen and B. Otzen; Sheffield: JSOT Press, 1984), 67–80; Alfred Jepsen, "*Ṣdq* und *Ṣdqh* im Alten Testament," in *Gottes Wort und Gottes Land* (FS H. W. Hertzberg; ed. H. Reventlow; Göttingen: Vandenhoeck & Ruprecht, 1965), 78–99.

presupposes the idea of order, an order encompassing the whole world and all humanity. It is the order the Creator established in the world by his will and then expanded in the course of history. But in addition to the idea of established order, justice includes a dynamic dimension, one that is expressed in action in accordance with the established order. Its effect is either to return to others what belongs to them or to restore them to their proper position according to the design of the Creator. In this regard, right order is something not established once and forever but something to be accomplished by both divine and human action.

1.1. Justice, order, right conduct, and saving action

It is first worth noting that the idea of justice as order, right conduct, and saving action is expressed in the Psalms, as in other OT books, through the terms *mišpāṭ*, *ṣedeq*, and *ṣĕdāqâ*, the meaning of which was explained in the earlier analysis of the book of Amos.[2] It is important to remember that *mišpāṭ* denotes "judgment," "legal sentence," "verdict," "legal complaint," "decree," "regulation," "order," and "custom," while both *ṣedeq* and *ṣĕdāqâ* may designate indiscriminately "order," "uprightness," and "justice," as well as "right conduct" and "saving action." Likewise, both *ṣedeq* and *ṣĕdāqâ*, each coordinated in a pairing with *mišpāṭ*, may form a hendiadys and designate the order established by God in human society, particularly in Israel. This is the order that people ought to observe in order to behave rightly, and it is up to the king to preserve it and rule in conformity with it so that the land may have peace, justice, and prosperity. In addition, we have to remember that these terms often are parallel to "steadfast love," "faithfulness," and "compassion" and thus have the connotation of gracious love and active compassion. Some examples illustrate the meaning of these terms in the Psalms. God loves order or righteousness *(mišpāṭ)* and justice *(ṣĕdāqâ*, Pss 33:5; 99:4), namely, the order God established in the world and expressed for his community. Hence, those who put into practice the order *(mišpāṭ)* and the justice *(ṣĕdāqâ)* expressed by God's will are blessed by the Lord (Ps 106:3). In Ps 72:1–2, the psalmist asks God to grant the king his *mišpāṭ* and *ṣĕdāqâ*, namely, the sense of order established by God, so that the king will judge with *ṣedeq* and *mišpāṭ*, that is, with uprightness. In Psalm 7, the suppliant beseeches the Lord, the judge of the nations, to judge him in accordance with his conduct, which proves his innocence (7:9[8]). Psalm 119:142 combines two concepts: "Your righteousness *[ṣĕdāqâ]* is order *[ṣedeq]*"; that is, it is upright. Other verses of the same psalm say that the decrees *(mišpāṭîm)* of the Lord are right or righteous *(ṣedeq)* (Ps 119:7, 62, 75), that is, represent the order God established for human beings. Likewise, many psalms associate justice with God's saving action (his help and deliverance). Thus Ps 40:10–11[9, 10] says,

> I have told the glad news of deliverance *[ṣedeq]* in the great congregation:
> see, I have not restrained my lips, as you know, LORD.
> I have not hidden your saving help *[ṣĕdāqâ]* within my heart,

---

[2] See above, ch. 5, §2.2.

> I have spoken of your faithfulness [ʾĕmûnâ] and your salvation [tesûʿâ];
> I have not concealed your steadfast love [ḥesed] and your faithfulness [ʾĕmet] from the great congregation.

In these verses, the psalmist gives thanks before the congregation because of the great action of justice the Lord showed on his behalf, setting him free from "the desolate pit" (40:3[2]). He describes this manifestation of saving justice as an expression of God's steadfast love and a sign of his faithfulness to the order he established in the world on behalf of his community. Likewise, in one of the hymns to Yahweh the king (Ps 145), the psalmist sings to the saving justice of God: "They shall celebrate the fame of your abundant goodness [tôb], and shall sing aloud of your righteousness [ṣĕdāqâ]. The LORD is gracious [ḥannûn] and merciful [raḥûm]" (Ps 145:6–8). In Psalm 143, the supplicant asks, "In your righteousness [ṣĕdāqâ] bring me out of trouble. In your steadfast love [ḥesed] cut off my enemies" (Ps 143:11b–12a). Reflecting on the same ideas, the psalmist praises the Lord: "The word of the LORD is upright, and all his work is done in faithfulness. He loves righteousness [mišpāṭ] and justice [ṣĕdāqâ]; the earth is full of the steadfast love [ḥesed] of the LORD" (Ps 33:4–5).

1.2. God, the source and model of justice

In the Psalms, God's justice reigns supreme. God not only establishes order but also judges rightly and shapes the model of right judgment, which includes steadfast love, fidelity, and compassion. Thus in Ps 82:3–4, God, as the one who possesses the supreme authority to judge the world and who establishes rules for right judgment, accuses earthly judges of being unjust and partial: "Give justice to the weak and the orphan; maintain the right of the lowly and the destitute. Rescue the weak and the needy; deliver them from the hand of the wicked." And the psalmist ends the psalm thus: "Rise up, O God, judge the earth; for all the nations belong to you" (82:8). Elsewhere the psalmist says, "He who disciplines the nations, he who teaches knowledge to humankind, does he not chastise?" (Ps 94:10–11). God is the ultimate source of authority and competence for judging rightly. From God comes the model of right judgment that earthly judges and rulers must imitate in order to have justice, peace, and prosperity in human society. In this vein, the psalmist prays,

> Give the king your justice, O God,
> and your righteousness to a king's son.
> May he judge your people with righteousness,
> and your poor with justice.
> May the mountains yield prosperity for the people,
> and the hills, in righteousness. (Ps 72:1–3)

1.3. Justice and the poor

In the Psalms, the poor stand out among all other people in their longing for justice and their gratefulness to God. The poor in the Psalms trust in God more than in human rulers. In time of need, they approach the Lord and request his saving action, his justice, and base their petition on the fact that the Lord is the one who delivers the weak and the needy from the hands of the powerful and the despoilers.[3] Once the poor experience the justice they have requested, their deliverance, they proclaim their gratitude in the congregation (Ps 40:11[10], 18[17]) and state that the Lord is the supreme judge who destroys the wicked and protects the needy; he is "a stronghold for the oppressed" and "does not forget the cry of the afflicted" (Ps 9:5[4], 10[9], 13[12], 19[18]). Psalm 22 attests to the conviction that one of the great qualities of God is the exercise of saving justice on behalf of the poor, and it points to this saving action as a gospel to be proclaimed to Israel and all the nations:

> I will tell of your name to my brothers and sisters;
> in the midst of the congregation I will praise you. . . .
> For he did not despise or abhor the affliction of the afflicted;
> he did not hide his face from me,
> but heard when I cried to him. . . .
> All the ends of the earth shall remember and turn to the LORD. . . .
> Future generations will be told about the LORD,
> and proclaim his deliverance to a people yet unborn,
> saying that he has done it (Ps 22:23[22], 25[24], 28[27], 31–32[30–31]).

1.4. Identification of the poor

The Psalms stand out among the books of the Bible in the number of references to the poor, and within the Psalter, the psalms of individual prayer, lament, and thanksgiving rank first in this regard. The variety of terms employed to designate the poor in these psalms is remarkable. The person who suffers poverty and affliction calls himself *anî wĕ'ebyôn*, which the NRSV translates as "poor and needy."[4] These terms also occur separately or parallel, used elsewhere to designate the poor.[5] In addition, there are several other names given to the poor, such as *dal* ("weak," e.g., Ps 41:2[1]), *ḥēlĕkâ* ("helpless," e.g., Ps 10:8), *rāš* ("destitute;" Ps 82:3), *dak* ("oppressed," e.g., Ps 10:18), and *šāpāl* ("lowly," Ps 138:6). The terms *ʿānî* and *ʾebyôn* are used most frequently, the others less often.

Since the middle of the last century, scholars have been puzzled by the interest toward the poor in the Psalms, and it was suggested that, within the religious society of ancient Israel, people of low social class, despoiled by rulers and powerful men, influenced the formation of the psalms.[6] A. Rahlfs published the first monographic work on the matter in 1891. In it he supported the idea that in ancient Israel there were two groups with similar names: the *ʿănāwîm*[7] and the

---

[3] See, e.g., Pss 18:27[26]; 35:10, 24, 27, 28; 91:3.
[4] Pss 40:18[17]; 70:6[5]; 74:21; 86:1; 109:22.
[5] See, e.g., Pss 9:19[18]; 69:34[33]; 82:3, 4.
[6] One may read a very fine historical summary on the theme in Norbert Lohfink, "Von der 'Anawim-Partei' zur 'Kirche der Armen': Die Bibelwissenschaftliche Ahnentafel eines Hauptbegriffs der 'Theologie der Befreiung,'" *Bib* 67 (1986): 153–75.
[7] See, e.g., Pss 10:12, 16; 22:27[26]; 25:9; 34:3[2]; 37:11.

ʿăniyyîm.⁸ The latter were economically poor and socially oppressed, while the former were members of a religious party that emerged during the exile, encompassing people from different social classes, poor and nonpoor, and whose distinctive feature was to foster a religious attitude of humility and docility before God. These people were active in the formation of the psalms, and their model was the Servant of the Lord in Second Isaiah.⁹

W. W. Graf von Baudissin in 1912 introduced a change in the designation of the group of the ʿănāwîm; he preferred to call them a "religious movement" instead of a "religious party."¹⁰ A. Causse in 1922 followed this idea and described the spirituality of the movement of the ʿănāwîm: these were farmers, shepherds, artisans, and common workers who lived in a religious, spiritual confraternity; they enjoyed union with God in fraternal love, possessed the power of divine inspiration, and composed the psalms of the poor.¹¹ A. Gelin in 1953 developed the idea of the spirituality of the ʿănāwîm and described them as pious Jews who fostered a humble and detached life, expressed submission to God and a willingness to accept suffering, and cherished the joy anticipated in the hope of the eschatological fulfillment.¹² According to Gelin, the prophet Zephaniah was the founder of this movement, and Jeremiah a major representative. Their most venerated figures were Job and the Servant of the Lord in Second Isaiah.¹³

The thesis that the ʿănāwîm were either a religious party or a movement of spirituality has been reconsidered by well-known scholars, such as S. Mowinckel,¹⁴ H. Birkeland,¹⁵ H.-J. Kraus,¹⁶ L. Delekat,¹⁷ J. D. Pleins,¹⁸ and N. Loh-

---

⁸ Examples of ʿăniyyîm in the Psalms follow the numbering of the Masoretic Text: Pss 9:13[12], 19[18]; 10:12; 12:6[5]; 72:2, 4; 74:19.

⁹ See Alfred Rahlfs, *Ani und Anav in den Psalmen* (Göttingen: Dieterich, 1892).

¹⁰ Wolf W. Graf von Baudissin, "Die alttestamentliche Religion und die Armen," *Preussische Jahrbücher* 149 (1912): 193–231.

¹¹ Antonin Causse, *Le "pauvres" d'Israël, prophètes, psalmistes, messianistes*. EHPhR 3; Strasbourg: Librairie Istra, 1922.

¹² Albert Gelin, *The Poor of Yahveh* (Collegeville: Liturgical Press, 1964).

¹³ Lohfink, "'Anawim-Partei,'" 165–70.

¹⁴ Sigmund Mowinckel, *The Psalms in Israel's Worship* (trans. D. R. Ap-Thomas; 2 vols.; New York: Abingdon, 1962), 1:197–203; 2:1–9; *Psalmenstudien* (2 vols.; Amsterdam: P. Shippers, 1961), 1:113–17; 2:58–65. Mowinckel holds that the ʿănāwîm had the misfortune of suffering under the power of witchcraft, a thesis that has not won wide acceptance. One great merit of Mowinckel's study, however, was to call attention to the contrast between the poor and their enemies.

¹⁵ H. Birkeland, *ʿĀnî und ʿĀnāw in den Psalmen* (Oslo: Dybwad, 1932); *Die Feinde des Individuums in der israelitschen Psalmenliteratur* (Oslo: Grøndahl, 1933); *The Evildoers in the Book of Psalms* (Oslo: Dybwad, 1955). Birkeland follows in the footsteps of Mowinckel, but he abandons Mowinckel's thesis of witchcraft; he retains, however, Mowinckel's idea that the poor were persons who, by reason of their utter poverty, were unable to fully participate in the society of which they were supposed to be a part.

¹⁶ Hans-Joachim Kraus, *Psalms 1–59: A Commentary* (trans. H. C. Oswald; Minneapolis: Augsburg, 1988), 92–94; *Theology of the Psalms* (trans. K. Crim; Minneapolis: Augsburg, 1986).

¹⁷ L. Delekat, "Zum Hebräischen Wörterbuch," *VT* 14 (1964): 35–49. Delekat rejects Rahlfs's distinction between these two groups and shows that ʿānāw/ʿănāwîm has the

fink.[19] The generally accepted conclusion is that the terms ʿănāwîm and ʿăniyyîm do not have different meanings (most probably they are two ancient linguistic or dialectical forms of the same word) and therefore ʿănāwîm does not merely encompass a spiritual attitude of humility and detachment but also a social and economic situation of poverty or destitution.[20] In effect, it is associated with or is parallel to terms denoting economic poverty (e.g., Isa 11:4; 29:19; Amos 2:7). A compelling argument that the ʿănāwîm of the Psalms designate those who are actually poor is that they are contrasted with the rich and powerful.[21] Within this context, they are called "righteous" because they trust God in their suffering and humiliation.[22] They are humble and submissive not because they accept poverty as a virtue but because they are not like their oppressors—they do not respond violently to their oppression. In their humiliation, they put their trust in God, the most High, and his saving action (Ps 37:5–19) because he judges the nations with justice and equity.[23] What the poor long for is not the reward of a tested virtue but the restoration of a violated order. When the poor beseech the protection of God Most High, the judge of heaven and earth, they are motivated by a universal hope shared by any human being who suffers destitution and oppression on earth.

By way of summary, the poor of the Psalms are persons who trust in God in the midst of their misery, suffering, and oppression and do not respond with violence to their aggressors.[24] The sad experience of their destitution causes them to

---

same range of meaning as ʿānî/ʿăniyyîm: both terms in the Psalms refer to socioeconomic poverty and designate people who are so dependent that they have insufficient resources by which to live. He emphasizes the fact that there are only three texts in the Bible in which ʿānî and ʿānāw refer to an attitude of humility instead of actual poverty understood in its socioeconomic sense: Num 12:3, Prov 3:34, and Zeph 2:3. These three passages are relatively late, from the postexilic epoch.

[18] J. David Pleins, "Poor, Poverty," ABD 5:403–14.

[19] Lohfink, "'Anawim-Partei,'" 170–75.

[20] The primary arguments Birkeland, Delekat, and Pleins use to demonstrate their thesis that ʿănāwîm is not an expression distinct from ʿăniyyîm are as follows: (1) Like ʿăniyyîm, ʿănāwîm includes the meaning of actual poverty, since it is found in a context of physical destitution or it is used together with or parallel to ʾebyônîm and dallîm, terms that indicate socioeconomic poverty. (2) The Masoretes understood the term ʿănāwîm in the same way. They introduced the system of kethib (what is written) and qere (what is to be said). In several texts (e.g., Ps 9:14[13]; Prov 3:34; 14:21; 16:19) where the kethib is ʿăniyyîm, they introduced ʿănāwîm as qere in a context of physical destitution. (3) Delekat and Pleins support the thesis that ʿănāwîm and ʿăniyyîm are dialectical variants of the same original word. They observe that the term ʿănāwîm is never seen together with or parallel to ʿăniyyîm. If they were, they would be different terms. According to their thesis, ʿănāwîm was the original plural of the ancient form ʿānîw, in which the early ending vav disappeared and became the well-known form ʿānî. The form ʿānāw, on the other hand, is a late formation after the structure of ʿănāwîm.

[21] See, e.g., Pss 10:2–6; 35:4–12; 37:1–2, 16–17; 49:5–6[4–5]; 92:7–9[6–8]; 119:23, 161.

[22] See, e.g., Pss 11:2–3, 5; 34:15–18[14–17]; 37:12, 16, 17, 21, 25, 29, 32, 39.

[23] See Pss 9:13[12], 19[18]; 10:12, 17; 72:2–4, 12–14; 147:6.

[24] Klaus Wengst, Humility: Solidarity of the Humiliated—the Transformation of an Attitude and Its Social Relevance in Graeco-Roman, Old Testament–Jewish, and Early Christian Thought (trans. J. Bowden; Philadelphia: Fortress, 1988), 21–24.

find support and hope in their religious faith. In some circles during postexilic times, this religious attitude became so synonymous with the concept of the poor that it seemed to eclipse the social and economic dimension (Num 12:3; Prov 3:34; Zeph 2:3).[25] The LXX translators followed suit, and thus, in the some of the Psalms, they employed the Greek word *praeis* ("meek") for the translation of ʿănāwîm, stressing the religious attitude. They did so only in isolated cases, but by doing so, they loaded the Greek term with a Hebrew meaning, which refers equally to social and economic dimensions also.[26] This is important to remember in connection with Matt 5:5.

The Dead Sea Scrolls are interesting concerning the meaning of ʿănāwîm; they witness that, in the Qumran community, poverty was associated with the experience of being oppressed and persecuted. So the quote from and commentary to Ps 37:11 (4QpPs 37) says,

> The poor [ʿănāwîm] shall inherit the land and enjoy peace in plenty. Its interpretation concerns the congregation of the poor who will tolerate the period of distress and will be rescued from all the snares of Belial. Afterwards, all who shall inherit the land will enjoy and grow fat with everything . . . of the flesh.[27]

1.5. The enemies of the poor

Mowinckel emphasized the importance of studying the poor in the Psalter in contrast to their enemies—an important observation even though his thesis, the tragedy of the poor was the result of witchcraft, is rejected by contemporary scholars.[28] It is clear that in the Psalms the poor have two enemies: (1) those who seek their ruin and (2) the illnesses that threaten their well-being. The former are persons who, from the oppressed's perspective, are powerful, aggressive, and very resourceful in carrying out their wicked plots. The poor call them "enemies,"

---

[25] Numbers 12:3 is probably postexilic; it belongs to the Priestly redaction. Proverbs 3:34 is part of a postexilic collection of sapiential utterances; according to A. Meinhold, *Die Sprüche* (ZBAT 16.1; Zürich: Theologisches Verlag, 1991), 39–40, 45, Proverbs 1–9 is from the fifth century B.C.E. Zephaniah 2:3 probably contains a postexilic insertion. See Ehud Ben Zvi, *A Historical-Critical Study of the Book of Zephaniah* (Berlin: de Gruyter, 1991), 144–50; Ronald E. Clements, *Isaiah 1–39* (New Century Bible Commentary; Grand Rapids: Eerdmans, 1980), 121–23; J. M. P. Smith, *Zephaniah* (ICC; Edinburgh: T&T Clark, 1911), 214–15.

[26] The LXX translated both ʿānî and ʿănāwîm by "meek" *(praüs/praeis)* in the following psalms: 24[Heb 25]: 9; 33[Heb 34]: 3; 36[Heb 37]: 11; 75[Heb 76]: 9; 146[Heb 147]: 6; 149:4. But the translators of the LXX were not consistent. They used the term *praüs/praeis* in only nine of the twenty-four instances in which the word ʿănāwîm occurs, and in only four of the thirty-one times in which the term ʿānî is found. The term the translators of the LXX used more frequently is *ptōchos* (one who depends upon another for subsistence), less frequently, *penēs* (indigent), and, more rarely, *tapeinos* (in low position or esteem).

[27] Florentino García Martínez, *The Dead Sea Scrolls Translated* (Leiden: Brill, 1994), 203–4; Norbert Lohfink, *Lobgesänge der Armen* (SBS 143; Stuttgart: Katholisches Bibelwerk, 1990), 32–33.

[28] See nn. 14, 15.

"foes," "wicked," "evildoers," and "persecutors."[29] They deceive, hate, ambush, strike, use false witnesses, and engage in murder. The poor view them as an attacking army.[30]

Birkeland illustrates the social and economic character of these enemies, whose interest is the economic exploitation of the poor.[31] His contrast between the afflicted poor and the despoiling enemy shows that the Psalms proclaim the poor's suffering and affliction as the result of social injustice. The oppression and destitution that the poor suffer are results of the action of powerful, greedy men who harass the poor and drag them to court to secure unjust verdicts for their own profit. Under these circumstances, the innocent poor realize that they do not have any chance for a fair trial from a human court but only from God.[32] Their despoilers bribe judges and the witnesses against them, thus mocking justice.[33] Often the powerless poor are forced to surrender their own property, as if they had stolen their own goods from themselves (Ps 69:5[4]).

But the plots of the powerful against the poor go beyond misusing the courts. Commenting on this the psalmist describes the evildoers.

> They sit in ambush in the villages;
> in hiding places they murder the innocent.
> Their eyes stealthily watch for the helpless;
> they lurk in secret like a lion in its covert;
> they lurk that they may seize the poor;
> they seize the poor and drag them off in their net.
> They stoop, they crouch, and the helpless fall by their might. (Ps 10:8–10)

The poor thus feel alone in an oppressive world, persecuted everywhere. In affliction and anguish, they approach the Lord, putting their trust in him (e.g., Pss 13:6[5]; 25:1–2), and promise to give thanks for the liberation they might receive (e.g., Pss 13:6b[6]; 22:22[21]). Occasionally poor people in the Psalms fear that the Lord may not help them because of their past sins. This is why they humble themselves and beg forgiveness so that God in his justice and steadfast love might relieve them of their present anguish and guard their lives (Ps 25:2–12, 15–21).

Attacks against the poor can originate not only from other peoples but also through life-threatening illnesses that, in their turn, provoke the anguish of an inevitable end.[34] Those afflicted with illness in the Psalms see their sickness as a manifestation of the powers of Sheol, intent on severing them from God forever.

---

[29] The translation of the Hebrew terms is taken from the NRSV. For "enemies" (*ʾōyĕbîm*), see, e.g., Pss 3:8[7]; 6:11[10]; 13:5[4]. For "foes" (*ṣârîm*), see, e.g., Pss 3:2[1]; 13:5[4]; 27:2. For "wicked" (*mĕreʿîm*), see, e.g., Pss 26:5; 37:9; 64:3[2]. For "wicked" (*rĕšāʿîm*), see, e.g., Pss 3:8[7]; 9:18[17]; 10:2, 3. For "evildoers" (*pōʿălê ʾāwen*), see, e.g., Pss 5:6[5]; 6:9[8]; 14:4. For "persecutors" (*rōdepîm*), see, e.g., Pss 31:16[15]; 119:150, 157.

[30] See, e.g., Pss 3:6–7[5–6]; 27:3; 56:2[1].

[31] See n. 15.

[32] See, e.g., Pss 7:1–11[1–10]; 9:4[3], 13[12]; 10:2–7; 11:3; 71:13; 82:2–4; 109:4–6, 26–31.

[33] See, e.g., Pss 15:5; 26:10; 27:12; 31:10–13[9–12]; 35:11; 50:19–20; 109:2–6.

[34] See, e.g., Pss 6:4–6[3–5]; 22:15–17[14–16]; 34:4[3], 19–20[18–19].

Hence, illness is frequently personified as an enemy seeking ruin and the psalmist employs mythic images to show it as a reincarnation of the primordial monster.

The psalmists use such mythic images not only for illnesses but also for personal enemies. The powers of chaos are manifested by "torrents of perdition" and "snares of death" (Ps 18:5–6[4–5]). In these descriptions, poor people find themselves caught up in a cosmic struggle between the power of the primordial monster and the power of Yahweh, who masters the tempestuous waters and "is enthroned over the flood" (Ps 29:10). These mythic images place the affliction of the poor on the battlefield of the cosmic war between the power of chaos and Yahweh, the God of order. This elevates the case of the poor to a transcendent dimension, inspiring great confidence in the one who suffers. This hope exists because the attacks on the poor are a direct challenge by the powers of evil to the sovereignty of Yahweh. The poor firmly believe that Yahweh cannot allow any power to threaten him; he is invincible. A defeat of Yahweh is impossible.

1.6. Reflections on the prosperity of the wicked

The psalmists reflect on the prosperity of the wicked and, for a while, remain puzzled.[35] Then, in pondering the reliability of wealth, they cease to be annoyed, because wealth cannot save one from death or be carried beyond the grave. Like all human beings, the wealthy shall die, leave their riches to others, and go to Sheol forever. The poor know that they will die, too, but they have the advantage of trusting in the living and eternal God, who is judge of the earth. In contrast, the wealthy in their foolishness think God does not exist (Ps 14:1) and therefore have nothing eternal in which to trust. The poor trust in God's faithfulness and cherish the idea that God is their eternal possession (Ps 73:25–28). In this light, the psalmist says, "God will ransom my soul from the power of Sheol, for he will receive me" (Ps 49:16[15]). These passages seem to contain the earliest glimmers of hope in an afterlife, a hope that probably started after the exile.[36]

The poor and afflicted not only realize that their idea of order and justice is contradicted by the reality of human society; they also suffer in themselves the consequences of the world's oppressive disorder. In anguish and pain, they ask God before the congregation to judge the world:

> Do not let the downtrodden *[dal]* be put to shame;
> let the poor and needy *[ʿānî wĕʾebyôn]* praise your name.
> Rise up, O God, plead your cause;
> remember how the impious scoff at you all day long. (Ps 74:21–22)

In considering the disorder of human society, the psalmists feel some relief and delight when they find an honest person who, with God's help, prospers and gives example of goodness, compassion, and generosity (Ps 112:1–9). They cele-

---

[35] See Pss 49:4–6[3–5], 17–18[16–17]; 73:3–17.
[36] See Bruce Vawter, "Intimations of Immortality in the Old Testament," *JBL* 91 (1972): 158–71.

brate the discovery of such a ray of light amid the darkness, an example for any person who seeks righteousness (Ps 112:4). Such compassionate conduct will motivate many others to improve the conditions of society so that the poor and afflicted might not be disheartened in their hope for justice and give themselves over to laziness, violence, and vice.

1.7. Eschatological expectations of the poor

Some of the psalms of prayer and thanksgiving, written or reedited in the postexilic period, extend the concept of the oppressed poor to the whole faithful community of Israel—an extension that provides these psalms with a social and political dimension that includes a call for the reunion of the tribes and the restoration of Israel as a nation free from the oppression of hostile powers. But in addition, these Psalms have an eschatological dimension, for in them the psalmists express a hope that God will intervene in a radical and final manner on behalf of his own people. They are so confident in the overwhelming intervention of Yahweh that they praise him now because of the certain victory of his liberating justice.[37] The deprivation, oppression, and persecution that the Jewish community suffered during the postexilic time motivated the extension of the concept of the poor to all of Israel. Third Isaiah had a great role in this; he specifically described his mission to Israel as a mission of liberation on behalf of the oppressed and afflicted poor (ʿănāwîm, Isa 61:1).

A set of these Psalms was placed at the end of the Psalter by the final editors to conclude the book with an offer of hope for oppressed Israel. This set, Psalms 146–150, forms a small collection of hymns of praise *(hallēl)* in the Psalter, each beginning and ending with the invitation to praise Yahweh *(halĕlûyâ)*. This small collection anticipates the praise for the wonderful deeds that Yahweh will carry out at the final restoration of Israel. Psalm 146, after its introductory invitation to the community to pray to the Lord, begins praising him in the first person singular but then proclaims happy those who hope in Yahweh, the Creator of the universe, because he is the God "who executes justice for the oppressed, gives food to the hungry, sets prisoners free, opens the eyes of the blind, watches over the strangers, upholds the orphan and widow, but the way of the wicked brings to ruin." The psalmist ends by addressing Zion, reassuring the city of its vindication by Yahweh, its God, who will reign forever.

Psalm 147, filled with reminiscences of Isaiah 40–60, praises Yahweh because Yahweh is present with his saving power to carry out the restoration of Jerusalem

---

[37] Thus Ps 102:15–17[14–16] refers to the time when the nations are converted and God listens to the prayer of the abandoned and does not disregard their requests. In Psalm 69, the affirmation that Yahweh listens to the poor is associated with God's intervention when he saves Zion and reconstructs the cities of Judah. See Brevard S. Childs, *Introduction to the Old Testament as Scripture* (Philadelphia: Fortress, 1979), 517–18, 522–23. On the eschatology of the Psalms, see Leopold Sabourin, *The Psalms: Their Origin and Meaning* (New York: Alba House, 1970), 141–56.

and the gathering of the outcasts of Israel (147:2). His distinctive actions are lifting up the downtrodden *(ʿănāwîm)* and casting the wicked to the ground (v. 6). Then the psalmist invites Zion to praise Yahweh because Yahweh had initiated his work of strengthening the city, blessing its children, and giving them peace and prosperity (vv. 12–14). Finally, the psalmist arouses in his congregation pride for being the people of God, reminding them that what Yahweh did for them, he did for no other nation (v. 20).

Psalm 148 praises Yahweh not only because of his wonderful creation but also because he is active in restoring Israel for the good of all believers. Psalm 149, in turn, praises Yahweh by anticipating the great and final vindication of Israel that God will carry out because "the LORD takes pleasure in his people; he adorns the humble *[ʿănāwîm]* with victory" (149:4). The psalmist looks at a future when Yahweh will execute his sentence against the nations and bind their kings with fetters to establish peace and glory for his faithful. Finally, Psalm 150 concludes the small *hallēl* with its eschatological orientation. In it, the psalmist sings praise to the Lord as if the singer were in a renewed world, where Israel is free from its enemies and enjoys peace and prosperity under Yahweh's protection.

The references to the future make these psalms a living voice addressing believers who belong to subsequent generations. They are a voice fostering the hope that God will show his liberating power in history and offering assurance that God will set free not only the person who suffers oppression but also the desolate nation, thrown into confusion by its inner crises and external oppression. The voice of these psalms nurtures the hope that God will help change the social and political structures that favor injustice and oppression in order to move humanity toward a life of peace and justice. It intensifies a desire for justice in the oppressed and calls people of goodwill to work toward fulfilling this desire. It assures the people that if they employ legitimate means to obtain justice, God is with them.

The Psalter provides models of prayer that help believers express praise and gratitude to the Lord, acknowledge their sinful condition, and bring their concerns and afflictions to the Lord. These psalms offer to the afflicted prayers shaped under the inspiration of the Spirit of God, through the recitation of which they can vent their anguish, raise their cry of protest before God, and strive to win God's favor for a speedy intervention. To this day those who are afflicted and oppressed can identify with those who first composed the psalms, feel the saving presence of God who strengthens them in the daily struggle to survive and better their lives, and experience the divine assistance that nurtures the hope of the yearned-for liberation.

2. The book of Proverbs

The book of Proverbs is an anthology comprising various collections of wisdom sayings from different periods in the history of ancient Israel.[38] The book

---

[38] See James L. Crenshaw, "Proverbs, Book of," *ABD* 5:513–20.

probably originated in an ancient collection of family teachings in wisdom style (Prov 10:1–22:16); then new collections were added, such as 25:1–29:27 and 22:17–24:22, until the whole of 10:1–29:27 was formed. This was later completed by the addition of the parental admonitions at the beginning of the book (1:1–9:18) and two small collections at the end (30:1–31:31). The final editing is dated to the postexilic period. In its formation, this book was influenced by the wisdom literature of surrounding countries. The Egyptian influence is particularly apparent in 22:17–24:22.[39]

The purpose of Proverbs is to teach the ruling order of the world and human society and to instruct people to behave accordingly. It imparts knowledge on "righteousness *[ṣedeq]*, justice *[mišpāṭ]* and equity *[mêšarîm]*," according to the NRSV (1:3). The personified Wisdom states, in 8:15–16, that her words teach the way in which people should act in order to be successful in their work or office: "By me kings reign, and rulers decree what is just *[ṣedeq]*; by me rulers rule, and nobles, all who govern rightly *[ṣedeq]*." The sages in this book insist that walking the path of *ṣĕdāqâ* brings security (12:28) and effects national prosperity (14:34). The path of injustice and disorder, however, leads to ruin. In defense of these values, the sages condemn the usage of false weights to cheat the poor,[40] censure the powerful who take advantage of the powerlessness of the poor to despoil them and seize their properties (22:22; 30:14), and reprimand those who remove the ancient boundary markers to appropriate the land of the poor (15:25; 22:28). They exhort those responsible for justice and order to despise bribes and maintain justice,[41] and urge them to defend the cause of the poor:

> Speak out for those who cannot speak,
> for the rights of all the destitute.
> Speak out, judge righteously *[ṣedeq]*,
> defend the rights of the poor and needy *[ʿānî wĕʾebyôn]*. (Prov 31:8–9)

Concern for the poor is a dominant theme in this book.[42] The sages emphasize that the Lord is the maker of both rich and poor, and offer assurance that he will bless those who are generous to the needy and judge them with equity (22:2, 9; 29:13–14). God is so committed to the poor that giving alms to the poor is the most solid investment because it means to "lend to the LORD, and he will repay in full" (19:17). The common origin of all people and their assurance of God's blessing are not the only incentives the sages adduce to persuade both rich and rulers to help the poor. They also threaten punishment as a way of persuasion:

---

[39] Nili Shupak, "The 'Sitz im Leben' of the Book of Proverbs in the Light of a Comparison of Biblical and Egyptian Wisdom Literature," *RB* 94 (1987): 98–119.

[40] See Prov 11:1; 16:11; 20:10, 23; Deut 25:13–16.

[41] See Prov 15:27; 17:8, 23; 28:21.

[42] See Roger N. Whybray, *Wealth and Poverty in the Book of Proverbs* (JSOTSup 99; Sheffield: JSOT Press, 1990); Norbert Lohfink, *Lobgesänge der Armen*; J. David Pleins, "Poor, Poverty"; "Poverty in the Social World of the Wise," *JSOT* 37 (1987): 61–78; J. van der Ploeg, "Les pauvres d'Israël et leur piété," *OTS* 7 (1950): 253–58.

> Do not rob the poor because they are poor,
> or crush the afflicted at the gate;
> for the LORD pleads their cause
> and despoils of life those who despoil them. . . .
> For their redeemer is strong;
> he will plead their cause against you. (22:22–23; 23:11)

The sages envision a time when God will judge evildoers and vindicate the poor and needy: God will cut off the wicked and treacherous from the land and establish the innocent poor in it.[43]

The sages in Proverbs regard wealth as good although they acknowledge that some people accumulate riches through dishonest and oppressive means (28:15–16; 30:14). Poverty, however, has no redeeming qualities. It is undesirable and bad. "All the days of the poor are hard" (15:15). The sages realize that some of the righteous are poor,[44] but they do not describe them as totally destitute. Rather, they have little income in contrast to the large income of the wealthy (16:8). Even so, this is an anomaly that will be remedied by divine judgment.[45] In the meantime, when deciding between wealth and wisdom, the sages advise one to opt for wisdom and uprightness (16:8, 16, 19).

In comparison with the prophets and the Psalms, Proverbs exhibits two salient features: its vocabulary in designating the poor and its attitude toward the extremes of wealth and poverty. While prophets and Psalms show preference for the terms ʿānî, ʿănāwîm, and ʾebyôn, Proverbs prefers *dal* ("weak" or "destitute"), *rāš* ("needy"), and *maḥsôr* ("indigence") to designate the poor. The term *dal* is employed in the prophets and Psalms, but less frequently than in Proverbs. The other two terms, often used in Proverbs, each occur only once in the Psalms, and never in the prophets. Proverbs not only has a distinctive vocabulary but also contains particular connotations related to laziness, negligence, and inefficiency as causes of poverty, connotations that result from its characteristic approach to the subject of wealth and poverty.[46] This approach showcases its second feature: its attitude toward the extremes of wealth and poverty.

The sages of Proverbs assume that wealth and poverty are normal elements of human society although they do not think class division is derived from the Creator. Unlike the prophets, who see poverty as a result of injustice, they do not offer only one explanation. From their point of view, poverty does not depend only on human injustice. They do mention the exploitation of the poor by the rich and powerful but insist that indigence is often a result of personal behavior. There are people who have fallen into poverty because of their laziness and negligence[47] and others who did so because of disordered behavior and bad habits.[48]

---

[43] See Prov 2:21–22; 10:30; 24:20; 28:19.
[44] Prov 15:15; 16:8, 16, 19.
[45] See Prov 2:21–22; 10:30; 28:19–20.
[46] Pleins, "Poverty in the Social World."
[47] Prov 6:6–11; 19:15, 24; 20:4; 24:30–34; 26:13–16.
[48] Prov 11:24; 13:25; 21:17.

In Proverbs, although the sages condemn injustices against the poor, they do not show the constant, passionate, and biting criticism of the prophets. They are practical, taking the world as it is and teaching men how to live in it, avoiding poverty, and prospering honestly; they inculcate a strong sense of responsibility and efficiency but do not instill a desire to change society's structure which favors oppression and discrimination. Part of their instruction is aimed at persuading people to help the poor because generosity will be rewarded by God.[49] They are teachers who belong to the upper middle class and impart instruction whereby people of their own kind can have success in the world.

In spite of its limitations, the book of Proverbs offers the teaching of Wisdom, imparting instructions on how to "walk in the way of righteousness, along the paths of justice" (8:20). Wisdom is the educator par excellence, who forms the conscience of the people in the fear of the Lord as the only path to true success. "The fear of the LORD is the beginning of wisdom" (1:7; 9:10), "the hatred of evil" (8:13) and "the fountain of life" (14:27). Such teaching, leading people to acquire intelligence and prudence (8:5–6, 12), offers important lessons valid for any season: the desire for an adequate education to develop personal talents, the need to form a strong sense of responsibility, and the need to practice moral virtues for the improvement of the individual and the good of the community. In this vein, the sages exhort us to avoid laziness and negligence, advise us not to squander but to save for the future, and encourage us to be efficient in our work.

In stressing personal responsibility as a cause of poverty, the sages provide a necessary supplement to the prophetic criticism, which emphasizes social injustice as a cause of oppression and destitution. The need for an adequate education (including the moral virtues) shows a concrete path to the transformation of the human condition which the prophets deemed necessary for a society of justice and peace. The sages' concern for education shows an increasing tendency to identify wisdom with the law, an identification that is conspicuous in Sirach and Baruch.[50]

3. The book of Job

The date of this book is debatable. It was probably written under Persian rule during the fifth or beginning of the fourth century B.C.E., when a serious social and economic crisis arose caused by a new tax system imposed by the Persian government. Under the new system, Jews had to pay taxes not by delivery of a percentage of their products but in Persian currency. Some people could not assemble enough cash to meet their obligations, because of bad harvests or low

---

[49] The advice that the sages give—that the poor should not be mistreated but rather helped—seems utilitarian, similar to the perspective that dominates the Instruction of Amen-em-Opet. See above, ch. 2.
[50] Sir 1:1–6; 19:20; 24:23; Bar 4:1.

market prices, and were forced to pawn their properties and families. The result for some was the loss of everything.[51]

This situation may have been the catalyst in shaping Job as a character. Job has fallen into miserable poverty, losing all his property, social standing, and reputation. His painful situation is intensified by a terrible and disgusting illness. In the book, he is the central character in a dialogue that seeks to understand the mystery of the suffering of an innocent person. Within the dialogue, Job's friends support the traditional teaching and suggest his terrible situation must be the result of some forgotten sin Job committed in the past. Job, however, is unshakable in his conviction that he is innocent and suffers unjustly. In listening to his friends, he reaches the conclusion that only God can explain his situation, and muses on how to approach God or even to file a suit against him. In Job's view, God established the bases of justice but does not secure the order God has created. Even more, God's conduct seems to contradict it (Job 21:27–34), since God delivers the righteous into the hands of the wicked (16:11) and Himself attacks an innocent man and dashes him to pieces (16:7–17).

In the first stages of his dialogue with his friends, Job is absorbed in his own tragedy. He feels himself an oppressed laborer under a hard yoke, without any respite; the shadow he longs for is the shadow of Sheol, and the wage he seeks is the release of death (7:1; 14:14). But then he emerges from his own absorption, opens himself to the consideration of others' suffering, and directs his attention to the despicable condition of the poor, oppressed by the rich and powerful. In doing so, he concludes that God does not answer the distressed cry of the poor who are unjustly treated: "From the city the dying groan, and the throat of the wounded cries for help; yet God pays no attention to their prayer" (24:12). While God does not answer the cry of the poor, God blesses the oppressive rich with a long and prosperous life (21:27–34; 24:22).

Pondering the tragedy of others, Job understands that his situation is not isolated but part of a larger picture of human reality. Observing others who suffer, he sees them as weak, powerless, and unable to make their case and raise their voice in protest. Then Job changes his attitude, no longer speaks only of himself, and becomes a voice for the voiceless. As a sage, he knows how to argue persuasively and to defend a claim before the court of elders (29:7–16). Knowing his abilities and moved by compassion, he identifies himself with the oppressed, takes up their cause, and becomes their spokesman. As an example of his persuasive power, Job offers a pathetic narration (24:2–12) describing a society in which the rich and powerful abuse and trample upon the poor and weak: "The wicked

---

[51] Frank Crüsemann, "Hiob und Kohelet: Ein Beitrag zum Verständnis des Hiobbuches," in *Werden und Wirken des Alten Testament: Festschrift für C. Westermann zum 70. Geburtstag* (eds. Rainer Albertz et al.; Göttingen: Vandenhoeck & Ruprecht; Neukirchen-Vluyn: Neukirchener Verlag, 1980), 373–93; Rainer Albertz, "Der sozialgeschichtliche Hintergrund des Hiobbuches und der Babylonischen Theodizee," in *Die Botschaft und die Boten: Festschrift für H. W. Wolff zum 70. Geburtstag* (ed. J. Jeremias and L. Perlitt; Neukirchen-Vluyn: Neukirchener Verlag, 1981), 349–72; Anthony R. Ceresko, *Psalmists and Sages* (IThSSup 2; Bangalore: St. Peter's Pontifical Institute, 1994), 195–204.

remove landmarks; they seize flocks and pasture them" (24:2). From dawn to sunset, the poor work for their oppressors and receive too little to survive. "They go about naked, without clothing; though hungry, they carry the sheaves. . . . They tread the wine presses, but suffer thirst" (24:10–11); "Like wild asses in the desert they go out to their toil, scavenging in the wasteland food for their young" (24:5). They suffer cold all night and cling to the rock for shelter. The rich and powerful appropriate everything they have, even their children. The ill-treated and powerless cry out, but nobody, not even God, listens to their groan (24:12).

Job identifies himself with those oppressed by men and abandoned by God but notices that in his ruinous situation he has fallen lower than they: he has descended to the condition of the pariahs,[52] who in turn make him feel worse in the depth of his misfortune because they despise him:

> But now they make sport of me,
> those who are younger than I,
> whose fathers I would have disdained
> to set with the dogs of my flock. . . .
> Through want and hard hunger
> they gnaw the dry and desolate ground,
> they pick mallow and the leaves of bushes,
> and to warm themselves the roots of broom.
> They are driven out from society;
> people shout after them as after a thief.
> In the gullies of wadis they must live,
> in the holes in the ground, and in the rocks. . . .
> A senseless, disreputable brood,
> they have been whipped out of the land. (30:1, 3–5, 8)

Although Job feels despised by the pariahs, he describes their subhuman condition in order to exhibit to the affluent an aspect of social reality they do not want to see or think about.

One of Job's friends, Eliphaz, argues that Job has fallen to such bitter misfortune because he had not helped the needy (22:6–9). In response, Job presents his final defense (29:1–31:40). In it he begins yearning for those days when he could help the poor and weak and defend them from their oppressors (29:12–16). He remembers that he assisted the poor, the orphans, and the widows and gave aid to the blind, the lame, and the stranger (29:12–16). Job concludes his defense with a confession of innocence, swearing solemnly that he fulfilled all ethical demands in accordance with the moral ideals of a righteous person (31:1–40). His oath mostly concerns ethical duties, and in particular assistance to the needy. Job thus swears that he aided the slave, the poor, the widow, the hungry, the orphan, and the naked (31:13–22). In this confession, Job explains that the motive for his generous conduct is the dignity the poor possess by creation: "Did not he who made me in the womb make them? And did not one fashion us in the womb?" (31:15).

---

[52] Ceresko, "Psalmists," 188–94.

Job's confession is so concentrated on the needy that it becomes testimony to his absolute identification with the poor. In all this, Job sees everything through the eyes of justice, and absorbed in this perspective, he accuses the Creator of neglecting the oppressed and blessing the oppressors.

Job wishes to meet God and argue his case. Finally, God answers Job out of the whirlwind (38:1–4:2; 40:6–41:26[40:6–41:34]). In his speeches, God addresses Job with authority, speaks of his creation, describes in detail some of his creatures, and shows full command over the wild beasts, especially the Behemoth and Leviathan, symbols of the chaotic powers. In doing so, God manifests that he is proud of his creation, loves it, and has full control over it. After listening carefully to what God had said and observing how God has spoken of the world, Job changes his attitude toward God and disowns what he had said (42:5–6). Now he sees God personally, hears God not through the tradition but directly, and understands that God is in the world with a mysterious, but powerful and loving, presence, taking care of his creatures. God does not explain the mystery of unjust suffering but makes Job feel that God is concerned about the situation of the oppressed and the needy and that God's love for his creatures is the love of the Almighty, the cause of hope for human beings. Job's hope is reinforced when God says that Job spoke well of God (42:7); in approving Job's words, God sides with him in defense of the poor and oppressed.

The author of Job guides the reader to conclude that in the midst of suffering the human person should look at the world not only through the eyes of human justice but also in light of the gracious love through which God created and governs the world, the powerful love of the Almighty that generates a hope of liberation in the oppressed.[53]

4. The book of Ecclesiastes

This book presents wise reflections on the sense of human existence; they are attributed to Solomon under the name of the Teacher, also called the Preacher by tradition. Written in the second half of the third century B.C.E., Ecclesiastes reflects the historical situation of Palestine under Ptolemaic rule, when Hellenistic cities were expanding, farming was intensifying in arable land, and the wealthy made great profits while most of the population lived in poverty. Some had a stable, although low, income, working for great landowners or for the governmental administration, but many languished in indigence. On the other hand, as Ecclesiastes notes, the administration of justice was bureaucratic and corrupt:

> I saw under the sun that in the place of justice *[mišpāṭ]*,
> wickedness was there, and in the place of righteousness *[ṣedeq]*,
> wickedness was there as well. . . .
> If you see in a province the oppression of the poor and the

---

[53] Gustavo Gutiérrez, *On Job: God-Talk and the Suffering of the Innocent* (trans. M. J. O'Connell; Maryknoll: Orbis, 1987), 51–92.

violation of justice and right, do not be amazed at the matter; for the high official is watched by a higher, and there are yet higher ones over them. (Eccl 3:16; 5:7[8])

The word the NRSV translates "watched by" means that the high and mighty take care of one another, so that the poor have no chance of justice. In this environment of corruption and injustice, the Teacher emphasizes that the rich man has an insatiable love of money (5:9–10[10–11]), that "a bribe corrupts the heart" (7:7), and that rulers appoint foolish people to high positions (10:5–6). Even in time of crisis and national danger, the rich do not turn to the wise man, who could save the nation (9:15). To allegations of corruption, greediness, and injustice, the Teacher adds foolishness and incompetence: "Better is a poor but wise youth than an old but foolish king, who will no longer take advice" (4:13). The Teacher, however, is compelled to admit the success of the Ptolemaic administration in many spheres—a fact that could remind Jewish people of the great works of King Solomon; but the Teacher sees them marked by the ephemeral and futile character of human achievement. Along this line of thought, the writer makes an indirect critique of the Ptolemaic achievements by presenting Solomon speaking of his success but adding at the end: "I considered all that my hands had done and the toil I had spent in doing it, and again, all was vanity and a chasing after wind, and there was nothing to be gained under the sun" (2:11).

The writer reflects not only on the concrete situation of his own time but also on the condition of human existence as a whole and on his own thinking. Two ideas are prominent: on the one hand, death is a factor that ends any human effort and enjoyment and equalizes all human beings in their final destiny (2:14–15; 3:19–20); on the other hand, a kind of determinism rules human existence to the extent that there is nothing new under the sun and everything is a repetition of the past (1:2–11; 3:2–9). These ideas guide the reflections of the Teacher on the vanity of everything—all is emptiness, futility, and meaninglessness, even the things that the Teacher holds in high esteem, such as wisdom and culture. "For in much wisdom is much vexation, and those who increase knowledge increase sorrow" (1:18). In line with this, he considers it useless for people to spend their lives acquiring wisdom and knowledge and toiling with skill, because in the end they will not enjoy their achievements, leaving all for others to enjoy (2:21). The Teacher observes the poor striving for the skills needed to succeed in their undertakings, but he sees all this toil as futile because the poor, like all other people, live only a few days, passing away like a shadow (6:8, 12). No human being, whatever effort he or she may make, can enjoy the result of his or her toil (2:22; 6:20) because the fate of humans is the same as the fate of animals—"all are from the dust, and all turn to dust again" (3:20).

In addition to the futility and uselessness of personal toil to determine human fate, the Teacher does not believe that human effort can achieve real change to better society:

What do people gain from all the toil
at which they toil under the sun?

> A generation goes, and a generation comes,
> but the earth remains forever....
> What has been is what will be,
> and what has been done is what will be done;
> there is nothing new under the sun. (1:3–4, 9)

Although the Teacher makes these statements with apparent certainty, he seems to guess or assume that there is something mysterious and unknowable that gives sense to creation: "He [God] has made everything suitable for its time; moreover he has put a sense of past and future into their minds, yet they cannot find out what God has done from the beginning to the end" (3:11).

It is worth noting, however, that the Teacher does not have the perspective of the biblical historians, nor the vision of the prophets, who say that God has a purpose in history and guides humanity to a future of justice and peace. The Teacher seems disconnected from the memory of the chosen people. "Memory enables both the community and the individual to recall and sequence significant events from the past in order to explain the present."[54] This disconnection implies a lack of vision capable of perceiving a future of hope for believers.[55] Still, in spite of his limitations, the Teacher leaves a lesson for believers who are still alive. In addition to the consideration of the transitory character of human existence, he draws attention to the presence of evil and destruction as recurrent elements in history; there is an assigned time for killing, breaking down, weeping, mourning, losing, tearing, and waging war (3:2–8). He invites people to be cautious in times of euphoria, when prosperity, peace, and well-being may give the impression of a permanent golden age. In these circumstances, the Teacher invites us not to forget the contingencies of history, in which people, inspired by selfish and exclusive ideologies, may cause suffering and destruction. But even in these circumstances, the Teacher is convinced that the believer is not abandoned to the arbitrary will of a blind destiny, because God mysteriously keeps control of this world and brings everyone into judgment (11:9); God will judge the righteous and the wicked (3:17). In this vein, the editor of the book added a final recommendation: "Fear God, and keep his commandments; for that is the whole duty of everyone. For God will bring every deed into judgment, including every secret thing, whether good or evil" (12:13–14).

---

[54] Leo G. Perdue, *Wisdom and Creation: The Theology of Wisdom Literature* (Nashville: Abingdon, 1994), 218.

[55] The author of Ecclesiastes esteems wisdom and appreciates the value of culture, but turns his attention to the vanity of all things. This insistence on negativity was well known in the international wisdom tradition. See "The Instruction of the Vizier Ptahhotep" 10, translated by J. A. Wilson (*ANET*, 412); "The Instruction of Amen-em-opet" 7:1–6, 21:15–16, translated by J. A. Wilson (*ANET*, 422–23); "Anksheshonq" 12:3; 22:25; 26:8; 26:14; "P. Insinger" 7:18; 17:2; 28:4; 30:15. For the last two documents, see Miriam Lichtheim, *Late Egyptian Wisdom Literature in the International Context* (OBO 52; Göttingen: Vandenhoeck & Ruprecht, 1983), 66–94, 194–234.

5. The book of Sirach

This book, called Ecclesiasticus in the tradition of the Latin church, was written in Palestine during the first decades of Seleucid rule, between 200 and 180 B.C.E. It contains the instructions of Ben Sirach, a wisdom teacher, addressed to a would-be disciple who wishes to be a sage. The book is a combination of instructions derived from ancient Near Eastern wisdom and religious Jewish tradition.[56] Among the many themes treated in this book, there are important passages devoted to the subjects of wealth, poverty, and social justice.[57] Sirach identifies various types of rich and poor people. There are rich people who have accumulated a fortune honestly (Sir 13:24) and remain blameless (31:8–11), but there are also rich men and women who are greedy and miserly (14:3–10), arrogant and deceptive, who despoil, scorn, and hate the poor (13:3–7, 20). Within the category of the poor there is also a broad range of people, extending from those of limited resources belonging to the lower middle class (29:21; 30:14) to the indigent without any income. The former live on their work, while the latter are beggars who live on charity (4:1–10). Within the society in which Sirach lives and teaches, in addition to freemen who work as retainers, there are also slaves who labor for their masters.[58]

Like Job (24:1–16), Sirach describes the sad condition of the poor. Speaking of them, he says, "Wild asses in the wilderness are the prey of lions; likewise the poor are feeding grounds for the rich" (13:19–20). The rich will maintain the poor as long as they can use them, but will abandon them as soon as they are in need because of sickness or family difficulty (13:4). The poor suffer insults and abuses and have to accept ill-treatment. They cannot raise a protest against their oppression. On the contrary, when abused, they have to apologize: "A rich person does wrong, and even adds insults; a poor person suffers wrong, and must add apologies" (13:3). A poor person may speak with good sense and wisdom, but nobody pays attention (13:22). If they are in trouble, no one comes to help them (13:22). "Should he stumble, they even push him down" (13:23). "He is an abomination to the rich" (13:20). Sirach's analysis of the condition of the poor coincides with the prophets' critique and with the approach on the subject found in the Psalter and in the book of Job.

In the society in which Sirach lived, there were various kinds of needy persons, reduced to poverty by different causes, some by tragic phenomena of nature or the volatility of the market and others by their own negligence, laziness, or bad habits; in addition, there were aliens and orphans or widows. Sirach encourages his readers to be generous toward them: "Do not reject a suppliant in distress, or

---

[56] See Alexander A. Di Lella, "Wisdom of Ben-Sira," *ABD* 6:931–45; Victor Tcherikover, *Hellenistic Civilization and the Jews* (trans. S. Applebaum; Philadelphia: Jewish Publication Society, 1959; repr., Peabody, Mass: Hendrickson, 1999), 142–51.
[57] See Sir 3:30–4:10; 13:1–24; 14:3–19; 31:1–11; 33:20–33; 34:18–35:24.
[58] See Sir 7:20–21; 23:10; 33:25–33.

turn your face away from the poor" (4:4), because it is a matter of justice that the Creator demands (4:6). A curse hangs over those who despise the poor, while a blessing is in store for those who help them: "You will then be like a son of the Most High, and he will love you more than does your mother" (4:10). On behalf of the generous person, there is a pledge: "As water extinguishes a blazing fire, so almsgiving *[eleēmosynē]* atones for sin" (3:30). The translation "almsgiving" for *eleēmosynē* is supported by the context, for in the following section (4:1–10), which describes charitable compassion, almsgiving has a prominent place. In addition, almsgiving is often encouraged by Sirach.[59] In several passages of this book, preserved in Hebrew,[60] the Greek word *eleēmosynē* renders the Hebrew term *ṣĕdāqâ* ("justice"); the word is thus loaded with biblical connotations, for in these texts almsgiving is regarded as one of the acts of saving or beneficent justice designed to reestablish the order set by the Creator.[61]

Sirach is not the kind of prophet who issues acrimonious critiques on society because of its abuses and injustices and who defends fearlessly the cause of the oppressed. Rather, he is a teacher of wisdom, enjoying the position of a person of the upper middle class, reflecting on the situation of people in society, and teaching young people of the same social condition how to be wise and succeed in life. Regarding material goods, he advises one to be satisfied with what is essential—food, clothing, house, family, health, and job—insisting that it is preferable to live on one's own work than to depend on others (29:21–28; 33:20–24; 39:26). In addition, education is necessary because, according to Sirach, it is essential for one's happiness to know and follow the ways of wisdom. While thinking that wealth is good, he criticizes the anxiety of the rich who toil to amass a vast fortune (31:1–3). Through this critique, he wishes to inspire trust in God, because "no evil will befall the one who fears the LORD, but in trials such a one will be rescued again and again" (33:1; 34:14–17).

Regarding slavery, Sirach advises masters to be demanding of their slaves, even to the point of applying punishment, if necessary, but with moderation (33:25–32). If a master has faithful slaves, he should treat them as brothers and should not withhold from them their freedom, in accordance with the law (7:21; 33:31). Sirach insists on the duties of social justice and, like the prophets, criticizes rituals disconnected from social obligations:

> The Most High is not pleased with the offerings of the ungodly,
> nor for a multitude of sacrifices does he forgive sins.

---

[59] Sir 7:10, 32–36;12:3–7; 14:13; 17:22; 18:15.

[60] See Sir 3:14; 7:10; 12:3.

[61] See Sir 3:14; 4:10; 7:10; 12:3; Dan 4:24[27]. These texts attest that, already in the last centuries before the Common Era, the word *ṣĕdāqâ* began to take on the meaning of almsgiving, though with biblical connotations, a meaning that will become common in the Talmud. See Cornelis van Leeuwen, *Le développement du sens social en Israël avant l'ère chrétienne* (Assen: Gorcum, 1954), 188–89; L. J. Prockter, "Alms and the Man," *JNSL* 17 (1991): 69–80. This development of the meaning of *ṣĕdāqâ* explains why Matt 6:1–2 places the practice of almsgiving *(eleēmosynē)* under the rubric of *dikaiosynē* (justice).

> Like one who kills a son before his father's eyes is the person who offers a sacrifice from the property of the poor. (34:23–24)

Sirach, however, does not imitate the prophets' audacity and fearlessness; he instead exercises caution and issues his critiques carefully, in accordance with the rules of prudence learned by experience. In this vein, he says:

> Do not contend with the powerful, or you may fall into their hands.
> Do not quarrel with the rich, in case their resources outweigh yours....
> Do not go to law against a judge, for the decision will favor him because of his standing. (8:1–2, 14)

Sirach is criticized these days on account of his immoderate and chauvinist comments on women (e.g., 25:16–26; 42:14). Such comments, although unpopular now, were suited to the social structure and mind-set of Sirach's time, when women were not considered autonomous individuals equal to men but, rather, subordinate to their fathers or husbands.[62] Sirach assumed that the social structures of his own time were permanent realities. Hence he did not consider the possibility of changing them. Like the book of Proverbs, however, Sirach pointed to elements essential for the improvement of society: education, a sense of responsibility, and discipline. These are components necessary to a proper society everywhere, but especially in underdeveloped countries or among discriminated minorities; they allow the growth of personal abilities, increase the awareness of one's dignity, foster respect toward others, and generate a desire to participate in community life, moving people to joint efforts to improve their own society.

6. Wisdom of Solomon

This book, attributed to Solomon, was probably written in Alexandria in the last half of the first century B.C.E. The occasion was a persecution of the Jewish community of Alexandria at the hands of the Greeks and Egyptians of the city.[63] The book exhorts the Alexandrian Jews to have pride in their traditional faith, emphasizing that their lifestyle, together with their worship of the true and living God, is far preferable to the conduct and religion of their adversaries; and it encourages them to remain steadfast to their faith, reminding them of the promise of immortality offered by God to those who seek true justice and practice it.

---

[62] See Warren C. Trenchard, *Ben Sira's View of Women: A Literary Analysis* (BJS 38; Chico, Calif.: Scholars Press, 1982); H. McKeating, "Jesus ben Sira's Attitude to Women," *ExpTim* 85 (1973–74): 85–87; K. E. Bailey, "Women in Ben Sirach and in the New Testament," in *For Me to Live* (ed. R. A. Coughenour; Cleveland: Dillon/Liederbach, 1972), 56–73.

[63] See David Winston, "Solomon, Wisdom of," *ABD* 6:120–27; *The Wisdom of Solomon* (AB 43; Garden City: Doubleday, 1979); John J. Collins, *Between Athens and Jerusalem* (New York: Crossroad, 1983), 182–86; George W. E. Nickelsburg, *Resurrection, Immortality, and Eternal Life in Intertestamental Judaism* (Cambridge: Harvard University Press, 1972), 48–90.

The book begins with an exhortation to the rulers of the nations to love justice and seek God with sincerity of heart (Wis 1:1) so that they may govern their people in accordance with the order Wisdom established in the world when God created it (1:6, 7; 11:17). This order shines in the world so that, by seeing it, human beings may know the one who made it (13:1–9). On the other hand, this order has such cohesion and strength that it punishes those who breach it and rewards those who observe it and suffer oppression on its account. The writer says, "One is punished by the very things by which one sins" (11:16; 16:1–2), and "through the very things by which their enemies were punished, they [the righteous] themselves received benefit in their need" (11:5). The author, formed by Alexandrian schools, introduces into biblical writing a concept of order derived from Greek thought, according to which the world is ruled by inner principles of cohesion and harmony. Hence, in his point of view, the cosmos is not simply ruled by the will of the Creator who defeated the power of chaos. It is also ruled by an inner order that the Creator put within the texture of the universe itself.[64] It is a combination of inner and outward order, but according to the writer, there is a subordination of the one to the other because the Creator, who made the inner order, remains present in the universe and in the history of humanity not only to secure the inner order, by punishing and rewarding, but also to guide humanity to its destiny of immortality.

The writer employs the two concepts of order in his reflection on history, but in his exhortation to the persecuted Jews, he insists on the personal presence of God in the cosmos as supreme assurance of the future vindication of the righteous oppressed by evildoers. In this, the writer is in line with the prophets and the Psalms, using their vocabulary and sharing their hope. The Jews are thus called righteous because they are oppressed on account of their faith—they acknowledge God as their Father, abide by God's will, and, through their conduct, reproach their adversaries' unrighteous and unjust behavior (2:10–15). These adversaries are the pagans who hate the Jews because of their lifestyle, their attitudes, and their teaching against pagan religious convictions (2:12–16). The writer emphasizes that such pagans have abandoned the principles of justice in which they were educated (2:12), and use violence and abuse as norms of government. He describes them saying,

> Let us oppress the righteous poor man;
> let us not spare the widow
> or regard the gray hairs of the aged.
> But let our might be our law of right,
> for what is weak proves itself to be useless (2:10–11).

Like the poor of the Psalms, the Jewish Alexandrian community trusts that God will set it free from its oppressors, but there is a difference. Whereas in the

---

[64] See John P. M. Sweet, "The Theory of Miracles in the Wisdom of Solomon," in *Miracles: Cambridge Studies in Their Philosophy and History* (ed. C. F. D. Moule; London: Mowbray, 1965), 115–26.

Psalms the motivation of a life after death is just a glimmer of hope present only in a few psalms, in this book the hope of immortality is well articulated and constitutes the predominant motivation encouraging the persecuted believers: "God created us for incorruption, and made us in the image of his own eternity" (2:23). The souls of the righteous, after being tested and purified, will be in the hand of God" (3:1) and "live forever, and their reward is with the LORD. . . . They will receive a glorious crown and a beautiful diadem from the hand of the LORD" (5:15–16). But the ungodly, those who despised the righteous, will be punished (3:10) without consolation (3:18).

Wisdom of Solomon embodies a new concept of life after death. In the preexilic period and the first centuries of the postexilic era, there had been no mention of expectation of reward in an afterlife. In addition, in the postexilic period, Job 14:10–12 and Eccl 3:19–21 denied any solid ground for such an expectation. Psalms 49 and 73 seem to offer the earliest glimmers of faith in an afterlife. The expectation developed during the Hellenistic period, moving in two directions: one trend believed in resurrection[65] and the other in the immortality of the soul.[66] Wisdom of Solomon seems to be more inclined toward the second.

The book employs the concept of immortality of the soul in speaking of the vindication of the righteous who have been oppressed. God will destroy the kingdom of evildoers by using the powers of nature, as God did in the book of Exodus, and will establish a new era in history, ruled by metahistorical powers under God's dominion. Then the souls of the righteous will be with God, enjoying immortal happiness (Wis 3:1–7; 5:15–16) and receiving royal power from God. They shall be his governmental agents and judges, ruling the nations: "They will govern nations and rule over peoples, and the LORD will reign over them forever" (3:8). This participation in divine ruling power resembles the dominion, found in Daniel, *4 Ezra,* and *1 Enoch,* that the glorified righteous will exercise over the nations of the earth.[67]

The writer speaks of the inexhaustible light of the Law, which Jews possess to illuminate the whole world. In this, he shares the idea, common in Jewish-Hellenistic tradition, that the acceptance of the Torah includes the obligation to spread its teaching to the Gentiles.[68] In line with this thought, the writer says,

> Their enemies [the Egyptians] deserved to be deprived of light and imprisoned in darkness, those who had kept your children imprisoned, through whom the imperishable light of the law was to be given to the world. (18:4)

Although the writer speaks of the imperishable light of the Torah and Israel's obligation to share it with the Gentiles, he does not apply an ability to transform society to this enlightening power, as Philo of Alexandria seemed to do in

---

[65] See *1 En.* 92:3; Dan 12:2; 2 Macc 7:9; 4Q521.
[66] See *1 En.* 22:1–14; 103:3–4; *Jub.* 23:31.
[67] Dan 7:22; 12:3; *4 Ezra* 9:97; *1 En.* 104:2.
[68] See, e.g., *4 Ezra* 7:20–24; *T. Levi* 14:4; *2 Bar.* 48:40.

developing the messianic character of the Torah.[69] The writer of Wisdom seems to be so overwhelmed by human injustice in society that he does not see the possibility of its transformation through the power that God installed in nature and history, such as the presence of divine Wisdom in creation (6:1–9:18) and the revelation given to Israel (18:4). To transform human society, he instead appeals to metahistorical factors, such as the immortal souls of the righteous, crowned in heaven with the royal diadem of divine sovereignty (3:8; 5:15–16). Through them, God creates order, justice, peace, and prosperity on earth. The vindication of the righteous and the dominion that will be bestowed on them constitute the principal motives the writer employs to encourage and strengthen those who seek justice and proclaim their ideals to a corrupt and oppressive society. Wisdom of Solomon offers a permanent message to those who suffer oppression, exhorting them to be steadfast in the midst of frustration, defeat, and even death. It instills in them the conviction that the oppressive earthly powers cannot destroy justice because God will overpower them on behalf of God's people.

Conclusion

The book of Psalms contains a moving description of the unshakable trust that the poor put in the saving and incorruptible justice of God. It also shares the prophetic hope that God has a plan of justice and peace that He will execute not only for the oppressed believers but also for Israel as a nation, giving the divine plan both an individual and a social dimension. The book of Proverbs sees poverty as a regular component of human society, urges believers to be generous toward the poor and teaches people to be active, efficient, and responsible. Although this book does not propose changes for society, it imparts a valid message for future generations by stressing the need for education, discipline, and personal and social responsibility.

Job, in the midst of his affliction, identifies himself with the poor and the pariahs and becomes their spokesman. He cries out for justice on behalf of those who suffer oppression, blames God for not listening to their prayers, and wishes to confront God to demand an explanation. Finally, God speaks to him, describing with enthusiasm and love what God has done in creation. After seeing God and listening to God's words, Job disowns what he himself had previously said

---

[69] See Peder Borgen, "Philo of Alexandria," *ABD* 5:336–37. Borgen deduces from his study of Philo that many Jews of Alexandria harbored the hope that the nations would recognize the law of Moses and the people of God, accepting the Jews as the center of the world. Among the Jews, there were two groups. One group was willing to use force if it became necessary. The other group thought that the Jews should overcome their neighbors by peaceful means, that is, by their religion, based on the laws given by the Creator, and by the growing prosperity of the Jewish community. Philo belonged to the second group. See Philo, *Mos.* 2.44, in *The Works of Philo: Complete and Unabridged* (trans. C. D. Yonge; Peabody, Mass.: Hendrickson, 1993), 494.

and understands that there is an important factor he failed to consider: the love of God for his creatures; a love that creates hope.

The author of Ecclesiastes introduces a skeptical note in his reflections on human life. In his understanding, poverty and injustice are evil parts of the present world, a situation that cannot be changed. He does not share the prophetic view of God's plan on behalf of God's people, nor does he have hope for fulfillment in an afterlife. In spite of his limitations, he has left us with ideas worth considering: the transitory nature of life and the presence of evil and destruction as recurrent elements in human history.

Sirach, like Job, describes the pathetic situation of the poor and, like Proverbs, emphasizes the need for education, discipline, and personal and social responsibility, things that are necessary for any human society, especially in underdeveloped countries and among discriminated minorities.

The Wisdom of Solomon applies the concept of the oppressed poor, found in the prophets and Psalms to Israel, and gives an answer to Job and Ecclesiastes by assuring divine vindication on behalf of the oppressed—glorious immortality after death and dominion over the nations. While Wisdom does not consider the possibility of improving society through the knowledge of the Torah, it does encourage those who seek justice and proclaim it to a corrupted society, promising them the coming of a new world under the rule of righteous souls, glorified in heaven.

Bibliography

Albertz, Rainer. "Der sozialgeschichtliche Hintergrund des Hiobbuches und der Babylonischen Theodizee." Pages 349–72 in *Die Botschaft und die Boten: Festschrift für H. W. Wolff zum 70. Geburtstag*. Edited by J. Jeremias and L. Perlitt. Neukirchen-Vluyn: Neukirchener Verlag, 1981.

Bailey, K. E. "Women in Ben Sirach and in the New Testament." Pages 56–73 in *For Me to Live*. Edited by R. A. Coughenour. Cleveland: Dillon/Liederbach, 1972.

Baudissin, Wolf W., Graf von. "Die alttestamentliche Religion und die Armen." *Preussische Jahrbücher* 149 (1912): 193–231.

Ben Zvi, Ehud. *A Historical-Critical Study of the Book of Zephaniah*. Berlin: de Gruyter, 1991.

Birkeland, H. *ʿĀnî und ʿĀnāw in den Psalmen*. Oslo: Dybwad, 1932.

———. *The Evildoers in the Book of Psalms*. Oslo: Dybwad, 1955.

———. *Die Feinde des Individuums in der israelitischen Psalmenliteratur*. Oslo: Grøndahl, 1933.

Borgen, Peder. "Philo of Alexandria." Pages 333–42 of vol. 5 of *Anchor Bible Dictionary*. Edited by D. N. Freedman. 6 vols. New York: Doubleday, 1992.

Causse, Antonin. *Le "pauvres" d'Israël, prophètes, psalmistes, messianistes*. Études d'histoire et philosophie religieuses 3. Strasbourg: Librairie Istra, 1922.

Ceresko, Anthony R. *Psalmists and Sages: Studies in Old Testament Poetry and Religion.* Indian Theological Studies Supplements 2. Bangalore: St. Peter's Pontifical Institute, 1994.

Childs, Brevard S. *Introduction to the Old Testament as Scripture.* Philadelphia: Fortress, 1979.

Clements, Ronald E. *Isaiah 1–39.* New Century Bible Commentary. Grand Rapids: Eerdmans, 1980.

Collins, John J. *Between Athens and Jerusalem.* New York: Crossroad, 1983.

Crenshaw, James L. "Proverbs, Book of." Pages 513–20 of vol. 5 of *Anchor Bible Dictionary.* Edited by D. N. Freedman. 6 vols. New York: Doubleday, 1992.

Crüsemann, Frank. "Hiob und Kohelet: Ein Beitrag zum Verständnis des Hiobbuches." Pages 373–93 in *Werden und Wirken des Alten Testament: Festschrift für C. Westermann zum 70. Geburtstag.* Edited by Rainer Albertz et al. Göttingen: Vandenhoeck & Ruprecht; Neukirchen-Vluyn: Neukirchener Verlag, 1980.

Delekat, L. "Zum Hebräischen Wörterbuch." *Vetus Testamentum* 14 (1964): 35–49.

Di Lella, Alexander A. "Wisdom of Ben-Sira." Pages 931–45 of vol. 6 of *Anchor Bible Dictionary.* Edited by D. N. Freedman. 6 vols. New York: Doubleday, 1992.

García Martínez, Florentino. *The Dead Sea Scrolls Translated.* Leiden: Brill, 1994.

Gelin, Albert. *The Poor of Yahveh.* Translated by K. Sullivan. Collegeville: Liturgical Press, 1964.

Gutiérrez, Gustavo. *On Job: God-Talk and the Suffering of the Innocent.* Translated by M. J. O'Connell. Maryknoll: Orbis, 1987.

Jepsen, Alfred. "Ṣdq und Ṣdqh im Alten Testament." Pages 78–99 in *Gottes Wort und Gottes Land.* FS H. W. Hertzberg. Edited by H. Reventlow. Göttingen: Vandenhoeck & Ruprecht, 1965.

Kraus, Hans-Joachim. *Psalms 1–59: A Commentary.* Translated by H. C. Oswald. Minneapolis: Augsburg, 1988.

―――. *Theology of the Psalms.* Translated by K. Crim. Minneapolis: Augsburg, 1986.

Leeuwen, Cornelis van. *Le développement du sens social en Israël avant l'ère chrétienne.* Assen: Gorcum, 1954.

Lichtheim, Miriam. *Late Egyptian Wisdom Literature in the International Context.* Orbis biblicus et orientalis 52. Göttingen: Vandenhoeck & Ruprecht, 1983.

Lohfink, Norbert. *Lobgesänge der Armen.* Stuttgarter Bibelstudien 143. Stuttgart: Katholisches Bibelwerk, 1990.

―――. "Von der 'Anawim-Partei' zur 'Kirche der Armen': Die Bibelwissenschaftliche Ahnentafel eines Hauptbegriffs der 'Theologie der Befreiung.'" *Biblica* 67 (1986): 153–75.

McKeating, H. "Jesus ben Sira's Attitude to Women." *Expository Times* 85 (1973–1974): 85–87.

Meinhold, A. *Die Sprüche.* Zürcher Bibelkommentar, Altes Testament 16.1. Zürich: Theologisches Verlag, 1991.

Mogensen, B. "Ṣĕdāqâ in the Scandinavian and German Research Tradition." Pages 67–80 in *The Productions of Time: Tradition History in Old Testament Scholarship.* Edited by K. Jeppesen and B. Otzen. Sheffield: JSOT Press, 1984.

Mowinckel, Sigmund. *Psalmenstudien.* 2 vols. Amsterdam: P. Shippers, 1961.

———. *The Psalms in Israel's Worship.* Translated by. D. R. Ap-Thomas. 2 vols. New York: Abingdon, 1962.

Nickelsburg, George W. E. *Resurrection, Immortality, and Eternal Life in Intertestamental Judaism.* Cambridge: Harvard University Press, 1972.

Perdue, Leo G. *Wisdom and Creation: The Theology of Wisdom Literature.* Nashville: Abingdon, 1994.

Pleins, J. David. "Poor, Poverty." Pages 402–14 of vol. 5 of *Anchor Bible Dictionary.* Edited by D. N. Freedman. 6 vols. New York: Doubleday, 1992.

———. "Poverty in the Social World of the Wise." *Journal for the Study of the Old Testament* 37 (1987): 61–78.

Ploeg, J. van der. "Les pauvres d'Israël et leur piété." *Oudtestamentische Studiën* 7 (1950): 236–70.

Pritchard, James B., ed. *Ancient Near Eastern Texts Relating to the Old Testament.* 3d ed. Princeton: Princeton University Press, 1969.

Prockter, L. J. "Alms and the Man." *Journal of Northwest Semitic Languages* 17 (1991): 69–80.

Rahlfs, Alfred. *Ani und Anav in den Psalmen.* Göttingen: Dieterich, 1892.

Sabourin, Leopold. *The Psalms: Their Origin and Meaning.* New York: Alba House, 1970.

Scullion, John J. "Righteousness (OT)." Pages 724–36 of vol. 5 of *Anchor Bible Dictionary.* Edited by D. N. Freedman. 6 vols. New York: Doubleday, 1992.

Shupak, Nili. "The 'Sitz im Leben' of the Book of Proverbs in the Light of a Comparison of Biblical and Egyptian Wisdom Literature." *Revue biblique* 94 (1987): 98–119.

Smith, J. M. P. *Zephaniah.* International Critical Commentary. Edinburgh: T&T Clark, 1911.

Sweet, John P. M. "The Theory of Miracles in the Wisdom of Solomon." Pages 115–26 in *Miracles: Cambridge Studies in Their Philosophy and History.* Edited by C. F. D. Moule. London: Mowbray, 1965.

Tcherikover, Victor. *Hellenistic Civilization and the Jews.* Translated by S. Applebaum. Philadelphia: Jewish Publication Society, 1959. Repr., Peabody, Mass.: Hendrickson, 1999..

Trenchard, Warren C. *Ben Sira's View of Women: A Literary Analysis.* Brown Judaic Studies 38. Chico, Calif.: Scholars Press, 1982.

Vawter, Bruce. "Intimations of Immortality in the Old Testament." *Journal of Biblical Literature* 91 (1972): 158–71.

Weinfeld, Moshe. *Social Justice in Ancient Israel and in the Ancient Near East.* Jerusalem: Magnes, 1995.

Wengst, Klaus. *Humility: Solidarity of the Humiliated—the Transformation of an Attitude and Its Social Relevance in Graeco-Roman, Old Testament–Jewish, and Early Christian Thought.* Translated by J. Bowden. Philadelphia: Fortress, 1988.

Whybray, Roger N. *Wealth and Poverty in the Book of Proverbs*. Journal for the Study of the Old Testament: Supplement Series 99. Sheffield: JSOT Press, 1990.

Winston, David. "Solomon, Wisdom of." Pages 120–27 of vol. 6 of *Anchor Bible Dictionary*. Edited by D. N. Freedman. 6 vols. New York: Doubleday, 1992.

———. *The Wisdom of Solomon*. Anchor Bible 43. Garden City: Doubleday, 1979.

CHAPTER SEVEN

JUSTICE IN APOCALYPTIC WRITINGS

Introduction

The previous chapter considered the theme of justice and poverty in Psalms and the Wisdom books. This chapter analyzes the same subject in the apocalyptic writings. First, one should distinguish between eschatology and apocalypse.[1] Eschatology deals with the final stage of humanity and the cosmos when, by God's definitive intervention, evildoers will be punished and the righteous rewarded forever. Apocalypse, on the other hand, is a literary genre that symbolically describes God's decisive action in the creation of a new world, a description that nurtures belief in an impending vindication of the righteous who are suffering oppression. To be more precise, apocalypse, as a literary genre, is a narrative about a divine revelation mediated by an angel to a human being through a vision or an otherworldly journey. The recipient, generally speaking, bears the name of a venerable person of the past. The actual addressee is a community that perceives itself as living in a time of stress and persecution. The revelation deals with the impending occurrence of final events that will end this historical time, which is under the power of evil. The final events are the last judgment, the destruction of evildoers, and the reward of the righteous in an afterlife.[2]

The apocalyptic writings studied in this chapter derive from the last centuries B.C.E. and the first century C.E. In addition to the canonical book of Daniel, this chapter includes four noncanonical writings; three are selected from the collection of *1 Enoch*, and the fourth is *4 Ezra*. The inclusion of noncanonical books is meant to place the book of Daniel within the broad setting of Jewish apocalyptic writings and thus to understand better its features and message. These

---

[1] See David Petersen, "Eschatology (OT)," *ABD* 2:575–79; Paul D. Hanson, "Apocalypses and Apocalypticism," *ABD* 1:279–82; John J. Collins, *The Apocalyptic Imagination: An Introduction to the Jewish Matrix of Christianity* (New York: Crossroad, 1984), 1–32; George W. E. Nickelsburg, "Social Aspects of Palestinian Jewish Apocalypticism," in *Apocalypticism in the Mediterranean World and the Near East* (ed. D. Hellholm; Tübingen: J. C. B. Mohr, 1983), 639–54.

[2] See Collins, *Apocalyptic Imagination*, 7.

noncanonical books are selected because they provide particularly illustrative material for the study of justice. Furthermore, it is worth noting that *1 Enoch* and *4 Ezra*, although they are not part of our canon, were held in high esteem within some Christian communities of the first centuries; *1 Enoch* was preserved and accepted as canonical by the Ethiopian church, while *4 Ezra* was appended to the Latin Vulgate. *First Enoch* is a collection of various traditions written over a long period of years, from the third century B.C.E. through the first century C.E. The collection includes five independent writings: the Book of the Watchers (*1 En.* 1–36), the Book of the Similitudes (37–71), the Book of Astronomical Writings (72–82), the Book of Dream Visions (83–90), and the Book of the Epistle of Enoch (91–107).[3] Selected for study in this chapter are the first, the second, and the fifth books. These writings, together with Daniel and *4 Ezra*, will be analyzed chronologically. Therefore the order in this chapter is: the Book of the Watchers, the Epistle of Enoch, Daniel, the Book of the Similitudes, and *4 Ezra*.[4]

This chapter studies the concept of justice in an apocalyptic setting, in which those who suffer oppression are both individuals and communities. They not only suffer in their social life and economic condition; their religious and political identity is also threatened.

1. The Book of the Watchers (*1 En.* 1–36)

Substantial parts of this book derive from the third and second centuries B.C.E., but it contains some earlier traditions dating to the end of the fourth century B.C.E. The book is related to the era of the Hellenistic rulers, successors to Alexander the Great.[5] The introduction (*1 En.* 1–5) describes Enoch's visions about the reward of the elect and the punishment of evildoers in the last judgment. These revelations are meant to encourage the community as it lives under unjust oppression. After the introduction, Enoch's revelations explain the cause of evil on earth: the rebellion of the watchers (6:11). The sexual union between the sons of God (the watchers) and the daughters of men in Gen 6:1–2, 4 is interpreted as a deliberate rebellion of the angels against God. The results of this union are the giants, a powerful and warlike race that claims divine attributes, plunders peoples' properties, and devours human beings. In their greed, they go so far as to

---

[3] See George W. E. Nickelsburg, "Enoch, First Book of," *ABD* 2:508–16; *Jewish Literature between the Bible and the Mishnah* (Philadelphia: Fortress, 1981), 46–55, 90–94, 145–51, 214–22; Matthew Black, *The Book of Enoch or I Enoch: A New English Translation* (SVTP; Leiden: Brill, 1985); Collins, *Apocalyptic Imagination*, 33–63, 142–80.

[4] The translation of these texts is that of James H. Charlesworth, ed., *Old Testament Pseudepigrapha* (2 vols.; Garden City: Doubleday, 1983–1985).

[5] See Marie-Theres Wacker, *Weltordnung und Gericht: Studien zur I Henoch 22* (2d ed.; FB 45; Würzburg: Echter, 1985); George W. E. Nickelsburg, "The Bible Rewritten and Expanded," in *Jewish Writings of the Second Temple Period* (ed. M. E. Stone; CRINT, sec. 2, vol. 2. Assen: Van Gorcum; Philadelphia: Fortress, 1984), 90–93; "Apocalyptic and Myth in *1 Enoch* 6–11," *JBL* 96 (1977): 383–405; Collins, *Apocalyptic Imagination*, 36–46.

turn against one another in fratricidal struggle (7:3–6). The oppressed people "cried and their voice reached unto heaven" (8:4; 9:3, 10).[6]

The archangels, seeing the bloody oppression upon the earth and hearing the cry of the oppressed reach the throne of God, bring the case before the Most High, naming the rebellious angels (the Watchers) as the culprits. In response, the Most High punishes the Watchers, causes the flood to destroy the pervasive corruption and oppression, and repopulates the earth through Noah's descendants. By divine command, the Watchers are arrested and condemned "to be sent into the fire on the great day of judgment" (10:6). They are held responsible for all the bloody injustices committed on earth. (*First Enoch* 10:6 offers the earliest testimony to a belief in Sheol as the place of torment for evildoers.)[7] God's judgment not only punishes evildoers but also rewards and renews God's people, making them "a plant of righteousness, truth, and of joy" (10:16).[8] The renewed people "shall inherit the earth" forever (5:7) and live there, free of internal and external oppression. They will be righteous and blameless (10:17–21), peacefully enjoying their boundless prosperity (10:19, 22).[9] All the nations will praise the chosen people and, seeing their life and prosperity, will worship and bless God (10:21).

The author of *1 Enoch* narrates this primordial history of violence, judgment, and restoration as an anticipation of the end of time. He sees in this story a benchmark for the interpretation of the events happening to his own community.[10] "The prayer of the angelic intercessors is in reality the bitter and desperate cry of the author's own people, who are querying about the problem of evil as they experience it at the hands of their enemies, the giants of the earth."[11]

The description of the giants as an oppressive and warlike race claiming divine honors reflects the time of Alexander the Great's successors. After his death in 323 B.C.E., the immense empire Alexander had conquered, from Egypt to India, remained in the hands of a small group of Macedonian generals (Lysimachus,

---

[6] The theme of the earth that cries out for vengeance owes its inspiration to the story of Cain and Abel. But the cry of the oppressed that rises to the heavens and moves God to intervene is not a motif of the primordial history. It is better seen as a motif that has its paradigm in the psalms of lamentation and in the exodus event. The author introduces his knowledge of angelology and assigns to archangels the role of intercessors between the heavens and the earth.

[7] See above, ch. 6, §6.

[8] On the "plant of righteousness," see Nickelsburg, "Social Aspects," 653.

[9] The text reads, "He who plants a vine upon her will produce wine for plenitude. And every seed that is sown on her, one measure will yield a thousand (measures) and one measure of olives will yield then measures of presses of oil" (*1 En.* 10:19).

[10] Paul D. Hanson, *The Dawn of Apocalyptic* (Philadelphia: Fortress, [1975]), 9–31, holds that, in apocalyptic literature, the myth of primordial struggle is applied to eschatological time. The establishment of order over chaos associated with the beginning of time is now used to describe the defeat of oppressive power at the end of time and to announce the foundation of a new world. In the Book of the Watchers, this primordial myth, however, has been augmented by the motif of the cry of the oppressed, who gain a hearing and obtain their liberation, a motif that is part of the paradigm of the exodus.

[11] Nickelsburg, "Bible Rewritten," 91.

Ptolemy, and Seleucus), aggressive and greedy personalities, each eager to increase his dominion at the expense of the others. "The world became the cockpit of a prolonged and ruthless struggle,"[12] in which Palestine was the bone of contention between the Ptolemies and the Seleucids. The Ptolemies were able to maintain their rule over Palestine until 198 B.C.E., when Antiochus III, a Seleucid king, defeated Ptolemy V. From then until the Roman period, the land remained under Seleucid rule.

Generally speaking, the successors of Alexander the Great ruled as despotic dictators. Eager for glory and power, they claimed divine honors. Alexander himself initiated his own deification. The Ptolemies and Seleucids followed suit. In describing the ideology, cruelty, and oppression of the giants, the writer has in mind these Hellenistic rulers. Through this identification, he offers his readers the assurance that the present oppressive powers will suffer the same destiny as the Watchers and their progeny. They will be destroyed, and the oppressed community will be vindicated forever. In applying the myth of the giants to the Hellenistic rulers, the writer raises the events of oppression and suffering of the community under Hellenistic rule to a mythological and metahistorical level, making them a paradigm for similar situations. "By telling the story of the Watchers rather than of the Diadochi or the priesthood, *1 Enoch* 1–36 becomes a paradigm which is not restricted to one historical situation but can be applied whenever an analogous situation arises."[13] Such a paradigm may be applied to the oppressive totalitarian regimes of our own century.

In the Book of the Watchers, the term *justice* is set against the oppression effected by the giants of the earth at every level of human existence: social, economic, political, and religious. Hence, the saving action expected from justice includes liberation from social, economic, political, and religious oppression. Through this liberation, the now oppressed community will bloom in its own land, serve freely the only true God, and enjoy peace, prosperity, and happiness. It will be "a plant of justice and joy" (10:16).[14] This book does not call the oppressed people to an armed revolt against the oppressing rulers. Written in apocalyptic code, it instead urges believers to hold firmly to their faith, maintaining their own identity as God's people and not bend to the wishes of the abusive rul-

---

[12] Tcherikover, *Hellenistic Civilization*, 8. The struggle among the Macedonian generals, which began after Alexander's death, abated somewhat with the battle of Ipsus in 301 B.C.E., after which the number of litigants decreased and the Middle East was divided into three parts: Lysimachus kept the western part of Asia Minor; Ptolemy obtained Egypt and Palestine; and Seleucus took Syria and Babylon. From 320 to 301 B.C.E., Palestine passed four times to the Egyptian dominion and remained the apple of discord between the Ptolemies and the Seleucids. The Ptolemies were able to secure their possession for several decades, but in 219 the war started up again and lasted intermittently until 198 B.C.E., the year in which Antiochus III took all the cities of Palestine and the land definitively became a part of the Seleucid dominion.

[13] Collins, *Apocalyptic Imagination*, 39.

[14] See M. H. Fiedler, "Dikaiosyne in der diaspora-jüdischen und intertestamentlichen Literatur," *JSJ* 1 (1970): 120–43.

ing powers. It encourages believers to do so on the basis that the imminent intervention of the Most High, who is the supreme and only master of the world and who has heard the cries of his people under oppression, is certain.

2. The Book of the Epistle of Enoch (*1 En.* 91–107)

This text reflects events of the first decades of Seleucid rule in Palestine, between 198 and 175 B.C.E.[15] During this time, some Jews became fervent supporters of Greek culture and practice to the point of harassing other Jews who clung to their ancestral traditions (1 Macc 1:11–15; 2 Macc 4:7–20). Unlike the Book of the Watchers, in which the conflict was between Hellenistic rulers and the Jewish community, this text depicts a conflict between two opposing Jewish groups: those who were hellenized, and the traditional Jews. The latter regarded themselves as poor, good, and righteous and felt themselves oppressed by the former, whom they perceived as rich, unjust sinners.[16] The traditional Jews blamed the hellenized Jews for neglecting the Law and even distorting it, and they reproached them for not feeling guilty for doing so. In principle, the traditional Jews criticized the hellenized Jews because the latter did not follow their interpretation of the Law.[17] Thus say the woes of Enoch:

> Woe unto you who would set at nought the words of the righteous ones!
> For you shall have no hope of life. . . .
> Woe unto you who alter the words of truth
> and pervert the eternal law!

---

[15] See George W. E. Nickelsburg, "Social Aspects," 651–54, and "The Apocalyptic Message of 1 Enoch 92–105," *CBQ* 39 (1977): 309–28; *Resurrection, Immortality, and Eternal Life in Intertestamental Judaism* (HTS 26; Cambridge: Harvard University Press, 1972), 112–30; Collins, *Apocalyptic Imagination*, 52–53. The Hasmoneans (the Jewish priestly family that revolted against the Seleucids in 167 B.C.E. and ruled Judea from 142 to 63 B.C.E.) very soon became powerful worldly politicians in competition with the Hellenistic political leaders, adopting their worst characteristics: a worldly life, a taste for exuberant luxury, an avidity for prestige and wealth, palace intrigues, and the exercise of absolute power. According to Josephus (*Ant.* 13.380), Alexander Jannaeus feasted with his concubines at the same time executioners were crucifying eight hundred prisoners of war. See Tcherikover, *Hellenistic Civilization*, 243–53.

[16] Members of the circle of Enoch are regularly designated, in the Greek translation of the work, as *dikaioi* ("just"), more rarely as *eusebeis* ("pious"), and only twice as *hosioi* ("devout"). The last two appellations raise the question whether this group had any relation to the *ḥasîdîm* of 1 Macc 2:42; 7:14 and 2 Macc 14:6. In addition, since fragments of two copies of the Epistle of Enoch were found among the Dead Sea Scrolls, the question of the relationship of this group with Qumran has been raised. See Nickelsburg, "Social Aspects," 653; M. Hengel, *Judaism and Hellenism* (trans. J. Bowden; 2 vols.; Philadelphia: Fortress, 1974), 1:180; *Jews, Greeks, and Barbarians: Aspects of the Hellenization of Judaism in the Pre-Christian Period* (trans. J. Bowden; Philadelphia: Fortress, 1980), 123–24.

[17] See Nickelsburg, *Resurrection*, 112–13. For the sociopolitical situation of Palestine in the first half of the first century B.C.E., Nickelsburg recommends Tcherikover, *Hellenistic Civilization*, 252–64.

> They reckon themselves not guilty of sin. . . .
> Woe unto you who reject the foundations and the eternal inheritance
> of your fathers. (*1 En.* 98:14; 99:2; 99:14)

The members of Enoch's community believed that they possessed a revealed wisdom that enabled them to interpret the Law correctly and to perceive the coming end of this age and the beginning of the new world (91:7–11; 104:12–13). They were proud to be the beneficiaries of eternal salvation (91:12–19; 93:1–14), firmly believing that "the spirits of those who died in righteousness shall live and rejoice" (103:4). Enoch solemnly assures believers, "Be hopeful, because formerly you have pined away through evil and toil. But now you shall shine like the lights of heaven" (104:2). The community for which Enoch was written strongly believed that God has everything under control and also that they themselves would be the agents of God's justice in the final destruction of evildoers and sinners. In this vein, Enoch says to the unrighteous, "Do know that you shall be given over into the hands of the righteous ones and they shall cut off your necks and slay you, and they shall not have compassion upon you" (98:12). Since the evildoers oppressed the righteous, their destruction was necessary for the liberation of the righteous. Thus, God's justice has two dimensions: on one hand, it punishes the oppressors, and on the other, it saves, restores, and exalts the oppressed.

It is remarkable that the Epistle of Enoch foresees a historical period of righteousness, before the end of the present age, followed by a period of wickedness and violence (91:12–17). This intermediate period of righteousness is the eighth in a sequence of ten. The tenth period is the time of judgment and final vindication of the righteous. This idea of a messianic kingdom within our history is also found in other books, such as *4 Ezra* 7:28, and finds an echo in the book of Revelation (Rev 20:4–6).

The Epistle of Enoch knows well that the differences between righteous and unrighteous go beyond social and economic concerns. But it describes the oppression specifically in those terms:

> We have become the victuals of the sinners and the oppressors; they have made their yoke heavy upon us. Those who hate us, while goading us and encompassing us, have become masters over us. We have bowed our necks to those who hate us, but they had no pity on us. . . . Then, in our tribulation, we brought a charge against them before the authorities, and cried out against those who were devouring us, but they (the authorities) neither would pay attention to our cries nor wish to listen to our voice. But (on the contrary) they were assisting those who were robbing and devouring us, those who were causing us to diminish. They (the authorities) conceal their (the offenders') injustice and do not remove the yokes of those who devour us, scatter us, and murder us; they (the authorities) cover up our murder; and they (the authorities) do not remember (the fact) that they (the offenders) have lifted up their hands against us. (*1 En.* 103:11–15)

The same theme is present in the woes in which Enoch condemns the abusive conduct of the powerful toward the weak and the poor:

> Woe unto those who build oppression and injustice
> Who lay foundations for deceit.

> They shall soon be demolished;
> and they shall have no peace. . . .
> Woe unto you, O rich people
> For you have put your trust in your wealth. . . .
> In the day of your affluence, you committed oppression. . . .
> Woe unto you, O powerful people!
> You who coerce the righteous with your power,
> the day of your destruction is coming! . . .
> Woe unto you who gain silver and gold by unjust means;
> you will then say, "We have grown rich and accumulated goods,
> we have acquired everything that we have desired." . . .
> Woe unto you, sinners, when you oppress
> the righteous ones, in the day of hard anguish,
> and burn them with fire!
> You shall be recompensed according to your deeds. (94:7, 8a, 9a; 96:8a; 97:8; 100:7)

In the Epistle of Enoch, the rich person is a sinner. Wealth is unjust both because of the way it is acquired and because of the way it is used. Wealth is so intertwined with oppression that the antagonism between rich and poor is impossible to reconcile. In the view of Enoch, the solution to the social problem is the extermination of the rich and powerful. He does not think social change is possible through the conversion of the wealthy. In his opinion, only God can effect it through a radical action to destroy the present society and create a new one. Enoch has an apocalyptic mind-set: evil is so identified with the oppressors that only through their extermination can God create a just and perfect society in history.

George W. E. Nickelsburg draws readers' attention to the similarities between the lamentations of the Epistle of Enoch and the lamentations of the third gospel in its address to the rich (Luke 6:24–26).[18] His observations are well taken. Certainly, the similarities are impressive, but the differences are no less noticeable. Unlike the Epistle of Enoch, which condemns the rich to destruction and sees the solution of the social problem in the elimination of the wealthy, the Gospel of Luke criticizes the rich in order to convert them and urges them to share their wealth with the poor. Luke's solution of the social problem, in other words, is not through elimination but through participation.

Worth noting also is a comparison that Victor Tcherikover draws between the Epistle of Enoch and Sirach.[19] He emphasizes the divergent perspectives of these approximately contemporary writings. While the Epistle of Enoch identifies wealth with sin, Sirach thinks that wealth can be justly acquired, and considers with pleasure the possibility that a poor person may be raised to a position of prominence through the study of wisdom. These two texts presuppose opposite experiences in society and address very different audiences. While the Epistle of

---

[18] George W. E. Nickelsburg, "Riches, the Rich, and God's Judgment in *1 Enoch* 93–105 and the Gospel according to Luke," *NTS* 25 (1979): 324–44.

[19] See Tcherikover, *Hellenistic Civilization*, 142–51, 259.

Enoch reflects an experience of poverty and oppression, Sirach belongs to the affluent middle class. The former addresses poor and oppressed people to offer them encouragement and consolation; the latter teaches middle-class young people, guiding them in the knowledge of wisdom and encouraging them to avoid poverty and strive for good positions in society. Tcherikover's comparison is most illuminating. It shows that the perception of reality expressed by an apocalyptic writer is not shared by all members of the community. Others in the same society may have a divergent perception of the situation. This observation serves two purposes in particular: first, it helps to balance the feelings and perceptions of the person under stress and oppression, and second, it guides the reader to moderate the apocalyptic perspective with the sage's viewpoint. Sirach serves as a corrective to the Epistle of Enoch.[20]

3. The book of Daniel

The name of Daniel was associated, during the Babylonian exile, with a legendarily wise and righteous man. To him stories and visions were attributed, some of which are preserved in Hebrew and Aramaic in the book of Daniel.[21] Chapters 1–6 were probably written in Babylon during the Hellenistic period before the reign of Antiochus IV Epiphanes (175–163 B.C.E.), and chapters 7–12 were composed in Judea in the years between Antiochus IV's return from his second military campaign against Egypt (167 B.C.E.) and his death in 163 B.C.E. The author or authors who composed these last chapters and edited the previous ones for inclusion in the book probably belonged to the group of wise teachers (*maskîlîm*) mentioned in Dan 11:33, 35; 12:3.[22]

The events that motivated the composition of Daniel 7–12 and the final compilation of the entire book are narrated in Daniel and in 1 and 2 Maccabees.[23] The dominant figure in the narrative is the oppressive ruler Antiochus IV. His cruelty and hostility toward Jerusalem were probably motivated by the rebellious resistance of the city under the influence of an anti-Seleucid party.[24] Antiochus's

---

[20] See Nickelsburg, "Social Aspects," 651.

[21] See John J. Collins, "Daniel, Book of," *ABD* 2:29–36; *The Apocalyptic Vision of the Book of Daniel* (HSM 16; Missoula: Scholars Press, 1977); Nickelsburg, *Jewish Literature*, 83–95.

[22] The identification of this group is controverted. Tcherikover (*Hellenistic Civilization*, 197) identifies them with the *ḥasîdîm*, who, according to him, were important scribes and interpreters of the Torah. Collins maintains, on the other hand, that the *maskîlîm* of Daniel practiced a wisdom that made them able to interpret mysterious dreams and signs. More than just a proverbial and legal wisdom, they practiced a mantic wisdom. Those who composed the first six chapters of Daniel would have been the ancestors of the *maskîlîm*. These, in their turn, fashioned the final composition of the book. See Collins, *Apocalyptic Vision*, 55–59.

[23] Dan 11; 1 Macc 1:10–6:17; 2 Macc 4:7–9:29.

[24] Tcherikover, *Hellenistic Civilization*, 186–96.

army intervened twice, first in 169 and again in 167 B.C.E., to subdue the rebellion; both military actions resulted in unrestrained killing and plunder.[25] In 167 B.C.E., to keep control over the city, Antiochus garrisoned Syrian troops, granting them residence rights (*katoikia*, 1 Mac 1:38).[26] This measure entailed new taxes, confiscation of property, and desecration of the temple by foreign worship. These abuses must have furthered the opposition and increased the religious hostility against the Seleucid regime. In response to the aggravated resistance, Antiochus issued a decree of prohibition against any practice of Jewish religion. In December 167 B.C.E., the king sent a delegate to Jerusalem to execute the decree, "to compel the Jews to forsake the laws of their ancestors and no longer to live by the laws of God; also to pollute the temple of Jerusalem and to call it the temple of Olympian Zeus" (2 Macc 6:1–2). Prohibited by the decree were the observance of the Sabbath, the celebration of Jewish feasts, and the rite of circumcision. In addition, the sacred books were burned and pagan altars erected (1 Macc 1:44–49). One of the new altars was dedicated to the Phoenician god *Baʿal šamen* ("the lord of heaven") and was built on the altar of burnt offerings. This action is described as the "desolating sacrilege" (Dan 11:31; 1 Macc 1:54).[27] The book of Daniel describes the attitude and actions of Antiochus in several passages:

> He shall speak words against the Most High,
> shall wear out the holy ones of the Most High,
> and shall attempt to change the sacred seasons and the law;
> and they shall be given into his power for a time, two times, and half a time.
> (Dan 7:25)

> He shall make sacrifice and offering cease;
> and in their place shall be an abomination that desolates. (9:27b)

> Forces sent by him shall occupy and profane the temple and fortress.
> They shall abolish the regular burnt offering
> and set up the abomination that makes desolate. (11:31)

> He shall exalt himself and consider himself greater than any god
> and shall speak horrendous things against the God of gods. (11:36)

---

[25] See 1 Macc 1:20–40; 2 Macc 5:11–26. According to the indication given in Dan 11:28, 30–31 and 1 Macc 1:20–28, 29–40, Antiochus IV attacked Jerusalem two times: after his first campaign against Egypt in 169 B.C.E., and the second time, after the second Egyptian campaign, in 167 B.C.E..

[26] By virtue of the institution of the *katoikia*, resident troops were entitled to citizenship in the city *(polis)*, with the consequent right to express their opinions in all the questions of civic life, even in religious matters. At the same time, because they were an occupying army, they could confiscate properties for their military or personal use, and they imposed taxes. See Tcherikover, *Hellenistic Civilization*, 186–96.

[27] The "desolating sacrilege," in Hebrew *šiqqûṣ mĕšômem* (Dan 11:31), is a deliberate deformation of *Baʿal šamen* to designate Zeus Olympios, whose statue Antiochus IV erected in the temple (1 Macc 1:54; see Matt 24:15). See L. Hartmann and A. DiLella, "Daniel," *NJBC* 417.

The book of Daniel emphasizes the religious aspects of the persecution against the Jewish community. But the persecution went beyond religious matters. It attacked the very existence of a people for whom religion and national identity were intimately bound. The text sees in the oppressive king, claiming divine honors, a representative of the primordial monster, who dares to challenge the sovereignty of the Most High and threatens to destroy the national and religious identity of the chosen people. The book attempts to deliver a message of hope and consolation to the oppressed community. To this effect, it resorts to the prophetic argument that the powers of the earth have a limited number of days, fixed by God, and will then be destroyed and replaced by God's kingdom.

The book employs the pattern of a sequence of kingdoms.[28] It is important here to distinguish between Daniel as a seer and Daniel as the book or author. As a seer, Daniel is a person of the past who envisions the consecutive kingdoms, which will rule the world until the end of time. As a seer, he is at the beginning of the sequence of kingdoms, contemporary to the first kingdom, and he predicts the doom of all the kingdoms seen in the vision, with special emphasis on the last, which is the oppressor of the community contemporary with the author. Along with the destruction of the oppressing power, the seer offers the assurance that the kingdom of God will be established on earth. By a literary fiction, Daniel the seer is made to live during the sixth century B.C.E. and to foresee the terrible suffering of the believing community under the rule of Antiochus IV. The purpose of such a prediction is to nurture in the community of the author's own day a strong sense of trust in the Most High as the supreme power who has everything under his control and guides history for the good of his people. It also reinforces the hope of the people because it assures them that they live in the last days, when the power of evil will be completely destroyed.

The author draws the pattern of the sequence of kingdoms from the Hellenistic environment, where the scheme was employed as a device for political criticism of the Macedonian kings, suggesting their impending collapse.[29] He draws a very

---

[28] The outline of the kingdoms occurs three times in the book of Daniel. It appears for the first time in the dream of the great statue (Dan 2:1–49); the second, in the vision of the four beasts (Dan 7:1–28); and the third, in the vision of the ram and the he-goat (Dan 8:1–27). These passages are parallel; they refer to the same sequence of kingdoms: the Babylonian, the Median, the Persian, and the Hellenistic. In the first two passages, the list is complete; the last, on the other hand, lacks the Babylonian kingdom. This omission is understood because the vision takes place in Susa, when the Babylonian kingdom was already extinct.

[29] The sequence of four periods is not original to Daniel. It already appears in Hesiod under the form of four eras symbolized by metals. But in the Hellenistic period, the scheme was applied to the kingdoms and was used as political propaganda against the Macedonian regimes, sending out the message that the Macedonians would succumb to extinction. Three documents from the ancient world demonstrate this sort of use. One is a fragment of the Roman chronicler Emilio Sura; another is the fourth *Sibylline Oracle* (*Sib. Or.* 4:49–101); and the third is the Persian document *Bahman Yasht*. This political use of the pattern illuminates its presence in Daniel. See Collins, *Apocalyptic Vision*, 36–43; J. W. Swain, "The Theory of the Four Monarchies: Opposition History under the Roman Empire," *CP* 35 (1940): 1–21; Hengel, *Judaism*, 1:181–83.

attractive scheme within the milieu of political resistance, adding to it mythological color and eschatological thrust. The earthly kingdoms are depicted as ferocious beasts, avatars of the primordial monster—consecutive avatars, each crueler than the previous, with the last the embodiment of the greatest cruelty that this world can produce. It fulfills the measure of iniquity allowed by the Most High and thus represents a sign of the end of this world and the beginning of God's kingdom.[30]

The intervention of God to liberate his oppressed people is a matter of justice; thus the text says that God comes "to bring in everlasting righteousness" (9:24), exercising a liberating justice that destroys the enemy and establishes the people in the position best suiting the order and design of the Most High. This justice goes beyond what the people deserve and creates a new reality through God's pure and generous goodness: the people who now suffer oppression under earthly powers will share the power of the eternal kingdom in a heavenly existence.

The vindication of the oppressed believers is symbolized by the exaltation of "one like a son of man" (7:13–14), which is probably not merely a corporate symbol but an angelic figure who represents the believers—a heavenly counterpart of the persecuted ones whose exaltation signifies their vindication and gives assurance of their triumph.[31]

Scholars have debated the identity of those vindicated by the liberating action of God. Daniel 7:13–14 says that "one like a son of man" is given eternal dominion over all peoples and nations. On the other hand, Dan 7:18, 22 identifies those who are given dominion as "the holy ones of the Most High." Likewise, Dan 7:27 states that "the kingship and dominion . . . shall be given to the people of the holy ones of the Most High." On the basis of these texts, many identify the "one like a son of man" with "the people of the holy ones of the Most High," understanding "people" to include the whole Jewish nation. This identification, however, is controversial, because, as Collins says, Daniel 11 distinguishes three groups within the Jewish people: "those who violate the covenant" (11:32), "the wise interpreters" *(maśkîlîm),* and the "many" *(rabbîm)* instructed by the "wise interpreters" (11:34).[32] The first group are the evildoers who, together with all the wicked of the earth, will "continue to act wickedly" (12:4, 10b) and therefore will be subject to everlasting contempt (12:2). Concerning the wise, some "shall fall by the sword and flame," and some "shall suffer captivity and plunder" (11:33–35), but all of them will be vindicated and "shall shine like the brightness of the sky . . . like the stars forever and ever" (12:3). And "the many," following the wise, will be refined and purified through suffering and then vindicated forever (11:35; 12:10a). In saying "many,"

---

[30] The sequence of four mythologized kingdoms became traditional in apocalyptic literature and was applied to the imperial power of Rome in the *Sibylline Oracles* (4:49–101), in *4 Ezra* (12:10), and in Revelation (13:1–2). The last book combined the four beasts of Daniel 7 to designate the Roman Empire.

[31] This is the opinion, among others, of Collins, *Apocalyptic Imagination,* 102–4; André Lacocque, *The Book of Daniel* (Atlanta: John Knox, 1979), 133; R. Hammer, *The Book of Daniel* (Cambridge: Cambridge University Press, 1979), 79; C. Rowland, *The Open Heaven: A Study of Apocalyptic in Judaism and Early Christianity* (New York: Crossroad, 1982), 178–82.

[32] Collins, *Apocalyptic Vision,* 166–79.

the author obviously speaks of a great multitude among the Jewish people that will remain faithful. This faithful multitude, together with the wise, makes up the people of the holy ones who will receive the eternal kingdom.

The book of Daniel speaks of the resurrection of the wise and their followers (12:1–3) but does not directly describe the restoration of Israel as a nation. It is true that this book focuses its attention on the vindication and exaltation of the wise and their followers. This does not, however, imply that Israel would be reduced to individuals or groups taken from this world and absorbed into the heavenly realm, with a loss of their identity as the children of Israel, the people of God.

A statement in the prophecy of the seventy weeks (9:20–27) contradicts this opinion of loss of identity, and the statement is not unique. It finds a parallel in the visions of the great statue and the four beasts. In the story of the prophecy of the seventy weeks, the angel Gabriel tells Daniel that his prayer has been heard and that now he has come to give him wisdom and understanding:

> Consider the word and understand the vision: "Seventy weeks are decreed for your people and your holy city: to finish the transgression, to put an end to sin, and to atone for iniquity, to bring in everlasting righteousness, to seal both vision and prophet, and to anoint a most holy place." (9:23–24)

Gabriel's explanation refers to the just action of God that will restore Israel, her city and temple. This action will produce the final and permanent restoration of God's community in fulfillment of the expectations of justice and peace, of which the prophets dreamed.

A similar promise of restoration is present in the story of the great statue of Nebuchadnezzar's dream and in the vision of the four beasts. The story tells of a stone that struck the statue and became a great mountain, filling the whole earth (2:35). In Daniel's interpretation, the mountain that filled the earth is the kingdom that God will establish on it, an indestructible and eternal kingdom composed of faithful Jews (2:44–45). The vision of the four beasts, in turn, shows the figure of one like a son of man to whom eternal and universal dominion is given so that all peoples, nations, and languages should serve him (7:13–14). The angel interprets the meaning of this figure: "The kingship and dominion and the greatness of the kingdom under the whole heaven shall be given to the people of the holy ones of the Most High . . . and all dominions shall serve and obey them" (7:27).

According to these texts, the faithful Israel will be the community of the final and everlasting kingdom of God on earth, with Jerusalem as the capital and the temple of God in it. Then Israel will enjoy the justice, peace, prosperity, and happiness the prophets dreamed about. How can this expectation be combined with the promise that "the wise" and "the many" will be exalted in heaven? The book does not explain. But in saying that "the wise" will shine as stars in the sky (12:3), it seems to suggest that they will rule over the earth just as the stars, in ancient belief, guided earthly events. The suggestion seems to include the idea that, in the fulfillment of God's kingdom on earth, the martyrs will occupy a special position of authority. The book of Daniel appears to have an image of the new earth similar to that in the book of Wisdom (studied in our last chapter). There are, however, some differences. While Daniel speaks of resurrection, the book of Wisdom seems rather to believe in the immortality of the soul. Furthermore, in the book of Wisdom, the whole people of God is in heaven, so that from there they are able to rule over all the nations on earth. In Daniel, instead, the people of God will have an earthly kingdom with Jerusalem as its capital. In it the martyrs seem to have special power to rule, exercised from heaven. In Daniel, it is not clear whether humanity will have an end terminating its existence on earth or will continue on a renewed earth without end. But in any circumstances, the faithful who die will rise and be glorified to share the kingdom in fullness.

The book of Daniel emphasizes that the destruction of the enemies is an exclusive action of God. The stone that struck the statue "was cut out, not by human hands" (2:34, 45). The oppressor king "shall be broken, and not by human hands" (8:25). On the other hand, "the wise" *(maskîlîm),* whose ideas the author shares, do not adopt a position of militant resistance as the Maccabees and the Hasideans did (1 Macc 2:42). They, rather, suffer persecution as servants of the Lord "so that they may be refined, purified, and cleansed" (Dan 11:35; 12:10), and teach the true understanding of the Scripture and the visions concerning the end of time (11:33; 12:10). They do offer positive resistance to the ideology and purpose of the persecutor, but it is not militant resistance; they do not rise up in arms, do not fight. The battle is carried out by the heavenly powers, by God and Michael, the great prince, the protector of the chosen people (12:1). The *maskîlîm* prepare themselves through suffering to be transformed into heavenly beings.[33] But they encourage people to continue rejecting the ideology of the overwhelming earthly power that oppresses them and to lead a life in contrast to the surrounding world. They are not apolitical mystics who seek only individual salvation through personal union with God. In addition to individual vindication, they foster a strong hope in the renewal of the faithful people on earth. They long for a flourishing community on a transformed earth, sharing the power of God's kingdom, with Jerusalem as the capital. Their longing both attests to the human drive for justice and happiness and witnesses to the belief that God is committed to the elect—not simply that they obtain their longing in the afterlife but that they also see justice flourishing on earth.

4. The Book of the Similitudes (*1 En.* 37–71)

This book, containing an introduction, three similitudes, and a twofold epilogue, was probably composed near the beginning of the first century C.E.[34] It

---

[33] Ibid., 205–10.
[34] For this study, see John J. Collins, "The Heavenly Representative: The 'Son of Man' in the Similitudes of Enoch," in *Ideal Figures in Ancient Judaism: Profiles and Paradigms* (ed. John J. Collins and George W. E. Nickelsburg; SBLSCS 12; Chico, Calif.: Scholars Press, 1980), 111–33; *Jewish Literature,* 214–23; *Resurrection,* 70–78; Collins, *Apocalyptic Imagination,* 142–54.

deals with visions that Enoch experienced during an ascent to heaven, assisted by an angelic interpreter. The visions relate to the transcendent and heavenly realm and the impending judgment of humanity, especially the fate of the righteous and the wicked.

A characteristic feature of apocalyptic literature is that earthly events are homologous to heavenly ones and, moreover, the heavenly events predetermine the earthly ones. Hence, it is very important to shed light on the darkness in which the righteous suffer on earth through the revelation of the otherworldly reality about the fates of the righteous and the wicked. The revelation concerns two groups and a central figure: the righteous, the wicked, and the Son of Man.

The righteous are oppressed and persecuted on earth, living in an iniquitous world (*1 En.* 47:1, 4). Unlike the wicked, the righteous are powerless people, without any social and political influence. They belong to the social category of the poor and dejected. But they "believe in the name of the Lord of the Spirits forever and ever" (43:4). They reject the wickedness of the world and lead their life according to the will of God. In their anguish and oppression, they cry to the Lord and receive the comforting assurance that their cry is heard in heaven (47:1, 4) and that they will be saved (48:7). After God's vindication, they will rest from the oppression of the wicked (53:7), enjoying the heavenly dwelling places with the angels (41:2; 51:4) and the pleasures of a renewed earth (45:5). The second similitude thus says,

> On that day, I shall cause my Elect One to dwell among them,
> I shall transform heaven and make it a blessing of light forever.
> I shall transform the earth and make it a blessing,
> and cause my Elect One to dwell in her.
> Then those who have committed sin and crime shall not set foot in her.
> For in peace I have looked upon my righteous ones and given them mercy. (45:4–5)

In contrast to the righteous, the wicked "commit sin and crime" (45:5). They are "kings and mighty ones" (46:4), "judges of the stars of heaven" (46:7), and "mighty landowners" (48:8; 62:1). All the wicked share something in common: they reject "the name of the Lord of the Spirit," and "their power depends on their wealth" (46:7), unjustly acquired (63:10). "They manifest all their deeds in oppression" (46:7), and in the judgment, they will be punished "on account of their deeds which (they performed) as messengers of Satan" (54:6, 10). Then they will no longer oppress the righteous (50:4) and will be "cast into the oppressive Sheol" (63:10).

The Son of Man, in turn, is a heavenly individual, looking like a human being (46:1, 3), associated with both the angelic world and the community of the suffering righteous. To him belongs righteousness (46:3). He is "the Righteous and the Elected one" (53:6; see 48:6; 49:2, 4; 62:1). He is the heavenly representative of the oppressed community, the heavenly embodiment of its hope. He is the revealer and the eschatological judge who will vindicate the suffering righteous and condemn the oppressive wicked.

In this context, justice is multifaceted. On the one hand, it opposes the oppression and iniquity exercised by the mighty ones, with their unbridled ambition for power. It is thus contrary to the attitude of those who put their trust only in wealth and power and reject the rule of life established by the Most High. On the other hand, justice is identified with the attitude of the righteous, who reject the views and conduct of this world and abide by their commitment to the Lord of Spirits. Furthermore, justice is identified with the conduct of the Son of Man, who, on the one hand, punishes the wicked and, on the other, vindicates the righteous, granting them participation in the glory of the angels and exclusive possession of the renewed earth (45:4–5).

The author of the Similitudes develops Daniel's figure of "the one like a son of man." In Daniel 7, the performance of "the one like a son of man" (Dan 7:13–14) is rather passive: his performance is limited to receiving the power of God's kingdom, whereas the Ancient One is he who judges and destroys the evil kingdoms. In the Similitudes, however, the Son of Man is clearly identified as an active individual. He sits on the throne of glory, passes judgment (*1 En.* 61:7), and removes the kings and the mighty ones (46:4). He reveals the divine wisdom (48:7) and is the "staff for the righteous," "the light for the Gentiles," and "the hope of those who are sick" (48:4). He will dwell among the believers in the transformed world (45:6). He is the messiah of the Lord of the Spirits (48:10). It is worth noting that Daniel's figure of "the one like a son of man" has two parallel developments: one occurs in the Book of the Similitudes and the other in the Synoptic Gospels—probably one independent of the other but moving in a similar direction, to an individual messianic figure.

The author of the Similitudes, in his role as apocalyptic thinker, is convinced that the present world cannot be mended because of its deep and pervasive wickedness. His hope rests in the restorative power of God and God's justice, which materializes in the person of the Son of Man in heaven as representative of the oppressed community. The Son of Man embodies the justice and glory the community longs for, and is the guarantee of its vindication, anchored in heaven. He will secure justice and peace in the new world.

5. The second book of Esdras

This book, called also the Apocalypse of Esdras (and its chs. 3–14 also called 4 Ezra), was written after the destruction of the temple by the Romans (70 C.E.) and probably during the reign of Domitian (81–96 C.E.).[35] It includes seven visions, narrated in a dialogue between Esdras and an angel. The basic themes are God's justice and Israel's fate.

---

[35] For a study of *4 Ezra*, see Michael E. Stone, "Esdras, Second Book," *ABD* 2:611–14; "The Way of the Most High and the Injustice of God in 4 Ezra," in *Knowledge of God in the Graeco-Roman World* (ed. R. van den Broeck et al.; Leiden: Brill, 1988), 132–42; repr. in *Selected Studies in Pseudepigrapha and Apocrypha* (SVTP 9; Leiden: Brill, 1991), 348–58; *Fourth Ezra* (Hermeneia; Minneapolis: Fortress, 1990); Collins, *Apocalyptic Imagination*, 156–69; A. L. Thompson, *Responsibility of Evil in the Theodicy of 4 Ezra* (SBLDS 29; Missoula: Scholars Press, 1977).

The visions can be interpreted in different ways. W. Harnisch and E. Brandenburger see Esdras as a skeptical Jew used by the writer as a mechanism to highlight the message conveyed through the angel.[36] M. E. Stone, in turn, reads the book as the odyssey of Esdras, who, in the fourth vision, embraces the message of the angel.[37] Following Stone, I understand Esdras as a spokesman for the heartbroken Jews after the war against the Romans (66–70 C.E.), which ended with the destruction of Jerusalem and its temple. In the aftermath, Judaism was in a critical situation: the temple was in ruins; Jerusalem had been destroyed and occupied by a Roman legion; most of the population was dead, one part of the survivors departed enslaved, and the other, though left in the land, was carrying the stigma of pain and humiliation; and the temple tax traditionally collected to pay for the upkeep of the temple of Jerusalem was now being collected to support the temple of Jupiter Capitolinus in Rome. The bitterness of this situation is reflected in Esdras's words:

> our sanctuary has been laid waste, our altar thrown down, our temple destroyed; our harp has been laid low, our song has been silenced, and our rejoicing has been ended; the light of our lampstand has been put out, the ark of our covenant has been plundered, our holy things have been polluted, and the name by which we are called has been almost profaned; our children have suffered abuse, our priests have been burned to death, our Levites have gone into exile, our virgins have been defiled, and our wives have been ravished; our righteous men have been carried off, our little ones have been cast out, our young men have been enslaved and our strong men made powerless. And, worst of all, the seal of Zion has been deprived of its glory, and given over into the hands of those that hate us. (*4 Ezra* 10:21–23)

In the visions, Esdras acts as a witness of this bitter situation; he expresses his pain and frustration in a long series of questions. He asks in the first vision "why Israel has been given over to the Gentiles in disgrace; why the people whom you loved has been given over to godless tribes, and the law of our ancestors has been brought to destruction and the written covenants no longer exist" (4:23). These impassioned questions are more than mere lamentations. They are uttered within the framework of a legal complaint. Indeed, after stating that what distresses him is the painful contrast between the desolation of Zion and the wealth of Babylon (3:1–3), Esdras addresses God and recites his mighty deeds (3:4–27). The purpose of this recital is not to praise God, as the psalmist did (Ps 136:5–25); nor is it to indict Israel because of its ungratefulness, as Ezekiel did (Ezek 20:1–32). The purpose is, rather, to establish God's responsibility for the events of history. Once God's responsibility has been identified, Esdras poses more pressing questions,

---

[36] See Wolfgang Harnisch, *Verhängnis und Verheissung der Geschichte* (FRLANT 97; Göttingen: Vandenhoeck & Ruprecht, 1969); Egon Brandenburger, *Die Verborgenheit Gottes im Weltgeschehen* (Zürich: Theologisches Verlag, 1981).

[37] This approach, introduced by H. Gunkel, is developed by Stone and is followed, among others, by Collins. See H. Gunkel, "Das vierte Buch Esra," in *Die Apokryphen und Pseudepigraphen des Alten Testaments* (ed. E. Kautzsch; 2 vols.; Tübingen: J. C. B. Mohr, 1900), 2:331–401; Stone, *Fourth Ezra*, 14–38; Collins, *Apocalyptic Imagination*, 195–209.

making serious charges against God's justice (*4 Ezra* 3:28–36). The charges may be summarized in the idea that God is patient with the godless but destroys God's own people (3:30). Esdras may agree that all are sinners, but he cannot understand why, while Israel is bitterly punished, the nations that are more sinful than the chosen people enjoy prosperity.

Esdras's questions to God remind the reader of God's questions addressed to Job (Job 38:4–27; 41:1–14). In Job, God questions a human being; in Esdras, a human being questions God and requests an answer, and his questions are categorical and incriminating. Because of their legal character, they are reminiscent of God's lawsuit against Israel in the prophetic writings (e.g., Jer 2:5–11), but there is a difference: the author of 2 Esdras (that is, the whole of *4–6 Ezra*) reverses the direction of the legal process. While the prophets mentioned God's mighty acts in favor of Israel in order to charge it with ingratitude, Esdras recites God's mighty acts to bring a charge against God, summoning him before his own tribunal. The one who was accused is now the plaintiff and accuser.

In his dialogue with the angel, Esdras begins with a harsh attitude but slowly moderates his stance. He does not find it difficult to admit the limitations of human knowledge, but he thinks that this does not apply in his case because what he wants to know lies within the purview of human knowledge. He wants to know something pivotal in the understanding of the meaning of human existence, namely, how God runs the world (*4 Ezra* 4:12). On the limitations of human knowledge, Esdras agrees with the angel in rejecting the idea that one may obtain revelation on the netherworld or paradise through mystical journeys or visions (4:5–9). In this the author takes a position contrary to the common current in the apocalyptic tradition.[38] Esdras admits likewise that the course of history is predetermined by God and that, in order to understand the sowing and the growth, one has to see the harvest (4:26–32).

In the second vision, Esdras is more composed and less accusatory. Now his questions seek knowledge and understanding (5:34), and he sees the destruction of Zion from another angle. His focus is no longer on the question of evil and justice within the scope of divine providence in the world but on the destiny of Israel in light of its divine election. Thus he offers this reflection to God: "If you really hate your people, they should be punished at your own hands" (5:30).

God asks Esdras if he loves Israel more than her maker does. In response, Esdras acknowledges that he does not love Israel as much as God loves her (5:32–33). Insisting on this, God says to Esdras, "You cannot discover my judgment, or the goal of the love that I have promised to my people" (5:40). With these words, Esdras understands that, as far as Israel is concerned, the weights of strict justice do not play any role; what matters is the weight of God's love. Esdras has to reinterpret his idea of justice, which he had conceived in the sense of strict distribution or retribution. He begins to understand that justice has become an instrument of God's love, ready to restore God's beloved people.

---

[38] See Stone, "The Way," 136–37.

In the third vision, Esdras is still impatient in his inquiry. Now his emphasis is on the theme of election and love. Stressing the idea of election, he addresses God: "If the world has indeed been created for us, why do we not possess our world as an inheritance? How long will this be so?" (6:59). In the course of the dialogue, Esdras understands that the promised inheritance does not belong to this world but one can have access to it through the sufferings of this life (7:1–18). Esdras is exhorted to consider not what is present but what is to come, and God reveals to him the coming of a temporary messianic kingdom: four hundred years of peace and justice on earth. At the end of those years, the Messiah will die, and humanity with him (7:28–29). Then will come the resurrection of the dead and final judgment. The righteous will share the splendor of the glory of the Most High forever, and the wicked will be thrown into the furnace of hell. The idea of a temporary messianic kingdom had appeared already in *1 En.* 91:12–17 and is shared by Rev 20:4–6.

After hearing from the angel that God made this world for the sake of many but the future one for the sake of only a few (8:1), Esdras asks God to be compassionate with his creation and adds, "O Lord, your righteousness and goodness will be declared, when you are merciful to those who have no store of good works" (8:36). In his argument, Esdras appeals to the power of God's saving justice, which does not consider what one deserves but the love God has for his creatures.[39] In his appeal, Esdras says, "Spare your people and have mercy on your inheritance, for you have mercy on your own creation" (8:45). In response, God reveals what God has in store for the righteous: an open paradise, the tree of life, a wide store of goods, the eternal city, rewarding rest, and perfect goodness and wisdom (8:52).

In the fourth vision, Esdras reaches the climax of his conversion and himself comforts the desolate Zion: "Shake off your great sadness and lay aside your many sorrows, so that the Mighty One may be merciful to you again, and the Most High may give you rest, a respite from your troubles" (10:42). The compassionate justice stemming from the Creator's love is ready to restore his beloved one.

Esdras's new attitude and mission develop through three visions: the woman in grief, the eagle, and the man from the sea. The vision of a woman in grief who suddenly is transformed into a glorious city with massive foundation (9:38–10:59) symbolizes the complete transformation of Esdras himself from skeptic to believer. The city is the future, restored Jerusalem, and Esdras becomes its herald. In the vision of the eagle (11:1–12:51), a lion denounces the eagle's injustice, oppression, and cruelty, and then the eagle is burned. The eagle, which is a reinterpretation of the fourth beast of Daniel 7, represents Rome, and the lion stands for the Messiah, the one "who will deliver in mercy the remnant of my people" (12:34). Through the destruction of the eagle, "the whole earth will be relieved . . . then it can hope for justice and the compassion of him who made it"

---

[39] This idea of justice is present in the prophets and Psalms, and Paul develops it particularly in his letter to the Romans.

(11:46). In the vision of the man from the sea (13:1–58), the Messiah is described like the figure of a man coming up out the heart of the sea to deliver the world and direct those who are left (13:26). Standing on the top of Mount Zion, he will judge the nations and gather the tribes that have been dispersed (13:35–40).

Through these three visions, Esdras changed his skepticism into faith and became the herald of consolation: "The Mighty One has not forgotten you in your struggle" (12:48). In the process, Esdras recovered the hope of the prophets and revived in himself the faith of the apocalyptic seers. While fostering the apocalyptic vision of the destiny of humanity to an eternal happiness, Esdras encourages people to persevere in their struggle for a better world on earth. In his vision, justice and peace on earth are part of the messianic expectation.

Conclusion

The five texts considered in this chapter have a common purpose: to encourage the oppressed community and revive its faith and hope for the future. They all strengthen the expectation of an impending action of God's justice, which will punish the oppressors and vindicate the oppressed. They describe a future when wickedness and injustice will be exterminated, death will be overcome by glorious resurrection, and the risen righteous will share the heavenly existence. These apocalyptic writers are not apolitical mystics, interested only in individual salvation through a personal union with God, to be fulfilled in the afterlife. They nurture a communitarian perspective, thinking themselves as part of a community longing for its realization in a renewed earth, in the new Jerusalem.

The apocalyptic writers do not think it possible to change present society because, in their perception, it is entirely overcome by evil powers. They are convinced of the need for divine intervention to change the created world radically, confident that God has prepared a new earth for the righteous now being oppressed. Distressed by the delay of God's intervention, however, they cry, "How long, O Lord," echoing the lament of Habakkuk and the psalmists. *Fourth Ezra* resumes the cry of lamentation in a particularly distressed manner. The cry increases over generations and is spread over the whole earth while the long-awaited justice remains elusive. Nevertheless, the cry of the believers is animated by an unshakable trust in God that helps the community keep its identity as the people of God in the midst of pain and oppression.

The message of the apocalyptic writers, valid for analogous circumstances, instills trust in God's justice and faithfulness and nurtures the conviction that God is ready to reassert his sovereignty over his created world in order to reshape it for the benefit of God's faithful ones. Their message is a call for believers to persevere and keep their identity under persecution. It is a call to grow and be refined through suffering, urging the chosen people to give testimony of their faith and hope in words and deeds.

The oft repeated message promising the impending coming of God's kingdom to vindicate his oppressed believers after a seemingly endless succession of persecutions shows that the essential point of the apocalyptic proclamation is not the actual and immediate destruction of the present world but the assurance that God is present in human history, has events under his control, and guides them for the benefit of his people. The purpose of the insistent announcement of the immediate intervention of God's justice is to urge people to assume or renew their commitment of faithfulness to God and maintain their faith until death.

The apocalyptic perspective should be balanced with the prophetic and sapiential viewpoints. In fact, the book of Daniel was accepted into the canon together with the prophetic and Wisdom books. The negative aspect of the apocalyptic writers concerning human society must be mitigated by the view of the prophets, who worked within the society in order to transform it, and the sages, who, engaged in dialogue with the world, drew their knowledge from human experience and treated society as the normal locale for the human person to develop.

Bibliography

Black, Matthew. *The Book of Enoch or I Enoch: A New English Translation*. Studia in Veteris Testamenti pseudepigraphica. Leiden: Brill, 1985.

Brandenburger, Egon. *Die Verborgenheit Gottes im Weltgeschehen*. Zurich: Theologisches Verlag, 1981.

Charlesworth James H., ed. *Old Testament Pseudepigrapha*. 2 vols. Garden City: Doubleday, 1983–1985.

Collins, John J. *The Apocalyptic Imagination: An Introduction to the Jewish Matrix of Christianity*. New York: Crossroad, 1984.

———. *The Apocalyptic Vision of the Book of Daniel*. Harvard Semitic Monographs 16. Missoula: Scholars Press, 1977.

———. "Daniel, Book of." Pages 29–36 in vol. 2 of *Anchor Bible Dictionary*. Edited by D. N. Freedman. 6 vols. New York: Doubleday, 1992.

———. "The Heavenly Representative: The 'Son of Man' in the Similitudes of Enoch." Pages 111–33 in *Ideal Figures in Ancient Judaism: Profiles and Paradigms*. Edited by John J. Collins and George W. E Nickelsburg. Society of Biblical Literature Septuagint and Cognate Studies 12. Chico, Calif.: Scholars Press, 1980.

Fiedler, M. H. "Dikaiosyne in der diaspora-jüdischen und intertestamentlichen Literatur." *Journal for the Study of Judaism in the Persian, Hellenistic, and Roman Periods* 1 (1970): 120–43.

Gunkel, H. "Das vierte Buch Esra." Pages 331–401 in vol. 2 of *Die Apokryphen und Pseudepigraphen des Alten Testaments*. Edited by E. Kautzch. 2 vols. Tübingen: J. C. B. Mohr, 1900.

Hammer, R. *The Book of Daniel*. Cambridge: Cambridge University Press, 1979.

Hanson, Paul D. "Apocalypses and Apocalypticism." Pages 279–82 in vol. 1 of *Anchor Bible Dictionary*. Edited by D. N. Freedman. 6 vols. New York: Doubleday, 1992.

———. *The Dawn of Apocalyptic*. Philadelphia: Fortress, 1975.
Harnisch, Wolfgang. *Verhängnis und Verheissung der Geschichte*. Forschungen zur Religion und Literatur des Alten und Neuen Testaments 97. Göttingen: Vandenhoeck & Ruprecht, 1969.
Hartmann, L., and A. DiLella. "Daniel." Pages 406–20 in *The New Jerome Biblical Commentary*. Edited by Raymond E. Brown et al. Englewood Cliffs: Prentice Hall, 1990.
Hengel, M. *Jews, Greeks, and Barbarians: Aspects of the Hellenization of Judaism in the Pre-Christian Period*. Translated by J. Bowden. Philadelphia: Fortress, 1980.
———. *Judaism and Hellenism*. Translated by J. Bowden. 2 vols. Philadelphia: Fortress, 1974.
Lacocque, André. *The Book of Daniel*. Atlanta: John Knox, 1979.
Nickelsburg, George W. E. "Apocalyptic and Myth in *1 Enoch* 6–11." *Journal of Biblical Literature* 96 (1977): 383–405.
———. "The Apocalyptic Message of 1 Enoch 92–105." *Catholic Biblical Quarterly* 39 (1977): 309–28.
———. "The Bible Rewritten and Expanded." Pages 89–156 in *Jewish Writings of the Second Temple Period*. Compendia rerum iudaicarum ad Novum Testamentum, sec. 2, vol. 2. Edited by M. E. Stone. Assen: Van Gorcum; Philadelphia: Fortress, 1984.
———. "Enoch, Book of." Pages 508–16 in vol. 2 of *Anchor Bible Dictionary*. Edited by D. N. Freedman. 6 vols. New York: Doubleday, 1992.
———. *Jewish Literature between the Bible and the Mishnah*. Philadelphia: Fortress, 1981.
———. *Resurrection, Immortality, and Eternal Life in Intertestamental Judaism*. Harvard Theological Studies 26. Cambridge: Harvard University Press, 1972.
———. "Riches, the Rich, and God's Judgment in *1 Enoch* 93–105 and the Gospel according to Luke." *New Testament Studies* 25 (1979): 324–44.
———. "Social Aspects of Palestinian Jewish Apocalypticism." Pages 639–54 in *Apocalypticism in the Mediterranean World and the Near East*. Edited by D. Hellholm; Tübingen: J. C. B. Mohr, 1983.
Petersen, David. "Eschatology (OT)." Pages 575–79 in vol. 2 of *Anchor Bible Dictionary*. Edited by D. N. Freedman. 6 vols. New York: Doubleday, 1992.
Rowland, C. *The Open Heaven: A Study of Apocalyptic in Judaism and Early Christianity*. New York: Crossroad, 1982.
Stone, Michael E. *Fourth Ezra*. Hermeneia. Minneapolis: Fortress, 1990.
———. "The Way of the Most High and the Injustice of God in 4 Ezra." Pages 132–42 in *Knowledge of God in the Graeco-Roman World*. Edited by R. van den Broeck et al. Etudes preliminaries aux religions orientales dans l'empire romaine. Leiden: Brill, 1988. Repr. in pages 348–58 of *Selected Studies in Pseudepigrapha and Apocrypha*. Studia in Veteris Testamenti pseudepigraphica 9. Leiden: Brill, 1991.
Swain, J. W. "The Theory of the Four Monarchies: Opposition History under the Roman Empire." *Classical Philology* 35 (1940): 1–21.

Tcherikover, Victor. *Hellenistic Civilization and the Jews.* Translated by S. Applebaum. Philadelphia: Jewish Publication Society, 1959. Repr., Peabody, Mass: Hendrickson, 1999.

Thompson, A. L. *Responsibility of Evil in the Theodicy of 4 Ezra.* Society of Biblical Literature Dissertation Series 29. Missoula: Scholars Press, 1977.

Wacker, Marie-Theres. *Weltordnung und Gericht: Studien zur I Henoch 22.* 2d ed. Forschung zur Bibel 45. Würtzburg: Echter, 1985.

CHAPTER EIGHT

JUSTICE IN THE MINISTRY OF JESUS OF NAZARETH

Introduction

The five preceding chapters examined the idea of justice in the OT and in apocalyptic writings, which was expressed in stories of God's mighty deeds, the oracles of prophets, the sayings of sages, the words of psalmists, and the writings of apocalyptic visionaries. Now we turn to justice in the NT. This chapter is devoted to the historical Jesus, an important subject of discussion among liberation theologians in Latin America, who seek the rehabilitation of the historical Jesus for contemporary theology.[1] The debates of the Jesus Seminar bear witness that the quest for the historical Jesus has received a new impetus in the last two decades.[2]

---

[1] See Jon Sobrino, *Christology at the Crossroads: A Latin American Approach* (trans. J. Drury; Maryknoll: Orbis, 1978), 9–14; J. Sobrino, *Jesus the Liberator: A Historical-Theological View* (trans. P. Burns and F. McDonagh; Maryknoll: Orbis, 1993), 45–63; Juan L. Segundo, *The Historical Jesús of the Synoptics* (trans. J. Drury; Maryknoll: Orbis, 1985), 45–188. These authors categorically affirm the importance of knowing the historical Jesus for liberation theology. In their contention, the historical Jesus experienced a situation very similar to that endured by the peoples of Latin America. They claim that, like the peoples of Latin America, Jesus lived in a land that was at the crossroads of conquering empires, and thus suffered the hardship of political and socio-economic problems, which were provoked and nurtured by oppressive powers. The result was an explosive social situation characterized by the impoverishment of the masses and the enrichment of a few. Contemporary scholars devoting their research to Palestine at the time of Jesus are somewhat critical of this claim: they find fault with the assertions that these theologians make with respect to the socio-political conditions of Galilee in times of Jesus (see Seán Freyne, *Galilee, Jesus, and the Gospels: Literary Approaches and Historical Investigations* [Philadelphia: Fortress, 1988], 15). Biblical exegetes, too, sometimes express reservations regarding the lack of critical academic rigor on the part of liberation theologians when they talk about Jesus of Nazareth. However, it would be fair to say that J. L. Segundo is more apt to use critical academic methodology to identify the words and deeds of the historical Jesus. See Ched Myers, *Binding the Strong Man: A Political Reading of Mark's Story of Jesus* (Maryknoll: Orbis, 1988), 469–72.
[2] See W. R. Telford, "Major Trends and Interpretative Issues in the Study of Jesus," in *Studying the Historical Jesus* (ed. B. Chilton; Leiden: Brill, 1994), 32–74; Raymond E. Brown, *An Introduction to the New Testament* (ABRL; New York: Doubleday, 1996), 817–30.

After an introduction on the quest for the historical Jesus, this chapter proceeds to the analysis of Jesus' historical and social context and a description of Jesus' social background and public ministry. The core of the chapter considers Jesus' expectation of the impending coming of the eschatological kingdom, predicted by prophets and longed for by apocalyptic writers. This analysis includes reflections on the social dimension of the kingdom expected by Jesus, his attitude toward women, and his exhortation against violence. All of these subjects are analyzed from the point of view of the biblical concept of justice.

To begin, it must be emphasized that Jesus was not a leader seeking the political and religious control of his country. He was, rather, a prophet and teacher. As a prophet, he foretold the coming of the eschatological kingdom of God and anticipated it through symbolic actions. And as a teacher, he imparted instructions about the demands of the kingdom on individual persons and society. Although Jesus was not a politician, we may say that his mission had social and political repercussions because, in foretelling the kingdom and teaching its demands, Jesus established principles for a new configuration of society.

1. The quest for the historical Jesus

The quest for the historical Jesus is an inquiry, beginning in the eighteenth century, to reconstruct the life of Jesus through modern critical methods.[3] The inquiry was deemed necessary given the conviction that the NT does not offer a historical treatise on Jesus of Nazareth but is, rather, an apostolic proclamation of Christ as perceived through his disciples' faith. The purpose of the inquiry was to free the life of Jesus from mythological elements and embellishments introduced by the faith of the church. This inquiry was guided from the beginning by rationalistic presuppositions that denied the possibility of the supernatural.

The pioneer in the quest for the historical Jesus was H. S. Reimarus, whose work was published posthumously in 1778.[4] He pictured Jesus as an unsuccessful Jewish revolutionary who failed to consolidate his dream of an earthly messianic kingdom. Several decades later, in 1835, D. F. Strauss also attempted to write a life of Jesus, but ended by confessing that such a project was an impossible task because the Jesus of the Gospels is a mythical interpretation by the faith of the church and very few fragments can be recovered from this mythical transformation.[5]

---

[3] For the history of the problem, with accompanying bibliography, see Brown, *Introduction*, 829–30; Bruce Chilton and C. A. Evans, eds., *Studying the Historical Jesus: Evaluation of the State of Current Research* (NTTS 19; Leiden: Brill, 1994); Marcus J. Borg, *Jesus in Contemporary Scholarship* (Valley Forge: Trinity Press International, 1994), 3–68; N. T. Wright, "Jesus, Quest for the Historical," *ABD* 3:796–802.

[4] Hermann S. Reimarus, *The Goal of Jesus and His Disciples* (trans. George W. Buchanan; Leiden: Brill, 1970).

[5] David F. Strauss, *Das Leben Jesu, kritisch bearbeitet* (2 vols.; Tübingen: C. F. Osiander, 1835–1836).

At the end of the nineteenth century, in 1896, M. Kähler surveyed the research made by scholars since Reimarus, and pointed out that the results of such research were confused, varying from one scholar to another.[6] He concluded that the quest for the historical Jesus was futile because the Gospels did not preserve material conducive to a reconstruction of Jesus' life. Moreover, he insisted that, irrespective of the results of research, the quest for the historical Jesus was irrelevant because what is important for Christian faith and theology is not the Jesus of history but the Christ proclaimed by the apostles.

At the turn of the century, in 1900, A. von Harnack published *What Is Christianity?*—a classical book of liberal Protestantism.[7] In it Harnack pictured the historical Jesus as a teacher of ethical principles and claimed that the essence of Christianity resides in certain ethical truths taught by Jesus: the fatherhood of God, the brotherhood of humanity, and the infinite value of the human soul. Harnack thought it possible to reconstruct a life of Jesus based on the evidence preserved in the Gospels, a view shared by many in the second half of the nineteenth century who wrote books on Jesus' life.

At the beginning of the twentieth century, two scholars, W. Wrede and A. Schweitzer, challenged such presuppositions from different angles. In *The Messianic Secret*, published in 1901, Wrede labeled as unscientific any project that attempted to recover the life of the historical Jesus.[8] In Wrede's view, Mark, like the other gospels, pictures Jesus not as a human being but as a completely divine figure. This divine exaltation was a creation of the early Christian community without any basis in the historical Jesus, who had never made any messianic claim. Schweitzer published *The Mystery of the Kingdom of God* in 1906 as a critique of Harnack.[9] He wrote it under the influence of J. Weiss, who in 1892 had analyzed the concept of the kingdom of God in Jesus' preaching and concluded that Jesus had announced the imminent end of the world.[10] On the basis of this apocalyptic perspective, Schweitzer argued against Harnack's thesis that the historical Jesus was a preacher of timeless ethical principles; in Schweitzer's view, Jesus was a noble but deluded fanatic, convinced that he was the Messiah and certain that his death would bring the present world order to an end.

Some years later, in 1921, R. Bultmann published his very influential work, *The History of the Synoptic Tradition*, which shows the assimilation of ideas from

---

[6] Martin Kähler, *So-Called Historical Jesus and the Historic Biblical Christ* (trans. C. Braaten; Philadelphia: Fortress, 1964; repr., Philadelphia: Fortress, 1988).

[7] Adolf von Harnack, *What Is Christianity?* (trans. T. B. Saunders; Philadelphia: Fortress, 1957; repr., Philadelphia: Fortress, 1986).

[8] William Wrede, *The Messianic Secret* (trans. J.C.G. Greig; Cambridge, U.K.: J. Clarke, 1971).

[9] Albert Schweitzer, *The Quest of the Historical Jesus: A Critical Study of Its Progress from Reimarus to Wrede* (trans. W. Montgomery; New York: Macmillan, 1910; repr., New York: Macmillan, 1964).

[10] Johannes Weiss, *Jesus' Proclamation of the Kingdom of God* (trans. Richard H. Hiers and David L. Holland; Philadelphia: Fortress, 1971).

various provenances.[11] Bultmann adopted Wrede's understanding of the non-messianic character of the historical Jesus and the form-critical insight that the early Christian community provided the creative genius that shaped the messianic figure of Jesus. These presuppositions guided him to declare unfeasible the reconstruction of Jesus' life. Bultmann fostered a syncretistic view of the origin of Christianity, emphasizing the gnostic influence in the NT writings. He owed this view to the history-of-religions school. Moreover, in the background of Bultmann's thought is the constant influence of the Lutheran concept of faith, albeit one imbued by an existentialist perspective—an influence that explains his disinterest in the historical Jesus. For Lutheran's, faith is an act not of the intellect but of the will, by which believers surrender to the word of God. In this approach, what is relevant is not Jesus' teaching but the kerygma. On the other hand, the only history found in the kerygma is the bare fact of the existence and death by crucifixion of Jesus of Nazareth.[12]

At the beginning of the second half of the twentieth century, scholars such as G. Bornkamm and E. Käsemann, in reaction to their mentor Bultmann, gave new momentum to the search for the historical Jesus.[13] For Bornkamm, the Gospels offer access to several genuine historical events, for instance, the call of the Twelve. Käsemann, in his turn, stressed that Christian faith requires a traceable connection between the Christ of faith and the historical Jesus; otherwise Christianity turns into a myth. Historical and literary criteria to discern Jesus' authentic words developed in connection with this approach.[14]

In the wake of the renewal of the quest, scholars have emphasized various aspects of Jesus' life. In the 1970s, the discussion of Jesus concentrated on his revolutionary influence, and it was fashionable to speak of Jesus as a political Zealot. Very influential in this regard was S. G. F. Brandon's *Jesus and the Zealots*.[15] Dur-

---

[11] Rudolph Bultmann, *The History of the Synoptic Tradition* (trans. John Marsh; New York: Harber & Row, 1963).

[12] See John S. Kselman and Ronald D. Witherup, "Modern New Testament Criticism," *NJBC* 1137–38.

[13] Günther Bornkamm, *Jesus of Nazareth* (trans. I. McLuskey, H. McLuskey, and J. M. Robinson; New York: Harper & Row, 1960); Ernst Käsemann, *Essays on New Testament Themes* (trans. W. J. Montague; SBT 41; London: SCM, 1964).

[14] The criteria of authenticity established by this movement are: dissimilarity (where a saying is different from both the Jewish background and the early church); consistency (with other material known to be authentic); multiple attestation (where a saying occurs in different traditions); and linguistic or cultural tests (where the saying appears to fit with Palestinian Judaism of the time). See John Riches, "Jesus, Words of," *ABD* 3:802–4; John P. Meier, *The Roots of the Problem and the Person*, vol. 1 of *A Marginal Jew: Rethinking the Historical Jesus* (New York: Doubleday, 1991), 21–40; J. P. Meier, "Jesus," *NJBC* 1317–18; E. P. Sanders, *Jesus and Judaism* (Philadelphia: Fortress, 1985), 1–58; Ben F. Meyer, *The Aims of Jesus* (London: SCM, 1979), 76–94; Norman Perrin, *Rediscovering the Teaching of Jesus* (New York: Harper & Row, 1967), 39–49.

[15] S. G. F. Brandon, *Jesus and the Zealots: A Study of the Political Factor in Primitive Christianity* (Manchester: Manchester University Press, 1967). For critical reaction, see especially Martin Hengel, *Was Jesus a Revolutionist?* (trans. W. Klassen; Philadelphia: Fortress, 1971); Hengel, *Victory over Violence* (trans. D. E. Green; Philadelphia: Fortress,

ing those years the Zealot model for the study of Jesus of Nazareth was very attractive to various exponents of liberation theology.[16]

The last two decades of the twentieth century have seen a renaissance of interest in Jesus of Nazareth.[17] This renewal encompasses numerous tendencies with their own presuppositions and agendas. We may distinguish two main trends. The first sees Jesus as a wisdom teacher, an itinerant preacher in the style of cynic philosophers (so J. D. Crossan, B. L. Mack, and F. G. Downing).[18] Members of the Jesus Seminar are in this line of thought. The second also regards Jesus as a wisdom teacher, but one in the Jewish tradition, and moreover it emphasizes Jesus' prophetic character. Within this second trend there are two groups. One sees Jesus as a prophet who established parameters to reshape and reorient the community of Israel and who announced the impending coming of the kingdom of God (so R. A. Horsley, J. P. Meier, B. F. Meyer, D. E. Oakman, E. P. Sanders, and G. Theissen).[19] The other group argues that Jesus was indeed a prophet intent on giving a new configuration to society but that he did not announce the imminent coming of the kingdom (M. J. Borg and N. Perrin).[20]

To be sure, the results of this search for the historical Jesus through the application of modern methods are limited and fragmentary, sometimes distorted by antisupernatural bias.[21] In this chapter, the intent is not to offer a reconstruction of Jesus' life but, rather, to evaluate the results of the quest as they impinge on issues of social justice and related matters. To this end, we will consider the position of theologians of liberation and other scholars who claim that Jesus was a revolutionary in the style of the Zealots, and the opinion of those who argue that

---

1973), 45–59; and Hengel, *Christ and Power* (trans. E. R. Kalin; Philadelphia: Fortress, 1977), 15–22; Ernst Bammel and C. F. D. Moule, eds., *Jesus and the Politics of His Day* (Cambridge: Cambridge University Press, 1985); Walter Wink, "Jesus and Revolution: Reflections on S. G. F. Brandon's *Jesus and the Zealots*," *USQR* 25 (1969): 37–59.

[16] Sobrino, *Christology*, 211–13; *The Liberator*, 214–15; Ignacio Ellacuría, *Freedom Made Flesh: The Mission of Christ and His Church* (trans. J. Drury; Maryknoll: Orbis, 1976), 60–68.

[17] See Borg, *Scholarship*, 160–81; Telford, "Major Trends."

[18] See John D. Crossan, *The Historical Jesus: The Life of a Mediterranean Jewish Peasant* (San Francisco: HarperSanFrancisco, 1991); Burton L. Mack, *A Myth of Innocence: Mark and Christian Origins* (Philadelphia: Fortress, 1988); F. Gerald Downing, *The Christ and the Cynics* (Sheffield: JSOT Press, 1998).

[19] Richard A. Horsley, *Jesus and the Spiral of Violence: Popular Jewish Resistance in Roman Palestine* (San Francisco: Harper & Row, 1987); Meier, *A Marginal Jew*, vol. 1: *Rethinking the Historical Jesus*; Ben F. Meyer, *Aims of Jesus*, and "Jesus Christ," *ABD* 3:773–96; Douglas E. Oakman, *Jesus and the Economic Questions of His Day* (SBEC 8; Lewiston, N.Y.: Edwin Mellen, 1986); E. P. Sanders, *Jesus*, and *The Historical Figure of Jesus* (London: Penguin, 1993); Gerd Theissen and Annette Merz, *The Historical Jesus: A Comprehensive Guide* (trans. J. Bowden; Minneapolis: Fortress, 1996); B. D. Ehrman, *Jesus: Apocalyptic Prophet of the New Millennium* (New York: Oxford University Press, 1999).

[20] Marcus J. Borg, *Conflict, Holiness, and Politics in the Teachings of Jesus* (SBEC 5; New York: Edwin Mellen, 1984); M. Borg, "Jesus Christ, The Teaching of," *ABD* 3:804–12; Norman Perrin, *Rediscovering*.

[21] See Brown, *Introduction*, 817–30.

Jesus was not a prophet proclaiming the coming of the kingdom but instead a moral philosopher.

Here the argument is offered that Jesus was both a prophet who announced the impending coming of the kingdom and a wisdom teacher who taught the requirements of the kingdom. It is important to consider the social and historical context of Jesus of Nazareth because, to a large extent, his image is conditioned by his background.

2. The social and historical context of Jesus of Nazareth

Jesus was born in the last years of Herod the Great's reign (37–4 B.C.E.) and spent most of his life in Galilee during Herod Antipas's rule (4 B.C.E.–39 C.E.); he exercised his ministry there, with some incursions into Judea and visits to Jerusalem, dying between 30 and 33 C.E., during the procuratorship of the Roman Pontius Pilate.

During the first century C.E., until the Jewish War against Rome, the political history of Galilee differed from that of Judea, since Galilee continued under the Herodian family's rule. Herod Antipas controlled Galilee until 39 C.E., after which Herod Agrippa ruled it until 44 C.E. Judea, however, did not enjoy such continuity because Archelaus, who succeeded his father, Herod the Great, was removed from office in 6 C.E., after which Judea was ruled by a Roman prefect until 41 C.E.

During the period 41–44 C.E., the whole territory of Palestine fell once more under Herodian rule in the person of Herod Agrippa. After this brief period, however, Palestine fell under Roman procuratorship until the Jewish War (66–70 C.E.). Agrippa's reign, though brief, divided the history of Palestine from the beginning of the first century through 66 C.E. into two periods: the pre-Agrippan and the post-Agrippan. The second period was distinguished by the social and political disturbances that led to the Jewish War. There is widespread belief that the first period (6–41 C.E.), during which Jesus lived, was as restless as the second (44–66 C.E.). This opinion is supported by R. A. Horsley and J. S. Hanson, among others.[22] They argue that during Jesus' lifetime Galilee was unstable. Inner social and economic pressures had impoverished the rural population and led to social unrest; as a result, Galilee was seething with revolutionary agitation.[23] Using this description of the social and political situation, some scholars have constructed an image of Jesus as a revolutionary leader, a prophet of social liberation.

However appealing this construction may be, it is not supported by recent research. J.-A. Morin and D. M. Rhoads, in their studies of Flavius Josephus, pointed out that important elements of social unrest, allegedly attributed to the

---

[22] Richard A. Horsley and J. S. Hanson, *Bandits, Prophets, and Messiahs: Popular Movements at the Time of Jesus* (San Francisco: Harper & Row, 1985), 35.

[23] This idea is found in: John Riches, *Jesus and the Transformation of Judaism* (New York: Seabury Press, 1982), 65–67. So Riches, "Jesus, Words of," 3:189; Sobrino, *Christology*, 12–14, 211–15.

pre-Agrippan period, actually appeared only in the following period.²⁴ Examples of these are the Sicarii and the Zealots. The Sicarii emerged for the first time at the beginning of Felix's procuratorship (52–60 C.E.), while the Zealots arose in Judea during the Jewish War, about 67–68 C.E. More recent studies have confirmed Morin's and Rhoads's research.²⁵ The Sicarii were violent revolutionaries who practiced political assassination, choosing their victims from the Jewish aristocracy. The Zealots were fanatics who had taken an oath to eliminate any person opposing their vision of ritual purity in regard to the law and the temple. Before the Jewish War, the term *zealot* was used for a person who fervently protected God's cause, but during the war, it designated those committed to the violent overthrow of the government.²⁶

The Sepphoris revolt, which scholars often cite as evidence of a state of early unrest in Galilee, actually happened upon the death of Herod the Great in 4 B.C.E. The revolt caused the Romans to intervene, and the legions destroyed the city of Sepphoris. But the new Sepphoris, rebuilt by Herod Antipas with a Jewish and gentile population, always maintained loyalty to Rome, even in the Jewish War.

To the absence of Sicarii and Zealots in the pre-Agrippan period, S. Freyne adds other arguments to support his thesis that this period experienced calm, arguments drawn from his studies on Flavius Josephus. First, he argues against Horsley that social banditry was a phenomenon distinctive to the post-Agrippan period. Social banditry requires the support of a poor and oppressed rural population in order to take reprisals against the exploiting classes in favor of the oppressed. This type of banditry did not exist in Galilee during the pre-Agrippan period. The bandits during this period were common robbers or plunderers living on the frontiers.²⁷

---

²⁴ J.-A. Morin, "Les deux derniers des Douze: Simon le Zélote et Judas Iskariôth," *RB* 80 (1973): 332–58; David M. Rhoads, *Israel in Revolution, 6–74 C.E.: A Political History Based on the Writings of Josephus* (Philadelphia: Fortress, 1976), 97–110. Rhoads reaffirmed the results of his studies in "Zealots," *ABD* 6:1043–54.

²⁵ See Raymond E. Brown, *The Death of the Messiah* (2 vols.; ABRL; New York: Doubleday, 1993), 1:689–73; John J. Collins, "Praeparatio Evangelica in the Work of Martin Hengel," *RelSRev* 15 (1989): 226–28; H. Guevara, *Ambiente político del pueblo judío en tiempos de Jesús* (Academia Christiana 30; Madrid: Cristianidad, 1985). Guevara concludes his analysis thus:

> This study shows the need to establish a clear distinction between the period of the divided Judea (6 B.C.E.–41 C.E.) and the period of the reunited Judea under the Roman procurators (44–66 C.E.). The latter was indeed a highly violent period, but not the former. It should be emphasized that the analyzed sources do not record, during the time of the divided Judea, any group under the name of Zealots, Sicarii, or bandits. (p. 257)

²⁶ On the meaning of the term *zealot* in the Hebrew and the Greek Bible, as well as in the targumic and rabbinic literature, see Guevara, *Ambiente político*, 185–212.

²⁷ See Seán Freyne, *Galilee*, 163–67; and Freyne, "Bandits in Galilee: A Contribution to the Study of Social Condition in First-Century Palestine," in *The Social World of Formative Christianity and Judaism: Essays in Tribute of Howard Clark Kee* (ed. J. Neusner et al.; Philadelphia: Fortress, 1988), 50–69.

Second, Freyne points out that when the revolt against the Romans broke out in 66 C.E. and the people of Galilee were called to arms by the Jerusalem revolutionary council, the rural population did not rise in arms and, in fact, showed no inclination to do so.[28] As a matter of fact, the revolt was restricted to a few urban centers, most of which capitulated upon the first Roman attack. It is worth noting that in Galilee the revolutionaries did not burn the governmental archives, as they did in Jerusalem, in order to destroy evidence of debt.[29] The situation would have been different had the population been seething with rebellion since the pre-Agrippan period. In Galilee during this period, poor families lived in both the country and the cities, but there is no evidence that the population was in a state of explosive unrest.

In Judea poverty was also a harsh fact in both urban and rural areas. Most of its population was rural, and the arable soil was modest in proportion to the number of inhabitants. The soil was not as fertile as in Galilee. In addition, in Judea political factors exacerbated social and economic conditions. Jerusalem, the home of the temple and the highest Jewish institutions, was the religious and political center of Judaism, a circumstance that exposed the city to clashes with Roman power that often had religious repercussions. Indeed, during the pre-Agrippan period, arrogant and abusive actions by the Roman rulers often offended the religious and nationalistic principles of the native population. In these instances, however, the resulting protests did not reach the level of revolt. Usually the conflict was resolved through diplomacy, and once pacified, people returned to their practical acceptance of the foreign rule.[30] When Tacitus, the Roman historian, discussed the Jewish-Roman relations in the first century, he wrote that "under Tiberius all was quiet."[31]

The situation changed in the post-Agrippan period (44–66 C.E.), primarily because of the incompetence of the procurators, their cruel actions, and their manifestations of insatiable greed.[32] As a result, at the beginning of Cumanus's procuratorship (48–59 C.E.), some isolated groups started violent opposition

---

[28] Freyne, *Galilee*, 163–67; "Bandits," 50–69. See Josephus, *J.W.* 4.84; S. J. Cohen, *Josephus in Galilee and Rome: His Vita and Development as an Historian* (Leiden: Brill, 1979), 91–100.

[29] For a description of the social situation in Galilee during the first century C.E., see Freyne, *Galilee*, 135–75; Cohen, *Josephus*, 91–100; Rhoads, *Israel*, 47–173.

[30] Rhoads, *Israel*, 61–64. Guevara analyzes Josephus' account:

> He narrates two episodes that created strained relations between Judea and Rome under Pontius Pilate's government, portraying the Jewish reaction as follows: (a) the Jews did not ignore Roman authority; (b) nor did they resort to violent means; (c) no revolutionary group emerged; (d) they did not try to regain their independence. Instead, using peaceful means, either they requested the annulment of the governmental measure that had caused a violation of the law or they laid down a protest against the consummated violation. (*Ambiente político*, 144)

[31] Tacitus, *Hist.* 5.9 (Moore, LCL). See P. W. Barnett, "Under Tiberius All Was Quiet," *NTS* 21 (1975): 564–71.

[32] For the social causes of the First Jewish Revolt (of 66–70 C.E.), see M. Aberbach, *The Roman-Jewish War* (London: R. Golub, 1966); Rhoads, *Israel*, 150–73.

against the Roman occupation. The resistance increased during Felix's tenure (52–60 C.E.) and burst into general revolt in 66 C.E.[33]

3. Jesus of Nazareth's social condition and public action

Before his public ministry, Jesus was neither a farmer, a landowner, a merchant, nor a wealthy man. On the other hand, he was not needy or a beggar. He was characterized as a *tektōn* ("carpenter" or "artisan"). This term did not designate someone who was indigent but, rather, a person who possessed skills that conferred a certain social identity, enabling one to work wherever his service was needed.[34] Neither were his disciples indigent. Some were fishermen who had laborers in their service (Mark 1:20). There was even a tax collector among them.

In his public ministry, Jesus chose poverty. He assumed the poverty of a traveling prophet and teacher, totally devoted to preaching the kingdom of God. He took lodging in the houses of those who believed in him, and lived on the donations of friends.[35] When he moved from Nazareth to Capernaum, he probably lodged at Peter's house. In his traveling, Jesus seemed to prefer small cities and villages and to avoid large cities, such as Sepphoris or Tiberias. The suggestion that the Gospels omitted Jesus' preaching in these cities because of his eventual failure is not compelling, since the Gospels mentioned Jesus' failure in cities such as Chorazin, Bethsaida, Capernaum (Matt 11:20–23; Luke 10:13–15), and Jerusalem (Matt 23:37; Luke 13:34–35). It is worth noting that Jesus did not confront the Galilean civil authorities as John the Baptist had done. Moreover, he preached to both poor and rich, and he did not foster a social revolution of the poor against the wealthy. Had he done so, he would have aroused strong political opposition from the Herodian authorities. In fact, the opposition Jesus experienced in Galilee did not derive from the civil or political authorities but from the religious ones, including some scribes from Jerusalem.[36]

In his miraculous healings, Jesus made no distinction between social classes; he healed anyone approaching him with faith. This attitude is also conspicuous in Jesus' teaching; he balanced his eschatological and social message in favor of the poor with a warning addressed to the wealthy in order to move them to conversion.[37] Thus Jesus taught the futility of riches and warned against the danger of

---

[33] Scholars emphasize three major sets of causes for the Jewish War against Rome: political, socioeconomic, and religious. On the complexity of this issue, see Rhoads, "Zealots," 6:1050–52.

[34] According to Ramsay MacMullen, the carpenters formed groups, akin to the unions that were organized in the villages and towns of Egypt. See Ramsay MacMullen, *Roman Social Relations, 50 B.C. to A.D. 284* (New Haven: Yale University Press, 1974), 17.

[35] See Gerd Theissen, "Wir haben Alles verlassen (Mc X,29): Nachfolge und soziale Entwurzelung in der jüdisch-palästinischen Gesellschaft der 1. Jahrhunderts n. Chr.," *NovT* 19 (1977): 161–97.

[36] See Freyne, *Galilee*, 241–47.

[37] See Sanders, *Jesus*, 229–31.

being enslaved by their lure (Matt 6:24//Luke 16:13). He exhorted the rich to employ their abundant resources to help the poor: "Sell your possessions, and give alms. Make purses for yourselves that do not wear out" (Luke 12:33//Matt 6:19–20). And he added strong motivation: "Give, and it will be given to you. . . . For the measure you give will be the measure you get back" (Luke 6:38). Jesus' message to the greedy and miserly was exemplified in the parable of the Rich Man and Lazarus (Luke 16:19–31).[38]

Jesus' own abandonment of material goods and his teaching on the subject showed both his total trust in God's providence (Matt 6:25–34//Luke 12:22–31) and his challenge to the conventional mindset, according to which land was a valuable possession that ought not to be surrendered. Jesus' conduct and attitude invited wealthy people to reconsider their present situation and to change their life in accordance with the new order that the kingdom of God would introduce.

Some scholars, such as Crossan, Mack, and Downing, think that, in their way of life, Jesus and his first disciples imitated Cynic philosophers, who abandoned their families and properties and became traveling preachers. But this is a controversial matter.[39] Those opposed to this view stress that it is far from certain that Galilee was extensively hellenized or that Cynic influence was strong there. They argue that although literary and archaeological data show that some cities of Galilee might have experienced the phenomenon of hellenization, the native Jewish population in towns and villages retained traditional religious customs and beliefs. The city of Sepphoris has been particularly important in this discussion because of its proximity to Nazareth, barely four miles away. Scholars long considered the Sepphoris of Jesus' time, the strongest city in Galilee according to Josephus, an especially hellenized and paganized city. More than fifteen years of archaeological excavations have, however, demonstrated that the Sepphoris of Jesus' time was not a pagan but a Jewish city.[40]

---

[38] For the authenticity of this parable, see Joseph A. Fitzmyer, *The Gospel according to Luke X–XXIV* (AB 28A; New York: Doubleday, 1985), 1125–30.

[39] See Willy Schottroff and Wolfgang Stegemann, *God of the Lowly: Socio-historical Interpretation of the Bible* (trans. Matthew J. O'Connell; Maryknoll: Orbis, 1984), 148–68; Wright, "Jesus," 3:800; Richard A. Horsley, *Social Conflict in the Synoptic Sayings Source Q* (Valley Forge, Pa.: Trinity Press International, 1996), 230–31; Paul R. Eddy, "Jesus as Diogenes? Reflections on the Cynic Jesus Thesis," *JBL* 115 (1996): 449–69.

[40] See Mark Chancey and Eric M. Meyers, "How Jewish Was Sepphoris in Jesus' Time?" *BAR* 26 (2000):18–33; Jonathan L. Reed, *Archaeology and the Galilean Jesus: A Reexamination of the Evidence* (Harrisburg, Pa.: Trinity Press International, 2000), 100–138. The results of the archaeological excavations have confirmed Josephus' information on the magnitude and Jewish character of the Sepphoris of Jesus' time (see *J.W.* 2.56, 68, 573–74; 3.31–32). According to the archaeological findings, in the Sepphoris of Jesus' time, there were no signs of pagan religion; it was a Jewish city. The presence of Jewish religion is indicated, for instance, by the presence of many Jewish ritual stone vessels and baths *(miqvaʾot)* and an almost complete absence of pig bones. The cultural and religious conditions of the city changed in the second century C.E., when it became strongly hellenized and paganized.

Moreover, the opponents of the Cynic thesis assert that there is no proof that Cynic philosophers taught in Galilean cities during Jesus' time. They emphasize that Jesus was indeed a teacher but his way of teaching was closer to that of Jewish sages than to that of the Cynic philosophers. A conspicuous example of this was his use of parables. Furthermore, unlike the Cynics, Jesus did not preach unrestrained freedom or hold in contempt the traditional norms and customs of Jewish life. Finally, Jesus was not only a teacher of wisdom but a prophet who proclaimed the coming of the kingdom and through healings anticipated its arrival.[41] The biblical tradition embodied examples of traveling prophets, as the stories of Elijah and Elisha show.

All these arguments against the Cynic thesis have substantial value. We should recall, however, that the Hasmonean period, also known as the Maccabean period (142–63 B.C.E.), was a time not only of reaction against Hellenistic religious practices but also of assimilation of many Hellenistic ideas and methods, especially in education and learning.[42] Important in this regard is M. Hengel's thesis that Palestinian Judaism was a Hellenistic Judaism.[43] The assimilation of ideas, methods, and fashions would not necessarily entail acceptance of foreign religious ideas. Similarities to Cynic philosophers need not imply a direct influence; some of these ideas and fashions could have been common knowledge in hellenized Palestine.

4. Jesus' expectation of the imminent coming of the eschatological kingdom

Referring to Jesus' preaching, the Synoptics employ the abstraction "kingdom of God" without adding any explanation, assuming an audience sensitive to its prophetic and apocalyptic background, in which Second Isaiah and Daniel are prominent.[44] Second Isaiah emphasized Yahweh's kingship over history and creation, in particular over Israel, God's elect people. Accordingly, God's royal program included the glorious restoration of Jerusalem, the reunion of the twelve tribes, and the submission of the nations to Yahweh, who would dwell in the holy city.[45] Hence, Second Isaiah's comforting message to Israel in captivity was, "Your God reigns" (Isa 52:7) and, "See, the LORD God comes with might, and his arm rules for him" (40:10).

---

[41] Eddy, "Jesus as Diogenes?"

[42] Lee I. A. Levine, "The Age of Hellenism," in *Ancient Israel* (ed. H. Shanks; Englewood Cliffs: Prentice Hall, 1988), 177–204.

[43] See William R. Long, "Martin Hengel on Early Christianity," *RelSRev* 15 (1989): 230–34. Martin Hengel, *Jews, Greeks, and Barbarians* (Philadelphia: Fortress, 1980), 49–82.

[44] See Meier, *Mentor, Message, and Miracle*, 237–88; Jürgen Becker, *Jesus of Nazareth* (New York: de Gruyter, 1998), 86–100.

[45] See Isa 40:10–11; 43:14–44:5; 51:17–52:12; 59:9–21; 60:1–29.

Daniel, in turn, set forth the idea that the kings of the earth rule by the power God entrusted to them.[46] But he went beyond this by announcing both the destruction of any evil and oppressive power and the establishment of God's universal and eternal kingdom (Dan 7:1–28). Unlike Second Isaiah, who spoke of God's ruling actions without using the abstraction "kingdom of God," Daniel employed both concrete and abstract terms regarding the future divine dominion.

Addressing an audience familiar with prophetic and apocalyptic ideas, Jesus centered his preaching on the coming of God's kingdom. In doing so, while underlining the saving dimension of God's rule, he showed that the kingdom of God is a reality both present and future, moving toward its completion in a near future. For Jesus, the present differs from the past in relationship to God's salvific activity. Unlike the past, the present joins the future as the outset of God's kingdom. Though seeing the full realization of the kingdom in an impending future, Jesus asserted his belief that the kingdom already acted through his words and deeds.[47] In his perception, the defeat of the kingdom of evil, expected in apocalyptic literature, was carried out through his exorcisms.[48] In his healings, Jesus saw the beginning of the restoration of humanity, a restoration to be completed in the consummated kingdom. In the parables, he showed the kingdom in action—the sown seed that represents the work of the kingdom germinates and grows now. In the Beatitudes, Jesus extended his comfort to the poor and afflicted with the assurance derived from his conviction that the kingdom of God is already at work. In accordance with this persuasion, he shared tables with sinners, receiving them into God's kingdom. "The Kingdom of God happens in the table-fellowship."[49] Through his words and deeds, Jesus enabled his audience to live "an experience of God by making God's eschatological nearness a present reality."[50]

Although Jesus spoke and acted in full awareness of the power of the kingdom working in the present, he was eager to see the kingdom as a consummated reality. Thus, in the prayer he taught his disciples, Jesus instructed them that the first thing they should request was that God might reveal his full power and establish his eternal kingdom over Israel and the world: "Hallowed be your name. Your kingdom come" (Matt 6:9–10//Luke 11:2). Concurrently Jesus proclaimed the Beatitudes, in which he predicted the radical alteration that the kingdom of God would introduce into the human condition (Matt 5:3–12//Luke 6:20–23). In the same vein, he assured the Twelve that they had been chosen to govern the renewed Israel (Matt 19:28//Luke 22:30) and that the pagans would come from the edges of the world to sit at the patriarchs' table in the consummated kingdom of

---

[46] Dan 2:37; 4:2, 17, 34–51; 5:18, 21.

[47] For Jesus' belief that the kingdom of God is both acting in the present and moving toward its final consummation, see Becker, *Jesus of Nazareth*, 100–224; Meier, *Mentor, Message, and Miracle*, 237–506; Bornkamm, *Jesus of Nazareth*.

[48] See Luke 10:18; 11:20//Matt 12:28; Dan 7:1–28; 1QM 11:6–17; 13:10–18; 14:6–18; *T. Dan* 5:10–13.

[49] Becker, *Jesus of Nazareth*, 161.

[50] Becker, *Jesus of Nazareth*, 217.

God (Matt 8:11–12//Luke 13:28–29). Jesus retained his hope in the coming of the kingdom even at the time of his death. Thus at the Last Supper he foretold that he would enjoy the eschatological banquet.[51]

We possess no words of Jesus about the impending coming of the kingdom that can be said to be absolutely authentic. His remarks related to this expectation seem to derive from early Christian prophets.[52] Nevertheless, certain data suggests that Jesus expected the imminent coming of the kingdom. For instance, the fact that he, before his public ministry, became a follower of John the Baptist, who was well known because of his preaching of the impending arrival of God's kingdom,[53] suggests that Jesus shared a similar expectation.[54] But the strongest suggestions in this regard appear in Jesus' actions: his total dedication to preach the kingdom; his request for his disciples to do the same; his call for a radical conversion because of the coming of the kingdom; the incisive warning he addressed to those who rejected his message; the urgent exhortation to the disciples to make the kingdom the first concern in their prayers; the appointment of the Twelve to govern the renewed Israel; and his recourse to the hope of the coming of the kingdom for consolation before his passion. These actions would not make sense if Jesus were not expecting the impending coming of the kingdom.[55]

He did not, however, know the exact time of its coming. He stated that such knowledge was reserved to his heavenly Father (Mark 13:32). One may argue that Jesus' concern for communal order is not consistent with the expectation of an imminent coming of the kingdom. The objection, however, is not compelling, as the analogy with the Qumran community shows. For this community both lived with an intense expectation of the final intervention of God and constructed a highly organized community life.

Meyer, studying Jesus' expectation of the impending dawn of the kingdom, has connected it with the nature of prophetic knowledge, which is not foreknowledge of future events but an awareness through symbols and images, that conveys the certainty that the power of God, which will bring the crisis to final resolution, is already active in the present. The prophet appeals to this certainty in urging his or her listeners to take the proper decisions at once because they will be judged in accordance with them. The present time offers the opportunity of salvation for the present generation. God, who speaks through the prophetic

---

[51] Matt 26:29//Mark 14:25//Luke 22:18. See Meier, *Mentor, Message, and Miracle*, 289–397.

[52] See, e.g., Matt 10:23; Mark 9:1; 13:30.

[53] The historical probability of an eschatological orientation in the preaching of John the Baptist, present in the synoptic accounts and in Q, is not weakened by the absence of any corroborating witness in Josephus's description of the Baptist. In a similar fashion, Josephus fails to mention any apocalyptic dimension to the thought of the Essenes, yet the Dead Sea Scrolls themselves bear ample witness to their eschatological interests. It appears that Josephus tailors his accounts of both the Baptist and the Essenes to suit his own perspective or perhaps the Hellenistic tastes of his readers.

[54] Sanders, *Jesus*, 91–93; Meyer, *Aims*, 115–22.

[55] Meier, *Mentor, Message, and Miracle*, 338.

symbolics, also conveys his message through historical events subsequent to the prophetic utterance. Meyer says that these subsequent events, understood in the light of faith, allow us to "decipher prophetic symbols, translating image into event, schematic sequence into actual sequence, and symbolic time into real time."[56]

Jesus expected a total renovation of the world, including a new Zion with the true and perfect temple, the restoration of Israel, the conversion of the nations, and the establishment of the final social order, which would exclude sinners and oppressors.[57] In Jesus' view, this renovation could not be achieved by simple repair of the present world. It required a total transformation, to be effected by the full and definitive application of God's power. Motivated by the certainty in God's intervention, Jesus exhorted his disciples to ask the heavenly Father to speed the full implementation of his kingdom and, in the meantime, to grant them the necessary sustenance to live on: "Father! May your name be sanctified! May your kingdom come! Give us this day our bread for subsistence" (Luke 11:2–3//Matt 6:9–11).[58]

5. Jesus and the social and familial dimensions of the kingdom

Jesus did not announce a purely interior kingdom within the individual. In his time, the concept that religion is only a matter of individual concern was totally alien. "In first century Palestine, religion was instead embedded within all sectors of the system as a whole."[59] Ancient societies interwove religion into the social, economic, and political texture of society. This broader context made the prophets' political involvement understandable. Since Jesus was a prophet, his message had social and political consequences. "The evidence in the gospel tradition—e.g., the political symbol of the 'kingdom of God' as his central message, the healing of bodies as well as souls as the activity for which he was most renowned—rather confirms . . . that Jesus was concerned with the whole of life, in all its dimensions."[60]

The concept of kingdom employed by Jesus is a social and political symbol that refers to a community over which God exerts his dominion. Jesus emphasized the kingdom's social dimension in the image of it as an eschatological banquet.[61] But the social dimension is not reserved for the future. Jesus anticipated it when sitting at table with sinners and tax collectors, to whom he offered divine forgiveness and a foretaste of the friendship to be developed in the kingdom. This

---

[56] Meyer, *Aims*, 247.
[57] Sanders, *Jesus*, 232.
[58] See Fitzmyer, *Luke X–XXIV*, 896–907.
[59] John H. Elliot, "Social Scientific Criticism of the New Testament: More on Methods and Models," *Semeia* 35 (1986): 16; see also Horsley, *Spiral*, 152–54.
[60] Horsley, *Spiral*, 153.
[61] See Matt 8:11–12//Luke 13:28–29; Matt 22:1–10//Luke 14:15–24.

anticipation also occurs in the healings and exorcisms, since through them Jesus restored human beings to the present society in preparation for their integration into the future, final community.

One of the characteristics of Jesus' concept of the eschatological kingdom is that God is not only a king but also a father. This is abundantly clear in his instruction to the disciples about how to pray; on the one hand, he stressed that the coming of the kingdom of God must be the first concern in their prayer, but on the other, he taught them to address the master of the kingdom with the title "our Father" (Matt 6:9//Luke 11:2). The God who will establish the kingdom is "our Father." Jesus allowed his disciples to share his own approach to God and indicated that the intimate relationship between his disciples and God is to resemble his own with the heavenly Father.[62] This becomes the basis for family relations among the members of the eschatological community. When the disciples pray to the Father, they anticipate their intimate relationship with God in the consummated kingdom and foster a spirit of familiarity rooted in the fact that all of Jesus' disciples, without discrimination, are children of the same heavenly Father. In this prayer, believers celebrate their common dignity, nurture an awareness of their nobility before God and the community, and repudiate any contempt for, or oppression of, the human person.

6. The social dimension of Jesus' sapiential sayings

We may expand our consideration of the social aspect of Jesus' mission by a close analysis of some of his sayings and deeds. His sayings fall into sapiential and prophetic categories. We turn first to the sapiential. As a teacher of wisdom, Jesus conveyed his message especially through parables and aphorisms. Speaking in parables, Jesus surprised his listeners, shattering their way of thinking, which was rooted in conventional wisdom, and moving them to look at reality from another perspective. He offered new parameters to shape community life, as the parables of the Prodigal Son (Luke 15:11–32) and the Good Samaritan (Luke 10:30–35) show. In the former, the elder son complains of his father's behavior toward his brother, who has returned after squandering the inheritance he had received. He complains because the father welcomes the dissolute son back and restores him to his familial rights. Here the elder son voices conventional wisdom, based on the model of reward and punishment, while the father voices a new approach, based on love and compassion.[63] The story of the Good Samaritan, in turn, shocks its Jewish audience because Jesus combines the concept of the Samaritan with the idea of goodness. The story leads the listeners to conclude that helping the needy

---

[62] See Fitzmyer, *Luke X–XXIV,* 898.

[63] Many commentators, such as A. Jülicher, R. Bultmann, J. M. Creed, F. Hauck, I. H. Marshall, E. P. Sanders, and J. A. Fitzmyer, consider the Prodigal Son, save for minor redactional changes, to be a parable dating from Stage I of the gospel tradition, i.e., dating back to the historical Jesus. See Fitzmyer, *Luke X–XXIV,* 1083–86.

and afflicted takes precedence over rituals and nationalities.[64] Helping others in need must extend beyond the boundaries of social classes, ethnic groups, and religious affiliations.

Among Jesus' aphorisms embodying a new concept of life are two that deserve special attention: that referring to the center of purity or holiness (Mark 7:15//Matt 15:11) and that inviting one to abandon family and to follow Jesus (Luke 14:26//Matt 10:37). The former says, "There is nothing outside a person that by going in can defile, but the things that come out are what defile" (Mark 7:15). In the synoptic tradition, this is Jesus' answer to Pharisees and scribes who accused his disciples of not washing their hands before meals. Many scholars, such as Käsemann,[65] N. Perrin,[66] J. Lambrecht,[67] and H. Hübner,[68] hold that this is a genuine aphorism in which Jesus criticized the Levitical laws on clean and unclean foods (Lev 11:1–47) and the Pharisaic practice of ritual purity. There are, however, serious objections to this opinion because, if Jesus had dispensed with biblical food laws, the debate in the early church on the issue would probably not have occurred.[69] In addition, had Jesus made this critique of the Torah, his opponents would have used it as an accusation in his condemnation, and there is no reference to such in the Gospels. These difficulties can be resolved if Jesus' saying is interpreted as an exhortation stressing the priority of the heart over external circumstances. The antithesis emphasizes the importance of one thing over the other without rejecting either. (A parallel antithesis is the prophetic saying (Hos 6:6) that emphasizes the primacy of morality over sacrifice. The saying does not exclude sacrifices but stresses the priority of moral behavior and makes ritual practices contingent upon moral life.) Similarly, Jesus would have understood his remark on things that defile as a question of priority, of what matters more before God—not so much what enters but what comes out makes a person unclean. In

---

[64] Commentators concur that Luke is responsible for integrating into a dialogue a traditional parable displaying Jesus' teaching in contrast to conventional Palestinian Jewish attitudes. The Jesus Seminar prints in red the parable of the Good Samaritan in recognition of the authenticity of Jesus' words preserved here. The Seminar concludes its analysis by saying, "As a metaphorical tale that redraws the map of both the social and the sacred world, the Seminar regarded this parable as a classic example of the provocative public speech of Jesus the parabler." Robert W. Funk et al., *The Five Gospels: The Search for the Authentic Words of Jesus* (New York: Macmillan, 1993), 324.

[65] Käsemann, *Essays*, 39.

[66] Perrin, *Rediscovering*, 150.

[67] Jan Lambrecht, "Jesus and the Law: An Investigation of Mk 7.1–23," *ETL* 53 (1977): 75–79.

[68] Hans Hübner, *Gesetz in der synoptischen Tradition: Studien zur These einer progressiven Qumranisierung und Judaisierung innerhalb der synoptischen Tradition* (2d ed.; Göttingen: Vandenhoeck & Ruprecht, 1986), 171–75. Among the supporters are Hans Hübner, "Markus 7, 1–23 und das 'jüdisch-hellenistische' Gesetzesverständnis," *NTS* 22 (1975–1976): 319–45; H. Merkel, "Jesus und die Pharisäer," *NTS* 14 (1967–1968): 205–6; W. G. Kümmel, "Äussere und innere Reinheit des Menschen bei Jesus," in *Das Wort und die Wörter* (FS Gerhard Friedrich; eds. H. Balz and S. Schulz; Stuttgart: Kohlhammer, 1973), 35–46; Bultmann, *History*, 105.

[69] See Acts 10:15, 28; Rom 14:14, 20; 1 Cor 8:1–12.

the early Christian church, however, Jesus' saying was interpreted in an exclusive sense—it is not what enters but what comes from the heart that makes the person unclean. The Synoptics testify to this understanding.[70]

An inclusive meaning would make more sense in the life of Jesus, who would have drawn attention to the preeminence of the heart over external circumstances. Without rejecting the practice of the purity laws, he would have exalted the heart as the center of moral action. Jesus would have made such a statement against extremist observers of ritual practices, which not only segregated Jews from pagans but also served to create divisions within the Jewish community.[71] Jesus thereby prepared the ground for a community that would give preference to a holiness that does not segregate people but embraces and unites them.

The second aphorism, containing a new perspective on life, says, "Whoever comes to me and does not hate father and mother, wife and children, brothers and sisters, yes, and even life itself, cannot be my disciple" (Luke 14:26). This saying, which prominent scholars accept as authentic,[72] sets loyalty to Jesus over natural family bonds. Like the previous aphorism, it has an inclusive sense implying a hierarchy of values—loyalty to Jesus transcends natural family loyalties. The aphorism does not imply that Jesus opposed the family. His stand on marriage and divorce showed that he cared for the historical and social structure of human beings. In his position against divorce, Jesus referred to God's original idea in setting up the institution of marriage (Mark 10:5–9//Matt 19:4–9), and in perfecting it in accordance with the new order he was proclaiming, Jesus restored women to their original dignity. In the saying on loyalty, when Jesus subordinated family to loyalty to his person, he reordered familial relations in accordance with the new spirit of fellowship, love, and compassion that he was introducing with the power of the kingdom.

7. The social aspect of Jesus' prophetic sayings and actions

The restoration of the community that Jesus envisaged is also shown in his prophetic sayings and actions. Examples of these are the Beatitudes related to the poor, mourners, and the hungry (Matt 5:3–6; Luke 6:20–21), in which Jesus announced the radical alteration of the present social situation. An impending divine intervention will make it possible for the afflicted to overcome their misery, recover their dignity, and have a share in the final kingdom of God. The

---

[70] See William D. Davies and Dale C. Allison, *A Critical and Exegetical Commentary on the Gospel according to Saint Matthew* (3 vols.; ICC; Edinburgh: T&T Clark, 1988–1997), 2:528–30; William R. G. Loader, *Jesus' Attitude towards the Law* (WUNT 2.97; Tübingen: Mohr, 1997), 75–79.

[71] Jerome H. Neyrey, "The Idea of Purity in Mark's Gospel," *Semeia* 35 (1986): 91–128; J. Neyrey, "A Symbolic Approach to Mark 7," *Foundations and Facets Forum* 4/3 (1988): 63–91.

[72] Perrin, *Rediscovering*, 141; Fitzmyer, *Luke X–XXIV*, 1061.

Beatitudes at the same time were public statements that honored the poor and afflicted, emphasizing their dignity and inviting people to extend their generous hands toward them.

The same purpose of restoration was manifested in Jesus' healings and exorcisms, through which he provided the afflicted with the physical and spiritual wholeness they should have in accordance with the divine plan, thus allowing them to be reintegrated into society. Jesus thereby anticipated the final restoration of the community in the kingdom of God.[73] Similarly, in casting out demons, Jesus effected the first victorious actions, preannouncing the final defeat of Satan's power in the world now ruled by violence, discrimination, and oppression.

Likewise, Jesus' eating with sinners (Luke 7:34) was a powerful symbol because it was a way of breaking the ritual boundaries of conventional holiness and offering salvation outside the law of Moses and the temple. In biblical times, sharing the same table was a sign of friendship, but for some strict Jews, there was a limitation to such friendship. Observance of specific rules of purity was required, and only those who observed them could sit at the same table. In this environment, by eating with sinners, Jesus made a shocking gesture. He broke down ritual fences and offered sinners his friendship, obtaining for them the benefits of the kingdom he was proclaiming.[74]

Symbolic also was Jesus' overturning the tables of the money changers and the seats of merchants in the temple district, a story related in all four gospels.[75] Although abrupt and brief, this action was a powerful gesture, probably symbolizing the destruction and replacement of the temple, since it was connected with another of Jesus' authentic sayings, referring to its destruction.[76] The saying on the destruction of the temple, also present in each of the four gospels, was a subject of puzzlement in the gospel tradition and has been reinterpreted in various ways.[77] It had prophetic antecedents: Jeremiah (7:14; 26:6) and Micah (3:2) also foretold the temple's destruction. Jesus' prophecy, however, has an apocalyptic character, since it associates the destruction of the present world with the creation of a new one, in which the renewed Israel would have a dominant place. Jesus' prophecy pointed to the heart of Jewish life, since the temple was the civic and religious center of Judaism. Its destruction would entail not only religious, but also social, economic, and political consequences because it would endanger the employment of the masses in Jerusalem, deprive priests of their livelihood and power, and destabilize the order that the Roman power was committed to support. Furthermore, Jesus' prophecy could have stirred suspicions about his re-

---

[73] See Meier, "Jesus," *NJBC* 1320; Meier *Mentor, Message, and Miracle*, 509–1038.

[74] See Meier, "Jesus," *NJBC* 1320; Meyer, "Jesus Christ," 3:782; Borg, *Scholarship*, 80–95.

[75] See Matt 21:12–13//Mark 11:15–19//Luke 19:45–48; John 2:13–22.

[76] See Brown, *Death of the Messiah*, 455; Sanders, *Jesus*, 61–70; W. W. Watty, "Jesus and the Temple—Cleansing or Cursing?" *ExpTim* 93 (1981–1982): 235–39.

[77] See Brown, *Death of the Messiah*, 434–60.

construction of society because people in authority recognized Jesus' mistrust of wealthy people, his option for the poor, and his emphasis on building a society based on total trust in God. It is understandable that Jesus' symbolic action of overturning the merchants' tables worried the Jerusalem authorities and finally served as a charge against Jesus at his trial.[78]

In Jerusalem, Jesus urged the people to take a position regarding his message. Realizing its rejection by the authorities, Jesus submitted himself to death as part of his mission. Jesus' death does not detract from his message of the coming of the kingdom, as some scholars have argued.[79] For, at the Last Supper, Jesus interpreted his violent death as a necessary step in the development of God's eschatological action to establish God's kingdom in the world, and assured his disciples that he would drink a new cup in the consummated kingdom (Mark 14:25). His disciples understood the celebration of Jesus' Last Supper as a legacy that he entrusted to them, as a memorial that would reenact the liberating power of his death and anticipate the celebration of the eschatological banquet in the completed kingdom.[80]

8. The promotion of women

Jesus set forth principles leading to the promotion of women, especially by relativizing the value of purity laws (Mark 7:15). These laws were important factors in structuring Jewish society and particularly affected women. By relativizing the value of rituals, Jesus relaxed the borders circumscribing women. Jesus' action in this regard made a great contribution to the renewal of the community because through it he invited everyone, even those most remote from the center of holiness (the temple and the law), to enter the community of the kingdom. He extended his invitation to those considered to be the most sinful, such as tax collectors and prostitutes, and offered them the same dignity of brothers and sisters in the community. Thus Jesus said,

> Truly I tell you, the tax collectors and the prostitutes are going into the kingdom of God ahead of you. For John came to you in the way of righteousness and you did not believe him, but the tax collectors and the prostitutes believed him; and even after you saw it, you did not change your minds and believe him. (Matt 21:31–32)[81]

Paradoxically, those remote from the center of holiness will be part of the kingdom of God, but those belonging to its very center will be distant from the kingdom. The reason is that entering the kingdom does not depend on something outside the heart of the person but on the sincere and internal decision to

---

[78] See ibid., 458–59.
[79] E.g., Sobrino, *Christology*, 218.
[80] See Robert O'Toole, "Last Supper," *ABD* 4:239; Meier, "Jesus," *NJBC* 1316–28; Theissen and Merz, *Historical Jesus*, 405–39.
[81] For the authenticity of these sayings, see Bultmann, *History*, 177.

accept God's will revealed in Jesus. When this condition is achieved, one is allowed to enter the new and eschatological community on an equal footing with all other members.

As a sign that the power of the kingdom of God was already active in the renewal of the human community, Jesus healed everyone, without discrimination. He healed both men and women who approached him with faith, and restored their physical and spiritual wholeness. He cured them not only to allow them to be reintegrated as healthy and active members into the community to which they traditionally belonged but also to prepare them to be members of the new community of the kingdom. Thus Luke says that Jesus had cured and liberated from Satan the women who followed him in his missionary journeys (Luke 8:2).

As stated, Jesus healed women on various occasions.[82] Thus he cured a woman who had been suffering from hemorrhages for twelve years and had spent all her money on unhelpful physicians (Mark 5:25–34).This woman's sickness made her constantly unclean, ritually impure (Lev 15:25–27). But her faith saved her. In spite of her contagion, she approached the one whose healing power crossed the boundaries of ritual holiness. She touched Jesus, in whom there was divine power to purify, embrace, and unite. In response, she received the comforting and re-creating words, "Daughter, your faith has made you well; go in peace, and be healed of your disease" (Mark 5:34). The peace that Jesus gave her involved the awareness of her restored integrity, wholeness, and purity. She felt the happiness of being reintegrated into the normal life of her family and society, and rejoiced at being addressed as daughter by the creator of a new family. She had a foretaste of the peace of the final kingdom.

Likewise Jesus restored to life a twelve-year-old girl, Jairus's daughter. He touched her although she was dead and contact with her body made people unclean (Num 19:11–13). Because Jesus had the saving power of the kingdom and the life-giving presence of God, by touching the dead body he restored the girl to life (Mark 5:41–42). Similarly, Jesus cured a woman afflicted by a spirit that had crippled her for eighteen years. This happened in a synagogue on the Sabbath (Luke 13:10–17).[83] Although it was a Sabbath day and the synagogue was the place where the Sabbath was strictly observed, Jesus performed the healing in accordance with his principle that rituals should not take priority over the life of a human being. It is very significant that the healed person was a woman; this shows Jesus' concern for her life and dignity: the life of a woman takes priority over the observance of the Sabbath. Jesus liberated the woman from the power of an evil spirit on the Sabbath because on this day Israel, according to Deut 5:15, celebrated its liberation from the Egyptian slavery. Jesus liberated the crippled woman from the slavery of the evil spirit to allow her to share in the full joy of the

---

[82] E. Schüssler Fiorenza, *In Memory of Her: A Feminist Theological Reconstruction of Christian Origins* (New York: Crossroad, 1985), 123–30.

[83] "The story itself probably reflects one of the real-life situations of Jesus' own ministry: a cure and debate over the Sabbath in Stage I of the gospel tradition" (Fitzmyer, *Luke X–XXIV*, 1011).

Sabbath by celebrating the liberation God had effected in her. The Sabbath was also the day on which men and women, created in the image of God, imitated God the Creator, who rested on the seventh day (Exod 20:8–11). Jesus cured the crippled woman on the Sabbath so that she, restored to her integrity and wholeness as a liberated image of God, might rest as God did.

Jesus' promotion of women appears also in the abolition of divorce, placing women in the same condition as men.[84] We may add Jesus' saying about the eunuchs (Matt 19:12), which, interpreted symbolically, refers to both men and women.[85] This opens to women possibilities transcending their traditional roles as wives and mothers; now they can be independent individuals, practicing celibacy, dedicated to the kingdom of God, and lending their services to the community.

9. Jesus and nonviolence

As we have seen, the social and political context of Jesus' time, as reconstructed by recent historians, was not as restless and violent as has often been claimed. In Jesus' time, there were no Zealots or Sicarii. Neither was there the social banditry that developed later in the post-Agrippan period. Most scholars today dismiss the view that Jesus was a political revolutionist, plotting to overturn an oppressive government.[86] A few decades ago, some of Jesus' sayings in the Gospels were regarded as vestiges of a revolutionary political program. Today, however, these sayings are studied within a different context and joined with Jesus' central declaration of nonviolence.[87]

Among the allegedly revolutionary sayings are three worthy of special attention. First, Jesus says, "Do not think that I have come to bring peace to the earth; I have not come to bring peace, but a sword" (Matt 10:34//Luke 12:51). That is, though acting with the power of the kingdom, Jesus does not bring the expected messianic peace. On the contrary, he introduces a time of confrontation and division because, through his words and actions, he causes conflict.[88] Fitzmyer, in his

---

[84] See Matt 5:32; 19:9; Mark 10:11; Luke 16:18.

[85] Bultmann (*History*, 76) includes the saying about the eunuchs among the authentic "sayings of the Lord." See also Joachim Jeremias, *Theology of the New Testament: The Proclamation of Jesus* (New York: Scribner's, 1971), 224.

[86] An exceptional example of this viewpoint is J. Pixley, who thinks that Jesus had a political agenda and that he planned to persuade the masses of workers to act against the authorities of the temple, who were considered oppressors of the people. But according to Pixley, the strategy of insurrection failed because the masses changed sides against Jesus, preferring the political leadership of Barabbas. See Jorge Pixley, "God's Kingdom in First-Century Palestine: The Strategy of Jesus," in *The Bible and Liberation* (ed. Norman K. Gottwald; Maryknoll: Orbis, 1983), 378–93.

[87] See Matt 5:38–48//Luke 6:27–30, 32–36.

[88] So Davies and Allison, *Saint Matthew*, 2:218–19; W. D. Davies, *The Gospel and the Land: Early Christianity and Jewish Territorial Doctrine* (Sheffield: JSOT Press, 1994),

commentary on Luke 12:51, mentions the aggressive opposition Jesus experienced on account of his preaching, and suggests as a parallel the situation of the founder of the Qumran community, who, in his psalms, refers to the persecution he suffers from wicked persons because of his faithfulness to God's will.[89]

The second text with an alleged revolutionary tone is Matt 11:12b//Luke 16:16c. Matthew's text, which seems to be more primitive than Luke's, has two possible translations: "The kingdom of heaven has been coming violently *[biazetai]*, and the violent take it by force *[harpazousin]*" or "The kingdom of heaven has suffered violence *[biazetai]*, and the violent take it by force *[harpazousin]*." What makes two translations possible is the verb *biazetai*, which can be understood either as a middle or a passive. The second translation, however, seems to be the better because *biazetai* is parallel to *harpazousin*, which refers to an action of which the kingdom is the object. Thus, Jesus' words seem to relate to the violence that the kingdom suffers rather than to violence that the kingdom will inflict. Thus E. Käsemann writes,

> A most enlightening passage in this connection seems to me to be the much puzzled over logion in Matt 11.25f., according to which the kingdom of God suffers violence from the days of the Baptist until now and is hindered by men of violence. (This is, in my opinion, the only interpretation which makes sense.)[90]

Perrin comments on Käsemann's statement:

> What we have here is the reverse of the situation envisaged in the interpretation of the exorcisms: there the Kingdom of Satan is being plundered, here that of God. What is envisaged is an aeon of conflict, of victory and defeat, of achievement and disappointment, of success and failure.[91]

The texts of Qumran refer also to a time of conflict and struggle in which the wicked oppress the righteous.[92] O. Betz states that the *biastai* ("violent") of Matthew correspond to the wicked of the psalms of Qumran. The kingdom is like a fortress assailed by enemies.[93]

The third text (Luke 22:35–36) is part of the story of the Last Supper, in which Jesus, addressing his disciples, reminds them of the times when he sent them out to preach "without a purse, knapsack, or sandals," and immediately adds that now the situation has changed. They must now carry a purse, a knapsack, and a sword. To Jesus' frustration, the disciples take the reference to the sword literally. Luke has Jesus referring to the prophecy of the servant of the Second Isaiah, which he is about to fulfill, a reference that excludes any militant resistance to the persecutors. In the Lukan context, the disciples are taught sym-

---

336–65; F. Hahn, *The Titles of Jesus in Christology: Their History in Early Christianity* (London: Lutterworth, 1969), 153.
[89] 1QH 2:11–12, 14–15, 32–33. See Fitzmyer, *Luke X–XXIV*, 994–97.
[90] Käsemann, *Essays*, 42.
[91] Perrin, *Rediscovering*, 77.
[92] See 1QH^a 2:11–12, 14–15, 32–33.
[93] Otto Betz, "Jesu Heiliger Krieg," *NovT* 2 (1958), 128–29.

bolically that from now on they have to equip themselves to carry out the preaching of the gospel and that the time of the church will see persecution. In Acts, Luke portrays how the disciples acted in their mission and how they reacted to persecutors; there is no reference to revolt or a militant resistance against the authorities.[94]

To understand the words of Jesus within the context of his ministry, we have to place them in conjunction with his basic declaration on nonviolence, which he exemplified in his saying "If anyone strikes you on the cheek, offer the other also, and from anyone who takes away your coat do not withhold even your shirt" (Luke 6:29//Matt 5:39–40). In the Lukan version, this saying follows Jesus' statement on love for one's enemies: "But I say to you that listen, love your enemies, do good to those who hate you" (Luke 6:27). Jesus exhorted his disciples not to restrict their signs of love to those inside the community, urging them to include in their manifestations of love those outside: "For if you love those who love you, what reward do you have? Do not even the tax collectors do the same? . . . Be perfect, therefore, as your heavenly Father is perfect" (Matt 5:46, 48//Luke 6:32, 35, 36).

Jesus' teaching on nonviolence is echoed elsewhere in NT writings. Paul admonished the Thessalonians not to repay evil for evil (1 Thess 5:15). Writing to the Corinthians, the apostle not only reprimanded Christians for entering lawsuits against other Christians but also criticized those who, having suffered injustice from fellow Christians, look for compensation through legitimate means within the community. Thus he says, "In fact, to have lawsuit at all with one another is already a defeat for you. Why not rather be wronged? Why not rather be defrauded?" (1 Cor 6:7). Entering lawsuits constitutes a failure to "inherit God's kingdom" (6:9). Similarly Paul wrote to the Romans, "Do not repay anyone evil for evil. . . . If your enemies are hungry, feed them; if they are thirsty, give them something to drink. . . . Do not be overcome by evil, but overcome evil with good" (Rom 12:17–20). So, too, the author of 1 Peter exhorted Christians, "Do not repay evil for evil or abuse for abuse; but, on the contrary, repay with a blessing. It is for this that you were called—that you might inherit a blessing" (1 Pet 3:9). The Book of Revelation (5:2–10) shows that Christ was able to open the sealed scroll and be the conquering lion of Judah because he is the glorious Lamb slaughtered for the redemption of humanity. Because he submitted himself to the violence that was unjustly inflicted on him, he has defeated the violence of the world.[95]

The words and deeds of Jesus, the example and the attitudes of early Christians, continue to inspire political and religious leaders in our own day. In the twentieth century, one of the most principled theoreticians and practitioners of nonviolent resistance to political, economic, and social oppression was Dr. Martin Luther King, Jr. At the dawn of the twenty-first century, we do well to remember his words:

---

[94] See Fitzmyer, *Luke X–XXIV*, 1432; Hahn, *Titles*, 153.
[95] See Jorge Mejía, *La cuestión social* (Buenos Aires: Paulinas, 1998), 216–24.

To our most bitter opponents we say: "We shall match your capacity to inflict suffering by our capacity to endure suffering. We shall meet your physical force with soul force. Do to us what you will, and we shall continue to love you. . . . Throw us in jail, and we shall still love you. Bomb our homes and threaten our children, and we shall still love you. Send your hooded perpetrators of violence into our community at the midnight hour and beat us and leave us half dead, and we shall still love you. But be ye assured that we will wear you down by our capacity to suffer. One day we shall win freedom, but not only for ourselves. We so shall appeal to your heart and conscience that we will win *you* in the process, and our victory will be a double victory."[96]

Conclusion

Jesus exercised his public ministry in Palestine during the pre-Agrippan period of Roman rule, a time that was not teeming with social and political unrest, as Palestine during the post-Agrippan period was. During his public ministry, Jesus was not a revolutionary leader seeking political power but a wisdom preacher and a prophet. As a wisdom preacher, he was not a Cynic philosopher but, rather, a Jewish teacher in the Palestinian Jewish tradition. As a prophet, he proclaimed the coming of the kingdom of God, which had been announced by prophets and apocalyptic writers. In his miraculous healings and exorcisms, he anticipated the benefits of the kingdom, and in his preaching, he announced the radical change that God would introduce into society by the final and permanent establishment of divine dominion over the world. Both his sapiential teaching and his prophetic activity sought to give a new image to society and a new spirit to interpersonal relationships. His aim was to create a community seeking peace and rejecting violence, fostering mutual service and living in love, practicing justice and exercising compassion. He prepared the ground in order to overcome the discriminating principles of ritual purity, stating that the heart is the center of holiness, and offered his help to liberate and transform human beings for the benefit of individuals and society. Through his sapiential teaching and prophetic action, Jesus urged people to make a commitment toward God and himself, assuring them that God was ready to make his final intervention and to judge human beings in accordance with their attitude toward his message.

Bibliography

Aberbach, M. *The Roman-Jewish War*. London: Golub, 1966.
Bammel, Ernst, and C. F. D. Moule, eds. *Jesus and the Politics of His Day*. Cambridge: Cambridge University Press, 1985.
Barnett, P. W. "Under Tiberius All Was Quiet." *New Testament Studies* 21 (1975): 564–71.
Becker, Jürgen. *Jesus of Nazareth*. New York: de Gruyter, 1998.

---

[96] Martin Luther King, Jr., *Strength to Love* (New York: Harper & Row, 1963), 40–41.

Betz, Otto. "Jesu Heiliger Krieg." *Novum Testamentum* 2 (1958): 116–37.
Borg, Marcus J. *Conflict, Holiness, and Politics in the Teachings of Jesus.* Studies in the Bible and Early Christianity 5. New York: Edwin Mellen, 1984.
———. "Jesus Christ, The Teaching of." Pages 804–12 in vol. 3 of *Anchor Bible Dictionary.* Edited by D. N. Freedman. 6 vols. New York: Doubleday, 1992.
———. *Jesus in Contemporary Scholarship.* Valley Forge: Trinity Press International, 1994.
Bornkamm, Günther. *Jesus of Nazareth.* Translated by I. McLuskey, H. McLuskey, and J. M. Robinson. New York: Harper, 1960.
Brandon, S. G. F. *Jesus and the Zealots: A Study of the Political Factor in Primitive Christianity.* Manchester: Manchester University Press, 1967.
Brown, Raymond E. *The Death of the Messiah.* 2 vols. Anchor Bible Reference Library. New York: Doubleday, 1993.
———. *An Introduction to the New Testament.* Anchor Bible Reference Library. New York: Doubleday, 1996.
Bultmann, Rudolph. *History of the Synoptic Tradition.* Translated by J. Marsh. New York: Harper & Row, 1963.
Chancey, Mark, and Eric M. Meyers. "How Jewish Was Sepphoris in Jesus' Time?" *Biblical Archaeology Review* 26 (2000): 18–33.
Chilton, Bruce, and C. A. Evans, eds. *Studying the Historical Jesus: Evaluation of the State of Current Research.* New Testament Tools and Studies 19. Leiden: Brill, 1994.
Cohen, S. J. *Josephus in Galilee and Rome: His Vita and Development as an Historian.* Leiden: Brill, 1979.
Collins, John J. "Praeparatio Evangelica in the Work of Martin Hengel." *Religious Studies Review* 15 (1989): 226–28.
Crossan, John D. *The Historical Jesus: The Life of a Mediterranean Jewish Peasant.* San Francisco: HarperSanFrancisco, 1991.
Davies, W. D. *The Gospel and the Land: Early Christianity and Jewish Territorial Doctrine.* Sheffield: JSOT Press, 1994.
Davies, William D., and Dale C. Allison. *The Gospel according to Saint Matthew.* 3 vols. International Critical Commentary. Edinburgh: T&T Clark, 1988–1997.
Downing, F. Gerald. *The Christ and the Cynics.* Sheffield: JSOT Press, 1988.
Eddy, Paul R. "Jesus as Diogenes? Reflections on the Cynic Jesus Thesis." *Journal of Biblical Literature* 115 (1996): 449–69.
Ehrman, B. D. *Jesus: Apocalyptic Prophet of the New Millennium.* New York: Oxford University Press, 1999.
Ellacuría, Ignacio. *Freedom Made Flesh: The Mission of Christ and His Church.* Translated by J. Drury. Maryknoll: Orbis, 1976.
Elliot, John H. "Social Scientific Criticism of the New Testament: More on Methods and Models." *Semeia* 35 (1986): 1–34.
Fitzmyer, Joseph A. *The Gospel according to Luke X–XXIV.* Anchor Bible 28A. New York: Doubleday, 1985.
Freyne, Seán. "Bandits in Galilee: A Contribution to the Study of Social Condition in First-Century Palestine." Pages 50–69 in *The Social World of Formative*

Christianity and Judaism: Essays in Tribute of Howard Clark Kee. Edited by J. Neusner et al. Philadelphia: Fortress, 1988.

———. *Galilee, Jesus, and the Gospels: Literary Approaches and Historical Investigations*. Philadelphia: Fortress, 1988.

Funk, Robert W., et al. *The Five Gospels: The Search for the Authentic Words of Jesus*. New York: Macmillan, 1993.

Guevara, H. *Ambiente político del pueblo judío en tiempos de Jesús*. Academia Christiana 30. Madrid: Cristianidad, 1985.

Hahn, F. *The Titles of Jesus in Christology: Their History in Early Christianity*. London: Lutterworth, 1969.

Harnack, Adolf von. *What Is Christianity?* Translated by T. B. Saunders. Philadelphia: Fortress, 1957. Repr., Philadelphia: Fortress, 1986.

Hengel, Martin. *Christ and Power*. Translated by E. R. Kalin. Philadelphia: Fortress, 1977.

———. *Jews, Greeks, and Barbarians*. Translated by John Bowden. Philadelphia: Fortress, 1980.

———. *Victory over Violence*. Translated by D. E. Green. Philadelphia: Fortress, 1973.

———. *Was Jesus a Revolutionist?* Translated by W. Klassen. Philadelphia: Fortress, 1971.

Horsley, Richard A. *Jesus and the Spiral of Violence: Popular Jewish Resistance in Roman Palestine*. San Francisco: Harper & Row, 1987.

———. *Social Conflict in the Synoptic Sayings Source Q*. Valley Forge, Pa.: Trinity Press International, 1995.

Horsley, Richard A., and J. S. Hanson. *Bandits, Prophets, and Messiahs: Popular Movements at the Time of Jesus*. San Francisco: Harper & Row, 1985.

Hübner, Hans. *Gesetz in der synoptischen Tradition: Studien zur These einer progressiven Qumranisierung und Judaisierung innerhalb der synoptischen Tradition*. 2d ed. Göttingen: Vandenhoeck & Ruprecht, 1986.

———. "Markus 7, 1–23 und das 'jüdisch-hellenistische' Gesetzesverständnis." *New Testament Studies* 22 (1975–1976): 319–45.

Jeremias, Joachim. *Theology of the New Testament: The Proclamation of Jesus*. New York: Scribner's, 1971.

Kähler, Martin. *So-Called Historical Jesus and the Historic Biblical Christ*. Translated by C. Braaten. Philadelphia: Fortress, 1964. Repr., Philadelphia: Fortress, 1988.

Käsemann, Ernst. *Essays on the New Testament Themes*. Translated by W. J. Montague. Studies in Biblical Theology 41. London: SCM, 1964.

King, Martin Luther, Jr. *Strength to Love*. New York: Harper & Row, 1963.

Kselman, John S., and Ronald D. Witherup. "Modern New Testament Criticism." Pages 1130–45 in *The New Jerome Biblical Commentary*. Edited by Raymond E. Brown et al. Englewood Cliffs: Prentice Hall, 1990.

Kümmel, W. G. "Äussere und innere Reinheit des Menschen bei Jesus." Pages 35–46 in *Das Wort und die Wörter*. FS Gerhard Friedrich. Edited by H. Balz and S. Schulz. Stuttgart: Kohlhammer, 1973.

Lambrecht, Jan. "Jesus and the Law: An Investigation of Mk 7. 1–23." *Ephemerides theologicae lovanienses* 53 (1977): 24–79.
Levine, Lee I. A. "The Age of Hellenism." Pages 177–204 in *Ancient Israel*. Edited by H. Shanks. Englewood Cliffs: Prentice Hall, 1988.
Loader, William R. G. *Jesus' Attitude towards the Law*. Wissenschaftliche Untersuchungen zum Neuen Testament 2.97. Tübingen: J.C.B. Mohr, 1997.
Long, William R. "Martin Hengel on Early Christianity." *Religious Studies Review* 15 (1989): 230–34.
Mack, Burton L. *A Myth of Innocence: Mark and Christian Origins*. Philadelphia: Fortress, 1988.
MacMullen, Ramsay. *Roman Social Relations, 50 B.C. to A.D. 284*. New Haven: Yale University Press, 1974.
Meier, John P. "Jesus." Pages 1316–37 in *The New Jerome Bible Commentary*. Edited by Raymond E. Brown et al. Englewood Cliffs: Prentice Hall, 1990.
———. *A Marginal Jew: Rethinking the Historical Jesus*. Vol. 1: *The Roots of the Problem and the Person*. New York: Doubleday, 1991. Vol. 2: *Mentor, Message, and Miracle*. New York: Doubleday, 1994.
Mejía, Jorge. *La cuestión social*. Buenos Aires: Paulinas, 1998.
Merkel, H. "Jesus und die Pharisäer." *New Testament Studies* 14 (1967–1968): 194–208.
Meyer, Ben F. *The Aims of Jesus*. London: SCM, 1979.
———. "Jesus Christ." Pages 773–96 in vol. 3 of *Anchor Bible Dictionary*. Edited by D. N. Freedman. 6 vols. New York: Doubleday, 1992.
Morin, J.-A. "Les deux derniers des Douze: Simon le Zélote et Judas Iskariôth." *Revue biblique* 80 (1973): 332–58.
Myers, Ched. *Binding the Strong Man: A Political Reading of Mark's Story of Jesus*. Maryknoll: Orbis, 1988.
Neyrey, Jerome H. "The Idea of Purity in Mark's Gospel." *Semeia* 35 (1986): 91–128.
———. "A Symbolic Approach to Mark 7." *Foundations and Facets Forum* 4/3 (1988): 63–91.
Oakman, Douglas E. *Jesus and the Economic Questions of His Day*. Studies in the Bible and Early Christianity 8. Lewiston, N. Y.: Edwin Mellen, 1986.
O'Toole, Robert. "Last Supper." Pages 234–41 in vol. 4 of *Anchor Bible Dictionary*. Edited by D. N. Freedman. 6 vols. New York: Doubleday, 1992.
Perrin, Norman. *Rediscovering the Teaching of Jesus*. New York: Harper & Row, 1967.
Pixley, Jorge. "God's Kingdom in First-Century Palestine: The Strategy of Jesus." Pages 378–93 in *The Bible and Liberation*. Edited by Norman K. Gottwald. Maryknoll: Orbis, 1983.
Reed, Jonathan L. *Archaeology and the Galilean Jesus: A Reexamination of the evidence*. Harrisburg, Pa.: Trinity Press International, 2000.
Reimarus, Hermann S. *The Goal of Jesus and His Disciples*. Translated by George W. Buchanan. Leiden: Brill, 1970.
Riches, John. *Jesus and the Transformation of Judaism*. New York: Seabury Press, 1982.

———. "Jesus, Words of." Pages 802–4 in vol. 3 of *Anchor Bible Dictionary.* Edited by D. N. Freedman. 6 vols. New York: Doubleday, 1992.
Rhoads, David M. *Israel in Revolution, 6–74 C.E.: A Political History Based on the Writings of Josephus.* Philadelphia: Fortress, 1976.
———. "Zealots." Pages 1043–54 in vol. 6 of *Anchor Bible Dictionary.* Edited by D. N. Freedman. 6 vols. New York: Doubleday, 1992.
Sanders, E. P. *The Historical Figure of Jesus.* London: Penguin, 1993.
———. *Jesus and Judaism.* Philadelphia: Fortress, 1985.
Schottroff, Willy, and Wolfgang Stegemann. *God of the Lowly: Socio-historical Interpretation of the Bible.* Translated by Matthew J. O'Connell. Maryknoll: Orbis, 1984.
Schüssler Fiorenza, E. *In Memory of Her: A Feminist Theological Reconstruction of Christian Origins.* New York: Crossroad, 1985.
Schweitzer, Albert. *The Quest of the Historical Jesus: A Critical Study of Its Progress from Reimarus to Wrede.* Translated by W. Montgomery. New York: Macmillan, 1910. Repr., New York: Macmillan, 1964.
Segundo, Juan L. *The Historical Jesus of the Synoptics.* Translated by J. Drury. Maryknoll: Orbis, 1985.
Sobrino, Jon. *Christology at the Crossroads: A Latin American Approach.* Translated by J. Drury. Maryknoll: Orbis, 1978.
———. *Jesus the Liberator: A Historical-Theological View.* Translated by P. Burns and F. McDonagh. Maryknoll: Orbis, 1993.
Strauss, David F. *Das Leben Jesu, kritisch bearbeitet.* 2 vols. Tübingen: C. F. Osiander, 1835–1836.
Tacitus. *The Histories and the Annals.* Translated by C. H. Moore and J. Jackson. 4 vols. Loeb Classical Library. Cambridge: Harvard University Press, 1937.
Telford, W. R. "Major Trends and Interpretative Issues in the Study of Jesus." Pages 32–74 in *Studying the Historical Jesus.* Edited by B. Chilton. Leiden: Brill, 1994.
Theissen, Gerd. "Wir haben Alles verlassen (Mc X,29). Nachfolge und soziale Entwurzelung in der jüdisch-palästinischen Gesellschaft der 1. Jahrhunderts n. Chr." *Novum Testamentum* (1977): 161–97.
Theissen, Gerd, and Annette Merz. *The Historical Jesus: A Comprehensive Guide.* Translated by J. Bowden. Minneapolis: Fortress, 1996.
Watty, W. W. "Jesus and the Temple—Cleansing or Cursing?" *Expository Times* 93 (1981–1982): 235–39.
Weiss, Johannes. *Jesus' Proclamation of the Kingdom of God.* Translated by Richard H. Hiers and David L. Holland. Philadelphia: Fortress, 1971.
Wink, Walter. "Jesus and Revolution: Reflections on S. G. F. Brandon's *Jesus and the Zealots.*" *Union Seminary Quarterly Review* 25 (1969): 37–59.
Wrede, William. *The Messianic Secret.* Translated by J. C. G. Greig. Cambridge, U. K.: J. Clarke, 1971.
Wright, N. T. *Jesus and the Victory of God.* Minneapolis: Fortress, 1997.
———. "Jesus, Quest for the Historical." Pages 796–802 in vol. 3 of *The Anchor Bible Dictionary.* Edited by David Noel Freedman. 6 vols. New York: Doubleday, 1992.

CHAPTER NINE

JUSTICE IN THE GOSPEL OF MARK

Introduction

The previous chapter was devoted to Jesus of Nazareth, who not only proclaimed the imminent coming of the kingdom of God, anticipated it by his miracles and prophetic actions, and taught his disciples its demands but also predicted the vindication of his death by God's power. After Jesus' death and resurrection, the disciples understood that by his resurrection Jesus was enthroned in God's kingdom, and they perceived themselves as living in an intermediate period between the beginning of the kingdom and its consummation. In faith and hope, the Christian community sought to anticipate in its life the values of God's kingdom. The NT writings are witnesses to this. We begin with the Synoptic Gospels, the earliest of which is most probably the Gospel of Mark, composed around 70 C.E., possibly in Rome.[1]

It is true that Mark does not use the term *dikaiosynē* ("justice") and only twice mentions the word *dikaios* ("just," or "righteous," in 2:17; 6:20), which he takes as a qualifier, opposite to "sinner" and parallel to "holy." Still, in spite of the absence of this vocabulary, the concept of justice is included in the new order of relations that Mark advocates for the Christian community.[2] He shows that Jesus

---

[1] Raymond E. Brown and John P. Meier, *Antioch and Rome: New Testament Cradles of Catholic Christianity* (New York: Paulist, 1983), 191–201; Paul J. Achtemeier, "Mark, Gospel of," *ABD* 4:541–57.

[2] For a study of Mark from the perspective of social justice, see Hisako Kinukawa, *Women and Jesus in Mark: A Japanese Feminist Perspective* (Maryknoll: Orbis, 1994); Herman C. Waetjen, *A Reordering of Power: A Socio-political Reading of Mark's Gospel* (Philadelphia: Fortress, 1989); Ched Myers, *Binding the Strong Man: A Political Reading of Mark's Story of Jesus* (Maryknoll: Orbis, 1988); Dieter Lührmann, *Das Markusevangelium* (HNT 3; Tübingen: Mohr, 1987); D. A. Lee-Pollard, "Powerlessness as Power: A Key Emphasis in the Gospel of Mark," *SJT* 40 (1987): 173–88; José Cardenas Pallares, *A Poor Man Called Jesus: Reflections on the Gospel of Mark* (trans. R. R. Barr; Maryknoll: Orbis, 1986); Dan O. Via, Jr., *The Ethics of Mark's Gospel in the Middle of Time* (Philadelphia: Fortress, 1985); John R. Donahue, *The Theology and Setting of Discipleship in the Gospel of Mark* (Milwaukee: Marquette University Press, 1983); Fernando Belo, *A Materialistic Reading of the Gospel of Mark* (trans. M. J. O'Connell; Maryknoll: Orbis, 1981); Howard C. Kee, *Community of the New Age: Studies on Mark's Gospel* (Philadelphia: Westminster, 1977).

restores human beings and promotes them to the kingdom he proclaims and inaugurates. The Markan Jesus, indeed, frees people from the slavery of Satan and the slavery of wealth. He sets them free from the restrictions imposed by the principle of legal purity and from the oppression derived from the despotic exercise of authority. He restores dignity to the lowly, the defenseless, and women. Moreover, Jesus creates a new family in which the liberated and restored people can lead a life in accordance with his teaching. Jesus' restoring actions invoke the biblical concept of justice to the extent that he frees people and places them in the position accorded by God's will. The disciples, in turn, by following Jesus' teaching and imitating his example, are able to show the justice God demands in the final period of history.

1. Jesus as Messiah, spokesman, and agent of God's kingdom

Mark entitles his book "the beginning of the gospel of Jesus Christ, the Son of God" (1:1). In the title, Jesus is called Messiah (Christ), the eschatological messianic king expected in some Jewish circles but understood by Mark in a specifically Christian sense. The expression "the Son of God," a variant witnessed by important manuscripts, was a title attributed to Jesus from the early years of Christianity. In the Markan tradition, besides the messianic role, the title "the Son of God" included also a unique relation with God the Father. The word "gospel" ("good news"), by which Mark describes his work, has a prophetic background but was also a term known in the Greco-Roman world. Second Isaiah uses it to announce the liberation of the exiles and the restoration of Zion (Isa 40:9–10). In the Greco-Roman world, the term recurs in the imperial propaganda to celebrate the birth of the emperor, the "son of God" and the "father of peace." Mark writes during the Pax Romana and thus alludes to the language of imperial propaganda. His use of such terminology, however, does not refer to the birth of a Roman emperor. For Mark, the "good news" refers to the actions of a Jewish person appointed by God as the spokesman and the bearer of a new kingdom: the universal kingdom of God.

In Mark's Gospel, an epigraph follows the title (Mark 1:2). A quotation introducing the theme of the Gospel,[3] it results from a combination of texts taken from Exodus, Malachi, and Second Isaiah. The epigraph reminds the reader that the entire story of this Gospel is anchored in the Scriptures and contains the idea of their eschatological fulfillment according to the Christian perspective.

Mark 1:2 includes several references. It refers both to the messenger promised to Israel in the journey to the promised land (Exod 23:20) and to the one whom, according to Malachi, God would send to purify the temple in preparation for the coming of the Lord (Mal 3:1). The Jewish tradition identifies this messen-

---

[3] See Robert M. Fowler, *Let the Reader Understand: Reader-Response Criticism and the Gospel of Mark* (Minneapolis: Fortress, 1991), 87–91.

ger with Elijah, expected to come at the end of time (Mal 4:5; Sir 48:10–12). Mark also identifies the messenger with the voice that, in Second Isaiah (Isa 40:3), proclaims the good news of the liberation from the Babylonian captivity and assures the restoration of Zion. According to Mark, John the Baptist is the messenger to whom this dense series of allusions refers. He comes to prepare for God's definitive intervention into human history in an eschatological exodus. He prepares the way for the advent of God in the person of Jesus. The identification of John the Baptist with the voice of Second Isaiah signals that John heralds the coming of God as king who is ready, through Jesus, to use his sovereign power for the salvation of God's people (Isa 40:10; 52:7). John designates Jesus as the bearer of the power of God's kingdom, thus evoking the mighty deeds God performed to liberate God's people from abusive powers and reassuring believers that God will definitively intervene to establish God's kingdom by destroying evil and creating the community in justice and peace.

After introducing John the Baptist, Mark inserts the episode of Jesus' baptism, in which the heavenly voice confirms what John's voice has already stated—namely, that Jesus is the eschatological messianic king ready to come into action (Mark 1:11; Ps 2:7). By confirming John's statement, the heavenly voice also warrants the authenticity of the title that Mark gives Jesus at the beginning of the Gospel: the Son of God. Subsequently, Mark portrays Jesus initiating his public ministry by proclaiming the good news of God: "The time is fulfilled, and the kingdom of God has come near" (Mark 1:15). With these episodes put at the beginning of his Gospel, Mark prepares the reader to understand Jesus' dignity and mission.

According to Mark, Jesus' proclamation of the kingdom accompanied manifestations of divine power. Mark's Jesus is both the herald of the kingdom and the bearer of the power proclaimed. Indeed, Jesus' power made a deep impression on the people, to the extent that they questioned who this man was.[4] But according to Mark, Jesus' great reputation among the people aroused suspicions in certain circles. The Pharisees, for instance, regarded him as so dangerous that they joined the Herodians in a plan to destroy him (3:6). Additionally, scribes coming from Jerusalem assumed that Jesus acted by the power of the devil (3:22). Still, in spite of the opposition of Pharisees, Herodians, and some scribes, the puzzling question of Jesus' mission and identity continued to fascinate the people at large. The narrator, accordingly, uses the recurring question of Jesus' identity to help the reader discover the true meaning of the divine mystery of Jesus in the midst of the fight of two kingdoms, the kingdom of God and the kingdom of Satan.

The tension around this question reaches a high point when Jesus himself asks the disciples about his own identity (8:27–29) and Peter identifies him as the expected messianic king. At this point, Jesus takes the opportunity to clarify the sense of his messianic role. He does not reject Peter's statement but corrects it by adding the first prediction of the passion. In it he states that, according to the divine will, the way of the messiah runs through the passion and death (8:31).

---

[4] See Mark 1:22, 27; 2:12; 5:20, 42; 7:37.

With this statement, Jesus reveals the mystery that gives sense to his life and mission. He rejects the political concept of a messiah who rules over a society and exercises his authority vertically—from the top of a pyramid, as it were. He rejects the concept of a messiah who administers the economy of the nation, maintains an army to support his power, collects taxes, and subsidizes a temple served by priests committed to keeping the order established by the royal administration. Instead, the Markan Jesus introduces the concept of a messiah who serves his people even to accepting death on their behalf, a messiah who exercises God's saving justice, offers forgiveness, and rehabilitates people so that they can share his kingdom. In this concept, the Messiah establishes a new social order of horizontal structure and equal dignity for its members, a social order in which a human being finds its realization both individually and corporately. In this type of society, those in administration do not lord it over others, tyrannizing them; rather, they serve them. Jesus does not reject the sociopolitical character of the Messiah. He does reject a certain political concept of power.

After his acceptance of the passion and death as the plan of God, Jesus invites his disciples to follow him in the way of suffering and martyrdom (8:34–38; 10:38–39). To his followers he offers life (8:35). To those who confess their loyalty before the human court, he promises his support before God's tribunal (8:38). To those who are fallen, he offers rehabilitation by the power of the saving justice of God. He takes the initiative to meet those who abandoned him and urges them to return.[5] To those who repent, he offers forgiveness (14:66–72; 16:7).

2. Jesus as the crucified Messiah and the cornerstone of the new community

On entering Jerusalem, Jesus was acclaimed as the expected Davidic king (11:9–10), but he did not take the opportunity provided by popular acclamation to take over the rule of the nation. In the following days, however, Jesus performed actions and issued statements tantamount to announcements of destruction and replacement—destruction of the present structures of the nation and their replacement by structures of a new order. It is worthwhile noticing the sequence of episodes in which Mark arranges Jesus' actions during his first two days in Jerusalem (11:11–21).

Mark says that on the first day Jesus "entered Jerusalem and went into the temple; and when he had looked around at everything, as it was already late, he went out to Bethany with the twelve" (11:11). Returning to Jerusalem the following day, Jesus looked for figs to eat on a fig tree near the road, but on not finding them, he was disappointed and cursed the tree (11:14). The narrator notes that "it was not the season for figs" (11:13) to alert the reader to the symbolic meaning of the action.

---

[5] See Mark 13:9–11; 14:50; 16:7.

Then Jesus entered the temple. After driving out buyers and sellers, he began to teach: "Is it not written, 'My house shall be called a house of prayers for all the nations'? But you have made it a den of robbers" (11:17). Jesus addressed his statement to an audience wider than the sellers and buyers. In fact, the chief priests and the scribes understood that Jesus also referred to the authorities of the temple and to the whole administrative and magisterial body of Jerusalem (11:18). Jesus blamed them for having distorted the religious meaning of the temple. For, according to the prophetic view, the temple was meant to be a perfect religious center attracting all the nations of the world.[6] Using Jeremiah's words (Jer 7:11), Jesus condemned the authorities for having turned the temple into a den of robbers because of their socioeconomic abuses. Jesus' words recall Jeremiah's condemnation of the inhabitants of Jerusalem for oppressing the alien, the orphan, and the widow, for shedding innocent blood, stealing, murdering, committing adultery, and swearing falsely (Jer 7:5–11).

The following day, Jesus and his disciples "saw the fig tree withered away to its roots" (Mark 11:20). The reader who follows the sequence of episodes cannot help but see that the fate of the fig tree anticipates symbolically that of the temple. The Jerusalem temple will lose its role as the center of mediation for the salvation of the nations and will give way to another center and another community.

A change is announced, and the announcement continues in the parable of the Wicked Tenants (12:1–12), which Jesus delivers on the third day of his stay in Jerusalem. In it he exposes the plots of his adversaries and foretells their criminal action and their subsequent punishment. On the one hand, they will kill the beloved son sent by God and throw him "out of the vineyard." On the other hand, God, the owner of the vineyard, will punish them and give the vineyard to others (12:8–9). This parable is reminiscent of the song of the vineyard in Isa 5:1–7. The difference is that, unlike Isaiah's vineyard, Mark's is not identified with Israel. The vineyard in Mark refers to the religious institution as mediator of salvation. Still, the responsible parties in both cases—in Isaiah's song and in Jesus' parable—are the same, the religious authorities in Jerusalem. The common denominator in the blame against them is that they did not bear the expected fruits of loyalty and justice. The judgment issued by Isaiah resounds in the background of the parable: "He [the Lord] expected justice, but saw bloodshed; righteousness, but heard a cry!" (Isa 5:7). The cry in Isaiah's song is the weeping of the defenseless who, exploited by the powerful, lost their lands and houses (5:8). In Jesus' parable, there is wrath on the part of the owner because, instead of good fruits, the tenants brought forth rejection and bloodshed. The outcome is that the religious authorities, responsible for the crime, will lose the religious mediating role entrusted to them. To complete the picture, Jesus introduces another metaphor: the rejected stone that becomes the cornerstone. Jesus is the stone rejected by the builders; the builders stand for the authorities in Jerusalem. They rejected Jesus, but God makes him the cornerstone of a new building, a new temple, the new and final

---

[6] See Isa 2:2–3; 56:7; 60:4–12; Mic 4:1–2; Zech 8:20–22.

community of God (Mark 12:10–11). The divine action shows two sides of God's justice. He both punishes the oppressor and the arrogant and vindicates the oppressed and the rejected.

When the parable comes to fulfillment and Jesus is arrested and condemned to death, he does not offer resistance; he surrenders to the authorities and submits himself quietly to the sentence of death. Outwardly, Jesus' death looked like the final defeat of his cause and the victory of his enemies. But as events turned out, the institution Jesus' enemies supported was ruined, and the order on which they lived was destroyed. Mark says that "the curtain of the temple was torn in two, from top to bottom" and the Roman centurion made his profession of faith in Jesus, the Son of God (15:38–39). The narrator tells the reader that the saving presence of God, dwelling in the temple of Jerusalem, broke the sacred barriers of the traditional institution and came to establish itself in Jesus, hanging on the cross outside the walls. The one thrown "out of the vineyard" turned out to be the mediator of salvation for the whole world, both for Jews and for Gentiles. The crucified person who was supposed to contaminate the land (Deut 21:22–23) became the genuine source of holy and everlasting life. By virtue of the one who died on the cross, a new community is born; a new order, God established a new justice for the salvation of the world.

3. Reordering power in the world

According to Mark, the power that Jesus displayed in his teaching and miracles had never before been seen by those who saw and heard him. The narrator explains that the audience's perception resulted from Jesus' way of teaching; unlike the scribes, he taught with authority (Mark 1:22). Mark graphically describes the authority of Jesus' words by juxtaposing to his teaching the healing of a possessed man, whom Jesus exorcised by the power of his command (1:21–28, 39; 3:11). This striking phenomenon needed explanation. Scribes came from Jerusalem, the center of Jewish religious authority, to account for it. Their opinion was that Jesus was able to cast out demons "by the ruler of the demons" (3:22). Therefore they found him dangerous. Mark pits the scribal opinion against the demons' own view. While scribes talk about a struggle for power among the demons, the demons themselves state in unison that Jesus is the Son of God who comes to destroy their kingdom (3:11; also 1:24; 5:7). Ironically, whereas scribes blame Jesus for collaborating with one party of demons, they themselves turn away from the Spirit of God (3:29) and, for all practical purposes, side with demons against Jesus.

Jesus states that the scribes' argument does not hold water. The struggle of demons among themselves would mean that the kingdom of Satan is divided; such a division would be a sign of an inner crisis foretelling the collapse of the satanic power (3:24–26). In his response, Jesus provides the true interpretation for what is going on. He himself is the stronger one who, by the power of the Spirit of God, deprives the less strong one (Satan) of his subjects (3:27). Jesus' liberating actions are acts of justice against Satan's usurped dominion; by destroying satanic forces, he reorders power in the world. Jesus' actions against Satan, though brief and occasional, symbolize and anticipate the liberation from the dehumanizing forces of evil, a liberation that the kingdom of God will bring to its fullness forever.

H. C. Waetjen holds that the demons expelled by Jesus stand for sociopolitical institutions that dehumanize humankind. He cites the text of *1 Enoch* 6–7 and 15, in which the giants, offspring of fallen angels, represent the Hellenistic rulers as oppressors of humanity. Waetjen points to the synagogue as an oppressive power that, under Satan's direction, rejects Jesus' teaching on the new order that God is inaugurating.[7] Similarly, P. W. Hollenbach finds an anti-Roman reference in the Latin name "legion" (Mark 5:9), a name that the unclean spirit applies to himself in the story of the Gerasene demoniac (5:1–20).[8]

It is true that *1 Enoch* regards the Hellenistic rulers as embodiments of the satanic giants. This sort of symbolism accords with an apocalyptic approach in times of persecution and suffering. The same approach appears in Daniel and Revelation when they identify empires with chaotic beasts. Mark, however, does not explicitly identify at least Jewish authority with satanic power. But he certainly shows a systematic opposition of Jewish authorities to Jesus from the beginning, a radical resistance that prompted them to plot against his life (3:6). The Markan Jesus saw in the opposition of his adversaries an unforgivable sin because they attributed to Satan a power that really comes from the Spirit of God (3:29–30). Mark seems to suggest that the Jewish authorities sided with the devil in their design to kill Jesus, since Jesus actually was the great adversary of Satan.[9] Their opposition did not stop with Jesus' death. It continued against Jesus' disciples, bringing them to court (13:9). In Mark's view, the Jewish authorities turn out to be an oppressive power, whose destruction by the divine action establishing the new order of salvation Jesus foretold (12:1–12; 13:2).

An anti-Roman reference in "legion" is deemed possible by many scholars.[10] In the context of Mark 5:1–20, the term "legion" designates a high concentration of demonic power, a concentration that, on the one hand, explains the amazing strength of the possessed man (5:4) and, on the other hand, prepares for the scene of unclean spirits entering two thousand swine (5:13). Moreover, the Gerasene demoniac stands for the disorder of the pagan world. This story contains elements reminiscent of the Greek text of Isa 65:3–5 and Ps 67:6. The text from Isaiah refers to pagan and unclean people who offer sacrifices to demons, eat pork, and dwell in

---

[7] Waetjen, *Reordering*, 81–82.

[8] Paul W. Hollenbach, "Jesus, Demoniacs, and Public Authorities: A Socio-historical Study," *JAAR* 49 (1981): 575–79.

[9] Mark 14:1, 43, 53; 15:1.

[10] Paul Winter, *On the Trial of Jesus* (SJ 1; Berlin: de Gruyter, 1961), 129; Gerd Theissen, *The Miracle Stories of the Early Christian Tradition* (trans. F. McDonagh; Edinburgh: T&T Clark, 1983), 254–59; Joachim Gnilka, *Das Evangelium nach Markus* (2 vols.; EKKNT II/1; Zurich: Benzinger, 1978), 1:205; Rudolf Pesch, *Das Markusevangelium* (2 vols.; HTKNT 2; Freiburg: Herder, 1977), 1:286, 294.

tombs and mountain caves; and the psalm speaks of God's action that frees those held in chains and those who dwell in tombs.[11] Thus, the demoniac exorcised by Jesus is a prototype of the pagan world, which Jesus's power frees from Satan's dominion and joins to God's kingdom. The sociopolitical meaning, on the other hand, may include a reference, in the legion of unclean spirits, to the unclean and oppressive foreign power that occupies the territory by force and does not want to leave. In this context, Jesus' exorcism may be interpreted as a sign of a future liberation of the land. But without doubt, the exorcised man, free from demons, prepares for the saving action of Jesus in the Decapolis (Mark 7:31–8:13) by announcing to the people of his district the action of saving justice performed on his behalf (5:20). In so doing, he follows Jesus' order: "Go home to your friends, and tell them how much the Lord has done for you, and what mercy he has shown you" (5:19). He gives testimony of his experience of the action of God's justice that has liberated and rehabilitated him, and encourages his people to open themselves to—indeed, to long for—God's saving action.

4. Power as a service for the community

In Mark, the third prediction of the passion (10:32–34) precedes the episode of James and John, sons of Zebedee, asking ambitiously for the highest places in the kingdom (10:35–45). As the story runs, Jesus denies the petition because only God the Father can award those positions (10:40). He instructs them, however, regarding the kingdom in which they desire to exercise power: they will have to follow him along the way of suffering, even to the point of death. In the meantime, the other disciples, moved by jealousy and envy, grow angry with the sons of Zebedee. So Jesus takes the opportunity to clarify a new concept of authority that he brings into the world and wants his disciples to practice in the Christian community. This new concept finds its ground in imitating Jesus, who "came not to be served but to serve, and to give his life as ransom for many" (10:45).

In this episode from Mark's Gospel, Jesus sees authority as a service for the good of others. He repudiates the practice of the rulers of the nations, who exploit their subjects in order to live in luxury and who require armies and police forces to maintain their power. Jesus rejects any abuse of authority, disapproves of its use for the profit of a few, and declines to use force against violence. He prefers to break the cycle of violence by dying as a silent and unresisting martyr, a victim of abusive force. Jesus' goal is to create a community free from oppressive power, a community in which those who preside are meant to serve. If there is a place for slaves in the community, those who rule should be their slaves.

This lesson on service and authority, which follows the third passion prediction in Mark, is consonant with the lesson Jesus gave after the second passion

---

[11] See Rudolph Pesch, "The Markan Version of the Healing of the Gerasene Demoniac," *EcumRev* 23 (1971): 349–76.

prediction, when the disciples discuss among themselves who the greatest is (9:33–34). In response, Jesus says to them, "If any one would be first, he must be last of all and servant of all" (9:35). He then teaches that status and honor mean serving the least in the community. To this effect, he places a child in their midst and tells them, "Whoever receives one such child in my name receives me; and whoever receives me, receives not me but him who sent me" (9:37). Those who shelter and serve the least significant of the community pay honor to Jesus and to the heavenly Father.

Jesus not only teaches lessons of service in the Gospel of Mark; he also gives an appropriate example, such as the service he renders to the hungry throng in the desert (6:30–44; 8:1–10). He feeds them by multiplying the few loaves and fish he finds, and commands his disciples to give them to the people (6:41; 8:6). Mark stresses the fact that Jesus, in teaching and in feeding the multitude, acts like the true shepherd who, moved by compassion, tends the sheep that lack a shepherd (6:34). In the reference to "sheep without a shepherd," Mark alludes to the prophet Ezekiel, who prophesied against the shepherds (civil and religious leaders) of Israel because they fed themselves by exploiting and harshly ruling over the sheep instead of tending and feeding them (Ezek 34:8). The sheep were scattered because of a lack of proper care. In his oracle, Ezekiel promised that God himself would gather the scattered and would feed them by an intervention of "saving justice."[12] In Mark's view, Jesus fulfills God's promise. He puts into action the saving justice of God. He gathers and organizes the scattered multitude (Mark 6:39–40), and feeds them with his teaching and his multiplied bread and fish. By alluding to Ezekiel, the narrator insinuates a critique of the Jewish leaders who oppress their own people in their denial of the true teaching that would lead them to accept the presence of the kingdom in the person of Jesus. Their oppression of the people is intensified by their corrupt administration of the temple.

The service of saving justice that Jesus renders to the hungry multitude, in contrast to the careless and abusive treatment by the authorities, teaches a significant lesson for the leaders of the Christian community. The Markan narrative, however, brings out a further lesson. The second multiplication of loaves takes place in pagan territory, in the hilly area of the Decapolis (7:31). This Markan geography indicates that the service Jesus renders to human beings goes beyond the national and religious borders of Judaism, encompassing the whole of humanity on equal terms.

5. Liberation from the slavery of wealth

In the parable of the Sower, the Markan Jesus says that the thorns choked the seed and prevented it from yielding grain (4:7), and then he explains that the

---

[12] "I will feed them with justice *[běmišpāṭ]*" (Ezek 14:14). The LXX translated the expression by *meta krimatos,* loading the Greek term *krima* with salvific connotations.

thorns stand for "the cares of the world, the delight in riches, and the desire for other things" (4:19). In other words, the attachment to a life of pleasure, to the enjoyment of status, to the social and political power that wealth creates, and to the avarice that these attachments in turn generate—all clash with the demands of God's kingdom. For wealth takes full possession of the person's heart and does not permit a radical commitment to the kingdom to develop. The all-absorbing demands of wealth appear clearly in the story of the rich man (10:17–22), which Mark takes from oral tradition. The rich man refuses to sell his properties and give the proceeds to the poor. In opposition to the rich man, whose heart is mastered by his attachment to wealth, Jesus contrasts the action of the poor widow, who contributes to the needs of others with "everything she had, her whole living" (12:44). While the rich man is encumbered by his attachment to wealth, the poor widow is free to reach out and help others.

This lesson of enslavement to wealth is extremely important in a world in which money, power, and pleasure are the only things that count. The demands of God's kingdom clash with this disposition of the human person. For the kingdom calls for the restoration of the human person in a community animated by justice and peace. The kingdom of God demands that the rich take care of the poor; they must employ their wealth in social service so that the poor may share in their well-being.

Following the synoptic tradition, Mark advocates liberation from the slavery of wealth. But he introduces something new. He does not just retain the call to abandon everything and to become an itinerant preacher, as do the traditions preserved in Q (Luke 14:26–27//Matt 10:37–38). Mark chooses to be in a family in which people live according to the spirit of Jesus' teaching.

6. A family of disciples on equal conditions

Mark contrasts Jesus' earthly family with his new and spiritual family. Members of his natural family look for Jesus because "people were saying, 'He has gone out of his mind'" (Mark 3:21), and they stand outside waiting for him (3:32). In contrast to the natural family, the new and true family are those who are *inside* the house *(oikia)*—his disciples. They are those who do the will of God (3:34–35). In the house, the disciples are able to know the will of God, explained by Jesus; they find support to live according to the demands of his teaching; and they receive the spiritual energy to resist the dehumanizing and alienating factors of the surrounding culture.[13]

The spiritual family is a community of brothers and sisters in which each member enjoys the support of all and the service of those who preside, according to Jesus' teaching on authority (10:41–45). This concept of community also seems to be hinted at by Jesus when he speaks of the reward the disciples would

---

[13] See Myers, *Binding,* 150–51, 181.

receive on earth because they have left everything and followed him. Jesus lists things the disciples left for his sake and that of the gospel, including house, brothers, sisters, mother, father, children, and fields (10:29). When Jesus refers to the reward the disciples will receive "now at this age" (10:30), he repeats the words of the description he makes of the things left behind (10:29), with one exception—he omits the word "father." This omission seems to indicate that the spiritual family of Jesus on earth does not share the concept of authority typical of the patriarchal culture of the Jewish or Greco-Roman household. Rather, the new community of Jesus is shaped according to the spirit of service and love, which makes people equal in dignity and mutually supportive, a spirit that flows from Jesus' sayings, according to which "whoever wants to be first must be last of all and servant of all" (9:35; 10:43–45). The same spirit guides everyone to welcome, embrace, and serve the least significant people in the community (9:36–37; 10:14–15).

Of course, belonging to the spiritual family of Jesus does not prevent Christians from having a natural family now, the time between the beginning of the kingdom and its consummation. For the community grows both by the addition of converts and by the birth of children of Christian parents. In effect, Mark validates Christian life within the social structure of marriage, children, and possessions, as is clear in his defense of marriage against divorce (10:1–12). The validation of Christian life within the structure of the natural family appears again in the general statement about missionaries: "There is no one who has left house . . . for my sake and for the sake of the gospel who will not receive a hundredfold now in this age" (10:29).[14] The statement refers not only to converts who leave their non-Christian families but also to those who leave their Christian households for the sake of the gospel. Were matters otherwise, the community would have had to recruit missionaries only from converts.

7. Reshaping the center of purity

In the Jewish social and religious world, the law of purity was a boundary marker distinguishing the Jewish people from other nations, and a criterion for membership in the community.[15] The lack of physical integrity, for instance, prevented an individual from having access to social or religious life. Jesus, however, does not employ physical defects and legal impurities as criteria for excluding people from the community. In the thought of Jesus, obstacles to participation in

---

[14] See Lührmann, *Markusevangelium*, 176.
[15] See Jerome H. Neyrey, "The Idea of Purity in Mark's Gospel," *Semeia* 35 (1986): 91–128; J. Neyrey, "A Symbolic Approach to Mark 7," *Foundations and Facets Forum* 4/3 (1988): 63–91; Marcus J. Borg, *Conflict, Holiness, and Politics in the Teachings of Jesus* (SBEC 5; New York: Edwin Mellen, 1984), 56–72, 96–109, 239–40; Bruce J. Malina, *The New Testament World: Insights from Cultural Anthropology* (Louisville: Westminster/John Knox, 1993), 159–62.

community life result not from external circumstances, but from the heart as the center of thoughts and free decisions. In this regard, Jesus makes an important statement addressing Pharisees and scribes who complained because his disciples, against the traditions of the elders, eat with defiled hands (7:1–15). In his response, Jesus establishes a new principle of purity: "There is nothing outside a person that by going in can defile, but the things that come out are what defile" (7:15). In Jesus' explanation what defiles includes such as things as "evil thoughts, fornication, theft, murder, adultery, coveting, wickedness, deceit, licentiousness, envy, slander, pride, and foolishness" (7:22).

Mark underlines the import of Jesus' statement for the Christian community by narrating that, immediately after his response to the Pharisees and scribes, Jesus meets his disciples "in the house" and gives them a special explanation on the matter (7:17–23). As the following context shows, Jesus' statement contains a basic norm for the admission of new members into the community and includes a criterion to avoid discrimination. If justice means the act of liberating people from obstacles that hinder their full expression and restoring them to their rightful place according to God's design, then by this statement Jesus abolishes any notion of justice that is exclusive and discriminatory and establishes one that is open, inclusive, liberating, and promoting.

The following context shows the consequences of Jesus' statement on the principle of purity.[16] It is the episode of the Syrophoenician woman who "begged Jesus to cast the demon out of her daughter" (7:26). This is an interesting episode because, first, it reflects the racial, cultural, and sociopolitical hostility between Jews and pagan neighbors[17] and, second, it indicates the difficulty Jewish Christians had accepting pagan converts into their community. In the Markan story, a pagan woman in a pagan territory approaches Jesus with a request that puts him in a difficult spot. Delicate social and cultural conditions advise him to proceed with caution. On the one hand, Jesus is expected to protect the national honor of his own people. On the other hand, he is moved by compassion and by the honor of the kingdom of God. To get out of the difficulty, Jesus first pleases his fellow Jews by speaking harshly with the pagan woman and then satisfies the pagans by granting her request. The episode shows the happy denouement of the interaction between Jesus, who proceeds with caution, and the woman, who urges him on with her unbreakable and persistent faith.[18] The woman asks for a reconsideration of the concept of strict justice that would reserve bread for the family's children alone. She requests compassion for those who do not belong to the family. As a result, Jesus transcends the barriers of strict justice and extends the power of his saving justice to the pagan woman. His action displays a paradigm for the Christian community: Jesus opens the door to the pagans, offering them the

---

[16] Enrique Nardoni, "Lo puro y lo impuro en Marcos 7:1–23: La respuesta del lector," *RevistB* 59 (1997): 135–54.

[17] Theissen, *Miracle Stories*, 254.

[18] See Kinukawa, *Women*, 51–61.

benefit of God's saving justice.[19] Jesus feeds the pagans with his bread, the bread of the Christian family.

A similar approach occurs in the second multiplication of loaves, which Jesus performs in the pagan territory of the Decapolis (8:1–9; 7:31). Jesus shows compassion toward the hungry multitude (8:2), just as he did in the first multiplication of loaves. In the first multiplication of loaves, however, Jesus fed Jews; while in the second multiplication, he feeds pagans. Both multiplications have eucharistic echoes (6:41; 8:6; 14:22). With these allusions in mind, the reader may find that Jesus set a precedent for Gentile Christians to sit with Jewish Christians at the same table of the Lord. Such a precedent gets its motivation and power from Jesus' death on the cross (15:37–39), a death that breaks down barriers imposed by cult, abolishes the concept of a closed and exclusive justice, and extends God's saving action to all humanity.

In Mark's Gospel, Jesus foresees that the disciples, inspired by his word and example, will extend God's salvation to the world by preaching the gospel to the nations (13:10). They will sow God's word, planting communities everywhere. Thus they will extend Christ's family over all the earth. Both Jews and Gentiles will sit together at the same table of the Lord. As Christ's family, Christians will witness to the world of a new way of life, in which the exercise of authority is a service to the community and relationships among members are animated by a spirit of mutual love and care. Following Christ's teaching, Christians will develop a strong sense of human dignity and justice. But Christians will also undergo persecutions for the sake of Christ's word (13:9–13) until the consummation of the kingdom. Indeed, Jesus foresees his disciples' future hardship and, using apocalyptic language, describes their suffering in a world under the sway of ambitious powers in competition, a world possessed by an irresistible passion for domination, exploitation, and pleasure. The disciples will be tempted to deny their own identity in such a world, but Jesus exhorts them to persevere in their mission of preaching the gospel (13:10). Justice will be done: sinners will be destroyed, and the elect will be gathered together (13:27) and rewarded with a new existence in a world free from oppression and suffering and will enjoy God's peace and happiness forever.

8. The dignity of women

Mark stresses the dignity of women on several occasions. He does so, for instance, when he uses a feminine character, the Syrophoenician woman, to announce salvation to the pagan world (7:24–30). He does so also in the manner in which Jesus phrases the prohibition of divorce: "Whoever divorces his wife and marries another, commits adultery against her; and if she divorces her husband and marries another, she commits adultery" (10:11–12). In the Markan text, there

---

[19] Kee, *Community*, 149.

is a balance of rights and obligations. The husband sins against her if he marries another woman, and the wife sins against him if she marries another man. Unlike the Jewish custom, Mark's view comes close to full equality and mutual responsibility between man and woman.[20] Neither of the spouses should consider his or her partner disposable.

Mark is not only interested in the acceptance of women in the community on equal footing with men. He also is concerned with the promotion of women in the Christian community, as exemplified in the episode of the woman who anoints Jesus' head (14:3–9). Mark places the episode between the plot of the chief priests and the scribes to kill Jesus (14:1–2) and the Last Supper (14:12–31). The position of the story within the narrative framework of Mark's Gospel highlights it. An unnamed woman pours a highly expensive perfume over Jesus' head. Some of the disciples deem the woman's action as too extravagant a gesture, complaining that the cost of the perfume amounts to a year's salary and that the money could have been used to support the poor. The narrator, however, considers the woman's gesture highly symbolic.[21] Jesus himself explains its meaning. He identifies the unnamed woman as a prophetess who anticipates the anointing for his burial. She performs a prophetic action of great scope: an anointing suited to a royal burial because of the high cost and fine quality of the perfume used.[22] By her action, she demonstrates that she possesses the sharp perception of a prophetess of exceptional caliber and that she is endowed with the faith of a true and enlightened disciple. This woman is the first Christian prophet. While none of the disciples understand the passion of Jesus as messianic suffering, she carries out the symbolic action of anointing Jesus as messianic king; she performed an anointing befitting the royal dignity that Jesus would obtain by his death and resurrection. In doing so, she turns out to be a giant figure in the history of salvation, so that she will be remembered "wherever the gospel is proclaimed in the whole world" (14:9).

Conclusion

In Mark, Jesus is the spokesman and agent of God's kingdom and the cornerstone of the new community. He is the Messiah, who reaches his fulfillment in his death on the cross. The Markan Jesus reorders power in the world by defeating the kingdom of Satan and putting into action the power of God's kingdom. By his action, he frees the oppressed from demonic power, which, for Mark, enslaves not only through physical and mental illness, but also through the violence of human customs, institutions, and actions. Jesus announces the destruction of abusive power represented by the authorities that would condemn him and persecute his

---

[20] Ibid., 155.
[21] Kinukawa, *Women*, 83–88.
[22] Josephus describes the custom of lavishly anointing the bodies of dead kings when he relates the account of the burial of Herod (*Ant.* 17.8.3).

disciples. He established a new and definite order grounded in God's will, the core of which are his teaching and the saving event of his death and resurrection. In the new order, the saving action of God reaches the whole of humanity without distinction of race, nation, sex, or degree of legal purity. The new order shatters the barriers of a discriminatory justice and opens the saving justice of God to everyone who believes in Christ.

Jesus formed a community whose members are of equal dignity. He gave them a spirit of fellowship and mutual service and offered himself as a model to imitate, for he did not come to be served but to serve, even until death. The disciples, bound by a spirit of fellowship and service, are called to help each other know and fulfill Jesus' teaching and to shape their character according to his spirit. Moreover, the community Jesus formed is meant to protect the disciples against the dehumanizing influence of the surrounding world and to help them give a countercultural testimony. Their testimony will include an implicit social protest and will offer a model to imitate. Living in a harsh world, the disciples are encouraged to nurture the certainty that Jesus protects them and will reward them forever when he comes to establish his kingdom in its fullness.

Bibliography

Achtemeier, Paul J. "Mark, Gospel of." Pages 541–57 in vol. 4 of *Anchor Bible Dictionary.* Edited by D. N. Freedman. 6 vols. New York: Doubleday, 1992.

Belo, Fernando. *A Materialistic Reading of the Gospel of Mark.* Translated by M. J. O'Connell. Maryknoll: Orbis, 1981.

Borg, Marcus J. *Conflict, Holiness, and Politics in the Teachings of Jesus.* Studies in the Bible and Early Christianity 5. New York: Edwin Mellen, 1984.

Brown, Raymond E., and John P. Meier. *Antioch and Rome: New Testament Cradles of Catholic Christianity.* New York: Paulist, 1983.

Cardenas Pallares, José. *A Poor Man Called Jesus: Reflections on the Gospel of Mark.* Translated by R. R. Barr. Maryknoll: Orbis, 1986.

Donahue, John R. *The Theology and Setting of Discipleship in the Gospel of Mark.* Milwaukee: Marquette University Press, 1983.

Fowler, Robert M. *Let the Reader Understand: Reader-Response Criticism and the Gospel of Mark.* Minneapolis: Fortress, 1991.

Gnilka, Joachim. *Das Evangelium nach Markus.* 2 vols.; Evangelisch-katholischer Kommentar zum Neuen Testament II/1; Zurich: Benzinger, 1978.

Hollenbach, Paul W. "Jesus, Demoniacs, and Public Authorities: A Socio-historical Study." *Journal of the American Academy of Religion* 49 (1981): 567–88.

Kee, Howard C. *Community of the New Age: Studies on Mark's Gospel.* Philadelphia: Westminster, 1977.

Kinukawa, Hisako. *Women and Jesus in Mark: A Japanese Feminist Perspective.* Maryknoll: Orbis, 1994.

Lee-Pollard, D. A. "Powerlessness as Power: A Key Emphasis in the Gospel of Mark." *Scottish Journal of Theology* 40 (1987): 173–88.

Lührmann, Dieter. *Das Markusevangelium*. Handbuch zum Neuen Testament 3. Tübingen: Mohr, 1987.
Malina, Bruce J. *The New Testament World: Insights from Cultural Anthropology*. Louisville: Westminster/John Knox, 1993.
Myers, Ched. *Binding the Strong Man: A Political Reading of Mark's Story of Jesus*. Maryknoll: Orbis, 1988.
Nardoni, Enrique. "Lo puro y lo impuro en Marcos 7:1–23: la respuesta del lector." *Revista biblica* 59 (1997): 135–54.
Neyrey, Jerome H. "The Idea of Purity in Mark's Gospel." *Semeia* 35 (1986): 91–128.
———. "A Symbolic Approach to Mark 7." *Foundations and Facets Forum* 4/3 (1988): 63–91.
Pesch, Rudolph. "The Markan Version of the Healing of the Gerasene Demoniac." *Ecumenical Review* 23 (1971): 349–76.
———. *Das Markusevangelium*. 2 vols. Herders theologischer Kommentar zum Neuen Testament 2. Freiburg: Herder, 1977.
Theissen, Gerd. *The Miracles Stories of the Early Christian Tradition*. Translated by F. McDonagh. Edinburgh: T&T Clark, 1983.
Via, Dan O., Jr. *The Ethics of Mark's Gospel in the Middle of Time*. Philadelphia: Fortress, 1985.
Waetjen, Herman C. *A Reordering of Power: A Socio-political Reading of Mark's Gospel*. Philadelphia: Fortress, 1989.
Winter, Paul. *On the Trial of Jesus*. Studia judaica 1. Berlin: De Gruyter, 1961.

CHAPTER TEN

JUSTICE IN THE GOSPEL OF MATTHEW AND THE LETTER OF JAMES

The present chapter discusses the nature of justice in the Gospel of Matthew and the Letter of James. Both writings share a similar attitude about Jewish Christians in the Christian polemic of the first century and express analogous ideas concerning justice with respect to one's duty to others. Both were composed by Christian authors around the same time, during the eighties or nineties of the first Christian century.[1] The Gospel of Matthew was probably written in Syrian Antioch, the Letter of James in Palestine or Rome.[2]

1. Justice in the Gospel of Matthew

In Matthew, the word *dikaios* ("just" or "righteous") occurs seventeen times, and the term *dikaiosynē* ("justice" or "righteousness") seven times.[3] Several of these references have parallels in Q and Mark, but Matthew increases their number considerably and gives them all a particular connotation in accord with their context. Some scholars hold that *dikaiosynē* in Matthew always relates to ethical conduct guided by God's will.[4] Others maintain that *dikaiosynē* in Matthew is not restricted to a single sense. The term is open to multiple meanings, referring either to divine saving action, or to human moral conduct, or to both. The meaning

---

[1] See John P. Meier, *Matthew* (New Testament Message 3; Wilmington, Del.: Glazier, 1985), 622–41; Raymond E. Brown and John P. Meier, *Antioch and Rome: New Testament Cradles of Catholic Christianity* (New York: Paulist, 1983), 11–86.

[2] See Sophie Laws, "James, Epistle of," *ABD* 3:621–28.

[3] For a study of justice in Matthew, see John H. P. Reumann, *Righteousness in the New Testament: Justification in the United States Lutheran–Roman Catholic Dialogue, with Responses by J. A. Fitzmyer and J. D. Quinn* (Philadelphia: Fortress; New York: Paulist, 1982), 125–35; Benno Przybylski, *Righteousness in Matthew and His World of Thought* (SNTSMS 41; Cambridge: Cambridge University Press, 1980), 77–123; Georg Strecker, *Der Weg der Gerechtigkeit: Untersuchungen zur Theologie des Matthäus* (FRLANT 82; Göttingen: Vandenhoeck & Ruprecht, 1962).

[4] So Jacques Dupont, *Les Béatitudes* (3 vols; EB; Paris: Gabalda, 1958–1973), 3:383–84; Strecker, *Weg der Gerechtigkeit,* 149–58.

has to be defined in each case according to the context.⁵ The question thus arises as to how to translate *dikaiosynē* in Matthew. The RSV and NRSV usually translate it "righteousness." In biblical quotations I follow the NRSV, but because of my approach to the term in other books of the Bible, I prefer to use the term "justice" in the general discussion.

I divide the treatment of justice in the Gospel of Matthew into five sections: the beatitudes (Matt 5:3–10); the antitheses (Matt 5:21–28); the trilogy of justice (Matt 6:1–18); the parable of the two sons (Matt 21:28–32); and the option for the poor and needy involved in healings, exorcisms, and care for others, such as sinners, the little ones, the dispossessed, and the oppressed.

1.1. Justice in the Beatitudes (Matt 5:3–11)

First, an introductory note on the controversial issue of the literary genre of the Sermon on the Mount. In the last decades, two theories have become prominent in scholarly circles. The first is that of W. D. Davies, which regards the Sermon as a Christian answer to Jamnia's teachers, who collected the oral traditions of the Jewish halakah after the fall of Jerusalem in 70 C.E. Their collection formed the core of what would become the Mishnah. Davies argues successfully that the evangelist's community was at odds with this expression of contemporary Judaism.⁶ What is controversial, however, is whether this contention can be proved from the Sermon alone, apart from the whole of the Matthean Gospel.⁷

The second theory is that of H. D. Betz. He argues that the Sermon on the Mount and the rest of Matthew contain different theologies, deriving from diverse environments. According to him, the Sermon was a pre-Matthean tradition, incorporated into the Gospel without major modification. Its literary genre is a summary of Jesus' theology, an epitome stemming from a conservative Jewish-Christian, anti-Pauline community.⁸ Betz's monumental scholarly work has received the admiration and respect of fellow scholars, but many remain unconvinced of his claim that the theological perspective of the Sermon is at odds with the rest of Matthew's Gospel. In their opinion, Matthew has shaped and reinterpreted the traditions at his disposal in the Sermon, following the same methods

---

⁵ John H. P. Reumann, "Righteousness (NT)," *ABD* 5:754–56; *Righteousness*, 125–35; John P. Meier, *Law and History in Matthew's Gospel* (AnBib 71; Rome: Pontifical Biblical Institute, 1976), 76–79.

⁶ See William D. Davies, *The Setting of the Sermon on the Mount* (Cambridge: Cambridge University Press, 1964; repr., Atlanta: Scholars Press), 256–315.

⁷ See Graham N. Stanton, *A Gospel for a New People: Studies in Matthew* (Edinburgh: T&T Clark, 1992), 294–95; and reviews of William D. Davies, *The Setting of the Sermon on the Mount*, by P. Benoit, *RB* 72 (1965): 595–601; Raymond E. Brown, *TS* 25 (1964): 640–43; Georg Strecker, *NTS* 13 (1966): 105–12.

⁸ See Hans D. Betz, *The Sermon on the Mount: A Commentary on the Sermon of the Mount, including the Sermon on the Plain (Matthew 5:3–7:27 and Luke 6:20–49)* (Hermeneia; Minneapolis: Fortress, 1995), 70–88.

and themes he developed elsewhere in his Gospel.⁹ J. D. Kingsbury, for instance, had earlier maintained that the Sermon is an organic part of the Matthean presentation of the story of Jesus.¹⁰ Similarly, support for the theory that the Sermon stems from an anti-Pauline community seems to be declining.¹¹ The Sermon on the Mount, as D. Senior argues, should be understood within Matthew's scope and purpose—he endorses the acceptance of Gentiles but requires them to accept the Jewish-Christian heritage.¹²

In the Beatitudes (Matt 5:3–12), the word *dikaiosynē* occurs only twice (5:6, 10), but its meaning pervades the whole passage.¹³ The Beatitudes in Matthew can be divided into two parts.¹⁴ The first part (5:3–10) addresses hearers in the third person plural ("Blessed are those who . . ."); and the second part (5:11–12), addresses them in the second person plural, pointing to the readers ("Blessed are you . . ."). The present study is concerned with the first part, which makes up a literary unit beginning and ending with the same phrase: "For theirs is the kingdom of heaven" (5:3b, 10b). This unit in turn can be divided into two subsections: the first (5:3–6) deals with the social change that God will bring about in the consummated kingdom on behalf of the poor and oppressed; the second (5:7–10) concerns the reward in store for those who now fulfill the demands of social justice. The first subsection encompasses four beatitudes:

> Blessed are the poor in spirit, for theirs is the kingdom of heaven.
> Blessed are those who mourn, for they will be comforted.
> Blessed are the meek, for they will inherit the earth.
> Blessed are those who hunger and thirst for righteousness *[dikaiosynēn]*, for they will be filled. (5:3–6)

The second subsection likewise includes four beatitudes:

> Blessed are the merciful, for they will receive mercy.
> Blessed are the pure in heart, for they will see God.
> Blessed are the peacemakers, for they will be called children of God.
> Blessed are those who are persecuted for righteousness' sake *[dikaiosynēs]*, for theirs is the kingdom of heaven. (5:7–10)

Both subsections conclude by blessing those who one way or another are involved in issues of *dikaiosynē* (5:6a,10a). The same word, *dikaiosynē*, occurs in

---

⁹ See Stanton, *Gospel,* 294–95, 307–25; and reviews of Hans D. Betz, *The Sermon on the Mount,* by A. C. Allison, *JBL* 117 (1998): 136–38; David Catchpole, *JTS* 49 (1998): 219–25; J. Topel, *CBQ* 59 (1997): 370–72.

¹⁰ Jack D. Kingsbury, "The Place, Structure, and Meaning of the Sermon on the Mount in Matthew," *Int* 41 (1987): 131–43.

¹¹ See Catchpole, review of Betz; Davies, *Setting,* 316–41; Stanton, *Gospel,* 293–318.

¹² Donald Senior, "Between Two Worlds: Gentile and Jewish Christians in Matthew's Gospel," *CBQ* 61 (1999): 1–23.

¹³ For a study of the Beatitudes, see Ingo Broer, *Seligpreisungen der Bergpredigt: Studien zu ihrer Überlieferung und Interpretation* (BBB 61; Bonn: Hanstein, 1986); Dupont, *Béatitudes,* 3:308–667.

¹⁴ This division of the text is taken from Mark A. Powell, "Matthew's Beatitudes: Reversals and Rewards of the Kingdom," *CBQ* 58 (1996): 460–79.

both cases, but with a difference of meaning. While in 5:6a the term refers to God's eschatological action that vindicates those who suffer affliction, in 5:10a it refers to the righteous conduct of Christians who fulfill God's will, striving for justice in human relations.

In the first subsection (5:3–6), there is something striking at the very beginning, in the first beatitude: the expression "poor in spirit" *(ptōchoi tō pneumati)*, a phrase unique to Matthew. Luke does not have it in the parallel verse (Luke 6:20); instead, he gives the word "poor" *(ptōchos)* without a qualifier. The qualification "in spirit" probably comes from Matthew himself, and its purpose is still under discussion.[15] According to the more common opinion, the phrase "poor in spirit" emphasizes the inner and religious attitude of the poor, recognizing that not every poor person is blessed but only the one who experiences weakness, who realizes the deceptive character of human promises, and who trusts in God.[16] Of the expression "poor in spirit," Dupont claims that "the spirit is not the cause by which one is poor, neither is it something one is deprived of. Rather, it defines a particular manner in which one is poor. It is the seat of an interiorized poverty."[17] Yet, as Davies and Allison note, "the economic realm is not altogether out of view; for the coming of the kingdom of heaven (5:3, 10) will certainly eliminate the evils that cause poverty in the present."[18] Although Luke does not use the expression "poor in spirit," he includes the religious attitude in his concept of the poor, as discussed in chapter 11, below. This understanding of poverty is part of the biblical tradition, present particularly in the Prophets and in the Psalms.[19]

A parallel to the Matthean expression "poor in spirit" has been found in the Dead Sea Scrolls. It is the *'anwê rûah* of 1QM 14:7, the precise meaning of which is controverted.[20] S. Légasse argues that the phrase emphasizes the moral and religious dimension in the situation of suffering and oppression present in 1QM 14:7. He identifies a similar background to the Matthean Beatitudes and concludes that Matthew likewise emphasizes the religious dimension of those who are actually poor and downtrodden.[21]

Many scholars have understood the expression "poor in spirit" to designate those who possess a spirit of poverty or are detached from riches, regardless of

---

[15] Dupont offers an extensive analysis of this discussion in *Béatitudes*, 3:386–471.

[16] Dupont, *Béatitudes*, 3:384–471; Simon Légasse, "Les pauvres en esprit et 'le volontaires' de Qumran," *NTS* 8 (1961–1962): 336–45; Broer, *Seligpreisungen*, 73–74; William D. Davies and Dale C. Allison, *A Critical and Exegetical Commentary on the Gospel according to Saint Matthew* (3 vols.; ICC; Edinburgh: T&T Clark, 1988–1997), 1:442–45; Ulrich Luz, *Matthew 1–7: A Continental Commentary* (trans. W. C. Linnss; Minneapolis: Fortress, 1992), 231–35.

[17] Dupont, *Béatitudes*, 3:297.

[18] Davies and Allison, *Matthew*, 1:444, n. 21. See also Broer, *Seligpreisungen*, 73–74.

[19] See, e.g., Isa 57:15; 66:2; Ps 34:17–19; Norbert Lohfink, "Von der 'Anawim-Partei' zur 'Kirche der Armen': Die bibelwissenschaftliche Ahnentafel eines Hauptbegriffs der Theologie der Befreiung," *Bib* 67 (1986): 153–75; Lohfink, *Lobgesänge der Armen* (SBS 143; Stuttgart: Katholisches Bibelwerk, 1990), 32–33. See above, ch. 5, §2.2–9; ch. 6, §1.4.

[20] See Davies and Allison, *Matthew*, 1:444.

[21] Légasse, "Les pauvres en esprit," 336–45. So also Broer, *Seligpreisungen*, 73–74.

their actual economic condition.²² But a closer examination of the context leads the reader in another direction, pointing to those who suffer actual poverty and who, in their suffering, trust in the Lord: the poor in spirit are placed parallel to those who actually mourn, who are oppressed, and who hunger and thirst. To all of these is promised not a reward for their virtue but the eschatological reversal of their present condition in the new world of the kingdom of God.²³

The second beatitude of Matthew (5:4), referring to those who mourn, finds its parallel in the third beatitude of Luke (6:21) and alludes to Isa 61:2. This beatitude deals with those who mourn not because, in their repentance, they regret their sins but because they suffer the bitterness of a social injustice in the midst of a society under the control of the wicked. "Those who mourn" cry out on account of their anguish and moan because the Lord's coming has been delayed. To them eschatological comfort is assured.

The third beatitude of Matthew (5:5), without a parallel in Luke, is a quotation taken from the Greek version of Ps 36:11.²⁴ The LXX, in this psalm, translated the Hebrew ʿănāwîm by *praeis*, a term understood in the sense of meekness or humility by many who considered its Greco-Roman meaning. As a result, the beatitude was understood to offer a reward to those who practiced gentleness and submission. Such an understanding, however, has to be revised in view of the fact that the Hebrew ʿănāwîm in the context of the psalm designates the powerless, the disenfranchised who are humiliated and oppressed by the wicked. The LXX loaded the Greek term *praeis* with Hebrew meaning, designating the oppressed and humiliated as those who in their affliction do not resort to violence but trust in the Lord. This seems to be the understanding that Matthew follows. In the renewed world (*palingenesia*, Matt 19:28) the oppressed, who are deprived of the right to the land but trust in the Lord, will possess the land. This understanding makes sense of the text itself and is confirmed by the context of Matt 5:3–6, in which the point is not the rewarding of virtue but an alteration of social condition.²⁵ This beatitude underlines the importance of the land as a symbol of the resources that contribute to the development of self-identity, stability, freedom, economic security, and dignity of both the individual and the family within a just society.

The fourth beatitude, "Blessed are those who hunger and thirst for righteousness" (5:6), finds its parallel in Luke 6:21: "Blessed are you who are hungry now, for you will be filled." In this beatitude, Matthew diverges from Luke in several details. Unlike Luke, who mentions only "hunger," Matthew employs the traditional biblical couplet "hunger and thirst"²⁶ and qualifies it by adding "for

---

[22] Among representatives of this opinion, see Alfred Durand, *Évangile selon saint Matthieu* (VS 1; Paris: Beauchesne, 1948), 67–68; Joseph Bonsirven, *Le règne de Dieu* (Paris: Beauchesne, 1957), 90–93; Francis J. McGarrigle, "The Humility of the Poor in Spirit," *AER* 144 (1961): 313–19. Also see above, ch. 6, §1.4.

[23] Powell, "Beatitudes," 463–64.

[24] Ps 36 of the LXX corresponds to Ps 37 of the Hebrew text.

[25] See Powell, "Beatitudes," 466; Davies and Allison, *Matthew* 1:449; Eduard Schweizer, *The Good News according to Matthew* (trans. D. E. Green; Atlanta: Knox, 1975), 89.

[26] See Amos 8:11; Isa 49:10; 2 Chr 32:11.

righteousness." Moreover, Matthew uses the third person instead of the second person plural, as Luke does. In the Matthean addition, the term "righteousness" or "justice" has been interpreted in two major ways. W. D. Davies and D. C. Allison as well as J. A. Ziesler argue for the sense of righteous conduct in accordance with the divine will.[27] They find a parallel meaning in two of Jesus' sayings: "Blessed are those who are persecuted for righteousness' sake" (Matt 5:10) and "But strive first for the kingdom of God and his righteousness" (6:33). Others, however, such as J. H. P. Reumann and J. P. Meier, maintain that "justice" in the present context refers to the divine vindication of believers who, under the oppression of the wicked, long for the definitive establishment of justice.[28] The eschatological character of this beatitude seems to tip the balance of probabilities in favor of the latter opinion. In effect, this beatitude (5:6) promises the final restoration of the right order of the covenant—"they will be filled" in the banquet of the kingdom (8:11). The tone of eschatological reversal, present in the fourth beatitude, characterizes indeed the whole first subsection, which promises a radical change on behalf of those who now suffer harsh social conditions but nevertheless trust in the Lord.

The second subsection of the Beatitudes (Matt 5:7–10) continues the eschatological tone of the first—this time with an emphasis not on the reversal of the social situation but on the reward in store for those who practice justice, namely, those who observe the will of God in society. The first beatitude in this set proclaims blessed those who practice mercy or compassion *(eleēmones)* toward their neighbors. Luke does not have a parallel beatitude, but he includes a related saying: "Be merciful, just as your Father is merciful" in Luke 6:36. Matthew, highly interested in the theme of compassion, emphasizes its practice as part of the core of Jesus' message.[29] With this emphasis in mind, Matthew places the theme of compassion into this set of beatitudes and, throughout his Gospel, exhibits Jesus' insistence on this matter. Compassion should extend to everyone, but especially to the social outcast (9:13). Compassion toward others is a duty imposed on us by the fact of God's compassion toward us. God's merciful conduct impels us to imitate him in our relations with our neighbors (Matt 6:12; 25:31–46). Practicing mercy both conforms us to God's conduct and gives our neighbors support for their new beginning and growth. In this sense, compassion or mercy is associated with justice in the broad biblical sense.

The practice of compassion is so far-reaching that Jesus summarizes the essence of law in the practice of justice, mercy, and faithfulness (23:23). In this approach to the law, the Matthean Jesus follows the prophetic tradition. In 23:23, he alludes to Mic 6:8: "What does the Lord require of you but to do justice, and to love kindness, and to walk humbly with your God?" He explicitly quotes twice

---

[27] Davies and Allison, *Matthew*, 1:452–53; John A. Ziesler, The *Meaning of Righteousness in Paul: A Linguistic and Theological Enquiry* (SNTSMS 20: Cambridge: Cambridge University Press, 1972), 133.

[28] Reumann, *Righteousness*, 128; Meier, *Law*, 41.

[29] See Matt 9:13; 12:7; 18:33, 35; 23:23; 25:31–46.

(Matt 9:13; 12:7) Hosea's saying that expresses the spirit of the covenant: "I desire mercy and not sacrifice" (Hos 6:6 LXX).[30] Consonant with such an approach, the Matthean Jesus shows a polemical attitude toward the scribes and Pharisees, accusing them of unfaithfulness toward God—they neglected the essence of the law because "what God demands is not so much activity directed Godward ('I desire . . . not sacrifice') but loving kindness benefiting other people ('I desire mercy')."[31] In line with the prophets, Matthew associates mercy with justice, following a biblical tradition in which mercy is indeed a dimension of justice—the saving and restoring justice that places people in the right position in accordance with God's will. Such restoration includes social vindication or reward in the new world of the kingdom of God.

The second beatitude in this set proclaims as blessed those who are pure in heart (Matt 5:8). This beatitude does not have a parallel in Luke. The pure in heart seek only one goal—to please God in relations to one's neighbor. This purpose seizes their whole heart—the center of their feelings, thoughts, and decisions. Through the mastery of the heart, the purpose inspires every action of the individual, so that the pure in heart will not practice duplicity or deception. This beatitude is reminiscent of the words of the psalmist: "Those who have clean hands and pure hearts, who do not lift up their souls to what is false, and do not swear deceitfully, will receive blessing from the Lord, and vindication [ṣĕdāqâ] from the God of their salvation" (Ps 24:4–5). The psalmist emphasizes that being pure in heart includes avoiding falsehood and deception in one's relationship to others. A parallel statement is present at the conclusion of the antithesis, where there is mention of oaths; this conclusion underlines the need for honesty and sincerity in one's mutual relations (Matt 5:37). A similar concept is also present in Jesus' criticism of the hypocrisy of the scribes and Pharisees (23:13–36). Thus, the beatitude of the pure in heart offers the assurance that an eternal reward awaits those who are honest and sincere with others and who practice justice toward their neighbors.

The third beatitude of this set blesses the peacemakers (5:9). It, too, is absent in Luke. The peacemakers are those who are committed to the positive work of reconciliation. Because of the social dimension of the Beatitudes, such reconciliation can hardly refer to our relations to God. Rather, it concerns relations among human beings. The peacemakers strive to establish permanent, harmonious relations among individuals, groups, and nations. These relations are based in the right order God desires for human beings in society. Working for peace means striving for order and harmony. Those who do so imitate the heavenly Father, the God of order and peace, and by this imitation they become children of God.

In our time it is clearer than ever that working for peace requires great dedication to the cause of justice. A true and solid peace is hardly possible in the absence of positive efforts to meet the legitimate aspirations of people for justice.

---

[30] See David Hill, "On the Use and Meaning of Hosea VI. 6 in Matthew's Gospel," *NTS* 24 (1977): 107–19.

[31] See Davies and Allison, *Matthew,* 1:455.

Peace is the fruit of a united effort to resolve degrading and anguishing conditions arising from national and international injustice, which threaten human society with violence and destruction. In a world in which part of humanity has reached a high level of cultural and technical development, underdeveloped people and nations must be freed from exploitation and discrimination and be enabled to share the benefits of human development on every level, if authentic peace is to be established. The higher the progress of one part of humanity, the stronger the need for the other part to share in it. Striving for peace includes the endeavor to make justice accessible to all, and striving after justice includes seeking progress for everyone without exclusion or discrimination.

Matthew concludes the second subsection (5:7–10) with the blessing of those persecuted for justice's sake (5:10). They fulfill God's will, striving to bring justice into human relations and establish grounds for a justice accessible to all. In so doing, they risk persecution by the dominant and abusive class, which is determined to do whatever is necessary to protect its position and pursue tactics of exploitation and oppression. The beatitude assures eschatological reward for those who suffer such persecution. Suffering persecution for justice's sake (5:10) is tantamount to suffering persecution "for my account" (5:11). Striving for justice on behalf of the needy and oppressed means undergoing suffering for the sake of Jesus, who identifies himself with the poor and the oppressed (25:31–46).

The conclusion of this subsection (5:10) has two interesting features. First, it repeats the phrase "for theirs is the kingdom of heaven," a phrase that occurs at the beginning (5:3) of the whole series of eight beatitudes. By doing so, it emphasizes the literary unity of 5:3–10. Second, its understanding of justice as obedience to God's will is made consistent with the other beatitudes of the same subsection (5:7–9).

Thus, in the eight beatitudes (5:3–10), Matthew offers two concepts of justice. In the first four (5:3–6), justice is the divine action ready to vindicate in God's kingdom the believers who now suffer deprivation and oppression. In the remaining beatitudes (5:7–10), justice is obedience to God's will and the corresponding reward that believers will receive for their obedience to God in their efforts on behalf of justice in human relations. These two concepts are related in God's kingdom—God's dominion not only motivates and demands the observance of justice in human relations; the kingdom will also implement the radical change needed for the definitive establishment of justice. The Beatitudes thus speak prophetically of the certainty that God will intervene. Their assurance guarantees us that God is involved in the course of the present history, that God has everything under his control, and that God has a plan on behalf of the destitute and oppressed. On the one hand, the proclamation of such assurances generates hope among the lowly and inspires concern and respect for them; on the other hand, it challenges the arrogance and selfishness of those who are rich and oppressive. Those who suffer from the delay of God's final intervention, in addition to receiving prophetic words of encouragement, also enjoy the presence of the one who died and rose to transform the world—a transformation that is designed not only to take place in heaven but also to be prepared for on earth.

1.2. Justice in the antitheses of the Sermon on the Mount (Matt 5:20–48)

The six antitheses of 5:21–48 are introduced by a remark that is, in effect, a title: "I tell you, unless your righteousness *[dikaiosynē]* exceeds that of the scribes and Pharisees, you will never enter the kingdom of heaven" (5:20). This statement resembles what rabbinic tradition called *kĕlāl*. This is an expository form beginning with a general principle and continuing to a set of particular cases *(pĕrātōt)* in which the principle is applied.[32] The cases are expressed by way of contrast: one assertion is set against another. In the Matthean text, the particular cases are enunciated in antithetical phrases in which the Jewish interpretation or practice of the law is confronted by the Christian stance.

In accordance with the *kĕlāl* structure, the introductory statement of Matt 5:20 asserts the principle of a superior justice or righteousness as a requirement for entrance into the kingdom of heaven, and the antitheses (5:21–48) establish norms for obtaining the benefits implied in the general principle. The antitheses reveal what constitutes superior justice. They portray a justice that results from Jesus' deepening, internalizing, and radicalizing of OT teaching by returning to the original will of God. In doing so, the Matthean Jesus teaches the final revelation of the will of God, establishing thereby a new order of justice, an order that perfects the Sinai covenant by bringing it to final fullness in the new covenant (26:28). In the new order, the disciples find instructions on how to seek and obtain the superior justice described in Jesus' teaching, a justice that Jesus calls the justice of the kingdom of heaven in his well-known saying: "Strive first for the kingdom of God and his righteousness, and all these things will be given to you as well" (6:33).

The requirements of the order expressed in the antitheses are highly social. The social dimension is evident in each antithesis. In the first (5:21–26), Jesus sharpens ethical sensitivity and instills a selfless and loving attitude toward others. He equates anger with murder and makes reconciliation a necessary condition for participation in worship. This may not have been altogether new in contemporary Judaism. It was not found in the OT, however, and in confronting the sacred text of the Pentateuch, Jesus took a provocative position that proved hard to forget and compelled people to wonder about his identity. What is remarkable in this attitude is that respect for another's life and dignity is so strong that Jesus bans anger without qualification and considers it incompatible with participation in worship.[33] It is worth noting that Jesus asserts the primacy of ethical considerations over ritual ones:

> So when you are offering your gift at the altar, if you remember that your brother or sister has something against you, leave your gift there before the altar and go; first be reconciled to your brother or sister, and then come and offer your gift. (5:23)

---

[32] David Daube, *The New Testament and Rabbinic Judaism* (London: Athlone, 1956), 63–66.

[33] See Davis and Allison, *Matthew*, 1:521.

In line with this injunction, the disciple must be so sensitive to the feelings of others that he or she seeks reconciliation not only when conscious of having offended others but also when, though unaware of wrongdoing, he or she knows a brother or sister feels injured. In his instruction on the primacy of ethical conduct, Jesus follows the prophetic tradition: "I desire mercy, not sacrifice."[34] This tradition is very dear to the Matthean Jesus. He quotes it in defense of his disciples against the Pharisees who accused them of having violated the Sabbath. He likewise refers to it to explain to his adversaries why he sat at dinner with tax collectors and sinners, social outcasts in the Pharisees' minds (9:11–13). By quoting it, Jesus not only justifies himself before the Pharisees. He also asserts that he is fulfilling God's primary demand according to the prophetic tradition, namely, the imitation of what is essential in God—God's compassion. Such imitation is precisely the core of the superior justice Jesus teaches to his disciples.

In the second and third antitheses (5:31–32), Jesus emphasizes marital faithfulness, to the extent of equating lust with adultery. He thereby internalizes and refines the obligation of justice that binds a man to his wife and commands respect for his neighbor's wife. In the fourth antithesis (5:33–37), Jesus stresses the importance of sincerity and faithfulness toward one's neighbor. In the fifth (5:38–42), he rejects the *lex talionis,* vengeance executed on a personal level, and teaches nonresistance to violence or physical harm, leaving open the possibility of moral and psychological resistance. He instills, at the same time, an open, patient, and generous attitude toward others. Finally, in the sixth antithesis (5:43–48), Jesus reaches the climax of his approach to love and compassion: "Love your enemies and pray for those who persecute you" (5:44). In extending love to his enemies, Jesus goes beyond the OT commandment (Lev 19:19) in which the neighbor is a fellow Israelite. Jesus requires unrestricted love in the superior justice of his disciples. This unrestricted extension must be kept in mind when one hears Jesus' quotation of the OT commandment of love (Matt 19:19; 22:39) and when, referring to the traditional golden rule, he says, "In everything do to others as you would have them do to you" (7:12).

The text of the six antitheses concludes, "Be perfect, therefore, as your heavenly Father is perfect" (5:48). The instruction to imitate the perfection of the heavenly Father imposes a serious task on Christians. Whatever its cost may be, this is the way the disciples can both seek the superior justice Jesus demands and develop their identity as children of God. According to Jesus' teaching, in rejecting violence and practicing love towards enemies, one imitates God and becomes a child of God. In rejecting violence and showing love, the believer does not practice a justice that repays evildoers in their own coin. On the contrary, the believer exercises a sort of justice that restores a deteriorated or lost relationship—a saving justice, distinguished by the fact that the one who is to take the initiative for reconciliation is not the one who severed the relationship and harmed the neighbor but, rather, the person who has been injured. In taking such an initiative, the

---

[34] See Hos 6:6; Matt 9:13; 12:7.

disciple does not act as a humiliated person with no other recourse but out of a generous nobility proper to a child of God—the disciple imitates the sovereign God, who shows kindness without discrimination and acts as a king who exhibits pity and forgiveness.[35]

In imitating God the Father, the disciples form a community different from the Jewish and pagan communities and resistant to worldly concerns. But the community of the disciples not only creates a contrast to the world; it also generates an attraction. Because of its practice of good works, the community elicits sympathy and appreciation. Christians have the mission to be the light of the world, a light that must "shine before others so that they may see your good works and give glory to your Father in heaven" (5:16). Their light shines in works of compassionate justice toward the needy. Such a concept is reminiscent of Third Isaiah's saying: "If you offer your food to the hungry and satisfy the needs of the afflicted, then your light shall rise in the darkness and your gloom be like the noonday" (Isa 58:11).

The superior justice the antitheses require is in character with the teaching of the second section of beatitudes (Matt 5:7–10), which calls the Christian community to strive effectively to combat the misery and oppression in society. The disciple should not wait passively for the coming of the Lord. One's trust in the promise of divine vindication must accompany an attitude of dedication to the poor and the oppressed. Such an attitude is necessary for worship to be authentic. "The Gospel cannot be heralded by word alone, and authentic evangelization must release energies tending to transform the world in which we live."[36]

1.3. Justice in the trilogy: almsgiving, prayer, and fasting (Matt 6:1–18)

This passage in the Sermon on the Mount shows the same *kĕlāl* structure as the antitheses in 5:20–48. An introductory statement (6:1) offers a general principle, which in turn is illustrated by particular cases (6:2–18). The general principle states, "Beware of practicing your piety *[dikaiosynēn]* before others in order to be seen by them; for then you have no reward from your Father in heaven" (6:1). The principle is applied to three particular cases—almsgiving, prayer, and fasting—and includes both a negative element, concerning the behavior of the hypocrites, and a positive one, stating what Christian conduct ought to be (6:2–18). The term *dikaiosynē* in 6:1 is translated in the RSV and the NRSV as "piety," and in the NIV as "acts of righteousness." The significance of this term harks back to 5:20, which states that Christian justice *(dikaiosynē)* must exceed that of the scribes and Pharisees. In 5:20–48, the concept was applied to the right observance of the commandments of the written law. Now, in 6:1–18, it is

---

[35] See Gerd Theissen, *Social Reality and the Early Christians: Theology, Ethics, and the World of the New Testament* (trans. M. Kohl; Minneapolis: Fortress, 1992), 130.

[36] Avery Dulles, "The Meaning of Faith Considered in Relationship to Justice," in *The Faith That Does Justice: Examining the Christian Sources for Social Change* (ed. J. C. Haughey; New York: Paulist, 1977), 32.

extended to the right observance of three practices of Jewish piety: almsgiving, prayer, and fasting. This extension is already found in the biblical tradition, for example, in Tob 12:8.

The general principle in Matt 6:1 teaches Christians to avoid practicing peity with an ostentation that looks for prestige and power, because the ambition for honor and domination contravenes the very nature of the community made of equals. As Jesus said, "You are not to be called rabbi, for you have one teacher, and you are all brethren. And call no man your father on earth, for you have one Father, who is in heaven. Neither be called masters, for you have one master, the Christ" (Matt 23:8–10 RSV). Those in the community who seek prestige and power through such ostentatious practices have already received in full their reward in the present world and have forfeited the reward that the Father will give to his faithful in the renewed world of the kingdom of God (6:1). An attitude of secrecy, in God's eyes, marks the right observance of pious practices (6:3, 6, 17–18). It is a mark of authenticity, ensuring that they are free of duplicity and manipulation. The requirement of this authenticity recalls the concept of "the pure in heart" in the sixth beatitude: "Blessed are the pure in heart, for they will see God" (6:8).

The application of the general principle of right observance to particular cases in 6:2–18 adds to the concept of *dikaiosynē* significant connotations derived from the concept of the community as God's household, in which all members share equally in the dignity of God's children. These connotations are also related to the fact that the dignity of God's children binds them to seek not their own but God's glory and moves them to provide a fair distribution of goods and to exercise compassion and forgiveness as the heavenly Father does. These connotations appear especially in the analysis of the practices of almsgiving and prayer.

Almsgiving *(eleēmosynē)* is the first of the three pious practices of justice *(dikaiosynē)* in the sequence of 6:2–18.[37] The association of almsgiving with *dikaiosynē* derives from Jewish tradition, in which the term *ṣĕdāqâ* (translated in the LXX by *dikaiosynē*) is used for almsgiving. Sirach had already attested this usage, as we saw when dealing with justice in that biblical book.[38] At the basis of this association lies the idea that almsgiving is an act of saving and beneficent justice. It is noteworthy that the Greek term for almsgiving is *eleēmosynē,* a term that relates to the term *eleos,* which means "compassion." Almsgiving is an act of compassion that in biblical and Jewish tradition is part of beneficent justice inasmuch as it helps the needy and restores them to the life of the community according to God's plan for human society. In addition to 6:1–2, Matthew elsewhere associates *dikaiosynē* with compassion toward others. He does so, for instance, in one of his prophetic lamentations against scribes and Pharisees: "Woe to you, scribes and Pharisees, hypocrites! For you tithe mint, dill, and cummin, and have neglected the weightier matters of the law: justice *[krisin],* and mercy *[eleos]* and faith

---

[37] Almsgiving was strongly emphasized in Judaism (e.g., Sir 29:8–13; Tob 4:7–10, 16; 12:8–9; *T. Job* 9:8; ᵓ*Abot* 5:13).

[38] See Sir 29:8–13.

[*pistin*]" (23:23). From the Matthean perspective, the concern that scribes and Pharisees showed for details of the law prevented them from observing the essence of the Sinai covenant, which was summarized in the triad of justice, mercy, and fidelity. Such a view has its foundation in Micah's saying: "He has told you, O mortal, what is good; and what does the Lord require of you but to do justice [LXX, *krima*], and to love kindness [LXX, *eleon*], and to walk humbly with your God?" (Mic 6:8). Matthew's citation coincides with Micah's text in the first two words of the triad, "justice" and "kindness." Both terms express duties toward others. He diverges from Micah in the third part of the triad, in wording, but not in meaning. "Fidelity" in the Matthean text corresponds to Micah's formulation, "to walk humbly with your God," since faithfulness to God includes, in the mind of the prophet, fidelity to one's neighbors.

Returning to justice in the trilogy of Matt 6:1–18, we see that prayer is the second pious practice of *diakaiosynē*. Prayer has a prominent place in the three particular cases given in 6:2–18 (almsgiving, prayer, and fasting) because Matthew takes the opportunity to reinforce the warning against ostentatious actions by introducing Jesus' prayer (6:9–13), which portrays the character of the Christian community and its primary concerns. The prayer begins by reminding the community that there is only one Father, God, and that Christians are members of a community of equals, all sharing the same dignity of children of God as brothers and sisters in God's household.

> "All men are brothers." How often we hear this refrain, the rallying call that strikes a response in every human heart. These are the words of Christ, "Call no man master, for ye are all brothers." It is a revolutionary call which has even been put to music. The last movement of Beethoven's Ninth Symphony has that great refrain—"All men are brothers." Going to the people is the purest and best act in Christian and revolutionary tradition and is the beginning of world brotherhood.[39]

According to Jesus' prayer, the concern of the disciples should be not their own but God's glory—the manifestation of God's power in establishing his kingdom and the universal acknowledgment of God's dominion by humanity. This is what "Hallowed be your name" (6:9) means. A drive for high position and the manipulation of religion for gaining power are excluded by the primary tasks that Jesus assigns to the community.

The same prayer invites the community to ask God to give each person food for daily life as God gave the manna every day to the community of the desert (Exod 16:4)[40] and provides rain and sunshine for the righteous and unrighteous (Matt 5:45). The community is invited not only to trust in God's providence but also to imitate his goodness: "Be perfect as your heavenly Father is perfect" (5:48). God's goodness in providing for the needs of the people is a model for the

---

[39] Dorothy Day, *The Long Loneliness: An Autobiography* (San Francisco: Harper & Row, 1952), 216.
[40] See Davies and Allison, *Matthew*, 1:607–10.

Christian. Accordingly, the community must strive for a fair distribution of goods for the satisfaction of all.

A special concern for Matthew is a need for mutual forgiveness in the community. Not only does he recite the petition, "Forgive us our debts, as we also have forgiven our debtors" (6:12), but after the prayer he reinforces it by adding, "For if you forgive others their trespasses, your heavenly Father will also forgive you; but if you do no forgive others, neither will your Father forgive your trespasses" (6:14–15). In the petition we ask God to exercise on our behalf a permanent jubilee of forgiveness as we do toward our neighbors. In saying it, we commit ourselves to put into practice a permanent jubilee of forgiveness toward others. Matthew confirms and extends the need of this commitment both in Jesus' answer to Peter's question about how often should we forgive (18:21) and in the appended parable of the Unforgiving Servant (18:23–25). While Jesus' answer to Peter states that Christian forgiveness knows no limits because God puts no end to his forgiveness toward us, the parable of the Unforgiving Servant emphasizes that compassion and forgiveness are essential parts of Christian ethics. The emphasis is especially conspicuous in the outburst that climaxes the parable: "You wicked slave! I forgave you all that debt because you pleaded with me. Should you not have had mercy *[eleēsai]* on your fellow slave, as I had mercy *[eleēsa]* on you?" (18:32–33). Practicing compassion and forgiveness is thus part of what we owe to our neighbor because God has shown compassion to us.

In conclusion, for the right observance (justice) of pious practices to be authentic, it must avoid the pursuit of status and the drive for positions of honor. To act otherwise will infringe upon the basic principles of the Christian community, since it has only one Father, God, to honor. Moreover, all members are siblings equal in dignity and qualified to share a proportionate and fair distribution of goods. All members of the community are obliged to the same primary duties: mutual care, compassion, and forgiveness.

1.4. Justice in the parable of the Two Sons (Matt 21:28–32)

The parable of the Two Sons, present only in Matthew, was delivered by Jesus during his ministry in Jerusalem. It is part of the last call to conversion that he addressed to Israel. In the parable, Jesus contrasts doing God's will with rendering God lip service and applies the contrast to tax collectors and prostitutes, on the one side, and to the scribes and Pharisees, on the other. The former repented and expressed their belief in John the Baptist, while the latter felt no need for repentance and failed to do God's will. Thus Jesus says, "For John came to you in the way of righteousness *[en hodō dikaiosynēs]* and you did not believe him, but the tax collectors and the prostitutes believed him" (21:32). Jesus asserts that John came "in the way of righteousness." What does this phrase mean? It may signify that John led a righteous life or that he taught right conduct. The latter meaning seems more likely, because in Wisdom literature "the way of righteousness" is associated with teaching right behavior (Prov 8:20; 12:28). Understood in this way, the phrase makes sense, because John's coming in the way of justice is associated with the acceptance or refusal of his teaching. It does not exclude, however, the idea that John's conduct influenced people's decisions. The understanding of the text with an emphasis on John's teaching is reinforced by the fact that Matthew underlines John's preaching and call to repentance, which resemble Jesus'. Matthew uses the same phrase for both: "Repent, for the kingdom of heaven has come near" (Matt 3:2; 4:17). Remarkably, the preaching of the kingdom in Matthew is associated with justice not only in the sense of God's vindication but also in the sense of right behavior on the part of the believer. Thus, we may say that preaching the coming of the kingdom includes teaching the conduct demanded by God's kingdom.[41] Unlike Luke, Matthew does not include extended material on the preaching of John the Baptist. While Luke shows the social dimension of John's message (Luke 3:10–14), Matthew does not describe his preaching in detail. He indicates its thrust, however, by associating it with that of Jesus, which has a noticeable social dimension.

Matthew includes another scene in which justice is associated with John's activity—the baptism of Jesus. In this episode, John objected to baptizing Jesus, but Jesus insists, "Let it be so now; for it is proper for us in this way to fulfill all righteousness *[plērōsai pasan dikaiosynēn]*" (3:15). The verb *plēroō* ("fulfill") in Matthew often refers to a prophetic fulfillment. Hence we may presume the same sense in the present scene. Indeed, the context supports such a meaning, since the heavenly voice (3:17) alludes to Ps 2:7 and Isa 42:1 as messianic prophecies fulfilled in the baptism of Jesus. On the other hand, the term *dikaiosynē* ("justice") in Matthew is often associated with moral conduct in accordance with God's will. Therefore we may presume that it has the same meaning in the present passage. Jesus, aware of the messianic prophecies, urges John to perform the duty marked out beforehand by God. By doing so, both John and Jesus fulfill all righteousness. "Because prophecy declares God's will, to fulfill prophecy is to fulfill righteousness."[42]

1.5. Justice in the option for the poor and the afflicted

As we have seen, Jesus taught the importance of justice, a term that most often refers to human conduct in accordance with God's will. Such justice will be practiced particularly on behalf of the poor, oppressed, weak, and sick—in other words, social outcasts, those deemed insignificant in the eyes of the world. In the Beatitudes, the antitheses, Jesus used the notion of superior justice to instruct his disciples to care for the poor and afflicted. But in addition to teaching, Jesus also took action on their behalf. Hence it is important to pay equal attention to his healings and exorcisms. Indeed, healing is one of the three distinctive actions of the Matthean Jesus: "[He] went about all Galilee, teaching in their synagogues and preaching the gospel of the kingdom and healing every disease and every infirmity among the people" (Matt 4:23; see also 9:35).

---

[41] Reumann, *Righteousness*, 132–33.
[42] Davies and Allison, *Matthew*, 1:327.

According to Matthew, in healing and casting out demons, Jesus fulfills the mission of the Servant of the Lord described in Second Isaiah. After summarizing Jesus' healing activity (12:15), Matthew introduces a quotation from the first song of the Servant with his distinctive formula, "This was to fulfill what was spoken by the prophet Isaiah" (12:17). Immediately after the quotation, Matthew describes the healing of a demoniac and a controversy about Jesus' power over Satan (12:22–32). The quotation from Isa 42:1–4 refers to the patient and compassionate care that the Servant gives to the broken, the wounded, and the disheartened, emphasizing his mission of justice. This Matthean quotation of Isaiah twice repeats the term "justice": the Servant must "proclaim justice *[krisin]* to the Gentiles" and "bring justice *[krisin]* to victory." According to Isaiah's text, the oppressed will go free and the oppressors will lose their power and pride through the Servant's teaching.[43] Remarkably, there is a reciprocity in meaning between the text from Isaiah and its context in Matthew. On the one hand, the Matthean context, stressing Jesus' liberating action in healing every disease and casting out demons, leads us to understand the word "justice" in the sense of liberation, restoration, and salvation. On the other hand, Isaiah's assertion that the mission of the Servant is to proclaim and bring forth justice to the Gentiles suggests that Jesus' saving action—healing the multitude in Israel—anticipates what he will do for the Gentiles.

In addition to the quotation of the first song of the Servant, Matthew, in an earlier chapter, quoted the fourth song in speaking of Jesus' healings. After a summary of exorcisms and healings in 8:16, Matthew had added, "This was to fulfill what was spoken by the prophet Isaiah, 'He took our infirmities and bore our diseases'" (8:17, quoting Isa 53:4). The evangelist elsewhere (Matt 20:28; 26:28) applies the last song of the Servant to Jesus' vicarious and sacrificial death (Isa 53:12). Strikingly, in 8:17 Matthew relates the song of the suffering Servant to Jesus' miraculous and liberating action on behalf of the sick and possessed. In so doing, Matthew suggests that Jesus' healings are the anticipated effects of the suffering that Jesus took upon himself for our redemption when he came "to give his life as ransom for many" (20:28, quoting Is 53:12). The liberating healings come from the compassion of the one who freely chose to be a victim for our rehabilitation. Such a saving mission was already indicated in the very two names given by the angel to the child to be born of Mary. He is Jesus, "for he will save his people from their sins" (Matt 1:21), and "Emmanuel, which means, 'God is with us'" (1:23), the saving God among us.

The awareness of his mission drew Jesus to assume his preferential concern for the sick and afflicted. Through his liberating healings, he anticipated the full

---

[43] In this quotation Matthew coincides with the LXX in using the term "justice" *(krisis)* twice but does not follow the LXX for the rest of the quotation. Matthew's citation of Isaiah is very close to the Masoretic Text, but it bears some differences, too. The Hebrew text does not say that "he will proclaim justice to the Gentiles" but "he will bring justice to the nations" (Isa 42:1). Neither does it say that "he will bring justice to victory" but, rather, "he will faithfully bring justice" (42:4).

liberation in the consummated kingdom—the restoration of the human being to integrity and fullness according to the divine plan. But Jesus' preferential concern was not only for the sick and the possessed. It reached out with particular care to social outcasts, such as the tax collectors and sinners (9:10–13). In Jesus' mind, his table fellowship with tax collectors and sinners fulfilled the divine will revealed through the prophet Hosea (9:13; Hos 6:6 LXX), whose oracles proclaimed the primacy of mercy over sacrifice, namely, the ritual demands of the Mosaic law. Jesus, endowed with the power of the kingdom of God, undertook compassionate actions that fulfilled the prophetic oracle. In doing so, he broke the boundaries of ritual and extended the divine forgiveness through his presence and words, a forgiveness that integrates outcasts into the eschatological community and allows them a foretaste of the banquet of the consummated kingdom (Matt 8:11–12). Jesus quoted the same prophetic oracle to defend his disciples from the attack of the Pharisees who despised them and charged them with the crime of violating the Sabbath (12:1–7).

Another group of people who attracted Jesus' preferential attention were the "little ones," namely, the simple and lowly members of the community. This is noticeable in the first part of the sermon to the community (18:1–9). There, on the one hand, Jesus exhorts leaders to avoid seeking honor and power and instructs them to be humble and low. On the other hand, he emphasizes that they should avoid despising the little ones and should tutor and take special care of them. Jesus repeats instruction to the leaders to avoid lusting after places of honor and public recognition in his criticism of the scribes and Pharisees (23:8–12). The reason given is that the Christian community is a community of brothers and sisters, everyone sharing the same dignity as a disciple of Christ.[44] As Jesus says: "For you have one teacher, and you are all disciples" (23:8).

The list of people who attracted Jesus' preferential attention concludes with those mentioned in the scene of the final judgment (25:31–46). Although it is not a comprehensive enumeration but an illustrative one, it is quite broad in its exemplary character. It includes people who are hungry, thirsty, strangers, naked, sick, and imprisoned. Moreover, this enumeration includes something distinctive; unlike the others, which refer to the people of Israel to whom Jesus devoted his public ministry (10:6; 15:24), the present listing includes peoples of all nations, and Jesus deals with them in his role as judge of the whole earth. What impresses the nations is that Jesus identifies himself with the poor, the afflicted, the outcast, and the oppressed in the world. In his public ministry, Jesus did associate himself with such persons in Israel, and Matthew suggested a sort of identification with them by applying to Jesus the words of Second Isaiah, "He took our infirmities" (8:17). In the present scene, the identification is emphasized and extended to all the poor, afflicted, outcast, and oppressed of the world.

---

[44] Among the Synoptics, Matthew most frequently places the term "brother" in the mouth of Jesus. This term is used especially when Jesus addresses the issue of the disciples' relationship with one another. See Joachim Gnilka, "Die Kirche des Matthäus und die Gemeinde von Qumrân," *BZ* 7 (1963): 51–57.

Some exegetes, such as J. R. Donahue, refer "the least of these who are members of my family" (*toutōn tōn adelphōn mou tōn elachistōn*, 25:40, 45) to Christians or Christian missionaries.[45] In this understanding, the nations are judged according to their conduct toward Christians. Such an interpretation, however, has raised strong objections from scholars. First, restricting "the least of these" to Christians deprives the scene of an essential component—its universal perspective. Second, the argument that "the least of these who are members of my family" is an expression used in Matthew to designate only Jesus' disciples (see 10:42; 18:6) is not compelling. As B. Viviano has convincingly argued, the term *adelphos* in Matthew, in addition to designating people related by blood as members of the same family, can signify either a member of the Christian community[46] or a human being as a subject of ethical obligation.[47] The universal character and the ethical perspective of the present text support the latter sense of the term. Finally, the expressions "little ones" *(mikroi)* and "the least ones" *(elachistoi)* are targeted at a particular aspect of human reality. They aim not at the condition of being a disciple or a member of the community but at the humble and low aspect of the human condition. In the universal context of the final judgment, Christ, on the one hand, calls *adelphoi* ("members of my family") any persons who anywhere in the world experience need, affliction, or oppression. On the other hand, he rewards any signs of active love shown toward the needy wherever they may be. As judge of the universe, Christ rewards them because these signals of love were shown to him. The face of the needy is the face of Christ.[48] With this identification in mind, the scene of the final judgment urges Christians to follow Jesus in his preferential option for the poor and the needy—participation in the kingdom depends on the practice of active love toward people in need.

Justice in Matthew has two basic meanings. First, it is the action of God that restores the oppressed and outcast to the condition proper to human beings in accordance with the divine design. Second, justice is a person's action in obedience to God's will concerning his or her relationship to others. God's will aims at reestablishing human beings in the position appropriate to them in accordance with the divine plan. One who does justice toward others imitates God's compassion. Doing justice while keeping one's relationship with God constitutes an expansion of that relationship. Christians have a twofold motive for practicing compassionate justice. First, by doing so, believers imitate God and become children of God; second, in doing compassionate justice, they show loyalty and love to Christ because he identifies himself with the poor, weak, sick, and outcast in the world.

---

[45] John R. Donahue, "The 'Parable' of the Sheep and the Goats: A Challenge to Christian Ethics," *TS* 47 (1986): 3–32.

[46] See Matt 12:48–50; 18:15, 21, 35; 23:8; 28:10.

[47] See Matt 5:22, 23, 24, 47; 7:3, 4, 5; Benedict T. Viviano, "The Gospel according to Matthew," *NJBC* 669.

[48] Meier, *Matthew*, 304.

2. Justice in the Letter of James

This letter has traditionally been attributed to James, the brother of the Lord (Gal 1:19), who became the leader of the church of Jerusalem (Acts 15:13; 21:18) and was martyred in the years before the Jewish War (66–70 C.E.). Its authorship and time of composition, however, remain uncertain. The majority of scholars supports the thesis that it was written by a pseudonymous writer in the last decades of the first century. The writer shows an excellent knowledge of Jewish life and a good mastery of the Greek language. He might have been an admirer of James, the brother of the Lord. It has been suggested that the author might have belonged to a Christian community made up of former "God-fearers."[49] The author calls himself "James, a servant of God and of the Lord Jesus Christ" and addresses his writing "to the twelve tribes in the Dispersion" (Jas 1:1). According to this description, the addressee is a Christian community regarded as the true Israel, the authentic people of God, a community in the Diaspora—namely, a religious minority scattered in an unbelieving world, with the consciousness of being alienated from it.[50]

The community is made up of rich, poor, and middle-class people. The rich are affluent landowners and prosperous merchants. The poor are not only the beggars, the naked, and the hungry but also day laborers and unskilled workers, retail merchants and craftsmen. Between the rich and the poor, there are minor landowners and retainers working in the civil administration or serving the rich. Included among this middle class are the leaders of the community holding the title of "elders" (5:14) and "teachers" (3:1).

The author reprimands people of the middle class and reserves harsh criticism for the rich, while admonishing and encouraging the poor. He reprimands the middle class of the community because they despise the poor (2:6). He denounces the favoritism shown by the leaders in the Christian assemblies, who give places of honor to the rich and humiliate the poor (2:2–4), and he declares that the one who practices discrimination against the poor commits sin and is "convicted by the law as transgressor"; although he may observe the other commandments of the law, he is "accountable for all of it" (2:9–10). According to the writer, such partiality is not permissible for one who believes that God created all

---

[49] For a study of the Letter of James, see Hubert Frankemölle, *Der Brief des Jakobus: Kapitel 1* (ÖTKNT 17/1; Gütersloh: Gütersloher Verlag-Haus, 1994); Elsa Tamez, *The Scandalous Message of James: Faith without Work Is Dead* (trans. J. Eagleson; New York: Crossroad, 1990); Pedrito U. Maynard-Reid, *Poverty and Wealth in James* (Maryknoll: Orbis, 1987); François Vouga, *L'épître de saint Jacques* (CNT 2, XIII, a; Geneva: Labor et Fides, 1984); Peter H. Davies, *The Epistle of James: A Commentary on the Greek Text* (NIGTC; Grand Rapids: Eerdmans, 1982); Reumann, *Righteousness*, 148–58; Sophie Laws, *A Commentary of the Epistle of James* (HNTC; San Francisco: Harper & Row, 1980); Bent Noack, "Jakobus wider den Reichen," *ST* 18 (1962): 10–25.

[50] In the book of Revelation, there is a similar identification of the Christian community with the twelve tribes of Israel (Rev 7:4–8; 14:1; 21:12).

human beings in God's own image (3:9) and who ascribes glory only to Christ (2:1)—Christ's universal and exclusive sovereignty is incompatible with any discrimination. Faith must remain free from the pressure of any group.[51] The member of the community who discriminates against the poor and weak professes a faith dissociated from Christian ethics (2:14–26). In effect, such discrimination breaks the commandment "You shall not murder" (2:8–11). In saying this, the author follows a biblical tradition according to which exploiting the poor and denying what is necessary for life is an indirect homicide.[52] The author of James reminds us of a tradition that, according to Matthew, goes back to Jesus himself (Matt 6:14–15; 18:23–35), who said, "For judgment will be without mercy to anyone who has shown no mercy; mercy triumphs over judgment" (Jas 2:13).

These recriminations are serious, but more serious are those leveled at the rich. The author denounces the rich's merciless exploitation of the poor and weak and strongly condemns their manipulation of the justice system (2:6; 5:6). In manipulating the courts for gain, the wealthy Christians dishonor their Christian name (2:7). The writer twice turns directly on the rich in an apostrophe, in the style of the Hellenistic diatribe: "Come now" (*age nyn*, 4:13; 5:1). Both apostrophes introduce invectives reminiscent of prophetic oracles as indictments for breaches of the covenant (4:13–17; 5:1–6).[53]

The first verbal assault addresses prosperous businessmen and merchants (4:13–17), who boast of their success and make plans as though they were absolute masters of their existence and of the movement of the economy. In this vein they say, "Today or tomorrow we will go to such and such a town and spend a year there, doing business and making money" (4:13). The writer warns them against such arrogant bragging—they "do not know what tomorrow will bring," and as for their life, they are like "a mist that appears for a little while and then vanishes" (4:14). What is wrong is that, in planning their business and profits, they fail to conduct themselves with full awareness of their precarious existence. There is no sin in doing business. Their sin lies in a grave omission: being able to do good for others, they fail to do so (4:15–17). According to the author, practicing good means to "fulfill the royal law according to the scripture, 'You shall love your neighbor as yourself'" (2:8), and loving your neighbor entails showing mercy toward him or her.

In the second verbal assault (5:1–6), James addresses the rich of every Christian community in the world, saying, "Come now, you rich people, weep and wail for the miseries that are coming to you" (5:1). The complaint goes on, listing miseries that will fall on the wealthy (5:1–6). First, the riches in which the wealthy trust are transitory and perishable. Not only have their riches rusted; they also corrode the wealthy and drive them mad with a compulsive lust for money. The wealthy keep hoarding treasures without sense, because humanity is in the last days (5:2–3). Second, riches foster greed and avarice and lead the wealthy to abu-

---

[51] See Vouga, *Saint Jacques*, 71.
[52] See Pss 10:7–10; 94:5–6; Job 24:14.
[53] See, e.g., Isa 1:2–20; 5:8–24; 9:8–10:4; 65:1–15.

sive conduct, such as fraudulently keeping back the laborers' wages. But the cry of the oppressed has already reached the ears of the Almighty (5:4). Third, the wealthy have lived in luxury and in pleasure; the rich man is ready, like a fattened animal, for the eschatological slaughter (5:5). Finally, riches gave the wealthy positions of power in administration and the courts of law. Such positions are an opportunity for them to do injustice in the name of justice—"You have condemned and murdered the righteous one" (5:6). The poor, in turn, lack resources for legal defense and cannot resist the pressure of the powerful (5:6). Their silence, however, is a bad omen for the rich man because the cry of the powerless has reached the ears of the Lord of hosts, whose coming is near.

Just as the author of the letter strongly criticizes the rich, so he holds the poor in high esteem and speaks for their cause. Because God honors the poor, the author requests that the community accord them the honor they have been denied. Thus he says, "Listen, my beloved brothers and sisters. Has not God chosen the poor in the world to be rich in faith and to be heirs of the kingdom that he has promised to those who love him? But you have dishonored the poor" (2:5–6). In opting for the poor, the author follows the prophetic tradition.[54] In a similar vein, he states, "Religion that is pure and undefiled before God, the Father, is this: to care for orphans and widows in their distress, and to keep oneself unstained by the world" (1:27). The writer concludes his discussion of the demands of true religion by exhorting the members of the community to resist the influence of the world because of its hostility to the poor. The world is hostile to God, the creator, who made every human being in his own image (3:9; 4:4–5). It is hostile to God inasmuch as it encourages one to assume sociopolitical power driven by arrogance and covetousness.

After referring to the suffering and oppression of the poor (5:6), the writer encourages them to practice "patience" *(makrothymia)* and "endurance" *(hypomonē)* in suffering (5:7–11), a suffering that derives from the oppression they experience under abusive rulers. Such a patience is not a passive or inactive attitude.[55] The term includes the determination to remain steadfast while waiting to attain the denied goal. The example of "the farmer who waits for the precious crop from the earth" well describes the attitude involved in patience (5:7). It is worth noting, however, that in the present context the term *makrothymia* and the corresponding verbal form *(makrothymein,* "have patience") are associated with *hypomonē* (5:11), a term that holds a more active meaning. It describes a resistance that does not yield to opposing force, the resistance of the martyr who does not succumb, even when facing torture and death. The term refers to the heroic endurance of the one who, even under torture, does not surrrender to the claim of the oppressor but instead keeps working on the mission entrusted to him.

James encourages the suffering members of the community to persevere in resisting the flattering suggestions of a world driven by satanic power (4:4, 7). Christians are called to enter upon the battlefield, submitting themselves to God

---

[54] See, e. g., Amos 5:21–24; Isa 1:10–17; 58:6; Mic 6:6–8.
[55] See Tamez, *Scandalous Message*, 52–55.

and resisting the devil (4:7). Such an attitude of resistance includes both rejecting the standards the world offers for human life and rendering the contrasting testimony of Christian faith. In doing so, Christians must be ready to suffer the persecution that their resistance and testimony may entail.

The author rejects war and class struggle. According to him, such a struggle reflects a lack of wisdom, and to join it is to yield to disordered desires. Where there is wisdom, there are peace, kindness, and justice (3:13–18). Anger and violence do not produce justice; they cannot establish the right social, political, and economic order on earth in accordance with the creator's design (1:20). Instead, the work of persuasion through dialogue is able to harmonize opposing poles. One who sows peace harvests justice (3:18). Incidentally, this is also the position of Pope Paul VI in the twentieth century: "The Church cannot accept violence, especially the force of arms—which is uncontrollable once it is let loose—and indiscriminate death as the path to liberation, because she knows that violence always provokes violence and irresistibly engenders new forms of oppression and enslavement which are often harder to bear than those from which they claimed to bring freedom."[56]

The author of James takes for granted that the world's present social and economic situation has been established as it has to ensure that the righteous will grow and mature spiritually through suffering. He does not nurture any hope for a change of social structures, and consequently he does not offer to the poor the promise of a radical change in their sad situation while they are on earth. But although the author does not announce a change on earth in a prophetic or apocalyptic style, neither does he favor a radical ethical stance demanding that the members of the community relinquish their family and possessions. He favors what one may call love patriarchalism, common in early Christianity. Such a patriarchalist stance sees social differences as integral parts of human society but smooths their harsh edges. On the one hand, such a stance requests that the rich show respect and active love to the poor and weak, and on the other hand, it urges the poor to show subordination, faithfulness, and honor to their rich masters.[57] The author exhorts his readers to build unity and harmony in the community by fostering a sense of mutual acceptance and solidarity. To this end, he shows the accord between the two commandments to love God and to love one's neighbor, and the intimate relationship between faith and ethics. He emphasizes that an effective love must be permeated by compassion and that compassion is the standard God uses to judge human conduct. Today's readers may inquire how to apply the Letter of James to a community, made up of poor and rich, in which the rich generously support programs on behalf of the poor. Should acknowledgment be denied to the generous rich? Raymond E. Brown asks, "Is it possible to

---

[56] Pope Paul VI, apostolic exhortation *Evangelii Nuntiandi* 37, in *On Evangelization in the Modern World: Apostolic Exhortation* (Washington, D.C.: United States Catholic Conference, 1976), 25.

[57] See Gerd Theissen, *The Social Setting of Pauline Christianity: Essays on Corinth* (trans. J. H. Schütz; Philadelphia: Fortress, 1982), 107–10.

live in this world and not show partiality?"[58] Balance and prudence should be exercised in a spirit of love and solidarity.

Bibliography

Allison, A. C. Review of Hans D. Betz, *The Sermon on the Mount*. *Journal of Biblical Literature* 117 (1998): 136–38.
Benoit, Pierre. Review of William D. Davies, *The Setting of the Sermon on the Mount*. *Revue Biblique* 72 (1965): 595–601.
Betz, Hans D. *The Sermon on the Mount: A Commentary on the Sermon on the Mount, including the Sermon on the Plain (Matthew 5:3–7:27 and Luke 6:20–49)*. Hermeneia. Minneapolis: Fortress, 1995.
Bonsirven, Joseph. *Le règne de Dieu*. Paris: Beauchesne, 1957.
Broer, Ingo. *Seligpreisungen der Bergpredigt: Studien zu ihrer Überlieferung und Interpretation*. Bonner biblische Beiträge 61. Bonn: Hanstein, 1986.
Brown, Raymond E. *An Introduction to the New Testament*. New York: Doubleday, 1997.
———. Review of William D. Davies, *The Setting of the Sermon on the Mount*. *Theological Studies* 25 (1964): 640–43.
Brown, Raymond E., and John P. Meier. *Antioch and Rome: New Testament Cradles of Catholic Christianity*. New York: Paulist, 1983.
Catchpole, David. Review of Hans D. Betz, *The Sermon on the Mount*. *Journal of Theological Studies* 49 (1998): 219–25.
Daube, David. *The New Testament and Rabbinic Judaism*. London: Athlone, 1956.
Davies, Peter H. *The Epistle of James: A Commentary on the Greek Text*. New International Greek Testament Commentary. Grand Rapids: Eerdmans, 1982.
Davies, William D. *The Setting of the Sermon on the Mount*. Cambridge: Cambridge University Press, 1964. Repr., Atlanta: Scholars Press, 1989.
Davies, William D., and Dale C. Allison. *A Critical and Exegetical Commentary on the Gospel according to Saint Matthew*. 3 vols. International Critical Commentary. Edinburgh: T&T Clark, 1988–1997.
Day, Dorothy. *The Long Loneliness: An Autobiography*. San Francisco: Harper & Row, 1952.
Donahue, John R. "The 'Parable' of the Sheep and the Goats: A Challenge to Christian Ethics." *Theological Studies* 47 (1986): 3–32.
Dulles, Avery. "The Meaning of Faith Considered in Relationship to Justice." Pages 10–46 in *The Faith That Does Justice: Examining the Christian Sources for Social Change*. Edited by J. C. Haughey. New York: Paulist, 1977.
Dupont, Jacques. *Les Béatitudes*. 3 vols. Echter Bibel. Paris: Gabalda, 1958–1973.
Durand, Alfred. *Évangile selon saint Matthieu*. Verbum Salutis 1. Paris: Beauchesne, 1948.

---

[58] Raymond E. Brown, *An Introduction to the New Testament* (New York: Doubleday, 1997), 746.

Frankemölle, Hubert. *Der Brief des Jakobus: Kapitel 1*. Ökumenischer Taschenbuch-Kommentar zum Neuen Testament 17/1. Gütersloh: Gütersloher Verlag-Haus, 1994.

Gnilka, Joachim. "Die Kirche des Matthäus und die Gemeinde von Qumrân." *Biblische Zeitschrift* 7 (1963): 51–57.

Hill, David. "On the Use and Meaning of Hosea VI. 6 in Matthew's Gospel." *New Testament Studies* 24 (1977): 107–19.

Kingsbury, Jack D. "The Place, Structure, and Meaning of the Sermon on the Mount in Matthew." *Interpretation* 41 (1987): 131–43.

Laws, Sophie. *A Commentary of the Epistle of James*. Harper's New Testament Commentaries. San Francisco: Harper & Row, 1980.

———. "James, Epistle of." Pages 621–28 in vol. 3 of Anchor Bible Dictionary. Edited by D. N. Freedman. 6 vols. New York: Doubleday, 1992.

Légasse, Simon. "Les pauvres en esprit et 'le volontaires' de Qumran." *New Testament Studies* 8 (1961–1962): 336–45

Lohfink, Norbert. *Lobgesänge der Armen*. Stuttgarter Bibelstudien 143. Stuttgart: Katholisches Bibelwerk, 1990.

———. "Von der 'Anawim-Partei' zur 'Kirche der Armen': Die bibelwissenschaftliche Ahnentafel eines Hauptbegriffs der Theologie der Befreiung." *Biblica* 67 (1986): 153–75.

Luz, Ulrich. *Matthew 1–7: A Continental Commentary*. Translated by W. C. Linnss. Minneapolis: Fortress Press, 1992.

Maynard-Reid, Pedrito U. *Poverty and Wealth in James*. Maryknoll: Orbis, 1987.

McGarrigle, Francis J. "The Humility of the Poor in Spirit." *American Ecclesiastical Review* 144 (1961): 313–19.

Meier, John P. *Law and History in Matthew's Gospel*. Analecta biblica 71. Rome: Pontifical Biblical Institute, 1976.

———. *Matthew*. New Testament Message 3. Wilmington: Glazier, 1985.

Noack, Bent. "Jakobus wider den Reichen." *Studia theologica* 18 (1962): 10–25.

Powell, Mark A. "Matthew's Beatitudes: Reversals and Rewards of the Kingdom." *Catholic Biblical Quarterly* 58 (1996): 460–79.

Przybylski, Benno. *Righteousness in Matthew and His World of Thought*. Society for New Testament Studies Monograph Series 41. Cambridge: Cambridge University Press, 1980.

Reumann, John H. P. *Righteousness in the New Testament: Justification in the United States Lutheran–Roman Catholic Dialogue, with Responses by J. A. Fitzmyer and J. D. Quinn*. Philadelphia: Fortress; New York: Paulist, 1982.

———. "Righteousness (NT)." Pages 754–56 in vol. 5 of Anchor Bible Dictionary. Edited by D. N. Freedman. 6 vols. New York: Doubleday, 1992.

Schweizer, Eduard. *The Good News according to Matthew*. Translated by D. E. Green. Atlanta: Knox, 1975.

Senior, Donald. "Between Two Worlds: Gentile and Jewish Christians in Matthew's Gospel." *Catholic Biblical Quarterly* 61 (1999): 1–23.

Stanton, Graham N. *A Gospel for a New People: Studies in Matthew*. Edinburgh: T&T Clark, 1992.

Strecker, Georg. Review of William D. Davies, *The Setting of the Sermon on the Mount*. New Testament Studies 13 (1966): 105–12.

———. *Der Weg der Gerechtigkeit: Untersuchungen zur Theologie des Matthäus*. Forschungen zur Religion und Literatur des Alten und Neuen Testaments 82. Göttingen: Vandenhoeck & Ruprecht, 1962.

Tamez, Elsa. *The Scandalous Message of James: Faith without Work Is Dead*. Translated by J. Eagleson. New York: Crossroad, 1990.

Theissen, Gerd. *Social Reality and the Early Christians: Theology, Ethics, and the World of the New Testament*. Translated by M. Kohl. Minneapolis: Fortress, 1992.

———. *The Social Setting of Pauline Christianity: Essays on Corinth*. Translated by J. H. Schütz. Philadelphia: Fortress, 1982.

Topel, J. Review of Hans D. Betz, *The Sermon on the Mount*. Catholic Biblical Quarterly 59 (1997): 370–72.

Viviano, Benedict T. "The Gospel according to Matthew." Pages 1–168 in *The New Jerome Bible Commentary*. Edited by Raymond E. Brown et al. Englewood Cliffs: Prentice Hall, 1990.

Vouga, François. *L'épître de saint Jacques*. Commentaire du Nouveau Testament 2, XIII, a. Geneva: Labor et Fides, 1984.

Ziesler, John A. *The Meaning of Righteousness in Paul: A Linguistic and Theological Enquiry*. Society for New Testament Studies Monograph Series 20. Cambridge: Cambridge University Press, 1972.

CHAPTER ELEVEN

JUSTICE IN THE GOSPEL OF LUKE AND THE ACTS OF THE APOSTLES

Introduction

The Gospel of Luke and the Acts of the Apostles were written by the same author, traditionally called Luke, in the years between 80 and 100 C.E.[1] The author was a Gentile Christian who showed special concern about Christian life within the Greco-Roman world, where an abysmal gap between rich and poor existed. His concern with the issue of poverty and wealth, apparent in both of his books, has attracted intense attention, especially since the rise of the historical-critical method. In particular, discussions of the early "communism" in the Acts of the Apostles and the "Ebionite" strain of the third Gospel have evolved over the last century.[2] The present chapter discusses the issue of justice in Luke and Acts from the viewpoint of the liberation of the human person in its various dimensions.

1. Jesus in the synagogue of Nazareth

Luke begins the story of Jesus' visit to his hometown, Nazareth, with his entrance into the synagogue on the Sabbath in order to attend the service there (Luke 4:16–30).[3] The action starts with Jesus reading the text of Isaiah and

---

[1] See Claus-Jürgen Thornton, *Der Zeuge des Zeugen: Lukas als Historiker der Paulusreisen* (WUNT 56; Tübingen: J. C. B. Mohr, 1991); Joseph A. Fitzmyer, "The Authorship of Luke-Acts Reconsidered," in *Luke the Theologian: Aspects of Theology* (New York: Paulist, 1989), 1–26.

[2] See John Donahue, "Two Decades of Research on the Rich and the Poor in Luke-Acts," in *Justice and the Holy* (ed. D. A. Knight and J. Peter; Atlanta: Scholars Press, 1989), 131.

[3] For a study of this passage, see Robert O'Toole, "The Kingdom of God in Luke-Acts," in *The Kingdom of God in 20th Century Interpretation* (ed. W. Willis; Peabody, Mass.: Hendrickson, 1987), 147–52; Sharon H. Ringe, *Jesus, Liberation, and the Biblical Jubilee: Images for Ethics and Christology* (OBT; Philadelphia: Fortress, 1985); Jerome Kodell, "Luke's Gospel in a Nutshell (Lk 4.16–30)," *BTB* 13 (1983): 16–18; S. G. Wilson, *Luke and the Law* (SNTSMS 50; Cambridge: Cambridge University Press, 1983); A. del Agua Pérez, "El cumplimiento del reino de Dios en la misión de Jesús: Programa del evangelio de Lucas (Lc, 4, 14–44)," *EstBib* 38 (1979–1980): 269–93; C. Escudero Freire, "Jesús profeta,

reaches its climax with his statement, "Today this scripture has been fulfilled in your hearing" (4:21). A comparison of this passage with the Markan parallel proves helpful. Remarkably, Luke substitutes this scene of Jesus reading the text of Isaiah for the Markan summary of Jesus' proclamation of the good news of the coming of the kingdom (Mark 1:15). Through this substitution, Luke indicates clearly, though not explicitly, that in the synagogue at Nazareth Jesus was speaking about the good news of the kingdom. This is confirmed by Jesus himself after leaving Capernaum, when he said, "I must proclaim the good news of the kingdom of God to other cities *also*" (Luke 4:43; italic added). Jesus' statement, "Today this scripture has been fulfilled," declares the beginning of his mission as both the herald of the kingdom of God and the bearer of its liberating action. "Today" begins the rescuing intervention of God, which is reserved for the final time.[4] The text Jesus read from Isaiah is the following:

> The Spirit of the Lord is upon me,
> because he has anointed me to bring good news to the poor.
> He sent me to proclaim release *[aphesin]* to the captives
> and recovering of sight to the blind,
> to let the oppressed free,
> to proclaim the year of the Lord's favor. (Luke 4:18–19)

This text in Luke is a combination of verses taken from the Greek version of Isa 61:1–2 and 58:6. He himself seems to have conflated the verses to emphasize the liberating aspect of Jesus' mission. In the text, two phrases of Isaiah are omitted, namely, "to bind up the brokenhearted" (61:1c) and "the day of vengeance of our God" (61:2b). The second omission is especially significant because it removes the negative aspect of the mission of Third Isaiah and focuses attention exclusively on the comforting and compassionate mission Jesus implements in his ministry. In addition to these omissions, there is also an insertion that underlines Jesus' liberating mission. The insertion is taken from Isa 58:6d, which says, "to let the oppressed free."[5]

The Greek text of Isaiah alludes to the remission of the Year of Jubilee (Lev 25:8–17). "The year of release/remission *[apheseōs]*" is a characteristic expression for such a year. In Isa 61:1–2, the prophet adapted the statute of the Year of Jubilee and converted the Levitical law into a promise. Instead of imposing upon the community the practice of remission in the Year of Jubilee as the book of Leviticus does, the prophet constructed a divine promise of liberation and declared

---

libertador de los hombres: Visión lukana de su ministerio terrestre," *EstEcl* 51 (1976): 463–95; James A. Sanders, "From Isaiah 61 to Luke 4," in *Christianity, Judaism, and Other Greco-Roman Cults: Studies for Morton Smith at Sixty* (ed. J. Neusner; 4 vols.; SJLA 12; Leiden: Brill, 1975), 1:75–106; M. Völkel, "Zur Deutung des 'Reiches Gottes' bei Lukas," *ZNW* 65 (1974): 57–70; J. Bajard, "La structure de la pericope de Nazareth in Luc IV.16–30," *ETL* 45 (1969): 165–71.

[4] Völkel, "Reiches Gottes."
[5] See Joseph A. Fitzmyer, *The Gospel according to Luke I–IX* (Anchor Bible 28; Garden City: Doubleday, 1981), 532.

that he had received the mission to proclaim and execute it.[6] The Lukan Jesus takes the text shaped by the prophet and in turn introduces changes to it. He reshapes and redirects it by giving the text an exclusively compassionate and saving character and providing it with an eschatological orientation toward the coming of the kingdom. A similar character and orientation animate the description Jesus gives of his own ministry in response to the messengers from John the Baptist: "Go and tell John what you have seen and heard: the blind receive their sight, the lame walk, the lepers are cleansed, the deaf hear, the dead are raised, the poor have good news brought to them" (Luke 7:22).

The text of Isaiah read by Jesus in the synagogue at Nazareth contains indubitable reminiscences of the remission of the Year of Jubilee (Lev 25:8–17).[7] These reminiscences, however, do not make the text a call to put the Jubilee law into practice.[8] There is no solid ground upon which to make such a claim. If such were the case, one would expect in Jesus' speech a reference to an essential component of the Jubilee law—the return of land to its original owner (Lev 25:10, 13). Furthermore, in the people's response there is nothing to suggest that they understood Jesus' words as a call to practice the Levitical Jubilee law. Finally, it is difficult to relate Jesus' conduct with a call to enforce the Jubilee law because, whereas the Jubilee law requires that the dispossessed return to their original property (25:10, 13), Jesus asks his disciples to abandon their possessions.[9] Although Jesus' words could evoke the remission of the Year of Jubilee in the Palestinian social environment or among people familiar with the Bible, the audience in the synagogue would not have understood his words as a proclamation of the Jubilee in the manner of Lev 25:8–17.[10] What Jesus did, rather, was to use expres-

---

[6] Isaiah 61 refers to the postexilic community in Palestine and speaks of a year of liberation that the Lord is going to inaugurate. See O. H. Steck, *Studien zu Tritojesaja* (BZAW 203; Berlin: De Gruyter, 1991), 106–18; W. Zimmerli, "Das 'Gnadenjahr des Herrn,'" in *Studien zur alttestamentlichen Theologie und Prophetie: Gesammelte Aufsätze II* (TB 51; Munich: Chr. Kaiser, 1974), 222–34.

[7] C. J. H. Wright, "Jubilee, Year of," *ABD* 3:1028; Robert B. Sloan, *The Favorable Year of the Lord: A Study of Jubilatory Theology in the Gospel of Luke* (Austin: Schola, 1977), 28–110.

[8] John H. Yoder and A. Trocmé maintain that, in his discourse in the synagogue, Jesus demanded that the law of Jubilee be put into effect immediately. They point to the proclamation of Melchizedek in the Dead Sea Scrolls (11QMelch 7) as a confirmation that people hoped for a celebration of the great final Jubilee. See John H. Yoder, *The Politics of Jesus: Vicit Agnus Noster* (Grand Rapids: Eerdmans, 1975), 34–36; A. Trocmé, *Jesus and the Nonviolent Revolution* (trans. M. H. Shank and M. E. Miller; Scottsdale: Herald, 1973), 27–52. Without a doubt, Qumran testifies to the hope in certain circles that Melchizedek would come as a judge at the end of time, in the day of the last Jubilee, in order to execute God's vengeance against his enemies and bring salvation to the just. In contradistinction to this eagerly awaited Melchizedek, however, Jesus in the synagogue of Nazareth is described not so much as a judge as an agent of a compassionate ministry of liberation.

[9] See Luke 5:11; 5:27–28; 9:59–62; 18:22, 28; David P. Seccombe, *Possessions and the Poor in Luke-Acts* (SNTSU B, 6; Linz: Studien zum Neuen Testament und seiner Umwelt, 1982), 54–56.

[10] J. Massyngbaerde Ford, *My Enemy Is My Guest: Jesus and Violence in Luke* (Maryknoll: Orbis, 1984), 55–60; Seccombe, *Possessions*, 54–55; Joseph A. Fitzmyer, *Essays on the*

sions reminiscent of the Jubilee remission to emphasize the liberating character of the kingdom he was announcing and bringing into action.

The text that Jesus read from Isaiah and applied to his ministry as a program to follow lists the beneficiaries of God's liberating action. The list begins with the poor and ends with the oppressed (Luke 4:18). It is important to clarify what it is to be poor, according to Luke. Poverty in Luke is not simply a matter of economic disadvantage. The poor also include those who are socially neglected or despised, or even outcast.[11] Indeed, the poor are mentioned together with the captive, the hungry, the afflicted, the excluded, the unjustly discredited, the blind, the lame, lepers, and the deaf.[12] From another angle, the poor are destitute, weak, and defenseless because they are deprived of the resources necessary to secure their own rights. As we can see in the Beatitudes, however, the poor in Luke's view are those who, in the midst of their afflictions, trust in God. It is to such people, according to Luke, that Jesus announces the message of consolation and brings liberation.

In Luke's understanding, Jesus' proclamation was foreshadowed by Third Isaiah, who comforted the postexilic faithful community by giving assurances of God's impending intervention on behalf of the poor and the oppressed (Isa 61:1–2). Jesus, however, brings a new eschatological consolation that is directed not only toward the Jews who believe in Jesus but also toward the Gentiles, who, by their conversion to the gospel, will share with the faithful Israel the promise of the kingdom. Luke indicates the universal scope of Jesus' mission by emphasizing the references Jesus makes to the prophets Elijah and Elisha. In Jesus' terms, Elijah was not sent to help the widows of Israel, although they were many, but only to a Gentile widow. Nor did Elisha heal the lepers of Israel, though many, but only a pagan leper (Luke 4:25–27). By means of these allusions, Jesus claims that the liberating action of the gospel will extend beyond the Jewish borders and will spread over the Gentile world, as Acts shows. Thus, Jesus proclaims and brings the final consolation to all the poor of the world.

The statement that Jesus was sent to proclaim the good news to the poor may appear to restrict his mission to the people of lowly condition. But this is not so, because Jesus' ministry is not exclusive. According to Luke, Jesus did not speak only to poor people. He addressed varied audiences—large multitudes (6:17; 7:29; 8:4, 40), the congregation in the synagogue (4:15, 16, 33, 44), scribes and Pharisees (5:17; 6:2–3, 30–31), and tax collectors (5:29–30). And when he sent out his disciples to proclaim the kingdom of God, they went through towns and villages (9:2, 6; 10:1). Such inclusive practices make Jesus' recriminations against

---

Semitic Background of the New Testament (London: Chapman, 1971; repr., Missoula: Scholars Press, 1974), 249, 256–57.

[11] John O. York, *The Last Shall Be First: The Rhetoric of Reversal in Luke* (JSNTSup 46; Sheffield: JSOT Press, 1991), 87–102; Bruce J. Malina, "Interpreting the Bible with Anthropology: The Case of the Rich and the Poor," *List* 21 (1986): 148–59; B. Malina, *The New Testament World: Insights from Cultural Anthropology* (Louisville: Westminster John Knox, 1993), 103–7; B. Malina, "Wealth and Poverty in the New Testament and Its World," *Int* 41 (1987): 354–67.

[12] See Luke 4:18; 6:20–22; 7:22; 14:13, 21.

entire cities understandable, because of their negative response to the preaching of the gospel (10:13–16).

Thus, the statement in Luke that Jesus was sent to proclaim the gospel to the poor does not restrict Jesus' preaching to a particular group. Rather, it underlines the special interest that Luke promotes in his Gospel: the pressing social problem created by the indifference of the rich toward the poor. In Greco-Roman society, the wealthy and the poor lived poles apart. There was no connection between them; if anything, the relationship was one of exploitation. Cicero, for instance, describes those of lowly birth and status as "the filth and dregs of the city."[13] What is striking, however, is that, despite Luke's interest in the social contrast between rich and poor, he refers more often to wealth and possessions than to poverty. It seems as though Luke's main point is to encourage the rich to share their wealth with the poor. He does not contrast poor and rich in order to foster class struggle. On the contrary, his purpose is to encourage the establishment of a communion of goods between them.

In his consideration of the poor, Luke does not restrict his attention to the social and economic aspect of poverty or to the physical affliction caused by sickness or oppression. He sees in Jesus' preaching and work a deeper and more universal dimension—the ultimate goal is to destroy the power of Satan and rescue humanity. In this regard, Luke provides two illustrative episodes. The first is the healing of a man with an unclean spirit (4:31–37), located in the Lukan narrative immediately after the episode in the synagogue at Nazareth. The story describes Jesus overpowering the unclean spirit and casting him out. The ancient world regarded physical and mental illness as a result of the influence of powers outside what was considered a good moral and religious order—a result of the powers of evil and death. In conjunction with this belief, the Synoptic Gospels attribute various illnesses to the influence of unclean spirits under Satan's leadership. In this context, Jesus' victory over the unclean spirits means the defeat of Satan, the prince of evil; Jesus' victory, then, has a cosmic dimension. And since Jesus' victory is made possible through the power of the kingdom of God, his triumph over the power of evil is a conquest by God's kingdom, anticipating its full establishment in the world. Hence the emphasis the writer places on the reaction of the multitude, which says, "What kind of utterance is this? For with authority and power he commands the unclean spirits, and out they come!" (4:36). Jesus himself will comment later, "But if it is by the finger of God that I cast out demons, then the kingdom of God has come to you" (11:20).

The second illustrative episode is the healing of a paralytic (5:17–26). Luke takes the story from the synoptic tradition, and through it he shows that Jesus' cure of the body is a sign of a deeper healing that affects the whole of the human being. In the scene with the paralytic, Jesus displays a divine power that heals the physical body of the lame person in order to convince the audience that he possesses an identical power to cure the inmost being of a sinner by forgiving his sins

---

[13] Cicero, *Att.* 1.16.11.

(5:22–25). For this healing, Jesus requires from the person who approaches him an acknowledgment of his sinful condition and a conversion to the saving God. As he ironically says to the scribes and Pharisees, "I have come to call not the righteous, but sinners to repentance" (5:32). He calls everyone to conversion, both the oppressors and the oppressed. The message is valid for both: "unless you repent you will all likewise perish" (13:3). Jesus, on the one hand, calls everyone to acknowledge his own sinful condition, and on the other hand, he offers the possibility of liberation from one's present predicament through the forgiveness of sin, and the acquisition of a new condition that includes the anticipation of the eschatological kingdom of God.

2. The Beatitudes

The way Luke arranges the Beatitudes (6:20–26) diverges from Matthew (Matt 5:3–12). Whereas Matthew has ten beatitudes, eight in the third person and two in the second, and all of them in the plural, Luke has a set of four beatitudes and a set of four lamentations set against one another, all in the second person plural. Luke contrasts the poor to the rich as Third Isaiah does (Isa 65:13–14), but he offers a distinctive diptych; in the first part of this diptych, he gives four beatitudes for the poor, and in the second, he issues four lamentations against the rich.[14] The dominant theme is the radical change of fortune: the exaltation of the poor and humiliation of the rich, a theme prepared in the Magnificat (Luke 1:47–55). This hymn, which expresses the exaltation of Mary, exemplifies the vindication of the lowly and the oppressed in the history of salvation, according to the divine design: "He has put down the mighty from their thrones and lifted up the lowly" (1:52). In the past, God effected instances of justice on behalf of his people who were humiliated and oppressed, instances that created in the believing community a strong hope for a full future divine intervention. Now, in vindicating Mary from her lowliness and humiliation, God inaugurates the expected era of justice and liberation. He acts through his son, Jesus, who from the heights of his dignity as "the Son of the Most High" and from "the throne of his ancestor David" (1:32), comes down to look after the poor and oppressed in order to restore them to the position befitting them in the order established by God.[15]

---

[14] In the Dead Sea Scrolls is a fragment of a manuscript (4Q525) that preserves four beatitudes. Presumably the original text contained a larger list of such sayings. These beatitudes proclaim the happiness of those who search for wisdom. They have a sapiential orientation, not an apocalyptic one like those of the Gospels. They do not offer the reversal of destiny as the gospel beatitudes do, nor do they contrast the lot of the poor with that of the rich. And of course, they have no relationship with the coming of the kingdom of God. See E. Puech, "4Q525 et les péricopes des Béatitudes en Ben Sira et Matthieu," *RB* 98 (1991): 80–106; B. T. Viviano, "Beatitudes Found among Dead Sea Scrolls," *BAR* 18/6 (1992): 53–55, 66.

[15] See York, *The Last*, 44–55. It has sometimes been thought that Luke is referring to a group of poor people who cultivated a special spirituality of detachment from temporal

Luke, unlike Matthew, does not explicitly qualify the category of poverty referred to in the Beatitudes. While Matthew says, "Blessed are the poor in spirit" (Matt 5:3), Luke asserts simply, "Blessed are you who are poor" (Luke 6:20).[16] Still, in spite of the lack of qualification, Luke shares Matthew's view of the poor referred to in the beatitude: they are the poor who trust in the Lord. The Lukan context supports such an understanding. First, the set of beatitudes ends with one that blesses the oppressed because of their loyalty to Jesus; such a religious commitment expressed at the end was intended to permeate the whole set. Second, in the Lukan diptych the poor are contrasted with the rich. It is helpful, therefore, to see how Luke describes the rich in order to grasp his perception of the poor. To be precise, the evangelist depicts the rich as those who ignore God and put their full trust in themselves and their wealth (12:16–21; 16:19–31). By contrast, we can conclude that the poor are those who place their whole trust in God.[17] Such a concept of the poor comes from the biblical tradition. We find it, for instance, in Third Isaiah. In fact, while this prophet in Isa 61:1–2 proclaims a change to benefit the poor and oppressed generally, later he specifies, in 65:13–14, that those who will experience the saving justice of God will be the servants of the Lord.

In the Beatitudes, Luke associates the poor with those who hunger, those who weep because of social and economic oppression, and those who suffer rejection, ostracism, and loss of their rights because of their loyalty to Christian life (Luke 6:20–23). This association shows, as we have already seen, that Luke has a broad sense of what the term "poor" encompasses. He also associates the poor with the blind, the leprous, and the lame (7:22; 14:13, 21). The reversal of conditions Jesus announces for the poor and oppressed might have reminded the Gentile Christians of the change that the goddess Fortuna, also known as Tyche, was believed to introduce into human life.[18] But the reversal Jesus proclaims is not produced by a capricious stroke of blind fate; rather, it is God who acts according to his plan to establish justice and peace in the new world of God's kingdom. God's judgment, however, depends on the acceptance or rejection of the demands of the gospel by humanity.[19]

In contrasting the destiny of the poor with that of the rich, Luke shows that God has decided to be the benefactor and patron of the poor and that Jesus follows suit.[20] As a result, in his ministry Jesus performs liberating actions that, though local and occasional, anticipates the full and universal liberation to be

---

goods and complete trust in God—the ʿanāwîm. The existence of such a group, however, does not appear to be historically verifiable. See also ch. 6, §1.4.

[16] See the discussion on Matt 5:3 above, ch. 10, §1.1.

[17] Raymond E. Brown, "The Beatitudes according to Luke," in *New Testament Essays* (Milwaukee: Bruce, 1965), 265–71.

[18] Already Third Isaiah (Isa 65:11) had referred to the trust society's powerful ones placed in Gad (Fortune) and Meni (Destiny), Syrian gods of luck.

[19] York, *The Last*, 181–82.

[20] Halvor Moxnes, "Patron-Client Relations and the New Community in Luke-Acts," in *The Social World of Luke-Acts: Models for Interpretation* (ed. Jerome H. Neyrey; Peabody, Mass: Hendrickson, 1991), 257.

executed in the world of the kingdom of God. Then, with their condition reversed, the poor will share the power of God's dominion.

In the Beatitudes, Luke promises this reversal, but he does not immediately say how God will accomplish it. He will discuss this later, in the course of his Gospel. In this regard, the scene of the transfiguration is most illuminating; there Moses and Elijah speak with Jesus about the exodus, the "departure, which he was about to accomplish in Jerusalem" (9:31). To achieve liberation, an exodus is necessary. Jesus' exodus—his death, resurrection, and ascension—will effect the changes that bring about the promised liberation. To accomplish the redemption, "was it not necessary that the Messiah should suffer these things and then enter into his glory?" (24:26).

In his parable of the Rich Man and Lazarus, Luke describes the situation following such a change (16:19–31). Lazarus, who was poor, despised, and suffered hunger on earth, has been transferred to the abundance and happiness of heaven (16:22) to share a table with Abraham in the kingdom of God (13:28–29). The rich man, who "dressed in purple and fine linen and who feasted sumptuously every day" (16:19), entered instead the torments of hellfire (16:23, 24). This description of final reversal, taken out of context, may mislead the reader into believing that Luke sees the possibility of reversal only in the afterlife. There is no doubt that there will be a final reversal after death, but the story is told to a community in which there are both rich and poor, in order to move the wealthy to accept the demands of the gospel now. The rich must change their selfish viewpoint and work for the improvement of the poor and oppressed. They are responsible for such improvement because they have the means in their own hands to relieve misery of any kind. The story is told to increase their awareness of their accountability to God and to move them to act at once.

Luke offers several cases of quick reaction to Jesus' call. Among the tax collectors, Levi (5:27–29) and Zacchaeus (19:1–19) provide good examples. The latter fits especially well with this line of argumentation. Luke sees in the Zacchaeus episode a fulfillment of Jesus' remark "The Son of Man came to seek out and to save the lost" (19:10). Likewise the "today" in the encounter of Jesus with Zacchaeus (19:9) will remind the reader of that "today" when, in the synagogue at Nazareth, Jesus proclaimed his gospel of liberation (4:21). "Today, salvation" (19:9) touched Zacchaeus's house and changed his life, an effect of Jesus' saving presence. It is the result of the action of the one anointed by the Spirit to proclaim and to introduce the liberation of the kingdom of God. The change in Zacchaeus was not only individual, directed to his own good. It was also social insofar as it changed the relationship between the tax collector and the taxpayers as well as between the tax collector and poor people. Jesus' liberating action freed Zacchaeus to conduct his affairs in accordance with the new order of God's kingdom. It not only moved Zacchaeus to compensate others for a damage according to the proportion established in Exod 22:1; it also motivated him to let the poor share his wealth. Zacchaeus redistributed his assets, saying, "Look, half of my possessions, Lord, I will give to the poor; and if I have defrauded anyone of anything, I will pay back four times as much" (Luke 19:8).

3. The rich man and the alternative offered him by Jesus

Like the synoptic tradition he inherited, Luke emphasizes the negative aspect of riches, but he develops this idea further. In his depiction of the rich, Luke sees them not only as an economic class but also as a social elite. Thus, in order to present a character contrasted with the poor Lazarus, the Lukan Jesus says, "There was a rich man who was dressed in purple and fine linen and who feasted sumptuously every day" (16:19). And to depict John the Baptist, Jesus describes his exact opposite: "What did you go out to see? Someone dressed in soft robes? Look, those who put on fine clothing and live in luxury are in royal palaces" (7:25). But Jesus does not only give a description of the rich man in social terms; he also attaches to wealth an ethical evaluation, linking the wealthy to avarice. To understand this evaluation, the modern reader should keep in mind that Luke belonged to a preindustrial culture with limited material resources. In such a context, an honest person was content with what he inherited or personally obtained to have a decent life befitting to his social status. Accumulation of goods was interpreted as a way of depriving others of access to limited resources. The common belief was that the rich person either possessed a wealth iniquitously acquired or else inherited a patrimony dishonestly accumulated. In this vein, the rich man was a powerful individual who dishonestly took what belonged to the weak. Hence, to be rich was tantamount to being oppressive, covetous, and avaricious.[21]

Luke describes the rich person mainly in his parable of the Rich Fool (12:16–21) and the parable of the Rich Man and Lazarus (16:19–31). In the first narrative, the rich man accumulates commodities and keeps them in his storage houses, waiting for years of bad crops and famine in order to make the most of the opportunity by selling his grain and goods at exorbitantly high prices. The rich man is driven by the selfish desire of accumulating wealth for himself and the dream of enjoying life regardless of the condition of the impoverished and oppressed. But God calls him a fool and demands his life on the very night when his dream becomes reality, and the writer draws a lesson for all "those who store up treasures for themselves but are not rich toward God" (12:21). This parable offers remarkable similarities with *1 En.* 97:8–10 and Sir 11:18–19. The similarity lies in the threat of unpredictable death that hangs over a person in spite of presumptuous efforts to achieve security based on the accumulation of wealth. This similarity derives from familiarity with the wisdom tradition, which often reflects on the destiny of the rich.[22]

In the parable of the Rich Man and Lazarus (Luke 16:19–31), the wealthy man enjoys life without any concern about the poor man who, starving and covered with sores, lies at the gate of his mansion, "longing [in vain] to satisfy his hunger with what fell from the rich man's table" (16:21). The rich man does not extend his

---

[21] Bruce J. Malina and Richard L. Rohrbaugh, *Social Science Commentary on the Synoptic Gospel* (Minneapolis: Fortress, 1992), 324.
[22] George W. E. Nickelsburg, "Riches, the Rich, and God's Judgment in 1 Enoch 92–105 and the Gospel according to Luke," *NTS* 25 (1979): 335.

hand in order to help the starving poor man. Contemptuously, he thinks that the man at his gate does not deserve his care. His five brothers share the same selfishness (16:28). The moral evaluation of the rich of the parable is given by God himself. Such a one deserves no relief in his agony in the midst of hades's flames.

Luke not only evaluates the moral aspect of the wealthy man's conduct but also analyzes the relationship between the rich man and his riches. He does so by describing wealth as the "mammon of dishonesty" (16:9). "Mammon," according to Fitzmyer, is "an aramaized loanword from Hebrew," the meaning of which is "that in which one puts trust," hence "money" or "possessions." The expression "mammon of dishonesty" does not mean so much wealth iniquitously acquired as "the *tendency* or iniquitous seduction of mammon to enslave those who pursue it and to lead to forms of dishonesty."[23]

The rich fool and the rich man of the two parables represent an enduring social problem. They embody a disordered, selfish, and monopolizing accumulation of wealth. In their activities, they do not foster an attitude toward wealth that allows the poor to share in the well-being of the affluent. Their exclusive interest is in using money as a tool of personal gain. The wealthy may represent an individual person, a group, a nation, or a global corporation. The result for the poor is the same: for their labor they receive less than a pittance. "Though hungry, they carry the sheaves. . . . They tread the wine press, but suffer thirst" (Job 24:10–11). Likewise the poor may represent an individual person, a social group, a nation, or an entire continent. The larger the amount of wealth accumulated with a motive of selfish profit, the larger the number of people exploited. The parable of the Rich Fool holds an important lesson for anyone who is selfish and oppressive. In greedy satisfaction, such a rich person boasts of not having room in his old barns to store his crops and brags of the need to build larger ones. "But God says to him: 'You fool. This very night your life is being demanded of you'" (Luke 12:20).

In contrast to the selfishness and the greed of the rich in these two parables, Luke tells the story of a rich man who, through Jesus' influence, becomes conscientious and generous toward others: the story of Zacchaeus (19:1–10). Zacchaeus is a tax collector, a rich man alienated from Jewish society. Somehow he is as much a stranger as the Samaritan of the parable. The irony is that both, though outcasts from Jewish religious society, offer a far-reaching lesson for the community of the kingdom of God. Luke places the story of Zacchaeus at the end of Jesus' journey to Jerusalem, after his healing of the blind man and before his entrance to the city. This story, placed at the close of Jesus' ministry, invites the reader to go back to previous pages, reread the parables of the Rich Fool and of Lazarus, and understand this new parable, in which a rich man makes a place at his table for the poor to share his well-being and happiness.[24] The parable offers to the rich people in the community a model for managing their wealth.

---

[23] Joseph A. Fitzmyer, *The Gospel according to Luke X–XXIV* (AB 28A; Garden City: Doubleday, 1985), 1109.

[24] Pope Paul VI, *Populorum Progressio 47*, in *The Papal Encyclicals, 1958–1981* (ed. Claudia Carlen; 5 vols.; Raleigh: McGrath, 1981), 5:191–92.

In addition to the lesson of Zacchaeus, Luke on several occasions shows Jesus calling on the affluent to extend a generous hand toward the poor. He invites them to escape the vicious circle of covetousness and greed and to free themselves from their attachment to riches, which enslaves them and leads to dishonest conduct. Jesus' call varies according to circumstances. On the one hand, he calls on the rich ruler to sell everything and give the proceeds to the poor (18:22); on the other hand, he calls on Zacchaeus to change his conduct without changing his profession. Generally speaking, Jesus exhorts the rich to avoid covetousness in earthly affairs: "Take care! Be on your guard against all kinds of greed; for one's life does not consist in the abundance of possessions" (12:15). In connection with this advice, he recommends almsgiving: "Sell your possessions, and give alms. Make purses for yourselves that do not wear out" (12:33). Likewise he says, "I tell you, make friends for yourselves by means of dishonest wealth so that when it is gone, they may welcome you into the eternal homes" (16:9).

4. A banquet for the poor and a call to share

In the Greco-Roman society of Luke's time, friendship was traditionally a powerful factor in obtaining access to the world of wealth, honor, and power. The upper classes cultivated bonds of friendship in their circles, and membership was reserved for people of their own kind. Such circles of friendship followed the principle of reciprocity: a favor must be repaid. The Lukan Jesus exhorts Christians to break this principle of reciprocity.[25] Thus he says to a leader of the Pharisees,

> When you give a luncheon or a dinner, do not invite your friends or your brothers or your relatives or rich neighbors, in case they may invite you in return, and you will be repaid. But when you give a banquet, invite the poor, the crippled, the lame, and the blind. And you will be blessed, because they cannot repay you, for you will be repaid at the resurrection of the righteous. (Luke 14:12–14)

Jesus illustrates this teaching with the parable of the Great Dinner (14:15–24), in which those who were invited excuse themselves at the last moment and do not come to the dinner. In response, the owner of the house becomes angry and says to his slaves, "Go out at once into the streets and lanes of the town, and bring in the poor and the crippled, the blind and the lame" (14:21). In this text, Jesus exhorts the rich to break the circle of reciprocity by inviting the poor to their homes. The invitation to the poor is not merely an example of people who cannot return the favor. The poor and the disabled must enter the circle of friendship and obtain the benefits of such a relationship without discrimination and without expectation of repayment. In this way, the poor can take advantage of the opportunities that such support may offer for their individual, familial, and social improvement. This teaching goes beyond the common Jewish practice of alms-

---

[25] See Bruce J. Malina and A. C. Mitchell, "The Social Function of Friendship in Acts," *JBL* 111 (1992): 255–72.

giving, for it requires the rich to invite the poor to share both their friendship and their abundant resources.

In addition to the principle of friendship, Luke also considers the relationship between patron and client in the Greco-Roman world, in which the rich patron acted as benefactor to people of various social levels. The objective was to gain acknowledgment, honor, and loyalty. The Lukan Jesus preaches that benefactors in the Christian community should not seek their own benefit. He asks for a transformation in the relation between patron and client.[26] Thus Jesus says,

> If you lend to those from whom you hope to receive, what credit is that to you? Even sinners lend to sinners, to receive as much again. But love your enemies, and do good, and lend, expecting nothing in return. Your reward will be great, and you will be children of the Most High; for he is kind to the ungrateful and the wicked. Be merciful as your Father is merciful. (6:34–36)

Giving without expecting anything in return represents a behavior that befits the dignity of children of God and reflects the compassion of the heavenly Father. Such a teaching finds graphic representation in the parable of the Good Samaritan. Seeing someone in need, the Samaritan helps him without first seeking his identity and insures his recovery without expecting anything in return. In mentioning this parable, Luke may have intended his readers to recall the altruistic example of benefactors in the Greco-Roman world, such as the physician Metrodoros, who served his community "without set fee, omitting nothing by way of personal interest and generosity,"[27] or the civic benefactor Opramoas, who "acted as though his own funds were public property."[28] For Christians, however, the motivation for such selfless service will be explicitly theological: "Be merciful as your Father is merciful" (6:36). Moreover, Jesus asks that contributions made to the community not be a means of gaining prestige and power.

In the Acts of the Apostles, similarly, Luke describes the early Christians of Jerusalem as forming a close-knit community with one heart and soul, holding everything in common (Acts 2:44–47; 4:32–37). This description is reminiscent of Greco-Roman traditions praising friendship for generating common bonds and leading to the sharing of material goods. In depicting the early community of Jerusalem as one of friendship, Luke seems to appeal to Greco-Roman ideals, but at the same time he shows how the Christian way of life has the potential to transform them—a transformation that is noticeable in the way in which Christians establish familial relations among people of different social classes and break the cycle of reciprocity characteristic of circles of friendship in the Greco-Roman world. The Christian spirit encourages the rich in the community to give without expecting anything in return, inspiring conduct that finds an outstanding example in Barnabas. The Acts of the Apostles tells the story of this

---

[26] Moxnes, "Patron-Client," 264.
[27] See Frederick W. Danker, *Benefactor: Epigraphic Study of a Graeco-Roman and New Testament Semantic Field* (St. Louis: Clayton, 1982), 63.
[28] Ibid., 333.

man, a rich landowner who "sold a field that belonged to him, then brought the money, and laid it at the apostles' feet" (4:37)—the apostles, who, sociologically speaking, were no more than fishermen of Galilee. Luke contrasts Barnabas's conduct to that of Ananias and Sapphira, who sold a piece of property and stated that they gave all the proceeds of the land to the community, when in fact they kept back part of the proceeds for themselves. Their generosity was vitiated by a spirit of deception. Was there a hidden desire to serve two masters?

Luke uses the description of the original community of Jerusalem to motivate the rich to imitate the generosity of the early Christians toward the poor. In his writings, he has in mind the social context of Greco-Roman society, in which the upper and the lower classes were poles apart. The poor, deprived of such basic necessities as food and shelter, received little or no help from civil authorities or private organizations. In his two books, Luke offers in many ways a challenge to the mind-set and values of the Greco-Roman world. "The Lukan Gospel imposes on the rich an indispensable requirement, quite at odds with the social values of their own society, to provide the destitute with food and the other necessities of life in this world."[29] The provision of food and other necessities has to be effected not only through almsgiving but also through the invitation of beggars and the disabled to the homes of the rich.[30]

In Luke's thought, those who embraced the gospel of the kingdom of God should develop a strong sense of sharing in community life, a drive to provide for the needs of the community, nurtured by a generous spirit of solidarity. The wealthy should tear down the barriers of social status and come down from their high position of power in order to accept generously the destitute, powerless members of the community and extend to them their warm care.[31]

Dorothy Day captures the spirit of the Lukan message well when she says,

> Going around and seeing such sights [people suffering exile, hunger, and imprisonment] is not enough. To help the organizers, to give what you have for relief, to pledge yourself to voluntary poverty for life so that you can share with your brothers is not enough. One must live with them, share with them their suffering too. Give up one's privacy, and mental and spiritual comforts as well as physical.[32]

Luke's message and Christian practice not only challenged the premises and values of Greco-Roman society. They also challenge many social practices of our own time. And the response by power holders is often negative, sometimes resulting in persecution. For Christians, however, suffering because of their dedication to the poor is suffering for the cause of the gospel, and such suffering is full of

---

[29] Philip F. Esler, *Community and Gospel in Luke-Acts: The Social and Political Motivations of Lukan Theology* (SNTSMS 57; Cambridge: Cambridge University Press, 1987), 199.
[30] Ibid., 187–200.
[31] Wolfgang Stegemann, "The Following of Christ as Solidarity between Rich, Respected Christians and Poor, Despised Christians (Gospel of Luke)," in *Jesus and the Hope of the Poor* (ed. L. Schottroff and Wolfgang Stegemann; Maryknoll: Orbis, 1986), 67–120.
[32] Dorothy Day, *The Long Loneliness: An Autobiography* (San Francisco: Harper & Row, 1952), 214.

hope and consolation. For those who suffer hatred, rejection, and ostracism on account of Jesus and his teaching will surely be rewarded in heaven (Luke 6:22–23). Such suffering is the price of entering the kingdom of God (Acts 14:22). The placement of the blessing of those persecuted for preaching the gospel (Luke 6:20–23) after the blessing of the poor, the hungry, and those who weep (6:20–21) is significant. After seeing Jesus' concern for the poor and destitute in the Gospel of Luke, the reader concludes that the persecution to which the beatitude alludes is, at least in part, the consequence of Christian testimony that calls upon the rich to share their wealth with the poor. Christians will continue to suffer such persecution in many regions of the world as long as they challenge, through words and deeds, those who, moved by unbridled greed and unrestrained ambition, hold or pursue power in society.

5. A new map of relationships

Peter's vision at Joppa before Cornelius's conversion (Acts 10:9–16, 28b) constructed the standard for a new map of relationships.[33] In the vision, Peter saw a large sheet with unclean animals on it and heard a voice from heaven ordering him three times to eat, with the explanation that "what God has made clean, you must not call profane" (10:15). Upon meeting Cornelius, Peter recognized that the vision was not simply about food, saying, "I truly understand that God shows no partiality, but in every nation anyone who fears him and does what is right is acceptable to him" (10:34–35). As a result, Peter understood that he had to alter the program of action restricted to the Jews (10:28a) and include in it all the uncircumcised as well.[34] The new map of relationships is inclusive and shows no discrimination. The guiding criterion is the inclusive and impartial attitude of God himself (10:34–35).

In his explanation, Peter in 10:34 refers to Deut 10:17–18 and reinterprets it. The text commands the Israelites to love the stranger, for God shows no partiality, "executes justice for the orphan and the widow, and loves the stranger." But while Deuteronomy speaks about the stranger who resides in Israel and understands God's impartiality as being confined to the land of God's people, Peter understands that God's impartiality encompasses all the people of the world. The new map has no national, racial, ritual, or religious borders. "In every nation anyone who fears him and does what is right is acceptable to him" (Acts 10:35). Hence Peter's comment: "You yourselves know that it is unlawful for a Jew to associate with or to visit a Gentile; but God has shown me that I should not call anyone profane or unclean" (10:38).[35] Peter understood the transcendent significance of

---

[33] Jerome H. Neyrey, "The Symbolic Universe of Luke-Acts: 'They Turn the World Upside Down,'" in *The Social World of Luke-Acts: Models for Interpretation* (ed. Jerome H. Neyrey; Peabody, Mass.: Hendrickson, 1991), 292–94.

[34] See Luke 10:28b, 34–35, 44–48; 15:7–11.

[35] See Thomas D. Hanks, "Poor, Poverty," *ABD* 5:417.

the vision at Joppa and the attendant episode of Cornelius's conversion; he used them in a telling argument during the discussion about circumcision at the council of Jerusalem (15:7–11). The vision at Joppa not only provides a new criterion for the admission of people into the community but also generates a new attitude toward people of other nations, races, and religions. Similarly, the parable of the Good Samaritan richly embodies this attitude, inviting readers to behave as a good neighbor toward anyone in need, without discrimination based on nationality, race, sex, or religion. Christians are called to imitate the good Samaritan's compassion and act with effective and generous love toward any person in need.

6. Promotion of women

In his Gospel and in Acts, Luke presents many episodes featuring a feminine character. In his Gospel, he delights in juxtaposing stories, parables, or sayings involving males and females. For instance, the annunciation to Zechariah (Luke 1:8–20) parallels the annunciation to Mary (1:26–38). The healing of a centurion's slave (7:2–10) is juxtaposed to the raising of the widow's son (7:11–12). The parable of the Good Samaritan (10:29–37) is followed by the story about Martha and Mary (10:38–42). The parable of a man and the lost sheep (15:3–7) is parallel to that of a woman and the lost coin (15:8–10). In Jesus' two accusations of the Pharisees as being more helpful on the Sabbath to an animal than to a human person, the first episode involves a crippled old woman (13:10–16), and the second a man with dropsy (14:2–6). These examples show the interest of the writer in addressing both men and women.[36] He exhibits sensitivity and concern for the instruction of both. Women are an essential part of the learning audience of the gospel and therefore an essential part of a community revolving around the ministry of the word.[37] One may contrast this inclusive approach to teach women as well as men to the way in which, in the book of Exodus, God gives the commandments: God teaches men. In ancient Israel and early Judaism, generally speaking, women's status was mediated by males; although they received and transmitted some basic religious education in the home, women were not allowed to be disciples of a great teacher. In the Greco-Roman world, the education of women varied from one locale to another. Roman society considered the education of women important and desirable. In this, Rome shared ideas and practices prevalent in Asia Minor, Macedonia, and Egypt.[38]

The Acts of the Apostles, like the third Gospel, emphasizes an important role for women in the Christian community. When Paul applied for permission to arrest Christians in Damascus, he requested permission to arrest women as well as

---

[36] See Constance F. Parvey, "The Theology and Leadership of Women in the New Testament," in *Religion and Sexism: Images of Woman in the Jewish and Christian Tradition* (ed. R. Radford Ruether; New York: Simon & Schuster, 1974), 117–49.

[37] Ibid., 138–49.

[38] Ben Witherington, "Women (NT)," *ABD* 6:957–61, here 957–58.

men (Acts 9:1–2). There are many examples of women active in the community, such as Dorcas (9:36–43), Lydia (16:14–16), Priscilla or Prisca (18:2, 18), and the daughters of Philip (21:8–9). But as E. Schüssler Fiorenza points out, while the Pauline Letters refer to some women as apostles, missionaries, coworkers, prophets, and leaders of communities, Luke does not mention any woman missionary or leader of a church. "He seems to know of such functions of women, as his references to Prisca or Lydia indicate, but his knowledge does not influence his portrayal of early Christian history."[39] M. R. D'Angelo suggests an explanation for the absence of women in positions of leadership in the Lukan writings. She thinks that the author was guided by an apologetic motive. In writing the history of Jesus and early Christianity, Luke wished to give the impression that Christian communities did not represent the dangers that Roman writers detected in oriental cults in which, in their view, women acted wildly and became factors of disorder in society.[40]

W. Carter and R. J. Karris, however, argue that Luke alludes to the leadership and ministry of women. Carter analyzes the episode of Martha and Mary (Luke 10:38–42), seeing them as representing people dedicated to the service and leadership of communities.[41] He bases his assertion on the meaning of terms used in the Lukan context. The story narrates that Martha "welcomed" Jesus. The verb "welcome" in the context does not simply mean to greet with pleasure and hospitality; it also means to accept the message and mission of the person being welcomed.[42] In welcoming Jesus, Martha thus acknowledges his dignity and mission. Furthermore, the text says that Martha "serves" Jesus, using the Greek terms *diakonia* and *diakonein*, terms that in Greek literature, as J. N. Collins shows, carry as their first meaning the idea of being an agent or emissary of the person whom one serves—the idea of accomplishing a mission. According to Collins, this meaning conforms well to such terms used in Lukan writings.[43] Applying these observations to this case, we may say that both Martha and Mary acknowledge Jesus' dignity and mission and both are his agents or emissaries; they represent those engaged in a mission of service in the Christian community. Martha takes care of many needs of the community, but she is so busy that she neglects the most important mission, of listening and preaching the word.

This story has an echo in Acts 6:1–7, when the apostles appointed seven men for service *(diakonia)* on behalf of the Hellenistic widows. The reason given was that "it is not right that we should neglect the word of God in order to wait [*diakonein*] at tables" (6:2). And then they added, "We, for our part, will devote

---

[39] Elisabeth Schüssler Fiorenza, *In Memory of Her: A Feminist Theological Reconstruction of Christian Origins* (New York: Crossroad, 1983), 50.

[40] Mary R. D'Angelo, "Women in Luke-Acts: A Redactional View," *JBL* 109 (1990): 451–61.

[41] Warren Carter, "Getting Martha out of the Kitchen: Luke 10:38–42 Again," *CBQ* 58 (1996): 264–80.

[42] See Luke 10:8, 10; 9:5.

[43] John N. Collins, *Diakonia: Re-interpreting the Ancient Sources* (New York: Oxford University Press, 1990), 173–91, 213–38.

ourselves to prayer and to serving the word *[diakonia tou logou]*" (6:4). The apostles decided to avoid the danger of neglecting the service of the word. The reader will understand that they took seriously the warning addressed to Martha and followed the example of Mary. What is remarkable in all this is that in order to give such an important lesson for the Christian community, two women were chosen as representatives.

Karris, even before Carter, argued that Luke does mention missions entrusted to women. He pointed out, for instance, that we ought to reconsider the critical text and meaning of Luke 8:3c, which is usually translated, "who provided for them *[diēkonoun autois]* out of their resources." In effect, the critical text offers two options: the service is rendered either "to them" *(autois)* or "to him" *(autō)*. In Karris's opinion, there are solid reasons to think that the singular "to him" *(autō)* is a better reading.[44] So understood, the text refers to the service women rendered to Jesus. Furthermore, referring to the verb *diēkonoun* ("they provided" NRSV), Karris (again earlier than Carter) drew the attention of scholars to the import of Collins's research on the matter. With this understanding in mind, the women to whom the text refers serve Jesus as his agents or emissaries. In accomplishing the missions assigned by Jesus, they used their own resources.

Karris likewise drew scholars' attention to the fact that women were the first to understand the message of Jesus' resurrection. According to 24:6–8, the angels said to them, "He is not here, but has risen. Remember *[mnēsthēte]* how he told you, while he was still in Galilee, that the Son of Man must be handed over . . . and on the third day rise again." The text goes on, "Then they remembered his words." According to Karris, "remember" in the Lukan writings does not simply mean to recollect the past. It includes the recollection of Jesus' word, a word capable of changing the human person. In this case, recalling Jesus' word helped the women to move from perplexity to the certainty that faith in the paschal mystery can provide. Consequently, once they understood the message, the women relayed the announcement "to the eleven and to all the rest" (24:9). According to Karris, the women not only made the announcement to the eleven and all the rest; they were also present when Jesus appeared to the disciples (24:36–49), and were included with those sent out to preach the gospel. He argues by comparing Luke 24 with Acts 1:8, 14; 2:1; 10:41; and 13:31. Karris's analysis deserves consideration. It seems to offer a coherent interpretation of the role of women in the last chapter of Luke's Gospel.[45] But the question remains, if Luke wished to indicate roles of leadership for women, why he did not explicitly do so in Acts? D'Angelo's thesis, referred to above, may provide an answer. Moreover, Luke's attitude on the matter may reflect circumstances in the Christian communities of his own time, when the family codes were held in high esteem. In those codes, generally speaking, women played roles restricted to the realm of the family.[46] Such

---

[44] Robert J. Karris, "Women and Discipleship in Luke," *CBQ* 56 (1994): 6–7.

[45] See Judith R. Wegner, *Chattel or Person? The Status of Women in the Mishnah* (New York: Oxford University Press, 1988), 120–21.

[46] See below, ch. 12, §5.

circumstances might have persuaded Luke to be cautious on the matter, using insinuation rather than open statements.

Conclusion

According to Luke, Jesus is God's anointed, endowed with the power of the Spirit, sent as the messianic king to proclaim the good news of liberation and to implement it through words and deeds. The first beneficiaries of his liberating action are the poor and the oppressed—both in Israel and in the world—all of whom trust in the Lord. The Lukan Jesus does not preach only a liberation that will be effected in heaven but one that also begins on earth. He does refer to God's judgment after death, but such a reference underlines the importance of putting the message of the gospel into practice in the present life. Jesus calls the rich and powerful to break the cycle of reciprocity distinctive to circles of friends and to relationships between patrons and clients in the Greco-Roman world. Luke has in mind a harmonious community, after the example of the early community of Jerusalem, and envisions a new map of relationships, where there is a place for any person who believes in the gospel, without any discrimination based on race, nationality, sex, social status, or religious tradition. In such a community, women live on an equal footing with men. Luke offers two stories that powerfully epitomize his message: Zacchaeus's story and the parable of the Good Samaritan. Zacchaeus offers an example of the rich man transformed by Jesus' liberating action who thus treats people with justice and kindness, allowing the poor to share his wealth. The good Samaritan encourages Christians to help their neighbors without discrimination, wherever and whenever they are in need.

Bibliography

Agua Pérez, A. del. "El cumplimiento del reino de Dios en la misión de Jesús: Programa del evangelio de Lucas (Lc 4, 14–44)." *Estudios bíblicos* 38 (1979–1980): 269–93.

Bajard, J. "La structure de la pericope de Nazareth in Luc IV.16–30." *Ephemerides theologicae lovanienses* 45 (1969): 165–71.

Brown, Raymond E. "The Beatitudes according to Luke." Pages 265–71 in *New Testament Essays*. Milwaukee: Bruce, 1965.

Carter, Warren. "Getting Martha out of the Kitchen: Luke 10:38–42 Again." *Catholic Biblical Quarterly* 58 (1996): 264–80.

Collins, John N. *Diakonia: Re-interpreting the Ancient Sources*. New York: Oxford University Press, 1990.

D'Angelo, Mary R. "Women in Luke-Acts: A Redactional View." *Journal of Biblical Literature* 109 (1990): 441–61.

Danker, Frederick W. *Benefactor: Epigraphic Study of a Graeco-Roman and New Testament Semantic Field.* St. Louis: Clayton, 1982.

Day, Dorothy. *The Long Loneliness: An Autobiography.* San Francisco: Harper & Row, 1952.

Donahue, John. "Two Decades of Research on the Rich and the Poor in Luke-Acts." Pages 129–44 in *Justice and the Holy.* Edited by D. A. Knight and J. Peter. Atlanta: Scholars Press, 1989.

Escudero Freire, C. "Jesús profeta, libertador de los hombres: Visión lukana de su ministerio terrestre." *Estudios eclesiásticos* 51 (1976): 463–95.

Esler, Philip F. *Community and Gospel in Luke-Acts: The Social and Political Motivations of Lukan Theology.* Society for New Testament Studies Monograph Series 57. Cambridge: Cambridge University Press, 1987.

Fitzmyer, Joseph A. *Essays on the Semitic Background of the New Testament.* London: Chapman, 1971. Repr., Missoula: Scholars Press, 1974.

———. *The Gospel according to Luke I–IX.* Anchor Bible 28. Garden City: Doubleday, 1981.

———. *The Gospel according to Luke X–XXIV.* Anchor Bible 28A. Garden City: Doubleday, 1985.

———. *Luke the Theologian: Aspects of Theology.* New York: Paulist, 1989.

Ford, J. Massyngbaerde. *My Enemy Is My Guest: Jesus and Violence in Luke.* Maryknoll: Orbis, 1984.

Hanks, Thomas D. "Poor, Poverty." Pages 414–24 in vol. 5 of *Anchor Bible Dictionary.* Edited by D. N. Freedman. 6 vols. New York: Doubleday, 1992.

Karris, Robert J. "Women and Discipleship in Luke." *Catholic Biblical Quarterly* 56 (1994): 1–20.

Kodell, Jerome. "Luke's Gospel in a Nutshell (Lk 4.16–30)." *Biblical Theology Bulletin* 13 (1983): 16–18.

Malina, Bruce J. "Interpreting the Bible with Anthropology: The Case of the Rich and the Poor." *Listening: Journal of Religion and Culture* 21 (1986): 148–59.

———. *The New Testament World: Insights from Cultural Anthropology.* Louisville: Westminster John Knox, 1993.

———. "Wealth and Poverty in the New Testament and Its World." *Interpretation* 41 (1987): 354–67.

Malina, Bruce J., and A. C. Mitchell. "The Social Function of Friendship in Acts." *Journal of Biblical Literature* 111 (1992): 255–72.

Malina, Bruce J., and Richard L. Rohrbaugh. *Social Science Commentary on the Synoptic Gospel.* Minneapolis: Fortress, 1992.

Moxnes, Halvor. "Patron-Client Relations and the New Community in Luke-Acts." Pages 241–68 in *The Social World of Luke-Acts: Models for Interpretation.* Edited by Jerome H. Neyrey. Peabody, Mass.: Hendrickson, 1991.

Neyrey, Jerome H. "The Symbolic Universe of Luke-Acts: 'They Turn the World Upside Down.'" Pages 271–304 in *The Social World of Luke-Acts: Models for Interpretation.* Edited by Jerome H. Neyrey. Peabody, Mass.: Hendrickson, 1991.

Nickelsburg, George W. E. "Riches, the Rich, and God's Judgement in 1 Enoch 92–105 and the Gospel according to Luke." *New Testament Studies* 25 (1979): 324–44.

O'Toole, Robert. "The Kingdom of God in Luke-Acts." Pages 147–52 in *The Kingdom of God in 20th Century Interpretation*. Edited by W. Willis. Peabody, Mass.: Hendrickson, 1987.

Parvey, Constance F. "The Theology and Leadership of Women in the New Testament." Pages 117–49 in *Religion and Sexism: Images of Woman in the Jewish and Christian Tradition*. Edited by R. Radford Ruether. New York: Simon & Schuster, 1974.

Pope Paul VI, *Populorum Progressio*. Pages 183–201 in vol. 5 of *The Papal Encyclicals*. Edited by Claudia Carlen. 5 vols. Raleigh: McGrath, 1981.

Puech, E. "4Q525 et les péricopes des Béatitudes en Ben Shira et Matthieu." *Revue biblique* 98 (1991): 80–106.

Ringe, Sharon H. *Jesus, Liberation, and the Biblical Jubilee: Images for Ethics and Christology*. Overtures to Biblical Theology. Philadelphia: Fortress, 1985.

Sanders, James A. "From Isaiah 61 to Luke 4." Pages 75–106 in vol. 1 of *Christianity, Judaism, and Other Greco-Roman Cults: Studies for Morton Smith at Sixty*. Edited by J. Neusner. 4 volumes. Studies in Judaism in Late Antiquity 12. Leiden: Brill, 1975.

Schüssler Fiorenza, Elisabeth. *In Memory of Her: A Feminist Theological Reconstruction of Christian Origins*. New York: Crossroad, 1983.

Seccombe, David P. *Possessions and the Poor in Luke-Acts*. Studien zum Neuen Testament und seiner Umwelt B, 6. Linz: Studien zum Neuen Testament und seiner Umwelt, 1982.

Sloan, Robert B. *The Favorable Year of the Lord: A Study of Jubilatory Theology in the Gospel of Luke*. Austin: Schola, 1977.

Steck, O. H. *Studien zu Tritojesaja*. Beihefte zur Zeitschrift für die alttestamentliche Wissenschaft 203. Berlin: De Gruyter, 1991.

Stegemann, Wolfgang. "The Following of Christ as Solidarity between Rich, Respected Christians and Poor, Despised Christians (Gospel of Luke)." Pages 67–120 in *Jesus and the Hope of the Poor*. Edited by L. Schottroff and Wolfgang Stegemann. Maryknoll: Orbis, 1986.

Thornton, Claus-Jürgen. *Der Zeuge des Zeugen: Lukas als Historiker der Paulusreisen*. Wissenschaftliche Untersuchungen zum Neuen Testament 56. Tübingen: J. C. B. Mohr, 1991.

Trocmé, A. *Jesus and the Nonviolent Revolution*. Translated by M. H. Shank and M. E. Miller. Scottsdale: Herald, 1973.

Viviano, B. T. "Beatitudes Found among Dead Sea Scrolls." *Biblical Archaeology Review* 18/6 (1992): 53–55, 66.

Völkel, M. "Zur Deutung des 'Reiches Gottes' bei Lukas." *Zeitschrift für die neutestamentliche Wissenschaft und die Kunde der älteren Kirche* 65 (1974): 57–70.

Wegner, Judith R. *Chattel or Person? The Status of Women in the Mishnah*. New York: Oxford University Press, 1988.

Wilson, S. G. *Luke and the Law*. Society for New Testament Studies Monograph Series 50. Cambridge: Cambridge University Press, 1983.
Witherington, Ben. "Women (NT)." Pages 957–61 in vol. 6 of *Anchor Bible Dictionary*. Edited by D. N. Freedman. 6 vols. New York: Doubleday, 1992.
Wright, C. J. H. "Jubilee, Year of." Pages 1025–30 in vol. 3 of *Anchor Bible Dictionary*. Edited by D. N. Freedman. 6 vols. New York: Doubleday, 1992.
Yoder, John H. *The Politics of Jesus: Vicit Agnus Noster*. Grand Rapids: Eerdmans, 1975.
York, John O. *The Last Shall Be First: The Rhetoric of Reversal in Luke*. Journal for the Study of the New Testament: Supplement Series 46. Sheffield: JSOT Press, 1991.
Zimmerli, W. "Das 'Gnadenjahr des Herrn.'" Pages 222–34 in *Studien zur alttestamentlichen Theologie und Prophetie: Gesammelte Aufsätze II*. Theologische Bücherei: Neudrucke und Berichte aus dem 20. Jahrhundert 51. Munich: Chr. Kaiser, 1974.

CHAPTER TWELVE

JUSTICE IN PAUL'S LETTERS

Introduction

While the three previous chapters were devoted to the analysis of the idea of liberating justice in the Synoptic Gospels, this chapter analyzes this concept in the Pauline Letters, locating Paul's teaching in their time and place. In the authentic Pauline Letters the social dimension of God's justice toward humanity affects believers individually and socially, and it has the potential power to change structures of human society, especially the condition of women and slaves. God's justice in Paul is most evident in the apostle's approach to the collection on behalf of the poor of the church of Jerusalem. The idea of justice also appears in Paul's dealing with obedience to civil government in which he adopts a philosophical concept worth consideration. Also important are Paul's allusions to the weakness of justice and peace promised in the Roman propaganda in comparison with the saving justice of the gospel. Along with the authentic Pauline Letters, one should consider the deuteropauline writings, examining their approach to the household codes that embody the Greek concept of order, a concept deriving from the natural structure of human society. This chapter will examine all these issues.

1. The Roman Empire in the first Christian century

Paul of Tarsus lived during the first two-thirds of the first Christian century, dying between 64 and 67 C.E. He lived during the period of the Pax Romana, inaugurated by the emperor Augustus (27 B.C.E.–14 C.E.), whom contemporaries credited with having brought history to its climax by ending the iron age and returning the golden age to the world.[1] Augustus was celebrated as a god-given ruler, "savior of the whole human race, who brought war to an end and established peace." His birthday was the birthday of a god, "the beginning of the gospel

---

[1] See Aelius Aristides, *Eulogy*, 106; Virgil, *Aen.* 6.791–95; *Ecl.* 4.4–10; Klaus Wengst, *Pax Romana and the Peace of Jesus Christ* (Philadelphia: Fortress, 1987), 7–9.

of peace."² But his was a peace won on the battlefield and maintained by the power of arms. "There was peace, but peace with bloodshed."³ In addition to the power of arms, however, Rome used other means to maintain its rule. Thus, for instance, the Roman magistrates gained the loyalty of the ruling classes of a conquered nation by bestowing special favors on them and allowing them to share in the benefits and pleasures of Roman culture.⁴ Rome was, in a word, elitist. Pliny reveals this when he advises, "Keep up the distinctions of rank and dignity. For to level and confound the different orders of mankind is far from producing an equality among them; it is, in truth, the most unequal thing unimaginable."⁵

In the course of its conquests, Rome boasted of its faithfulness *(fides)* to the treaties it contracted with other people, and it knew how to reward its allies. Thus Julius Caesar acknowledged the support of the Jews in his struggle for the conquest of Egypt (48–47 B.C.E.), granting special privileges to Jewish communities resident in Greek cities, privileges that Augustus later endorsed.⁶

In the first Christian century, Judaism spread over all the Roman Empire. It was an international phenomenon.⁷ During this period, "very few cities of the eastern side of the Mediterranean and few of the great cities of the empire did not have a community of resident Jews."⁸ The best known, outside Palestine, were the Jewish communities in Rome and Alexandria.⁹

2. Paul of Tarsus and his background

Paul was born at Tarsus, near the southeastern coast of Asia Minor, of a Jewish family. He was a genuine Pharisee. Pharisees were educated people, the retainers who served the governing class, performing the functions of judges and

---

²These are quotations from the inscriptions of Priene and Halicarnassus, both in Asia Minor. See *OGIS*, 2:458; G. Hirschfeld, *Knidos, Halikarnassos and Branchidae* (vol. 4 of *The Collection of Ancient Greek Inscriptions in the British Museum;* London: British Museum, 1893), no. 894.
³Tacitus, *Ann.* 1.10.4.
⁴See Wengst, *Pax Romana*, 24–26, 40–43.
⁵Pliny the Younger, *Ep.* 9.5 (Melmouth and Hutchinson, LCL).
⁶Among these privileges were the following: taxes were reduced; Jewish territories were exempted from the usual obligation of providing auxiliary troops; and Jews were granted the right to practice their ancestral laws and customs, to exercise juridisdiction over their own communities, to hold communal banquets, and to establish communal financial institutions. See Josephus, *Ant.* 14, 10; Graeme W. Clarke, "Religio Licita," *ABD* 5:665–67; Bo Reicke, *The New Testament Era: The World of the Bible from 500 B.C. to A.D. 100* (Philadelphia: Fortress, 1975), 87–89.
⁷See J. Andrew Overman and William S. Green, "Judaism (Greco-Roman Period)," *ABD* 3:1037–54.
⁸E. Mary Smallwood, The *Jews under the Roman Rule from Pompey to Diocletian* (SJLA 20; Leiden: Brill, 1976), 122.
⁹See Steven D. Fraade, "Judaism (Palestinian)," *ABD* 3:1054–61; Romano Penna, "Judaism (Rome)," *ABD* 3:1073–76; Peder Borgen, "Judaism (Egypt)," *ABD* 3:1061–72.

teachers and holding auxiliary positions in governmental administration. They associated with one another, helping each other to lead lives of strict observance of the traditions of the elders, and to improve the social environment. They nurtured reforming ideals along with some revolutionary tendencies (although not of violent character), depending on their apocalyptic beliefs.[10] Generally speaking, they nurtured a messianic expectation of a new world, rooted in justice: they longed for a time in which foreign domination would end, the exiles would return to their land, the wicked would be exterminated, and the messianic kingdom would be established over a new world, with Jerusalem as its capital. The Pharisees were politically realistic, assuming a sort of apocalyptic view in which the rise and fall of empires were part of a plan written in heaven.[11] Paul as a Pharisee was thus exposed to a certain apocalyptic mentality, as some of his letters, especially 1 Thessalonians and 1 Corinthians, seem to indicate.[12]

Most scholars agree that Paul was reared and educated at Tarsus, a city well-known for its culture and learning. There he got his training in writing, rhetoric, and dialectic. Although Paul does not seem to have had any extensive knowledge of Greek literature, his way of debating, as well as his style of argumentation and exhortation, shows some familiarity with the literary and philosophical writings of Greek moralists, who used a mixture of philosophical ideas as street preachers.[13] He must have been exposed to miscellaneous compendia of sayings from different philosophers on the subject of morals. H.-D. Betz and A. J. Malherbe have emphasized the importance of Cynic philosophy in the understanding of Paul and his intellectual context.[14]

3. Paul as apostle of Christ

Paul understood the appearance of the risen Christ to him as the revelation of God the Father concerning his Son. Thus he says to the Galatians, "God ... was pleased to reveal *[apokalypsai]* his Son to me" (Gal 1:15–16). In this statement, Paul brings out the apocalyptic character of the revelation in order to emphasize

---

[10] Anthony Saldarini, *Pharisees, Scribes, and Sadducees in Palestinian Society* (Wilmington, Del.: Glazier, 1988), 200–220; Gedalia Alon, *Jews, Judaism, and the Classical World: Studies in Jewish History in the Times of the Second Temple and Talmud* (trans. I. Abrahams; Jerusalem:: Magnes, 1977), 34.

[11] Neil Elliot, *Liberating Paul: The Justice of God and the Politics of the Apostle* (Maryknoll: Orbis, 1994), 163; E. Rivkin, *The Hidden Revolution: The Pharisees' Search for the Kingdom Within* (Nashville: Abingdon, 1978); J. Bowker, *Jesus and the Pharisees* (Cambridge: Cambridge University Press, 1973).

[12] William D. Davies, *Paul and Rabbinic Judaism: Some Rabbinic Elements in Pauline Theology* (2d ed.; New York: Harper & Row, 1953), 10–11.

[13] Abraham J. Malherbe, *Paul and the Popular Philosophers* (Minneapolis: Fortress, 1989), 81.

[14] See Hans-Dieter Betz, *Der Apostel Paulus and die sokratische Tradition* (BHT 45; Tübingen: J. C. B. Mohr, 1972); Malherbe, *Paul*.

that it deals with the unveiling of the mysterious plan of God for the final salvation of humanity, and to assure his readers that God's plan has been put into action by Christ's death and resurrection. Jesus, who appeared to him, is the enthroned Lord, who puts an end to this world and establishes a new humanity in a renewed world. For Paul, the reign of Christ is a clear indication that the time allotted to the powers of this world has expired. Now comes the eschatological time of the proclamation of the gospel to humanity in order to offer to every human being the opportunity to accept God's salvation through Christ. But Paul does not just describe the eschatological and urgent character of God's offer of salvation; he also pictures it with the images drawn from Jewish apocalyptic tradition. He does so when, speaking of Christ's return, he mentions the voice of the archangel, the sound of the last trumpet, Christ's descending from heaven, the instant transformation of the dead and the living, their escape into the clouds, the destruction of the powers of this world, and the establishment of the consummated kingdom of God.[15]

In an effort to convey his conviction about the impending end of this world, Paul not only employed images from Jewish apocalyptic literature; he also adapted Hellenistic concepts. The notion that the structure of the cosmos rested in pairs of opposite elements was widespread in the Greco-Roman world. This concept included the idea that if the cosmic polarity were destroyed, the structure of the world would collapse. Paul seems to apply this concept to those who appropriate the saving benefits of Christ's death and resurrection through faith and baptism (3:28).[16] For those united with Christ, the major pairs of opposite elements in humanity (circumcised/uncircumcised; Jew/Greek; free/slave; male/female) no longer serve as primary criteria for admission to the community or for positions within it (6:15; 3:27–29). For those who have been baptized into Christ's death, such distinctions are no longer valid: the baptized belong to a re-created humanity in which membership in God's family by union with Christ matters most. Instead of the opposing pairs, the ground of the new reality is being "one in Christ Jesus," a reality that unifies people (3:28). By implying the termination of the primary role of opposites in human society, Paul conveys the conviction that this world is about to end and give way to a new creation.

4. The social dimension of God's justice

In the Letter to the Romans, Paul describes the eschatological action of God, performed by Christ, as the result of God's justice or righteousness *(dikaiosynē)*. He states this in advancing the theme of his letter:

---

[15] See 1 Thess 4:14–17; 1 Cor 15:24–28, 51–57.
[16] See J. Louis Martyn, "Apocalyptic Antinomies in Paul's Letter to the Galatians," *NTS* 31 (1985): 410–24; Ben Witherington, "Rite and Rights for Women—Galatians 3.28," *NTS* 27 (1981): 539–604.

> For I am not ashamed of the gospel; it is the power of God for salvation to everyone who has faith, to the Jew first and also to the Greek. For in it the righteousness of God *[dikaiosynē theou]* is revealed *[apokalyptetai]* through faith for faith; as it is written, "The one who is righteous will live by faith." (Rom 1:16–17)

As stated earlier, the term *dikaiosynē* holds multiple connotations within a rich biblical background. It is difficult to suggest in English a single word that encompasses all these connotations. Usually it is translated as "uprightness," "righteousness," or "justice." Whatever word we choose, needs clarification, however. The NRSV prefers "righteousness" here, but following my approach to this term in other books of the Bible, I prefer the term "justice." In Paul's statement, the cause that moves the saving action of the gospel is God's justice; in other words, the saving power of God through the gospel is an active display of the justice of God. Such a display is an apocalyptic manifestation *(apokalyptetai)* that reveals in the present time that the mysterious and saving plan of God for the final period of history is already in action.

Most exegetes today think that in 1:16–17 Paul understands the justice of God as a divine attribute.[17] Paul contrasts it with the wrath of God (1:18), and later he associates it with God's faithfulness *(pistis theou,* 3:3), truthfulness *(alētheia theou,* 3:7), and mercy *(eleos theou,* 11:31–32). In this context, God's justice is a divine quality, but it is dynamic, not static. It proves its power by absolving people and saving them, thereby demonstrating God's honesty and faithfulness. This saving action of God is just or righteous because in it God conforms his conduct to his promises and commitments.

God's justice in turn creates justice in believers. In Paul's thought, the divine justice puts believers in the right position toward God, liberates them from obstacles encumbering that proper relation to the Lord, and provides the means for people to conduct themselves in a fashion that pleases the divine will. This concept of saving justice finds its background not in the Greco-Roman culture but in the OT, particularly in the Psalms and the Prophets, where "righteousness" is parallel to "faithfulness," "steadfast love," and "salvation."[18]

For Paul, what motivates the saving justice of God is not only God's faithfulness to himself and the promises to the ancestors of Israel, but also God's creative and redemptive design toward all of humanity. Even more, because God created not only humanity but also the whole universe, God's care and faithfulness extend toward the whole which will share a destiny of glory. "For the creation waits with eager longing for the revealing of the sons of God . . . because the creation

---

[17] For a discussion of the concept of justice in Paul, see Ernst Käsemann, "'Righteousness of God' in Paul," in *New Testament Questions of Today* (Philadelphia: Fortress, 1969), 168–82; John H. P. Reumann, *Righteousness in the New Testament: Justification in the United States Lutheran–Roman Catholic Dialogue, with Responses by J. A. Fitzmyer and J. D. Quinn* (Philadelphia: Fortress; New York: Paulist, 1982), 48–77; S. K. Williams, "The 'Righteousness of God' in Romans," *JBL* 99 (1980): 241–90; John A. Ziesler, *The Meaning of Righteousness in Paul* (SNTSMS 20; Cambridge: Cambridge University Press, 1972).

[18] See above, ch. 5, §2.8.

itself will be set free from its bondage to decay and obtain the glorious liberty of the children of God" (8:19, 21).[19] In Paul's thought, the active justice of God enters history and claims all of creation under God's dominion and sovereignty.

God's justice frees the human person from oppression. In setting human beings free, God restores their dignity in accordance with the image given in the creation (3:23), an image perfected by Christ (2 Cor 3:18; 4:4). This divine restoration promotes men and women to the dignity of divine filiation. It puts all human beings on the same level, since it gives every believer the same dignity as a child of God and allows each to share in the same divine inheritance.[20] Paul describes the oppression from which God liberates humanity as cosmic powers whose influence touches both individual persons and society and its institutions.[21] The apostle calls these powers *hamartia* ("sin") and *thanatos* ("death"). "Sin" is the personified cosmic power that drives human beings away from their creator; "death" is also a personified cosmic power, but one in the service of "sin." Its specific role is to sever forever any connection between God and the human being under the power of "sin"; it severs the relationship with humanity's only source of life. These cosmic powers entered human history through Adam's transgression and exercise their deadly influence in individuals who accept the enticement of "sin" by committing personal sin. But the power of "sin" is not limited to the individual person. Through the sin of the individual, "sin" affects the social, political, and economic life of humanity. "Sin" stamps its own mark on human culture, institutions, and communication. It creates "the present evil age."[22]

According to Paul, a distinctive feature of *hamartia* and the behavior it inspires is *adikia*, the opposite of *dikaiosynē*. The term *adikia* designates the systematic violation of the right order established by God in creation. It is often translated as "wickedness," "injustice," or "unrighteousness" (Rom 1:18, 29). "Sin" includes a hostile and violent drive to shatter and destroy the submissive attitude of the human being toward God. It manipulates feelings and ideas in order to master human beings and make them its servants, instruments of injustice or wickedness (6:13, 16–20). This leads sinners to totally improper behavior, which Paul illustrates in a long list of vices:

> They were filled with all manner of wickedness, evil, covetousness, malice. Full of envy, murder, strife, deceit, malignity, they are gossips, slanderers, haters of God, insolent, haughty, boastful, inventors of evil, disobedient to parents, foolish, faithless, heartless, ruthless. (1:29–31)

Paul calls such vices "the work of the flesh," the acts of the human person under the power of "sin" without the help of the Spirit (Gal 5:19). "Sin" leads hu-

---

[19] See Joseph A. Fitzmyer, *Romans* (AB 33; New York: Doubleday, 1993), 504–11.
[20] See Gal 3:29; 4:5–7; Rom 8:14–17.
[21] See Rom 5:12–21; 6:9, 12–14.
[22] Rom 12:2; Gal 1:4; Phil 2:15. See Fitzmyer, *Romans*, 640–41; R. Alan Culpepper, "God's Righteousness in the Life of His People: Romans 12–15," *RevExp* 73 (1976): 451–63; Jeremy Moiser, "Rethinking Romans 12–15," *NTS* 36 (1990): 571–82.

manity to do the opposite of what the righteousness or justice of God moves it toward, since, while the former leads to wicked conduct, the latter guides people to works of righteousness, the fruit of the Spirit.[23] Thus there are two opposite services: the service to "sin" and its "injustice," and the service to justice or righteousness. The justice that the believer serves is the new order established by Christ's death and resurrection (Rom 8:1), an order regulated by the law of Christ (Gal 6:2), in which "the commandments are summed up in this sentence, 'You shall love your neighbor as yourself.'" Love under the guidance of the Spirit "is the fulfillment of the law."[24] Through this guidance, the Spirit provides the knowledge of God's will and empowers one to fulfill it.

God's justice, which justifies by faith, thus redirects the believer toward God. But in the process, it does not lead to separation or isolation from other human beings; nor does it leave the believer passive while waiting for the Lord to come. The saving justice of God makes those who have been justified members of Christ's body. It removes them from the evil in which they are complicit and makes them members of a new community enabling them through the Spirit to serve the common good. The believer is a member of a new body, living and working for the good of the other members and the whole body (1 Cor 12:4–31).[25]

To enliven relations with others, the Spirit pours into the believer the gift of selfless and creative love that drives human beings to serve others.[26] In Paul's words, such a love "does not insist on its own way; it is not irritable or resentful; it does not rejoice at wrong, but rejoices in the right. Love bears all things, believes all things, hopes all things, endures all things" (13:5–7). According to Paul, this unreserved and devoted love is a debt that each believer pays continuously to the neighbor (Rom 13:8). It includes all the duties demanded by commutative or distributive justice (13:8–10; Gal 5:14), but it goes beyond them in terms of quantity and quality. On the one hand, Christian love exceeds the limits of strict justice, which regulates only a part of the huge number of relations that bind people together. On the other hand, Christian love has an intensity that transcends the cold requirements of strict justice, becoming a vibrant manifestation of care and support, animated by a warm esteem that looks for the other person's good and rejoices in his or her achievements.

Hence, it is understandable that the justification effected by God's justice in the individual person would have far-reaching social consequences in the Christian community. Aware of such consequences, Paul confronted Peter at Antioch. In Paul's understanding, Peter, under pressure from people from Jerusalem, had agreed to consider ritual regulations as criteria for sharing the community table (Gal 2:11–14). This premise was unacceptable for Paul, since for him the deciding factor for Christians to share in community life was not adherence to dietary laws but faithfulness to Christ and a love for others that tears down fences, unifies

---

[23] See Rom 6:13, 18–20; Gal 5:22–23.
[24] Rom 13:8–10; 8:5, 9, 14; Gal 5:13–14, 22–26.
[25] See Nils A. Dahl, *Studies in Paul* (Minneapolis: Augsburg, 1977), 95–120.
[26] See Rom 5:5; 12:9–11; 15:7; 1 Cor 13:1–13.

people, and enables them to serve for the benefit of all. Paul employed the same criterion elsewhere to settle issues that were disrupting unity in Christian communities. He used it in the Corinthian community when he addressed the divisions created by various parties and the unrest caused by the "pneumatics." Thus he wrote to the Corinthians, "To each is given the manifestation of the Spirit for the common good" (1 Cor 12:7). Paul also employed this criterion when he wrote to the Roman church, giving advice concerning the division between the "weak" and the "strong": "Let us then pursue what makes for peace and for mutual upbuilding" (Rom 14:19).

The expectation of a new world through the power of God's justice—a justice that ends division, binds people together, and promotes all on the same level—is experienced intensively in liturgical celebrations, an experience that anticipates the eschatological consummation. In such celebrations, Christians—masters and slaves, males and females, Romans and barbarians, circumcised and uncircumcised—all together, animated by the same Spirit, feel themselves children of the same Father, God, acknowledge the one and only Lord, Christ Jesus, and wait for the same eternal inheritance. For Paul, however, the liturgical celebration does not help Christians escape from this world, but rather, energizes and motivates them to bring the values of the new order to bear on the daily life of this world.

5. God's justice and the dignity of women

Paul developed in both the men and the women of his churches an awareness of what it meant for their lives to be justified by faith and baptism.[27] Men and women share equally the positive, beneficial action of God's justice. Both have received the same Spirit, who moves them to call God their Father and energizes them to be faithful to the one and only Lord. Both are children of God who share the same inheritance and take part in communal worship without any distinction based on gender. Both men and women pray and prophesy (1 Cor 11:4–5). Several women labored side by side with Paul in the apostolic work. Women worked and struggled for the propagation of the gospel on an equal footing with men. Paul employs two verbs to express the collaboration of women: to "labor" *(kopiaō)* and to "struggle" *(synathleō)*. Both in the Pauline context designate the work of preaching the gospel.[28] As associates in his apostolic work Paul mentions several women, including Euodia, Syntyche (Phil 4:2–3), Prisca (Rom 16:3–5),

---

[27] On women in the letters of Paul, see Brendan Byrne, *Paul and the Christian Woman* (Collegeville: Liturgical Press, 1989); Victor P. Furnish, *The Moral Teaching of Paul* (Nashville: Abingdon, 1979), 84–114; Ben Witherington, "Women (NT)," *ABD* 6:957–61; B. Witherington, *Women in the Earliest Churches* (SNTSMS 59; Cambridge: Cambridge University Press, 1988); Susanne Heine, *Women and Early Christianity* (trans. J. Bowden; Minneapolis: Augsburg, 1988); Elisabeth Schüssler Fiorenza, *In Memory of Her* (New York: Crossroad, 1983), 205–41; Krister Stendahl, *The Bible and the Role of Women* (Philadelphia: Fortress, 1966).

[28] See 1 Thess 5:12; Gal 4:11; 1 Cor 15:10; 16:16; Phil 1:22; 2:16; 4:3.

Mary (16:6), Junia (16:7), Tryphaena, Tryphosa, and Persis (16:12). Junia is called "apostle" in the broad sense that this word had in the early Christian communities.[29] Some women discharged significant leadership roles in local churches: Phoebe was a "minister" *(diakonos)* in the church of Cenchreae (16:1), and Paul further describes her as a *prostatis* (16:2), a term that is sometimes translated as "helper" (RSV) or "benefactor" (NAB) but is probably better rendered as "patron(ess)."[30] Prisca, along with her husband Aquila, was Paul's colleague in preaching and teaching the gospel, and her house was a church in which Christians met for worship (16:5).

Many regard the text of Gal 3:28 as the Magna Carta of human equality: "There is no longer Jew or Greek, there is no longer slave or free, there is no longer male and female; for all of you are one in Christ Jesus."[31] Through this text, they say, Paul abolished distinctions based on race, nationality, social status, and sex. Doubtless, Paul's statement might have struck many as revolutionary in so discriminatory an environment as the Greco-Roman world. A saying variously attributed to Thales or Socrates was well known: "I thank Tyche that I was born a human being and not an animal, a man and not a woman, a Greek and not a barbarian."[32] The same discriminatory spirit is attested by Rabbi Jehuda ben Elai (ca. 150 C.E.): "Three thanksgivings must be said every day: Praised [be God] . . . that he has not made me a woman. Praised be God that he has not made me ignorant. Praised be God that he has not made me a *goy* [Gentile]."[33]

Paul in Gal 3:28 seems to utter a rhetorical statement similar to what M. Fishbane calls haggadic exegesis, in which what is negated is not actually abolished but becomes secondary to what is positively stated.[34] In this vein, B. Witherington makes his clarifying remark that the text of 3:28 does not deal with the abolition of ethnic, national, social, or sexual differences.[35] He states that, rather, it refers to the role of these differences: they ceased to be criteria for admission of people into the Christian community. They do not bear on salvation. The text of 3:26–28, however, refers not only to criteria for admission into the community but also to the status and dignity of those who are in it. In my opinion, Galatians includes the concept that the position of Christians in the community does not

---

[29] For the term "apostle" as designating a circle wider than that of the Twelve, see 1 Cor 15:7; Acts 14:14. Today it is widely accepted among scholars that the names Andronicus and Junia (Rom 16:7) refer to a man and a woman respectively, probably a couple. In the past, some commentators have tried to account for the name Junia as a variant of the masculine Junias. Junias as a masculine name, however, is nowhere otherwise attested, while the feminine Junia is a common Roman name. See Fitzmyer, *Romans,* 737–38.

[30] Ancient inscriptions and papyri support the translation of *prostatis* as "patron(ess)" rather than the simple "helper." See *NewDocs* 4 (1987): 242–44.

[31] See Stendahl, *Role of Women,* 32–37.

[32] See Wolfgang Speyer, "Barbar," *JAC* 10 (1967): 257; M. Hengel, *Jews, Greeks, and Barbarians* (Philadelphia: Fortress, 1980), 78–79.

[33] See Str-B 3:611 (trans. by the author).

[34] See M. Fishbane, *Biblical Interpretation in Ancient Israel* (Oxford: Clarendon, 1991), 300–307.

[35] Witherington, "Rights for Women," 593–94.

depend on their ethnic, national, social, or sexual circumstances. Still, the equality received through justification by faith does not exclude diversity of service in the community. Service, in turn, may include the subordination of one member to another in the ecclesial body, since charism is not contrary to authority. Such subordination, however, does not rest on race, nationality, social status, or sex but on the free gift of God.[36]

In addition to the opportunities for women's leadership in the Christian communities, we must also keep in mind the significance of the liberation and promotion of women in Paul's advice on celibacy (1 Cor 7:25–35). The apostle advises both men and women to consider the possibility of remaining celibate so that they might render service to the community. Instead of being "anxious about the affairs of the world," Paul advises them to be "anxious about the affairs of the Lord" (7:34). Such advice is revolutionary, especially for women, for remaining celibate clashed with the design of Roman law and the character of the contemporary culture in general.[37]

The picture of the dignity and role of women that we draw from Paul's statements and practice seems incompatible with two Pauline texts, namely, 1 Cor 11:2–16 and 14:33b–36. In the first instance, Paul speaks of the order to be kept in liturgical meetings. He advises the Corinthians to follow the traditional mores: men with head uncovered and women with head covered. Actually, the apostle does not deal with the role of women in the assembly but with a custom of dress that distinguished women from men. He preserves the symbols that show the identity of sex against a tendency purporting to destroy this identity by fusing the feminine into the masculine.[38] In support of his position, Paul turns to biblical references.[39] In doing so, he seems to employ the concept of woman being subordinate to man. Thus he states that "the husband is the head of his wife" (7:3), a statement that seems to imply the dependence of women on men. But in the process, Paul feels uncertain of the strength of his argument, for at the end he says,

> Nevertheless, in the Lord woman is not independent of man or man independent of woman. For just as woman came from man, so man comes through woman; but all things come from God. (11:11–12)

Thus Paul ends his discussion by stating the mutual dependency of man and woman. By such a statement, Paul amends the tradition on woman's subordination and emphasizes that all are one in Christ, each possessing different gifts and accomplishing different roles.[40]

In the second text (14:33b–36), Paul again takes up the issue of subordination of women in mentioning the instruction that women be silent in churches.

---

[36] See 1 Cor 12:28–30; 16:16; Enrique Nardoni, "The Concept of Charism in Paul," *CBQ* 55 (1993): 68–80.
[37] See Schüssler Fiorenza, *Memory*, 225.
[38] See Byrne, *Paul*, 49–51.
[39] See Gen 1:27; 2:18, 21–23; Sir 17:3; Wis 2:23.
[40] See Furnish, *Teaching*, 95–102.

This instruction, however, is not in character with Paul's statement in 11:5 or with his praxis of accepting women as preachers of the gospel and leaders of communities (Rom 16:1–12; Phil 4:2–3). The prohibition seems more in keeping with the view of the deuteropauline writings, which assimilated Hellenistic household codes as guides for conduct in the Christian community. For this very reason, several exegetes regard this instruction as a later, non-Pauline, addition to 1 Corinthians.[41] Such an addition must have been made very early, however, because no manuscript witnesses the text without the instruction.

6. God's justice and slavery

Paul discusses the issue of slavery in both 1 Corinthians and the Letter to Philemon. The apostle approaches it from the perspective of God's justice, which justifies graciously by faith and elevates every justified person to the same dignity. Paul's statements and praxis concerning slavery should be understood within the framework of Greco-Roman law and custom. In Rome's imperial economy, slavery was an essential element, for every kind of work, especially manual labor, was performed by slaves. Work was not considered suitable for free people. K. Hopkins has noted that physicians, teachers, scribes, clerks, bookkeepers, inspectors, secretaries, captains—were all slaves.[42]

In the Greco-Roman world, slavery was not in general a permanent social condition. It was, rather, a stage through which many persons went for various reasons. Manumission of slaves was common. The practice of liberating slaves is very well documented and was motivated by many reasons.[43] The process of manumission, however, could not be initiated by slaves themselves. The slave could hardly even foresee it. Such liberation rested totally on the will of the master, hence Paul's advice that Corinthian slaves should seize advantage of the opportunity for freedom that would be eventually offered by their masters. Thus, in the best translation of this passage, the apostle says, "Were you a slave when called? Do not be concerned about it. But if you can obtain freedom avail yourself of the opportunity" (1 Cor 7:21).[44]

The Letter to Philemon deals with a concrete case in which Paul supported the manumission of a slave. The apostle intercedes with Philemon on behalf of Onesimus, who was probably not a runaway or fugitive slave, as has been suggested in the past, but, rather, a slave who was in serious trouble for having

---

[41] See ibid., 91–92; Jerome Murphy-O'Connor, "The First Letter to the Corinthians," *NJBC* 811–12; Byrne, *Paul*, 62–64.

[42] Keith Hopkins, *Conquerors and Slaves* (New York: Cambridge University Press, 1978), 123.

[43] See S. Scott Bartchy, *Mallon Chresai: First Century Slavery and the Interpretation of 1 Cor 7:21* (SBLDS 11; Missoula: Scholars Press, 1973), 65–73.

[44] See ibid., esp. 183; cf. Peter Trummer, "Die Chance der Freiheit: Zur Interpretation des *mallon chresai* in 1 Kor 7.21," *Bib* 56 (1975): 344–68.

wronged his master and who approached Paul for help. It was a documented Roman practice that in these circumstances the slave could turn to an influential person for support.[45] This seems to be the case with Onesimus, who had resorted to Paul and meanwhile had also converted to Christianity. In Paul's letter, he put Philemon in a quandary—either continue being Onesimus's master or else become his brother and colleague in the new social relationship that Christianity provides. Paul asks Philemon not to remember the damage done by Onesimus and beseeches him not to delay the slave's manumission, arguing that Onesimus as a freedman would be a great benefit to him because Philemon would lose a slave but gain a beloved and faithful brother.

In the Letter to Philemon, Paul shows an exquisite ability to reconcile opposing parties and to generate solidarity, always inspired by the ideal of the new social reality that Christianity can create. Nevertheless, Paul does not deliver a manifesto demanding that slavery be abolished in the Roman Empire. Rather, he persuades. On the one hand, the apostle presents an attitude that contrasts with the mind-set of the surrounding world. Although he is a free man and a Roman citizen, Paul labors and toils, working day and night, to earn his living (1 Thess 2:9), instructs Christians to do the same (4:11), and encourages people in his communities to develop their own ability for productive work in order to earn their living and help others. Moreover, the apostle exhorts Christians to be responsible for their own support and encourages them to develop a sense of civic responsibility to the society to which they belong. On the other hand, Paul employs all the rhetorical skill at his disposal to persuade Christian masters to reflect on the equality created by our incorporation into Christ and to be generous in practicing manumission. Simultaneously he strives to persuade slaves to accept the manumission eventually offered to them and to face the risks that free life may entail.[46]

Later NT writings, such as the deuteropauline writings and 1 Peter, instruct wives to be obedient to their husbands, and they urge slaves to respect and obey their masters.[47] Despite the fact that the wisdom literature of the OT already contained instructions on the duties of household members, scholars commonly hold that these NT texts reflect the influence, both in form and substance, of contemporary catalogues of ethical responsibility originating in Greek philosophy and propagated through Greco-Roman culture.[48]

Such household codes, as they are known today, were originally composed as collections of ethical norms regulating relations among the various members of the household *(oikos/oikia)* in order to preserve order and authority in the family.

---

[45] See S. Scott Bartchy, "Philemon, Epistle to," *ABD* 5:305–10; Peter Lampe, "Keine 'Sklavenflucht' des Onesimus," *ZNW* 76 (1985): 135–37.

[46] See Bartchy, "Philemon," 5:308.

[47] See Col 3:18–4:1; Eph 5:22–6:9; 1 Pet 2:11–3:12; 1 Tim 2:8–15; 5:1–2; 6:1–2; Titus 2:1–10; 3:1.

[48] For a study of these household codes, see Balch, *Let Wives Be Submissive;* David C. Verner, *The Household of God: The Social World of the Pastoral Epistles* (SBLDS 71; Chico: Cal.: Scholars Press, 1983); Ulrike Wagener, *Die Ordnung des "Hauses Gottes."* (WMANT 2.65; Tübingen: Mohr, 1994).

In adapting such schemes of ethical teaching, Christians did not undermine the patriarchal structure of the Greco-Roman culture with its emphasis on subordination to the authority of the head of the household *(paterfamilias)*. Nevertheless, they introduced new motivations animated by a new concept of authority—authority as service—and a new view of the dignity of those previously considered insignificant. These new motivations pointed to a new spirit of reciprocal love that is to govern relations between the members of the family. As a result of the new spirit, the Christian household codes rejected, for instance, abuse of slaves and the absolute subordination of wives to their husbands on religious matters.[49] Christianity presented enormous potential for liberating people from oppressive customs and institutions. But it was a long time before this potential came to be realized. For instance, it took many centuries for slavery to be abolished. Abolition was achieved only after the long and harsh experience of many enslaved human beings, an experience that was finally condemned in the light of an increasing awareness of the dignity of the human person and a deeper understanding of the spirit of the gospel.[50]

New Testament experts disagree on which factors motivated Christians at the end of the first century to emphasize the Greco-Roman household codes. D. L. Balch expresses the opinion that Christians were moved by an apologetic purpose.[51] On the one hand, the household codes served to encourage Christian wives and slaves who had pagan husbands and masters to exemplify the virtues that Greco-Roman culture held in high esteem. The encouragement of such virtues was intended to exhibit a kind of living testimony to refute pagan calumnies against Christians, who were unjustly slandered as immoral, antisocial, subversive, and atheistic. On the other hand, the emphasis on the household codes could foster virtuous conduct on the part of Christians according to the accepted ethical norms of Greco-Roman culture, a virtuous way of life that would make Christianity attractive to pagans and win their respect and even their conversion.

J. H. Elliot agrees with Balch's explanation in many respects but believes that it misses the inner motives of Christians in adapting the household codes, motives that were necessary for the survival of the small groups of Christians scattered in the Greco-Roman world.[52] Small groups living in contrast to the society at large, as Christian communities did, are described by sociologists as sectarian. They urgently need to consolidate an inner cohesion in order to survive in a hostile environment. The household codes met this need precisely because they

---

[49] See Col 4:1; Eph 5:25–30; 6:9; 1 Pet 3:7. These texts favor love patriarchalism, which, on the one hand, requests that the rich show respect and active love to the poor and weak and, on the other, urges the poor to show subordination, faithfulness, and honor to their rich masters. See Gerd Theissen, *The Social Setting of Pauline Christianity: Essays on Corinth* (trans. M. Kohl; Philadelphia: Fortress, 1982), 107–10.

[50] See John T. Noonan, "Development in Moral Doctrine," *TS* 54 (1993): 662–77.

[51] See David L. Balch, "Household Codes," *ABD* 3:318–20; D. Balch, *Let Wives Be Submissive*, 130–80.

[52] John H. Elliot, *A Home for the Homeless: A Sociological Exegesis of 1 Peter, Its Situation and Strategy* (Philadelphia: Fortress, 1981), 208–20.

fostered and strengthened social bonds, thus providing a sense of belonging and moral support. Strengthening mutual relations within the basic unit—the family—was tantamount to consolidating the cohesion of the whole Christian community. The First Letter of Peter is an outstanding case in which the author encourages Christians to stand firm and persevere as the household of God within an unfriendly society. The letter exhorts Christians to overcome the experience of being strangers and resident aliens by tightening their bonds as the community of God and practicing virtues that reinforce their inner cohesion.

In order to understand the importance of both the family unit *(oikos)* and the household codes, one has to keep two things in mind. First, in the Greco-Roman world, belonging to a family was essential, for it provided the individual person with identity, protection, shelter, acknowledgment, and love. Deprived of a family, the individual person was isolated, lost, and socially alienated. Second, it was an honor for each member to fulfill his duties in the family and a shame to neglect them. Honor and acknowledgment, in turn, brought the esteem of the whole group. Thus the right conduct of each member in the household contributed to tightening the family bonds.

Incidentally, such patriarchal centralization as the type found in the Pastoral Letters has had an enormous influence in the Christian church. The countermovement of depatriarchalization was supported officially for the first time in the Catholic Church only in 1965 by the Second Vatican Council's Pastoral Constitution on the Church in the Modern World, which in one of its most important passages states, "Forms of social or cultural discrimination in basic personal rights on the grounds of sex, race, color, social conditions, language or religion, must be curbed and eradicated as incompatible with God's design."[53]

7. God's justice and the Pax Romana

In his First Letter to the Thessalonians, Paul refers to the insecurity and suffering that the preaching of the gospel and a Christian way of life entail for believers who live and work in a non-Christian world (1 Thess 1:6–7; 2:2, 14). Paul contrasts such insecurity and suffering with two types of security. The first is the true and eternal security that the impending return of the Lord will bring to believers. At his return, the Lord will end injustice and corruption and free believers from their insecurity and suffering forever (1:10; 4:15–17). The second type of security is pretentious, fragile, and transitory, a security created by the Pax Romana and praised by imperial propaganda. It is mentioned by Paul in his exhortation to the Thessalonians: "When they say, 'There is peace and security,' then sudden destruction will come upon them, as labor pains come upon a pregnant woman, and there will be no escape!" (5:3). Paul's reference to the imperial propaganda is clear for "peace and security" was a slogan of the Roman Empire after Augustus

---

[53] Second Vatican Council, *Gaudium et Spes* §29, in *Vatican Council II: The Conciliar and Post Conciliar Documents* (ed. Austin Flannery; Collegeville: Liturgical Press, 1975), 929.

had ended civil war and consolidated universal peace.⁵⁴ Also 5:3 and surrounding verses use other terms, loaded with political-imperial connotations. Thus in 4:15, 17, two such terms occur—*parousia* ("coming") and *apantēsis* ("meeting"), both of which are used on the occasion of solemn visits of the emperor, the bearer of salvation.⁵⁵ Moreover, in the same context we find the title *kyrios* (4:15, 17), a title given to Caesar in imperial worship.⁵⁶

These references are more pointed if one bears in mind that Thessalonika was a city devoted to Rome and proud of praising Roman power. Thessalonika had integrated the Roman pantheon into the religion of the city and even given the gods of Rome a special place of honor. Consistent with its religious and political conduct, Thessalonika acclaimed Caesar as "god" and dedicated a temple to him. It worshiped Augustus under the title "Son of God" and engraved the emperor's head on its coins rather than Jupiter's. Proud of its fidelity to the emperor, Thessalonika imposed on its citizens an oath of total loyalty to Caesar. In return for such honors, the city received from Rome important privileges.⁵⁷

Paul, however, regarded the security offered by Roman power as fragile and deceitful. For him, when the Lord returns—an event he expected to occur in his own generation—Rome's imperial power will collapse along with all the powers of this world.⁵⁸ It will be the day of wrath (1:10), a day that will expose everything to light, unmask deception, and establish the truth. Arrogance will crash and injustice end. The power of light will destroy darkness. In 5:8 Paul alludes to Third Isaiah, who says that when God saw the lack of justice on earth, he was displeased and decided to intervene as in a holy war, wearing the breastplate of justice and the helmet of salvation (Isa 59:17). Paul believes that Christians, children of light, wear God's suit of armor; they wear "the breastplate of faith and love and for helmet the hope of salvation" (1 Thess 5:8). They are strengthened by the power of three Christian virtues: faith, love, and hope. So equipped, they shine as a light in the world and contribute to the defeat of the powers of injustice (5:4–5). Paul develops these ideas to encourage Christians in their sufferings, heightening the awareness of their final destination: they are called to be with the Lord forever (5:10) and enjoy the true and eternal peace and security.

In the Letter to the Romans, Paul similarly employs terms that, while having a biblical grounding, also echo imperial and political language. In Rom 1:16–17, advancing the theme of the letter, the apostle uses the words *euangelion* ("gospel" or "good news"), *sōtēria* ("salvation"), and *dikaiosynē* ("justice"). In 3:3 he speaks of *pistis* in the sense of "loyalty"; and in 5:1 he emphasizes the concept of *eirēnē* ("peace"). Remarkably, this series of terms was employed in the theology of

---

⁵⁴ Wengst, *Pax Romana*, 19–21, 77–78.
⁵⁵ See A. Oepke, "Παρουσία, πάρειμι," *TDNT* 5 (1967): 858–71; E. Peterson, "ἀπάντησις," *TDNT* 1 (1964): 380–81.
⁵⁶ Karl P. Donfried, "The Cults of Thessalonica and the Thessalonian Correspondence," *NTS* 31 (1985): 336–56.
⁵⁷ Ibid.
⁵⁸ See 1 Thess 1:10; 4:15–17; 5:2.

imperial politics. Imperial propaganda proclaimed the great gospel as the proclamation of the good news of the birth of Augustus, son of god, savior of humanity, bearer of a new world, and restorer of the golden age.[59] Augustus was the creator of a realized eschatology. *Fides* ("loyalty"), the Latin equivalent of *pistis,* was the loyalty of Rome toward its allies, acknowledged by the nations.[60] *Iustitia,* the equivalent of *dikaiosynē*, was one of the four attributes of Augustus, the virtue that Augustus held enthroned in his mind.[61] *Pax* ("peace") was the slogan that proclaimed the great deeds of Augustus, a slogan repeated when the emperor restored order and tranquility.[62]

Paul contrasts the vocabulary of Roman propaganda with that of Christian faith. He never uses the term "justice" in the Hellenistic sense of virtue (which stresses human achievement) to describe the moral demands of the Christian life. (Only later, in the Pastoral Letters [1 Tim 6:11; 2 Tim 2:2], will the word occur in this sense; indeed, these letters show the distinctive influence of the vocabulary of Greco-Roman thought.)[63] Paul instead makes use of the political connotations of the words, first, to invalidate the arrogant character of Roman propaganda and to expose the deceitful, transitory, and fragile condition of the imperial peace and justice; and second, to emphasize the trustworthy, definitive, and indestructible character of God's desire for peace and justice on behalf of humanity. The comparison relativizes imperial power and encourages Christians to intensify their sense of identity and their appreciation of belonging to Christ's community. It spurs them to resist the viewpoint and lifestyle fostered by imperial ideology, inciting them to face the hardships that the Christian life entails.

8. Paul and civil government

Even though Christians believe themselves to possess heavenly citizenship, and long for the second coming of the Lord, they still live in a human and earthly society. Although this society is doomed (Rom 13:11–12; 1 Cor 7:29–31), it im-

---

[59] See above notes 1 and 2; Wengst, *Pax Romana,* 7–10; Dieter Georgi, *Theocracy in Paul's Praxis and Theology* (trans. D. E. Green; Minneapolis: Fortress, 1991), 28–29; D. Georgi, "Who Is the True Prophet?" in *Christians among Jews and Gentiles: Essays in Honor of K. Stendahl on His Sixty-Fifth Birthday* (ed. George W. E. Nickelsburg and George W. MacRae; Philadelphia: Fortress, 1986), 100–127.

[60] See *Res Gestae Divi Augusti: The Achievements of the Divine Augustus* (ed. P. A. Brunt and J. M. Moore; Oxford: Oxford University Press, 1967), 32. This example of imperial propaganda, composed during Augustus's reign, claims that the nations, which once had been enemies of Rome, now acknowledged the honesty and faithfulness *(fides)* of the Roman authorities to their pledges. During this time the word *fides* also began to occur frequently on the imperial coins, and there was a renaissance of the ancient Latin cult of the goddess Fides. See W. Eisenhut, "Fides," *KlPauly* 2:545–46.

[61] See Ovid, *Pont.* 3.6.23–29; *Res Gestae,* 34.

[62] See *Rex Gestae,* 12, 13, 26; Virgil, *Aen.* 6.791–95; *Ecl.* 4.4–10; Wengst, *Pax Romana,* 7–10.

[63] See G. Schrenk, "δίκαιος," *TDNT* 2:210.

poses demands on its members. In his Letter to the Romans, Paul directly addresses the demands of the civil authority and the corresponding duties of Christians because they remain part of this world with its laws and order. He was probably motivated to write on the subject by disturbances in Rome caused by popular discontent with abuses committed by tax collectors. Such discontent forced the emperor Nero in 58 C.E. to reform the tax system.[64] Considering the demands of the civil government, Paul in Rom 13:1–7 explains why Christians should obey civil authorities and asserts the obligation of paying taxes:

> For the same reason you also pay taxes, for the authorities are God's servants, busy with this very thing. Pay to all what is due them—taxes to whom taxes *[phoron]* are due, revenue *[telos]* to whom revenue is due, respect to whom respect is due, honor to whom honor is due. (13:6–7)

Paul seems to distinguish between direct taxes *(phoros)* and indirect taxes *(telos)*. The former is collected by government employees, the latter by a group of individuals, the *societas publicanorum*, composed principally of Romans of the equestrian order.[65] Paul states the obligation of Christians to pay all taxes.

These directives on one's duties toward the civil government in 13:1–7 do not seem to be truly Pauline.[66] Some have called them "an alien body in Paul's exhortation," since they do not show the christological or eschatological perspective so distinctive of the authentic Pauline texts. Most scholars, however, find no real evidence that the text is an interpolation. Paul merely discusses a secular issue using a rational and philosophical way of argumentation, similar to the teaching of Wis 6:1–8 and the *Let. Aris.* 224. This is precisely that rare case in which Paul uses the Greco-Roman concept of justice, which roots the relations between the citizens and the government in the very nature of human society. In general, Paul does not derive norms for human conduct from a consideration of the inner laws that govern nature and society. Rather, he draws them from the will of God revealed in Christ.

In Rom 13:1–7, Paul does not speak directly of the Roman Empire but of the authority of human society at large. He states that civil authority has been instituted by God, since there is no authority on earth that is not derived from God. Governors have received authority from above and are responsible before God to serve their fellow men and women for the common benefit of all in the society. One of the governors' duties is to enforce the observance of the law. Hence, when they punish a crime according to the law, they fulfill their obligations as servants

---

[64] On the connection between Rom 13:1–7 and the discontent of the Roman people during the reign of Nero at the abuses of the tax collectors, see Furnish, *Teaching*, 131–35; J. Friedrich, W. Pöhlmann, and P. Stuhlmacher, "Zur historischen Situation und Intention von Röm 13,1–7," *ZTK* 73 (1976): 131–66.

[65] John R. Donahue, "Tax Collector," *ABD* 6:337–38.

[66] See Elliot, *Liberating Paul*, 218–26; Fitzmyer, *Romans*, 661–76; Wolfgang Schrage, *The Ethics of the New Testament* (Philadelphia: Fortress, 1990), 235–39; Furnish, *Teaching*, 115–39; Marcus Borg, "A New Context for Romans xiii," *NTS* 19 (1972–73): 205–18; Byrne, *Romans* (Sacra pagina 6; Collegeville, Minn.: Liturgical Press, 1996), 385–93.

of God. Since governors hold this authority as God's servants, Christians owe them respect and obedience. Part of this obedience is to pay taxes. Paul describes it as an obligation of conscience rooted in justice, according to which one has to pay to all what is due (13:7). By paying taxes, Christians as members of civil society contribute to the treasury administered by the government for the common benefit of the society. In discussing this matter, Paul exhorts Christians to develop a sense of social responsibility so that all people might be aware of their duties toward government and society. Such an exhortation confronts anyone who evades the payment of taxes. (Tax evasion occurs everywhere, but it seems especially ingrained in people of the upper and middle classes in developing or third-world countries—a practice that is highly detrimental to the community.)

Paul, in any case, sees the civil authority as transitory, part of a world that is passing away (13:11–14; 1 Cor 7:31). But even though this world is transitory, it is governed by a God-given order for the common benefit of society, and Christians cannot disregard it and certainly cannot sabotage it. Complying with civil authority is a duty of justice. But however straightforward he may be, Paul does not offer a systematic or comprehensive view on the subject. For instance, he does not consider the eventuality of totalitarian or tyrannical governments oppressing their citizens. He states that authority must benefit all of society but does not define its limits, although he knows well that the obedience due to the government is not unrestricted. He would not obey, for instance, a government forbidding him to preach the gospel. Neither would he worship Caesar as god, no matter how strongly the emperor's command was enforced.[67] It is remarkable that while Paul advises one not to resist the civil authority established by God (Rom 13:2), he emphasizes that the believer has to avoid adopting a worldly way of thinking and behaving (12:2). Such resistance is a challenge that the world takes seriously, and in response it imposes suffering and hardship on Christians. In his First Letter to the Thessalonians, Paul alluded to such a suffering in which the believers become imitators of the crucified Lord (1:6).

9. God's justice and the collection for the Jerusalem church

The Jerusalem council asked Paul to "remember the poor" of the church of Jerusalem, the mother church (Gal 2:10). In response, he organized collections in his churches. He saw in this process something more than a simple donation to alleviate extreme poverty. He understood the collection to be a generous undertaking under the influence of God's grace *(charis tou theou)*,[68] a ministry *(diakonia)* for the benefit of the whole church,[69] a gift of God (2 Cor 9:15), a work of grace, an action inspired by the favor of God the Father, and a "manifestation of the Spirit for the common good" (1 Cor 12:5–7). Such an undertaking brought

---

[67] See Schrage, *Ethics*, 138.
[68] See 2 Cor 8:1, 4, 6, 7, 9; 9:15.
[69] See 2 Cor 9:1, 12, 13; Rom 15:31; 1 Cor 12:5–7.

the Pauline churches together in a willingness to minister to the "saints," the Christians of Jerusalem, an action that helped establish an equilibrium between the "plenty" of the Pauline churches and the "shortage" of the mother church, an equilibrium by participation inspired by a principle of equity *(isotēs)*. Since equity is a basic notion in both Greek and Hellenistic thought,[70] one might expect Paul to use some secular texts for rhetorical purposes. Instead, as usual, he resorts to biblical tradition: "As is written, 'The one who had much did not have too much, and the one who had little did not have too little'" (2 Cor 8:14–15; Exod 16:18). This is equity, a fair balance consistent with the justice God wants us to implement in our community.

God's grace made it possible for Paul's churches to come together and fulfill this ministerial contribution to the poor among the saints.[71] Grace creates such a *koinōnia* (2 Cor 8:4)—it moves believers to exhibit love that signifies and effects the unity of the church. The Letter to the Romans associates the action of God's grace in its saving character with the action of God's justice or righteousness,[72] for God's justice is God's fidelity to his promises and commitments, his trustworthiness, and his reliable favor that frees and restores people and makes of them a new community. In the Pauline view, the saving action of the gospel receives its power from God's justice or righteousness (Rom 1:16–17). In the final analysis, Paul regards the collection as inspired and moved by God's grace or favor, which derives from God's justice. On the other hand, God's grace became visible in Christ and took the image of his attitude and conduct, and so God's grace became in Christ a concrete motif and model for Christians to follow. Paul refers to such an image of grace when he encourages the Corinthians to be generous toward the poor of the mother church: "For you know the generous act of our Lord Jesus Christ, that though he was rich, yet for your sakes he became poor, so that by his poverty you might become rich" (2 Cor 8:9).

Paul sees in such a generous undertaking a flow of thanksgiving to God, from whom all good things come. The collection inspires a thanksgiving to God both from the mother church, because of the material help received, and from the Pauline churches, because the collection heightened their awareness of the grace of faith received from the mother church. "For the rendering of this ministry not only supplies the needs of the saints but also overflows with many thanksgivings to God" (2 Cor 9:12). But the collection not only arouses feelings of thanksgiving toward God; it will also establish, Paul hopes, bonds of mutual acknowledgment between the Pauline churches and the mother church. On the one hand, Paul sees in the financial contribution of his churches a sign of their acknowledgment of the church of Jerusalem, whose spiritual blessings they were allowed to share (Rom 15:27). On the other hand, he hopes that the church of Jerusalem, in

---

[70] Dieter Georgi, *Remembering the Poor: The History of Paul's Collection for Jerusalem* (Nashville: Abingdon, 1992), 85.
[71] See Rom 15:25, 27; 2 Cor 8:1, 4, 6, 7, 9; 9:1.
[72] See Rom 3:21–24; 4:16; 5:15, 17, 20, 21.

receiving the financial donation to alleviate its poverty, will forget in gratitude whatever difficulties it might have experienced with the Pauline churches.

In addition, the financial support will help the mother church in fulfilling two missions: testifying to the paschal mystery in the very center of Judaism; and carrying on a challenging mission to the world at large—Jerusalem is the eschatological community of the poor, longing for the Lord's coming and offering her spiritual riches to a world that builds its security only upon material goods.

Paul's collection put in motion a circulation of spiritual goods. It is remarkable that wealth, which in a disproportionate accumulation generates discrimination, separation, and injustice, can, under the power of God's grace, balance duties and unite people. By putting into motion material wealth, grace makes it possible for the needy to develop their talents, fulfill their mission, and create riches that benefit the donors and the whole community. "The collection has now been transformed into a paradigm for ecumenical communal exchange in the form of a financial communication."[73]

10. Justice and the exercise of authority in the Pauline Letters

In Greco-Roman society, exercise of authority lay in the hands of established classes, characterized by wealth and education, and the possession of authority was tantamount to honor. In a society animated by an intensive love of honor, high positions were targets of hard competition. Candidates for office would establish connections with influential people in society and praise their own skills and social profile. The rich, through munificent gifts, would win the loyalty of their clients, who, in turn, would flatter their patrons to increase their favor. Those in authority, in turn, would exercise all their skills and manipulations in order to strengthen their position and secure their power base.

Some critics today argue that Paul, in exercising his leadership, practiced the manipulation of authority common in the surrounding pagan society.[74] They claim to see Paul doing so in his metaphor of fatherhood, the title of apostle, and the injunctions to imitate his example. In response to this contention, I shall consider first Paul's attitude toward those who in his communities indulge in competition for social status, and then Paul's exercise of authority.[75]

Paul realized that members of his communities competed for positions of honor, such as those who in Corinth exalted their own wisdom and power (1 Cor

---

[73] Georgi, *Remembering*, 152.

[74] See Graham Shaw, *The Cost of Authority: Manipulation and Freedom in the New Testament* (London: SCM Press, 1983), 29, 41, 62; Elizabeth Castelli, *Imitating Paul: A Discourse of Power* (Literary Currents in Biblical Interpretation; Louisville: Westminster/John Knox, 1991), 24.

[75] In this response I am indebted to Andrew D. Clarke, *Serve the Community of the Church: Christians as Leaders and Ministers* (First-Century Christians in the Graeco-Roman World; Grand Rapids: Eerdmans, 2000), 209–47; James D. G. Dunn, *The Theology of Paul the Apostle* (Grand Rapids: Eerdmans, 1998), 571–79.

1:26) or boasted of their superior charismas (14:12, 37), as well as those who were proud of their preachers and baptizers, regarding them as their great benefactors and reciprocating with loyalty to the extreme of creating factions within the community (1:12). Similarly, in the Galatian churches some bit and destroyed one another for rivalry (Gal 5:15), and among the Philippians others acted from selfish ambition or conceit (Phil 2:3), seeking honor and prestige according to the standards of the surrounding society.

Paul challenged those engaged in competition by undermining the bases of their claim. The factionalist claim goes against the grain of the very nature of God's community because there is only one benefactor who gives life to the community—God through Christ. Paul and Apollos are no more than servants to God's life-giving action, as Paul asserts: "For we are God's servants, working together; you are God's field, God's building" (1 Cor 3:9). Then he concludes by saying, "So let no one boast about human leaders. For all things are yours, whether Paul or Apollos or Cephas or the world or life or death or the present or the future—all belong to you, and you belong to Christ, and Christ belongs to God" (3:21–23).

Paul returns to the issue of factions and rivalries when he discusses the claim of those who consider themselves superior because of the spiritual gifts they possess (12:1–31). Paul recognizes a great variety of gifts in the community. Any gift has the potential for leadership. The gifts, since they are services for the common good (12:7), should not be a matter of competition whereby one might gain social status or secure a basis of power. All who share leadership must work together, following the Lord's example in his selfless service on behalf of all. They must listen to the Spirit, who is the source of all gifts and whose purpose is to generate unity, harmony, and solidarity (12:4–5). Similarly, in his Epistle to the Galatians, Paul challenges those who indulge in competition and rivalry. After indicating that their practices are works of the flesh (Gal 5:15, 20), he invites them to bear the fruit of the Spirit (5:22–23) and concludes his exhortation by saying, "Let us not become conceited, competing against one another, envying one another" (5:26). In his Letter to the Philippians, the apostle addresses those who indulge in factionalism, looking for vainglory and moved by selfish ambition in order to establish their own status (Phil 2:5; 3:19). He exhorts them to follow the model of Christ, who, "though he was in the form of God, did not regard equality with God as something to be exploited, but emptied himself, taking the form of a slave" (2:6–7).

Paul's approach to competition and rivalry in his communities allowed him to define the purpose and goal of Christian leadership. His approach on this matter is important for the understanding of his metaphor of fatherhood, of the title of apostle, and of the injunctions to imitate his example. Regarding the metaphor of father, Paul conceives the Christian community as one of siblings. Approximately a hundred times he addresses his people as brothers and sisters. They, in turn, foster their awareness of being siblings in their prayer, "Abba! Father!" (Rom 8:15; Gal 6:1). Nevertheless, Paul sometimes uses the metaphor of father to describe his relationship to his communities.[76] In doing so, he usually does not emphasize the authority of the paterfamilias but the care and respect of an affectionate father. Thus he says to the Thessalonians, "As you know, we dealt with each one of you like a father with his children, urging and encouraging you and pleading that you lead a life worthy of God" (1 Thess 2:1–12). The same mood of affection appears in his Second Letter to the Corinthians (2 Cor 6:13; 12:14–15). In the First Letter to the Corinthians, however, Paul blends affection with authority. First, he criticizes those in the community who used the names of the apostles as a pretext to create factions and establish their status (1 Cor 1:11–12; 3:4). Paul calls their attention to the fact that the apostles, like Paul himself and Apollos, are no more than "servants of God and stewards of God's mysteries" (4:1) and live in pitiful conditions because of the gospel while those who use their names for their own reward revel in prestige and honor (4:8–13). In this context, Paul introduces the metaphor of fatherhood, emphasizing that the Corinthians have many pedagogues but few fathers (4:15). The apostles are their fathers, and Paul enjoys a special place among them because he founded the community. Paul resorts to this metaphor in order to move the readers to gratitude and affection toward those who preached the gospel to them, especially toward Paul the apostle-founder, and to convince them not to use the reputations of their apostles-fathers as a pretext for their own selfish purposes. But there is another purpose to Paul's metaphor. He wants to remind the Corinthians that his words are not the simple instructions of a pedagogue but the authoritative injunctions of a father (4:21). His authority resided in the creative power of the gospel that he possessed and by which he begot communities of children. He, of course, applied the principles of biblical ethics (5:1–12; Gal 5:14; Rom 13:19) and urged others to follow the Lord's commands (1 Cor 7:10–11) but was careful to distinguish his own advice from what has been received as commands (1 Cor 7:25). Paul's regular way of leading his churches was not through decrees but through persuasion. While guiding his people to know how to discern and make their own decisions, Paul kept them aware that his words were those of their apostle-founder.

Paul's primary title was apostle of Christ, with full awareness of being sent out by Christ himself. Paul was commissioned not only to proclaim the gospel but also to gather believers in communities. He was aware that his apostolic authority did not end with the believers' response of faith, but continued in the community during its time of growth. His apostolic mission was harsh work and brought him stress and pain. In Thessalonika, to his grief, Paul was blamed for using his apostolic mission for selfish purposes, accused of deception and greed (1 Thess 2:3, 5–6). In response, he wrote to them, "You are witnesses, and God also, how pure, upright, and blameless our conduct was toward you believers" (2:10). The allegation of exploitation of the community returned often to Paul's mind. He reminds the Corinthians that he declined to be supported by the community he had founded (1 Cor 9:1–18; 2 Cor 11:7–11). He states that his great re-

---

[76] See 1 Cor 4:14; 2 Cor 6:13; 12:14–15; Gal 4:11; 1 Thess 2:11.

ward is making the proclamation of the gospel free of charge (1 Cor 9:18). Thus Paul's letters say that his exercise of apostolic mission was characterized by generous dedication, integrity, and selfless service.

Paul is unique among the NT writers in proposing himself as a model for his communities to imitate, but he does not claim to be the sole model. He also exhorts his community to imitate Christ, other colleagues, and other churches. For instance, Paul praises the Thessalonians because their faith has become an example to other churches and they, in turn, became imitators of Paul, of Timothy, of the churches of Judea, and of the Lord inasmuch they endured persecution because of their faith (1 Thess 1:6–7; 2:14). When Paul describes his lifestyle as a model for the Thessalonians, he asks them to imitate his disinterested dedication to the community (1:5; 2:1–6). He reminds them that he worked day and night so that he might not be a burden to others (2:1–9).

It seems ironic that Paul emphatically portrays himself as an object of imitation in the First Letter to the Corinthians (1 Cor 4:16; 11:1), a letter that criticizes personality cults. The imitation motif becomes understandable, however, given the aspect of his lifestyle that Paul asks others to imitate. He clarifies with this statement: "Give no offense to Jews or to Greeks or to the church of God, just as I try to please everyone in everything I do, not seeking my own advantage, but that of many, so that they may be saved" (10:33–11:1). In the Letter to the Philippians, Paul develops the foundation of the imitation motif. Christ is the primary model to imitate: Christ did not seek to hold power but became a servant so that all may recognize the glory of God (Phil 2:2–11). Paul's basic concern is to imitate Christ (3:10–16). When he proposes himself as an object for his community to imitate (3:17; 4:9), he intends others to emulate his lifestyle inasmuch it reflects Christ's.

To summarize, Paul claimed apostolic authority over the churches he founded but his style of authority was not one of domination and exploitation. On the contrary, he preferred persuasion to command. He distinguished clearly what derived from the Lord and what was his own opinion. He exercised authority as a service for the community. He did not charge the churches for his work. He lived by his own professional efforts. He left a lesson of extraordinarily selfless care and dedication to others, warning us against seeking honor and position in the church or fostering cults of personality.

Conclusion

Paul holds a theological concept of justice, although on occasion, when referring to the relationship between believers and the civil government, he uses a philosophical concept of order rooted in the nature of things. Nevertheless, the theological concept predominates in his view. Accordingly, God's justice frees those whom it justifies, elevates them, and puts them on an equal footing. Moreover, it gathers them together in a familial bond, making them members of the same body, Christ. It makes them active, bestowing on them the gifts of the Spirit in service to others. The justifying justice of God invalidates differences of race, nationality, sex, and social status in the Christian community. Such differences ceased to be controlling factors for admission into the community or for gaining positions within it. God's justice frees women from discrimination and allows them to share in Christian activities on an equal footing with men. It establishes the basis for the manumission of slaves. With a sense of equality, it motivates each believer to be responsible for himself or herself and for the good of others. God's justice is grace that moves individuals and groups to put into circulation material and spiritual goods for the common benefit of all. God's justice moves those in authority to use their position for the service of the community.

Bibliography

Alon, Gedalia. *Jews, Judaism, and the Classical World: Studies in Jewish History in the Times of the Second Temple and Talmud.* Translated by I. Abrahams. Jerusalem: Magnes, 1977.

Balch, David L. "Household Codes." Pages 318–20 in vol. 3 of *Anchor Bible Dictionary.* Edited by D. N. Freedman. 6 vols. New York: Doubleday, 1992.

———. *Let Wives Be Submissive: The Domestic Code in 1 Peter.* Society of Biblical Literature Monograph Series 26. Chico, Calif.: Scholars Press, 1981.

Bartchy, S. Scott. *Mallon Chresai: First Century Slavery and the Interpretation of 1 Cor 7:21.* Society of Biblical Literature Dissertation Series 11. Missoula: Scholars Press, 1973.

———. "Philemon, Epistle to." Pages 305–10 in vol. 5 of *The Anchor Bible Dictionary.* Edited by David Noel Freedman. 6 vols. New York: Doubleday, 1992.

Betz, Hans-Dieter. *Der Apostel Paulus und die sokratische Tradition.* Beiträge zur historischen Theologie 45. Tübingen: J. C. B. Mohr, 1972.

Borg, Marcus. "A New Context for Romans xiii." *New Testament Studies* 19 (1972–73): 205–18.

Borgen, Peder. "Judaism (Egypt)." Pages 1061–72 in vol. 3 of *The Anchor Bible Dictionary.* Edited by David Noel Freedman. 6 vols. New York: Doubleday, 1992.

Bowker, J. *Jesus and the Pharisees.* Cambridge: Cambridge University Press, 1973.

Brunt, P. A. and J. M. Moore, eds. *Res Gestae Divi Augusti: The Achievements of the Divine Augustus.* Oxford: Oxford University Press, 1967.

Byrne, Brendan J. *Paul and the Christian Woman.* Collegeville: Liturgical Press, 1989.

———. *Romans.* Sacra pagina 6. Collegeville, Minn.: Liturgical Press, 1996.

Castelli, Elizabeth. *Imitating Paul: A Discourse of Power.* Literary Currents in Biblical Interpretation. Louisville: Westminster/John Knox, 1991.

Clarke, Andrew D. *Serve the Community of the Church: Christians as Leaders and Ministers.* First-Century Christians in the Graeco-Roman World. Grand Rapids: Eerdmans, 2000.

Clarke, Graeme W. "Religio Licita." Pages 665–67 in vol. 5 of *The Anchor Bible Dictionary.* Edited by David Noel Freedman. 6 vols. New York: Doubleday, 1992.

Culpepper, R. Alan. "God's Righteousness in the Life of His People: Romans 12–15." *Review and Expositor* 73 (1976): 451–63.

Dahl, Nils A. *Studies in Paul.* Minneapolis: Augsburg, 1977.

Davies, William D. *Paul and Rabbinic Judaism: Some Rabbinic Elements in Pauline Theology.* 2d ed. New York: Harper & Row, 1953.

Dittenberger, Wilhem, ed. *Orientis graeci inscriptiones selectae: Supplementum sylloges inscriptionum graecarum.* 2 vols. Hildesheim: G. Olms, 1960.

Donahue, John R. "Tax Collector." Pages 337–38 in vol. 6 of *The Anchor Bible Dictionary.* Edited by David Noel Freedman. 6 vols. New York: Doubleday, 1992.

Donfried, Karl P. "The Cults of Thessalonica and the Thessalonian Correspondence." *New Testament Studies* 31 (1985): 336–56.

Dunn, James D. G. *The Theology of Paul the Apostle.* Grand Rapids: Eerdmans, 1998.

Elliot, John H. *A Home for the Homeless: A Sociological Exegesis of 1 Peter, Its Situation and Strategy.* Philadelphia: Fortress, 1981.

Elliot, Neil. *Liberating Paul: The Justice of God and the Politics of the Apostle.* Maryknoll: Orbis, 1994.

Fishbane, M. *Biblical Interpretation in Ancient Israel.* Oxford: Clarendon, 1991.

Fitzmyer, Joseph A. *Romans.* Anchor Bible 33. New York: Doubleday, 1993.

Flannery, Austin, ed. Second Vatican Council, *Gaudium et Spes* §29, in *Vatican Council II: The Conciliar and Post Conciliar Documents.* Collegeville: Liturgical Press, 1975.

Fraade, Steven D. "Judaism (Palestinian)." Pages 1054–61 in vol. 3 of *The Anchor Bible Dictionary.* Edited by David Noel Freedman. 6 vols. New York: Doubleday, 1992.

Friedrich, J., W. Pöhlmann, and P. Stuhlmacher. "Zur historischen Situation und Intention von Röm 13,1–7." *Zeitschrift für Theologie und Kirche* 73 (1976): 131–66.

Furnish, Victor P. *The Moral Teaching of Paul.* Nashville: Abingdon, 1979.

Georgi, Dieter. *Remembering the Poor: The History of Paul's Collection for Jerusalem.* Nashville: Abingdon, 1992.

———. *Theocracy in Paul's Praxis and Theology.* Translated by D. E. Green. Minneapolis: Fortress, 1991.

———. "Who Is the True Prophet?" Pages 100–127 in *Christians among Jews and Gentiles: Essays in Honor of K. Stendahl on His Sixty-Fifth Birthday.* Edited by George W. E. Nickelsburg and George W. MacRae. Philadelphia: Fortress, 1986.

Heine, Susanne. *Women and Early Christianity.* Minneapolis: Augsburg, 1988.

Hengel, M. *Jews, Greeks, and Barbarians.* Philadelphia: Fortress, 1980.

Hirschfeld, G. *Knidos, Hilikarnassos and Branchidae* (vol. 4 of *The Collection of Ancient Greek Inscriptions in the British Museum*). London: British Museum, 1893.

Hopkins, Keith. *Conquerors and Slaves.* New York: Cambridge University Press, 1978.

Horsley, G. H. R. and S. Llewelyn. *New Documents Illustrating Early Christianity.* North Ryde, N.S.W., 1981–.

Käsemann, Ernst. " 'Righteousness of God' in Paul." Pages 168–82 in *New Testament Questions of Today.* Philadelphia: Fortress, 1969.

Kittel, G., and G. Friedrich, eds. *Theological Dictionary of the New Testament.* Translated by G. W. Bromiley. 10 vols. Grand Rapids: Eerdmans, 1964–1976.

Lampe, Peter. "Keine 'Sklavenflucht' des Onesimus." *Zeitschrift für die neutestamentliche Wissenschaft und die Kunde der älteren Kirche* 76 (1985): 135–37.

Malherbe, Abraham J. *Paul and the Popular Philosophers.* Minneapolis: Fortress, 1989.

Martyn, J. Louis. "Apocalyptic Antinomies in Paul's Letter to the Galatians." *New Testament Studies* 31 (1985): 410–24.

Moiser, Jeremy. "Rethinking Romans 12–15." *New Testament Studies* 36 (1990): 571–82.

Murphy-O'Connor, Jerome. "The First Letter to the Corinthians." Pages 798–815 of *The New Jerome Bible Commentary.* Edited by Raymond E. Brown et al. Englewood Cliffs: Prentice Hall, 1990.

Nardoni, Enrique. "The Concept of Charism in Paul." *Catholic Biblical Quarterly* 55 (1993): 68–80.

Noonan, John T. "Development in Moral Doctrine." *Theological Studies* 54 (1993): 662–77.

Overman, J. Andrew and William S. Green. "Judaism (Greco-Roman Period)." Pages 1037–54 in vol. 3 of *The Anchor Bible Dictionary.* Edited by David Noel Freedman. 6 vols. New York: Doubleday, 1992.

Penna, Romano. "Judaism (Rome)." Pages 1073–76 in vol. 3 of *The Anchor Bible Dictionary.* Edited by David Noel Freedman. 6 vols. New York: Doubleday, 1992.

Reicke, Bo. *The New Testament Era: The World of the Bible from 500 B.C. to A.D. 100.* Philadelphia: Fortress, 1975.

Reumann, John H. P. *Righteousness in the New Testament: Justification in the United States Lutheran–Roman Catholic Dialogue, with responses by J. A. Fitzmyer and J. D. Quinn.* Philadelphia: Fortress; New York: Paulist, 1982.

Rivkin, E. *The Hidden Revolution: The Pharisees' Search for the Kingdom Within.* Nashville: Abingdon, 1978.

Saldarini, Anthony. *Pharisees, Scribes, and Sadducees in Palestinian Society.* Wilmington, Del.: Glazier, 1988.

Schrage, Wolfgang. *The Ethics of the New Testament.* Philadelphia: Fortress, 1990.

Schüssler Fiorenza, Elisabeth. *In Memory of Her.* New York: Crossroad, 1983.

Shaw, Graham. *The Cost of Authority: Manipulation and Freedom in the New Testament.* London: SCM Press, 1983.

Smallwood, E. Mary. *The Jews under the Roman Rule from Pompey to Diocletian.* Studies in Judaism in Late Antiquity 20. Leiden: Brill, 1976.

Speyer, Wolfgang. "Barbar." *Jahrbuch für Antike und Christentum* 10 (1967): 257.

Stendahl, Krister. *The Bible and the Role of Women.* Philadelphia: Fortress, 1966.

Strack, H. L., and P. Billerbeck. *Kommentar zum Neuen Testament aus Talmud und Midrasch.* 6 vols. Munich: C. H. Beck, 1922–1961.

Theissen, Gerd. *The Social Setting of Pauline Christianity: Essays on Corinth.* Translated by M. Kohl. Philadelphia: Fortress, 1982.

Trummer, Peter. "Die Chance der Freiheit: Zur Interpretation des *mallon chresai* in 1 Kor 7.21." *Biblica* 56 (1975): 344–68.

Verner, David C. *The Household of God: The Social World of the Pastoral Epistles.* Society of Biblical Literature Dissertation Series 71. Chico, Calif.: Scholars Press, 1983.

Wagener, Ulrike. *Die Ordnung des "Hauses Gottes."* Wissenschaftliche Untersuchungen zum Neuen Testament 2.65. Tübingen: J. C. B. Mohr, 1994.

Wengst, Klaus. *Pax Romana and the Peace of Jesus Christ.* Philadelphia: Fortress, 1987.

Williams, S. K. "The 'Righteousness of God' in Romans." *Journal of Biblical Literature* 99 (1980): 241–90.

Witherington, Ben. "Rite and Rights for Women—Galatians 3.28," *New Testament Studies* 27 (1981): 539–604.

———. "Women (NT)." Pages 957–61 in vol. 6 of *The Anchor Bible Dictionary.* Edited by David Noel Freedman. 6 vols. New York: Doubleday, 1992.

———. *Women in the Earliest Churches.* Society for New Testament Studies Monograph Series 59. Cambridge: Cambridge University Press, 1988.

Ziegler, Konrat., and Walther Sontheimer. *Der kleine Pauly: Lexicon der Antike.* 5 vols. Stuttgart: Druckenmüller, 1964–1975.

Ziesler, John A. *The Meaning of Righteousness in Paul.* Society for New Testament Studies Monograph Series 20. Cambridge: Cambridge University Press, 1972.

CHAPTER THIRTEEN

JUSTICE IN THE JOHANNINE WRITINGS

Introduction

This chapter deals with the writings attributed to the Apostle John in the NT, namely, the Fourth Gospel, the Johannine Letters, and the book of Revelation. In these writings, the term "justice" has a broad range of meaning revolving around the basic idea that one must give to humans, either individually or collectively, what is proper in accordance with the divine order and design. The variety of meanings derives from the fact that, in these writings, Christians experience rejection, hostility, and persecution and feel themselves unjustly oppressed. Thus the community of the Fourth Gospel suffers expulsion from the Jewish synagogue; the communities of the Johannine Letters undergo the contempt and opposition of separatists; and the churches of the book of Revelation endure persecution from supporters of the imperial cult. Under these circumstances, the concept of justice is applied not only to external but also to internal relations of the community, for the violation of justice stems from both the outsiders and the insiders.

1. The Fourth Gospel

The present text of the Fourth Gospel probably is the result of a long period of formation, reaching its final shape at the end of the first century.[1] It reflects the debate of the Johannine community with "the Jews" and other outside groups

---

[1] Francis J. Moloney, *The Gospel of John* (SP 4; Collegeville: Liturgical Press, 1998), 1–20; Robert Kysar, "John, Epistles of," *ABD* 3:900–12, and R. Kysar, "John, The Gospel of," *ABD* 3:912–31, here 900–922; Martin Hengel, *The Johannine Question* (London: SCM, 1989), 102–8; Howard M. Teeple, The *Literary Origin of the Gospel of John* (Evanston, Ill.: Religion and Ethics Institute, 1974), 150, 152; Raymond E. Brown, *The Gospel according to John I–XII* (AB 28; Garden City: Doubleday, 1970), lxxx–lxxxvi; Barnabas Lindars, *Behind the Fourth Gospel* (London: SPCK, 1971), 42–43; Rudolph Schnackenburg, *The Gospel according to St. John* (trans. K. Smyth; 3 vols.; New York: Crossroad, 1982), 1:101–4.

and manifests the community's distress at the expulsion of several of its members from the synagogue. This gospel twice employs the word *dikaiosynē* ("justice" or "righteousness," John 16:8, 10) and includes a passage in which the terms *eleutheroō* (to "make free") and *eleutheros* ("free") are repeated three times (8:32, 33, 36). Although these expressions in this gospel do not seem at first to refer, at least directly, to the idea of justice that concerns us, nevertheless it is worth inquiring into any bearing they may have on our subject. This chapter will also examine the oppression the community experiences and its inner response to rejection by the world. This inner response includes the strengthening of mutual relations among its members and the concern that the lives of its members be animated by Christian love as a binding, promoting, and equalizing factor.

1.1. An oppressed community, confident of divine vindication

The Johannine community, aware of being under stress, feels itself unjustly oppressed and persecuted. The Fourth Gospel describes this situation as predicted by Jesus at the Last Supper: "The world hates you. Remember the word that I said to you, 'Servants are no greater than their master.' If they persecuted me, they will persecute you" (15:19c–20). The persecution the disciples suffer from Jewish authorities is an extension of the one undergone by Jesus; as the persecution against Jesus was unjust (15:25), so is the persecution against the disciples. Jesus predicted that the hatred of "the Jews" against him "was to fulfill the word that is written in their law, 'They hated me without cause'" (15:25). Referring to the law, Jesus includes more than the five books of Moses, since the text quoted belongs to the Psalms (Pss 35:19; 69:4).[2] He refers to "their law" to emphasize that the very scripture "the Jews" claimed as their own proves their wrongdoing toward Jesus. In addition, the quotation from the Psalms includes the idea that the suffering of Jesus—and by extension that of the disciples—follows the pattern of the suffering of the poor, the weak, and the needy in the Psalms, their experience of persecution and their trust in God.[3] Moreover, the quotation gives the assurance that the persecution unleashed against Jesus and his disciples is foreseen in the design of God the Father, who is committed to deliver God's people from their oppressors.

In addition to the general statement on the persecution stemming from the hostility of the world (John 15:19c), including under the term "world" the Jewish authorities, three references (9:22; 12:42; 16:2) point to the expulsion from the synagogue as the basic cause for the suffering of the community.[4] The expulsion

---

[2] Jesus cites the text with a preterite indicative verb ("hated"), although both the Hebrew text and the LXX version of Pss 35:19 and 69:4 put the verb in participial form, connoting present tense. The change in tense serves to emphasize the prophetic character of the passage.

[3] Pss 35:10, 19, 24; 69:4, 33.

[4] On anti-Judaism in the Fourth Gospel, see Robert Kysar, "Anti-Semitism and the Gospel of John," in *Anti-Semitism and Early Christianity: Issues of Polemics and Faith* (ed. A. Craig et al.; Minneapolis: Fortress, 1993), 113–27; U. C. von Wahlde, "The Gospel of

referred to by the Fourth Gospel does not necessarily presuppose the existence of the *birkat ha-mînîm,* a Jewish curse on those regarded as religious deviants. Indeed, the inclusion of this curse in the Eighteen Benedictions, a prayer used in synagogue services, may have occurred later than the last decade of the first century.[5] This gospel retrojects the expulsion, which seems to have occurred in the late 80s or early 90s, back to the time of Jesus. A similar retrojection occurs in the high Christology developed in the Johannine community. Thus Jesus' opponents in the Fourth Gospel accuse him of "making himself equal to God" (5:18). The observation that this gospel moves episodes and ideas of the time of the community back to the time of Jesus leads many contemporary scholars to read the history of the community behind Jesus' story.[6]

The expulsion from the synagogue deeply troubled the Johannine community, largely composed of Jewish Christians, because their separation from the Jewish community entailed the loss of identity and patterns of life. The separation caused, first of all, a religious dislocation: exclusion from synagogue meetings, religious services, Jewish feasts, traditional observances, and the synagogal interpretation of the Scriptures. The Johannine Christians were severed from the environment of Jewish ideas and perceptions that constituted their world. Consequently, they had to face the difficult task of building their own identity without traditional religious connections. In addition to this religious dislocation, the Johannine Christians experienced a social separation with economic consequences. In effect, the expulsion from the synagogue was a sort of ostracism from family and friends, accompanying a loss of economic position within the Jewish

---

John and the Presentation of Jews and Judaism," in *Within Context: Essays on Jews and Judaism in the New Testament* (ed. D. Efroymson et al.; Collegeville: American Interfaith Institute and Liturgical Press, 1993), 67–86; George M. Smiga, *Pain and Polemic: Anti-Judaism in the Gospels* (New York: Paulist, 1992), 134–73; D. Moody Smith, "Judaism and the Gospel of John," in *Jews and Christians: Exploring the Past, Present, and Future* (ed. J. H. Charlesworth; New York: Crossroad, 1990), 76–96; J. T. Townsend, "The Gospel of John and the Jews: The Story of a Religious Divorce," in *Antisemitism and the Foundations of Christianity* (ed. A. Davies; New York: Paulist, 1979), 72–97.

[5] The date of the curse's insertion in the Eighteen Benedictions and its interpretation are debated by contemporary scholars. See R. Kimelman, "*Birkat ha-Minim* and the Lack of Evidence for an Anti-Christian Jewish Prayer in Late Antiquity," in *Jewish and Christian Self-Definition* (ed. E. P. Sanders; 3 vols.; Philadelphia: Fortress, 1981), 2:266–44; William Horbury, "The Benediction of the *Minim* and Early Jewish-Christian Controversy," *JTS* NS 33 (1982): 19–61; David Flusser, "The Jewish-Christian Schism: Part II," *Imm* 17 (1984): 32–33; repr. in *Judaism and the Origins of Christianity* (Jerusalem: Magnes, 1988), 637–38; Raymond E. Brown, *An Introduction to the New Testament* (ABRL; New York: Doubleday, 1997), 374.

[6] So, among others, Brown, *Introduction to the New Testament;* Kysar, "John, The Gospel of"; J. L. Martyn, "Glimpses into the History of the Johannine Community," in *L'Évangile de Jean; sources, rédaction, théologie* (ed. M. de Jonge; BETL 44; Gembloux: Duculot, 1977), 259–99; Francis J. Moloney, *The Gospel of John* (SP 4; Collegeville, Minn.: Liturgical Press, 1998); David Rensberger, *Johannine Faith and Liberating Community* (Philadelphia: Westminster, 1988); Klaus Wengst, *Bedrängte Gemeinde und verherrlichter Christus: Ein Versuch über das Johannesevangelium* (Munich: Kaiser, 1990).

community. Finally, the expulsion brought negative consequences for Christians with respect to the Roman administration because, in losing their membership in the Jewish community, they also forfeited privileges granted to Jewish communities, such as the exemption from worshiping the gods of Rome and the right to have their own assemblies.[7] Under these circumstances, the community was grateful to find in Jesus' words the strength necessary to endure a situation that threatened its existence within human society at large.

The Fourth Gospel refers three times to repercussions caused by the expulsion from the synagogue. The first (9:22) alludes to the decision, issued by Jewish authorities under the Pharisees' leadership, to expel believers in Jesus from their community (9:13, 15, 16, 40). The decision was already in effect when the Johannine text was composed, and caused an atmosphere of fear among believers in Jesus and his sympathizers within the Jewish community (9:22). From a Jewish perspective, Jesus and his followers were sinners (9:24, 31), having lost their way to salvation. From the Christian perspective, however, Jesus was the one sent by God to liberate humanity from sin, and his disciples were made free from sin. Jesus was the bearer of God's truth, and his disciples were the beneficiaries of the truth. Both Jesus and his disciples suffered oppression by the children of Satan, the father of lies (8:32, 34, 44).

The second reference to expulsion (12:42) mentions the decision by the Pharisees to oust Christians from the synagogue, a decision that provoked fear even among the authorities *(archontes)* who believed in Jesus. The ouster of Christians prevented these authorities from professing their faith publicly. The writer disapproves of the hesitation of these crypto-Christians to make a public witness of their faith: "They loved human glory more than the glory that comes from God" (12:43). The power of this attachment to human esteem becomes more understandable in light of the religious and social consequences of expulsion from the synagogue.

The third reference (16:2) is a text containing Jesus' words related to the future suffering of his disciples. The immediate context (16:1, 4) emphasizes Jesus' prediction in order to strengthen the disciples' faith, giving them assurance that God is ready to vindicate their cause. The suffering foreseen by Jesus includes the expulsion from the synagogue and the death that some of the disciples would suffer from Jewish authorities. This is a suffering that the community has already experienced and will continue to endure in the future. Under these circumstances, Jesus' words are most comforting: "But I have said these things to you so that when their hour comes you may remember that I told you about them" (16:4). K. Wengst suggests that the death of some of these disciples might have been caused by lynch mobs permitted by Jewish authorities.[8] R. E. Brown alludes to the Mishnaic practice that allowed zealots to slay people for religious offenses but suggests that the matter could have been more complex. There might have been

---

[7] Rensberger, *Johannine Faith*, 26–27, 110–11; G. W. Clarke, "Religio Licita," *ABD* 5:665–67.

[8] Wengst, *Bedrängte Gemeinde*, 88.

cases of denunciation to the Romans. Since Christians were no longer considered Jews, they might have been accused of failing "to adhere to pagan customs and to participate in emperor worship."[9] Under such circumstances, Christians could suffer confiscation of their properties, ostracism, and even martyrdom because of loyalty to their religious conscience, informed by Christian faith. Those who underwent death were martyrs for the sake of religious freedom. Their option to suffer death rather than betray their faith shows a developed moral conscience.[10]

After predicting their expulsion from the synagogue and announcing their death on account of their faith, Jesus promised to his disciples the coming of the Paraclete (16:7), explaining what he will do for them:

> When he comes, he will prove the world wrong about sin and righteousness and judgment: about sin, because they do not believe in me; about righteousness, because I am going to the Father and you will see me no more; about judgment, because the ruler of this world has been condemned. (16:8–11)

This is a summary of the accusations the Paraclete will level against the world.[11] At the core of these accusations is the world's refusal to believe in the truth that Jesus is the only Son of the Father, sent to be the center of the saving action on behalf of humanity, the center of the order of the new and final world. This refusal of the world to believe is aggravated by its opinion that Jesus' death irrefutably proved the fallacy of his claims. The Paraclete will prove the world wrong. Jesus' apparent defeat was vindicated by God. The world did not realize that Jesus was not destroyed by death. His death was, rather, the destruction of the ruler of the present world; Jesus lifted up to the cross was the sentence of this ruler's condemnation (12:31–32). On the one hand, the Paraclete will show that the ruler of this world, who is ultimately responsible for the rejection of Jesus and the oppression of Christians, will die. On the other hand, the Paraclete will also exhibit the justice of Jesus as the mediator of liberation and salvation for humanity and thus justify the existence and mission of the Christian community.

---

[9] Raymond E. Brown, *The Community of the Beloved Disciple* (New York: Paulist, 1979), 42–43.

[10] This is a point that the Second Vatican Council addressed in its Declaration on Religious Liberty, a document that introduced a new position into the common teaching of the Catholic Church:

> The Vatican Council declares that the human person has a right to religious freedom. Freedom of this kind means that all men should be immune from coercion on the part of individuals, social groups and every human power so that, within due limits, nobody is forced to act against his convictions in religious matters in private or in public, alone or in associations with others (*Dignitatis Humanae* 2, in *Vatican Council II: The Conciliar and Post Conciliar Documents* [ed. Austin Flannery; Collegeville: Liturgical Press, 1975], 800).

[11] See Gary M. Burge, *The Anointed Community: The Holy Spirit in the Johannine Tradition* (Grand Rapids: Eerdmans, 1987), 208–11; Ignace de la Potterie, *La verité dans saint Jean* (AnBib 73; Rome: Biblical Institute Press, 1977), 396–421; Raymond E. Brown, *The Gospel according to John XIII–XXI* (AB 29A; Garden City: Doubleday, 1970), 703–17.

The Paraclete will display his forensic role (16:8–11) on behalf of the community and exercise it in the inner forum of believers. Indeed, the Paraclete will grant the disciples both understanding and assurance of Jesus' victory in their trials. Thus enlightened and strengthened, they will bear witness, challenging the world's interpretation of Jesus' trial and proclaiming his justice (15:27). The action of the Paraclete will include a defense of the Christian community.[12] In contrast to the interpretation and attitude of the world, the Paraclete grants the disciples the right understanding of their trials and endows them with the strength necessary to endure tragedy and to maintain their adherence to Christ, who makes them free.

1.2. An oppressed community experiencing Christ's liberation

The Johannine community, in its experience of oppression and rejection, withdraws into itself but without despairing. It finds the support and comfort of the Paraclete and the peace and joy stemming from the awareness of being a community liberated through adherence to Christ (8:32, 36). As Jesus said, "If you continue in my word, you are truly my disciples; and you will know the truth, and the truth will make you free" (8:32).[13] The truth that makes people free is Christ in his character of the only Son who came from the Father to save humanity. The adherence to Christ frees the disciple from the slavery of sin, the dominion of the devil, and death.[14]

The issue is not simply liberation from individual sins or sin in general. The matter of great concern is with the radical sin of unbelief, which is a power that, in a kind of eschatological dualism, struggles against the revelation of the Son coming from the Father.[15] Such sinful power, on the one hand, enslaves one to Satan through an ideology of deception, violence, and death (8:37, 40, 44) and, on the other hand, closes the way to the life that the Son brings from the Father. Contrarywise, faith in Jesus establishes a living relationship with the one who is "the way, the truth, and the life" (14:6).

The devil has a far-reaching undertaking. He enslaves not just individuals but all humanity, including authorities and institutions. The devil rules the social and cultural world of the present time (12:31; 16:11). He infiltrates the thoughts

---

[12] De la Potterie, *Verité*, 410–16; M.-F. Berrouard, "Le Paraclet, Défenseur du Christ devant la conscience du croyant (Jo. XVI, 8–11)," *RSPT* 33 (1949): 361–89; Raymond E. Brown, "The Paraclete in the Fourth Gospel," *NTS* 13 (1966–1967): 113–32.

[13] On "the truth will make you free," see J. O. Tuñí, *La verdad os hará libres (Jn 8,32): Liberación y libertad del creyente en el cuarto evangelio* (Barcelona: Herder, 1973); H. Lona, "Wahrheit und Freiheit in Jo 8, 31–36 und die 'Theologie der Befreiung' in Lateinamerika," in *Biblische Randbemerkungen* (FS R. Schnackenburg; ed. H. Merklein and J. Lange; Würzburg: Echter, 1974), 300–313; I. Ellacuría, *Freedom Made Flesh: The Mission of Christ and of His Church* (Maryknoll: Orbis, 1976). See also the extensive bibliography in de la Potterie, *Vérité*, 789.

[14] See John 8:33–37, 44, 51–52.

[15] See John 8:21, 24, 40–43; 9:41; 17:3.

and actions of the people with his principles and leads them to destruction and death (8:44). A world ruled by the devil hates and persecutes Jesus and his disciples (15:19–20; 17:14) and cannot receive the Paraclete (14:17). This world will be judged, and its ruler condemned (12:31; 16:11).

In contrast to the slavery the devil pursues and exercises, Jesus offers his liberation, which takes the believing person in his or her inmost being and in his or her relations to others. In freeing human beings, Jesus confers on them a new life that comes from God the Father, thereby providing them with a destiny in the heavenly world (1:11; 3:3–6). The life that Jesus gives is like the sap of a vine, which enlivens its branches (15:1–5). The gift of new life makes the disciples branches of the divine vine, as it were, ready to bear good fruits of love for God, Christ, and other human beings (15:4, 8, 12, 16).

This new life includes the Spirit (7:38–39), who enables believers to love their neighbors with the intensity of Christ's love for us, a love so committed that the believer is ready to give his or her own life for others (10:17; 15:12, 13). Thus believers are spiritually energized to respond to Jesus' call to follow his example (13:34; 15:12). The power of love moves them to bear good fruits by serving their brothers and sisters in need, respecting their dignity, helping to restore it if it has been impugned, and furthering their enjoyment of a life lived in justice and peace.

Such works of love motivated by Christ's example are the opposite of those inspired by the devil, whose ideology includes deception, violence, injustice, war, and destruction. Jesus' liberation involves a pedagogical action; it makes believers aware of their dignity of being united with him and their capacity to love. This understanding of liberation develops in believers a strong sense of responsibility in accord with their dignity.

In John's Gospel, submission to God and Christ liberates the believer.[16] To be free is to be Christ's disciple. The acceptance of liberation includes the commitment to observe the commandments, but now animated by the spirit of the new commandment of love. This notion of being free for the service of God and neighbor echoes the theology of Exodus. A comparison can be established: just as for the Israelites liberation meant both emancipation from slavery and acceptance of the law of God given at Sinai, so liberation for Christians includes obedience to the word of Christ, submission to the truth in order to serve others. This idea of service is included in the new commandment of love given by Christ (13:34). Thus the person made free through his docility to Christ is able to serve

---

[16] Referring to the Christian paradox of freedom through submission, Romano Guardini wrote,

> Man's freedom is a created freedom and it therefore develops essentially before God and in subordination to Him—all the more, too, since God is not only creator of being but also ground of truth and source of good. In consequence, obedience to God does not signify subjection to superior power but the fulfillment of what is right and good.... God is not "an other" but that Being in whom my existence is established, my truth preformulated, and the significance of my existence contained. If I come to God in knowledge, love, and activity, I discover myself in Him. (*Freedom, Grace, and Destiny* [New York: Pantheon, 1961], 81)

the transcendent God, who is present in the Christian's brothers and sisters. Docility to Christ's voice generates unity and harmony and liberates in believers the energy to serve others.[17]

1.3. An oppressed community fostering inner solidarity and equality

The liberated community is urged to observe Jesus' commandments,[18] which include the duties of justice of the Mosaic covenant but go beyond their ethical norms, as John sees them, since the spirit of love that animates Jesus' commandments not only provides a new motivation but also generates in believers an attitude of care and compassion, with an unrestricted generosity. The spirit of love is so important in Jesus' commandments that they can be summarized in the new commandment of love. This new commandment is not merely an extension of the Mosaic commandment "You shall love your neighbor as yourself" (Lev 19:18), because here Jesus enjoins his disciples to do something new: "I give you a new commandment, that you love one another. Just as I have loved you, you also should love one another" (John 13:34). This commandment is new because Jesus confers the power to fulfill it and he provides a model of following it. He loved his people to the end (13:1), and he, like the good shepherd, laid down his life for his sheep (10:11). This love, which characterizes the community of the new covenant, originates ultimately in God the Father, who "so loved the world that he gave his only Son, so that everyone who believes in him may not perish but may have eternal life" (3:16). Jesus' new commandment is exemplified by his symbolic action of washing his disciples' feet: "If I, your Lord and Teacher, have washed your feet, you also ought to wash one another's feet. For I have set you an example, that you also should do as I have done to you" (13:14–15).[19] In this scene, Jesus made himself a slave in serving his disciples by washing their feet. The Johannine Jesus thereby offers a far-reaching lesson of loving service, which is central in the new order established by Jesus for his community. A member of the community must imitate Jesus. Since conforming one's conduct to the order established by God is doing justice in the biblical sense, the loving service Jesus requires from his disciples is a duty of justice. This is also the way in which Paul understood the commandment of love: "Owe no one anything, except to love one another; for the one who loves another has fulfilled the law" (Rom 13:8).

The Johannine community is characterized by a noticeable equality among its members. The two favorite images to describe the community—the flock and the vine—are very telling in this regard. The image of the flock underlines the

---

[17] On this, I am indebted to de la Potterie, *Verité*, 844–66.
[18] See John 14:15, 21; 15:10.
[19] W. Schrage, *The Ethics of the New Testament* (trans. D. E. Green; Philadelphia: Fortress, 1990), 314. For an analysis of the washing of the feet in John 13, see John C. Thomas, *Footwashing in John 13 and the Johannine Community* (Sheffield: JSOT Press, 1991); Arland J. Hultgren, "The Johannine Footwashing (13.1–11) as Symbol of Eschatological Hospitality," *NTS* 28 (1982): 539–46; Sandra M. Schneiders, "The Foot Washing (John 13:1–20): An Experiment in Hermeneutics," *CBQ* 43 (1981): 76–92.

personal and intimate relationship of each sheep to its shepherd and the total dedication of the shepherd to his sheep. The image of the vine, in turn, underscores the idea that each member belongs to the center from which the sap, or life, is derived. Unlike the Pauline image of the body, these Johannine images make no distinction of categories in membership. In accord with this concept of equality, in the Fourth Gospel the term "apostle" is missing. Instead the writer employs the word "disciple." In this gospel, all are disciples on an equal footing. The one who excels among all is called the Beloved Disciple, "the disciple whom Jesus loved." Love, not charism or function, is what makes distinctions in the Johannine community. Thus, in his perceptions, the beloved disciple surpasses Peter because he loves Jesus more than Peter. In a late stage of the formation of this gospel, the community highlighted the special role of Peter but did so by using Johannine categories. On the one hand, John 21 describes the function of Peter using the image of a shepherd who knows his sheep and readily lays down his life for them (John 21:19). On the other hand, the same pericope emphasizes love *(philia, agapē)* as a necessary condition of leadership (21:15, 16, 17).[20] This is why Jesus asked Peter to make a profession of love before appointing him as a shepherd to the church. Still, although the Johannine community accepted the special role of Peter in the church, it insisted that the bestowal of authority on Peter does not include the transfer of ownership. The flock continues to belong to the Lord.

Those who belong to this community are full members on an equal footing anywhere they may live. True worship is not confined to any particular geographic place (4:23). The Paraclete comes to every Christian in any place and at any time he or she may live: "If you love me, you will keep my commandments. And I will ask the Father, and he will give you another Paraclete to be with you forever" (14:15–16). In the Johannine community—whether men or women, Jews or Gentiles, rich or poor—all equally are Jesus' disciples, possess the same Spirit, and share the same duty of service. There are no second-class Christians. Women are on an equal footing with men, both in showing love to Christ and in proclaiming the truth.[21] Martha makes the profession of faith (11:27) that the Gospel of Matthew reserves for Peter (Matt 16:16–17). The Samaritan woman preaches and makes converts among the people of her own town (John 4:39), just as the apostles do in the book of Acts. Mary Magdalene is the first person to make the paschal announcement (2:17–18); this is why she was called "the apostle to the apostles" *(apostola apostolorum)*.[22]

What elevates all Christians to the dignity of Christ's disciples is that Jesus came down to us to raise us up. The scene of Jesus washing his disciples' feet—an

---

[20] The Greek text shows a variation of terms for love. There is a stylistic play between *phileō* and *agapaō*. Although in classical and Hellenistic Greek these terms included different nuances, in the Fourth Gospel the terms are interchangeable in meaning. See Brown, *John XIII–XXI*, 1103.

[21] See Brown, *Community*, 183–98.

[22] See Raymond E. Brown, *The Churches the Apostles Left Behind* (New York: Paulist, 1984), 94–95.

anticipation of his death as service for the life of the world—shows that Jesus through his self-humiliation takes us from our low and sinful condition up to his divine friendship. The self-humiliation of Jesus at the Last Supper is a concrete and particular case exhibiting the great abasement of the Logos, who became flesh to elevate humanity and thus allows it to share his divine fullness. D. Rensberger points to the dualistic perspective of the Fourth Gospel, in which logos is superior to flesh *(sarx)*. Logos is spirit and "spirit gives life, the flesh is useless" (6:63). Greco-Roman culture identified logos with spirit and flesh with matter, and this distinction and identification had social connotations. Logos was associated with free people of the ruling class, and flesh or matter was related to people of lower condition, such as slaves and women. Logos represented rulers and those in positions of power, and flesh stood for retainers and servants. In saying that "Logos became flesh," the Fourth Gospel makes a social statement, shocking to the ears of the upper classes in Greco-Roman culture. The Logos takes on the fleshly condition and abases himself to inject strength and new life into the flesh. The master abases himself to promote the servant. The Logos thereby shows his great esteem for the oppressed and abject; he comes down to give them freedom and dignity.[23] The conduct of the Logos is a paradigm for the disciples: "I set you an example, that you also should do as I have done to you" (13:15). Christians always have been urged to follow the example of the Logos in taking care of the lowly, the oppressed, and the abject, but there are times and places in which the imitation of the Logos is more urgent because people live in subhuman conditions.[24]

In today's circumstances, disciples who enjoy the benefits of culture and social well-being should help the poor escape their miserable condition and offer them an opportunity to develop their cultural and economic abilities so that they may participate in the life and well-being of a developed society.

---

[23] See David Rensberger, "Sectarianism and Theological Interpretation in John" (paper presented at the annual meeting of the AAR/SBL, Chicago, November 20, 1994), 7–12 (summary in *AAR/SBL Abstracts* [Chicago: Scholars Press, 1994], 334).

[24] In recent times, for instance, Pope Paul VI has insisted on the necessary connection between faith and justice:

> The Church . . . has the duty to proclaim the liberation of millions of human beings—many of whom are her own children—the duty of assisting in the birth of this liberation, of giving witness to it, of ensuring that it is complete. This is not foreign to evangelization.
>
> Between evangelization and human advancement—development and liberation—there are in fact profound links. These include links of an anthropological order, because the man who is to be evangelized is not an abstract being but is subject to social and economic questions. They also include links in the theological order, since one cannot dissociate the plan of creation from the plan of redemption. The latter plan touches the very concrete situations of injustice to be combatted and of justice to be restored. . . . How in fact can one proclaim the new commandment without promoting in justice and in peace the true, authentic advancement of man?

Pope Paul VI, apostolic exhortation *Evangelii Nuntiandi* 30–31, in *On Evangelization in the Modern World: Apostolic Exhortation* (Washington, D.C.: United States Catholic Conference, 1976), 3, 22–23.

2. Justice in the Johannine Letters

The Johannine Letters were probably written after the Fourth Gospel, by the writer whom the second and third letters call "the elder."[25] The elder was the leader of the Johannine churches, which were probably made up of a mother church and several affiliated congregations. The elder was in charge of the mother church, with some sort of supervisory responsibilities over the affiliated congregations. ("Johannine community" here stands for both the Johannine mother-church and its affiliated congregations.) In these letters, the community has already recovered from the trauma caused by the expulsion from the synagogue. The attention is no longer focused on debates with the Jews. The concern now is about an inner crisis, and the debate deals with Christians who abandoned the elder's community. The theological center of discussion is not Jesus' divine dignity, as it is in the Fourth Gospel, but his human condition. The opponents, the secessionists, seem to minimize the import of Jesus' human nature for the salvation of human beings. What mattered for them was that Christ as God's Son has made it possible for us to share in the divine sonship. Their lack of esteem for Jesus' human nature was matched by a neglect of human duties. The secessionists severed their relations with the communities led by the elder and refused to contribute toward their needs. These circumstances moved the elder to deal with the themes of justice and love.

2.1. The saving justice

The Johannine Letters employ the terms "just/righteous" *(dikaios)* and "justice/ righteousness" *(dikaiosynē)* several times. The former occurs four times; the latter, three times. The adjective "righteous" is applied to God (1 John 1:9), to Jesus (2:1, 29; 3:7), and to Christians (3:7), while the noun "justice/righteousness" refers only to Christians and is used in the phrase "[the one] who does right," which is repeated three times (2:29; 3:7, 10). It is worth noting that the word "just," as applied to God, is coupled with the term "faithful." The syntagma "faithful and just" is present in the phrase "If we confess our sins, he who is faithful and just will forgive us our sins and cleanse us from all unrighteousness" (1:9). The text's connection of the concept "God who is faithful and just" with forgiveness calls to mind other biblical texts related to the covenant (Deut 32:4; Ps 111:7). In this connection, the justice of God is obviously the opposite of sin, but the text underlines in particular its forgiving and saving aspect. God's saving action is called "justice" because God, in saving people, conforms himself to his commitment sealed in the covenant. Thus the book of Deuteronomy relates to God's faithfulness and justice the mighty deeds God performed on behalf of Israel, namely God's victories over enemies and the establishment of Israel in the land

---

[25] Raymond E. Brown, *The Epistles of John* (AB 30; Garden City: Doubleday, 1983), 14–35; *Community,* 93–144; Kysar, "John, Epistles of."

allotted to Jacob (Deut 32:4, 9). The triumphs of God on behalf of Israel were actions of justice (Judg 5:11; Exod 12:12). In the same vein, the psalmist relates divine justice to God's graciousness and mercy (Ps 111:3–4; Exod 34:6–7) and then, pointing to God's mighty deeds on behalf of Israel, says, "The works of his hands are faithful and just" (Ps 111:7). The association of God's justice with God's grace and faithfulness is common both in the Psalms[26] and in the Prophets.[27] Saint Paul also employs this connection of concepts in the Letter to the Romans (Rom 3:5, 7).

In any case, the First Letter of John applies the concept of saving justice to Christ: "If anyone does sin, we have an advocate *[paraklēton]* with the Father, Jesus Christ the righteous" (1 John 2:1). Because he is just, Christ protects and defends his believers before the Father. Therefore Christians can be sure that he will defend their cause. The ability of Christ "the just" to save rests in the fact that "he is the atoning sacrifice for our sins, and not for ours only but also for the sins of the whole world" (2:2).[28] Through his atoning sacrifice, Christ has established a new order, in which justice serves forgiveness. The First Letter of John thus exhorts believers to keep their adherence to Christ so that at the Parousia they "may have confidence and not be put to shame" (2:28). Knowing that Christ is just gives confidence to believers that he will welcome them at his second coming.

2.2. Righteous works, product of God's children

Christians who produce just works obtain from the just Christ the certainty that they are born of God: "If you know that he is righteous, you may be sure that everyone who does right *[dikaiosynēn]* has been born of him" (2:29). Since each one produces fruits in accordance with his or her nature, only God's children can produce just works. The children of the devil instead can produce only evil works (3:8). Those who produce just works imitate Christ (3:7), because they share in his eternal life. Such participation gives them not only the possibility but also the responsibility to produce righteous works: "Whoever says, 'I abide in him,' ought to walk just as he walked" (2:6). In accomplishing this responsibility, believers develop the life they share in Christ, with the understanding that Christ is for them not only the source but also the living model of justice. The writer of the Johannine Letters sometimes employs the expression "to do justice" or "to do right" in a polemical sense. Each member of his community does right (2:29; 3:7, 10). The one who belongs to the opposing group "commits sin," "is guilty of lawlessness," and "is a child of the Devil" (3:4, 8). The polemical attitude derives from

---

[26] See above, ch. 6, §1.1.

[27] See above, ch. 5, §2.3.

[28] The NRSV translates the Greek *hilasmos* as "atoning sacrifice." Although scholars debate the exact meaning of *hilasmos* in the NT, in all probability it does not express the idea of placating God, for Christ is not the target of God's wrath but the manifestation of his love for humanity (1 John 4:8; John 3:16; Rom 3:24–25; 5:8). What *hilasmos* means, rather, is the removal of sin by cleansing, and hence reconciliation of humanity to God (Brown, *Epistles*, 217–22).

the fact that the group faithful to the elder suffers harm and affliction from the opposing party.

The phrase "to do justice," applied to the conduct of believers, occurs in the book of Proverbs, in the Psalms, in Ezekiel, and in Third Isaiah. The contrast between the works of justice and the works of lawlessness is distinctive, however, to the Psalms.[29] The psalmists identify themselves with those who practice justice and feel themselves persecuted by evildoers. This similarity with the Psalms is very helpful in understanding the expression "doing justice" in First John. Especially important is Psalm 15, which sets up the conditions necessary for the Israelite to approach God properly in the temple. The worshipper must do justice, that is, respect the order of relationships stipulated by God in the covenant. The psalmist specifies the demands of the covenantal order, explaining what is included in the practice of justice, and answers the question, who are those who practice justice?

> Those who walk blamelessly, and do what is right,
> and speak the truth from their heart;
> who do not slander with their tongue,
> and do no evil to their friends,
> nor take up a reproach against their neighbors; . . .
> who stand by their oath even to their hurt;
> who do not lend money at interest,
> and do not take a bribe against the innocent. (Ps 15:2b–5b)

The psalmist combines the duties of worship with ethical obligations. Practicing justice means fulfilling all the requirements for the human person to be in the proper position in the covenantal order. Therefore doing justice includes obedience to all the cultic and ethical demands stipulated by the Sinai covenant. It is obedience in fullness.

The First Letter of John adopts the notion of doing justice in obedience to the conditions of the covenant but introduces relevant changes. Whereas the psalmist speaks of the demands of the Sinai covenant, 1 John points to the new covenant, with Christ's commandments, which includes the ethical demands of Sinai covenant but transfers them to the personal relationship with Christ, animated by active love. In Christ's demands, duties toward neighbors are so central that they constitute a new commandment and the basic rule of the new covenant. Not two commandments sum up the whole law, but only one: the command to love one's neighbor. In addition, instead of listing the duties in the practice of justice, as Psalm 15 does, 1 John points to the imitation of Christ: "Whoever says, 'I abide in him,' ought to walk just as he walked" (1 John 2:6). Christ's dedicated and generous love led him to give his life for us (1:7; 4:10). Hence, the justice Christians ought to practice has to include full obedience to Christ, imitating him in their generous service to their neighbors.

---

[29] See, e.g., Pss 5:5; 6:8; 14:4; 15:3.

Finally, while Psalm 15 focuses on the person who approaches the temple in the present, the writer of 1 John has an apocalyptic point of view and considers the practice of justice, set against the practice of lawlessness, as a component of the events of the final time. And for him his age is the last hour (2:18); consequently, he identifies evildoers as the manifestation of the mystery of lawlessness *(hē anomia)*, expected to be revealed at the end of times (3:4b). With this viewpoint, the writer sees in his opponents, "the evildoers," the presence of the antichrist (2:18). For him, the present crisis of the community is part of the final battle between the followers of the devil and those of Christ. This apocalyptic framework gives special urgency to his exhortation to imitate Christ and practice that justice which requires generous manifestations of love toward one's neighbors.

The reason 1 John gives such importance to the practice of justice, particularly in its expression of generous love toward members of the community, rests in the need for the community to tighten the bonds of fellowship, in order to resolve domestic problems, retain believers within the community, and prevent them from going over to the secessionists. The crisis facing this community is serious: it has lost more than a few of its members, some of whom were wealthy. As a result, the community lost essential financial resources, especially those necessary for taking care of the poor. This attitude explains the accusation the elder levels against them: they do not fulfill the fundamental commandment Jesus has left to the church. He accuses them of hating their brothers and sisters (2:9–11) and thus of not doing what is right (3:10). For the elder, this hatred and injustice demonstrate that they are not of God: "How does God's love abide in anyone who has the world's goods and sees a brother or sister in need and yet refuses help?" (3:17). The elder sees the basis for Christian conduct in Christ's example: "We know love by this, that he laid down his life for us—and we ought to lay down our lives for one another" (3:16).

To be sure, the Johannine Letters, in speaking of love for brothers and sisters, refer to members of the Christian community. The letters deal with the inner crisis of the community and the need for active love among believers. But what is their approach to the outside world? In this respect, the writer seems to set forth contradictory statements. On the one hand, he claims that Christians should not love the world because God rejects its lawless desires (2:25). On the other hand, the writer maintains that the Father has sent his Son to save the world and has provided it with Christ's atoning sacrifice for the forgiveness of sins (2:2; 4:14).

This seeming contradiction demands further exploration. In his first claim, the writer means that believers cannot accept the lawless principles ruling the world. The world is sinful, and the people in it are sinners. But in his second claim, the author of the Johannine Letters reminds his readers that God's own attitude toward the world has consequences for his children's conduct. Children should imitate their Father by working for the salvation of the world.

It is undeniable that these letters see the world from the viewpoint of an apocalyptic dualism that sets up a clear division between good and evil. Good is on the side of believers, and evil on the side of unbelievers. Moreover, the world is mired in its lawlessness, and the writer sees this fixed attitude as a distinctive sign of the final battle between light and darkness (2:18–27; 4:1–6). The author of these letters, however, seems to employ an apocalyptic perspective as a rhetorical device in his polemical approach to his adversaries. In fact, he does not deny the possibility of salvation for people in the world. Indeed, he emphasizes it: Christ "is the atoning sacrifice for our sins, and not for ours only but also for the sins of the whole world" (2:2). "The main expression of God's love was his giving them [the people of the world] eternal life. Similarly, the believer should love the world by communicating the message of life and love."[30]

2.3. Equality in the community

The community is animated from inside by a strong sense of equality. The foundation for such equality is that the community as a whole and each person possess the anointing of the Spirit, who teaches and assures the right knowledge of Christ, necessary for each believer to conduct a Christian life (2:20, 27). Each possesses the Spirit as his or her teacher and does not need any human authority to teach.[31] The elder himself supports this idea: his letter does not so much impose his own authority as it encourages believers to follow the guidance of the inner teacher. In the present crisis created by secessionists, however, a tendency toward establishing an authority to safeguard tradition and unity seems to emerge. This tendency is most noticeable in the case of Diotrephes, who, as the leader of an affiliated congregation, rejects letters of recommendation written by the elder and denies hospitality to approved missionaries. Diotrephes probably sought to establish his own authority in a local church (3 John 9–11).[32]

The emerging tendency toward the establishment of authority is also noticeable in the final stage of the formation of the Fourth Gospel, in John 21. Here Jesus appoints Peter to be shepherd of the whole church. This event shows that the Johannine churches at the end of the century accepted a principle of authority, albeit with the distinctive characteristics of the Johannine concept of church. Despite the critical situation brought on by the absence of authority, the Johannine communities witness to an essential component of the Christian church: all Christians are disciples in Christ's church on an equal footing.

3. Justice in the book of Revelation

This chapter includes a discussion of the book of Revelation because of its similarities with the Fourth Gospel in ideas and vocabulary, although its style and intellectual perspectives are different.[33] It was written after the destruction

---

[30] J. G. van der Watt, "Ethics in First John: A Literary and Socioscientific Perspective," *CBQ* 61 (1999): 510–11.

[31] See Brown, *Epistles,* 341–49, 369–76.

[32] See Brown, *Epistles,* 107, 732–38.

[33] See Henry B. Swete, *Commentary on Revelation* (Grand Rapids: Kregel, 1977), clxxxii–clxxxv; Robert H. Charles, *The Revelation of St. John* (2 vols.; ICC; Edinburgh: T&T Clark, 1971), 1:xxix–l.

of Jerusalem, probably during Domitian's persecution between 90 and 96 C.E.[34] The writer calls himself John without any title or qualification (Rev 1:4, 9). Traditionally, he has been identified with John the apostle. He was almost certainly not an apostle but a Christian prophet of the end of the first century, also called John.

3.1. The critical situation of Christians

The book of Revelation has an epistolary framework. It begins with a salutation in the style of the Pauline Letters (1:4–5) and ends with a typical epistolary conclusion (22:21). It is addressed to seven churches of Asia Minor. Although each of them faced its own inner social situation and difficulties, all experienced the same trouble from outsiders: first, hostility from Jews and popular pagan opinion; and, second, the threat from local authorities, since, now separated from the synagogue, they did not enjoy Jewish privileges but, according to Roman law, belonged to a nonauthorized religion.

The letters to Smyrna and Philadelphia refer to Jewish denunciations of Christians before Roman officials, followed by arrests and interrogations (2:9–10; 3:9). Those accused might have been Jewish Christians who sought protection on the basis of their connections to the Jewish community or made themselves appear as sympathizers of Judaism in order to win immunity from the religious demands of pagan social life. Seeking protection in Judaism was understandable, since Jewish religion was authorized by Roman law as a *religio licita,* so that any Jew was exempted from the pagan religious obligations that Rome imposed on subject peoples within the empire. But at the end of the first century, Christians who used to seek protection in the name of Judaism were in trouble because Jews developed a hostile attitude against Christians and in some cases denounced them to Roman officials. This practice finds an antecedent in the behavior of the Achaian Jews who brought Paul to the Roman tribunal (Acts 18:12); such indictments are likewise reflected in the story of the Jews of Smyrna accusing Bishop Polycarp before the Roman proconsul.[35]

In addition to Jewish hostility, Christians in Asia Minor experienced the opposition of public opinion among pagans, who regarded Christians as depraved people, accusing them of abominable acts such as incest and cannibalism.[36] Such blame was intended to move local authorities to take repressive measures. The local authorities of Asia Minor, in particular, were inclined to act against Christians, since traditionally they were devoted to the emperor cult and used to flatter

---

[34] See Brown, *Introduction,* 805–9; Gregory K. Beale, *The Book of Revelation: A Commentary on the Greek Text* (NIGTC; Grand Rapids: Eerdmans, 1999), 4–36.

[35] *Mart. Pol.* 12:2; 13:1. See also Colin J. Hemer, *The Letters to the Seven Churches in Their Local Setting* (JSNTSup 11; Sheffield: JSOT Press, 1986), 67, 161–63; Adela Yarbro Collins, "The Political Perspective of the Revelation to John," *JBL* 96 (1977): 241–56; Collins, "Revelation," *ABD* 5:694–708, here 705.

[36] See G. E. M. de Ste. Croix, "Why Were the Early Christians Persecuted?" *Past and Present* 27 (1964): 6–38.

Caesar with divine titles in order to win his favor.[37] In fact, they had already acted against Christians. As a result, the church of Pergamum had a martyr among its members, Antipas (Rev 2:13). In addition, John was on the island of Patmos, probably banished there because of his testimony of faith (1:9). Such persecutory actions were bad omens for Christians who remembered Nero's terrible persecution in Rome.

The churches of Asia Minor also faced inner problems. They suffered the social gap between rich and poor. While Christians of Smyrna endured the hardship of poverty (2:9), those of Laodicea enjoyed security and prosperity (3:17). In addition, some Christians seemed to accept pagan lifestyles, unlike others who resisted pagan influence. Such acceptance seems to have been supported by the so-called Balaamites, Nicolaitans, and followers of Jezebel (2:14–15, 20). Most Christians suffered the tension between Christian faith and hope, on the one hand, and the actual world in which they lived, on the other. They certainly believed in Christ, enthroned at the right of the Father, endowed with supreme power over the universe, and they awaited his impending return, which would implement his full conquest. But they also lived in a world mastered by an opposing power, which appeared to be unshakable and invincible. Such tension caused frustration in Christians. The agonizing and impatient cry "how long?" burst from oppressed believers, a cry that reached its climax when imperial power unjustly and violently shed Christian blood. A reference to this cry occurs when the Lamb breaks the fifth seal and John sees the souls of those slaughtered for the testimony of their faith and hears them crying with a loud voice, "Sovereign Lord, holy and true, how long will it be before you judge and avenge our blood on the inhabitants of the earth?" (6:10).

3.2. Revelation's purpose and approach

The writer of the book of Revelation responds to this situation. To this end, he composes his work in an apocalyptic code. Thus John describes three septets of visions: the seven seals, the seven trumpets, and the seven bowls, all showing symbolic scenes of judgment and salvation. The judgment thus rendered punishes those opposed to the sovereignty of God and Christ; the salvation thus bestowed rewards those who have remained faithful to the Lord. The septets include parallel visions, each ending with the final manifestation of the wrath of God and the Lamb and the salvation of the oppressed believers. The repetition of these septets generates in the reader the conviction that God masters the events of history, rejects the arrogance and injustice of those who oppose his rule, and vindicates those who suffer for the sake of their faith.

---

[37] See S. R. F. Price, *Rituals and Power: The Roman Imperial Cult in Asia Minor* (New York: Cambridge University Press, 1984), 243–48; Thomas B. Slater, "On the Social Setting of the Revelation of John," *NTS* 44 (1998): 232–56; Leonard L. Thompson, *The Book of Revelation: Apocalypse and Empire* (New York: Oxford University Press, 1990), 97–109.

John describes the suffering of Christians as the result of the outbreak of the final battle between two cosmic powers: the great dragon and the Lamb. In the apocalyptic description of current and future events, the writer employs symbolic images with mythical connotations. Through these images, he enters into the dark thicket of human history, identifying deep and transcendent powers working in it.

In so doing, the writer shows a strong trust in God's faithfulness and justice; he is confident in the victory of good over evil. Through mythical descriptions, he pursues a rhetoric of persuasion: he comforts, encourages, and exhorts. He strengthens Christians' faith and hope, giving them the divine assurance that the current social and cultural world will no longer continue and will very soon collapse. But he does not just make a negative announcement of destruction; he also offers the alternative of a better world. This offer has a practical purpose: he intends to persuade believers to renew and strengthen their commitment, to conduct their lives in accordance with the new world God is about to create. The book of Revelation in presenting a new order to which Christians may conform their lives, speaks of a justice to be fulfilled.

The book sees the world under the power of a primordial monster, called the great dragon, the ancient serpent, alias the Devil and Satan (12:9; 20:2). According to John's apocalyptic perspective, the dragon rules the world through an attractive but destructive ideology and makes his presence visible through the Roman power, characterized by a frantic ambition for conquest, a ravenous exploitation of nations, and a set of idolatrous demands. The Roman power, the dragon's puppet, plays the role of an apocalyptic beast. It is "the first beast" (13:1–10) in the setting of this book. The beast receives from the dragon authority to persecute and destroy Christianity (13:4–8) and is so ferocious in its undertaking, ambitions, and demands that it unites in itself all the terrible features of the four beasts of Daniel's vision (13:2; Dan 7:3–8). This first beast employs a second beast. The second beast probably represents the local authorities of Asia Minor, who willingly serve the desires of the Roman power. The second beast's mission is to make people worship the first beast (Rev 13:11–17). In this apocalyptic setting, the figure of the Roman power swells beyond its historical reality, reaching gigantic, cosmic size, since it is the visible prototype of an invisible, universal, and metahistorical power ruling the world. A power of such cosmic pretensions represents a direct challenge to God's supreme sovereignty and universal dominion. The book of Revelation sees the persecution of Christians as part of this challenge against God's sovereignty. From this perceived connection, it derives its certainty that God is resolved to intervene on behalf of his people because God cannot allow the satanic challenge against his sovereignty to go unpunished. This conviction underlies the book's exhortations and symbolic actions of judgment and salvation.

The book of Revelation intends to instill comfort, strength, and hope into a community under stress. To this end, the lamentation over the fallen Babylon is dramatically effective. The proclamation from heaven that Babylon has fallen, along with the ensuing dirge of kings, merchants, and mariners (18:1–20), is a moving call for the oppressed community to renew its resolve, to reject any temptation to compromise with an idolatrous world, and to strengthen its pledge of allegiance to Christ. The action of a mighty angel throwing into the sea a great millstone symbolizing Babylon (18:21) gives assurance of the oppressive power's downfall with the certainty of an apotropaic ritual. And the hallelujah of victory sung by the great multitude of heaven (19:1–8) generates the most intense jubilation that a vibrant liturgical celebration may convey.

3.3. Revelation's alternative to the Roman Empire

The overwhelming opponent to Satan is God. In the apocalyptic setting, the dragon finds his deadly enemy in the Lamb, or Christ, who through his death and glorious resurrection won the victory and sovereignty over the universe (5:9–14). "He has won a legal victory over Satan in the heavenly court through his testimony and death. This legal victory makes him *worthy* to overcome Satan by carrying out the sentence against him."[38] The Lamb is the invincible warrior, ready to destroy the power of the dragon and his subservient beasts and to liberate Christians from oppression. His intervention is imminent, since the prayers and cries of the oppressed Christians claiming justice have reached the throne of God.[39] Christ will come soon to avenge the oppressed and make them share the power of God's kingdom. In his coming, he will renew the heavens and the earth, and faithful Christians will constitute a new society in the new Jerusalem coming down from heaven. They will be a new society in the renewed earth, a society made indeed by God (21:2), in which there will be no longer any suffering or death, oppression or slavery, or any dehumanizing powers. In God's kingdom all will serve the Lord. And in serving God, they will share the royal power and function as royal priests.[40] Like the OT high priest (Exod 28:36; 39:30), all of them will have the name of God written on their foreheads (Rev 14:1). All of them will be high priests in the new Jerusalem. But unlike the OT high priest, who could enter the holy of holies only once a year, they stand before the divine presence in perpetuity, since God will be with them forever (21:3). All this will be possible because the Lamb submitted himself as a sacrificial victim to the violence that the world unjustly inflicted on him. Thus the four living creatures and the twenty-four elders sing before the Lamb,

> You are worthy to take the scroll and to open its seals,
> for you were slaughtered and by your blood you ransomed for God
> saints from every tribe and language and people and nation;
> you have made them to be a kingdom and priests serving our God,
> and they will reign on earth. (5:9–10)

The book of Revelation rereads the story of Exodus within its new context. Just as the blood of the lamb meant the liberation of the Israelites from Egyptian

---

[38] Adela Yarbro Collins, *The Apocalypse* (New Testament Message 22; Wilmington, Del.: Glazier, 1979), 41–42.
[39] See Rev 5:8; 6:9–10; 8:3.
[40] See Rev 1:6; 5:10; 20:6.

slavery, so the blood of Christ, the Lamb, makes Christians free from the bondage of this world. And just as liberation in the book of Exodus included the formation of Israel as "a priestly kingdom, a holy nation" (Exod 19:6), so Christ's blood makes of the redeemed community a priestly kingdom. Just as the Israelites, after crossing the sea, celebrated the power of the rescuing God by singing the song of Moses (Exod 15:1), so Christians, rescued by the Lamb, celebrate the victory over the beast. Standing before the sea, they sing the song of Moses, the servant of God, and the song of the Lamb (Rev 15:2–3). Christian martyrs, having crossed the sea of blood by the power of the Lamb's blood, reach the other side and sing Moses' song, which now is transformed into the song of Christ the Lamb.

The martyrs are symbolically promised vindication in many ways.[41] One in particular has exercised the imaginations of readers over the centuries—the thousand years of Satan's imprisonment and the millennial reign of the martyrs (20:1–6). Scholars debate whether the span of the thousand years refers to a period before or after the second coming of the Lord.[42] In all probability, it refers to a time prior to the Parousia. In any case, the scenario is envisioned as follows: Satan is imprisoned for a thousand years, after which he is loosed. He deceives the nations, marshaling their forces for the final war against the saints (20:7–10). The vision of this ultimate battle of the nations parallels the previous vision (19:11–21), in which the rider of the white horse, the Word of God, the King of kings, fights the final battle against the kings of the earth whom Satan deceived. The Lord destroys them utterly, and "all the birds gorge themselves on their flesh" (19:21).

These two parallel visions refer to the same final war. The imprisonment of Satan, described as an event placed between the two visions, goes back to a time before the final battle, and Satan's release prepares the final war. But how far back does the imprisonment go? The term "a thousand years" is a symbolic number—as are all the numbers in the book of Revelation. It connotes a long time, as opposed to a few days or months. In a similar fashion, the imprisonment of Satan is also a figure of speech. The Gospels help to shed light on it. According to the Gospel of John, the ruler of this world is judged and driven out at Jesus' death and exaltation (John 12:31; 16:11), and it is then that Jesus begins to attract people to himself (12:32). In the Synoptics, Jesus binds Satan in his public ministry (Mark 3:27; Matt 12:29; Luke 11:22). To be imprisoned, to be driven out, to be bound are three different figures of speech that all seem to express the same idea—that Satan has been ousted and placed in subjection to Christ's power. They express the conviction that Satan's activity has been restricted. He cannot prevent people

---

[41] See Rev 6:9–11; 7:9–17; 11:16–18; 12:11; 14:1–5. The term "martyr" in the book of Revelation does not have the technical meaning it later gained. Here the term designates a believer who witnesses to Christ by rejecting a way of life that leads to idolatry and who is ready to die for the faith if necessary.

[42] See Beale, *Revelation*, 972–1021; M. Eugene Boring, *Revelation* (Interpretation; Louisville: John Knox, 1989), 200–208; Wilfrid J. Harrington, *Revelation* (SP 16; Collegeville: Liturgical Press, 1993), 195–202.

from coming to Jesus, and he cannot threaten the salvific security of the true church, although he can harm it physically.[43]

The binding of Satan seems to correspond to the dragon's defeat, when he is thrown down from heaven by Michael and his angels at the exaltation of the messianic child (Rev 12:7–9).[44] In this context, it is sound to argue that the period of Satan's imprisonment (20:1–3) begins at Jesus' death and exaltation; the period of the martyrs sharing in Christ's kingdom begins as soon as they imitate the Lord's own death in their martyrdoms. The long period of exaltation accorded the martyrs—the thousand years—stands in sharp contrast to the brief time of their suffering, symbolically described as a period of ten days (2:10). A thousand is the third power of ten.[45]

After the final defeat of Satan and the judgment of the dead, the new heaven and the new earth begin, and the new Jerusalem descends from heaven. Who will be the citizens of the new city? The martyrs, of course. But the city also numbers among its citizens those who now are poor and afflicted and trust in God (2:9–10), those who turn away from their attachment to riches (3:17–19), those who renounce pagan ways of life (2:14–16; 20–21), and all who repent of their evildoing.[46] Moreover, the nations, converted to Christ, will benefit from the city and serve God who dwells in it (21:24).

On the one hand, the dramatic action expressed through mythical images shows the existence of a transcendent world; on the other hand, as A. Yarbro Collins says, using Aristotelian categories, it produces a cathartic effect in the audience "in the sense that it clarifies and objectifies the conflict. Fearful feelings are vented by the very act of expressing them, especially in this larger-than-life and exaggerated way."[47] In addition to providing a catharsis, the dramatic action strengthens Christian faith and motivates followers of Jesus to persevere in their hope. It conveys the certainty that the present social and cultural world, in which the believers are suffering, will be destroyed, and offers the vision of another empire, more powerful than the present one, the just and eternal kingdom of God.

---

[43] The idea of divine protection combined with exposure to persecution is also found in the vision in which the inner court of the temple is measured, cordoned off, and thus secured (Rev 11:1). The outer court, by contrast, is neither measured nor secured (11:2). Both the inner court and the outer court represent the community of the faithful. The distinction between what is inside and what is outside, applied to the same community, expresses the idea that it is at one and the same time protected by God and exposed to Satan's attacks.

[44] The woman is said to be transferred to the wilderness for protection for "one thousand two hundred and sixty days" while her children are attacked by the great dragon for holding the testimony of Jesus (12:6, 17). The number of days, equivalent to forty-two months (11:2), emphasizes the limited span of time assigned for the suffering of believers. Numbers in Revelation express not only quantity but also quality of duration. Thus the period of the church can be indicated by a time of a thousand years to emphasize the happiness of those who, like the martyrs, remain faithful to the Lord.

[45] See Beale, *Revelation*, 1017–21.

[46] See Rev 2:4–5, 16, 22; 3:3, 19.

[47] See Adela Yarbro Collins, *Crisis and Catharsis: The Power of the Apocalypse* (Philadelphia: Fortress, 1984), 153.

The book of Revelation encourages Christians to identify themselves with God's kingdom and see in it their liberation and the fulfillment of their expectations.

3.4. Christian participation

Christian participation in the kingdom of God is a future reality, though near at hand. Participation in the kingdom is a divine promise, but it must be deserved. The letters to the seven churches make this clear. This is the time for Christians to conform their conduct to God's will and thus merit participation in the kingdom. They have to undergo tribulation.[48] It is a time when Christians' patient endurance *(hypomonē)* is tested and forged.[49] The one who conquers will be rewarded and will share the power of the kingdom.[50] The conquest at issue is not the victory of a revolutionary movement or a guerrilla war against Roman power but the victory of perseverance in Christian faith and conduct, in contrast to the pagan way of life and the demands of its institutions. It is the victory of those who practice justice (22:11) by conforming their life to the order established by the kingdom of God and who reject the pleasures offered by Roman power in return for accepting its religious demands.

The present is a time for Christians to live their lives in contrast to a power that embodies international oppression and slaughters not only Christians but also other peoples in conquered nations: "In you was found the blood of prophets and of saints, and of all who have been slaughtered on earth" (18:24). The lives of Christians must also contrast with that of an empire that accumulates fabulous wealth at the expense of human slavery (18:13). The contrasting Christian life should anticipate the future society that the kingdom of God will implement—a society that, instead of dehumanizing, allows human beings to reach their fulfillment and, instead of exploiting, gives life and power. Christians are called to conquer, going through the purification that faithfulness requires, willing and ready, if necessary, to suffer martyrdom. They are called to believe in the revealed wisdom that discovers another dimension of reality, at variance with that presented by the world. In so believing, they can transcend their own death and become conquerors.

The book of Revelation transforms the historical situation of a local and transitory persecution into a cosmic and metahistorical event. The community's experience of alienation is understood as God's ultimate struggle with the destructive power of primordial beasts, reincarnated in history. Through this transformation, the book gives a message of hope to all Christians who find themselves in a similar situation in any period of history. They are encouraged to trust—even in the midst of suffering—in the protecting presence of God, since the persecution is part of a cosmic struggle in which God has the upper hand: "Take courage; I have conquered the world!" (John 16:33). This trust in the power of the Lamb is so strong that it is able to generate in the readers of the book of Revelation the conviction that the

---

[48] See Rev 1:9; 2:9, 10, 22; 7:14.
[49] See Rev 1:9; 2:2, 3, 19; 3:10; 13:10; 14:12.
[50] See Rev 2:7, 11, 17, 26; 3:5, 12, 21.

present world is fast running toward its end. Its destruction is imminent. Indeed, according to the perspective of this book, the present world, together with its ruler, is wholly undermined by Christ's victory. The divine power that destroys evil is already activated and has already begun to imperil the very existence of evil. The present is the time for believers to strengthen their trust; and even though they live under oppression and persecution, they should renew their faithfulness to Christ and give the testimony of an authentically Christian life.

In reading this book, one has to remember that it was accepted into the canon, but in conjunction with the writings of other NT communities of faith. Its negative ideas about the present world must be balanced by other perspectives found in the NT. In fact, Jesus taught us to love our enemies. Indeed, he employed the image of a Samaritan to model the sort of Christian love that reaches out to any needy person without discrimination. And Paul's mission to the Gentiles was based on an understanding that all peoples everywhere are invited to come to Christ and have their lives transformed.

The book of Revelation does, however, deliver a valid message to Christians who experience oppression and suffering for sake of the gospel, like the churches of Asia Minor. This message is one of trust in the Lord and patient endurance in the midst of afflictions. Nevertheless, the reading of this book should not dishearten those who, enlightened by the gospel and inspired by Jesus' command of love, struggle against oppression and strive to renew earthly society in accordance with the order that the creator has established in this world. Although the church is aware that suffering persecution is part of its mission, it must practice love of enemies and teach its members to work for the common good of the present society. The image of the new Jerusalem descending from heaven to a renewed earth encourages Christians to work for peace and justice, knowing that their efforts help develop the order the creator imprinted on the world and humanity and prepare the final transformation of human society. Their efforts anticipate the new city. The image of a heavenly Jerusalem in a renewed earth, with which the book of Revelation closes, is not a symbol of the present world's destruction but a hopeful sign of its transformation and fulfillment. This sort of sign points to the abiding presence of God among his people and testifies to the faith these early Christians had that God is the author of their history.

Such convictions are not confined to first-century Christians. For example, the fathers at the Second Vatican Council were likewise convinced that the hope of a new world compels Christians to work for progress here and now:

> Far from diminishing our concern to develop this earth, the expectancy of a new earth should spur us on, for it is here that the body of the new human family grows, foreshadowing in some way the age which is to come. That is why, although we must be careful to distinguish earthly progress clearly from the increase of the kingdom of Christ, such progress is of vital concern to the kingdom of God, insofar as it can contribute to the better ordering of human society.[51]

---

[51] Second Vatican Council, *Gaudium et Spes* 39, in *Vatican Council II* (ed. Flannery), 938.

Conclusion

The Christians for whom the Fourth Gospel was written, though expelled from the synagogue, nevertheless experience the consolation of the Paraclete. They feel the effect of being liberated by the truth of the gospel and are aware of their ability, by following Jesus' teaching, to serve the transcendent God, present in the members of the community. The community develops a strong sense of equality among its members: every one of them is a disciple, and all are equally servants. The equality is rooted in the incarnation, according to which the Logos became human so that humanity might share in the divine fullness. John's message of equality and service is embodied in the scene in which Jesus washes his disciples' feet and urges them to follow his example.

In the Johannine Letters, the community has experienced an inner crisis: an important group has severed relations with the mother church and refused to help the community in its time of need. Under these circumstances, the author of the letters urges his correspondents to practice justice in accordance with the demands of the new covenant—namely, to serve others in the community to the point of giving their own lives for them, following the example of Christ. Practicing this justice is a sign that a member of the community is actually born of God.

In the book of Revelation, likewise, the community experienced both Jewish and pagan hostility as well as persecution from local governments. The book is designed to strengthen faith and to nurture hope in oppressed Christians. It assures them of the imminent destruction of the oppressive powers and gives them certainty that they will share with Christ the power of God's kingdom in the new Jerusalem coming down from heaven to a renewed earth. The book urges Christians to exhibit a conduct at variance with pagan mores and to be ready, if necessary, to undergo martyrdom. Their attitude and conduct must contrast with the dictatorial and satanic power that oppresses in the effort to dominate, enslaves in the effort to exploit, and slaughters in the effort to conquer.

By transforming a local and transitory persecution into a cosmic and metahistorical event, the book of Revelation gives a message of hope, valid for any Christian in the world who may experience similar oppression. This negative perspective of the world must be balanced by the viewpoint of other books of the NT that consider the gospel a power for transforming humanity.

Bibliography

Beale, Gregory K. *The Book of Revelation: A Commentary on the Greek Text*. New International Greek Testament Commentary. Grand Rapids: Eerdmans, 1999.

Berrouard, M.-F. "Le Paraclet, Défenseur du Christ devant la conscience du croyant (Jo. XVI, 8–11)," *Revue des sciences philosophiques et théologiques* 33 (1949): 361–89.

Boring, M. Eugene. *Revelation*. Interpretation. Louisville: John Knox, 1989.

Brown, Raymond E. *The Churches the Apostles Left Behind.* New York: Paulist, 1984.
———. *The Community of the Beloved Disciple.* New York: Paulist, 1979.
———. *The Epistles of John.* Anchor Bible 30. Garden City: Doubleday, 1983.
———. *The Gospel according to John I–XII.* Anchor Bible 28. Garden City: Doubleday, 1970.
———. *The Gospel according to John XIII–XXI.* Anchor Bible 29A. Garden City: Doubleday, 1970.
———. *An Introduction to the New Testament.* Anchor Bible Reference Library. New York: Doubleday, 1997.
———. "The Paraclete in the Fourth Gospel." *New Testament Studies* 13 (1966–1967): 113–32.
Burge, Gary M. *The Anointed Community: The Holy Spirit in the Johannine Tradition.* Grand Rapids: Eerdmans, 1987.
Charles, Robert H. *The Revelation of St. John.* 2 vols. International Critical Commentary. Edinburgh: T&T Clark, 1971.
Clarke, Graeme W. "Religio Licita." Pages 665–67 in vol. 5 of *Anchor Bible Dictionary.* Edited by D. N. Freedman. 6 vols. New York: Doubleday, 1992.
Collins, Adela Yarbro. *The Apocalypse.* New Testament Message 22. Wilmington, Del.: Glazier, 1979.
———. *Crisis and Catharsis: The Power of the Apocalypse.* Philadelphia: Fortress, 1984.
———. "The Political Perspective of the Revelation to John." *Journal of Biblical Literature* 96 (1977): 241–56.
———. "Revelation." Pages 694–708 in vol. 5 of *Anchor Bible Dictionary.* Edited by D. N. Freedman. 6 vols. New York: Doubleday, 1992.
Ellacuría, I. *Freedom Made Flesh: The Mission of Christ and of His Church.* Maryknoll: Orbis, 1976.
Flannery, Austin, ed. Second Vatican Council, *Dignitatis humana.* Pages 799–812 in *Vatican Council II: the Conciliar and Post-Concilir Documents.* Collegeville: Liturgical Press, 1975.
Flusser, David. "The Jewish-Christian Schism: Part II." *Immanuel* 17 (1984): 30–39. Repr. pages 635–44 in *Judaism and the Origins of Christianity.* Jerusalem: Magnes, 1988.
Guardini, Romano. *Freedom, Grace, and Destiny.* New York: Pantheon, 1961.
Harrington, Wilfrid J. *Revelation.* Sacra pagina 16. Collegeville: Liturgical Press, 1993.
Hemer, Colin J. *The Letters to the Seven Churches in Their Local Setting.* Journal for the Study of the New Testament: Supplement Series 11. Sheffield: JSOT Press, 1986.
Hengel, Martin. *The Johannine Question.* London: SCM, 1989.
Horbury, William. "The Benediction of the *Minim* and Early Jewish-Christian Controversy." *Journal of Theological Studies* 33 NS (1982): 19–61.
Hultgren, Arland J. "The Johannine Footwashing (13.1–11) as Symbol of Eschatological Hospitality." *New Testament Studies* 28 (1982): 539–46.

Kimelman, R. "*Birkat ha-Minim* and the Lack of Evidence for an Anti-Christian Jewish Prayer in Late Antiquity." Pages 266–44 in vol. 2 of *Jewish and Christian Self-Definition*. Edited by E. P. Sanders. 3 volumes. Philadelphia: Fortress, 1981.

Kysar, Robert. "Anti-Semitism and the Gospel of John." Pages 113–27 in *Anti-Semitism and Early Christianity: Issues of Polemics and Faith*. Edited by A. Craig et al. Minneapolis: Fortress, 1993.

———. "John, Epistles of." Pages 900–12 in vol. 3 of *Anchor Bible Dictionary*. Edited by D. N. Freedman. 6 vols. New York: Doubleday, 1992.

———. "John, The Gospel of." Pages 912–31 in vol. 3 of *Anchor Bible Dictionary*. Edited by D. N. Freedman. 6 vols. New York: Doubleday, 1992.

Lindars, Barnabas. *Behind the Fourth Gospel*. London: SPCK, 1971.

Lona, H. "Wahrheit und Freiheit in Jo 8, 31–36 und die 'Theologie der Befreiung' in Lateinamerika." Pages 300–313 in *Biblische Randbemerkungen*. FS R. Schnackenburg. Edited by H. Merklein and J. Lange. Würzburg: Echter, 1974.

Martyn, J. Louis. "Glimpses into the History of the Johannine Community." Pages 259–99 in *L'Évangile de Jean: sources, rédaction, théologie*. Bibliotheca ephemeridum theologicarum lovaniensium 44. Edited by M. de Jonge. Gembloux: Duculot, 1977.

Moloney, Francis J. *The Gospel of John*. Sacra pagina 4. Collegeville: Liturgical Press, 1998.

On Evangelization in the Modern World: Apostolic Exhortation. Washington, D.C.: United States Catholic Conference, 1976.

Potterie, Ignace de la. *La verité dans saint Jean*. Analecta biblica 73. Rome: Biblical Institute Press, 1977.

Price, S. R. F. *Rituals and Power: The Roman Imperial Cult in Asia Minor*. New York: Cambridge University Press, 1984.

Rensberger, David. *Johannine Faith and Liberating Community*. Philadelphia: Westminster, 1988.

———. "Sectarianism and Theological Interpretation in John." Paper presented at the annual meeting of the AAR/SBL, Chicago, November 20, 1994. Summary in *AAR/SBL Abstracts* (Chicago: Scholars Press, 1994), 334.

Schnackenburg, Rudolph. *The Gospel according to St. John*. Translated by K. Smyth. 3 vols. New York: Crossroad, 1982.

Schneiders, Sandra M. "The Foot Washing (John 13:1–20): An Experiment in Hermeneutics." *Catholic Biblical Quarterly* 43 (1981): 76–92.

Schrage, W. *The Ethics of the New Testament*. Translated by D. E. Green. Philadelphia: Fortress, 1988.

Slater, Thomas B. "On the Social Setting of the Revelation of John." *New Testament Studies* 44 (1998): 252–56.

Smiga, George M. *Pain and Polemic: Anti-Judaism in the Gospels*. New York: Paulist, 1992.

Smith, D. Moody. "Judaism and the Gospel of John." Pages 76–96 in *Jews and Christians: Exploring the Past, Present, and Future*. Edited by J. H. Charlesworth. New York: Crossroad, 1990.

Ste. Croix, G. E. M. de. "Why Were the Early Christians Persecuted?" *Past and Present* 27 (1964): 6–38.
Swete, Henry B. *Commentary on Revelation.* Grand Rapids: Kregel, 1977.
Teeple, Howard M. *The Literary Origin of the Gospel of John.* Evanston, Ill.: Religion and Ethics Institute, 1974.
Thomas, John C. *Footwashing in John 13 and the Johannine Community.* Sheffield: JSOT Press, 1991.
Thompson, Leonard L. *The Book of Revelation. Apocalypse and Empire.* New York: Oxford University Press, 1990.
Townsend, J. T. "The Gospel of John and the Jews: The Story of a Religious Divorce." Pages 72–97 in *Antisemitism and the Foundations of Christianity.* Edited by A. Davies. New York: Paulist, 1979.
Tuñí, J. O. *La verdad os hará libres (Jn 8,32): Liberación y libertad del creyente en el cuarto evangelio.* Barcelona: Herder, 1973.
Wahlde, U. C. von. "The Gospel of John and the Presentation of Jews and Judaism." Pages 67–86 in *Within Context: Essays on Jews and Judaism in the New Testament.* Edited by D. Efroymson et al. Collegeville: American Interfaith Institute and Liturgical Press, 1993.
Watt, J. G. van der. "Ethics in First John: A Literary and Socioscientic Perspective." *Catholic Biblical Quarterly* 61 (1999): 491–511.
Wengst, Klaus. *Bedrängte Gemeinde und verherrlichter Christus: Ein Versuch über das Johannesevangelium.* Munich: Kaiser, 1990.

CHAPTER FOURTEEN

OVERALL CONCLUSION

On this journey through the biblical world, we have established contact with those who searched for justice and those who taught us how to search for it, and we have endeavored to understand the ancient texts in their own contexts and to perceive their lessons for us. We are now in a position to present overall conclusions.

In the ancient Near East, especially in Mesopotamia and Egypt, we found even in their early history a concern for the poor, the orphan, and the widow, a concern that later would be a relevant theme in the Bible. Accordingly, the ancient Near Eastern people introduced social reforms and regulations, practiced philanthropic aid, and were concerned with a fair administration of justice. Thus, they issued measures that were meant to help the poor, to free the oppressed, and to restore them to the social level that was theirs according to the divine design.

Ancient Israel shared these concerns and expressed them in concepts and terms inherited primarily from ancient Mesopotamia. Obviously, it assimilated and developed them according to its own concept of God and its own idea of an order established by Yahweh, the ruler of the world and savior of his own people. Thus, biblical Israel not only fostered charity toward the poor and taught giving each person what each deserves but also instilled into the people the ideal of imitating God. Israel endeavored to show to its poor and afflicted the creative compassion that Yahweh manifested for his people under Egyptian slavery. According to ancient tradition, the beginning of Israel as a free society was the consequence of Yahweh's own saving justice, by which God brought Israel out of oppression and gave the newly liberated people a new social structure in order to live in freedom and justice. Israel was called to imitate the saving conduct of God by carrying out actions of saving justice toward the poor, the orphan, the widow, and the foreigner. The divine conduct as a model for action was part of God's covenant with Israel. The covenant had an educational dimension for the people. It helped the Israelite community to be aware of its own dignity, destiny, and religious and moral duties. Furthermore, the covenant fostered a sense of individual and social responsibility. The covenant also included God's commitment to make his creative power active in history on behalf of God's people, as he had done in Egypt. By virtue of this divine commitment, the exodus from Egypt became a paradigm in similar situations requiring an exodus—a prototype of God's intervention in history, in other words, meant to vindicate God's sovereignty against any presumptuous power that dares to impose slavery on any human being, the masterpiece of God's creation. Hence, the exodus from Egypt lays the foundations of hope and serves to inspire people who suffer abuse and oppression in various ways. The Exodus narratives, and the entire Moses narrative in the Pentateuch as well, look to the future of the community. They present an opening to the future that allows the reader to transfer to his or her own situation the religious and moral spirit that animates the norms of the Sinai covenant. The image of Moses himself inspires future generations. After he conveys the will of God to his people, Moses raises his eyes toward the future, the promised land, a place that mediates life and social well-being and is an expression of identity, freedom, and dignity for his people. The image of Moses gazing at the land is an enduring inspiration to anyone who strives for a society of justice and peace.

In its social, economic, and political development, Israel adopted a monarchical structure, common in the ancient Near Eastern world. But it also adapted the institution of kingship in keeping with its own religious perspectives. In the Israelite understanding of kingship, the monarch was the dispenser of justice and the protector of the poor, the orphan, and the widow. Great hopes lay in the king's performance. Centralized government, however, brought abuses of power that gave the prophets plenty of occasion to issue oracles of condemnation. The prophets were the consciences of kings and governors, and they issued their guiding word at key historical moments. Denouncing and censuring crimes in times of abuse of power, the prophets also comforted and encouraged the people in times of suffering and destruction. They stressed kindness, faithfulness, and compassion as essential elements of justice. They condemned social injustice as the cause of people's poverty and destitution. They proclaimed the practice of social justice as a necessary condition for practicing an acceptable worship of God. Amos's oracle is well known: "Let justice roll down like waters, and righteousness like an ever-flowing stream" (Amos 5:24). Most of the prophets fostered a vision of hope for the future, and they envisioned social and political structures under rulers who would guide the community to a life of justice and peace. They insisted on the need to change not only external social structures but also the inmost being of the people—including a transformation of the heart that they deemed necessary in order to have a free and just society. Animated by an unbreakable trust in God's presence in human history, they shaped the messianic hope and forged the vision of a new Jerusalem, a center of justice and peace. From their midst came the Servant of the Lord, a prophetic figure who, although innocent and peaceful, suffered violent death for the liberation and restoration of his people and became a model for everyone who works on behalf of the poor and the oppressed.

In their frustrations, sufferings, and oppressions, the people of Israel turned to God. Their prayers expressed their pain and full confidence in God's protection. This fact is obvious in the psalms of petition and lamentation. In these poetic hymns, believers—mainly the poor and the afflicted—show an unshakable trust in the saving justice of God. By reciting or singing them, subsequent generations of poor and afflicted people identify themselves with the supplicants of the Psalms: they find their souls encouraged and their hope strengthened. The Psalms convey the same vision the prophets set forth—a vison of the just world that God has in store for the poor and afflicted.

The book of Proverbs sees poverty as a regular part of human society. It exhorts its readership to be generous toward the poor in order to alleviate their sad situation. Although it does not indicate the need for a change of social structures, it does insist on the need for education in order for the human person to shape the sense of individual responsibility and to form a habit of discipline and consistency necessary for success in one's work and the development of familial well-being. The book offers an important lesson to help the human person avoid poverty, ignorance, laziness, slackness, and a lack of personal and social responsibility. By stressing the need for education, Proverbs provides a necessary supplement to the prophetic critique against injustice as the cause of poverty. By including the "fear of the Lord" as part of education, this book offers a remarkable contribution to the transformation of the heart that the prophets themselves deemed necessary for a just and harmonious society.

Job not only laments his own affliction but also identifies himself with the poor and the outcast and makes himself their spokesman. He cries out for justice on behalf of those who suffer unjustly and who blame God for all their misfortunes. When he sees God, however, he retracts what he has said, and he begins to understand that there is something else he must ponder, namely, God's hope-giving love for his creatures.

Ecclesiastes does not show the prophetic vision of God's plan for the good of God's people. But this work offers something valuable by alerting people to the danger posed by overextended euphoria in prosperous times, for in the movement of history negative powers may emerge and produce suffering and destruction. Sirach assumes that the distinction between poor and rich is a permanent and unchangeable reality, but exhorts his readers to help the poor. Like the book of Proverbs, Sirach emphasizes education and the development of personal and social responsibility, which are very important in any human society, especially for people of underdeveloped countries and minorities against whom discrimination exists.

The book of Wisdom applies to the persecuted people of Israel the concept of the poor and afflicted individual. It provides an answer to the questions raised by Job and Ecclesiastes, in the sense that it offers the afflicted an assurance of divine vindication—namely, immortality and happiness after death and a share in rule over the nations from their heavenly existence. It offers the assurance of a change in the afterlife. But surprisingly, it does not consider the possibility of change in earthly society through the light of the Law revealed to the Jewish people.

The book of Daniel, like the other apocalyptic writings studied in chapter 7, addresses a community under oppression. Daniel offers assurance that his people's cause is God's cause because their oppressor dares to challenge God's sovereignty. God is poised to intervene, Daniel says, in order to change both Israel's destiny and that of the entire world. God will establish his kingdom, and those now under oppression will overcome death by obtaining immortality; they will share the power of the eternal kingdom in a new earth. Daniel's negative opinion of the present world should be amended by following the perspective of the prophets, who strive to transform the society in which they live, and by following the attitude of the sages, for whom society is the proper place for the human person to grow.

The NT associates the concept of justice with Jesus' saving words and deeds, with his death as an act of serving love, with God's love manifested in the giving of God's Son for the salvation of the world, with the incarnation of the Logos meant to elevate human beings and make them equal, and with Christ, who will come in glory to punish the unrighteous and the oppressor and reward the righteous and oppressed. The NT does not, however, direct Christian hope solely toward heaven. On the contrary, it commits the believer to strive for the transformation of the present world. The believer has to prepare for the heavenly dwelling by building the earthly city. We can see this approach in Jesus of Nazareth, in the Synoptic Gospels, in the Pauline Letters, and in the Johannine writings.

Jesus of Nazareth proclaims the coming of God's kingdom, announced by the prophets and the apocalyptic writers, and teaches its requirements. His prophetic words and deeds, as well as his sapiential teaching, sought to reshape human society. With this goal in mind, Jesus gives a model in the new family he creates. His miracles are liberating deeds in anticipation of the future kingdom. In his teaching, Jesus breaks the ritual fences that separate the clean from the unclean and proclaims that the human heart is the ethical center of the human person, the place from which moral growth develops. Jesus favors social change without violence and offers his teaching and power to liberate human beings from evil. Jesus transforms human life for the good both of the individual person and of society at large.

In the Gospel of Mark, Jesus is the crucified Messiah, the spokesman and agent of God's kingdom, and the cornerstone of the new community. He reshapes the image of power in the world, defeats Satan by the action of God's kingdom, and liberates the human person from the dehumanizing elements of the present world. Jesus liberates people without discrimination and makes them members of a new community animated by the Christian spirit, a community in which a sense of equality, mutual service, and inner freedom are fostered in contrast to the ideals of the surrounding world. Jesus offers the model: "The Son of Man came not to be served but to serve, and to give his life as ransom for many" (Mark 10:45).

In the Gospel of Matthew, compassion is an outstanding feature of the saving justice of God. Believers must imitate God's compassion and serve Christ, who is identified with the destitute, the sick, and the outcast in accordance with his statement "Truly I tell you, just as you did it to one of the least of these who are members of my family, you did it to me" (Matt 25:40). The Letter of James teaches that true religion means to care for the needy and to avoid the discriminating and dehumanizing mentality of the world. It emphasizes that what generates justice is not violence but peace.

According to Luke, Jesus is God's anointed, who proclaims eschatological liberation. The first beneficiaries of the saving justice are the poor, the disabled, and the oppressed, who trust in the Lord. Jesus calls the rich to break the closed circle of reciprocity that characterized both friendship and the relationship between patrons and clients in the Greco-Roman world. He exhorts us to share our goods with the poor without expecting repayment. From Luke the reader retains two impressive images—Zacchaeus and the good Samaritan.

For Paul, God's justice, proclaimed by the gospel, is meant to restore the human person to the right position according to the divine design. The effect is to elevate human beings to the dignity of God's children. The divine justice raises them up and makes them equal in dignity. In the Christian community, God's justice renders differences in sex, race, nationality, culture, social status, or economic situation absolutely irrelevant. As Paul says, "There is no longer Jew or Greek, there is no longer slave or free, there is no longer male and female; for all of you are one in Christ Jesus" (Gal 3:28). The apostle promotes women and lays the groundwork for the manumission of slaves. He requires the formation of individual and social responsibility and motivates all people, be they rich or poor, to develop their abilities to work both for their own good and for that of others. God's justice is a grace that motivates people to put into circulation spiritual and material goods for the common benefit. Paul uses the Hellenistic concept of order, derived from the inner nature of the cosmos, only once. He does so in dealing with the relations of believers to the state. This concept will appear later in the codes of family duties referred to in the deuteropauline letters and in the instructions of the Pastoral Letters.

The community of the Fourth Gospel, suffering the expulsion of its members from the synagogue, experiences the consolation and support of the Paraclete. Under its guidance, the community enjoys the certainty that by Christ's truth it is liberated from the slavery of Satan and from the power of sin and death. By being docile to Christ's truth, humans can escape selfishness and serve the transcendent God present in one's neighbor. The liberating truth of Christ allows a deep sense of equality to develop in the disciples. The equality among the disciples finds its foundation in the incarnation, in which the Logos assumed human nature in order to allow it to participate in the divine fullness. In one thing only the disciples may look for superiority: in love of Christ, a love that includes service to one's neighbors. Jesus, who lowers himself and serves his disciples by washing their feet, remains an everlasting example for the disciples to follow.

In the Johannine Letters, the community suffers an inner crisis. The author of the First Letter identifies his community with those who practice justice—namely, with those who obey fully Christ's words, which in turn demands a generous dedication, even unto death, to the brothers and sisters in need. In the book of Revelation, the community experiences Jewish and pagan hostility and suffers oppression from the local government. The author of the book encourages Christians under persecution by assuring them that Christ has conquered the world.

The author exhorts them to act without violence in contrast to the majority culture and encourages them to be ready to face—even to the point of martyrdom—the dictatorial and satanic power that oppresses, enslaves, and murders in order to conquer and consolidate its dominion. To strengthen his congregation's hope, the author describes the Christian future in the new Jerusalem coming down from heaven to a renewed earth. Their motto has to be Christ's words: "Take courage: I have conquered the world" (John 16:33). The negative opinion of this book concerning the present state of the world should be amended by reference to the apostolic teaching, according to which the gospel represents the divine power designed to transform the present world.

In our journey through the biblical world, we have been like spectators witnessing both the misery and anguish of many oppressed peoples and the hope of a few who spoke and labored on their behalf. As spectators, we perceive a misery that arouses our moral and religious indignation because such a human plight is "contrary to the plan of the Creator and to the honor that is due him."[1] Although, perhaps, we have become indignant, we may feel comfortable in being just spectators. The biblical texts, however, call us to be transformed from bystanders into participants. The misery of millions of humans, manifest in so many ways—hunger, oppression, poverty, illiteracy, chronic disease—challenges our Christian commitment to the new commandment of love. We do well to recall the pointed question of Pope Paul VI: "How in fact can one proclaim the new commandment without promoting in justice and in peace the true, authentic advancement of man?"[2] The lessons derived from the biblical writings continue to inspire especially two communities who long for justice, both motivated by the hope inherited from their ancestors. On the one hand, there are the Jewish people, who, strengthened by their faith in the creator and the redeemer of Israel, keep uttering the cry shouted by the prophet Habakkuk, the psalms of lamentation, and Second Esdras: "O Lord, how long?" Journeying from one holocaust to another, the believing Israel, servant of the Lord, hopes that its life of suffering will turn into a life of justice and peace in a new world. Thus it prays on the feast of Rosh Hashanah, "May this day add meaning to our lives. Let the shofar's sound awaken the voice of conscience, our common worship unite us in love, our memories of bondage impel us to help the oppressed."[3]

The Christian community, on the other hand, believes that it lives between the beginning of the establishment of God's kingdom on earth and its final consummation. It received the commandment to love and to serve from Jesus' teaching in the washing of his disciples' feet. It is committed to care for any person in

---

[1] *Puebla Document* 28, in *Puebla and Beyond: Documentation and Commentary* (ed. J. Eagleson and P. Schaper; Maryknoll: Orbis, 1979), 128.

[2] Pope Paul VI, apostolic exhortation *Evangelii Nuntiandi* 31, in *On Evangelization in the Modern World: Apostolic Exhortation* (Washington, D.C.: United States Catholic Conference, 1976), 22–23.

[3] C. Stern, ed., *Shaarei Tesuvah, Gates of Repentance: The New Union Prayerbook for the Days of Awe* (New York: Central Conference of American Rabbis, 1978), 64.

need, following the lesson of the good Samaritan. It works, exhorts, and prays that Zacchaeus may have many followers so that the impoverished Lazarus may sit at the rich man's table. It strives to give an example of participation, offering its material, intellectual, and spiritual riches for people to share. The Christian community firmly believes in the saving power of "the ferment of the Gospel [that] has aroused and continues to arouse in the hearts of men an unquenchable thirst for human dignity."[4] In the face of the elusive character of justice, the Christian community does not lose hope because it trusts deeply in the power of the Spirit, who dwells in the community and is acting in the world quietly and patiently, but effectively.

Bibliography

Eagleston, J., and P. Schaper, eds. *Puebla Document* 28, in *Puebla and Beyond: Documentation and Commentary*. Maryknoll: Orbis, 1979.

Flannery, Austin, ed. *Vatican Council II: The Conciliar and Post-Conciliar Documents*. Collegeville, Minn.: Liturgical Press, 1975.

On Evangelization in the Modern World: Apostolic Exhortation. Washington, D.C.: United States Catholic Conference, 1976.

Stern, C., ed. *Shaarei Tesuvah, Gates of Repentance: The New Union Prayerbook for the Days of Awe*. New York: Central Conference of American Rabbis, 1978.

---

[4] Second Vatican Council, *Gaudium et Spes* 26, in *Vatican Council II: The Conciliar and Post Conciliar Documents* (ed. Austin Flannery; Collegeville: Liturgical Press, 1975), 927–28.

GLOSSARY OF FREQUENTLY-USED ANCIENT WORDS

ʿănāwîm: (Heb.) the poor; those who are afflicted in any way

ʿānî: (Heb.) poor

ʿăniyyîm: (Heb.) the poor; dialectical variant of ʿănāwîm

andurārum: (Akk.) liberty or liberation in ancient Mesopotamia, including the emancipation of slaves and the abolition of debt; acts of *andurārum* were the prerogatives of the kings

awīlum: (Akk.) upper echelon of Mesopotamian society; comparable to patricians in Republican Rome

dak: (Heb.) oppressed

daʿat: (Heb.) knowledge

dĕrôr: (Heb.) jubilee; an amnesty encompassing the material and spiritual, economic and social levels of human existence

dikaiosynē: (Gk.) justice, righteousness

ʾebyôn: (Heb.) oppressed

ʾebyônîm: (Heb.) the innocent poor

eleēmosynē: (Gk.) almsgiving; frequently translates the Hebrew ṣĕdāqâ

ʾĕmet: (Heb.) faithfulness

ʾĕmûnâ: (Heb.) faithfulness

ENSI: (Sum.) term used to designate the ruler or governor of any ancient Mesopotamian city-state

gērîm: (Heb.) the resident alien, non-citizen

gōʾēl: (Heb.) redeemer, liberator

ḫāpiru: (Peripheral Akk.) lower class, generally referred to as those revolting from authority

ḥesed: (Heb.) goodness; compassion; loving-kindness

ḥēlĕkâ: (Heb.) helpless

ka: (Eg.) moving and animating energy

kittum: (Akk.) the justice done by the Babylonian king as an expression of his capacity to bring about social order as a gift from the gods; related to the concept of *mīšarum*

maat: (Eg. m3ᶜt) term used in ancient Egypt for order, goodness, justice, wisdom, truth and knowledge

maḥsôr: (Heb.) indigence

maśkîlîm: (Heb.) wise teachers

mina: (Akk. *mīnum*) unit of currency mentioned in the Code of Hammurabi; smaller than a *shekel*

mīšarum: (Akk.) specific acts accomplished by the Babylonian king which bring about public order and the common good; related to the concept of *kittum*

mišpāṭ: (Heb.) judgment, verdict, decree, bylaw, order or custom

muškēnum: (Akk.) lower echelon of Mesopotamian society; comparable to Roman plebeians

praeis: (Gk. *praos*) meek; the translators of the LXX used this term to translate the Hebrew ᶜănāwîm

raḥămîm: (Heb.) compassion

rāš: (Heb. *rôš*) destitute

rāṣaḥ: (Heb.) intentional and malicious violence

rîb: (Heb.) lawsuit

šāpāl: (Heb.) lowly

ṣĕdāqâ: (Heb.) order, uprightness, equity justice or right conduct; righteousness

ṣedeq: (Heb.) that which brings about order, uprightness, equity, justice or right conduct; an action related to these things

śĕkîrîm: (Heb.) day-laborers

shekel: (Akk. *šiqlum*) unit of currency mentioned in the Code of Hammurabi; larger than a *mina*

tôšabîm: (Heb.) assimilated aliens

wardum: (Akk.) slaves in ancient Mesopotamia

INDEX OF MODERN AUTHORS

Aberach, M., 180, 196
Achtemeier, Paul J., 201, 215
Agua Pérez, A. del, 242, 259
Ahlström, Gösta W., 54, 62
Albertz, Rainer, 136, 147
Allison, A. C., 219, 239
Allison, Dale C., 189, 193, 197, 220, 221, 222, 223, 225, 229, 231, 239
Alon, Gedalia, 265, 286
Amit, Yairah, 14, 18, 55, 62, 87, 88, 89, 90
Anderson, Gary, 57, 62
Andrew, M. E., 70, 93
Anthes, Rudolph, 23, 39
Assmann, Jan, 22, 39
Aubert, Jean-Marie, 75, 91

Bailey, K. E., 143, 147
Baines, John, 21, 26, 39
Bajard, J., 243, 259
Balch, David L., 274, 275, 286
Bammel, Ernst, 177, 196
Barnet, P. W., 180, 196
Barré, Michael L., 57, 62, 101, 118
Bartchy, S. Scott, 273, 274, 286
Barton, George A., 5, 16, 18
Barton, J., 103, 118
Batto, Barnard F., 45, 58, 62
Baudissin, Wolf W. Graf von, 126, 147
Baum, Gregory, 72, 91
Beale, Gregory K., 305, 309, 310, 313
Becker, Jürgen, 183, 184, 196
Belo, Fernando, 201, 215
Ben Zvi, Ehud, 128, 147
Bendor, Shunya, 55, 62
Benoit, Pierre, 218, 239
Berge, Kaare, 49, 62
Berrouard, M.-F., 295, 313
Betz, Hans-Dieter, 218, 239, 265, 286

Betz, Otto, 194, 197
Bird, Phyllis A., 56, 62, 70, 78, 91
Birkeland, H., 126, 147
Black, Matthew, 152, 170
Blenkinsopp, Joseph, 48, 49, 62, 99, 118
Boadt, Lawrence, 110, 118
Boecker, Hans J., 1, 3, 7, 8, 9, 18
Bonsirven, Joseph, 221, 239
Booij, T., 57, 63, 101, 118
Borg, Marcus J., 174, 177, 190, 197, 211, 215, 279, 286
Borgen, Peder, 146, 147, 264, 286
Boring, M. Eugene, 309, 313
Bornkamm, Günther, 176, 184, 197
Bottéro, Jean, 4, 5, 6, 9, 12, 15, 19
Botterweck, G. J., 91, 118
Bowker, J., 265, 286
Brandenburger, Egon, 166, 170
Brandon, S. G. F., 176, 197
Breasted, James H., 37, 39
Bright, John, 56, 63
Broer, Ingo, 219, 220, 239
Brown, Raymond E., 63, 173, 177, 179, 190, 191, 197, 201, 215, 217, 218, 239, 248, 259, 290, 292, 294, 295, 298, 300, 304, 305, 314
Brueggemann, Walter, 43, 60, 63
Brunt, P. A., 278, 286
Buccellati, Giorgio, 96, 118
Bultmann, Christoph, 81, 91
Bultmann, Rudolph, 176, 187, 188, 191, 193, 197
Burge, Gary M., 294, 314
Byrne, Brendan J., 270, 272, 273, 286

Cardascia, Guillaume, 8, 12, 18
Cardellini, Innocenzo, 81, 91
Cardenas Pallares, José, 201, 215

Carroll, Robert P., 110, 118
Carter, Warren, 257, 259
Castelli, Elizabeth, 282, 286
Castellino, Giorgio R., 15, 18
Catchpole, David, 219, 239
Causse, Antonin, 126, 147
Cazelles, Henri, 11, 12, 13, 18, 21, 22, 23, 39, 49, 52, 63, 96, 97, 101, 118
Ceresko, Anthony R., 114, 118, 136, 137, 148
Chancey, Mark, 182, 197
Chaney, Marvin L., 96, 118
Charles, Robert H., 304, 314
Charlesworth, James H., 170
Childress, J., 61, 63
Childs, Brevard S., 131, 148
Chilton, Bruce, 174, 197
Clark, Andrew D., 282, 286
Clarke, Graeme W., 264, 286, 293, 314
Clements, Ronald E., 126, 148
Clifford, Richard, 84, 91, 114, 118
Cohen, Shaye J. D., 180, 197
Collins, Adela Yarbro, 305, 308, 310, 314
Collins, John J., 103, 118, 143, 148, 155, 158, 161, 163, 165, 166, 170, 179, 197
Collins, John N., 257, 259
Contenau, Georges, 4, 18
Coote, Robert B., 49, 63, 96, 119
Couturier, Guy P., 110, 119
Creed, J. M., 187
Crenshaw, James L., 22, 39, 132, 148
Croatto, J. Severino, 50, 51, 53, 55, 56, 57, 58, 63, 72, 91
Crossan, John D., 177, 197
Crüsemann, Frank, 136, 148
Culpepper, R. Alan, 268, 287

Dahl, Nils A., 269, 287
Dandamayev, Muhammad A., 56, 63, 80, 91
D'Angelo, Mary R., 257, 259
Danker, Frederick W., 253, 260
Daube, David, 225, 239
Daumas, François, 26, 39
Davies, G. I., 53, 55, 63
Davies, Peter H., 235, 239
Davies, William D., 189, 193, 197, 218, 220, 221, 222, 223, 225, 229, 231, 239, 265, 287
Day, Dorothy, 229, 239, 254, 260
Day, John, 53, 63, 104, 119
Delekat, L., 126–127, 148
Dever, William G., 54, 63
Di Lella, Alexander A., 141, 148, 159, 171

Dittenberger, Wilhelm, 287
Dohmen, Christoph, 70, 91
Donahue, John R., 201, 215, 234, 239, 242, 260, 279, 287
Donfried, Karl P., 277, 287
Downing, F. Gerald, 177, 197
Dozeman, T. B., 74, 91
Dulles, Avery, 227, 239
Dunn, James D. G., 282, 287
Dupont, Jacques, 217, 220, 239
Durand, Alfred, 221, 239

Eagleston, J., 322, 323
Eddy, Paul R., 182, 183, 197
Ehrman, B. D., 177, 197
Eisenhut, W., 278
Eissfeldt, Otto, 114, 119
Ellacuría, Ignacio, 177, 197, 295, 314
Elliot, John H., 186, 197, 275, 287
Elliot, Neil, 265, 279, 287
Epzstein, Léon, 1, 8, 18, 22, 26–27, 34, 35, 39
Escudero Freire, C., 242–43, 260
Esler, Philip F., 254, 260
Evans, Craig A., 174, 197

Fager, Jeffrey A., 89, 91
Fendler, Marlene, 100, 102, 119
Fensham, Frank C., 21, 39
Fiedler, M. H., 154, 170
Finet, André, 8, 10, 19
Finkelstein, Jacob J., 5, 6, 14, 18, 74, 87–88, 91
Fishbane, Michael A., 57, 58, 63, 101, 119, 271, 287
Fitzmyer, Joseph A., 182, 186, 187, 189, 192, 194, 195, 197, 242, 243, 244–45, 251, 260, 268, 271, 279, 287
Flannery, Austin, 75, 91, 276, 287, 294, 312, 314, 323
Flusser, David, 292, 314
Ford, J. Massyngbaerde, 244, 260
Fowler, Robert M., 202, 215
Fraade, Steven D., 264, 287
Frankemölle, Hubert, 235, 240
Freedman, David N., 53, 55, 63
Fretheim, Terence E., 49, 60, 63, 64, 105, 119
Freyne, Seán, 173, 179, 180, 181, 197–98
Frick, Frank S., 96, 119
Friedman, Richard E., 49, 64
Friedrich, G., 288
Friedrich, J., 279, 287
Fritz, Volkmar, 54, 64

Funk, Robert W., 188, 198
Furnish, Victor P., 270, 272, 279, 287

Gamberoni, J., 73, 91
García Martinez, Florentino, 128, 148
Gelin, Albert, 126, 148
Georgi, Dieter, 278, 281, 282, 287
Gerstenberger, Erhard, 70, 91
Ginzberg, Eli, 88, 91
Globe, A., 53, 64
Gnilka, Joachim, 207, 215, 233, 240
Goodfriend, Elaine A., 76, 91
Gottwald, Norman K., 50, 51, 52, 53, 54, 55, 58, 64
Grayson, A. Kirk, 81, 91
Green, William S., 264, 288
Greengus, Samuel, 6, 18, 74, 92
Guardini, Romano, 296, 323
Guevara, H., 179, 198
Gunkel, H., 166, 170
Gunn, Battiscombe, 37, 39
Gutiérrez, Gustavo, 52, 58, 64, 138, 148

Hahn, F., 194, 195, 198
Halpern, Baruch, 54, 64, 97, 119
Hamilton, Jeffries M., 14, 19, 82, 83, 92
Hammer, R., 161, 170
Hanks, Thomas D., 255, 260
Hanson, J. S., 178, 198
Hanson, Paul D., 151, 170
Harnack, Adolf von, 175, 198
Harnish, Wolfgang, 166, 171
Harrington, Wilfrid J., 309, 314
Hartmann, L., 159, 171
Harvey, John, 104, 119
Hasel, Gerhard E., 71, 92
Hauck, F., 187
Hayes, John H., 56, 65
Heine, Susanne, 270, 287
Helck, W., 22, 24, 39
Hemer, Colin J., 305, 314
Hendel, Ronald S., 56, 64
Hengel, Martin, 155, 160, 171, 176–177, 183, 198, 271, 287, 290, 314
Hiebert, Theodore, 74, 92
Hill, David, 223, 240
Hillers, Delbert R., 108, 119
Himes, Kenneth R., 76, 92
Hirschfeld, G., 264, 287
Hobbs, T. Raymond, 74, 92
Hoffner, Harry A., 78
Holden, Lynn H., 37, 40
Hollenbach, Paul W., 207, 215
Hopkins, Keith, 273, 287

Horbury, William, 292, 314
Horsley, G. H. R., 288
Horsley, Richard A., 177, 178, 182, 186, 198
Horst, F., 103, 119
Hossfeld, Frank-Lothar, 92
Houten, Christiana van, 81, 92
Hübner, Hans, 188, 198
Huffmon, Herbert B., 100, 104, 119
Hugues, G. R., 21
Hultgren, Arland J., 297, 314

Jacobsen, Thorkild, 16, 19
Jenks, Alan W., 49, 64
Jenni, E., 119
Jepson, Alfred, 101, 102, 119, 122, 148
Jeremias, Joachim, 193, 198
Jones, Douglas R., 110, 119
Jülicher, A., 187

Kähler, Martin, 175, 198
Karris, Robert J., 258, 260
Käsemann, Ernst, 176, 188, 194, 198, 267, 288
Kee, Howard C., 201, 213, 214, 215
Kimelman, R., 292, 315
King, Leonard W., 11, 19
King, Martin Luther, Jr., 196, 198
King, Philip J., 54, 64, 65
King, Robert, 54
Kingsbury, Jack D., 219, 240
Kinukawa, Hisako, 201, 212, 214, 215
Kittel, G., 288
Knohl, Israel, 85, 92
Kochavi, Moshe, 109, 119
Kodell, Jerome, 242, 260
Kramer, Samuel, 16, 19
Kraus, Fritz R., 12, 14, 19
Kraus, Hans-Joachim, 126, 148
Krauss, R., 21, 40
Kremers, Heinz, 73, 92
Kruse, H., 57, 64, 101, 119
Kselman, John S., 176, 198
Kümmel, W. G., 188, 198
Kysar, Robert, 290, 291, 292, 300, 315

Lacocque, André, 161, 171
Lalouette, Claire, 23–24, 26, 27, 32, 33, 40
Lambert, Maurice, 2, 3, 4, 19
Lambrecht, Jan, 188, 199
Lampe, Peter, 274, 288
Langan, John, 61, 64, 75, 92
Larrson, Goran, 46, 64
Laws, Sophie, 217, 235, 240
Lee-Pollard, D. A., 201, 215

Leeuwen, Cornelis van, 142, 148
Légasse, Simon, 220, 240
Lemaire, André, 70, 92
Lemche, Niels P., 2, 13, 14, 19, 51, 53, 54, 64, 96, 119
Lenski, Gerhard, 55, 64
Levine, Lee I. A., 183, 199
Lewy, Julius, 87, 92
Lichtheim, Miriam, 22, 25, 28, 29, 32, 33, 37, 38, 40, 140, 148
Liedke, G., 101
Limet, Henri, 7, 19
Lind, Millard C., 74, 92
Lindars, Barnabas, 290, 315
Lipinski, Edward, 53, 64
Liverani, Mario, 27, 40
Llewelyn, S., 288
Loader, William R. G., 189, 199
Lohfink, Norbert, 9, 19, 38, 40, 46, 65, 81, 92, 125, 126, 127, 128, 133, 148, 220, 240
Lona, H., 295, 315
Long, William R., 183, 199
Lührmann, Dieter, 201, 211, 216
Luz, Ulrich, 220, 240

Macholz, G. C., 98, 120
Mack, Burton L., 177, 199
MacMullen, Ramsay, 181, 199
Malamat, Abraham, 86, 92
Malherbe, Abraham J., 265, 288
Malina, Bruce J., 211, 216, 245, 252, 260
Marcus, Ralph, 23, 40
Marshall, I. E., 187
Marshall, Jay W., 79, 92
Martyn, J. Louis, 266, 288, 292, 315
Mathys, Hans-Peter, 86, 92
Mattha, G., 21
Mauchline, J., 103, 120
Maynard-Reid, Pedrito U., 235, 240
Mazar, Amihai, 54, 65
McCarter, P. Kyle, 53, 55, 65
McEvenue, Sean, 49, 65
McGarrigle, Francis J., 221, 240
McKeating, H., 143, 148
Meier, John P., 176, 177, 183, 184, 185, 190, 191, 199, 201, 215, 217, 218, 222, 234, 239, 240
Meinhold, A., 128, 148
Mejía, Jorge, 195, 199
Mendenhall, George E., 58, 65, 96, 120
Merkel, H., 188, 199
Merz, Annette, 177, 191, 200
Meyer, Ben F., 176, 177, 185, 186, 190, 199
Meyer, Eric M., 182, 197

Milgrom, Jacob, 85, 92
Millard, A. R., 56, 65
Miller, James Maxwell, 56, 65
Miller, Patrick D., 60, 65, 74, 93
Miranda, José P., 56, 65
Mitchell, A. C., 252, 260
Mogensen, B., 101, 102, 120, 122, 149
Moiser, Jeremy, 268, 288
Moloney, Francis J., 290, 292, 315
Moore, J. M., 278, 286
Moortgat, Anton, 3, 19, 27, 28, 40
Moran, William L., 78, 86, 93
Morenz, Siegfried, 22, 40
Moret, A., 22, 40
Morin, J.-A., 179, 199
Moscati, Sabatino, 8, 19
Moule, C. F. D., 177, 196
Mowinckel, Sigmund, 126, 149
Moxnes, Halvor, 248, 253, 260
Murphy, Roland E., 23, 40, 49, 53, 56, 60, 65
Murphy-O'Connor, Jerome, 273, 288
Myers, Ched, 173, 199, 201, 210, 216

Nardoni, Enrique, 212, 216, 272, 288
Nasuti, Harry P., 82, 93
Neufeld, Edward, 87, 93
Neyrey, Jerome H., 189, 199, 211, 216, 255, 260
Nicholson, Ernest W., 53, 55, 65, 104, 120
Nickelsburg, George W. E., 143, 149, 152, 153, 155, 157, 158, 163, 171, 250, 261
Noack, Bent, 235, 240
Noonan, John T., 275, 288
North, Robert, 54, 65, 87, 93

Oakman, Douglas E., 177, 199
Oepke, A., 277
Olley, John W., 114, 120
O'Toole, Robert, 191, 199, 242, 261
Otto, E., 39
Overman, J. Andrew, 264, 288

Parvey, Constance F., 256, 261
Paul, Shalom M., 79, 93
Penna, Romano, 264, 288
Perdue, Leo G., 140, 149
Perlitt, Lothar, 53, 65
Perrin, Norman, 176, 177, 188, 189, 194, 199
Pesch, Rudolph, 207, 208, 216
Petersen, David, 151, 171
Peterson, E., 277
Petschow, H., 12, 19

Pflüger, Kurt, 34, 35, 40
Phillips, Anthony, 70, 73, 76, 84, 93
Pintore, Franco, 4, 7, 19
Pixley, Jorge V., 50, 51, 52, 53, 55, 57, 58, 65, 193, 199
Pleins, J. David, 127, 133, 134, 149
Ploeg, J. P. M. van der, 87, 93, 133, 149
Pöhlmann, W., 279, 287
Pope John Paul II, 72, 75, 89, 93
Pope Paul VI, 238, 251, 261, 299, 322
Potterie, Ignace de la, 294, 295, 297, 315
Powell, Mark A., 219, 221, 240
Price, S. R. F., 306, 315
Pritchard, James B., 19, 40, 66, 93, 149
Prockter, L. J., 142, 149
Przbyslski, Benno, 217, 240
Puech, E., 247, 261
Pury, Albert de, 49, 66

Rad, Gerhard von, 52, 60, 66
Rahlfs, Alfred, 126, 149
Ramlot, Léon, 22, 40
Reed, Jonathan L., 182, 199
Reicke, Bo, 264, 288
Reimarus, Hermann S., 174, 199
Rendtorff, Rolf, 49, 66
Rensberger, David, 292, 293, 299, 315
Reumann, John H. P., 217, 218, 222, 231, 240, 267, 288
Reviv, Hanoch, 98, 99, 120
Rhoads, David M., 179, 180, 200
Riches, John, 176, 178, 199–200
Ricoeur, Paul, 53, 66
Ringe, Sharon H., 242, 261
Ringgren, H., 91, 118
Rivkin, E., 265, 288
Roberts, Jimmy J. M., 96, 120
Rohrbaugh, Richard L., 250, 260
Römer, Thomas, 49, 66
Rowland, C., 161, 171

Sabourin, Leopold, 131, 149
Sadek, A. I., 37, 40
Saggs, H. W. F., 2, 19
Sakenfeld, Katharine D., 86, 93
Saldarini, Anthony, 265, 288
Sanders, E. P., 176, 177, 181, 185, 186, 187, 190, 200
Sanders, James A., 243, 261
Schaper, P., 322, 323
Scharff, Alexander, 3, 19, 27, 28, 40
Schmid, Hans H., 22, 24, 40, 105, 120
Schmitt, John J., 57, 66
Schnackenburg, Rudolph, 290, 315

Schneiders, Sandra M., 297, 315
Schottroff, Willy, 182, 200
Schrage, Wolfgang, 279, 280, 288, 297, 315
Schrenk, G., 278
Schüssler Fiorenza, Elizabeth, 192, 200, 257, 261, 270, 272, 288
Schweitzer, Albert, 175, 200
Schweizer, Eduard, 221, 240
Scullion, John J., 56, 66, 101, 102, 120, 122, 149
Seccombe, David P., 244, 261
Seebass, Horst, 49, 66
Segundo, Juan L., 173, 200
Senor, Donald, 219, 240
Sesboüé, Bernard, 45, 66
Seux, Marie-Joseph, 16, 17, 19
Shaw, Graham, 282, 288
Shirun-Grumach, I., 22, 41
Shupak, Nili, 22, 41, 133, 149
Simpson, William K., 31, 41
Slater, Thomas B., 306, 315
Sloan, Robert B., 244, 261
Smallwood, E. Mary, 264, 288
Smiga, George, M., 292, 315
Smith, D., Moody, 292, 315
Smith, H. S., 36, 41
Smith, J. M. P., 128, 149
Smith, Mark S., 44, 47, 66
Sobrino, Jon, 173, 191, 200
Soggin, J. Alberto, 85, 93, 96, 120
Sontheimer, Walther, 289
Speiser, Ephraim A., 7, 11, 19, 48, 59
Speyer, Wolfgang, 271, 288
Spiegel, J., 27–28, 41
Spohn, William C., 52, 61, 66
Sprinkle, Joe M., 79, 93
Stamm, Johann J., 70, 93
Stanton, Graham N., 218, 219, 240
Ste. Croix, G. E. M. de, 305, 316
Steck, O. H., 244, 261
Stegemann, Wolfgang, 182, 200, 254, 261
Stendahl, Krister, 270, 271, 288
Stephens, Ferris A., 3, 20
Stern, C., 322, 323
Stoebe, H. J., 101, 120
Stone, Lawson G., 55, 66
Stone, Michael E., 165, 166, 167, 171
Strauss, David F., 174, 200
Strecker, Georg, 217, 241
Stuhlmacher, P., 279, 287
Stuhlmueller, Carroll, 113–14, 120
Swain, J. W., 160, 171
Sweet, John P. M., 144, 149
Swete, Henry B., 304, 316

Tamez, Elsa, 235, 237, 241
Tcherikover, Victor, 141, 149, 154, 155, 157, 158, 159, 172
Teeple, Howard M., 290, 316
Telford, W. R., 173, 200
Théodoridès, Aristide, 21, 24, 41
Thiessen, Gerd, 177, 181, 191, 200, 207, 212, 216, 227, 238, 241, 275, 289
Third General Conference of Latin American Bishops, 61, 66
Thomas, John C., 297, 316
Thompson, A. L., 165, 172
Thompson, Leonard L., 307, 316
Thompson, Thomas L., 56, 66
Thornton, Claus-Jürgen, 242, 261
Tobin, Vincent A., 37, 41
Topel, J., 219, 241
Tournay, R., 4, 19
Townsend, J. T., 292, 316
Trenchard, Warren C., 143, 149
Trocmé, A., 244, 261
Trummer, Peter, 273, 289
Tuñí, J. O., 295, 316

Unterman, Jeremiah, 44, 66

Valadier, Paul, 75, 93
Van Seters, John, 49, 56, 66
Vandier, J., 24, 41
Vaux, Roland de, 6, 20, 57, 66, 71, 81, 84, 88, 93
Vawter, Bruce, 100, 120, 130, 149
Vercoutter, J., 27, 41
Vermeylen, Jacques, 49, 66
Verner, David C., 274, 289
Via, Dan O., Jr., 201, 216
Viviano, Benedict T., 234, 241, 247, 261
Völkel, M., 243, 261
Vouga, François, 235, 236, 241

Wacker, Marie-Theres, 152, 172
Waetjen, Herman C., 201, 207, 216

Wagener, Ulrike, 274, 289
Wahlde, U. C. von, 291–292, 316
Watt, J. G. van der, 304, 316
Watty, W. W., 190, 200
Wegner, Judith R., 258, 261
Weinfeld, Moshe, 36, 41, 53, 55, 67, 83, 93, 100, 102, 106, 120, 122, 149
Weiss, Johannes, 175, 200
Wengst, Klaus, 127, 149, 263, 264, 277, 278, 289, 292, 293, 316
Wente, Edward F., 24, 41
Westbrook, Raymond, 13, 14, 20, 88, 93
Westendorf, W., 39
Westermann, Claus, 56, 67, 120
Whitelam, Keith W., 96, 97, 98, 99, 121
Whybray, R. N., 114, 121, 133, 150
Wildberger, Hans, 107, 121
Williams, S. K., 267, 289
Wilson, John A., 30, 34, 41
Wilson, Robert R., 55, 67
Wilson, S. G., 242, 262
Wink, Walter, 177, 200
Winston, David, 143, 150
Winter, Paul, 207, 216
Wiseman, D. J., 56, 65
Witherington, Ben, 256, 262, 266, 270, 271, 289
Witherup, Ronald D., 176, 198
Wrede, William, 175, 200
Wright, Christopher J. H., 15, 20, 55, 67, 73, 78, 88, 94, 244
Wright, N. T., 174, 182, 200

Yaron, Reuven, 6, 8, 20
Yoder, John H., 244, 262
York, John O., 245, 247, 262

Zaccagnini, C., 81, 94
Ziegler, Konrat, 289
Ziesler, John A., 222, 241, 267, 289
Zimmerli, Walther, 70, 94, 244, 262
Zobel, H.-J., 101

Index of Ancient Sources

OLD TESTAMENT

Genesis
1:31   46
2:1–3   46
2:2–3   71
6:1–2   156
6:4   156
9:5b–6   75
9:6   75
15:1   44
15:13–21   44
17:2–8   44
20:3   76
20:9   76
31   55
38   55
39:9   76

Exodus
1:1–13:16   43
2:23–4:17   48, 49
3:1–3   44
3:1–12   44
3:7–8   48
3:7–10   44
3:8   45, 48
3:10   44, 49
3:11   44
3:12   44
3:13–15   49
3:16–17   48
3:17   44, 48
3:19–20   44, 48
3:20   44
4:10–17   48
5:1–21   44

6:1   48
6:6–8   44
7:8–11:10   44
12:1–28   46
12:12   45, 301
12:14   45, 48
12:29   48
12:30   45
13:17–15:21   44
14:1–15:19   45
14:13–14   48
14:15–18   48
14:15–31   45
14:19–21   48
14:22–23   48
14:24–25   48
14:26–27   48
14:27   48
15:1   309
15:1–18   45
15:18   45
15:22–40:38   44
16:4   229
16:18   281
19:1–25   48, 49
19:4–6   69
19:5   49, 68
19:5–6   45, 69, 85
19:6   47, 309
19:8   69
20:1–2   70
20:1–17   45, 69, 70
20:2   68
20:5   70, 78
20:6   70
20:8   71
20:8–11   70–72, 197

20:11   71
20:12   72–73
20:13   73–76
20:14   76
20:15   77
20:16   77
20:17   78–79
20:22–23:33   79
20:23–26   79
21:1–11   57
21:1–22:19   79
21:1–23:19   45
21:2–11   80, 83, 87
21:15   73
21:17   73
21:20–21   80
21:26–27   80
22:1   249
22:1–4   77
22:20–23:19   79
22:21   81
22:21–22   81
22:21–24   81
22:23–24   81
22:25   81
22:26–7   81
23:1–3   81
23:6–8   81
23:9   81
23:10–11   81, 83, 86
23:11   87
23:20   202
23:21   70
23:25–26   69
23:27–31   68
24:1–11   45
24:1–14   48, 49

24:3   69
24:7   68, 69
25:1–31:18   45
28:36   308
31:17   71
32:1–35   47, 48
32:1–34:35   49
32:7–10   49
32:10   46
32:11–14   46
32:14   49
32:30–34   49
32:31–32   47
33:12–17   46
33:19   46
34   48
34:1–35   49
34:6–7   70, 301
34:6–13   46
34:7   70
34:10–26   69
34:11   48
34:18–26   48
34:21   72
36:8–40:33   46
37:6–9   46
39:30   308
39:43   47

Leviticus
11:1–47   188
15:25–27   192
17–26   85, 111
18:20   76
18:24–25   76
19   86
19:2   86
19:2–18   111
19:3a   86
19:3b–8   86
19:9–18   87
19:10   86
19:13   86
19:14   86
19:15   86
19:18   297
19:18b   86
19:19   226
19:32   86
19:33   86
19:34   86
19:39   86
20:10–12   76
25   85, 86, 87

25:1–7   86, 87
25:2   87
25:6   88
25:8–17   86, 87, 116, 243, 244, 252
25:10   244
25:13   244
25:23–55   86, 87
25:39   85, 87
25:39–41   80
25:44–46   80
25:44–46a   85
25:46b   85
25:47   86

Numbers
12:3   128
19:11–13   192
31:9–18   57, 80
31:32–35   80
35:33   75

Deuteronomy
4:8   85
4:44–28:68   82
5:6–21   69, 70
5:9   70
5:10   70
5:12   71
5:12–15   70–73
5:16   72–73
5:17   73–76
5:18   76
5:19   77
5:20   77–78
5:21   78
10:12–13   84
10:17–18   84, 255
10:19a   84
10:19b   84
14:28–29   83
15:1   83
15:1–6   83
15:1–11   87
15:4–5   83
15:7–11   83
15:11   84
15:12   83
15:12–14   83
15:12–18   88
15:13–14   83
15:14–15   83, 84
16:11–14   83
16:18   84

16:19   84
16:20   84, 86
19:18   77
19:19–21   79
21:15–16   57
21:18–21   73
21:22–23   206
22:22–24   76
23:19–20   83
24:19–21   83
25:14–15   84
26:12–15   83
28:1–14   85
30:15–20   85
32:4   301
32:9   301

Judges
5:5   54
5:8   54
5:11   53, 301
5:13   53

1 Samuel
8:11–18   99

2 Samuel
11:1–25   100
14:1–24   98
15:1–6   99

1 Kings
3:28   99
21:1–16   77
21:1–29   100

2 Chronicles
19:4–11   98, 99

Job
7:1   136
14:10–12   145
14:14   136
16:7–17   136
16:11   136
21:27–34   136
22:6–9   137
24:1–16   141
24:2   137
24:2–12   136
24:10–11   137, 251
24:12   136, 137
24:14   74

24:14–15   76
24:22   136
26:13   45
29:1–31:40   137
29:7–16   136
29:12–16   137
30:1   137
30:3–5   137
30:8   137
31:1–40   137
31:13–22   137
31:15   137
38:1–4:2   138
38:4–27   167
40:6–41:26   138
41:1–14   167
42:5–6   138
42:7   138

Psalms
2:2   97
2:7   203, 231
7   123
7:8   123
9:4   125
9:9   125
9:12   125
9:18   125
10:8   125
10:8–10   129
10:18   125
13:6   129
14:1   130
15   302, 303
15:2b–5b   302
18:4–5   130
22   125
22:21   129
24:4–5   223
25:1–2   129
25:2–12   129
25:15–21   129
29:10   130
33:4–5   123
33:5   123
35:19   291
37:5–19   127
36:11 (LXX)   221
37:11   128
40:2   124
40:9–10   123–24
40:10   125
40:17   125
41:1   125

45   99
45:6   97
45:7   97
49   145
49:15   130
67:6 (LXX)   207–8
69:4   291
69:5   129
72   99
72:1–2   97, 123
72:1–3   124
72:3   97
72:4   107
73   145
73:25–28   130
74   58
74:11–13   59
74:21–22   130
82:3   125
82:3–4   124
82:8   124
89   53
89:14   23
94:5–6   74
94:6   74
94:10–11   124
99:4   123
103:6   58
103:7   58
104   34
106:3   123
110:4   97
111:3–4   301
111:7   300
112:1–9   130
112:4   131
119:7   123
119:62   123
119:75   123
119:142   123
122:5   97
136:5–25   166
138:6   125
143:11b–12a   124
145   124
145:6–8   124
146   131
147   131
147:2   132
147:6   132
147:12–14   132
147:20   132
148   132
149   132

149:4   132
150   132

Proverbs
1:1–9:18   136
1:3   136
1:7   135
1:8–9   73
3:34   128
6:19   77
8:5–6   135
8:12   135
8:13   135
8:15–16   133
8:20   135, 230
9:10   135
10:1–22:16   133
10:1–29:27   133
12:28   133, 237
14:25   77
14:27   135
14:34   133
15:15   134
15:25   133
16:8   134
16:12   23, 97
16:16   134
16:19   134
19:17   133
22:2   133
22:9   133
22:17–24:22   133
22:22   133
22:22–23   134
22:28   133
23:11   134
25:1–29:27   133
25:5   97
28:15–16   134
29:13–14   133
30:1–31:31   136
30:14   133, 134
31:8–9   133

Ecclesiastes
1:2–11   139
1:3–4   139–40
1:9   140
1:18   139
2:7   80
2:11   139
2:14–15   139
2:21   139
2:22   139

3:2–8   140
3:2–9   139
3:3   75
3:8   75
3:11   140
3:16   138–39
3:17   144
3:19–20   139
3:19–21   145
3:20   139
4:13   139
5:8   139
5:10–11   139
6:8   139
6:12   139
6:20   139
7:7   142
9:15   139
10:5–6   139
11:9   140
12:13–14   140

Isaiah
1:10–15   106
1:10–17   106
1:12–15   57
1:16–17   106
1:21–23   107
1:25–26   109
1:26   107
1:26–27   107
3:1–18   107
3:13–15   106, 108
5:1–7   205
5:7   106, 205
5:8   79, 106, 109, 205
5:23   106
5:26–30   107
6:3   106
6:5–7   106
9:7   107
10:1–2   106
11:4   127
11:4–5   107
29:19   127
40–55   111
40–60   135
40:1–2   112
40:3   203
40:9–10   208
40:10   183, 203
41:10   112
42:1   231
42:1–4   232

43:15–17   114
44:24–45:13   112, 113
44:26   113
44:28–45:7   114
45:8–9   113
45:15–17   112
51:1   114
51:1–8   115
51:1–52:16   116
51:2   115
51:3   114
51:4–5   113
51:6   114
51:8   114
51:9   45, 112
51:9–10   48
51:9–11   59, 112
52:7   183, 209
52:13–53:12   114
53:3–10   114
53:4   232
53:5   114
53:8   114
53:10–11   114
53:12   232
55:3   113
56:1   115
57:1   115
57:14–19   116
58:6   243
58:6–7   115–16
58:6–9   117
58:9–10   116
58:10–14   115
58:11   227
59:17   277
60:1–14   116
60:17   116
60:17–22   116
61:1   131, 243
61:1–2   243, 245, 248
61:1–3a   116
61:2   221, 243
61:10   116
62:3   116
65:8   116
65:11–12   116
65:13   116
65:13–14   247, 248

Jeremiah
2:5–11   167
2:9   109
2:34   110

5:1   110
5:4–5   109
5:26   110
5:28   110
7:5–6   110
7:5–11   205
7:11   205
7:14   190
7:21–23   110
9:2   76
12:1   109
22:3   110
22:16–17   110
23:5–6   110
26:6   190
31:31–34   110
32:18   70
33:15–16   110
34:8–9   98

Ezekiel
11:19   111
11:20   111
18:5–9   111
18:14–17   111
20:1–21   113
20:1–32   166
22:1–12   111
22:6–7   111
22:9   111
22:12   111
34:8   209
36:25–27   111
36:27   111
37:24–28   111
37:27   111
40–48   111
43:7   111
43:9   111

Daniel
1–6   158
2:34   163
2:35   162, 163
2:44–45   162
2:45   167
7   165, 168
7–12   158
7:1–28   184
7:3–8   307
7:13–14   161, 162, 165
7:18   161
7:22   161
7:25   159

7:27 161, 162
8:25 167
9:20–27 162
9:23–24 162
9:27b 159
11:31 159
11:32 161
11:33 158, 163
11:33–35 161
11:34 161
11:35 158, 161, 163
11:36 159
12:1 163
12:1–3 162
12:2 161
12:3 158, 161, 162
12:4 161
12:10 163
12:10a 161
12:10b 161

Hosea
2:9–13 105
4:1–3 104, 106, 108
4:3 104
6:1–2 105
6:6 57 (LXX), 58, 105, 106, 188, 233 (LXX)
10:12 105
12:6 105
14:9 106

Amos
1:3–2:16 103
2:6–7 103
2:7 127
2:12 102
3:1–2 101, 103
3:9–10 101
5:7 103
5:12 102
5:15 102, 103
5:18–20 103
5:21–22 101
5:21–23 57
5:21–24 106
5:24 101, 102, 103, 318
6:11 103
9:1 103
9:11–15 103

Micah
2:1–2 108–9
2:2 79

2:4–5 109
3:2 190
3:2–4 109
3:12 110
4:4 109
4:6–7 110
5:1–3 108
6:1–8 108
6:8 222, 229
7:18–20 109

Zephaniah
2:3 128

Malachi
3:1 202
4:5 203

NEW TESTAMENT

Matthew
1:21 232
1:23 232
3:2 231
3:15 231
3:17 231
4:17 231
4:23 231
5:3 220, 224, 248
5:3b 219
5:3–6 189, 219, 220, 221, 224
5:3–10 219, 224
5:3–12 184, 218–24, 225, 247
5:4 221
5:5 131, 227
5:6 221–22
5:6a 219, 220
5:7–9 224
5:7–10 219, 222, 224, 227
5:8 223
5:9 223
5:10 220, 222, 224, 230
5:10a 219, 220
5:10b 219
5:11 224
5:11–12 219
5:16 227
5:20 225, 227
5:20–48 225–27

5:21–26 225
5:21–28 224
5:22–26 74
5:23 225–26
5:28–30 76
5:31–32 226
5:33–37 226
5:37 223
5:38–42 226
5:39–40 195
5:43–48 226
5:44 226
5:45 229
5:46 195
5:48 195, 226, 229
6:1 227, 228
6:1–2 228
6:1–18 224, 227–30
6:2–18 227, 228, 229
6:3 234
6:6 228
6:8 228
6:9 187, 229
6:9–10 184
6:9–11 186
6:9–13 229
6:12 222, 229
6:14–15 230, 236
6:17–18 228
6:19–20 182
6:21 227
6:24 182
6:25–34 182
6:33 222, 225
7:12 226
8:11 222
8:11–12 184, 233
8:16 238
8:17 232, 233
9:10–13 233
9:11–13 226
9:13 105, 222, 223
9:35 231
10:6 233
10:34 193
10:37 188
10:37–38 210
10:42 234
11:12b 194
11:20–23 181
12:1–7 233
12:7 105, 223
12:15 232
12:17 232

12:22–32 232	5:1–20 207	11:14 204
12:29 309	5:4 207	11:17 205
15:11 188	5:7 206	11:18 205
15:24 233	5:9 207	11:20 205
16:16–17 298	5:13 207	12:1–12 205, 207
18:1–9 233	5:19 214	12:8–9 205
18:6 234	5:20 208	12:10–11 206
18:21 230	5:25–34 192	12:44 210
18:23–25 230	5:34 192	13:2 207
18:23–35 236	5:41–42 192	13:9 207
18:32–33 230	6:20 207	13:9–13 213
19:4–9 189	6:30–44 209	13:10 213
19:12 193	6:34 209	13:27 213
19:19 226	6:39–40 209	13:32 185
19:28 184, 221	6:41 209, 213	14:1–2 214
20:28 232, 239	7:1–15 212	14:3–9 214
21:28–32 230	7:15 188, 191, 212	14:9 214
21:31–32 191	7:17–23 212	14:12–31 214
21:32 230	7:22 212	14:22 213
22:39 226	7:24–30 212–13	14:25 191
23:8 233	7:26 212	14:66–72 204
23:8–10 228	7:31 209, 213	15:37–39 213
23:8–12 233	7:31–8:13 208	15:38–39 206
23:13–36 223	8:1–9 213	16:7 204
23:23 222, 228–29	8:1–10 209	
23:37 181	8:2 219	**Luke**
25:31–46 222, 224, 233	8:6 209, 213	1:8–20 256
25:40 234, 320	8:27–29 203	1:26–38 256
25:45 234	8:31 203	1:32 247
26:28 225, 232	8:34–38 204	1:47–55 247
	8:35 204	1:52 247
Mark	8:38 204	3:10–14 231
1:1 202	9:33–34 208–9	4:15 245
1:2 202	9:35 209, 211	4:16 245
1:11 203	9:36–37 211	4:16–30 242
1:15 203, 243	9:37 209	4:18 245
1:20 181	10:1–12 211	4:18–19 243
1:21–28 206	10:5–9 189	4:21 243, 249
1:22 206	10:11–12 213–14	4:25–27 245
1:24 206	10:14–15 211	4:31–37 246
1:39 206	10:17–22 210	4:33 245
2:17 207	10:29 211	4:36 246
3:6 203, 207	10:30 211	4:43 243
3:11 206	10:32–34 208	4:44 245
3:21 210	10:35–45 208	5:17 245
3:22 203, 206	10:38–39 204	5:17–26 246–47
3:24–26 206	10:40 208	5:22–25 246–47
3:27 206–7, 309	10:41–45 210	5:27–29 249
3:29 206	10:43–45 211	5:29–30 245
3:29–30 207	10:45 208, 320	5:32 247
3:32 210	11:9–10 204	6:2–3 245
3:34–35 210	11:11 204	6:17 245
4:7 209	11:11–21 204	6:20 220, 248
4:19 210	11:13 204	6:20–21 189

6:20–22   252
6:20–23   184, 248, 255
6:20–26   247–49
6:21   221
6:22–23   262
6:24–26   157
6:27   195
6:29   195
6:30–31   245
6:32   195
6:34–36   253
6:35   195
6:36   195, 222, 252
6:38   182
7:2–10   256
7:11–12   256
7:22   244, 248
7:25   250
7:29   245
7:34   190
8:2   192
8:3c   258
8:4   245
8:40   245
9:2   245
9:6   245
9:31   249
10:1   245
10:13–15   181
10:13–16   245
10:29–37   256
10:30–35   187
10:38–42   256, 257
11:2   184, 187
11:2–3   186
11:20   246
11:22   309
12:16–21   248, 250
12:20   252
12:21   250
12:22–31   182
12:33   182, 252
12:51   193–94
13:3   247
13:10–16   256
13:10–17   192
13:28–29   184, 249
13:34–35   181
14:2–6   256
14:12–14   252–53
14:13   248
14:15–24   252–53
14:21   248, 252
14:26   188, 189

14:26–27   210
15:3–7   256
15:8–10   256
15:11–32   187
16:9   250, 251, 252
16:13   182
16:16c   194
16:19   249, 250
16:19–31   182, 248, 249, 250, 258
16:21   250
16:23   249
16:24   249
16:28   250, 251
18:22   252
19:1–10   251
19:1–19   249
19:8   249
19:9   249
19:10   249
19:18   257
22:30   184
22:35–36   194–95
24   266
24:6–8   258
24:9   258
24:26   249
24:36–49   258

John
1:11   296
2:17–18   298
3:3–6   296
3:16   306
4:23   298
4:39   298
5:18   292
6:63   299
7:38–39   296
8:32   291, 293, 295
8:33   291
8:34   293
8:36   291, 295
8:37   295
8:40   295
8:44   293, 295, 296
9:13   293
9:15   293
9:16   293
9:22   291, 293
9:24   293
9:31   293
9:40   293
10:11   297

10:17   296
11:27   298
12:31   295, 296, 309
12:31–32   294
12:32   309
12:42   291, 293
12:43   293
13:1   306
13:14–15   297
13:15   299
13:34   296, 297
14:6   295
14:15–16   298
14:17   296
15:1–5   296
15:4   296
15:8   296
15:12   296
15:13   296
15:16   296
15:19–20   296
15:19c-20   291
15:25   291
15:27   295
16:1   293
16:2   291, 293
16:4   293
16:7   294
16:8   291
16:8–11   294, 295
16:10   291
16:11   295, 296, 309
16:33   311, 322
17:14   296
21   298, 304
21:15   298
21:16   298
21:17   298
21:19   298

Acts
1:8   266
1:14   266
2:1   266
2:44–47   253
4:32–37   253
4:37   253–54
6:1–7   257
6:2   257
6:4   257–58
9:1–2   256–57
9:36–43   257
10:9–16   255
10:15   255

10:28a 255
10:28b 255
10:34–35 255
10:38 255
10:41 266
13:31 266
15:7–11 256
15:13, 235
16:14–16 257
18:2 257
18:12 305
18:18 257
21:8–9 257
21:18 235

Romans
1:16–17 266–67, 277, 281
1:18 267, 268
1:29 268
1:29–31 268
3:3 267, 277
3:5 301
3:7 267, 300
3:23 268
4:23 298
4:39 298
5:1 277
6:13 268
6:16–20 268
8:1 269
8:15 283
8:19 267–68
8:21 267–68
11:19 46
11:27 298
11:31–32 267
12:2 280
12:17–20 195
13:1–7 279–80
13:2 280
13:6–7 279
13:7 280
13:8 269, 297
13:8–10 269
13:11–12 278
13:11–14 280
13:19 284
14:19 270
15:27 281
16:1 271
16:1–12 273
16:2 271
16:3–5 270
16:5 271

16:6 271
16:7 271
16:12 271

1 Corinthians
1:11–12 284
1:12 283
1:26 282–83
3:4 284
3:9 283
3:21–23 283
4:1 284
4:8–13 284
4:15 284
4:16 285
4:21 284
5:1–12 284
6:7 195
6:9 195
7:3 280
7:10–11 284
7:21 273
7:25 284
7:25–35 272
7:29–31 278
7:31 280
7:34 272
9:1–18 284
9:18 284–85
10:33–11:1 285
11:1 285
11:2–16 272
11:4–5 270
11:5 273
11:11–12 272
12:1–31 283
12:4–5 283
12:4–31 269
12:5–7 280
12:7 270, 283
13:5–7 269
14:12 283
14:33b–36 272–73, 281
14:37 283

2 Corinthians
3:18 268
4:4 268
6:13 284
8:4 281
8:9 281
8:14–15 281
9:12 281
9:15 280

11:7–11 284
12:14–15 284

Galatians
1:15–16 265–66
1:19 235
2:10 280
2:11–14 269
3:26–28 280
3:27–29 266
3:28 266, 271–72, 321
5:14 269, 284
5:15 283
5:19 268
5:20 283
5:22–23 283
5:26 283
6:1 283
6:2 269
6:15 266

Ephesians
5:25–30 275
6:9 275

Philippians
2:2–11 285
2:3 283
2:5 283
2:6–7 283
3:10–16 285
3:17 285
4:2–3 270, 273
4:9 285

Colossians
4:1 275

1 Thessalonians
1:5 285
1:6 280
1:6–7 276, 285
1:10 276, 277
2:1–6 285
2:1–9 285
2:1–12 284
2:2 276
2:3 284
2:5–6 284
2:9 274
2:10 284
2:14 276, 285
4:11 274
4:15 277

4:15–17   276
4:17   277
5:3   276
5:4–5   277
5:8   277
5:15   195

1 Timothy
6:11   278

2 Timothy
2:2   278

James
1:1   235
1:20   238
1:27   237
2:1   236
2:2–4   235
2:5–6   237
2:6   235, 236
2:7   236
2:8   236
2:9–10   235
2:13   236
2:14–16   236
3:1   235
3:9   236, 237
3:13–18   238
3:18   238
4:4   237
4:4–5   237
4:7   237–38
4:13   236
4:13–17   236
4:14   236
4:15–17   236
5:1   236, 243
5:1–6   236, 243
5:2–3   236
5:4   237
5:5   237
5:6   236, 237
5:7–11   237, 244
5:11   237
5:14   235

1 Peter
3:7   275
3:9   195

1 John
1:7   302
1:9   300

2:1   300
2:2   301, 303, 304
2:6   301, 302
2:9–11   303
2:18   303
2:18–27   303
2:20   304
2:25   303
2:27   304
2:28   301
2:29   300, 301
3:4   301
3:4b   303
3:7   300, 301
3:8   301
3:10   300, 301, 303
3:17   303
4:1–6   303
4:10   302
4:14   303

3 John
9–11   304

Revelation
1:4   305
1:4–5   305
1:9   305, 306
2:9   306
2:9–10   305, 310
2:10   310
2:13   306
2:14–15   306
2:14–16   310
2:20   306
2:20–21   310
3:9   305
3:17   306
3:17–19   310
5:2–10   195
5:9–10   308
5:9–14   308
6:10   306
12:7–9   310
12:9   307
13:1–10   307
13:2   307
13:4–8   307
13:11–17   307
14:1   308
15:2–3   309
18:1–20   307
18:13   311
18:21   308

18:24   311
19:1–8   308
19:11–21   309
19:21   309
20:1–3   310
20:1–6   309
20:2   307
20:4–6   156, 168
20:7–10   309
21:2   308
21:24   310
22:11   311
22:21   305

APOCRYPHA

1 Maccabees
1:11–15   155
1:38   159
1:44–49   159
1:54   159
2:42   163

2 Maccabees
4:7–20   155
6:1–2   159

Sirach
3:1–16   73
3:30   142
4:1–10   141, 142
4:4   141–42
4:6   142
4:10   142
7:21   142
8:1–2   143
8:14   143
11:18–19   250
13:3   141
13:3–7   141
13:4   141
13:19–20   141
13:20   141
13:22   141
13:23   141
13:24   141
13:25   145
14:3–10   141
25:16–26   143
29:21   141
29:21–28   142
30:14   141

31:8–11   141
33:1   142
33:20–24   142
33:25–32   142
33:31   142
34:14–17   142
34:23–24   142–43
39:26   142
42:14   143
48:10–12   203

Tobit
12:8   228

Wisdom
1:1   144
1:6   144
1:7   144
2:10–11   144
2:10–15   144
2:12   144
2:12–16   144
2:23   145
3:1   145
3:1–7   145
3:8   145, 146
3:10   145
3:18   145
5:15–16   145, 146
6:1–8   279
6:1–9:18   146
11:5   144
11:16   144
11:17   144
13:1–9   144
16:1–2   144
18:4   145, 146

PSEUDEPIGRAPHA

2 Baruch
48:40   145

1 Enoch
1–36   152–55
6–7   207
6:11   152
7:3–6   153
8:4   153
9:3   153
9:10   153
10:6   153
10:16   135, 154
10:17–21   153
10:19   153
10:22   153
15   207
37–71   163–65
41:2   164
43:4   164
45:4–5   165
45:6   165
46:1, 3   164
46:4   165
46:7   164
47:1   164
47:4   164, 165
48:6   164
48:7   164, 165
48:8   164
48:10   165
49:2   164
50:4   164
51:4   164
53:6   164
53:7   164
61:7   165
62:1   164
63:10   164
91–107   152, 155–58
91:7–11   156
91:12–17   156, 168
94:7, 8a, 9a   156–57
96:8a   156–57
97:8   156–57
97:8–10   250
98:12   156
98:14   155–56
99:2   156
99:14   155
100:7   156–57
103:4   156
103:11–17   156
104:2   156
104:12–13   156

2 Esdras
165–69

4 Ezra
3:4–27   166
3:30   166
4:12   167
4:23   166
5:30   167
5:32–33   167
5:34   167
5:40   167
6:59   168
7:1–18   167
7:28–29   167
8:1   168
8:36   168
8:45   168
8:52   168
9:38–10:59   168
10:21–23   166
10:42   168
11:1–12:51   168
11:46   168–69
12:34   168
12:48   169
13:1–58   169
13:26   169
13:35–40   169

Jubilees
23:31   145

Letter of Aristeas
224   279

Sibylline Oracles
4:49–101   160, 161

Testament of Dan
5:10–13   184

Testament of Levi
14:4   145

Testament of Job
9:8   228

DEAD SEA SCROLLS

Dead Sea Scrolls

1QH
2:11–12   194
2:14–15   194
2:32–33   194

1 QH^a
2:11–12   194
2:14–15   194
2:32–33   194

1QM
11:6–17   184
13:10–18   184
14:6–18   184
14:7   220

4Q521
145

4Q525
247

4QpPs37
128

11QMelch7
244

OTHER JEWISH WRITINGS

'Abot
5:13   228

Josephus

Jewish Antiquities
13.380   155
14.10   264
17.8.3   214

Jewish War
2.56   182
2.68   182
2.573–574   182
3.31–32   182
4.84   180

Philo

De Vita Mosis
2.44   146

GREEK AND ROMAN AUTHORS

Aristides, Aelius

Eulogy
106   263

Cicero

Epistulae ad Atticum
1.16.11   246

Ovid

Epis. Ex Ponto
3.6.23–29   278

Pliny the Younger

Epistulae
9.5   264

Res Gestae Divi Augusti
12   278
13   278
26   278
34   278

Tacitus

Annales
1.10.4   264

Historiae
5.9   180

Virgil

Aeneid
6.791–95   263, 278

Eclogae
4.4–10   263, 278

CHURCH FATHERS

Martyrdom of Polycarp
12:2   305
13:1   305